Praise for *El Norte*

"Torpedoes a popular understanding of North American history by searching beyond the Anglo-centric lens through which it's often taught . . . *El Norte* traces an underrepresented history of north America in accessible terms, all while doing some serious narrative-busting." —*Jezebel*

"Ambitious . . . Overflows with rich detail, revealing often startling truths that this reviewer, for one, never encountered in the textbooks of his adolescence." —*Washington Independent Review of Books*

"A diligent, informative, and highly readable chronicle." —*Washington Times*

"An ambitious history of the U.S. that focuses on the country's often overlooked Hispanic origins . . . Gibson's exhaustively researched and well-written chronicle is an essential acquisition for all American history collections." —*Booklist* (starred review)

"A sweeping and accessible survey of the Hispanic history of the U.S . . . Unusual and insightful . . . Provides a welcome and thought-provoking angle on the country's history, and should be widely appreciated." —*Publishers Weekly* (starred review)

"Enlightening and exhaustively researched . . . Her narrative is far reaching, vividly detailed, and a gift to assessing the American experience and evolving identity."
—Jack E. Davis, author of *The Gulf: The Making of an American Sea*, winner of the 2018 Pulitzer Prize for History

"An epic history which will significantly change the way we look at American history, from the Georgia in which she grew up to the California coast . . . Her research is meticulous in detail and her writing propels the reader through 500 years to transport them to today."
—Richard Parker, author of *Lone Star Nation: How Texas Will Transform America*

"A sweeping story of our Hispanic roots that links the dreamers of the Conquest with the Dreamers of the present, ranging across a continent's history from first contacts in Florida to intersecting empires on Vancouver Island. In connecting places across the United States with their Hispanic pasts, Carrie Gibson connects our America with what one Cuban called Nuestra América, blurring borders at a time when others are building them up." —Paul Gillingham, author of *Cuauhtémoc's Bones*

Also by Carrie Gibson

Empire's Crossroads

EL NORTE

The Epic and Forgotten Story of Hispanic North America

CARRIE GIBSON

Grove Press
New York

Maps by Martin Lubikowski, ML Design, London.

Image credits are as follows: Images 1.1 and 1.2: Courtesy of the author. Images 2.1 and 2.2: Library of Congress, Prints & Photographs Division. Images 3.1, 3.2, and 3.3: Library of Congress, Prints & Photographs Division. Image 4.1: Library of Congress, Prints & Photographs Division, HABS FLA,55-SAUG,1—13. Image 4.2: Library of Congress, Prints & Photographs Division. Image 5.1: Library of Congress, Prints & Photographs Division. Image 5.2: Courtesy of the author. Image 5.3: Library of Congress, Prints & Photographs Division. Image 6.1: Courtesy of the author. Image 6.2: Library of Congress, Prints & Photographs Division. Image 6.3: Courtesy of the author. Image 7.1: New Mexico State University Library, Archives and Special Collections. Image 7.2: Library of Congress, Prints & Photographs Division. Image 8.1: Library of Congress, Prints & Photographs Division. Image 8.2: Filippo Costaggini. "American Army Entering the City of Mexico." Frieze of American History in rotunda of U.S. Capitol building. Architect of the Capitol. Image 8.3: Library of Congress, Prints & Photographs Division. Image 9.1: James Gillinder & Sons (American, 1860-1930s). Compote, "Westward Ho!" Pattern, ca. 1880. Glass, 11 1/2 x 8 3/4 x 5 1/2 in. (29.2 x 22.2 x 14 cm). Brooklyn Museum, Gift of Mrs. William Greig Walker by subscription, 40.226.1a-b. Image 9.2 and 9.3: Courtesy of the author. Image 10.1: The New York Public Library. Image 10.2 and 10.3: Library of Congress, Prints & Photographs Division. Image 11.1: Library of Congress, Prints & Photographs Division. Image 11.2: Courtesy of the author. Image 12.1: The New York Public Library. Image 12.2: The Getty Research Institute. Image 13.1, 13.2, and 13.3: Library of Congress, Prints & Photographs Division. Image 14.1: Mural: © 2012 Artists Rights Society (ARS), New York/SOMAAP, Mexico City; Photo: The Getty Research Institute, Los Angeles. Image 14.2: Courtesy of the Author. Image 15.1: "Seven Latino men, arrested in zoot suit clash, seated in Los Angeles, Calif. courtroom in 1943," Los Angeles Daily News Negatives (Collection 1387). Library Special Collections, Charles E. Young Research Library, UCLA. Image 15.2: Courtesy of the author. Images 16.1 and 16.2: Courtesy of the author.

Published simultaneously in Canada
Printed in the United States of America

Designed by Norman E. Tuttle of Alpha Design & Composition
This book was set in 11.75-pt. Dante with New Baskerville.

First Grove Atlantic hardcover edition: February 2019
First Grove Atlantic paperback edition: February 2020

Library of Congress Cataloging-in-Publication data is available for this title.

ISBN 978-0-8021-4836-0
eISBN 978-0-8021-4635-9

Grove Press
an imprint of Grove Atlantic
154 West 14th Street
New York, NY 10011

Distributed by Publishers Group West

groveatlantic.com

20 21 22 23   10 9 8 7 6 5 4 3 2 1

A Matteo: amigo, guía y hermano

"How will we know it's us without our past?"
—John Steinbeck, *The Grapes of Wrath*

Contents

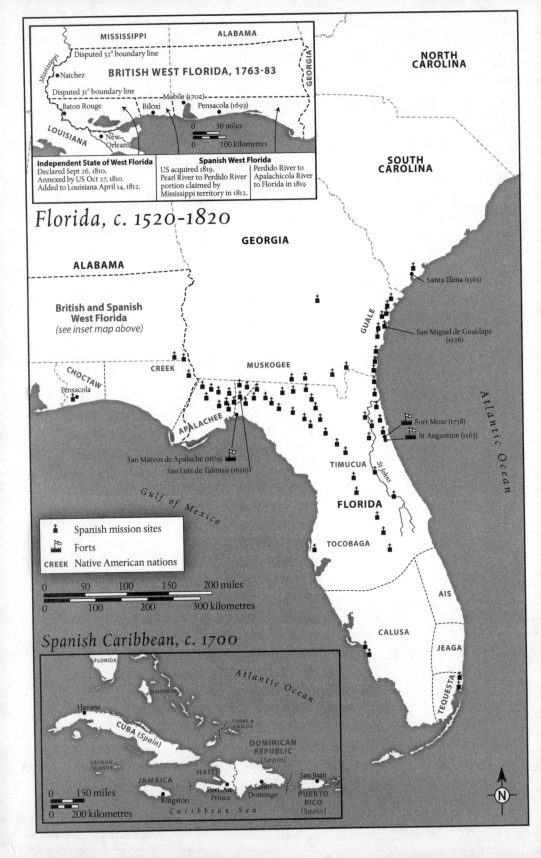

British West Florida, 1763–83

MISSISSIPPI | ALABAMA | GEORGIA

Disputed 32° boundary line

- Natchez

Disputed 31° boundary line

Mobile (1702)

Baton Rouge | Biloxi | Pensacola (1693)

LOUISIANA

- New Orleans

0   50 miles
0   100 kilometres

Independent State of West Florida
Declared Sept 26, 1810.
Annexed by US Oct 27, 1810.
Added to Louisiana April 14, 1812.

Spanish West Florida
US acquired 1819.
Pearl River to Perdido River portion claimed by Mississippi territory in 1812.

Perdido River to Apalachicola River to Florida in 1819

Florida, c. 1520–1820

NORTH CAROLINA

SOUTH CAROLINA

GEORGIA

ALABAMA

British and Spanish West Florida
(see inset map above)

Santa Elena (1565)

GUALE

San Miguel de Gualdape (1526)

CHOCTAW

CREEK

MUSKOGEE

Pensacola

APALACHEE

Fort Mose (1738)

St Augustine (1565)

San Marcos de Apalache (1679)

San Luis de Talimali (1656)

TIMUCUA

St Johns

Atlantic Ocean

Gulf of Mexico

FLORIDA

TOCOBAGA

- Spanish mission sites
- Forts
- **CREEK** Native American nations

0   50   100   150   200 miles
0   100   200   300 kilometres

AIS

CALUSA

JEAGA

Spanish Caribbean, c. 1700

FLORIDA

Atlantic Ocean

BAHAMAS

Havana

CUBA (Spain)

TURKS & CAICOS

CAYMAN ISLANDS

JAMAICA

HAITI

Kingston | Port-au-Prince | Santo Domingo

DOMINICAN REPUBLIC (Spain)

San Juan

PUERTO RICO (Spain)

Caribbean Sea

TEQUESTA

0   150 miles
0   200 kilometres

N

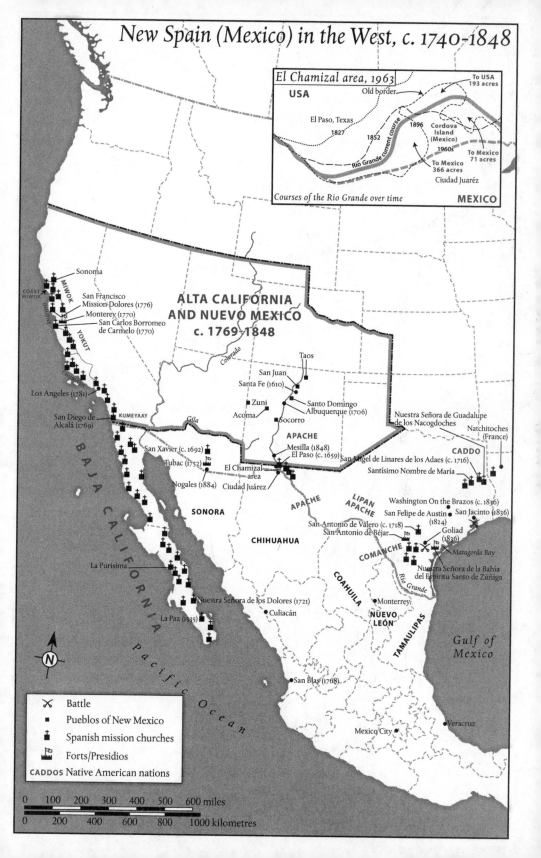

New Spain (Mexico) in the West, c. 1740–1848

El Chamizal area, 1963

USA

Old border
To USA 193 acres

El Paso, Texas
1827

1852
Rio Grande Current course

1896
Cordova Island (Mexico)

1960s
To Mexico 71 acres

To Mexico 366 acres

Ciudad Juaréz

MEXICO

Courses of the Rio Grande over time

ALTA CALIFORNIA AND NUEVO MEXICO c. 1769–1848

Sonoma

COAST MIWOK

MIWOK

San Francisco
Mission Dolores (1776)
Monterey (1770)
San Carlos Borromeo
de Carmelo (1770)

OHLONE

YOKUT

Colorado

Taos
San Juan
Santa Fe (1610)
Santo Domingo
Albuquerque (1706)

Los Angeles (1781)

KUMEYAAY

Zuni
Acoma
Socorro

Gila

APACHE

Nuestra Señora de Guadalupe
de los Nacogdoches

San Diego de
Alcalá (1769)

San Xavier (c. 1692)
Tubac (1752)

El Chamizal
area
Nogales (1884)
Ciudad Juárez

Mesilla (1848)
El Paso (c. 1659)

San Migel de Linares de los Adaes (c. 1716)

Natchitoches
(France)

CADDO

Santísimo Nombre de María

SONORA

APACHE

LIPAN
APACHE

Washington On the Brazos (c. 1836)
San Felipe de Austin
(1824)

San Jacinto (1836)

BAJA CALIFORNIA

CHIHUAHUA

San Antonio de Valero (c. 1718)
San Antonio de Béjar

Goliad
(1836)

Matagorda Bay

La Purisima

COMANCHE

COAHUILA

Nuestra Señora de la Bahía
del Espiritu Santo de Zúñiga

Nuestra Señora de los Dolores (1721)

Rio Grande

Monterrey

La Paz (1535)

Culiacán

NUEVO
LEÓN

TAMAULIPAS

*Gulf of
Mexico*

N

San Blas (1768)

Legend

✕ Battle
■ Pueblos of New Mexico
✝ Spanish mission churches
⚑ Forts/Presidios
CADDOS Native American nations

Mexico City

Veracruz

Pacific Ocean

```
0   100   200   300   400   500   600 miles
0     200     400     600     800   1000 kilometres
```

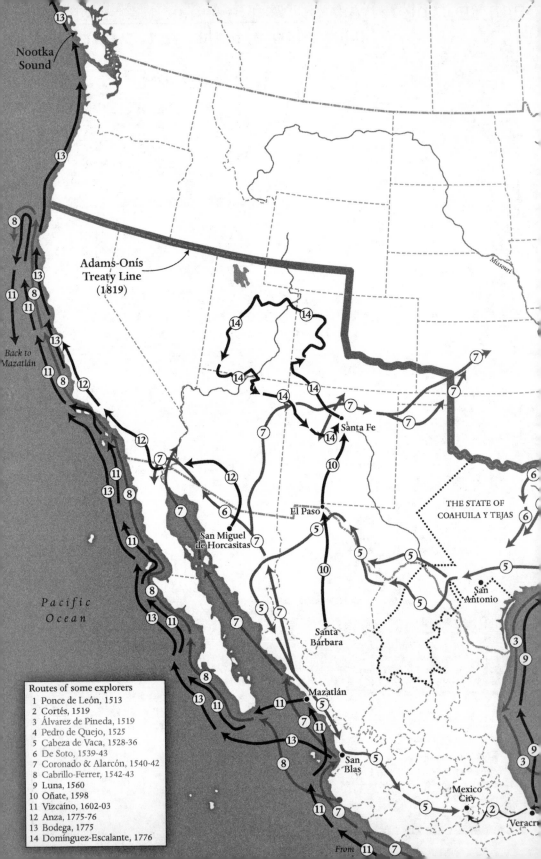

Nootka
Sound

Adams-Onís
Treaty Line
(1819)

Back to
Mazatlán

Pacific
Ocean

San Miguel
de Horcasitas

El Paso

Santa Fe

THE STATE OF
COAHUILA Y TEJAS

San
Antonio

Santa
Bárbara

Mazatlán

San
Blas

Mexico
City

Veracruz

Missouri

Routes of some explorers
1 Ponce de León, 1513
2 Cortés, 1519
3 Álvarez de Pineda, 1519
4 Pedro de Quejo, 1525
5 Cabeza de Vaca, 1528-36
6 De Soto, 1539-43
7 Coronado & Alarcón, 1540-42
8 Cabrillo-Ferrer, 1542-43
9 Luna, 1560
10 Oñate, 1598
11 Vizcaíno, 1602-03
12 Anza, 1775-76
13 Bodega, 1775
14 Domínguez-Escalante, 1776

From

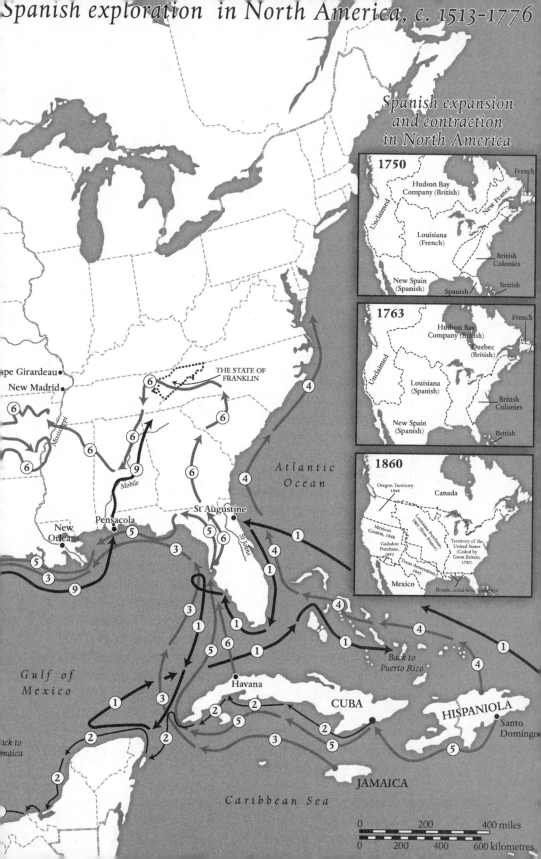

Spanish exploration in North America, c. 1513-1776

Spanish expansion and contraction in North America

1750
Hudson Bay Company (British)
Undaimed
New France
Louisiana (French)
New Spain (Spanish)
British Colonies
Spanish
British

1763
Hudson Bay Company (British)
Quebec (British)
Undaimed
French
Louisiana (Spanish)
New Spain (Spanish)
British Colonies
British

1860
Oregon Territory 1846
Canada
Mexican Cession, 1848
Louisiana Purchase 1803 (from France)
Territory of the United States (Ceded by Great Britain, 1783)
Gadsden Purchase, 1853
Texas Annexation 1845
Mexico
Florida, ceded from Spain 1819

pe Girardeau
New Madrid
THE STATE OF FRANKLIN
Mississippi
Mobile
Pensacola
New Orleans
St Augustine
St Johns
Atlantic Ocean

Back to Puerto Rico

Havana
CUBA
HISPANIOLA
Santo Domingo

Gulf of Mexico

ck to maica

JAMAICA

Caribbean Sea

0   200   400 miles
0   200   400   600 kilometres

Author's Note:
The Search for *El Norte*

MY JOURNEY TO *El Norte* was a circuitous one, taking me via England and, later on, through the islands of the Caribbean before ending not far from where I began, in Dalton, Georgia. This sleepy, mostly white Appalachian town had a dramatic transformation when I was in high school. In 1990, my freshman year, the school consisted of a majority English-speaking student body, with only a handful of people in the English as a Second Language (ESL) classes. By the time I was a senior, the morning announcements were made in English and Spanish, and the ESL classes were full. Thousands of workers and their families, mainly from Mexico, moved to Dalton to work, for the most part, in the carpet mills that dominated the town's economy. I graduated in 1994, only months after the North American Free Trade Agreement (NAFTA) came into force. We were twelve hundred miles from the border, but Mexico had come to us. Today, my old high school has a student body that is about 70 percent Hispanic, and the town is around 50 percent.

The complexity of what I experienced then and in the two decades since is what informs this book. What started in my Spanish-language classes was augmented by the arrival of people who could teach me about *banda* music and *telenovelas*. Later, I added to this mix by spending a decade researching a PhD that involved the colonial histories of Cuba, the Dominican Republic, and Puerto Rico. Finally, my experience has been filtered through two decades of living in one of the world's most multicultural cities, London, England.

My family moved away from Dalton years ago, as have many of my high school friends, and I hadn't really thought about the town, or the question of immigration in the United States, in any serious way until the 2012 election. I was in Washington, D.C., while working on my history of the Caribbean, *Empire's Crossroads*. As I watched and read the coverage, I was struck by the general tone of the media conversation. The way Hispanic people were depicted surprised me because the language seemed unchanged from the rhetoric of more than a decade earlier. The subtexts and implications were the same—there was little recognition of a long, shared past, and instead the talk was of border-jumpers, lack of documentation, and the use of "Mexican" as shorthand for "illegal immigrant." It was jarring because the reality of who was coming to the United States had long been more complex, not least because plenty of immigrants and citizens have roots in all the distinct nations of Latin America. The simmering anxieties about the Spanish-speaking population that such rhetoric exposed exploded in the 2016 presidential race, during which chants of "build that wall" between the United States and Mexico could be heard at campaign rallies for Donald Trump. When I started this project, that election was still years away.

This book is still concerned with the questions that arose in 2012, but they are now given new urgency: there is a dire need to talk about the Hispanic history of the United States. The public debate in the interval between elections has widened considerably. The response to frank discussion about issues such as white privilege at times appears to be a vocal resurgence of white nationalism. For quite some time the present has been out of sync with the past. Much of the Hispanic history of the United States has been unacknowledged or marginalized. Given that this past predates the arrival of the Pilgrims by a century, it has been every bit as important in shaping the United States of today.

I realized, watching my Mexican schoolmates, that if my surname were García rather than Gibson, there would have been an entirely different set of cultural assumptions and expectations placed upon me. I, too, had moved to the South—I was born in Ohio—because my father's job necessitated it. We were also Catholic, my grandmother didn't speak English well, and I had lots of relatives in a foreign country. Yet my white, middle-class status shielded me from the indignities, small and large, heaped upon non-European immigrants. Like most people in the United States—with the obvious exception of Native Americans—my people are from somewhere else. In fact, I'm a rather late arrival. The majority of the motley European mix of Irish, Danish, English, and Scottish on my father's side dates from the 1840s onward. My maternal grandparents, however, came to the United States from Italy in the period around the Second World War—before, in the case of my grandfather; and afterward, for my grandmother. The pressure to "Americanize" was great in the 1950s, and my grandmother, who never lost her heavy Italian accent, felt it necessary to raise my mother in English. She died before I could learn any of her Veneto *dialecto*. My Anglo-Saxon name belies my recent immigrant roots. What continued to bother me was: why had I—and other Italian-Americans—been able to transcend this but not those with Hispanic names? There are plenty of Hispanic Americans who have a much deeper past in the United States than I do: so why are they *still* being treated as strangers in their own country?

Language, belonging, community, race, nationality: these are difficult questions at the best of times, but they are especially fraught with pain at the moment. This book is an attempt to make some historical sense of the large, complex story of Hispanic people in the United States. There have been more than two hundred years of wars, laws, and social attitudes that inform the contemporary situation, in addition to an earlier three centuries of an entangled colonial history.

Much of this project also involved plugging the gaps in my own knowledge, as well as connecting the dots of what I have learned, from my Mexican-infused adolescence to my scholarly work on the Spanish Caribbean. However, there was a gulf in the middle. I had crossed the Mississippi only a few times in my life, so as part of my research I set out to experience the vast space of El Norte, a slang term for the United States, yet a phrase heavy with meaning. I covered more than ten thousand miles, from Florida to northwest Canada, stopping at everything from taco trucks to university library special collections, national parks, and historical monuments. My aim was to have a tangible sense of the wide terrain of the Hispanic past and present. The landscape of this historical inquiry often felt as endless and overwhelming as the sky on an empty Texas road. Really, though, it was just the starting point of a much longer journey.

The poet Walt Whitman, writing in 1883 to decline an invitation to speak at the anniversary of the founding of Santa Fe, meditated on the country's Spanish past. "We Americans have yet to really learn our own antecedents, and sort them, to unify them," he wrote. "Thus far, impressed by New England writers and schoolmasters, we tacitly abandon ourselves to the notion that our United States have been fashioned from the British Islands only, and essentially form a second England only—which is a great mistake." Whitman believed that understanding the nation depended on knowing its Hispanic past, and that "to that composite American identity of the future, Spanish character will supply some of the most needed parts."[1]

Introduction
Nogales, Arizona

T HE DRIVE DOWN Interstate 19 in Arizona from Tucson to Nogales is everything a passenger might expect from a trip through the desert. It is a flat, dusty affair. Craggy mountains seduce from a distance, while scrubby bush blurs past. As the road nears the small city, the flatness gives way to a gentle undulation. Houses appear, dotting one steep hillside in bright pinks, blues, and oranges. Then, when the road rounds a corner, something else comes into view—the sudden shock of it is like seeing a snake in the bushes. It is long and copper-colored, slithering along the hills. It is the United States–Mexico security fence, visible from miles away.

As the presidential election campaign of 2016 made clear, a section of the U.S. public felt this barrier was no longer sufficient. There are in fact two cities called Nogales, one on each side of the border, separated by a fence consisting of giant poles. These allow families to see each other—though the addition of mesh panels along parts of the fence now stop them from reaching through—making it feel like a large outdoor prison. Nogales, Mexico, like many other places along the *frontera*, has seen the arrival of drug gang–related violence and the departure of tourists, giving it an air of quiet resignation. Even the colorful Mexican tiles and crafts sold in the shops near the border crossing do not banish the gray atmosphere.

For someone standing at the fence, it is difficult to imagine what Nogales was like before the 1880s, when the city was a celebrated connection point between the Sonora Railway and the Arizona and New Mexico Railway, linking the two nations. In some ways Nogales was a victim of its own success. By the turn of the twentieth century, there was so much movement back and forth that the town was divided by a sixty-foot cleared strip of land which permitted authorities on both sides to better monitor the comings and goings of residents and visitors alike.[1] Those people would have been not just Mexicans or Americans, but an international mix, including people from Europe and China, who came to work on the rails or in nearby mines, as well as Native Americans. Their lives may well have involved crossing the border on a regular, perhaps daily, basis. Borderlands by their nature are zones of interaction. Some of it is positive—trade, cultural exchange, linguistic innovation—while other aspects are less desirable, not least illicit commerce, racism, and violence. Borders require certain kinds of flexibility, among them the ability to speak multiple languages, calculate more than one currency, or assume different identities. They also, at times, demand demarcation and even militarization. Borders can be a potent reminder of power and possession. These divisions are also, as Juan Poblete has pointed out, something people can carry within as they go about their everyday life, an "internalized border zone."[2]

Today the security fence cuts across that old clearing, with Nogales, Arizona, a city of about twenty thousand, on one side, and its southern Sonoran neighbor, now more than ten times larger, spreading out to the south. This stretch of fence is a physical reminder of the long and often troubled history between the two nations, calling to mind the blunt assessment by the Nobel Prize–winning Mexican author Octavio Paz that the United States and Mexico are "condemned to live alongside each other."[3] Or, in the more graphic description of the scholar and poet Gloria Anzaldúa, the border is *"una herida abierta"*—an open wound—and a place set up "to distinguish *us* from *them*."[4]

Given that the entirety of the Americas was shaped by the arrival of Europeans, the demographic demolition of indigenous communities, and the use of African slavery, what constitutes *us* and *them*? Lines on a map? Catholicism against Protestantism? The Spanish language instead of English? The myth of "American exceptionalism" has for too long eclipsed other ways of contemplating the trajectory of U.S. history, even down to the use of "American." As the Spanish historian José Luis Abellán explained in his book *La idea de América* (The Idea of America), when a Spaniard used the term "America," it traditionally referred to

Latin America—as it also did for people living there—but "when an American speaks of America, he refers to his own country, the United States."[5]* Now that usage of "America" dominates, but a return to its old meaning might be useful. Some historians have long argued that the United States is part of wider Latin America, in studies ranging from Herbert Eugene Bolton's "Epic of Greater America" in the 1930s to Felipe Fernández-Armesto's more recent assessment that the United States "is—and has to be—a Latin American country."[6] Thinking about the United States in this way can help make sense of a past that goes far beyond the boundary markers at the United States–Mexico border and instead focuses on the longer hemispheric connections, from Canada to the tip of Chile.

Even when we accept that the United States is part of a larger Latin American community, this still leaves the question of who is Hispanic and, correspondingly, who is American. The term "Hispanic" is being employed here in part to express a sense of continuity, as the word reaches back to the Roman past (*Hispania*) and forward to the census-taking present. It is at once a panethnic label—the worlds of Europeans, Africans, Asians, and Amerindians were all transformed by the arrival of the Spanish in the Americas—as well as one that today serves as a marketing category.[7] It has a long past, yet its current incarnation is the product of constant reinvention.

For the most part, people from Latin American countries identify themselves by their nation of birth: Cuban, Colombian, Venezuelan. As soon as they come to the United States, they often find themselves categorized as Hispanic or Latino/a, or the more inclusive Latinx.** This

---

* This book will use the term "Anglo" when referring to white, English-speaking people within the United States. Also, whenever possible, specific Native American names will be used, with the term "Indian" employed to convey a more general sense.

** There is a long and heated debate about nomenclatures, with Hispanic falling out of favor. There has been some criticism of the word "Hispanic," the most serious being that it is exclusionary because it leaves out people of African, Asian, and indigenous origin. At the same time some people think it covers anyone with roots in a Spanish-speaking nation. Interestingly, a 2017 book, *Keywords for Latina/o Studies*, which has sixty-three short essays about a single term, omits the word "Hispanic" altogether, with perhaps the closest term being a chapter on Latinidad/es, though as this essay's author points out, this word, too, has come under fire for homogenizing the diversity of an entire hemisphere.

modern usage is in large part an identity created in the United States and one that brings a certain uniformity—though also vital political clout—to a diverse group of people. Even the assumption that people in Latin America are Spanish-speakers is misplaced, as there are a wide variety of Amerindian languages spoken across the continent. The use of the term "Hispanic" in this book is a way to pick at, challenge, and understand its meaning, and examine the historical forces that formed its linguistic evolution and social context.

Yet for those of Spanish-American origin who have long been in the United States, a reverse question could be asked: at what point are you allowed to *not* be Hispanic? People who are identified by the census as "Hispanic" might have a grandparent who arrived from Mexico or Cuba two generations ago, or might speak only a smattering of Spanish, but this is often met with an expectation that as recent arrivals they should be knowledgeable about their "heritage" and "traditions," which, by implication, are not Anglo-American.

Language, in particular, is no small matter. Are you Hispanic if you don't speak Spanish? The share of Hispanic people who speak Spanish at home has declined, with 73 percent speaking it in 2015, against 78 percent in 2006, according to a Pew Research Center study. Despite this drop, another poll of Hispanic people in 2015 found that for 71 percent of respondents, it was not necessary to speak Spanish in order to be considered Latino.[8] Despite these shifts, the overall number of Spanish-speakers in the United States remains a source of anxiety to those for whom "becoming American" means speaking English. Some 440 million people are native Spanish-speakers, while around 370 million are native English-speakers, and at least the same number again speak English as a second language. The United States is now second only to Mexico in the number of its Spanish-speakers, with 41 million speakers and nearly 12 million who say they are bilingual.* At the same time, thirty-one states—including Florida, Arizona, and California—have declared English their official language. There is a great deal of silence

---

* The U.S. Census Bureau estimates there will be 138 million Spanish-speakers by 2050, out of an overall population of around 430 million. The languages Spanish and English more or less dominate the Americas, with Portuguese running a close third at around 200 million people, and French a distant fourth. These are followed by a wide range of indigenous languages from across the hemisphere.

about this particular aspect of the Hispanic past, as if prohibiting the use of Castilian will somehow erase that history as well as resolve the contemporary issues. "We are never as steeped in history," the Haitian anthropologist Michel-Rolph Trouillot wrote in his classic *Silencing the Past*, "as when we pretend not to be."[9]

Alongside language is a question that permeates every pore of contemporary American life: race. In this seemingly endless obsession with physiognomy, a toxic hangover from slavery and Jim Crow, is "Hispanic" just another way of saying "not white"? Although scientific notions of "race" have been discredited, as a social force it continues to order society, placing hierarchies in everything from the organization of labor to the distribution of rights. Creating "whiteness" and granting access to it were—and remain—ways to create power and exert social control.[10] As the historian Nell Irvin Painter pointed out in *The History of White People*, race has no scientific basis and so "is an idea, not a fact, and its question demands answers from the conceptual rather than factual realm."[11] Race, at its most basic level, as sociologists Michael Omi and Howard Winant point out, is a way of "making up people." To them, the social development of the United States had been shaped by what they call "racialization," a process by which "racial meaning" is extended to "a previously racially unclassified relationship, social practice or group," in this case, Hispanic people.[12]

Historians, activists, novelists, and people in everyday life are trying to make sense of race, while the practice of putting people into racial categories continues. This is not unique to the United States. All Latin American nations share in the colonial legacy of racism, as, too, does Canada. In some places, including Mexico, it is a question of a person looking more indigenous or European. In others, like the Dominican Republic, it is about "blackness."[13] Even seemingly positive trends toward multiculturalism, or in Mexico *mestizaje*, have led to criticism that such color blindness continues to obscure structural inequalities and ongoing racism. A glance across the powerful and wealthy in Latin America shows the lightest-skinned often at the top. These different whitenesses sometimes do not translate, however, and many people find they go from being white in their home nation to being "Hispanic" or "brown" in the United States. "Brown confuses," Richard Rodriguez wrote in his memoir about race. "Brown forms at the border of contradiction," though with its mixture of Indian, African, and European, to Rodriguez brown is the true "founding palette."[14]

Equally muddied is the issue of "ethnicity," which overlaps with markers such as language or food. There is no clear consensus on where Hispanic people lie on this spectrum, or even how to pinpoint ethnicity. To the historian Alan Gallay, an ethnic identity "becomes apparent only when people are faced with an external threat that draws them together," a conclusion drawn from his research on Native Americans in the seventeenth century. For Gallay, ethnicity is "relational and situational" and thus there can be no "pure" ethnicities because even elements like religion or language are mutable.[15] In the context of Mexican-Americans, the historian George J. Sánchez has described ethnicity as being "not a fixed set of customs surviving from life in Mexico, but rather a collective identity that emerged from daily experience in the United States."[16] For the Californian journalist Carey McWilliams, writing in 1948, the terms "Anglo" and "Hispano" were simply "the heads and tails of a single coin, a single ethnic system; each term has a meaning only as the other is implied."[17]

Today, ethnicity remains as puzzling as race, and it, too, is often shaped by stereotypes. Are you still "Hispanic" if you speak only English, are Protestant, and don't care for tacos? Language, race, and ethnicity also overlap with the question of citizenship, and so inform one of the key underlying issues: belonging. This can lead to what the legal historian Mae Ngai has called "alien citizens," which she defined as "persons who are American citizens by virtue of their birth in the United States but who are presumed to be foreign by the mainstream of American culture and, at times, by the state." To Ngai, a type of foreignness can exist in one's own homeland, where one group, such as Hispanics, is deemed "illegitimate, criminal, and unassimilable." Despite being citizens, they are told they don't belong.[18]

Now turn this around: who does belong? Who is allowed to be American? Although it is a nation that puts an immigrant narrative at its core—a story that immediately shunted aside the history of black and Native American people—many of the groups who came to the United States in significant numbers have faced some sort of prejudice. Benjamin Franklin, for instance, was wary of the Germans, asking, "Why should

Pennsylvania, founded by the English, become a Colony of Aliens who will shortly be so numerous as to Germanise us?"[19] However, in the earliest days of nationhood—itself a political experiment—the United States needed to craft an identity. In some ways this was a reaction to Europe of the seventeenth and eighteenth centuries, which was a kaleidoscope of often warring kingdoms, city-states, and principalities.[20] For the fledgling United States, identity was also an existential question. Survival apart from the British empire depended on some sort of unity, not least because the strip of thirteen colonies along the Atlantic was surrounded by Native American nations and the encroaching Spanish and French. In formulating what the United States would be, one founder, John Jay, had this vision of the nation: "Providence has been pleased to give this one country to one united people, a people descended from the same ancestors, speaking the same language, professing the same religion."[21]

Like whiteness, being "American" was designed at some level to be exclusionary; it was built on Anglo and northern European ancestry, Protestantism, and, for the most part, speaking English. There was no place for the Indians or the enslaved Africans, or even southern Europeans. To J. Hector St. John de Crèvecoeur, a French immigrant who arrived in 1759 and was writing around the time of the American Revolution, "Americans" were "a mixture of English, Scotch, Irish, French, Dutch, Germans, and Swedes." Crèvecoeur, whose *Letters from an American Farmer* enjoyed a wide readership in Europe, considered these people to be "melted into a new race of men, whose labours and posterity will one day cause great changes in the world."[22]

By the nineteenth century, during a time of widespread Eastern and southern European immigration, southern Mediterraneans such as Italians and Greeks were considered not quite "white." Yet by the early twentieth century, Mexican laborers, who were in demand, were allowed, up to a point, to be "white." White, it appears, was a gray area. Italians are now considered white, but Mexicans usually are not. Like many of the categories that are bandied about—race, ethnicity, black, white, Latino—"American" is a social construction, supported by a scaffolding of historical precedent, tradition, legal structures, and government legislation. For all the talk of the melting pot or the salad bowl, for all the protests, Twitter feuds, and talking heads, the question of who is allowed to be American remains unresolved.

This book, then, is devoted to examining the construction of the Hispanic past. The story it outlines is an epic one. It could easily run into many volumes, so there will be no promises of an exhaustive account. There is also no glorification: the Spanish had plenty to be ashamed about. Not every event will be outlined; not every policy of every president will be dissected in detail. For the most part, Spain, Mexico, Cuba, and Puerto Rico are the places of focus, as they dominated the United States' relationship with its southern neighbors until the 1950s. Likewise, the stories of Native Americans, African-Americans, and Asian-Americans, who are an important part of this history, are necessarily curtailed, as is the connection with Brazil and Portuguese-speakers. Nor is there scope to consider the more mutual aspects of these long connections, namely the extent of U.S. influence in Latin America. However, the full bibliography (available at carriegibson.co.uk) offers a guide to more detailed reading.

In general, the route I take through this dense history has two parallel tracks. An interstate offers a narrative history of events and people from the arrival of the Spanish in the early sixteenth century to the present day. This is the story of *El Norte*. The back road, so to speak, is the cultural one. Dotted throughout the book are some observations about how the story of the Hispanic past is remembered, forgotten, or reinvented, reflecting its ever-shifting place in the nation's wider collective memory.

El Norte is organized chronologically, with four overlapping sections. The first starts with the arrival of the Spanish in North America. After all, for much of its early history, the United States was not a dominant power. It was a small, though troublesome, English-speaking fringe in a world that was dominated by Spain.[23] From there, the book moves into a second section, the independence period, as Spain's colonies became nations, looking at the relationship of the young United States with these new republics—especially Mexico—throughout the nineteenth century. This was a time of great upheavals, not least the Texas Revolution, the Mexican-American War, and the Spanish-American-Cuban War that closed out the nineteenth century.

The third part looks at the early decades of the twentieth century, especially immigration, as Mexicans, Cubans, and Puerto Ricans arrived in significant numbers. This is the period when the paths to the present become more recognizable, as stereotypes harden and parts of the social structure begin to shut out Hispanic people. This overlaps with the final section, which considers the changes in wider public attitudes and ideas about immigration after the Second World War—in which Hispanic-Americans played an important part—and the Cuban Revolution, the onset of NAFTA, and the current political climate.

T HE FIRST STOP, however, is not in El Norte, but on the small Bahamian island of San Salvador, where Christopher Columbus is thought to have landed in 1492. Although he is both admired and reviled across the continent, there is no telling the story of Spain in the Americas without Columbus.[24]

The Genoese navigator presented his plan for an expedition to the east to the powerful monarchs of Castile and Aragon, Isabel and Fernando, at an opportune moment. They had just finished a drive in Andalusia to expel what was left of the Moorish kingdoms from the Iberian Peninsula, and their victory in Granada in early 1492 ended the centuries-long Muslim era in Spain. The monarchs were buoyed by this triumph, and also interested in possible new sources of revenue to cover their costs.

Columbus, an experienced navigator, had been trying for years to raise money. He believed his calculations would eventually deliver him to the east—even though he would be sailing west—and to Cipangu, as Japan was labeled on early maps. There he would encounter all the riches this part of the world was said to contain. He finally secured the backing of the Catholic monarchs, organized his ships, and set sail, not realizing that he was thousands of miles off in his calculations. Rather than arriving in Japan, he spotted the Bahamas in October 1492. His initial encounter with the people there did not inspire him to linger—the sandy isle did not match his expectations of great eastern cities—and so his three ships pushed on, landing on Quisqueya. He claimed it for the crown, and renamed it Española (also called Hispaniola, today's Dominican Republic and Haiti). There he found enough evidence of gold to convince him to search for more.[25] Columbus had also been on a trading mission, and he would have been familiar with the sort of transactions between Africans and Portuguese that had been taking place for decades at the trading posts that dotted the West African coast, including exchanges of cloth, gold, weapons, and humans.

The arrival of Columbus and his men sowed the seeds of destruction for the indigenous way of life, and the initial friendliness and curiosity on the part of the people of Quisqueya soon turned to hostility and fear, as Columbus and his men started to enslave them or they fell ill with unfamiliar diseases. Columbus wanted to establish a colony and implement what became known as the *encomienda*.[26] This entitled the leaders of a successful expedition who had been given a grant, known as *encomenderos*, the right to collect tribute from the vanquished. In the case of Hispaniola, this required making deals or using force to exact tribute from the indigenous chiefs, whom the Spanish called *caciques*. Although some of it went into the crown's coffers, there could also be a vast personal reward for raising an expedition. Initial anger at the behavior of the Spanish was thought to have led to the disappearance of La Navidad, the first colony, on the north coast of the island, named to reflect its founding near Christmastime. Columbus had left thirty-nine men there and returned to Spain in January 1493 to show the king and queen what he had found, as well as to resupply. By the time he came back to Española in November 1493, the settlement was empty. Undeterred, Columbus moved farther east along the coast and established La Isabela, in honor of the queen, which survived.

Gold was not the only concern: there was also God. In exchange for the tribute the people of Quisqueya paid, the Spaniards offered them protection from any enemy and conversion to Christianity. To the minds of the crown and the conquistadores, this was a legitimate transaction; these Spaniards, as one historian put it, could "serve God, country, and themselves at the same time."[27]

Religious conversion was bound up with the colonization project for Spain and Portugal from the beginning. In 1493, Pope Alexander VI issued the bull *Inter Caetera*, which outlined this spiritual dimension, stipulating that on these voyages to non-Christian lands there must be "worthy, God-fearing, learned, skilled, and experienced men, in order to instruct the aforesaid inhabitants and residents in the Catholic faith."[28] The document also gave Spain and Portugal spheres of influence, and these demarcations were confirmed in 1494 by the Treaty of Tordesillas, which put the limit of the Portuguese boundary at 370 leagues (around 1,185 nautical miles) west of the Cape Verde Islands. Spain was given everything to the west of that line, which was the vast majority of the American landmass, with only the easternmost part of Brazil falling to the Portuguese. When these documents were being drawn up, the size of the area was speculative and the number of possible converts could scarcely have been imagined.[29] Although it is thought that no priests were on Columbus's first voyage, by the second, in September 1493, two or three Franciscans were aboard. From then on, religious orders became intimately involved in the conversion of the Americas.[30]

While the term "Spanish" is used as shorthand to describe Columbus's men, they were anything but; calling them Europeans—or at least Mediterraneans—is more accurate. Columbus, although long associated with Spain, had grown up in Genoa and spent much of his seafaring life sailing out of Portugal. The geographical boundaries of the Iberian Peninsula contained a broad mix of people, many of whom, including Catalans, Basques, and Galicians, as well as the Portuguese, would become part of the imperial project in the New World. Spanish, as an identity, did not exist in 1492. It developed over time, as crowns and kingdoms consolidated.[31] Indeed, as explorers pushed into new territories on the Central and South American landmass, they added to what were then considered kingdoms—not colonies—under the crown of Castile.[32] Part of what it meant to be a Spanish subject was forged in the colonies of the growing empire, as Catholicism and the use of Castilian (rather than other languages, such as Basque or Catalan) became integral to that identity. Also, within the space of Columbus's four voyages between 1492 and 1502, Spanish and indigenous people began to mix sexually, by desire, force, or pragmatism, and a group of people known as mestizos were born, blending together these worlds.

The Spanish managed to survive in Hispaniola, despite ongoing attacks from the island's indigenous communities, while the crown became alarmed by reports of conquistadores' abuse of the Amerindians.* Even Columbus fell afoul of the monarchs by granting land to men on the island without royal permission, and in 1499 Francisco de Bobadilla was dispatched to Hispaniola to replace Columbus as governor. The following year, in 1500, the crown issued a royal *cédula* (decree) that freed any Amerindian slaves who had been brought to Spain, although native people in the Caribbean could continue to be enslaved if they resisted conversion to Christianity.

Columbus died in Spain in 1506, clinging until the end to the belief that he had found the east, and never acknowledging what he had discovered. Perhaps this helps explain how it was the name of the Florentine navigator Amerigo Vespucci that began to appear on European maps. Vespucci, who explored in the late 1490s, challenged Columbus's claims. He also coined the phrase "New World" in his pamphlet *Mundus Novus*, in which he claimed there was undiscovered territory south of the equator.[33] His discoveries informed the 1507 map *Universalis Cosmographia*, attributed to the German cartographer Martin Waldseemüller, which labeled the landmass across the southern Atlantic "America."[34] Whatever the name, Europeans now had a foothold in these new lands.

---

* Accounts from the fifteenth century call the people of Hispaniola Taino, but this is possibly based on a misunderstanding of what they called themselves. Likewise, some of the inhabitants of the other islands were called Caribs. Both of those terms are still in use today, but more contemporary scholarship identifies them as members of the Arawak people.

Chapter 1

Santa Elena, South Carolina, ca. 1492–1550

At the southern tip of Parris Island, South Carolina, in the center of a silent grove of trees heavy with Spanish moss, sits a simple white monument. It reads:

Here stood
Charlesfort
Built 1562
By Jean Ribaut
For Admiral Coligny
A Refuge
For Huguenots
And to the
Glory of France

Reaching this point requires driving through the Carolina low country to the Marine Corps Recruit Depot that takes up most of the island. At the far southern end of the base, beyond a golf course, a tree-lined road connects the clubhouse to a small park. Just over a wooden footbridge that spans a dry creek bed is the shady spot where the monument stands. Erected in 1925, this historical marker was later joined by others dotted around the area, explaining how the Spanish spotted this bit of land in 1521, named it Santa Elena in 1526, and fought over it against the French, who arrived three decades later. Parris Island, where the Broad and Beaufort Rivers converge, is surrounded by tidal creeks, mosquitoes, and the dense, wet smell of alluvial mud. It seems an unlikely location to begin the story of the Spanish in North America, and in some ways it was.

The Spanish path to Santa Elena can be traced from Spain to Hispaniola, bouncing from island to island in the Caribbean, until it reaches Veracruz, Mexico. By the early 1500s, three men whose lives would be bound up with the creation of Spain's American empire had arrived in Hispaniola: Bartolomé de Las Casas, in 1502; Hernando Cortés, in 1504; and Juan Ponce de León, who had been part of Columbus's second voyage in 1493. They all had complicated journeys to the Americas and through life: Las Casas would undergo a famous conversion over the treatment of indigenous people; Cortés would take a gamble that had an unimaginable payoff; and Ponce would die a failure, though his exploits would live on, misunderstood and misremembered.

Ponce's career had an auspicious start. As a young man in Spain, where he was born in the Valladolid province sometime around 1474, he participated in the successful campaign against the Moors in Granada before joining Columbus. From there he became involved in the suppression of an indigenous uprising on Hispaniola, in Higüey in 1504, for which he was rewarded by being put in charge of the eastern territory.[1]

In 1507 Ponce asked Nicolás de Ovando, who had replaced Bobadilla as governor, for permission to make an expedition to a nearby island, Borikén (sometimes spelled Borinquén) or San Juan Bautista, as Columbus named it on his second voyage, which is today's Puerto Rico.[2] Ponce met with local chiefs and explored the coastline before returning to Hispaniola, where he obtained the necessary permissions to colonize the island. In doing so, he was entitled to a share of what was discovered— and he struck gold. Deals were soon made with *caciques* to force their people to work prospecting in the rivers or digging in mines, as well as growing crops in the fields to support the Spaniards, and so began the *encomienda* on that island.[3]

In 1509 Ponce was named governor of the island, a post he kept until it was contested by Diego Columbus, the admiral's son, who had convinced the courts in Madrid of his claim to his father's title of admiral and viceroy of the New World. With his newfound powers, he pushed Ponce out in 1511.[4] This was coupled with a large indigenous uprising in Puerto Rico, which killed at least two hundred Spaniards.[5] By this point Ponce had amassed enough wealth to undertake another expedition, and in 1512 he secured a royal grant for the right to colonize what was thought to be the island of Bimini, though once again Spanish geography would prove inaccurate.[6]

The impetus for Ponce's trip was to explore, but also to raid neighboring islands looking for Amerindians to enslave, a profitable enterprise.[7] As was customary, Ponce put up his own money. He gathered men in three ships, making their way from Puerto Rico to the Atlantic side of today's Florida. There are uncertainties about where they landed, but the consensus is somewhere between Ponte Vedra, just south of modern Jacksonville; and Melbourne, near modern Cape Canaveral, among the Ais (Ays) people.[8]

They arrived in April 1513 around the time of the Easter feast of flowers, Pascua Florida, so Ponce named the spot La Florida. This was the first known European encounter on this part of mainland North America, though other explorers, slavers, and shipwreck survivors very likely washed up before Ponce did. Initially he thought he was on an island, though he realized it was not the one he was seeking because it did not match his idea of Bimini's size. All the same, he claimed the territory for Spain.[9]

Ponce and his men then sailed south past Biscayne Bay, down to the Keys, rounding the tip of Florida, ending up in the Gulf of Mexico. Along the way they encountered the fierce currents of the Gulf Stream—the European discovery of which Ponce was later credited with making.[10] They landed in an area belonging to the Calusa people, around modern Fort Myers.[11] Although they stayed there a few weeks, the reception was hostile, resulting in a number of small skirmishes that were unpleasant enough to impel Ponce and his men to leave.

Some historians have suggested that Amerindians from Cuba who had fled during the Spanish colonization of that island in 1511 went to Florida, so Ponce and his men were not so foreign after all—the native peoples of Florida had been warned. Some of the earliest, albeit secondary, accounts of indigenous-European encounters in Florida back this up, claiming there were Native Americans who could speak Spanish. It would have meant that the Calusa had some inkling about what these foreigners wanted, and what they were capable of doing.[12] In this particular case, they wasted little time in driving Ponce and his men back to the Caribbean.

Ponce reported a version of his efforts in 1514, even sending the king
some gold from Puerto Rico to give the impression that the Florida expedition had been a success.[13] The ruse worked, and Ponce was granted the
title of *adelantado* (frontier governor) of La Florida the following year.
This name was a hangover from the *Reconquista* era—literally meaning
one who advanced troops or invaders, signifying the advance of the
Christian frontier and driving out the Moors. In the Americas, it granted
the right to organize an expedition to unknown lands, and then claim
and govern them for Spain. Ponce started making plans for his return.

HERNANDO CORTÉS, LIKE Ponce, flourished after leaving Hispaniola.
He was born around 1484 and grew up in the western Extremadura
region of Spain, the son of an hidalgo, or minor nobleman. He studied
law in Salamanca but later quit and sailed to Hispaniola around 1504.
Once on that island, he obtained the post of notary in Azúa, about
seventy miles west of Santo Domingo.[14] He stayed there for a few years
before joining Diego Velázquez de Cuéllar, who had also been on Columbus's second voyage, on an expedition to Cuba in 1511. Columbus had
sailed along the coast of the island he called Juana on his first voyage,
probably in honor of Princess Joanna (Juana). This name was inter-
changed with and eventually superseded by mentions of Cuba, coming
from Columbus's interpretation of what he thought the indigenous
people called the island. Soon *Cuba* began to appear on maps.[15]

Velázquez erected a settlement on the southeastern edge of the
island, near today's Baracoa, though the headquarters was moved to
a place they named Santiago de Cuba, on the southernmost coast.
Cortés served as secretary to Velazquéz for a few years and was later
a magistrate, or alcalde, in Santiago by 1517.[16] As had been the case
in Hispaniola and Puerto Rico, the indigenous people of Cuba had a
complex relationship with the Spanish, often leading to bloody clashes.
Subduing them was a formidable task, and the early colonial years
were brutal. Although Queen Isabel had attempted to temper the treatment of the Amerindians, considering them vassals who could not be
enslaved, violence was rife. Loopholes in the decrees the crown had

issued could be exploited, not least the enslavement of anyone who resisted conversion to Christianity.

Isabel died in 1504, and eight years passed before King Fernando turned his attention to how the indigenous people were being treated. The result was the 1512 Laws of Burgos.[17] These required that *encomenderos* treat the Indians who worked for them well, not beating them and ensuring they had enough to eat. To support more systematic efforts of Christian conversion, they also called for new Indian settlements to be put near Spanish towns, a practice that would cause a significant disruption to traditional patterns of living.[18]

With the fledgling colonies located so far from official oversight, abuses continued. The gap between what the crown wanted and what was happening on the ground was filled by a concept that developed in these early decades, known as *obedezco pero no cumplo*, "I obey but I do not comply," meaning that mandates from Spain were accepted but not followed to the letter, allowing officials to be flexible—in positive and negative ways—in dealing with orders coming from thousands of miles away by monarchs and advisers who never saw for themselves the challenges of this New World.

Around 1517, Governor Velázquez sent expeditions from Cuba to the nearby Yucatán Peninsula, to the west of the island. One party went ashore, in part to explore but also to find water, and they met the Maya who lived there. Although the Spanish might have been hoping to enslave some of them, the resulting encounter led to the death of fifty Spaniards and the capture of two. A second expedition landed on Cozumel, an island off the coast of the Yucatán, in 1518, with around two hundred men. Although they were attacked, they continued exploring the coast before returning to Cuba to report what they had seen.[19] It appeared to Velázquez that this land might be suitable for settlement, so he wrote to the crown to obtain the necessary permission.[20] In 1519, Velázquez ordered Cortés to further explore the Yucatán, but only to explore and trade, not colonize.[21] Cortés obeyed, but he was not necessarily going to comply. He had other ideas and, gathering some five hundred men, he set sail in eleven ships.

Cortés was taking a gamble. By not waiting for royal permission—doing so would have revealed his plans to Velázquez, who had the same goal—he risked forfeiting everything he thought he might find.[22] He first sailed to Cozumel and soon discovered two Spaniards living on the mainland. Gonzalo Guerrero had married a local woman and had no interest in returning to life with Europeans, while Jerónimo de Aguilar could speak Yucatec Mayan and joined Cortés, his skills as a translator later proving an important asset.[23]

They had a rocky start. A battle against the Maya ensued and cost Cortés some thirty-five soldiers, but in the end he received gifts of loyalty, including a female slave thought to be named Malintzin. She could speak Chontal Mayan and Nahuatl, and would become far more to Cortés than just his translator.* She, along with Aguilar, provided critical linguistic links as Cortés continued to explore along the Gulf coast, now some way south and west of the Yucatán Peninsula.[24] He came to a stop on Good Friday in April 1519, at a promising harbor near an island the Spanish called San Juan de Ulúa. Cortés and his men went ashore, and they were met within the first couple of weeks by representatives of Moteuczoma, the ruler of the Mexica confederacy, which later accounts described as the "Aztec empire."[25]

This confederacy consisted of many different groups, but at its core was a triple alliance among the Nahuatl-speaking Mexica people, whose rise to power began in the fifteenth century, and the people of Texcoco and Tlacopan.[26] The Maya and Mixtec-speaking people to the south were also connected, and the confederacy had a wide reach. These societies had their aristocracies and, like European kingdoms, complex social hierarchies. A powerful emperor was elected from within the alliance, though tradition dictated it was a Mexica man. Cortés quickly found out, however, that there was no uniform loyalty or support across the confederacy, something he learned after speaking to the Totonac people he had landed among.[27]

During this time, Cortés and his men set up a camp on land near where they met with the Mexica representatives. Although various accounts of Moteuczoma written by Europeans claim the emperor had seen prophecies that involved the arrival of a white-skinned god, called Quetzalcóatl, or that there had been other cosmological portents indicating the fall of the Mexica, they may well have been later embellishments.[28] There is much

---

* She was later enshrined in history as Marina, her Spanish name, but also known as La Malinche.

uncertainty about what Moteuczoma knew, why he made the decisions that he did, and how the Spanish chose to interpret them. In some tellings, Mexica representatives found Cortés and brought him gifts, staying among his men for about two weeks, in part to find out more about these strangers. Other interpretations cast this as an effort to get rid of the Spanish, while some consider this visit a prelude to meeting the emperor in the capital.[29]

As Cortés explored, his men were fracturing. Some wanted to stick to the letter of Velázquez's original order to only explore and trade, while others were more ambitious.[30] Cortés decided to establish a settlement in late June, naming it Villa Rica de la Vera Cruz (today's Veracruz), or Rich Town of the True Cross, after the Good Friday landing. He appointed judges, councilmen, a sheriff, and a treasurer who, in turn, appointed Cortés the captain and chief justice under the authority of the king, a shrewd way to establish his legitimacy. By July, there was a rudimentary town in place, and a ship was dispatched for Spain, bearing the "royal fifth," treasures they had obtained of fine cotton cloth, feathers, and objects crafted of gold for the king. Also being carried to the court was a narrative of the expedition and the petition of the town council seeking royal confirmation of its actions.[31] After that vessel sailed, some of the uneasy members of the expedition began to plan a return to Cuba. Once Cortés heard what was afoot, he ordered the remaining ships to be dismantled. There would be no turning back.[32]

By early August, Cortés began his overland trek to the capital city Tenochtitlán (today's Mexico City). Over the months that followed, he and his men encountered various Mesoamerican peoples, confirming their suspicions that the empire was not as unified at it might have seemed. The Totonac were not the only disgruntled subjects: the Mexica confederacy had been built on the conquest of other peoples. They were forced to pay tribute but, crucially, local leaders and regimes were left in power. What had held the confederacy together was force. It was believed to have the power to enforce its political will, as embodied by the emperor. Cortés saw the weaknesses, but he needed to win over allies. He faced a tough battle with the Tlaxcalteca people, who were hostile to the Mexica but also suspicious of the Spanish. In the skirmishes and ambushes that followed, Cortés saw the skill of their army as the Spanish casualties mounted. He realized they needed to be on the same side and eventually brokered a peace.[33] From there, Cortés headed with around five thousand

Tlaxcaltec soldiers to Cholula, where the Spanish faced wary Cholulteca, whom Cortés hoped to bring onside. Around this time, rumors arose of a plot involving Mexica troops aiming to massacre Cortés and his men, so he attacked first, killing thousands, though this is the Spanish version of events. Subsequent interpretations have revealed no such plan, though the end result was a firm alliance with the Tlaxcalteca.[34]

Cortés arrived in Tenochtitlán on November 8, 1519, and the world he entered was on a much larger and more urbanized scale than anything he had yet encountered. For a start, Tenochtitlán was a wonder in itself, sitting on an island on placid Lake Texcoco in the verdant Valley of Mexico, surrounded by mountains and more than a mile above sea level. The thin, cool air would have been a marked change from the always-present pressure of tropical humidity at sea level. The city was connected to the land around the lake by a system of causeways that could be removed to stop invasions. The capital was estimated to have a population of around 150,000 by the time the Spanish arrived, making it far larger than any European city—Seville, for instance, numbered around forty thousand people at the time.[35] The Valley of Mexico was home to an estimated 1 million to 2.65 million people.[36]

In October 1520, Cortés reported to the crown that he "[could] not describe one hundredth part of all the things which could be mentioned" about Tenochtitlán, before later attempting to relate the scale of the markets:

> There is also one square twice as big as that of Salamanca, with arcades all around, where more than sixty thousand people come each day to buy and sell, and where every kind of merchandise produced in these lands is found: provisions as well as ornaments of gold and silver, lead, brass, copper, tin, stones, shells, bones, and feathers. . . . Finally, besides those things which I have already mentioned, they sell in the market everything else to be found in this great land, but they are so many and varied that because of their great number and because I cannot remember many of them nor do I know what they are called I shall not mention them.[37]

Cortés was also at the beginning of what would be a great biological exchange—he had no vocabulary for much of what he saw, and likewise the Mexica were not yet familiar with the wheat, cattle, pigs, and horses the Spaniards brought from Europe. Nor would they have names for the unfamiliar invisible and deadly microbes that accompanied the Spanish.[38]

After arriving in the city, Cortés accepted an offer to meet Moteuczoma and was taken to the court, a vast compound of palaces, apartments, libraries, warehouses, and even a zoo.[39] Cortés was received with much courtesy and was shown the wonders of the capital by the emperor. In return, the Spaniard decided to take Moteuczoma hostage.[40] Kidnapping a high-profile, non-Christian prisoner was a tactic that Spaniards had earlier used against Muslims.[41] To Cortés, this was the final part of a legitimate imperial transfer of power from Moteuczoma to Spain's Carlos V, Holy Roman emperor and successor to Fernando II who died in 1516.[42]

Into this delicate situation came Pánfilo de Narváez. Velázquez sent him in the spring of 1520 to arrest Cortés for insubordination after hearing what had happened from the crew on the ship that had left Veracruz, which had called at Cuba on its way to Spain. Cortés was forced to leave Moteuczoma under guard and settle matters with Narváez. In the end, Cortés convinced many of Narváez's nine hundred men to join him, but while he had been away, Pedro de Alvarado, who had been left in charge, launched an attack on an unarmed crowd in the Great Temple during Toxcatl, a religious celebration.[43] By the time Cortés returned to the capital he found the Spaniards under siege. In an attempt to stop the assault, he convinced Moteuczoma to appear in front of his people. According to some accounts, a stone thrown by a person in the crowd struck the emperor on the head, and he died three days later; other accounts pin his death on the Spanish.[44] There was little left for Cortés to do but retreat. On June 30, 1520, as they made their way out of the capital, he and his men, including Tlaxcalteca allies, faced an onslaught which the Spanish later called la Noche Triste (the Night of Sorrows) because some four hundred Spaniards and thousands of Tlaxcalteca soldiers were killed. Cortés survived but he and his men retreated to Tlaxcallan, roughly today's state of Tlaxcala, which is east of Mexico City, to regroup.

The Tlaxcalteca, over the subsequent centuries, were reduced to historical bit players, though they had leading roles in the events that followed, not least their contribution of more than thirty thousand soldiers.[45] The Huexotzinca, Cholulteca, and Chalca provided another thirty thousand.[46] While Cortés did not have the numbers among his own men, he did have technology, including cannons and guns. At the same time, European diseases began to spread, giving Cortés a silent and unrealized weapon.[47] Indeed, a smallpox outbreak killed Moteuczoma's successor, his brother Cuitláhuac, in October, leaving the next emperor, Cuauhtémoc, to prepare for war.[48] Thousands of other people in the Valley of Mexico soon succumbed to diseases that would eventually kill millions.*

By May 1521, the offensive by Cortés and his allies had begun in earnest. It is not clear how many troops he had, but estimates range from one hundred thousand to five hundred thousand. Cortés was also aided by a plague sweeping through the capital. One indigenous account later described the outbreak as lasting "for seventy days, striking everywhere in the city and killing a vast number of our people. Sores erupted on our faces, our breasts, our bellies; we were covered with agonizing sores from head to foot."[49] Before long, Cortés and his men had reentered Tenochtitlán; they held it under siege until the surrender came on August 13, 1521. After justifying his actions to a Spanish crown that grudgingly accepted the conquest, Cortés acquired some of the largest landholdings in Mexico, which would become a source of immense wealth. This, however, was not enough to calm his restlessness, and the years to come would find him searching for another Tenochtitlán.[50]

Spain soon placed this territory firmly in the constellation of its kingdoms, calling it Nueva España, or New Spain. By 1526, a decree had put all the land under the crown, the mining of silver deposits had begun, and taxes and Indian tribute were collected.[51] Shortly before this, in 1524, a Council of the Indies had been formally established to advise the king on governing these new lands. In addition, the Casa de Contratación (House of Trade), which had been established in Seville earlier, in 1503, now controlled with a firm grip all the trade to the Americas.[52]

In New Spain, the military was now bolstered by the Tlaxcalteca, former members of the Mexica confederacy, as well as Maya, Zapotecs, and other groups, which they needed because only about half of the estimated two thousand Spaniards with Cortés managed to survive.[53] Besides, these Spaniards had little interest in being soldiers: they were looking to become

---

* Mexico's population before the arrival of the Spanish was thought to be around ten million, though some estimates reach as high as twenty-five million; within a century, it would drop below one million.

landowners, as Cortés had done. In these early years, a bureaucracy also took shape, one that would wield far more power with its pens than the conquistadores did with their swords, over both Spaniards and Indians.[54] A judicial *audiencia* was set up and a president appointed by 1528, and layers of official posts were created for the towns and cities.[55] In 1535 New Spain was proclaimed a vice-royalty, with the viceroy—appointed from Spain for a term that varied in length—to represent the king. New Spain was not a colony but part of the Spanish crown.[56]

Alongside the political world, the physical one also changed. During his final push, Cortés razed much of the capital. Soon, stone by stone, the Spanish placed their present atop the Mexica past.[57] In the capital, the Templo Mayor, dedicated to the gods of rain and war, Tláloc and Huitzilopochtli, was destroyed. Next to this sacred site rose a Catholic cathedral, which today sits on the main plaza, known as the Zócalo, in Mexico City.[58]

Although Tenochtitlán provided the Spanish with a useful foundation for their city, it was Santo Domingo, the capital of Hispaniola, that had become the model for the urban colonial center. In general, cities and towns were to be the cornerstone of conquest. The built environment of these places, and the many administrators who governed them, reflected the Spanish familiarity with urban living, as well as a preoccupation with keeping order. The maze-like narrow streets of Muslim Andalusian cities, such as Seville or Granada, were thought to be counterproductive for such aims. Instead, a grid system was deemed more useful. This had been employed with success in Santo Domingo, and so it became the template—refined and adapted over time—for Spanish cities in the Americas, whose number began to grow throughout the sixteenth century.[59] Not surprisingly, Cortés's exploits had spurred other conquistadores to search for their own Tenochtitláns in South America. Francisco Pizarro began his campaign against the Inca empire in Peru in 1530, and within fifty years, Spain claimed the length of the continent for itself, from the Caribbean coast through the Andes Mountains and into Chile and Argentina. The way cities were built across these diverse areas followed a form that was later enshrined in Spain's *Laws of the Indies*. Urban settlements were to have a main plaza, around which would be a grid of streets. The governor's house, administrative offices, and a church would occupy the plaza, and the most prominent families lived nearby.

The lower members of society—often indigenous—lived the farthest away from the plaza in houses made of wood or other poorer materials.[60]

The conversion of souls to Catholicism continued to be a priority, and it, too, would be an important pillar used to reinforce colonial authority. In keeping with the religious nature of conquest, Cortés requested missionaries to come to New Spain.[61] By 1524, a symbolic 12 Franciscans had arrived in Veracruz, growing to around 380 by 1550.[62] Dominicans followed in 1526, and Augustinians in 1533. By 1559, there were around eight hundred friars in New Spain.[63] The Franciscans were part of what is known as the regular clergy—from the Latin *regula*, meaning rule— who were priests and friars of religious orders. They were joined by the secular clergy—from *saeculum*, signifying of the world, or not living in cloisters—consisting of parish priests up to bishops and archbishops. In addition, the Spanish crown and not the pope made appointments of bishops and archbishops to the Americas, and it could collect the Church's tithe income.

At first, the majority of missionaries were from religious orders, though the number of secular clergy rose as more dioceses were established. Although the orders were united in their efforts to convert, they had diverse reasons for doing so. Some Franciscans, for instance, believed that once the "last Gentiles" were found and converted—and the Mexica people fitted the bill—this would trigger the end-times, followed by a postmillennial heaven on earth.[64] Whether they were secular or regular, conversion was difficult work for priests, hampered by many factors, not least linguistic ones. In order to swell the numbers of converts, mass baptisms were performed—sometimes on hundreds or even thousands of people at once, who may or may not have been clear on what was taking place.[65] Priests tried to learn indigenous languages, such as Náhuatl, and some even wrote grammars and catechisms in these languages, while the new Christians were required to attend services and learn certain prayers.[66] Amerindians may have lived in or near missions, but under the sixteenth-century policy of *reducción*, they were expected to form Christian, indigenous towns; Spain's way of exerting control over often disparate groups was to forcibly resettle hundreds of thousands of people.

Despite all these changes, some indigenous beliefs and practices took longer to eradicate. Religious objects, such as small statues that depicted or symbolized Mexica deities, were considered pagan and often destroyed, and spiritual leaders who practiced banned rituals were punished. Yet indigenous forms proved adaptable. Perhaps one of the best-known examples of this in Mexico is the Virgin of Guadalupe. According to the myth, in 1531 an Indian peasant named Juan Diego claimed to have experienced an apparition in the countryside near Mexico City. The woman said she was the Virgin Mary and asked for a church to be built there. Diego reported what he saw to the bishop, who asked for miracles as proof. Diego gathered flowers that were not typical of the area and put them in his cape to take to the bishop. Once the blooms fell to the ground, the cape was left with an image of Mary; this is now a national symbol of Mexico. The church today is built upon the Mexica shrine to Tonantzin, the goddess mother of the earth.[67] This incarnation of Mary was later interpreted as an embodiment of Mexicanness—that she was a unique symbol of the nation and this merging of ancient and modern, Catholic and indigenous.[68]

THE LEGACY OF Bartolomé de Las Casas in the Americas was no less dramatic than that of Cortés or Ponce, but his odyssey was spiritual. Las Casas's father, Pedro, joined Columbus on his second voyage in 1493, when Bartolomé was a boy of nine.[69] Pedro returned in 1498 and by 1502, Bartolomé was on his way to Santo Domingo, sailing in Nicolás de Ovando's fleet.[70] Las Casas began to oversee the encomienda his father had set up, though at the same time he had started the religious journey that would later lead him into the priesthood.[71] Las Casas could not fail to see the brutality the Spanish were inflicting on the people of Hispaniola. He witnessed for himself the 1504 slaughter of the Indians in Higüey that Juan Ponce de Léon had participated in, later writing that the Spanish conquistadores were each "trying to top the others on novel ways to spill blood."[72] He was not alone in his discomfort. The Dominicans who had arrived on the island in 1510 were growing concerned. In 1511, the Dominican friar Antonio de Montesinos delivered a scathing indictment of Spanish behavior toward the island's inhabitants, asking the congregation in Santo Domingo: "Are these Indians not men? Do they not have rational souls? Are you not obliged to love them as yourselves!"[73] The sermon stirred instant controversy on the island and within Las Casas, whose transformation was well under way and who may have already been ordained by this point.[74]

In 1512, Las Casas joined an expedition to Cuba led by Diego Velázquez, later ending up with Pánfilo de Narváez, who was also taking part. He wrote about this period much later in his life, reflecting that "these people [Spaniards] never abandoned a place until they had laid it waste and killed off the Indians."[75] Las Casas spent two years with Narváez, as he described it, "securing the island," which for him meant trying to convert people peacefully. At the same time, Velázquez kept rewarding him with Indians for his *encomienda*.[76] He saw the hypocrisy of his own position and began to renounce his holdings as an *encomendero*, deciding instead by 1514 to devote himself to ending the scourge of violence the Spanish had inflicted on Amerindians, an effort that later earned him the title "Protector of the Indians."

Las Casas, like many of the friars, was concerned that indigenous people were often characterized as enemies of Christianity; he deemed this unfair given that they had never heard of the faith.[77] In one attempt to address this, the crown had issued the Requirement (*Requerimiento*) in 1512. This legal concoction was to be read out loud by conquistadores to any future subjects. The document was supposed to explain to the Indians the Catholic and monarchist world of the Spaniards and the perils of not submitting to it. If the Indians were thus informed and did not acquiesce, then any fighting could be considered a just conflict, the vanquished could be taken as slaves, and their property could be seized. This document was put to use as the Spanish continued their march into Central and South America.[78]

It was not enough for Las Casas, and burning with desire for reform, he left for Spain in 1515, accompanied by Montesinos, with the intention of gaining an audience with the ailing king Fernando to convince him that the practice of *encomienda* needed to stop.[79] By the end of the year, he had related to the king the brutalities that were taking place on the island, despite the Laws of Burgos. Fernando listened, but nothing resulted from that meeting, and the king died soon afterward.[80] The following year, 1516, Las Casas wrote a *Remedio*, or Remedy, for the Indians, while he had the attention of two powerful advisers and regents to the sixteen-year-old king Carlos V: Adrian of Utrecht, who would become pope in 1522, and Cardinal Francisco Ximénez de Cisneros.[81] Las Casas laid out his vision for saving the Indians, though one of those suggestions would come back to haunt him. In that "remedy" he suggested that "blacks, or other slaves" be used in the mines instead of Indians.

In the same manner that the first conquistadores had enslaved Amerindian people and brought some of them to Spain to work or be sold, the Portuguese had done so with Africans from the west coast of the continent since the mid-1400s. Muslim North Africans—often referred to as Moors—had been a precursor to this, as they had been captured on the basis of not being Christian.[82] This continued into the sixteenth century, and West Africans bought and sold on the Iberian Peninsula began to appear in Hispaniola by 1502. This was followed by licensing of such a trade in 1513, by which point it is likely enslaved people were brought directly from West Africa to the Caribbean, contravening the existing trade rules. By 1518, licensing for the direct transport of slaves was in place, and thousands of enslaved people could now be taken to all parts of Spain's growing empire.[83] Such were the growth and scale of African slavery that by 1547 Las Casas was forced to speak out against the slave trade, though this required another personal conversion.[84] This time, it was triggered by his reading chronicles of Portuguese involvement in Africa. He realized that the enslavement there was not under the "just" conditions he had assumed. It occurred to him that he could not call for an end to Indian bondage without doing the same for Africans; he later wrote that he "regretted the advice" he gave the king.[85] Between 1514 and 1600, some 250,000 enslaved Africans were forced to disembark in Spain's Caribbean and mainland colonies, with many destined to work in gold and silver mines during this period.[86] By the 1570s, Mexico City alone had at least eight thousand enslaved Africans.[87]

Long before his change of heart about African slavery, Las Casas had returned to the Americas in 1516, and he spent much of the following decades traveling back and forth to Spain, drawing attention to the plight of the indigenous people. Although his intention was to end their suffering, he often discussed Amerindians in paternalistic terms, as did other writers at this time, describing them as "the simplest people in the world—unassuming, long-suffering, unassertive, and submissive," as well as being "among the least robust of human beings," with "delicate constitutions."[88] Yet he was livid about the abuses they suffered. Las Casas wrote to Carlos V in 1542 about their treatment in his *Brevísima relación de la destrucción de las Indias* (*Short Account of the Destruction of the Indies*). He minced no words in explaining how Spanish conquistadores "forced their way into native settlements, slaughtering everyone they found there . . . they hacked them to pieces, slicing open their bellies with swords as though they were so many sheep herded into a pen."[89] Those who survived often fared little better as laborers, where "the men died down the mines from overwork and starvation, and the same was true of the women who perished out on the estates."[90]

The crown was moved to issue the 1542 *New Laws of the Indies* (*Las Leyes Nuevas*), which was intended, once again, to promote better treatment of the indigenous people. Furthermore, the laws aimed to phase out the *encomienda* when the titleholder died and free any Indians on it.[91] This legislation was unsurprisingly not popular among *encomenderos* and triggered a revolt by a group of them in Peru, leading to the decapitation of the viceroy. Parts of the *New Laws* were later amended to stave off similar rebellions elsewhere, including New Spain. Despite the weakening of the legislation, the *encomienda* system gradually declined over the course of the seventeenth century.

At the same time, Spain's enemies read Las Casas's account with as much interest as Carlos V, but for a very different reason: it exposed the cruelty of Catholic Spaniards. The *Short Account* was published in Spain in 1552, and the text circulated around Europe, with the first Dutch translation appearing in 1578, and the English in 1583.[92] By 1598, the Latin edition, published by Theodore de Bry in Germany, included a number of engravings depicting violent scenes, such as native people being hanged and burned.[93] The Habsburg monarchy, which now controlled Spain and its colonies, also included parts of Italy, the Netherlands, and, for a time, Portugal (1580–1640).[94] When Felipe II came to the Spanish throne in 1556, he ruled over a vast but troublesome realm.*

The mixture of religious tension, imperial envy, and the vivid account painted by Las Casas helped to lay the basis of what became known as the *leyenda negra*, or "Black Legend," a concept that would color the

---

* His uncle Fernando took the title of Holy Roman emperor and ruled over the Habsburg lands in Austria and Germany.

exploits of conquistadores and darken Spain's reputation for centuries. In its simplest form, it was the allegation that Catholic conquistadores were uniquely evil and bloodthirsty—an accusation which overlooked similar abuses committed by Protestant Europeans in the Americas— but it also took issue with the reach of Felipe II's powers, and with the Catholic orthodoxy defended by the Spanish Inquisition, an institution one English observer described as a "dreadful engine of tyranny."[95]

The writings of Las Casas gave Spain's opponents plenty of ammunition, such as his claim that "the real reason the Christians have murdered on such a vast scale is purely and simply greed. They have set out to line their pockets with gold."[96] The Dutch took a particular interest in the Black Legend, in part because by the 1560s they were growing increasingly frustrated with Felipe II. In 1568 the Eighty Years' War began, and these images of brutal conquistadores helped fuel propaganda against Spain. Pamphlets likened subjects of Felipe II in the Low Countries to the indigenous slaves in the Americas. As the conflict wore on, some of the writings by the Dutch expressed a fear that they, too, would meet a violent end, as the Amerindians had.[97]

Las Casas returned to New Spain to take up the post of bishop of Chiapas in 1545. A few years later, however, he crossed the Atlantic once again and by 1550 he found himself defending the Amerindians in front of the Royal Council, in Valladolid, Spain. The issue of legitimate conquest was still unresolved and continued to attract the leading legal minds in Spain.[98] Juan Ginés de Sepúlveda was one such scholar, and he defended Spain's behavior in his *Democrates Alter* of 1547, though he had never crossed the Atlantic.* *Democrates Alter* espoused a belief in a "natural" order, whereby "the perfect and most powerful rule over the imperfect and weaker."[99] In arguing that "there [be] some who by nature are masters and others who by nature slaves," Sepúlveda implied the Indians could be enslaved, not least because they were "barbarous and inhumane peoples."[100] Such a view incurred the angry criticism of Las Casas and his supporters. In the resulting furor, the publication of the work was halted—it had originally been circulated in manuscript form—and a formal debate was arranged at Valladolid,

---

* *Democrates Alter* was not published until two centuries after Sepúlveda's death.

where Las Casas and Sepúlveda would present their respective cases, though not in front of each other.[101]

Las Casas took his turn before the fourteen jurists assembled in August 1550 and argued over five days—to Sepúlveda's three hours the day before—that people who had not been exposed to Christianity should not be punished for it, going on to point out that despite the "enormous and extraordinary crimes" the Spanish perpetrated against the native people, many still "embraced Christian truth very willingly," which he considered "a great miracle."[102] There was another session in the spring of 1551, but, in the end, it was an intellectual draw with no clear victor.[103] The great moral and intellectual question of the day remained unanswered.

Las Casas also devoted a great deal of his life to his monumental history of the Indies (*Historia de las Indias*), which he stipulated was to be published forty years after his death.[104]* By the time he died, in 1566, the contours of colonialism were changing. The destruction of the native populations and the continued arrival of Africans had transformed the West Indies, while Spanish settlement continued through Central America and the Andean regions of South America. One area, however, remained undisturbed: the impenetrable Florida.

———

PONCE'S FIRST ATTEMPT to establish a settlement in La Florida ended in failure, but this did little to deter others from exploring the coastline and carrying out slaving missions. Indeed, at one point in his capacity as *adelantado* of Florida, Ponce filed a lawsuit against Diego Velázquez for illegally bringing back three hundred slaves from his territory.[105] In 1519, the Spanish explorer Alonso Álvarez de Pineda sailed from Jamaica, then still a Spanish colony, and traveled around the Gulf coast of Florida, Alabama, Mississippi, and New Spain. He may have been the first European to see the Mississippi River, which he called the Espíritu Santo, a name that was used on maps for a time.[106] While another century would pass before more accurate guides emerged, each successful voyage

---

* It would take much longer than that—the manuscript, with its unflattering descriptions of Spanish imperialism, did not see the light of publication until 1875.

brought explorers one step closer to understanding the unknown land to the north. On the 1519 map of the Gulf that is attributed to Álvarez de Pineda, the outline of La Florida and its connection to a larger mainland are clear, ending the notion of its being an island.[107] Álvarez de Pineda may have also encountered, some 350 miles north of Veracruz, a river which became known as the Pánuco River, returning there to put a settlement near what would later be the city of Tampico, though this initial effort was destroyed by the local Huastec people.[108]

Ponce was drawn back to Florida in 1521, organizing another expedition of two ships, paid for once again with his own money. In a letter to Carlos V, he explained, "I am returning to that island [Florida] to settle, with great pleasure and the will of God."[109] He returned to Florida's southwest coast and, as on his previous attempt, he was soon fighting with the Calusa. This time, however, Ponce was wounded by an arrow and taken to Cuba, where he developed gangrene and died in July 1521. That was not the end of Ponce, of course. He lives on in the still popular myth that he was on the hunt for a magical wellspring that would provide the waters of eternal life. Despite all tales to the contrary, Ponce was not looking for this Fountain of Youth. The legend, however, started early, in Spanish chronicler Gonzalo Fernández de Oviedo y Valdés's *Historia general y natural de las Indias* in 1535, and from there became forever associated with Ponce.[110]

Around the same time as Ponce's final venture, a Spanish ship landed near Winyah Bay (near present-day Myrtle Beach), on the feast of John the Baptist in June 1521.[111] It was under the charge of Pedro de Quejo, who first spotted land. He waited for the caravel commanded by Francisco Gordillo to join him. The men and some of the crew went ashore, where they were met by a group of Indians. The Spaniards captured some of these people and took them on board their ships—they had, after all, intended this to be a slaving mission.[112] When Gordillo and Quejo returned to Hispaniola, they had with them a young man who was probably from the Catawba people and whom they named Francisco de Chicora.[113] El Chicorano, as he was sometimes called, was quick to learn Spanish and he also was baptized. He was taken to Spain where he regaled the court, including the chronicler Peter Martyr, about his homeland, a place that would take on mythical dimensions.[114] El Chicorano told them how it was fertile and full of riches, including gold, whetting the Spaniards' appetite to establish a colony in this place, which they called Chicora.

Lucas Vázquez de Ayllón, a member of the judicial *audiencia* in Santo Domingo and the organizing force behind the expedition that had brought Francisco de Chicora to the island, echoed these claims, describing it as "new Andalusia." He managed to obtain the necessary contract for exploration and settlement by 1523.[115] While he was making preparations, he sent Quejo to reconnoiter the area in 1525. On that voyage, Quejo reached as far north as modern Cape Fear, North Carolina, naming on the way Río de la Cruz, today's Savannah River.[116] He stopped and met some of the Muskogean-speaking people there before pushing on. He also returned to the site of his 1521 landfall and named it Punta de Santa Elena. Its exact location remains unclear, but it is thought to correspond to the present-day Port Royal Sound.[117]

The success of Cortés in Mexico had inspired other explorers to turn south to see what they could find, but the information that had been gleaned from El Chicorano was enough to propel Ayllón to head north instead. In 1526, with six hundred eager colonists and some reluctant slaves, as well as Francisco de Chicora, the expedition left Puerto Plata in Hispaniola. Ayllón's six ships were loaded with horses, livestock, and many of the goods needed to build a permanent colony in Chicora. Las Casas happened to be in Hispaniola and was in the crowd to see them off—on board was his friend Father Montesinos, one of three friars tasked with the spiritual colonization.[118]

Almost as soon as they landed in Winyah Bay, Francisco de Chicora and the other Indians on board fled, never to be seen again. Meanwhile, the three scouting parties that had been sent out were having trouble locating a good base, so a decision was made to sail a bit farther south, perhaps around Sapelo Sound in present-day Georgia, though the landing point is still debated.[119] By then, one ship had run aground and many of the supplies had been lost.[120] People fell ill and needed to disembark, so one party traveled overland to the site and the ships later joined them. Despite not knowing the terrain, they managed to survive, foraging as they went.[121] A rudimentary colony, named San Miguel de Gualdape, was established in the late summer of 1526; it was the first Spanish settlement in this part of North America, nearly two thousand miles to the north of Mexico. It was named for St. Michael the archangel, whose feast day, September 29, was close at hand.[122] Being coastal, it was hot, sandy, and marshy, and a poor choice for a colony. Ayllón died on October 18, and the fragile settlement fell into chaos.[123] The colonists never developed a good trading relationship with the local Guale Indians, and some black slaves who had been brought on the expedition rebelled as well. As winter set in, the survivors, who numbered around 150 and included Montesinos, returned to the Caribbean.[124] The riches of Chicora that the Spanish kept seeking were, in the end, intangible. San Miguel de Gualdape was another Florida debacle. However, for a time, it remained all that was known about this area, and a 1529 map by Diego Ribero labeled this part of the coast the "Land of Ayllón."[125]

Ayllón's failure did not deter would-be *adelantados*. In 1527, the year after the survivors returned to the West Indies, Pánfilo de Narváez—the one-eyed conquistador who had been part of the invading force on Cuba and later failed to arrest Cortés in Mexico—set out from Spain with a royal contract to explore and settle the area between Florida and the unknown lands to the west.[126] The expedition began on a bad note: while it was in Cuba, a hurricane destroyed two ships, killing sixty people and twenty horses.[127] By February 1528, Narváez was on his way, with five vessels and a few hundred men, as well as eighty horses.[128]

Narváez landed around modern Tampa Bay, though he failed to make any alliances with the Tocobaga people. They did, however, tell him about a place that Narváez believed might have gold—as well as corn, as food was already running low—in the province of Apalachee.[129] It was a considerable distance north from the Tocobaga, who may well have made up the story to get rid of these bearded interlopers; perhaps, too, the Apalachee were their enemies at this time, and the arrival of Narváez would be an unwelcome surprise.[130] Narváez sent some of his men by land, while others sailed along the coast, with both groups aiming to make their way along it toward the Pánuco River in Mexico, now a part of New Spain. This division proved to be a terrible decision for Narváez in part because of the serious miscalculations about where they were and where they wanted to be. Even the pilots could not agree.[131]

Second in command on this expedition was Álvar Núñez Cabeza de Vaca, who came from a family of conquistadores. He grew up in Andalusia, near Jérez, though he left as a young man to participate in military campaigns in Europe, after which he received a royal appointment to go on the Florida expedition.[132] Little could he imagine at the time that this voyage would take him well beyond the boundaries of the known world.

Cabeza de Vaca went on foot with Narvaéz, and for the first two weeks they walked north from today's Tampa Bay. Along with them on the expedition were fellow conquistadores Andrés Dorantes and Alonso del Castillo Maldonado, as well as an enslaved black man known only as Estevánico (the Moor). The three figured in the resulting report Cabeza de Vaca would write many years later. As they walked in the months that followed, they met the various groups who lived along the coastal region—at one point spending time with the sought-after Apalachee people—and discovering there was no sign of gold in their villages. Before long, however, skirmishes, accidents, and hunger began to drain the expedition. The remaining 242 men divvied themselves up across five makeshift barges fashioned from palmettos, on which they set sail from a cove in Apalachicola Bay, drifting for a month along the coast in search of the open sea. Desperate for water and battered by a storm, the men took refuge with some coastal Indians who seemed friendly but who attacked them that night, forcing them to flee. In the days that followed, the barges became separated, and one sank. The men on Cabeza de Vaca's barge "had fallen over on one another, close to death," but they continued on until they landed at another shore, later taking refuge with local Indians after their raft was sunk by violent waves.[133] A short time later, Cabeza de Vaca was reunited with Dorantes and Castillo after the Indians had told them of the presence of the other Spaniards. One of the surviving barges needed repairs, and they also decided that four men would be sent to try to reach New Spain, while the others waited out the winter somewhere around the coast of Texas, on an island they called *Malhado*, or Island of Doom.[134]

The number of survivors dwindled from one hundred to four men after disease, starvation, and attacks killed the rest, including Narváez, leaving only Cabeza de Vaca, Estevánico, Dorantes, and Castillo. Cabeza de Vaca later recounted, "We were in such a state that our bones could easily be counted and we looked like the picture of death."[135] The four men continued west on foot, through what would be today's Texas, later crossing the Río Grande, encountering many chiefdoms of Native Americans. At times they were captives, but Cabeza de Vaca and the others were later apparently transformed into healers, called upon to "bless the sick, breathe upon them, recite a *Pater Noster* and *Ave Maria*, and pray earnestly to God our Lord for their recovery."[136]

After what seemed to be an endless time spent walking—by this point they had been on the expedition for eight years and covered something approaching six thousand miles—around March 1536 they encountered "four Christians on horseback" who were puzzled by the four men on the road, as they were not Indian and yet did not seem to be Spanish. Cabeza de Vaca later recalled that "they were dumbfounded at the sight of me, strangely undressed and in the company of Indians. They just stood staring for a long time." He had to request that they "take me to your captain," who was Diego de Alcaraz, then in charge of the town of Culiacán.[137] The men had walked all the way from Florida to northwest New Spain. In losing themselves they had found an overland connection in this seemingly endless New World.

Once his contact with Spaniards was secure, Cabeza de Vaca's journey came to an end, though he still had to make his way to Mexico City and then Veracruz, where his attempt to return to Spain was ruined by a storm that capsized his ship. His account of his adventures in North America, initially titled *La Relación* and published in 1542, is a fascinating document, but not an anthropological one. Although it has its modern uses in efforts to piece together a picture of Native American life, its language is mystical, dwelling on Cabeza de Vaca's own transformation from a captive to a miracle worker. It is nonetheless an epic tale, of suffering and violence, but also of mythic proportions, with startling reversals of fortune keeping the four men alive while they walked through the valley of death.*

---

* One of the difficulties in making sense of this period is that so much of what is known—and indeed often taken as historical truth—is legend or otherwise dubious. Accounts that attempt to explain the New World, such as Bernardino de Sahagún's *Florentine Codex* (ca. 1569), Peter Martyr's *Of the New World* (1530), or Gonzalo Fernández de Oviedo's *General and Natural History of the Indies* (ca. 1535), came out of a pre-Enlightenment tradition. Much as early maps were spiritual in nature, with Jerusalem at their center, these early accounts had crown and church at the core of their narratives. These accounts can at times read like tales of the supernatural. This is further complicated by official documents from this period that contain the writings of unreliable narrators—Cortés, for instance, had to polish his story to make his rule-breaking acceptable to the king.

His years of tribulations were still not enough to diminish Florida's lure. Not long after Cabeza de Vaca's return to Spain in 1537, Hernando de Soto wanted to set sail for La Florida.[138] De Soto was an experienced conquistador, having been involved in exploits in Peru, and in 1538 was named the governor of Cuba and given the *adelantamiento* of Florida.[139] He, too, was convinced that the land held secret riches, and fell upon clues such as the account of Cabeza de Vaca, who at one point had been given "five emerald arrowheads," though scholars think the stone was the less valuable malachite.[140] In fact, de Soto tried—and failed—to convince Cabeza de Vaca to join him.[141]

De Soto set out from Spain with around 840 people and nine ships, with all the necessary tools and weapons for settlement.[142] They stopped in Cuba, and then headed north, landing at *Bahía Honda* (Deep Bay), around present-day Tampa Bay, in May 1539. Writing from his ship on July 9, de Soto said the natives told him about the "many merchants among them, and much trade and abundance of gold and silver and many pearls. I pray to God that it is so, because I do not believe anything that I do not see . . . since they know and have had it told to them that if they lie to me it will cost them their lives."[143]

De Soto soon heard of Juan Ortiz, a man who had been captured during the Narváez expedition more than a decade earlier.[144] He dispatched his men to find Ortiz, who they discovered could speak to the Uzita and Mocoso people of the area.[145] Ortiz became de Soto's translator, and the men spent the winter of 1539–40 relying on the goodwill of the people they encountered around today's Tallahassee. De Soto saw large villages and temple mounds, and survived on corn, game, and fish. He was not on a cultural mission, however—he pillaged crops, enslaved Indians, and launched attacks. He and his men moved up through Florida, battling the Apalachee, then into Georgia and South Carolina, where he was lured into a hunt for the chiefdom of Cofitachequi.[146] It is thought that de Soto crossed the southern Appalachian Mountains, encountering the Muskogean-speaking people. He moved into Alabama, meeting the Choctaw. At one point, lured by chief Tuscaluza, they reached Mabila, in central Alabama, where they were attacked and many Spaniards were killed.[147] From there, they also spent time among prosperous and settled people, such as the Caddo and Creeks, in Mississippi. They met the Chickasaw and Tupelo and may have crossed the Mississippi River in 1541.

Pushing on, de Soto was clearly searching for more than just a place to put a settlement—he wanted to find more wealth.[148] He also was on the lookout for the still elusive shortcut to the east.[149] Finding neither, he remains one of the first known Europeans to wander through great swaths of North America. During the course of his wanderings he drained much of his fortune and, perhaps, his sanity. He decided to turn back but fell ill and died, it is believed somewhere in Arkansas or Louisiana near the Mississippi River, around May or June 1542. The rest of his party turned south, hoping to return to New Spain, ending up spending the winter building boats near today's Natchez, Mississippi. Finally, the three hundred men headed down the Mississippi River, reaching the Gulf of Mexico in September 1543; it is possible they were the first Europeans to sail on that river.[150]

By the mid-1550s, claims began to circulate that the explorer Giovanni da Verrazzano, who had been in the service of France's king, had reached the northern part of La Florida, around modern North Carolina, in 1524. Now the French were planning some sort of venture to that area and Spain's Council of the Indies was eager to prevent such an encroachment from taking place. In late 1557 it approved a plan to send a large fleet from Mexico to establish a settlement on the Gulf coast. The Spaniards would go overland to Santa Elena, which would be the site of another colony, and from there they could construct a road along which they could put missions and towns, in theory, connecting La Florida to New Spain.[151]

In 1559, the expedition was put under the leadership of Tristán de Luna y Arellano, who had been appointed governor of Florida. Spanish-born Luna had come to New Spain, where his cousin, Antonio de Mendoza, was viceroy in the 1530s. By the time he left for Florida, Luis de Velasco had become viceroy and was heavily involved in the plan's preparations. In June, fifteen hundred people, including five hundred soldiers, one hundred artisans, and six Dominican friars, departed from Veracruz.[152] They landed around Pensacola Bay, on Florida's western panhandle, in August.[153] At first they saw only a few fishermen's huts on the beach, and Luna sent men to further scout along the coastline.[154] Then, on September 19, disaster struck as a hurricane roared into the harbor, destroying most of Luna's fleet and ruining much of their year's supply of provisions. Hunger set in among the settlers, and some members of the party searched for people who could help.[155] The Spanish squabbled among themselves; most wanted to return to New Spain. By spring 1560, reinforcements had arrived from the capital, and they set up a makeshift camp among the Nanipacana, who soon fled, leaving the settlers subsisting on foraged food such as acorns. Luna continued to send scouting parties into the interior to find food, and other people who might help them, later encountering the Coosa.[156] Another relief supply ship arrived that summer but by August the situation remained desperate, and Luna dispatched some of the men to sail around to the Atlantic coast to begin work on the Santa Elena colony. They first set off for Cuba to provision the ship, but it was destroyed in a hurricane.[157] The viceroy was angered at the chaos in Florida, and he stripped Luna of his governorship, sending vessels to evacuate the settlers in early 1561 with Ángel de Villafañe now governor. Luna left for Spain, via Havana, in April, and Villafañe was also in Cuba, resupplying a ship on its way to Santa Elena. Villafañe never arrived, however, as storms destroyed many of his ships in June. He managed to survive and return to Pensacola to remove the remaining settlers. Such expeditions could be exercises in frustration for the viceroy, as so many factors—hurricanes or Indian attacks—could completely put an end to their efforts. It could also take quite some time to hear about why a mission had failed and, if need be, extract a more complete recounting of events through the judicial system.[158]

For almost fifty years following Ponce's initial 1513 voyage, no one from the Spanish empire had been able to make anything stick in La Florida. It was a very different world from the one Cortés found in Mexico. Though some people lived in settled villages, many of the natives of Florida were mobile, and implementing a tributary system like the *encomienda* would have been difficult if not impossible.[159] In addition, the soil was sandy, and the weather veered from sweltering to freezing. Everything about La Florida seemed designed to foil the conquistadores. Mexico was fast becoming the hub of a wealthy empire, and the Caribbean islands were now strategic outposts after their gold supplies had been exhausted.[160] A frustrated Felipe II decreed in 1561 that he would grant no further permissions for these expensive and embarrassing expeditions to colonize Florida. His ruling, however, meant nothing to the French.

Chapter 2

St. Johns River, Florida, ca. 1550–1700

THERE WAS ANOTHER route to Santa Elena, though it was forged not by Spanish Catholic conquistadores but by French Protestants. The roots of their enterprise stretch back to the small German town of Wittenberg, where the disgruntled Augustinian friar Martin Luther formulated his Ninety-Five Theses in 1517. The religious controversies and conflicts that were part of the subsequent Protestant Reformation spread disorder throughout European Christianity, reaching as far as the nascent Spanish colonies. Many Protestant English, Dutch, and French nobles and explorers were, by the mid-1550s, no longer willing to abide by the rules of the papacy, including papal bulls supporting the new lands Spain and Portugal had claimed. They, like thousands of other Europeans, were enraptured by tales of great riches. This was a battle over more than just religious ideology; the Dutch, along with Protestants elsewhere in Europe, including the English and French Huguenots, were seeking to justify their own involvement in the Americas and their right to explore, conquer, plunder, and enslave. Such desires found expression in the works of prominent thinkers such as the Dutch jurist Hugo Grotius, who argued for free navigation of the seas, as the Dutch were trying to extend their trading networks throughout the globe, including North America and the West Indies.

Many enterprising mariners were well aware of the Spanish treasure fleet, ferrying gold and silver to Europe, and it did not take long for these "Lutheran corsairs," as the Spanish called them, to descend on the Americas. With Protestant piracy on the rise, the Spanish islands turned to fort-building: in Puerto Rico, for instance, work on Castillo San Felipe del Morro began in 1539, along the north coast of the island, near the city of San Juan, which had been founded in 1521. Such forts were meant to protect the haul of empire on the ships that went to Spain and returned with European wares for the settlers. The *flota* would set off twice a year, leaving Seville (and, later, Cádiz once the river in Seville became too silted) for Veracruz, while another fleet, the *Tierra Firme* or *galeones*, sailed to Cartagena, Colombia, and onward to Portobelo, Panama. Goods from Peru would come up to Panama and be taken overland to Portobelo; the same would happen with silks and other luxury goods from the east that arrived in Acapulco and traveled overland to Veracruz.

Then, in the spring, the ships would return, uniting in Havana before crossing the Atlantic. Such a system had many vulnerabilities: shipwrecks around the Florida Keys were common, as were the hurricanes that wiped out whole fleets, but piracy was one of the most persistent problems.[1] England, the Low Countries, and France at varying times were enemies of Spain and so these corsairs, often armed with letters of marque, granting permission from their respective monarchs, considered it legal to attack Spanish ships. Individual pirates, with no religious or political connection, were also willing to risk death to get their hands on just one of the treasure-laden vessels.

Other Protestants were seeking not riches but sanctuary from the religious wars erupting in Europe. One such eager group was the French Calvinists, known as Huguenots, who faced mounting persecution by the 1560s. They imagined these new lands might offer a peaceful place to live and worship. A scheme to place a settlement on the other side of the Atlantic won the backing of the crown, with Catherine de Médicis supporting the idea on behalf of her young son, Charles IX. It also was popular with Gaspard de Coligny, a French admiral and himself a Huguenot.[2]

The waterways that spread out like veins in the South Carolina lowlands could have guided the vessels of the first French expeditions from Port Royal Sound to a landing spot on the edge of Parris Island in May 1562, but this was not their initial stopping point. Farther to the south, they called instead at the mouth of the St. Johns River, in the north of Florida, which runs into the Atlantic Ocean not far from today's Jacksonville. The French named it the Rivière de Mai, marking the month of their arrival.[3] The two ships were led by Jean Ribault, and he erected a small column to mark France's claim.

Ribault was an experienced sailor, born around 1515 in the port city of Dieppe, Normandy, to a family of minor nobility. For a time, he served England's King Henry VIII, which was not unusual for Norman sailors in the 1540s, as the king was trying to bolster English maritime defenses.[4] During this period, his experiences were wide-ranging, from a brief imprisonment for espionage charges to working under the navigator Sebastian Cabot. Ribault returned to France in the mid-1550s and fought in sea battles against the Flemish, Spanish, and English, securing his reputation as a skilled mariner.[5]

Once ashore, the French did not take long to make contact with the Timucua people near the coast and present them with gifts.[6] Ribault's second in command, René Goulaine de Laudonnière, later described their landing spot as a place "so pleasant it was beyond comparison."[7] However, Ribault wanted to explore farther to the north, arriving a couple of weeks later at an inlet that they named Port Royal. It was here that he established Charlesfort, named in honor of Charles IX.

It was not the most advantageous time of year to start such an enterprise, with the heat and humidity at a peak in July and August. In front of them stretched an endless yellow-green sea of tidal grass, a world of natural wonders from tiny mud-burrowing crabs to soaring ospreys and herons that fished for food in the creeks to unfamiliar flowers and plants all around. They built a rudimentary fort and began to make contact with the nearby Orista and Guale peoples. The Orista lived along the coast around the Edisto River valley, which forms its namesake island around forty miles south of Charleston, South Carolina, while the Guale were farther south, scattered around the coastal estuaries between the Ogeechee and Altamaha Rivers.[8] The Guale territory was divided into about thirty or forty villages, each ruled by a chief, and the total population is estimated to have ranged from thirteen hundred to about four thousand.[9]

The entire Florida region Spain initially claimed was diverse in terms of its people, climate, and landscape, and distinct from the Caribbean and New Spain. Living near the shores and rivers were coastal communities, such as the Orista and Guale, that subsisted on fishing. Inland to the north and west were the people the Europeans would later call the

Creeks, who were related to the wider Muskogean-speaking people of the region and whose nation covered parts of the modern states of Georgia, Alabama, Tennessee, Mississippi, and Louisiana, as well as Florida. Along today's Florida panhandle were Apalachee people, while to the east, and into Florida's peninsula, lived the Timucuan-speaking people, who were organized into about twenty-five different—and not always amicable—chiefdoms.[10] Farther south, along the east coast, were the Ais, while on the west were the Tocobaga. Living in the southernmost part were the Calusa and the Tequesta, among other, smaller groups.[11] Overall, the precontact population estimates of all Native Americans in Florida have a wide range, from as low as ten thousand to as high as four hundred thousand.[12]

Their settlements took a variety of forms, influenced by their environment. For instance, the Calusa of the south were sedentary and relied on fishing and, increasingly, trade with passing Europeans or scavenging from shipwrecks. The coastal Guale and Orista looked to the sea and rivers for their survival, though they did spend parts of the year hunting and growing crops. The Timucua also lived on a combination of hunting, gathering, and growing. Crops such as corn and squash made up a large part of their diet, but the soil in north Florida was not as fertile as in lands to the north, such as those where the Apalachee lived, which supported a greater reliance on agriculture.[13]

The Spanish had quickly learned that the Florida Indians' communities were not suited to the *encomienda* system, in part because their villages often did not have enough people to use as a labor force, nor did their social structure lend them to it. Overall, these were not tributary societies as the members of the Mexica confederation had been, though it is thought the Calusa in the south may have exacted tribute from some of the other chiefdoms.[14] In these early days, however, the challenge for the Spanish and French was simply to make sense of the relations between these groups and figure out how to gain their trust and assistance.[15]

Ribault did not stay long in Charlesfort, leaving for France by early June 1562 to stock up on supplies for the colony. The twenty-eight men he left behind were instructed to continue building the fort with logs and clay, backbreaking labor in the summer heat. They carried on, working with the expectation that reinforcements would soon appear, yet by January

1563 there were still no ships, and hunger was stalking the colony.[16] The desperate colonists spent the winter building a sloop to take them back to France, and they left in April 1563. They were later picked up by an English ship, with many on board near death as their vessel had run out of food and water.[17]

Ribault, for his part, arrived in France at the start of what would become the long-running Wars of Religion between Catholic and Protestant. From there, he left for London, where he wrote about his experiences in Florida. A translated English version of his *Whole and True Discoverye of Terra Florida* surfaced, printed by Thomas Hacket around 1563. In his account, Ribault painted a vivid picture of what he referred to as the "land of Chicore [Chicora] whereof some have written." Like some of the Spanish reports, his also noted that Florida was "a country full of havens, rivers and islandes of such frutefullnes as cannot with tonge be expressed," no doubt described as such to entice backers to fund a larger expedition "where in shorte tyme great and precyous comodyties might be founde."[18] Ribault's account helped secure him an audience with Queen Elizabeth I. Royal support looked promising at one point, but the plans collapsed. He was accused of being a spy and was even briefly imprisoned over claims that he was plotting to steal English ships and take them to France.[19]

While Ribault was in England, a Spanish ship had been dispatched from Havana in 1564, under the command of Captain Hernando Manrique de Rojas, to destroy the French settlement in Florida. After a number of stops along the coast, the Spaniards found two Indians who indicated "from their signs" that there had been "ships of Christians" in that harbor, but they could see no evidence of the fort.[20] The Spaniards continued sailing along the coast and by June came across a "Christian, clothed like the Indians of that country, who declared himself to be a Frenchman."[21] Manrique de Rojas questioned the man, who said his name was Guillaume Rouffi and that he had not wanted to join the others on the makeshift sloop sailing back to France. He told them the location of the now abandoned fort, which the Spanish burned before returning to Havana.[22]

While Manrique de Rojas was exploring the area, another French expedition slipped past him. This group of around three hundred people was led by Laudonnière, who had joined Ribault on the return journey to France. Laudonnière had departed France in April 1564 with three ships: a three-hundred-ton galleon as the flagship, and two smaller vessels. They arrived in June at the St. Johns River.[23] This time, Laudonnière decided not to return to Charlesfort, instead establishing Fort Caroline on a bluff overlooking the river. Laudonnière believed he was on good terms with the Timucuan people, which was crucial as he considered them good fighters who were "brave in spirit."[24]

The French were under the misguided impression that the Timucua were growing plenty of food and so the colonists could simply trade to meet their own needs. Rather than plant, they set about building their new fort. It was a deadly misunderstanding; the Timucuan chiefdoms grew only what they needed and there was not enough to feed their villages as well as the French.[25] It soon was too late to grow any more crops, and the food supply among the French began to dwindle, while tempers frayed, leading to a mutiny by the end of 1564. As Laudonnière tried to rein in angry settlers, a reprieve appeared on the horizon: the English slave trader and explorer John Hawkins called at the St. Johns River in August 1564, allowing them a chance to obtain provisions.[26]

By this point, Ribault had been released from prison in England, and he left Dieppe for Florida in May 1565.[27] Following close behind in June was Pedro Menéndez de Avilés, a Spaniard from the mountainous Asturias, on Spain's northern coast. Like many men from this region, he sought his fortune at sea, where, in his case, he established his reputation fighting French corsairs in the Bay of Biscay. Menéndez later commanded fleets to the Indies, entering the lucrative trade between the colonies and Spain.[28] He profited, but his successes were not consistent. A hurricane in 1563 cost him more than his fortune when a vessel sank and his son was also lost in the storm, possibly shipwrecked somewhere near Florida. Later that year, the king summoned Menéndez to Spain, concerned about reports of French activity in Florida. While in Spain, Menéndez had a dispute with some merchants and found himself under house arrest in 1564 until the claims were settled.[29] Eager to clear his name, Menéndez negotiated a contract with the crown to place a colony in Florida, and he left Spain. He had organized an expedition of nineteen ships, with some fifteen hundred soldiers and settlers. His plan was for some of the fleet to meet in the Canary Islands, with a few of the vessels following later.[30] Menéndez had a troubled start, however, as some of the ships never arrived in the Canaries, and a hurricane destroyed most of the rest. One of his caravels was blown so far off course it was later captured by French corsairs. In the end, he managed to limp into San Juan, Puerto Rico, in his flagship, the *San Pelayo*.[31]

Despite the setbacks, Menéndez regrouped and managed to arrive somewhere near Cape Canaveral just after Ribault returned to the St. Johns River, in late August 1565. When Menéndez discovered the whereabouts of the French fleet, a brief skirmish broke out between the Spanish and French ships, the latter managing to block the entrance to the mouth of the river. Menéndez decided to head south to an inlet he had spotted earlier. Once he and his men reached shore, they claimed Florida—again—for the king, and named this stopping point St. Augustine, as they had first sighted land on August 28, the feast day of that saint.[32] A sandbar lay across the inlet, and while this meant the flagship had to be anchored farther out, the harbor would help protect them from attack.[33] As Menéndez and his men were setting up camp, Ribault sent four ships and most of his men at Fort Caroline to attack the Spanish. This plan was left in tatters after another hurricane struck. Ribault was not able to spot the Spanish ships, and this caused him to sail too far south. The ferocity of the storm left his own ships wrecked just below St. Augustine.[34]

Menéndez determined that rather than waiting for Ribault to return for a sea battle, the Spaniards should attack Fort Caroline by land. After almost four days of marching through heavy rains, Spanish troops reached it by September 20. They had no trouble capturing the fort, and around 140 of the French were killed, while 45 managed to escape. Another 50 women and children were taken captive.[35] After securing the fort, Menéndez returned to St. Augustine to fight Ribault, not realizing what had happened to him until local Indians told him that French castaways had washed up in a nearby inlet, about fifteen miles south of St. Augustine. Menéndez found them, and they surrendered. He ordered his troops to kill them anyway, with the exception of any Catholics in their group. This bloody execution was the genesis of the name given to that site, which it bears to this day: *Matanzas* (Massacre) Inlet. A few weeks later, more survivors from the shipwreck arrived near the same spot, this time including Ribault, and they, too, met the same fate. One final group washed up that November. Some of them fled, though this time the captives' lives were spared, and they were put in a small fort under Spanish guard, near Cape Canaveral.[36]

———◦———

ONE MAN WHO managed to flee the Fort Caroline attack was Jacques le Moyne de Morgues, a cartographer and engraver who, upon returning to Europe, published an account of his experiences and provided illustrations of the Timucuan people, as well as the flora and fauna of the region. He lost most of his work during his escape but re-created it from memory; it was later reproduced and published by Theodore de Bry, who bought le Moyne's images and written account from his widow in 1588. Laudonnière also escaped the attack on Fort Caroline, fleeing to the St. Johns River where he and other survivors sailed on two ships to France.[37] He ended up in Swansea, Wales, where he began his *Notable History of Florida*, before returning to France, where it was published in 1586, with le Moyne's work following in 1591. These two books were translated and read throughout Europe, showing many people for the first time images of Native American life. Laudonnière provided one of the earliest European accounts of the Timucuan people, describing the men as being "olive in colour, large of body, handsome, well proportioned, and without deformities," and noting their deerskin loincloths and tattoos, which "ornament their bodies, arms, and thighs with handsome designs."[38] Le Moyne's images reflected Laudonnière's descriptions. His pictures show fierce, muscular, tattooed men, and women of similar stature, tall and strong, with long hair and bare breasts.

Now the Spanish would try to assert their authority in this part of Florida. They took control of Fort Caroline in 1565 and renamed it San Mateo.[39] Later that year, Menéndez began to explore the rest of Florida from St. Augustine, attempting to make alliances with the Native Americans. He erected more forts, including San Antón de Carlos on the west coast in the Calusa territory of Mound Key (south of modern Fort Myers) and outposts in the Tocobaga and Tequesta lands, although none of these fortifications survived past 1569.[40]

Gonzalo Solís de Merás, Menéndez's brother-in-law, joined in the *adelantado*'s exploits in Florida and later wrote about his experiences.[41]

Solís was with Menéndez when they encountered Calusa people in southwest Florida in 1566. Their party was searching for a rumored group of shipwrecked Spaniards who had been held captive for more than twenty years. They found some of them, and a meeting was arranged between Menéndez and the Calusa chief. At first there was an exchange of gifts and food and then, according to Solís, "the *Adelantado* told him that the King of Spain, his Lord, sent him for the Christian men and women that he had, and if he did not bring them to him, he would order him killed."[42] The captives were handed over and more gifts exchanged. The chief, for his part, apparently had earlier adopted the name Carlos after his captives told him that Emperor Carlos V was the king of all the Christians. In another display of respect, Carlos tried to give Menéndez his sister to marry. Solís recounted the exchange:

> The chief told him that he should go sleep in a room that was there, with his sister, since he had given her to him as a wife, and that if he did not do so, that his Indians would be upset, saying that they were laughing at them and at her, and that he regarded her poorly. And there were more than 4,000 Indian men and women in the town. The *Adelantado* [Menéndez] showed a little perturbation, and told him through the interpreter that Christians could not sleep with women who weren't Christian.[43]

Thrust into a complicated social situation, Menéndez tried to explain Christian practices; the chief said he would accept and even permitted his sister to be baptized. She became known as Doña Antonia.[44] This "marriage"—even though Menéndez had a wife in Spain—would seal a sort of brotherhood between the two men, and a long, extravagant feast followed.

Tales of Indian women being "given" to the Spanish abound in reports from conquistadores from across the empire, presenting only one side of the story. These women, be they slaves or princesses, often functioned as linguistic and social translators. Few Spanish women had been taken to Florida, and so the men were left to seek relationships with indigenous women, sometimes by force. Many native women were used as domestic servants and concubines, entrapped in servitude and sexual slavery. This was not unique to Florida, and throughout Spanish

America, the subsequent offspring of these relationships were known
as mestizos. An elaborate *casta* (caste) system of racial hierarchy took
shape, ranking the mixtures of people, with the most "Spanish" being
at the top and the most indigenous or African at the bottom. These
racialized ideas were connected to an older concept from the Iberian
Peninsula—*limpieza de sangre*, or "purity of blood"—that was concerned
with a person's possible Jewish or Muslim ancestry. Since some of the
Spanish who came to the Americas had converted Jewish (*converso*) or
Muslim (*morisco*) ancestry, these preoccupations crossed the Atlantic as
well.[45] How deeply ingrained such racial ideas were in Spanish Florida
in this period is difficult to ascertain; indigenous communities were
too scattered, the Spanish colonists too few, and the records too scant
to allow a detailed picture of the extent of *mestizaje* and the state of
emerging *casta* hierarchies.

Menéndez and Carlos continued to spend time together, with Carlos
later asking Menéndez to help him attack the Tocobaga people, who
lived to the north of the Calusa. Menéndez declined to involve himself
in the conflict, though he did broker a peace between the two groups.[46]
In his dealings with the Calusa, he met a captive, Hernando de Escalante
Fontaneda, who had been shipwrecked in south Florida and who knew
of Menéndez's son; it had transpired that he had not survived. Escalante
served as an interpreter for the Spanish and later left for Cuba in 1569.[47]
He also wrote a *Memoria* of his experiences, a rare written record of a
prolonged period spent with the indigenous people of Florida. Escalante's
work contains a mix of admiration and prejudice, and at times seems
to make a negative assessment of the prospects in Florida—a sharp
contrast to conquistadores' letters to the crown extolling the virtues of
this corner of empire. He might have been making, in a roundabout
way, the case against further settlement in Florida, to spare the Indians
any more European incursions, writing:[48]

> As I have stated, they [Ais and Jeaga people] are rich from the sea, and
> not from the land. From Tocobaga up to Santa Elena, which will be
> about six hundred leagues of coastline, there is no gold or even less
> silver naturally from the land, but rather it is what I have said, from
> the sea. I do not wish to say if there is land to inhabit, since the Indians

live in it. It is plentiful for livestock and for agriculture in their vicinity. . . . In all these provinces that I have declared about, from Tocobaga-chile up to Santa Elena, they are great fisherfolk . . . they are great archers, and traitors, and I hold it for very certain that they will never be at peace, and even less Christian.[49]

Yet such inferences were ignored. Menéndez's efforts had finally allowed the Spanish to entrench themselves on the edge of Florida. Menéndez also discovered that if he hugged the eastern coastline rather than battling the Gulf Stream, a smoother journey could be made to Havana. Before long, the main settlement in Florida was St. Augustine, not Santa Elena, which was another two hundred miles up the coast.[50] However, Felipe II wanted a presence in Santa Elena to forestall any future arrivals of the French, and so in April 1566, Menéndez and 150 soldiers went there and established Fort San Felipe close to the old Charlesfort location.[51]

After the fort was finished, Menéndez returned to St. Augustine, leaving the colony and around a hundred men under the supervision of Esteban de Las Alas. By the summer Santa Elena was in trouble: sixty of the men mutinied when a supply ship from St. Augustine stopped there, commandeering it to Cuba. Another twenty men disappeared into the interior, leaving about twenty-five, who were now forced to rely on the goodwill of Native Americans for survival.[52]

Not long after the runaways fled, Captain Juan Pardo arrived from Spain in July with supplies and around three hundred men. Las Alas and Pardo worked to improve the fort in time for Menéndez's return in August 1566. Pleased at the result, Menéndez named Las Alas governor—Menéndez still held this power as the *adelantado*—and for a brief moment, Santa Elena appeared to have stabilized.[53] At the end of 1566, Pardo left on an expedition into the interior, searching for the elusive overland path to link Florida with New Spain, which formed part of Menéndez's instructions from the crown.[54] Menéndez was optimistic enough to believe that he would also find a waterway to the Far East from Florida.[55]

Pardo headed west into North Carolina and went as far as Tennessee, meeting many Native Americans along the way and setting up two more forts, one of which was Fort San Juan near the Indian village of Joara (sometimes Joada), near modern Morganton, North Carolina. Pardo returned to Santa Elena a few months later, in 1567, and discovered that while he had been away, relations between his men and the local Indians had soured. Despite the tensions, he made plans to leave again later that year.[56]

Menéndez, for his part, had won the crown's favor with his success in Florida and wanted to take advantage of the situation by returning to Spain to enjoy his accolades, leaving in May 1567. Pardo set out on his second expedition inland in September, returning to Santa Elena by March 1568. Once again, the colony had been beset by more problems in his absence, not least a lack of food, as well as continued Indian attacks.[57]

To complicate matters, French corsairs arrived in April 1568, intent on revenge. Reports from the few survivors who returned to France had begun to circulate, revealing the scale of France's disaster in Florida.[58] Dominique de Gourgues, who had earlier been imprisoned among the Spanish, organized a retaliatory expedition from Bordeaux. Aided on their arrival by about four hundred Timucua Indians, they headed to the site of the first large massacre, Fort Caroline (San Mateo), on the St. Johns River.[59] Upon learning of their impending arrival, the hundred or so Spanish troops there tried to flee to St. Augustine, leaving Gourgues to destroy the fort before returning to France. Santa Elena, however, was left unharmed.

More colonists arrived in Santa Elena by 1568; at its peak some four hundred people lived there. By 1571, Menéndez secured for Florida a subsidy, known as the *situado*, to ensure its growth and protection.[60] Other parts of the empire, such as Cuba and Puerto Rico, which had little or no mineral wealth remaining but provided strategic importance, also received a share of silver, often delivered at erratic intervals.

Menéndez's plan was to put soldiers, settlers, and missionaries along the length of Florida, which the Spanish considered to be from the tip of the peninsula up to around the Chesapeake Bay, or the Bahía de Santa María, as it was called.[61] That bay was particularly important because it was thought to connect to the fabled Northwest Passage, which would link Spanish America to Asia.[62] Menéndez had gone some way toward realizing this vision by the time of his death in 1574, which occurred in Spain while he prepared for another trip to Florida.

While Menéndez had managed to drive off the French and establish rudimentary garrisons during his time in Florida, the territory remained fragile for the Spanish. By 1576, Santa Elena was falling apart. The colony's leaders turned violent, demanding tribute from the Orista and committing brutal acts, including the killing of two Guale chiefs, prompting an uprising of five hundred Orista and Guale, who attacked Fort San Felipe.[63] The Spaniards decided to abandon it and retreated to St. Augustine.[64]

Assessing indigenous hostility or cooperation in regard to the Spanish and even among themselves is complicated in this period. Written accounts or testimonies from the Spanish about attacks or ambushes often come from judicial proceedings and reflect Spanish beliefs and prejudices.[65] While there were also periods of calm around Santa Elena, this had not been the case along the coast near the St. Johns River, where the chiefdoms of Seloy and Saturiwa, both part of the larger community of Timucuan-speakers, were more consistently hostile to the Spanish. There had been skirmishes from the outset, as these chiefdoms tried to expel the Spanish from St. Augustine, with soldiers retaliating through the late 1560s.[66]

Efforts to bolster Santa Elena continued when, in 1577, Menéndez's nephew, Pedro Menéndez Márquez, arrived with orders to rebuild it. Up went Fort San Marcos, with a garrison of fifty men and artillery that included three cannons.[67] Menéndez Márquez tried to negotiate peace with the Guale and Orista, and he also discovered there were some French living among them on the coast.[68] Clashes with the Native Americans and their French allies took place throughout the 1570s, but settlement also continued. The relationship with the Guale broke down once more, and in 1579 the Spanish burned some of their villages and maize fields. Menéndez Márquez managed to stop aggression from some of the chiefdoms around Santa Elena by 1580, though relations with the Guale and Orista remained troubled.[69] Spanish officials, however, had decided to base themselves in St. Augustine, in part because they had finally brokered a peace with the hostile Timucua chiefdoms, as evidenced by records of Indians having been baptized around this time, as well as the establishment of two Indian villages near the town.[70]

In the end, it was neither Orista nor French attacks that ended Santa Elena, but those of the English. Francis Drake's assault on St. Augustine in 1586 was an impetus for Menéndez Márquez to bring the Santa Elena settlers to that town to help rebuild it and shore up its defenses, even though Drake had been unable to find Santa Elena and so it was left unharmed. In the face of much protest, the governor forced the settlers to leave in 1587, and the fort was dismantled.

———⌒———

THE COMPLEX NEGOTIATIONS and often violent confrontations that took place over the course of establishing settlements in Florida constituted one part of the colonizing story. Running in parallel were the efforts of the religious orders, ready to build churches and convert the native peoples, creating conflict of a different nature. Evangelization in Florida presented basic but serious challenges. The first was the priests' very survival. Like the conquistadores, the friars had numerous false starts, such as the ill-fated voyage of the Dominican friar Luis Cáncer in 1549.

Cáncer had met Bartolomé de Las Casas, who by this point was the bishop of Chiapas, in Mexico. Like Las Casas, Cáncer wanted to convert people in Florida by peaceful means. He arrived in the Tampa area in 1549, and some of the people there captured a few of the friars, forcing the remaining ones, including Cáncer, to sail on.[71] When he stopped again, he was clubbed to death within a matter of minutes after stepping onshore.[72]

Nearly two decades passed before another concerted effort was made, and it came only after Menéndez drove out the French. He reached out to the new Society of Jesus (Jesuit) order, which had been founded in 1540; the Jesuits were dedicated to evangelization and education, and Menéndez wanted them to work among the Florida Indians.[73] The Jesuit experience in the Americas was limited, with the order having gone only to Brazil in 1549, but they were enthusiastic. Like the Dominicans, they, too, were concerned about how the secular habits and worldly vices of soldiers and colonists were influencing the spiritual conquest of these lands. It would be up to the religious orders to provide a successful and lasting conversion to Christianity.[74]

In 1570 a small party of Jesuits and soldiers set forth from Santa Elena, sailing north to the Bahía de Santa María, to a land they believed to be named Ajacán or Axacán. Along with them was a man called Don Luis de Velasco, though he was not a Spaniard but a Native American whose original name was Paquiquineo. He claimed he was from Ajacán and in 1561 had been taken on board the Spanish ship *Santa Catalina*, which may have been on an exploratory mission around the area, or perhaps been blown off course.[75] On board, he was baptized and given the name of the then viceroy of New Spain, going on to spend almost a decade in Cuba, New Spain, and Spain, where he attracted the favor of Felipe II.[76] Velasco told many stories about his homeland and regaled the court with descriptions of its abundance, helping to reignite the king's interest in La Florida.[77]

Around 1565–66 he and Menéndez finally met, and the two went on voyages between Cuba and La Florida. This was around the time when Menéndez wanted to put a settlement in the Bahía de Santa María, and his interest in Ajacán was intensified in part by his conversations with Velasco. Menéndez also mentioned the possibility of the existence of a waterway to the east in his correspondence with the king.[78] Velasco, however, now having spent years among Spaniards, could not help noticing how they behaved in their American territories. Whatever he really thought, Velasco appeared to be enthusiastic about Christianity and plans for the expedition, which left in August 1566, taking Dominican friars and soldiers to Ajacán. As they sailed near the bay, Velasco tried to direct them, but he could not—or did not want to—find the proper entrance for Ajacán. They were forced to give up and turn back.[79]

Despite the suspicious circumstances surrounding Velasco's failure to navigate what should have been familiar waters, another attempt was organized in 1570, this time with the Jesuits. There were no soldiers with them, only Velasco, eight priests, and a young boy named Alonso de Olmos, a Spaniard born in the Americas. This time, they arrived in Ajacán by September and were soon in Velasco's village. His friends and family thought he had returned from the dead; yet it seemed to the priests that these people were half-alive themselves, as there were signs of food shortages, not the promised abundance.[80] Velasco was meant to act as a translator for the Jesuits, but he soon abandoned them, leaving the priests to fend for themselves.

By the time a ship carrying supplies arrived in the spring of 1571, it was too late. The sailors noticed that the Indians near the shore were dressed in the clothing of priests, and they became alarmed. They took two hostages (one jumped overboard) and returned to Cuba to extract the full story. What they heard was that Velasco had left the priests, but the Jesuits were soon forced to return to his village because they could not find enough food to survive and they had trouble communicating with other Indians. When three priests arrived asking to speak to Velasco, he killed them and went on to murder the other five men who were waiting at an encampment.[81]

Menéndez, who was in Havana at that point, organized an immediate campaign of retaliation and to rescue the one survivor, young Alonso de Olmos. Menéndez sailed to Ajacán in 1572 and, luring some of the native people onto his ship, he ambushed them, killing twenty. He managed to have Olmos released from captivity. Menéndez also demanded that Velasco be brought to him, but in his absence Menéndez hanged some of the Indian captives.[82] After that, the Jesuit authorities decided that no more of their order should go to Florida. They were replaced by Franciscans, with Father Francisco del Castillo arriving in Santa Elena in 1573, and soon after him, Father Alonso Cavezas, who went to St. Augustine.[83]

The priests showed up just as Felipe II issued new legislation that aimed to change the nature of conquest across the Americas. Menéndez had written to him in 1573 asking permission to enslave Florida Indians if the circumstances of a just war arose against those who had "broken the peace many times, slaying many Christians."[84] A reply came that same year in the form of the king's ordinances of discovery (*Ordenanzas de descubrimiento, nueva población y pacificación de las Indias*), stipulating that now "discoveries are not to be called conquests since we wish them to be carried out peacefully and charitably."[85] He ordered that the missionaries—not *adelantados*—lead this effort, with the military now charged with defending the missions.[86]

The second challenge for the priests—once they had ensured their own survival—was the actual task at hand: converting the native people to Christianity, a process that could be hindered by cultural misunderstanding and linguistic incomprehension. In the 1580s, the Franciscans began to place small missions—*doctrinas*—where the friars instructed the locals in Catholic doctrine. Because of what had happened in Ajacán, as well as the abandonment of Santa Elena in 1587, these missions reached only as far north as San Diego de Satuache, by the Ogeechee River, south of today's Savannah.[87] Others were dotted southward along the coast, in places such as St. Catherines Island, then known as Santa Catalina de

Guale, all the way to St. Augustine. By 1596, there were nine *doctrinas* and a dozen friars, and they would continue to spread south and west.[88] They had less success in south Florida, among the Calusa or Tequesta (near Miami).[89] Where these missions had taken root, especially among the Timucua and Apalachee, conversion was received with some degree of enthusiasm. There was one known case of a Timucua chief even requesting that friars come to his village, a change of heart that may have had more to do with using an association with Spanish power to boost his authority than with a spiritual transformation.[90]

The priests were also forced to try to understand the people they wanted to convert. Francisco Pareja learned the Timucuan language to help with conversions at the San Pedro de Mocama mission, which had been set up in 1587 amid the Tacatacuru chiefdom on Cumberland Island.[91] Pareja arrived in 1595 and his efforts to communicate have preserved what little was known about the Timucuan language and at least nine of its dialects. His method was straightforward: Pareja turned Timucuan into a written language, spelling out Timucuan words as they sounded. By doing this, he was able to translate religious doctrines into Timucuan, though this was only a sliver of the linguistic world of Florida. It included the Guale language and the inland Apalachee, both of them related to Muskogean, but Timucuan was distinct from them all.[92]

If peaceful relations could be established, followed by a willingness to submit to the practices of the Church, a third challenge remained: how to make a mission survive and even thrive. This often required trying to tie people to the land. The Guale and Orista people would go inland for part of the year, no doubt at times to be free of the missionaries, which worried the priests because it meant the Indians might go a long time without hearing Mass.[93] As one Jesuit, Juan Rogel, wrote in a 1570 letter, this "wandering" was the core of the problem. "If we are to gather fruit, the Indians must join and live in settlements and cultivate the soil."[94] Yet not all the people subsisted solely on agriculture, in part because of the diverse environment of Florida. It was more complicated to plant crops in southern Florida, as the sandy soil and swamps were not suitable. Although St. Augustine and many of the early missions were near the coast, the assistance of Indians who lived farther inland and had more developed agriculture helped them survive.[95]

Even when crops were planted, mission life could be difficult. The structures were often basic. The friars in Florida had to contend with wattle-and-daub or oyster-shell tabby as a building material, palm thatching for roofs, and earthen floors. A typical mission had a chapel, a kitchen, and living quarters for the priests, built around a courtyard, with some including military garrisons for protection.[96]

Some of the Native Americans who had converted to Christianity worked for the religious orders as laborers or farmers, often living in small villages near the mission. For many groups, this was a lasting and significant transformation from their seasonal nomadic movements. With Christianity came settlement. Despite this change, the biggest threat to any sort of longevity was the possibility of an Indian revolt, which could destroy years of work. In 1597 the Guale uprising, also known as Juanillo's Revolt after Don Juan, its leader, who was heir to a chieftaincy, set back the Franciscan effort. Although uprisings and rebellions could be triggered for many reasons, what is known about this particular incident from the remaining accounts is that both Indians and Spaniards experienced a wide range of challenges and frustrations.[97] For instance, the accepted cause of the revolt, at Nuestra Señora de Guadalupe de Tolomato (near today's Darien, Georgia), and the subsequent beheading of Father Pedro de Corpa, may have been the alleged attempts by the priest to curb Don Juan's polygamous behavior; at the same time, underlying struggles among the chiefdoms also fed into these events.[98]

Corpa had been stationed in Tolomato, the Guale town with one of the most important chiefs, known to the Spanish as Don Francisco. The priests had managed the conversion of several thousand people, so it took Corpa by surprise when a group of warriors burst in on his morning prayers. The chief's son, Juanillo, had Corpa killed on the spot. Juanillo then summoned other Guale chiefs to Tolomato, from which they raided other missions, including Santa Catalina de Guale and Santa Clara de Tupiqui, killing five more friars and setting buildings and chapels on fire.[99] From there they planned to move south, toward the missions near San Pedro, among the Mocama people, but on the morning of October 4, 1597, they discovered an unexpected number of Spanish soldiers, whose brigantine happened to have called at the island. Many of the Guale turned back and, while a few struck anyway, neither of the two friars there was hurt.[100] One of the surviving friars wrote to the governor in

St. Augustine pleading for help, and men arrived by October 17.[101] Once the attacks had been quelled, Governor Gonzalo Méndez de Canzo began to look for answers, interrogating people as well as conducting punitive raids. While the Spanish were concerned with their own safety, structures and property belonging to other chiefs were also attacked, indicating that wider power struggles may have been taking place.

The investigation took years. By 1600, Méndez began negotiating peace treaties with many of the *caciques*.[102] He also sent the chief of the Asao village, Don Domingo, on a mission to capture Don Juan in 1601—this despite Don Domingo's own involvement in the initial 1597 uprising. Méndez, however, was more interested in reestablishing alliances with Guale leaders, including Don Domingo, who now had considerable power.

Don Domingo had made a visit to St. Augustine and told Méndez who was behind the attacks. He also brought some laborers to work in the Spanish maize fields, and in exchange Méndez gave him some woolen cloth.[103] After this, Don Domingo led a party of other chiefs and uncovered Don Juan at a fortification in Yfusinique. They killed Don Juan, as well as the male members of his family who were with him. Don Domingo sent Don Juan's scalp to Méndez, who then considered the matter closed.[104] Other chiefs now pledged or reaffirmed their loyalty and obedience to the Spanish crown. Don Domingo continued to stay in the governor's good graces, and when the Franciscans returned to build a new mission, it was placed in Asao in 1606 and called Santo Domingo de Asao.[105] The Guale uprising indicates how complex these overlapping relationships were, not only between the Spanish and Native Americans, but also among the Indian chiefdoms, where the balance of power was continually shifting.[106]

By the beginning of the 1600s, the Florida missions had been repaired, and in 1606 the bishop of Cuba, Juan de las Cabezas Altamirano, decided to inspect them. Within a few decades, the priests began to move inland, and the first Franciscan mission was placed among the Apalachee people of the Florida panhandle in 1633, taking advantage of the fertile terrain ideal for larger-scale agriculture, since St. Augustine needed a steady supply of basic foodstuffs.[107] Overland trails soon connected the settlement to the missions, a journey that could take around two weeks.[108] The Apalachee missions were mostly small, but some, such as San Luís de

Talimali, in today's Tallahassee, were substantial. San Luís, for instance, produced surplus wheat, cattle, and corn that could be distributed to St. Augustine or even exported elsewhere.[109]

It took more than half a century, but the Spanish managed to put a settlement in Florida, drive out the French, win Indian alliances, and even have thousands of converts by the early 1600s. The lands of Ayllón and Chicora did not yield hoped-for gold, but those initial explorers had been following mental maps, driven by imaginings as much as by navigational reality. Although by the early seventeenth century a small part of Florida was now firmly in Spain's orbit, there were only a few hundred people living in St. Augustine, precariously positioned on the fringes of both the Spanish empire and a much larger indigenous world that they had barely penetrated and could scarcely imagine, which stretched west from Florida for thousands of miles.

Chapter 3

Alcalde, New Mexico, ca. 1540–1720

FLORIDA PROVED TO be a mirage for the Spanish, but it was only half of their North American story. While Menéndez and others had come up from the Caribbean, conquistadores in the west were traveling through the unknown northern reaches of New Spain. They, too, were hunting for yet another mythical land, though in this region the search was necessarily conducted on foot and horseback, over miles of scrubland and desert, under an often hot and unforgiving sky. In such a vast space, legends could know no limits. Rather than a single island of riches, this territory was said to hold seven treasure-laden cities: the Seven Cities of Cíbola.[1]

The legend of Cíbola was given some credence by the pen of Father Marcos de Niza, who had been sent on a mission in 1539 to explore the frontier by the viceroy of New Spain, Antonio de Mendoza. The viceroy, like many others, including Hernando Cortés, had heard the wild tales of Cabeza de Vaca's adventures in the *tierra adentro* (inland) and wanted to believe there was another Tenochtitlán. Underneath this was an older story, the Seven Cities of Antilia, a legend involving seven Portuguese bishops who fled Muslim Spain long before the *Reconquista*. They supposedly crossed the ocean and established these cities. In some variations they did so on an island, in others they were far inland. Whatever the provenance, the fabled wealth of the cities grew exponentially over the decades.[2] The vast areas unknown to European mapmakers allowed imaginations to run free, and Spanish explorers colored in the gaps with their desires.

By 1531, Nuño de Guzmán—the head of the judicial *audiencia* and a conquistador—had forged a brutal and bloody extension of the Spanish frontier northwest toward the Pacific and up to Sinaloa, founding in 1531 the town of San Miguel de Culiacán, which would become a base for further expeditions to the north. It was also where Cabeza de Vaca and the other three survivors were taken after their epic wanderings. This region was still considered remote, and, unlike the settled Indians of southern Mexico, including those in and around the capital, the people of the north were mostly nomadic. These groups posed many problems for would-be conquistadores, on top of any resistance or attack: signs of their wealth might not be immediately evident, and their labor would be far more difficult to exact. Still, some Spaniards were willing to push north, though it would take decades, if not centuries, for settlement to happen at the northernmost edges of New Spain.[3]

Father Marcos de Niza left from Culiacán with the now veteran explorer Estevánico—the African who had survived along with Cabeza de Vaca— as well as some indigenous scouts to look for these fabled seven cities.[4] After weeks of slow travel from Culiacán, Estevánico and a few others went in advance of Niza. When they were about a day away from Hawikuh, one of the largest towns of the Zuni people (also Zuñi)—today just under two hundred miles west of Albuquerque—Estevánico relayed back a message encouraging the party to join him. Before they could, another messenger arrived with grim news: Estevánico had been killed.[5] It is possible that he had been too demanding with these Native Americans in searching for valuables, or that they had mistaken him for a spy.[6] Niza hurried back to New Spain, though he later claimed that he had seen the rich kingdom of Cíbola from a hilltop, declaring it "larger than the city of Mexico."[7] In another telling, it is possible that the name of Cíbola was just the name for Zuni in one of the local indigenous languages.[8]

Whatever the genesis, Niza reported that he had met a "citizen of Cíbola," a man of "good disposition," who told him that "Cíbola is a big city, that it has a large population and many streets and squares, and that in some parts of the city there are very great houses, ten stories high, in which the chiefs meet on certain days of the year."[9] The priest wrote a glowing account of the place, describing it as "a beautiful city, the best that I have seen in these parts."[10] Niza said he was told about another of the seven cities, Ahacus, and reported that the richest was Totoneac. He crowned his imaginary achievements by claiming for Spain all seven cities and the "kingdoms of Totoneac and Ahacus and Marata."[11]

Inspired by the friar's report and having no way to know the extent of its exaggeration, Mendoza sent a much larger exploration party. This time he put twenty-nine-year-old Francisco Vázquez de Coronado in charge, with some three hundred soldiers, eight hundred Indian allies from New Spain, fifteen hundred horses and mules, and six Franciscan friars, including Niza. Also with him was the young Tristán de Luna, twenty years before his disastrous expedition to establish a colony in Florida. They set off from Compostela, near the coast in the Jalisco region, in February 1540.[12] Coronado left by land, while Hernando de Alarcón took two ships from nearby Acapulco to attempt a maritime route.[13] They managed to navigate the vessels as far as the Gulf of California and today's Colorado River, reaching the Gila River before having to turn back. This western expedition was taking place at the same time that Hernando de Soto was encamped among the Apalachee, in the middle of his ill-fated exploration of Florida.[14]

Niza guided Coronado back to the supposed cities of Cíbola, coming first to the town of Hawikuh. Although it was impressive, with its multistoried adobe houses, there was little sign of gold. The Zuni were also wary of these visitors, not wanting them to enter the town, and the result was a brief battle, in which Coronado was wounded and the Spanish raided the Zuni food supply.[15]

The Zuni were one group out of a much larger and diverse community that the Spanish categorized together under the umbrella term "pueblo," the Castilian word for town or village. They used it because the people in this area were sedentary and resided in what the Spanish considered to be recognizable towns. Pueblo villages were dotted along the Río Grande valley in New Mexico, reaching to the west and north into today's northern Arizona. The people of the pueblos had common ancestral roots in the Anasazi, who lived in the region around AD 1000. By the time of the Spaniards' arrival, they were gone and their descendants had diversified, reaching an estimated population of around sixty thousand.[16] Spread across a wide area, they encompassed five broad language groups. Along the Río Grande were the Tanoan, who included the Tiwa, Towa, Tewa, and Piro. Farther up the river valley were the Keresans, who also stretched to the west and included the

Acoma. West from there were the Zuni, and beyond that to the north and west were the Hopi. In addition, some people would have spoken some Navajo and Apache because of contact through trade networks. However, these language groups and related dialects were for the most part mutually unintelligible, and the Spanish would have been forced to rely on multilingual translators.[17]

The landscape was as diverse as the people, with the scrubby Chihuahuan Desert giving way to the Río Grande basin. From there, the river valley rises up beyond ten thousand feet, into the mountains and toward the Colorado Plateau, an otherworldly terrain of red rocks and skies of piercing blue. The higher altitudes were colder at night, while lower down could be baking hot, and rain mostly fell in seasonal cycles. Many of the Pueblo towns had the right conditions for agriculture, and so for the most part they were settled farming communities, growing crops such as maize.

Their societies were organized by clan, usually with matrilineal descent, though men were often polygamous. Families lived in adobe homes, frequently extending them into compounds as a family grew. These dwellings could reach multiple stories and were accessed by a system of ladders.[18] The houses in the towns were often built around a plaza, with *kivas*, sacred buildings used for religious rituals and community functions. Despite these general similarities, the broad linguistic groups among the Pueblo considered themselves socially and culturally different from one another, though there were points of overlap, one of which would be the shared experience of dealing with the Spanish.

These settled pueblos were surrounded by nomadic people, including the Apache, Navajo, and Ute. The Apache traded with the pueblos, bringing valuable buffalo meat and hides to towns; they were also feared for their violent raids.[19] The Plains Indians went as far west as the Taos Pueblo in order to trade.[20] To the south, in today's southern Arizona, which the Spanish called Pimería Alta, were the Tohono O'odham people, the Yuma, and the Sobaipuri; and farther into New Spain were the Opata, Pima Bajo, Seri, Concho, Lipan, and Tarahumara.[21] This region was rich and diverse, though not in the way Coronado and his men might have hoped.

Coronado occupied the Hawikuh pueblo for six months, using it as a base of exploration, with his men venturing to Acoma and Hopi territory, continuing to search for signs of precious metals.[22] One band of men, led by Hernando de Alvarado, went north to the Hopi territory, and from there east to the Río Grande and beyond, to what was later called "land of the buffalo." On their way they encountered the Acoma people, whose village was perched on top of a high, flat rock outcrop known as a *mesa* (Spanish for table), allowing them to see visitors or invaders from miles away.

Alvarado's men reached the Pecos pueblo—east of modern Albuquerque—where an Indian man they called "the Turk" told them about riches in a distant place called Quivira, which turned out to be the land of the Wichita people.[23] Trusting the tale, the Spanish appear to have overlooked the possibility that he might have been making up such a story to get rid of these violent, corn-thieving strangers.

While Alvarado continued to explore, some of the other men were preparing to spend the winter among the Tiwa pueblos, which were near Río Grande and to the west of Pecos. However, the Spaniards' behavior, including their demands for food, guides, and women, incited a rebellion in the nearby Arenal pueblo that ended up spreading to at least twelve other villages, triggering what was later called the Tiguex War, as Coronado had called the area the "Tiguex province."[24] During this time Coronado and his men managed to put thirteen of the fifteen Tiwa towns under siege and killed some two hundred men by burning them at the stake.[25]

By spring, Coronado was ready to head east to find Quivira. He and his men wandered along the modern New Mexico–Texas border, often losing their direction on the flat plains, where there were few trees to serve as landmarks.[26] At last, Coronado realized he had been deceived. He turned on the Turk, who was traveling with the party, and demanded to know the truth. The Turk said that he had been asked to lead Coronado astray, and he was killed for his confession.

Coronado no doubt had visions of glimmering cities, but they eluded him. He was forced to write a dispiriting report: "[Marcos de Niza] has not told the truth in a single thing he said, but everything is the opposite of what he related, except the name of the cities and the large stone houses."[27] Coronado returned to Mexico in the spring of 1542. Despite having covered thousands of miles passing through what are now the states of Arizona, New Mexico, Texas, Oklahoma, and Kansas, he was empty-handed. The whole expedition was such a fiasco that he was hauled before a tribunal.[28]

⌐◝‿◜¬

Before embarking on the expedition, Coronado had been the governor of Nueva Galicia, a province the Spanish created near Guadalajara. A few months after Coronado departed, an uprising known as the Mixtón War (1541–43) began among the Caxcanes people in the Zacatecas and Jalisco regions, 350 miles to the northwest of Mexico City. A number of factors were behind the rebellion, including resentment of the *encomienda* and a rejection of Christianity.[29] It took the Spanish some time to quell because the Indians had placed themselves on top of cliffs (one of which was named Mixtón), that gave them a tactical advantage. With the aid of some thirty thousand Texcoco and Tlaxcalan warriors, the Spanish wrested back control of the territory.[30] Not long afterward, silver was found in nearby Zacatecas, and three large veins had been discovered by 1548.[31]

Indigenous laborers from other parts of New Spain were brought there to work in the mines, as well as grow crops for the booming population.[32] At first the silver deposits could be mined from the surface of the slopes of the hills around Zacatecas, but those were soon exhausted. This was followed by opencast mines, and later deeper excavation, making silver extraction increasingly dangerous.[33] The establishment of the mines also disrupted the entire region, and before long regional nomadic groups, including the Zacateco, Chichimeca, Guachichil, and Guamare, attacked Spanish miners and merchants. The Chichimeca, who later had their own war against the Spanish in the 1550s, lived to the north of Zacatecas, and that area turned into hostile and dangerous terrain.[34] Further exploration and mapping were now perilous, but the lure of silver meant other mining towns continued to spring up, including a new northernmost base in 1567: Santa Bárbara, in the modern state of Chihuahua.

At the same time, the religious orders had been deepening their involvement. The Franciscans arrived in Zacatecas by the 1550s, moving north from their base in Michoacán, about three hundred miles to the south; the first Jesuits arrived in 1574.[35] Like their secular counterparts, priests and friars would also venture to the outer limits of New Spain. In 1581, Franciscan Agustín Rodríguez set off on one such mission, though by this point it had been a considerable interval since Coronado's failed effort. Rodríguez was accompanied by two other priests, as well as Captain Francisco Sánchez and a handful of soldiers. They reached the Río Grande and continued into Pueblo territory. They traded and had peaceful interactions with the people they met, and Rodríguez named the territory San Felipe del Nuevo México around this time. However, they were still looking for Cíbola— throughout the trip, Sánchez and the soldiers kept searching for silver.[36] Eventually, the soldiers left for Santa Bárbara, and Rodríguez decided to stay on in one of the Tiwa pueblos. One of the other missionaries wanted to return as well but was killed on the way back to New Spain. The soldiers, now worried about the fate of the two remaining priests, organized a rescue party, led by the Franciscan Bernardino Beltrán and Antonio de Espejo, who brought fourteen men for protection.[37]

They left in November 1582 and, upon reaching the pueblos, discovered that the friars were dead.[38] However, after he returned to Santa Bárbara, Espejo wrote a report in 1583 recommending the Río Grande valley for Spanish colonization, with a plea for permission to settle the area.[39] Felipe II authorized it in 1583. Espejo had been eager to lead such an expedition, but he died in Havana where he had stopped en route to Spain. The viceroy's search for a suitable replacement took more than a decade, not least because a candidate needed to have the personal means to pay for such an expedition.[40]

This, however, did not stop illicit ventures such as that of Gaspar Castaño de Sosa, who took a few hundred settlers without permission to New Mexico in 1590–92 before he was discovered. He was followed in 1593 by Francisco Leyva de Bonilla, who left New Spain and is thought to have reached as far northeast as Nebraska. During the expedition, Leyva de Bonilla and his deputy, Antonio Gutiérrez de Humaña, had a disagreement and Gutiérrez de Humaña murdered his colleague; he in turn was later killed by Plains Indians.

Finally, the viceroy and the Council of the Indies agreed on someone to colonize this part of New Spain: Juan de Oñate. He was a man of the Americas, a creole (or *criollo*), meaning he was born in New Spain to Spanish parents, in his case around 1550. His family had made their fortune from silver in Zacatecas and their numerous *encomiendas*. Oñate married Isabel de Tolosa Cortés, Hernando Cortés's granddaughter and

Moteuczoma's great-granddaughter, putting himself in the highest tier of the Mexican elite.[41] He had the money to pay for the enterprise and so he would be the *adelantado*. Although this was arranged in 1595, it took three years of review before he started, in part because a new viceroy was appointed: Gaspar de Zúñiga, who wanted to go over every detail of the arrangement.[42] Oñate was aware of the risks—he heard in 1598 about Leyva de Bonilla and Gutiérrez de Humaña's disastrous attempt from an Indian guide who had been with them—but he also knew of the potential rewards.[43]

Although Oñate would be allowed to administer only a limited *encomienda*, he was instructed to "treat the Indians well; they [settlers and soldiers] must humor and regale them so they come in peace and not in war . . . this is very important for the success of such an important undertaking."[44] He was not to force them to work and was to exact only minimal tribute.[45] In addition, the Franciscan missionaries who joined him would receive a subsidy as part of the *patronato real* (royal patronage), which was now supporting their work.

Serving as Oñate's captain was Gaspar Pérez de Villagrá, a fellow creole who would later write an epic poem about his experience with Oñate, his *Historia de la Nueva México* (1610).[46] Villagrá believed they were going to conquer a "new" Mexico, like Cortés had done some seventy years earlier, writing, "That prodigy immense which we did find / When taking road, uncertain and unknown / for that New Mexico."[47]

The party left in January 1598 from the Valley of San Bartolomé, an area close to Santa Bárbara, then part of a larger region called Nueva Vizcaya, or New Biscay—an ironic toponym given that the damp maritime climate of Spain's northern Basque region was almost the exact opposite of the dry extremes in the desert through which Oñate would spend months traveling. Accompanying him were around five hundred people, including soldiers, settlers, and missionaries, along with the goods they would use to establish settlements, distributed among some eight wagons and carts.[48] By April they had arrived at the Río Grande, and continued north. Oñate passed through what became known as the Jornada del Muerto (Dead Man's Journey), a sixty-five-mile section of dusty trail with no source of water. Though dangerous and difficult—some of Oñate's supply carts had to be left behind during their six-day trek—it was a useful shortcut around the longer route following the bend in the Río Grande.[49]

Once the river came back into view, Oñate was close to the pueblos. The nearest were inhabited by the Piro-speaking peoples, who had been alerted about the arrivals and fled. Oñate tried to send gifts to reassure people, and when the Spaniards reached one pueblo, Teypana, the chief gave them a gift of corn. In return they called the pueblo Socorro, which means "help" or "aid."[50] Oñate continued on, reaching in early July a pueblo of the Keres-speaking people he had known about from Castaño de Sosa's trip; the Spanish renamed this pueblo Santo Domingo. Two Mexican Indians, Tomás and Cristóbal, had decided to stay there, and they served as translators for Oñate. He asked them to explain to the people of Santo Domingo and from other pueblos who were present that they needed to pledge their loyalty to the king, in effect issuing the *Requerimiento*.[51] When this had been seemingly secured, they pushed on.

Farther north, Oñate was at first welcomed by the Ohkay Owingeh people, and he called their town San Juan de los Caballeros. The Spaniards stopped in nearby Yunque, which Oñate renamed San Gabriel and which would serve for a time as the capital for the Spanish. Oñate divided up the area into six districts and sent priests into each. He also handed out *encomiendas* and attempted to exact tribute, though the Pueblo Indians did not have these types of labor or taxation systems, and this quickly became the source of many disagreements.[52]

By October 1598, Oñate was ready to try to find the yet undiscovered passage to the Pacific, still a preoccupation for the Spanish. Along the way, he sent out instructions, including some to his nephew, Juan de Zaldívar, asking him to join the expedition. Oñate did not wait for Zaldívar, however, and soon arrived at the Acoma pueblo that Coronado had earlier visited, some sixty miles west of the other villages.[53] Oñate informed the Acoma they were now vassals of the crown and tried to trade. However, a plot was afoot to kill Oñate—whom the Acoma did not trust—which involved trying to lure him into a ceremonial prayer *kiva* where he could be murdered. For whatever reason, Oñate declined to enter the *kiva*, and in the end the Acoma leaders, some of whom had misgivings about the plan, did not follow through.[54] Oñate continued on his way but would soon receive disturbing news about this pueblo.

Juan de Zaldívar had been traveling west to catch up with his uncle. Zaldívar also called on the Acoma, sending some of the thirty men who were with him ahead to ask for food and water. The men stopped at the foot of the Acoma mesa and set up camp. The Acoma invited them up, as they had done with Oñate. The men who had arrived ahead of Zaldívar had obtained the food they sought, but by the time Zaldívar arrived the mood had shifted and the Acoma were angry. Varying accounts say the Spaniards tried to seize some priests or that they were stealing food, or that they harassed or even raped an Acoma woman. In the end, the Acoma attacked the Spanish, killing Zaldívar and around ten other men, hurling their bodies off the top of the mesa, while the rest scurried down the rock face and hurried off to find Oñate.[55]

Oñate sent the younger brother of the murdered Zaldívar, Vicente, to lead a retaliatory mission. On January 21, 1599, they returned to the mesa and demanded that the Acoma hand over the people who killed their men. The Acoma responded with arrows, spears, and jeers.[56] The Spanish then tried to distract them by climbing one side of the mesa, while troops on the other side brought up a cannon. They fired on the village, and, in the end, some eight hundred Acoma were killed and another six hundred taken prisoner.[57] The prisoners were later put on trial because, Oñate said, they were judged as having broken their loyalty to the king. The sentences were severe: men over the age of twenty-five were to have their right foot amputated and to be put into servitude; younger men and women were to be put into twenty years of service to the Spaniards; and children were divided between the missionaries (girls) and direct supervision by Vicente de Zaldívar (boys).[58]

Some settlers thought the punishment was too harsh, and the viceroy was notified of what had taken place, leading to an investigation.[59] Oñate, in the meantime, left on another mission to search for the Pacific Ocean. On his return to the Pueblo region in 1605, he carved his name on a rock outcrop now known as El Morro, not far from the modern New Mexico–Arizona state line, with the inscription: "The Adelantado Don Juan de Oñate passed by here from the discovery of the South Sea, on the 16th day of April 1605."[60] While this sounds as if he were returning from a successful venture, he was hundreds of miles away from the Pacific, having reached only the lower part of the Colorado River.

Oñate was recalled to Mexico City and gave up his governorship in 1607, having spent an estimated 400,000 pesos of his own money, with little to show for it.[61] He returned to Zacatecas around 1613, but in 1614 he was charged and found guilty by the viceregal court in Mexico City for the violent suppression of the Acoma. He spent much of the remainder of his life trying to clear his name, traveling to Spain in 1620 to make his case. He was appointed the mining inspector of Spain in 1624 and spent his final years on the peninsula before his death in 1626.[62] The poet Villagrá, too, faced banishment for his involvement in the brutalities and was exiled from New Mexico for six years.[63] His *Historia de la Nueva México* ends with a detailed account of the attack on the Acoma, with Villagrá concluding:

> Of all that is total misery,
>> Grief, sadness, ultimate destruction.
>> Let's leave the histories, so full
>> Of thousand sad events, now done,
>> And let us look at this ruined heathen,
>> Loosed, unshielded, now abandoned
>> By so holy, divine, and lofty hand.[64]

By 1610 a new governor, Pedro de Peralta, was in charge of New Mexico, and the capital moved from San Gabriel, where the Río Grande and the Río Chama meet, to a location some 40 miles south, a settlement known as La Villa Real de la Santa Fé de San Francisco de Asís. The Spanish population in New Mexico remained small in the early seventeenth century; twenty years after its founding, Santa Fe was little more than a frontier outpost, with only about 1,000 settlers—250 Spanish, 750 mestizos, and about 25 friars.[65] Although some priests were in the new capital, the official spiritual center, or *custodia*, was elsewhere: by 1616 it was in the Santo Domingo pueblo, about twenty-five miles to the south.[66] Missions spread out across the region, though the friars often had trouble placing them in the center of Pueblo life, in either a physical or a spiritual sense. Because the pueblos were towns with existing buildings and plazas, the new missions were pushed to the margins.[67] In a similar vein, although many people agreed to conversion, Christian beliefs did not easily supplant existing ones. Broadly speaking, Pueblo religious practices had much in common with those of other Mesoamerican cultures, drawing from the weather and seasons, using medicine men or healing priests, with rituals devoted to the fertility of people and the land. Some of the indigenous and Catholic rites overlapped, such as the use of water in baptism and singing during services. Likewise, certain symbols could have multiple meanings; for instance, a cross was interpreted as an important type of prayer stick.[68] Priests tried to root out Pueblo beliefs, but many people continued to conduct their own ceremonies, though they were forced to do so away from the prying eyes of the missions.[69] Modern archaeological research has uncovered physical evidence of this, such as Pueblo idols hidden under church altars.[70]

Missions had another, more secular, dimension: harnessing the economic power of the Pueblo people through their labor. As had been the case in Florida, at times the survival of the priests depended on it.[71] Most of the food was produced by Pueblo hands, and the churches and other mission buildings were built by them, too. From roughly a dozen churches in 1616, by the 1650s the friars had fifty churches and *conventos* (priests' quarters).[72]

A typical day at a mission would begin with the tolling of the church bells, calling people to Mass and then on to work. Later there might be religious instruction. As missions grew, some Pueblo took on non-religious roles in the church, for instance as *fiscales*, a job that involved helping to maintain the church while also disciplining those people who fell afoul of Christian doctrine.[73] Aiding this was often the whip—at times administered by a *fiscal* trying to police his own people.[74] Through this, the Franciscans were able to incorporate many of the Pueblo people into mission life. Some priests, indeed, had quite personal ties to the mission: mestizo children were living proof that the friars were not necessarily keeping their vows of celibacy. One priest reported in New Mexico "all the pueblos are full of friars' children."[75]

Another priest who was in New Mexico around this time, a Portuguese Franciscan named Alonso de Benavides, wrote a long *memoria* to the Spanish crown in 1630 about his travels in New Mexico. He revised his account in 1634 and this time sent Pope Urban VIII a copy, which was later translated into Latin, French, Dutch, and German.[76] Benavides arrived in Santa Fe in January 1626, after a long journey from Mexico City. His report, like many of this time, glossed over some of the complex realities of mission life on the frontier, but it also presented a surreal and often mystical picture of the people and the landscape. This was especially the case in his description of the miraculous appearance of María de Ágreda, later known as the Blue Lady, who was a member of the Order of the Immaculate Conception, which has a special devotion to Mary, the mother of Jesus. Benavides claimed she "visited" some of the pueblos in the early 1620s through bilocation, or divine translocation—not in the flesh. According to his account, there were reports of Pueblo people seeing this "lady in blue," who urged them—in their own languages—to convert to Christianity.[77] He made estimates, no doubt generous, of the number of converts but pointed out that much work remained. At one pueblo, a man Benavides described as a "sorcerer" confronted him, saying: "You Spaniards and Christians are lunatics. You live like crazy people, and you want to teach us to be crazy as well."[78] Benavides dismissed his words, putting them down to the "devil who was fleeing, confused by the virtue of the Holy Word."[79]

In addition to their own sustenance, the friars had to contend with other matters of the world, including their often troubled relationship with the colonial officials. New Mexico had not produced much of the abundance that had been expected, leaving the two groups squabbling over what few resources they did have.[80] Colonists, meanwhile, were often not pleased by the small tribute they could exact, usually paid in cloth or corn.[81] Despite being on the fringes of the Spanish empire, New Mexico was still part of the wider imperial economy. Settlers had begun to raise sheep and livestock and there was some trade with the capital, in part because the Spanish had no access to imported foodstuffs such as wine. Goods had to travel from Mexico City northward for some fifteen hundred miles along the Camino Real, or Royal Road, and back again.

The fractures between Spanish officials and the clergy widened throughout the 1600s. There were disagreements at times over quite fundamental issues, such as the treatment of the Pueblo people. The Franciscans felt they were acting in line with the king's dictates and converting nonbelievers using peaceful means. Officials wanted their *encomienda* and were eager to enslave unwilling converts, and even the willing were not immune from occasional raids on mission workers, despite the royal orders prohibiting this behavior.[82]

In terms of administration, a governor was in control of the territory, though for quite a long time he had few subordinates, with only two lieutenant governors being posted to jurisdictions about twenty miles to the north and south of Santa Fe before 1680.[83] Although the Franciscans did not have much civil authority, they were in charge of the local Inquisition and thus could charge colonists, though not the mission Indians, with all manner of offenses, including blasphemy, bigotry, and heresy, which could lead to trial in Mexico City and the loss of all property and perhaps even life. It gave the thirty or so friars crucial leverage against the colonial authorities.[84] At the same time, officials could make friars' tasks more complicated, as when Governor Juan de Eulate (1618–25) refused to provide military guards for priests who wanted to visit new pueblos looking for converts. Eulate even encouraged the Taos people to ignore the priests and took little interest in indigenous idols or practices. He was far more concerned about gaining the trust of the Pueblo in order to later exploit or even enslave them.[85]

The Church and state were not able to put up a unified front, and as the seventeenth century wore on there was a growing resentment among the Pueblo at both administrators and friars. Then, by the 1660s and 1670s, a situation developed that no one could control: drought.[86] Around this time the Franciscans had some sixty mission *estancias*—farms of arable land—in the Río Grande valley where grain was grown and stored.[87] In general, during times of shortages when there was a need for distribution, a bell would toll to signal the handing out of rations.[88] By the 1660s and 1670s, however, the missions had little to spare. At the same time there were increased raids by the Navajo and Apache, who were also experiencing famine. The Apache, in particular, had proved adept at learning to use a tool introduced by the Spanish: the horse, which transformed them into an even more fearsome enemy.[89]

All of this took place against a backdrop of rising infectious diseases. The Pueblo, like most of the Amerindian people who encountered Europeans, suffered at the hands of unfamiliar microbes. By 1638 the Pueblo population was around forty thousand—by 1660 it had fallen to twenty-four thousand, and twenty years later to seventeen thousand. However, the deadliness of new diseases was somewhat mitigated by the arid climate, high elevations, and sparse settlement of Spaniards. The Spanish and mestizo population had grown only from two thousand to three thousand in the twenty years leading up to 1680.[90] Few settlers could be enticed to this remote region, and much of the population rise resulted from intermarriage.[91]

As the drought worsened, so did relations between the Spaniards and Pueblo. The Spanish were failing to live up to their end of the colonial pact. A Franciscan missionary wrote that in New Mexico "in the past year, 1668, a great many Indians perished of hunger, lying dead along the roads, in the ravines, and in their huts."[92] Catholicism could not bring rain, nor could these settlers offer adequate protection from raiding enemies. The Pueblo people began to return to their own religious customs in the hope of ending their suffering, but the Spanish intervened and punished them, only provoking more anger.[93]

Governor Juan Francisco Treviño, in an attempt to assert his authority over the missionaries and further repress Pueblo religious practices, had forty-seven medicine men from the Tewa arrested in 1675. They were tortured and admitted under duress that they were involved in "witchcraft," a common charge leveled at indigenous practices, such as ceremonial dances.[94] Three were hanged and the rest were sold into slavery after being flogged. The incident outraged the Tewa and a group of them marched to Santa Fe to demand the release of the prisoners. The Pueblo had run out of patience.

One of the men who had been involved in the original incident, a religious leader named Po'pay, became a key organizer of a mass uprising in 1680 that united most of the pueblos against the Spanish.[95] Po'pay wanted to bring other Pueblo leaders together in what would later be called the Pueblo Revolt, and unite the six thousand warriors they had among themselves—they still outnumbered the Spanish five times over—as well as involve the Apache.[96] In addition some mestizos, as well as people of Indian-African origin—a small number of enslaved Africans came with the Spanish to New Mexico—were also involved.[97] The plan was fraught with challenges, not least communication across the diverse pueblos. Po'pay and other leaders found ways around this problem, for instance by transferring messages about when to attack in the form of knotted cords.[98]

The plot was almost uncovered at various points, for example on August 9, 1680, when messengers carrying knotted string were picked up by Spanish soldiers and tortured until they confessed, though the Spanish did not anticipate the scale of what was to come. Antonio de Otermín, then governor of New Mexico, later explained that "there was some negligence in that no one really believed the uprising was going to happen."[99] As soon as the Pueblo leaders heard about the capture of the runners, they sent out another message, and the next day around five hundred Indians attacked Santa Fe, later reinforced by the arrival of another twenty-five hundred, laying siege to the town for nine days and killing 380 colonists and 21 missionaries.[100] Priests were not spared; indeed, they were often targeted. Many of the Pueblo tore down churches in their villages with the intention of replacing them with their own religious *kivas*.[101]

With around five hundred people dead, the Spaniards were forced to retreat south of the Río Grande, around modern El Paso/Ciudad Juárez.[102] The Pueblo emerged victorious, though not every pueblo had decided to join in the fight; some opted to remain loyal to the Spanish. When the Spanish left, members of the Piro and Tompiro people, who lived southwest of Santa Fe, went with them.[103] El Paso del Norte would now serve as the Spanish base for New Mexico and a small *presidio* was built for defense, as was a later mission church, Corpus Christi de la Ysleta del Sur, by the Tigua Indians in 1682.

Otermín attempted to take back the territory in 1681, when he and his men set fire to eight pueblos and captured more than three hundred people, but it was a brief retaliation, not a sustained recolonization. However, at the same time, the pueblo communities were fracturing. For instance, the Tewa and Picuris were allied against the Jemez, Taos, Zia, Santo Domingo, and other Keresan-speaking communities. This was happening while the Apache were attacking a number of the pueblos, and the Ute were fighting the Jemez, Taos, Picuris, and Tewa.[104] Leadership tussles continued in the aftermath of the revolt. Po'pay remained in charge after the rebellion but was later ousted by the Keres, Taos, and Pecos after he tried to exact tribute.[105]

The next governor, Domingo Jironza Petrís de Cruzate, spent much of his time shoring up the El Paso settlement before venturing north to see if some of the Pueblo people were willing to resume relations. In August 1689, he led an expedition along the Jemez River, a tributary of the Río Grande, where they attacked the Zia Pueblo, killing six hundred people and taking some seventy prisoners. A fragile peace was then brokered, but the Spanish were still unable to reassert their authority until

the next governor, Diego de Vargas, arrived in 1691.[106] Vargas succeeded
where the others had failed, but not without fights and compromises.
By the autumn of the following year, Vargas reported to the crown that
Santa Fe and a dozen other pueblos were once again under Spanish rule.
That September, he had made an *entrada* in Santa Fe, carrying a standard
with the Virgin Mary on it, confronting the Indians there:

> After sunrise, I approached about twenty paces closer with the inter-
> preter, my secretary of government and war, and the captain of the
> *presidio*, telling them I had come, sent from Spain by his majesty, the
> king, our lord, to pardon them so they might again be Christians, as
> they had been, and the devil would not lead them astray.[107]

Soon afterward, people from neighboring pueblos arrived and he had
trouble communicating his message, writing, "I come to pardon them,
as I have told them. They were rebellious and did not heed my kind
words." They opted instead to make what Vargas interpreted as war
preparations, as more Pueblo people continued to arrive, while some
were held under siege in the town's fortress. Eventually, they agreed that
if the Spanish would take their weapons and leave, they could negotiate
a peace, which they did. As Vargas described it: "The Indians, although
frightened, began to come out to give me the peace, which I gave them
all, with all my love."[108]

In this way, and also using any lingering divisions among the Pueblo
to his advantage, Vargas visited the pueblos, negotiating with leaders
while the priests baptized children and offered absolution.[109] It would not
last, and matters once again turned violent, with another large rebellion
breaking out on June 4, 1696. The fighting lasted for months, with priests
killed and missions attacked, including those in Tewa, Tano, and Jemez
pueblos.[110] Eventually, the Pueblo capitulated in November 1696.[111]

These years of violence left the region transformed. Some towns
were abandoned, which was a strategy often employed to put distance
between the Pueblo and an enemy, be it the Spanish or the Apache.[112] In
one case, the Jemez left their land and moved to live among the Acoma,
Hopi, Zuni, and others. The Zuni, for their part, had seen their six pueblos reduced to one. The Piro, Tompiro, Southern Tiwa, and Southern
Tewa people were absorbed by larger towns.[113]

As the eighteenth century began, a racial *casta* hierarchy had also emerged in New Mexico: the elite colonial officials sat on top, followed by landed peasants who were mostly mestizo, though they often called themselves *españoles* so as not to be identified as Indian. Below this sat the *genízaros*, detribalized people who were treated little better than slaves. A *genízaro* could be a Pueblo person who refused to submit to Spanish rule or Christianity and was subsequently pressed into domestic service; the term could also signify a non-Pueblo captured by the Spanish, such as an Apache.[114] The Spanish also bought enslaved Indians from among Apache captives and other non-Pueblo, all of whom were considered to be justly enslaved, so the Spanish would barter or pay a ransom for them.[115] From 1700 to 1850, some three thousand ransomed people were brought into New Mexican society.[116] Although Indian slavery was no longer permitted by the crown, local officials often turned a blind eye to what was taking place in this remote frontier.

The Pueblo people represented a fourth group.[117] After the rebellions, they were permitted to continue in their own communities, with less interference than before. The Franciscans could not wield as much power so they reduced their "civilizing" activities, such as trying to teach trades like blacksmithing or forcing the Pueblo to work in the fields planting European crops.[118] After more than a hundred years of attempting to settle this region, the Spanish in New Mexico remained on the fringes not only of their empire but of a world still dominated by Native Americans.[119]

FARTHER WEST, THE exploration and settlement of California had evolved in fits and starts over the course of a century. In the early 1530s the Spanish were still puzzling over the size of the North American landmass and any potential water routes that might connect the Atlantic to the Pacific Ocean, which had been first explored for Spain by Vasco Núñez de Balboa some twenty years earlier. Hernando Cortés was also eager to have a second haul of good fortune and so funded a couple of expeditions to explore the north by sea. The first left Acapulco in 1532, and its wreckage was found the following year. The next, in 1533, departed from the west coast and was led by Fortún Jiménez after a brief mutiny, reaching the southern tip of Baja California by late December. Jiménez and some of his men were attacked and killed when they went ashore, but the survivors returned to New Spain claiming they had found an island with a large quantity of pearls. Around this time the area started to be referred to as California.[120]

For once, the Spanish name came from mythology rather than Catholicism. "California" is thought to be based on the imaginary island of the same name, which was under the rule of Queen Calafia, a character from a tale written around 1510 by Garci Rodríguez de Montalvo. *Las Sergas de Esplandián* is a story of this island, located "due east of the Indies," which was "populated by black women, with no men among them, for they lived in the fashion of Amazons."[121] They displayed "ardent courage and great strength," not least by feeding any men on the island—including any they gave birth to—to their terrifying griffins.[122] The island was also famed for its "abundance of gold and precious stones."[123] The story was set in the context of fighting between Christians and Muslims where Calafia wades into battle and in the end marries and converts to Christianity.

Legends aside, the report of pearls was enough to convince Cortés to make the journey himself, and, setting sail from Acapulco, he landed in Baja around 1535. His settlement around modern La Paz, almost directly across the Gulf of California from Culiacán, lasted less than two years.[124] Despite its failure, Cortés sent Francisco de Ulloa on another expedition, and in 1539 Ulloa navigated around the Gulf of California. After Ulloa, Juan Rodríguez Cabrillo left from the small port of Navidad, on the Pacific coast about 450 miles northwest of Acapulco, in 1542, sailing into a natural harbor he called San Miguel, later renamed San Diego.[125] Cabrillo and his men continued along the coast, but he died during the voyage and the ships returned to New Spain. Enthusiasm for further costly exploration diminished as silver was found inland and trade boomed with the establishment of the Spanish in the Philippines in 1565. California, for the moment, fell by the wayside.

Indeed, its next visitor would be not Spanish, but English. Francis Drake, aboard the *Golden Hind*, arrived in 1579 at a bay to the north of modern San Francisco, after months of raiding the ports along the Pacific coast of South America. He, too, was seeking the Northwest Passage to the Atlantic. He spent around five weeks in Northern California, naming the territory Nova Albion (New England); it is thought he reached as far north as today's Alaska before sailing to the Philippines and onward back to England via the Cape of Good Hope.[126] Drake later continued to pester the Spanish, this time in the West Indies, raiding, among other spots, St. Augustine in Florida in 1586.

With the growing Pacific trade between Manila and New Spain, Drake's foray was a cause for concern. In 1587, Spanish ships returning from Manila were ordered to reconnoiter some of the California coast. While doing so, they were attacked and looted by another English pirate, Thomas Cavendish. He set the galleon *Santa Ana* on fire before departing, but the Spanish crew managed to return to Acapulco in the burned and blackened remains of the ship, sending a clear message about the growing threat in the Pacific.[127]

The next serious attempt to explore California's coastline did not come until 1594. As had been the case in 1587, the exploration was to happen on a return voyage from Manila. This time it was led by the Portuguese merchant Sebastián Rodríguez Cermeño, who reached the same harbor as Drake and claimed it for Spain in 1595. He also went ashore, meeting the Miwok people there, but a storm later destroyed his vessel and he was forced to make his way back to New Spain in a salvaged launch.[128]

Using the ships on return from Manila had proved costly, so the next undertaking originated in Acapulco. This one, in 1602, was led by Sebastián Vizcaíno, who had spent time in Manila and had already sailed around parts of Baja California.[129] On this voyage, he reached as far north as Cape Mendocino before bad weather forced him to return, naming San Diego and the bay of Monterey, the latter in honor of the viceroy of New Spain who had sent him on the journey: Gaspar de Zúñiga Acevedo y Fonseca, the fifth Count of Monterrey. He reported to the viceroy in December 1602 that the harbor of Monterey was "well situated" and "secure against all winds," with a ready supply of pine trees nearby, making it an ideal stopping point for the ships coming from the Philippines; he said it was "thickly peopled by Indians and is very fertile, in its climate and the quality of the soil resembling Castile, and any seed sown there will give fruit, and there are extensive lands fit for pasturage, and many kinds of animals and birds."[130]

Despite the glowing report, there was no further exploration of California for another eighty years, it being too remote and expensive to be a wise use of New Spain's resources. When initial settlement did happen, it was spearheaded by the Jesuits. They began to establish remote missions in Baja California in 1684.[131] Leading the effort was perhaps the best-known Jesuit from this period, Eusebio Kino, who was accompanied by Juan María de Salvatierra. They were not Spaniards but rather from northern Italy, and Kino had been sent by the order to New Spain, arriving in 1681. By 1683 he was exploring the Baja Peninsula, having sailed there from the Pacific port of Chacala. Later, under his leadership, the mission of Nuestra Señora de los Dolores (Our Lady of Sorrows) in Sonora was set up in 1687. From there he moved into the Gila and Colorado River basins.[132] Like the missionaries in New Mexico, Kino and his men faced resistance from Native Americans, including a 1695 rebellion in which two priests were killed and the mission of San Pedro y San Pablo del Tubutama, now in the modern Mexican state of Sonora, about seventy miles south of the U.S. border, was attacked. Spanish troops became involved in the retaliation, and the fighting lasted for four months.[133] Despite the threats, Kino walked or rode thousands of miles, covering the land and meeting numerous Native Americans, many of whom ended up building the priest's missions, until his death in 1711.

Kino's legacy can be seen about ten miles south of Tucson, Arizona, where the "white dove of the desert" rises out of the bleak browns and muted patches of green, the gleaming towers of the church contrasting with their flat setting, as if the entire structure had been dropped down from the sky. San Xavier del Bac sits around a mile from Kino's original 1692 site and, unlike the mission of Tumacácori to the south, it remains intact. Today its ornate carved facade is not crumbling, and its interior, framed by an elaborate gilt altarpiece, signals its continued use as a place of worship and as a historical site, a spiritual link between Kino's world and today's, as does its continued connection with the Tohono O'odham people.*

Many other reminders exist of the long seventeenth century that transformed these outer limits of El Norte. San Miguel, in Santa Fe,

---

* San Xavier was rebuilt by the Franciscans in 1783.

claims that its foundation dates back to 1610—making it the oldest church in the continental United States. Even the rebellious Acoma preserved San Estevan del Rey, and its smooth facade and towers continue to over-look the far edge of the Sky City. Some Spanish and Pueblo ruins have become park sites, and tourists in New Mexico can walk among the former villages and missions of San Gregorio de Abó, Gran Quivira, and Quarai, all of which date back to the 1620s and today make up the Salinas Pueblo Missions National Monument. Even Unesco has stepped in, deeming the multistoried brown houses of the Taos pueblo a World Heritage Site. The diverse complexity of the world that Oñate, Kino, and thousands of Spaniards found themselves in lives on. The legacy of what took place there, however, remains contested.

Just outside the sleepy village of Alcalde, New Mexico, heading north along Highway 68, is a man on horseback. Juan de Oñate sits tall on his bronze steed, riding over rough grass and tall weeds. Behind the statue are bare flagpoles and a faded pink building named Oñate Monument and Visitor Center. The statue sits diminished by these surroundings, as if Oñate had taken a wrong turn. Many people in the area might argue that he had.

The statue came to national attention in 1998—the four-hundredth anniversary of Oñate's arrival in New Mexico—when the *New York Times* reported that a group of Acoma people had sneaked into the site and taken a saw to Oñate's right foot, seeking vengeance for the punishment meted out to their ancestors.[134] This act embodied the region's competing histories: for the Hispanic population, the Oñate statue was an emblem of their heritage, while to the Acoma it was an insult. Today this statue of Oñate has both feet—for now.

An even larger seventeen-ton statue of Oñate greets passengers just outside the El Paso airport, with his mighty horse rearing back, ready to head for the horizon. Yet this statue does not bear his name, after Native American groups convinced the city council to call it *The Equestrian*.[135] Dedicated in 2007, the work "commemorates the shared history of Spain, Mexico and the United States at El Paso del Norte."

Despite the controversies, the conquistador era continues to loom large in New Mexico. Santa Fe has an annual three-day celebration, the Santa Fe Fiesta, which dates back to 1712 and was established in honor of Diego de Vargas's *entrada* in 1692. People wear period costumes, attend religious processions, and commemorate the events of more than three hundred years ago, though the fiesta also attracts protests.[136] The New Mexican town of Española, about ten miles south of Alcalde, holds a three-day Fiesta del Valle de Española every June, a festival dating to around 1933 that also commemorates the arrival of the Spanish. This fiesta begins with the naming of a Don Juan de Oñate and the coronation of a queen, La Reina. Oñate is attended by young men dressed as conquistadores, while the queen has her female court, which includes Native American members.[137]

In places like the Coronado National Memorial south of Tucson—a forest named in honor of the Spanish explorer—such overlaps and contrasts are more solemn. A sign at the entrance to the park, across from one that bears an illustration of a conquistador, presumably Coronado, on his horse, says: "Smuggling and/or illegal entry is common in this area due to the proximity of the international border." People who today follow in the Spaniards' footsteps, moving from south to north through the park's 4,750 acres, face a similar range of natural threats, such as bears and extreme temperatures in the Huachuca Mountains. Now the additional prowl of the Border Patrol, whose SUVs, complete with built-in holding cells, race up and down the road, acts as a reminder that this region's past remains complicated by the demands of the present.

Chapter 4

Fort Mose, Florida, ca. 1600–1760

W HILE THE SPANISH were pushing into New Mexico and the West, the English and Dutch had been lured to the Atlantic coast of North America. They, too, wanted to see what they could find—at the very least there might be a Spanish ship to capture, though many people persisted in the belief that there would be precious metals. The geographer and colonial enthusiast Richard Hakluyt thought the earlier writings from adventurers and explorers, like Jean Ribault's account of Florida, held clues. Hakluyt wrote in his 1584 *Discourse of Western Planting* that there was "in the lande golde, silver and copper." These were metals that, argued Hakluyt, would be in colonies rightfully claimed by Queen Elizabeth I, a territory stretching "from Florida northward to 67 degrees, (and not yet in any Christian princes actual possession)."

Hakluyt supported the planting of English colonies in North America for a number of reasons, not least because it would "be greatly for thinlargment [*sic*] of the gospel of Christe." Perhaps more important, it would benefit trade, it would bring "manifolde imployment of nombers of idle men." Such a colony would also allow the English to find the Northwest Passage, and, perhaps best of all, it would humiliate Felipe II because "the lymites of the kinge of Spaines domynions in the west Indies be nothing so large as ys generally ymagined."[1]

The English were already familiar with such enterprises—before they started looking across the Atlantic, they had focused on Ireland. More than one hundred thousand people, mainly Protestants from England, Wales, and especially Scotland, left for Ireland in the seventeenth century,

setting up "plantations"—a system that rewarded them with land ownership and altered the dynamics of social and political relations to the
detriment of the Catholic Irish. The island had been made a part of Henry
VIII's kingdom in 1541, but the settlement process accelerated under
James I's Plantation of Ulster, in 1609. These developments, however,
met with periods of fierce Irish resistance and required the presence of
tens of thousands of soldiers.

Settlement expeditions were costly, and so would-be colonizers had
to possess the money themselves or raise it through crown-sanctioned
joint-stock companies.[2] The first serious attempt to place a colony in
North America was promoted by the adventurer Walter Raleigh, who was
also an Irish landowner. He received a charter from Elizabeth I to put a
settlement in what the Spanish considered to be Florida but the English
thought of as being "not inhabited by Christian people."[3] A place was
found in 1585 between the long stretch of barrier islands along modern
North Carolina's Outer Banks and the mainland, near the Albemarle
Sound. These English settlers lived among the Roanoke people, and so
the place adopted that name, in an area they called Virginia, thought to
be named in honor of the Virgin Queen, though perhaps also inspired
by a powerful local chief, Wingina. Although Raleigh did not join the
settlers, he hoped the spot would prosper as a base for privateering
attacks on the Spanish fleet. Indeed, Francis Drake sailed there after his
May 1586 sacking of St. Augustine.

The colonists survived through one winter, but they faced many of
the same difficulties as the French in Florida had twenty years earlier,
especially food shortages and deteriorating relations with the Native
Americans. By the time Drake arrived in June 1586, the settlers wanted
to return to England and the colony was abandoned. A new batch of
hopeful colonists was sent out in 1587, but because of ongoing naval hostilities between England and Spain—a period that included the English
defeat of the Spanish Armada in 1588—no resupply ships could reach
the colony. When they finally did arrive in 1590, they found no survivors.

This failure did not dim English enthusiasm for overseas colonies, and
plans to try again were aided by the 1604 Treaty of London. This accord
ended, for the time being, the hostilities between Spain and England,
and trading resumed. James I had come to the English throne in 1603,
and his counterpart in Spain, Felipe III, had ascended in 1598. Although

James I wanted to improve relations with Spain, many of the English remained distrustful of Catholic Spaniards, while some of the Spanish were wary of England's designs on the Americas. There were plenty of good reasons to harbor suspicions, as Pedro de Zúñiga, Spain's ambassador to England, discovered.

Zúñiga arrived in England in July 1605 and by 1607 was relaying his intelligence about plans "made in great secrecy" to send ships to Virginia and Plymouth.[4] Zúñiga managed to gain an audience with James I in October that year, when he reiterated the claim that Virginia "is a part of the Indies belonging to Castile." James I rejected this, saying such measures were not outlined in the 1604 treaty. Zúñiga reported that "he [James I] had never known that Your Majesty had a right to it [Virginia], for it was a region very far from where the Spaniards had settled." He told Zúñiga that the participants in these voyages undertook them at their own risk, and so could not complain if the Spanish did capture and punish them. Their meeting ended with a final plea from Zúñiga that "a remedy be found for the Virginia affair," though none was forthcoming.[5]

Zúñiga continued to worry about the implications for Spain, telling his king in 1609 that he understood the settlements were considered to be "so perfect (as they say) for piratical excursions that Your Majesty will not be able to bring silver from the Indies." Zúñiga's advice in dealing with the settlements was to "command that they be crushed as quickly as possible."[6] Felipe III sent Francisco Fernández de Écija, a captain who had served with Governor Menéndez when St. Augustine was founded, to find out more. Although by this point in his sixties, Écija sailed from St. Augustine in June 1609 to gather information about Virginia.[7] His report detailed his travels along the coast, including the area around Santa Elena, and his meetings with Native Americans. He sailed near the ruins of the Roanoke Colony, which the Spanish had known about, before heading up to Chesapeake Bay, where his men finally caught sight of an English vessel that "carried two topsails and a great flag at the masthead." They did not escape detection, and an English ship followed them for a while.[8] Once out of the line of attack, the Spaniards continued their investigation, before returning to St. Augustine by late September.[9]

By the time of Écija's report, the Virginia Colony had been well established, with its settlers arriving in 1607. Although at least one hundred thousand Spaniards had emigrated to Spain's colonies by 1600, with some estimates reaching three hundred thousand, few of them were living anywhere near Virginia—most were in New Spain or farther south—leaving an area the Spanish considered to be theirs undefended.[10] The English settlement, organized by the Virginia Company, was farther north than Roanoke, in the Chesapeake Bay area. To the Spanish this had been the ill-fated land of Ajacán that they had abandoned a century earlier, but to the English it was Jamestown, named for James I. In the same year that ships departed for Virginia, other vessels headed farther north, funded by the Plymouth Company, which also had a charter. Those settlers established the Popham Colony in 1607, on the Kennebec River in today's Maine, and built a small fort. However, after a year—including a harsh winter—its colonists returned to England.

Virginia struggled on, and its early years were precarious. The settlers died in droves from disease and hunger—some ten thousand people arrived between 1607 and 1622, but only around two thousand were alive by 1622.[11] The crown, however, realized that this colony could be a useful place to send the potentially troublesome as well as the poor, for instance shipping some two hundred impoverished children there in 1618–19.[12] Attacks from Native Americans on the colony required constant vigilance. Yet like the French, the English also depended on Indian support for survival, though like the Spanish, they were quick to dispossess Native Americans of their territory. They were aided in this as illnesses threatened peoples of the Algonquin-speaking Powhatan confederacy, whose numbers in Virginia plummeted; there were around twenty-four thousand at the time of the first encounter with the English, but this figure was reduced to two thousand by 1669.[13] The English colonies also had lower levels of *mestizaje*—in their case Anglo-Indian—than Spain's. While the Spanish crown had permitted, and in the earliest years even encouraged, marriage between Amerindians and Spaniards, the English did not follow suit. Despite this, one of the most important foundational stories of English settlement remains how Pocahontas, a Powhatan chief's daughter, was said to have saved the life of Captain John Smith, a member of the initial voyage, though she was later held captive by the English. By 1614, however, she married John Rolfe and through her actions temporarily mitigated the growing animosity between the two groups. Pocahontas was an exception and remained so. As more

Englishwomen traveled to join the colony, concubinage or cohabitation with Native Americans was increasingly frowned upon.[14]*

Any hope of finding mineral wealth faded in Virginia's early years. Captain Smith, in writing his account of Virginia, had much to say about the natural wonders of the colony, though less about such riches. His 1612 *The Description of Virginia* praised its forests of oak, walnut, and elm trees; the wide range of fruits that grew there; and the birds and fish that abounded: "no place is more convenient for pleasure, profit, and mans sustenance."[15] On the matter of extractable riches, he was more circumspect, claiming that "concerning the entrailes of the earth little can be saide for certainty . . . only this is certaine, that many regions lying in the same latitude, afford mines very rich of diverse natures."[16]

The rise of tobacco reinforced the English belief that the land itself was capable of providing wealth through the production of an exportable commodity, and, to this end, unused land meant a loss of potential profit. The English puzzled over Algonquin land management and often claimed that land was not being "used," as a justification for trying to buy, barter, or take it away from the Indians. To work the land was to own it, and this pattern was repeated throughout the Tidewater region.[17] The English philosopher John Locke, who would go on to become a secretary to one of the Lords Proprietors of Carolina and a shareholder in the slave-trading Royal African Company, believed that laboring to "improve" land was at the heart of the colonizing project. He wrote much later in his 1690 *Two Treatises of Government* that "as much land as a man tills, plants, improves, cultivates, and can use the product of, so much is his property," arguing that "the extent of the ground is of so little value without labour."[18]

After some deliberation, the Council of the Indies in Spain finally recommended an attack on Virginia in 1611, though the expedition never materialized. In its place were diplomatic complaints and a slight expansion of the St. Augustine garrison, because it was the closest point to the English.[19] The crown did not want to risk another long, costly conflict

---

* By 1691 the Virginia General Assembly had passed a law forbidding marriages of whites to Native Americans, as well as to black and mulatto people.

with England. Spain's unwillingness to act may have avoided problems for the time being, but the longer-term ramifications were profound: it allowed the English to cement their place in North America and the wider Atlantic world. Not long after the establishment of Jamestown, other colonies were placed on islands with little or no Spanish presence, including St. Kitts in 1623 and Barbados in 1627. The English also later took Jamaica as a consolation prize from the Spanish in 1655 after a failed attempt to capture Santo Domingo.

Where the English went, other Europeans soon followed. French privateers were already roaming the West Indies. The Dutch also engaged in piracy, but they, too, began using joint-stock companies to fund American colonies, putting one in what they called New Amsterdam (New York), by 1625, as well as a few in the islands of the Caribbean, including, in 1634, Curaçao, which would become a hub of the African slave trade.

Trade and wealth were not the only goals of the English colonists; they also had their minds on God. Christianity was a crucial factor in colonization, but for reasons distinct from those of the Spanish. Protestants did not have the equivalent of the Jesuits or Franciscans to minister to Native Americans, nor did English edicts demand conversions. While settlers like Captain Smith believed, as he wrote, that colonists could "bring such poore infidels to the true knowledge of God and his holy Gospell," Protestant Christianity would have its own trajectory in the Americas.[20] At first, religion provided many settlers with their reason for being in North America. John Rolfe described the English presence there as a sign of being "marked and chosen by the finger of God."[21] New England became a beacon for Protestants escaping the often fatal uncertainties of the English Reformation; and while the initial Plymouth Colony may have been a failure, English Protestants continued to eye the shores of North America.

Although Henry VIII had broken with Rome in 1533, the particulars of English Protestantism were in no way settled. The Puritans, who followed the teaching of John Calvin, pushed for further changes in the Anglican Church; indeed the term "Puritan" was initially meant as an insult by Anglicans who viewed them as extremists. There was much disagreement within Puritan circles on how changes should be accomplished, but in general their aims included the creation of a more direct relationship with God and a less formal worship service. Such dissent, however, was interpreted in different ways by subsequent monarchs, and so at times Puritan beliefs could be perilous.[22] They were tolerated under James I, though some uneasy Puritans began to seek religious refuge across the Atlantic. The most famous group of dissenters, the Pilgrims, were the first to make that crossing. They were also Calvinists but were more extreme than other Puritans in their demands. Their ship, the *Mayflower*, arrived in 1620; they landed on the easternmost hook of modern Massachusetts before crossing the bay and establishing their Plymouth Colony.

When Charles I took the throne in 1625 more serious issues emerged, not least that he was married to a Catholic and had sympathies with English Catholics. Indeed, Cecilius Calvert, the second Lord Baltimore, received a charter in 1632 that would become the colony of Maryland, which was intended to be a place of tolerance and refuge for Catholics who faced discrimination in England, though the initial settlers in 1634 also included Protestants.[23] By this time, the Puritans were leaving England in droves, having established the Massachusetts Bay Colony near the Pilgrim settlements in 1630. Some thirty thousand Puritans, many of whom had been middle-class merchants in England and would be so again, migrated over the course of the 1630s.[24]

Unlike Virginia, where tobacco plantations were forming, New England became a land of small farmers, craftsmen, and merchant houses. From here, the Puritans could build their "city upon a hill" and engage in a form of worship they could not practice in England.[25] These settlements also faced hardships early on and many were very rudimentary in comparison with parts of the Spanish empire. Mexico City, for instance, had a population of at least 150,000 by 1620, a university, and a cathedral.[26] The town of Boston, some thirty years later, in 1650, hovered around only 2,000 souls.[27]

Although other parts of Spanish America were urban and populated, St. Augustine lagged. The dream of thriving missions throughout Florida had not materialized, though by 1655, seventy friars were ministering to some twenty-six thousand people in the region, working across four mission provinces: Guale, Timucua, Apalachee, and Apalachicola.[28] This modest success, however, could do little to stem the decline of the indigenous population by the middle of the 1600s. There were a number of factors involved, with significant outbreaks of smallpox and measles, but also changes in diet and land use brought on by the missions, as well as serious rebellions, including an eight-month uprising in 1656 of the Timucua, and raids from other Native Americans.[29] The Spanish settler and mestizo population remained small, while the Timucua would see virtual eradication, dropping from around ten thousand in 1600 to fourteen by 1727, and the Apalachee population was halved to around ten thousand over roughly the same period.[30] Some Florida Indians moved north and west, often joining with other indigenous communities.[31] Others looked south, seeking Spanish help and protection; for instance, the Guale people headed to St. Augustine around 1680.[32] As these groups moved, the number of laborers dropped and the missions struggled to sustain themselves.

Another factor in these shifts in Florida was the English, who were inching closer. As Virginia had prospered, there was growing pressure within the colony to push south, both to expand and, it was claimed, to defend Jamestown from any Spanish incursions.[33] In 1663, Charles II issued a grant to a group of investors—who were also supporters of his restoration to the throne after the English Civil War—for a settlement to be called Carolina. Soon English ships were exploring the waterways around Santa Elena, though the main port, Charles Town (modern Charleston, South Carolina), was placed a bit farther north, around the Ashley River, in 1670. That same year, England and Spain hammered out the terms of the Treaty of Madrid, drawn up to ease tensions between the two brought about by a number of attacks between English and Spanish ships in the Caribbean. It was a turning point in Anglo-Spanish relations, finally granting official recognition to British claims on Jamaica and Virginia and placing the boundary of Spanish Florida at N 32°30′, with Charles Town sitting just north of this border.

Around the same time, in 1672, the Royal African Company was granted a monopoly on all English trade between the west coast of Africa, the Caribbean, and the North American colonies, and English ships joined those of the Portuguese, Spanish, and Dutch in violently forcing the migration of Africans. Within thirty years, some sixty-six hundred people lived in Carolina, of whom thirty-eight hundred were settlers and twenty-eight hundred slaves.[34]

Africans were the other significant group of arrivals in the seventeenth century. These were not the first Africans in North America—the Spanish had enslaved and freed people with them from their sixteenth-century expeditions onward—but the English drove up this number. According to the Trans-Atlantic Slave Trade Database, between 1670 and 1700, some 8,600 Africans, many from the western region of the continent, disembarked in North America. Most of them went to either the Virginia territory (4,504) or Maryland (2,917).³⁵ Their numbers continued to rise as the colonists wanted more workers for the expanding plantations and Africans replaced white or Indian laborers. The use of enslaved people had also spread throughout the British colonies in the West Indies, where Africans were put to work in the sugar fields of islands such as Barbados.

However, not all slaves were African. Native American enslavement remained a significant component of labor throughout the English colonies at this time, and into the eighteenth century. The English considered conflict with the Indians a "just war," and so any captivity or enslavement was deemed fair. Native Americans made up the majority of nonwhite labor in New England before 1700, with some thirteen hundred people enslaved at this time.³⁶ The definition of slavery was also nebulous in this period, with servitude and unfair indenture contracts leading to a form of enslavement, even after 1700 when Indian enslavement was made illegal.³⁷ The Virginia colonists also enslaved Indians throughout the seventeenth century, for instance after a number of conflicts with the Powhatan. Some were kept to work in Virginia, while others were exported—often at a handsome profit—to other English colonies.³⁸

Carolina, with its proximity to the Native American communities of Spanish Florida, was heavily involved in this slave trade. The colony's officials made alliances with the Westo—also called the Rickahockan—who had migrated in the mid-1600s to an area around the Savannah River, and who had pushed the Guale off their land. The Westo were critical to Indian enslavement in Carolina, and they were offered English goods, such as guns, tools, or cloth, in exchange for captives. This made raiding potentially far more lucrative than hunting or farming, but it also introduced a particular dilemma for the English, in that in this trading configuration there was a distinct lack of a "just war."³⁹

The raids into neighboring chiefdoms and Spanish territory spelled the end of the Spanish mission system in Florida, as the priests could no longer offer protection when the Westo assailed sites in Timucua and Apalachee. The situation was such that by the 1690s the Spanish found it necessary to keep troops in a small fort at the San Luis de Apalachee mission and in the surrounding area.[40] By the first years of the 1700s, the chain of missions linking the Guale territory to St. Augustine had disintegrated, bringing more than a century's worth of evangelical effort to a close.[41]

While these attacks destroyed a crucial part of Spanish Florida, they were foundational in the development of the Carolina plantation economy. That colony's leaders tried to keep the trade for themselves, using the profits from Indians sold to other English colonies to buy the tools and African slaves needed to develop the land, as well as the manufactured goods to exchange for more slaves.[42] The entire situation was fragile, however, and there were wars between the English and the Westo in the 1670s and 1680s.[43] The Carolina planters were forced to find allies beyond the Westo, for instance, with the Yamasee, a confederation of smaller chiefdoms from Georgia and South Carolina that raided Apalachee in 1684–85.[44] Some raiders even brought back slaves from as far west as modern Texas, and this practice continued well into the next century.[45]

In addition to these raids, sea-based hostilities continued between the English and Spanish. English privateers attacked Florida in 1668 and again throughout the 1680s. One attack, in 1682, destroyed the small fort of San Marcos, located near the convergence of the Wakulla and St. Marks Rivers, near the northern Gulf Coast of Florida. The Spanish were under orders not to retaliate, however, because it would violate their peace deal with the English.[46] This frustrated the governors of Florida and Cuba, who used a Spanish privateer, Alejandro Tomás de Léon, to organize a retaliation on their behalf. The expedition left St. Augustine in May 1686 and burned down a settlement known as Stuart Town (or Stuart's Town), south of Charles Town, before going on to attack and plunder plantations along the coast.[47] Such back-and-forth raids continued by land and sea throughout the later part of the seventeenth century.

Throughout this turbulent time, the Spanish in St. Augustine were working on a new fort, spurred into action by an attack in 1668. They broke ground on the Castillo de San Marcos fort in 1672, though its completion would take another couple of decades. It was designed to be another link in Spain's extensive defense system, connecting San Marcos to the older forts, including San Juan de Ulúa in Veracruz, and the Castillo San Felipe del Morro in San Juan, Puerto Rico. San Marcos was more modest than these other fortifications, though a vast improvement on its predecessor. Each of the fort's four corners featured a diamond-shaped bastion, with rounded sentry boxes, called *garitas*, on each of them. Although its style was in line with the design of the other forts, San Marcos's materials were unique: it was built using coquina, a type of limestone rock consisting of tiny compressed shells. The true test of the fortress's strength would come soon enough.

WHILE THE ENGLISH and Dutch were making inroads along the Atlantic seaboard, the French had changed direction. Huguenots in Spanish Florida had been only one arm of France's involvement in the Americas; as early as 1534, Jacques Cartier explored around Newfoundland and the St. Lawrence River, claiming the area for France, though his attempts to set up a trading post failed. After further intermittent efforts, the French finally enjoyed some success in 1608, when Samuel de Champlain erected a settlement at Quebec.

From there, they spread in two directions. First, they moved into what they called New France, along the Gulf of St. Lawrence and toward the Great Lakes, where they were trapping animals and trading lucrative furs; they also went into the southern part of the Mississippi valley. In addition, as the English and Dutch had done, they took some Caribbean islands, including Martinique (1635), Guadeloupe (1635), and, by the end of the seventeenth century, Saint-Domingue (1697), which was the eastern third of Spanish Santo Domingo.

Spain may have been successful driving the French out of Florida but now faced a similar problem in the Gulf of Mexico. The Spanish had explored much of the Gulf and considered it part of their territory, though it remained sparsely settled. Thus, when René-Robert Cavelier, Sieur de La Salle, decided to start his travels on the Mississippi River in February 1682, there was no Spaniard to stop him. La Salle, who traversed much of French America, also believed in the dream of a passage to the Pacific. Hoping to find it, his party of twenty-two Frenchmen and eighteen Native Americans, seven of whom were women, set out from where the Illinois and Mississippi Rivers meet, just north of modern

St. Louis. On their way south, they passed today's Missouri, Ohio, and Arkansas Rivers, before arriving near the mouth of the Mississippi in April.[48] There was no obvious route west, but undeterred, they claimed the area that surrounded the Mississippi River for Louis XIV, calling it La Louisiane.

La Salle had returned to France the following year to make his case to the crown for settlement in this territory, departing once again in 1684 with four ships and some three hundred people. Navigational miscalculations in the Gulf of Mexico put the project in jeopardy: rather than landing at the mouth of the Mississippi in 1685, La Salle arrived at present-day Matagorda Bay, Texas, some four hundred miles west. The French built a rudimentary fort, and La Salle spent the next two years exploring the region by land and sea, trying to find the location of the Mississippi River, as well as now looking for the overland route to the celebrated silver mines of northern Mexico.[49]

The settlement scarcely survived, and resentment festered as La Salle was absent for long periods. In March 1687 a group of men with La Salle on another of his journeys mutinied and killed him. Some of the survivors of this expedition returned to France, while the remaining handful of people at the settlement were attacked by the local Karankawa people the following year.[50] The Spanish made five attempts to look for La Salle after hearing what the French were doing and in 1689 found the ruins of Fort St. Louis. Upon further exploration, the Spanish found two survivors living among the Native Americans. One survivor and mutineer, Jean l'Archevêque, told the Spanish what had happened and was later imprisoned.[51] After his release, however, he turned his loyalty to Spain and worked as a translator and soldier, later appearing in New Mexico.

The next significant French expedition came under the leadership of Pierre Le Moyne d'Iberville, who managed to find the mouth of the Mississippi River and navigate through its maze of channels. He established a settlement in Biloxi Bay in 1699 and, near the coast, a small military outpost, Fort Maurepas, which would serve as the first capital for the Louisiana territory.[52] In 1702, they moved northeast to a bluff overlooking the Mobile River and established Fort Louis de la Louisiane, though that lasted only a few years. In 1711, the residents were uprooted once again to start a settlement twenty-five miles south, building another Fort Louis, which would be renamed Fort Condé in

1723.[53] The French by this point were under the leadership of Iberville's brother, Jean Baptiste Le Moyne, the Sieur de Bienville, who governed the Louisiana territory until 1740.

French objectives in North America were not unlike those of the Spanish and the English: exploration, trade, and profit. However, French interaction with Amerindians was markedly different from that of the Spanish. Rather than using an *encomienda*-style labor system like the Spanish, or developing plantations along the lines of the English, many of the French started their commercial exploits by trading furs, such as beaver. French traders often resided at close quarters with Native Americans and, over time, they were able to build intimate ties with many chiefdoms, partnering with indigenous women and having children, who were known as *métis*. Profitable furs were sent to France, and guns and manufactured wares were shipped over to be sold to the Indians.

That is not to say the French eschewed more spiritual activities. Although the earliest French settlers in Santa Elena were Huguenots, Catholicism remained the dominant faith for the seventeenth-century arrivals, among them a number of Jesuits who began to appear in North America in the early 1600s. These priests left extensive accounts of their time among the people along the modern U.S.-Canadian border, including the Iroquois and Algonquin. Like the traders, the Jesuits often lived within Indian villages, where they continued to attempt to convert these "heathen" people.[54] Some Jesuits also participated in exploration missions, such as Jacques Marquette, who was a member of the party that in 1673 discovered a route from Lake Michigan to the Mississippi River, which La Salle would travel all the way down nine years later.[55]

The French activity in the Mississippi valley unsettled Spanish administrators in Florida, so in 1698 they erected a small defensive settlement, Santa María de Galve, near the waters of Pensacola Bay. Around the same time, in northern New Spain, the Spanish continued their attempts to broker alliances with the Native Americans west of the Mississippi River, including the Caddo-speaking Hasinai people, with the aim of buffering any French advances into that territory.

The Hasinai were part of the larger Caddo confederacy, which spread out in East Texas and western Louisiana. Although there were some twenty-five different chiefdoms, their ways of life had certain shared characteristics. They were mostly agricultural, growing crops like maize and squash, supplemented by the hunting of bison and other animals. They were also sedentary, living in grass homes in villages that also included temple mounds.[56] The Spanish began to call this region *Tejas*, also spelled Texas, after the Hasinai word for "friends" or "allies," *ta-sha*.[57] Priests tried to put missions among the Hasinai, building San Francisco de los Tejas, just east of today's Augusta, Texas, in 1690, which was followed by Santísimo Nombre de María, located around twelve miles northeast on the Neches River, in the same year. A smallpox epidemic descended not long afterward, killing about three thousand people. The Hasinai blamed the Spanish for the devastation and drove them out of the territory. San Francisco de los Tejas was abandoned by 1693, and Santísimo Nombre de María was destroyed in an earlier flood in 1692. With little to show for these efforts, in 1694 the viceroy of New Spain, at this point struggling with a number of other concerns, abandoned any further activity in this part of Texas, for the time being.[58]

T HE EIGHTEENTH CENTURY opened with a crisis in Europe. Spain's Hapsburg king, Carlos II, died in 1700 with no heir. The prospect of the Spanish throne passing to a French Bourbon, Philippe d'Anjou, the grandson of María Theresa—Carlos's half sister and the first wife of Louis XIV—left the rest of the continent with serious concerns about the balance of power if France and Spain were united. England, Holland, and Austria went to battle against Spain and France in the War of the Spanish Succession, a conflict that spilled into the colonies and was known in North America as Queen Anne's War (1702–13).

Some of the opening shots of this conflict were fired at the recently finished San Marcos fort in St. Augustine, as the English, aided by Indian allies and led by the South Carolina governor James Moore, attacked the Spanish in 1702. They had worked their way down from South Carolina, destroying a Spanish fort on Amelia Island and fortifications near the St. Johns River. By the time the English arrived in St. Augustine, the townspeople had taken refuge inside the fort, waiting out a siege that lasted around seven weeks. The fort's coquina walls held out until a fleet from Havana arrived in late December and chased away the English, but not before they had set fire to the town.

The French had limited resources to contribute to the conflict; in 1708 French Louisiana consisted of fewer than three hundred settlers, including 122 soldiers.[59] However, a plan was organized to make use of the sea power of French privateers, and in 1706 a joint force of the Spanish in Florida and French corsairs attacked Charles Town, though the city remained in English hands.[60] The war ended in 1714, with Philippe, now Felipe V, on the Spanish throne after renouncing his French claims. The British—as they had become when the Acts of Union created Great Britain by uniting England and Scotland in 1707—emerged victorious from the negotiations of the Treaty of Utrecht. They were ceded much of France's territory in Canada, including Newfoundland, Nova Scotia, and Hudson Bay. In addition, within Europe, Spain was forced to turn over Gibraltar and the island of Minorca to Britain. Also as significant, the British won the lucrative *asiento*, a contract that granted its traders an exclusive right to supply African slaves to Spanish America.

North American colonists had to contend with changing power balances on two fronts: the rivalries and wars of Europe and those in the Native American world. The disease, enslavement, and migration that forced Native Americans into new lands or confederations in the late 1600s meant that by the early 1700s there were a number of recent alliances and animosities among Indian groups. Among the most powerful groups to emerge in this period were the Creeks, also known as Musk-ogee. The Upper Creeks, as the Europeans called them, lived along the Tallapoosa and Coosa Rivers that feed into the Alabama River—near modern east Alabama and west Georgia. The Lower Creeks, as they were known, were situated along the Apalachicola River in Florida, and as far north as the Chattahoochee and Flint Rivers.[61] There was a constant jostle for influence, trade, and alliances among the Upper and Lower Creeks with the British and Spanish. It was a situation that each side could exploit. For instance, the Creeks helped the British fight the Spanish—for example, during a devastating attack on the mission Santa Fé de Toloca among the Apalachee in 1702—but the Spanish at various points played to the Creeks' anxieties by telling them they might be enslaved by the British.[62] Relationships could be fragile and subject to quick changes.

The Creeks also participated in slave raids for the British, who had started giving them goods—including arms and alcohol—on credit, allowing them to run up large debts. Because the Spanish missions in Florida had been abandoned by the early 1700s, few Indians were left to enslave. They had to turn to deerskin to pay the British and became indebted to the tune of about one hundred thousand skins by 1711, something that would require years of labor to produce. The Creek people were angry about their treatment—not only what they considered trickery in allowing the debts to accumulate, but also the British habit of punishing indebted Indian men with humiliating public floggings.[63]

The Creeks were not the only people with grievances, and in April 1715 some Yamasee people executed a few English traders, triggering a conflict known as the Yamasee War (1715–17). A number of Native American nations, including the Upper Creeks and the Chickasaw, joined the Yamasee in attacking English settlements, and even some runaway black slaves joined the effort.[64] After months of fighting, the British faced defeat, until they managed to enlist the help of the Cherokee people, who drove the Yamasee out of the Carolina territory and into Spanish Florida.[65]

Conflict also spread around the Gulf of Mexico. In 1718, Governor Bienville claimed for France a small crescent of land near where the Mississippi River fans out into the Gulf, calling it La Nouvelle-Orléans, after the Duke of Orléans.[66] Although its climate was brutal—hot and sticky in the summer and prone to flooding and hurricanes—it was well positioned for trade, and a handful of settlers arrived. The French had also continued exploring north along the Mississippi River, building a small outpost in 1716 near the Red River, a tributary of the Mississippi that meanders from Louisiana through northeast Texas. This was close to the Natchitoches chiefdom, a group that was also part of the larger Caddo confederacy, with whom the French were eager to trade. The Natchitoches also distrusted the Spanish, in part because of their failed attempt at planting missions among the Hasinai in the 1690s.[67] This territory had not come under any European dominance, but as the French leaned west, the Spanish were drawn back to Texas. They were spurred into action after French traders arrived at the outpost of San Juan Bautista, near the Río Grande (by today's Guerrero, in the Mexican state of Coahuila), in July 1714.[68] They responded with a flurry of building in East Texas, constructing a small fort in 1716 along with four wooden churches.[69] Two Franciscan missions were also built just to the west of Natchitoches—Nuestra Señora de los Dolores de los Ais and San Miguel de Linares de los Adaes, near San Augustine, Texas, and Robeline, Louisiana, respectively—in an attempt to establish a boundary between Spanish and French spheres of influence among Native Americans. In 1718, farther south, a presidio was placed near the headwaters of the San Antonio River, with the name San Antonio de Béxar. A mission—San Antonio de Valero—was built there in the same year and it would later be known as the Alamo.[70] Four more missions were later added, strung southward along the San Antonio River.

In the same year, hostilities in Europe resumed, this time in the War of the Quadruple Alliance, which pitted Spain against France, England, Holland, and Austria. The French in Natchitoches used the opportunity to attack and capture San Miguel de Linares de los Adaes, as well as ambush the Spanish fort in Pensacola in May 1719.[71]

While plans were being made for a Spanish attack on Louisiana, the larger conflict ended, in 1720. Spanish officials in Texas took the opportunity to reinforce the frontier, with the most significant addition being a presidio near the Los Adaes site in 1721; it garrisoned around a hundred men and would become the capital of Spanish Texas from 1729 to 1773.[72] Farther away from Louisiana, also in 1721, the presidio of Nuestra Señora de la Bahía de Espíritu Santo de Zúñiga was built on the Gulf, on the site of the earlier failed La Salle expedition.

Meanwhile, in New Mexico, Governor Antonio Valverde y Cosío had launched an attack in 1719 against the Ute and Comanche when he heard that the French were nearby and living among the Pawnee and Jumanos.[73] In June 1720, Valverde y Cosío's lieutenant, Pedro de Villasur, was dispatched with around one hundred men, among them the Frenchman Jean l'Archevêque, who had earlier survived at the Matagorda Bay colony and pledged his allegiance to Spain.[74] They set off to the northeast from Santa Fe, reaching the Río de Jesús María (today's Platte River, in Nebraska), which they followed to the Rio San Lorenzo (today's Loup River). They found the Pawnee people, but their attempts to communicate with them foundered. Villasur and his men set up camp nearby and the following morning were woken by a volley of gunshots—no doubt from French weapons—as the Pawnee ambushed them. Villasur and l'Archevêque were among those killed, with only a few Spaniards escaping.[75]

Despite a number of losses and setbacks in the first two decades of the eighteenth century, the Spanish managed to build up their presence in Texas to around 250 soldiers and ten missions, though they amounted to little more than specks on a landscape still dominated by Native Americans. While the French had been warded off, the lack of settlers in Texas was a growing concern because it hampered Spain's ability to maintain control of its frontier.[76] One Franciscan friar wrote to the king in 1716 asking for "Galicians and [Canary] Islanders" to come to Texas to take advantage of a fertile paradise with a climate 'similar to that of Castile.'"[77] Attacks by local Native Americans—who were proving resistant to conversion—were a constant threat. Although official land grants were made, it was difficult to farm in many of the areas and there were few indications of any new mines. To many in New Spain, going to the frontier was dangerous, and it did not seem that the risks were worthwhile. Still concerned about poor settlement, the crown agreed in 1723 to permit and pay the passage for two hundred isleños from the Canaries to immigrate to Tejas, though in the end the scheme was hampered by an eight-year bureaucratic delay, after which only fifty-six people, in fifteen families, came over. Although the isleños were, in theory, welcome additions, in practice they found it difficult to carve out a place for themselves between the missions and the military garrisons. The friars ensured that the settlers could not hire Indian labor, because it provided the missions with crop surpluses. The Canary Islanders found it hard to compete, opting instead to try to raise cattle or work as merchants.[78] Yet, at the same time, the isleños had created their own town, San Fernando, with its own civilian government, laying claim to valuable lands earlier irrigated by soldiers—again causing friction, this time with the military. This led to frustrated attempts to secure permission from the viceroy to hire Indians—a move foiled by the friars—while the military governors prohibited soldiers from buying from local isleño merchants.[79] In 1745 the viceroy of New Spain described the isleños as people who "maintain themselves quite comfortably by trading," though many might have begged to differ.[80] The three-way feud continued for years, while other settlers stayed away, leaving Texas as a Spanish outpost.

In 1725, THE governor of Florida, Antonio de Benavides, wrote a letter to one of his superiors seeking clarification about a group of runaway slaves that had been on his mind, noting that over the "eight months more or less we find ourselves in this *Presidio* seven blacks, that on two separate occasions have fled the City of Carolina."[81] The arrival of runaways was a familiar issue for Benavides, as it had been for governors before him.

The first reported instance of slaves fleeing from the plantations of South Carolina was in 1687. The Spanish baptized them as Catholics and gave them sanctuary. Word of this spread, causing many more slaves to make their way to Florida. Officials in St. Augustine were forced to ask the crown for guidance, and by 1693 a royal decree granted these refugees their freedom through conversion to Catholicism and a pledge to the crown. This helped Spain in two ways, by depriving the English of their labor force and by populating the frontier with people loyal to Spain.[82]

At issue for Benavides, more than two decades later, was that the most recent group of runaways had arrived during a pause in the ongoing animus between Spain and Britain.[83] He was willing to pay 200 pesos for each runaway, but the planters rejected this offer and threatened to come to Florida and take their slaves back. Forced to make a decision before receiving official instructions, he sold a total of ten runaways at a public auction in St. Augustine and paid off the disgruntled Carolina planters with the proceeds.[84]

The hiatus with the British was brief. Even before Benavides's slave dilemma, the British had built Fort King George in 1721, near where the Altamaha River runs into the Atlantic Ocean, by today's Darien, Georgia. The fort sat along a crucial route for defense and trade, near the site of the abandoned Santo Domingo de Talaje mission. The Spanish were by now accustomed to living with the ongoing British threat, and in 1728 Benavides had requested more men.[85] Into this already volatile mix entered another English colony, though it would not follow the same path as Virginia or South Carolina. Instead, Georgia was to be a place for the "worthy poor" of Britain, according to the English social reformer James Edward Oglethorpe, who founded the colony, named for George II, with the intention of giving debtors in prison a new life.

Oglethorpe had served in the military and as a member of Parliament, where the squalor of British jails was brought to his attention. His goal was to establish a colony in North America in which to place those whose crime was often that of simple poverty, and by 1730 he had chosen a site by the Savannah River, with South Carolina to the north and Spanish Florida to the south. Oglethorpe presented the colony as a possible buffer zone between the two rivals—the people sent there could protect as well as work the land—and gambled on this being the key to winning government support. The royal charter he was granted in 1732 permitted him to establish the colony on land between the Savannah and Altamaha Rivers, and he joined the first ship to Georgia in October of that year, arriving in early 1733. Later that year, as part of his campaign, he wrote a pamphlet, *A New and Accurate Account of the Provinces of South-Carolina and Georgia*, laying out his case. In it, he argued that the poor and prison-bound could "relieve themselves and strengthen Georgia, by resorting thither, and Great Britain by their Departure." In addition, the colony would not permit the labor of enslaved Africans, at least not at first.[86]

While the British made alliances and traded with the Native American groups in the region, the Spanish reinforced their defenses and asserted their claim on the Georgia coast.[87] Francisco del Moral Sánchez arrived to take up a post as governor of Florida in 1734 and was aghast at the "deplorable state" of St. Augustine, lamenting that the "fort has been left defenseless by its deterioration," and "it is impossible to provide in defense, or offence that Plaza with the small number of troops it has."[88]

An engineer named Antonio de Arredondo traveled over from Cuba in 1736 to assist with the building works in St. Augustine and was also dispatched to settle the land claims between Florida and Georgia. Arredondo met with Oglethorpe, and they agreed that the British would dismantle an outpost they had put near the St. Johns River, which they continued to claim was the boundary. In the same year, however, Oglethorpe built the small but well-placed Fort Frederica on St. Simons Island. Arredondo continued to investigate the claims of both sides and in 1742 produced an extensive report detailing Spain's right to the Georgia coast, writing that "the fact that the Spaniards after the year 1702, in which they abandoned those lands, had never occupied or cultivated them . . . does not take away from the crown of Spain the right of ownership in them, as every reasonable person knows."[89]

While Oglethorpe was arguing with the Spanish over the limits of his colony, he also became caught up in the debate over whether slavery should be permitted in Georgia. One of the colonists' concerns was that slaves might be quick to run away to Spanish Florida. Still, the prosperity in South Carolina was seductive, and the ban on slavery in the Georgia colony was a tense issue throughout the 1730s. One faction, in New Inverness, a part of Georgia settled by a group of Scots, made its case to Oglethorpe against slavery in 1739. The prospect of runaways was a crucial component of their reasoning, as they explained: "The Nearness of the Spaniards, who have proclaimed Freedom to all Slaves, who run away from their Masters, makes it impossible for us to keep them, without more Labour in guarding them, than what we would be at to do their Work." The petitioners also outlined other reasons for eschewing slavery, such as their own industriousness, and the possibility of financial ruin through being "debtors for Slaves."[90]

The issue of runaway slaves within Florida had not been settled, either. Spain still permitted slavery, and the policy was not uniform. For instance, although the black militia helped to defend St. Augustine against the English in 1728, some of its members remained enslaved. Indeed, the leader of the black militia, Francisco Menéndez, made the case for his freedom and that of another thirty people in the years that followed, claiming that they had been unjustly enslaved. The next governor, Manuel de Montiano, investigated their claims and in 1738 granted them their freedom. The crown confirmed this decision, and also ordered that any future fugitives from the English colonies should be given their liberty.[91] Menéndez sent a letter in June 1738 thanking the king, explaining that "all the Black people who escaped from the English plantations, obedient and loyal slaves to your majesty, declare that Your Majesty has done us true charity in ordering us to be given freedom" and in exchange promised "whenever the opportunity arises, we will be the cruelest enemies to the English."[92]

Later that year, a settlement for free people was established to the north of St. Augustine; it was known as Gracia Real de Santa Teresa de Mose. Some hundred people lived there, including Native Americans. The community sat strategically on the shores of Robinson Creek, just up the North River from St. Augustine, also near the Indian trails that connected to an outpost on the St. Johns River or, heading west, to the

Apalachee settlements. A small fortification was put there, built with the carpentry and stoneworking skills of the people in Mose, and Menéndez remained in charge of the settlement and the soldiers.[93]

The issue of runaway slaves continued to irritate Oglethorpe, who encouraged raids by the Creeks on Spanish Florida throughout 1738. The previous year he had requested and been given permission from London to raise a regiment of soldiers for the defense of the southern boundary of Georgia, claiming Georgia was at constant risk from Spanish invasion.[94] By 1739 he had a legitimate reason to attack the Spanish, as the War of Jenkins' Ear began between the two rivals.[95] The colorful name came from the severed ear of British captain Robert Jenkins, who lost it during naval skirmishes with the Spanish in the Caribbean and was alleged to have displayed it in the House of Commons in 1738. The conflict concerned the long-running animosities between Britain and Spain over privateering, contraband trade, and the seizure and searches of each other's ships in the Atlantic and Caribbean. Britain was quick to score a victory in the 1739 Battle of Portobello, though the conflict would have no firm conclusion as it melded into the wider War of the Austrian Succession, which would last until 1748. Closer to home, the British in South Carolina had been rattled by a rebellion of around sixty to one hundred slaves at Stono River, on September 9, 1739, which was suppressed only after the death of about forty slaves and twenty settlers.

In the spring of 1740 in the Georgia-Florida borderlands, Oglethorpe, with his troops and Indian allies including the Creeks and Chickasaw, captured three small Spanish forts: San Diego, near the coast; and Pupo and Picolata, on the St. Johns River. This prompted Governor Montiano to make hasty reinforcements to St. Augustine in preparation for an attack, and he also urged the villagers of Fort Mose to join the town's other two thousand residents in the Castillo de San Marcos for protection.[96] By June, Oglethorpe, aided by Royal Navy warships, had blockaded St Augustine, and occupied Fort Mose. On June 26, the Spanish counterattacked, surprising the British at Fort Mose, where Spanish forces—including Menéndez—killed around seventy-five British fighters, prompting the British to later refer to it as "bloody Mose."[97] By July 15 the siege was over. The defeat at Fort Mose and the well-timed arrival of reinforcements from Cuba led to the retreat of the British, and Menéndez won praise for his bravery during the fighting.[98] The fort, however, had suffered much damage—British soldiers had taken off the gate and breached some of the walls, and the village was left uninhabitable.[99]

After the siege, Governor Montiano decided another fortification was needed, and in 1740 work began on Fort Matanzas, near the site of the violent 1565 massacre of the French. It sits on an islet, known today as Rattlesnake Island, and was tasked with watching ships approaching St. Augustine from the south, via the Matanzas River. It was one of Spain's smallest forts, with five guns and space for about seven soldiers. Its one small *garita* peered out over a marshy landscape, with the nearest neighbors being the ospreys and tortoises that lived there. The closest the troops ever came to seeing action there was in 1743, when a potential attack was foiled by rough waters. Now a U.S. national monument, it stands in the silence that has mostly surrounded it since its completion.

That was not quite the end of the fighting, though, and in the summer of 1741 the Spanish sent Mose militia members into the borderland area to give arms to slaves who would be willing to attack their British masters.[100] By July the following year, some fifteen hundred soldiers led by Montiano sailed to St. Simons Island, though it was the British who won the Battle of Bloody Marsh, in July 1742, forcing the Spanish to retreat before the month was out. Battles and raids continued along the border until the Treaty of Aix-la-Chapelle in Europe in 1748 brought the War of the Austrian Succession to an end and confirmed British control of Georgia.[101] Oglethorpe, for his part, had returned to England in 1743. Eight years later the prohibition against slavery in Georgia had been removed and in 1752 the colony reverted from its status as a trusteeship to control by the crown.

In Florida, Governor Fulgencio García de Solís, who was appointed in 1752, took a different view of freed people in St. Augustine from that of his predecessor. After the destruction of Fort Mose, its residents lived in or around the main city. García thought the former slaves, in addition to their Indian allies, had the potential to cause social disorder in the town, so he ordered the reconstruction of the settlement. The fort was rebuilt, and many of the original residents moved back, though others were now accustomed to the relative security of urban life and did not want to return to the uncertainty of the frontier. In order to convince them otherwise, he punished two leaders who were resisting the move, threatening to do likewise to anyone else who would not go. The new fort, with a moat and six small cannons, was also located on Mose Creek.[102] This time Franciscans were assigned to minister to the sixty-seven villagers in twenty households, according to the 1759 census. The parish register illustrates the wide diversity of the former slaves, who identified themselves by where they were from in Africa; in this period there were people in Mose who identified as Mandinga—as Menéndez had done—Fara, Arará, Congolese, Carabalí, and Mina, among others.[103]

García de Solís and his successors remained concerned about the lack of Spanish settlers, and there were attempts to lure people from the Canary Islands, with around seventy-five people arriving by the late 1750s.[104] St. Augustine continued to struggle and although Florida was considered strategic because of its proximity to the Caribbean, the city never developed into a port on the scale of San Juan or Havana. The coast remained difficult for growing crops, and settlers stayed away. The low-lying areas of Georgia and South Carolina, however, proved to be more fertile. With the introduction of enslaved labor, the region was soon a center of agricultural production and trade, through the port of Charles Town. By 1760, Georgia had a population of around six thousand British and another thirty-six hundred slaves, far more than the three thousand people in Florida.[105] Within a few years, another global battle would upend Spanish Florida, sending it reeling and leaving Fort Mose abandoned once more.

Chapter 5

New Madrid, Missouri, ca. 1760–90

THE FIRST HALF of the eighteenth century saw a rush of settlers to the colonies of British North America, and by 1760 more than a million Europeans had staked out new lives there.[1] The bulk of the immigrants were English, Scottish, and Protestant Irish (Scots-Irish), but other Europeans also came over, with groups like the Swedes settling in Delaware and people from Germanic kingdoms fanning out across New York, New Jersey, and Pennsylvania.[2] Many were driven by poverty out of their own place of birth and lured by the prospect of land in North America. Not all were in a position to be landowners, and many people came at first as indentured servants, though indenture declined as tens of thousands of Africans were brought in. By the 1770s, the number of enslaved people, from Africa and born within the colonies, reached nearly half a million.[3]

Spain had no equivalent surge in its North American lands. Estimates vary, but between 1506 and 1650 some 250,000 to 400,000 people made the voyage from various parts of Spain to the Americas, with more than half going to Peru or New Spain, joining the surviving indigenous peoples and the growing creole and mestizo population. Other Europeans, mostly Catholics, also arrived in Spanish America, including people from France, Portugal, and Italy, but their numbers were small; in New Spain only fifteen hundred non-Spaniards were estimated to have come between 1700 and 1760.[4] Few gravitated to the frontiers of either Florida or New Mexico. The number of enslaved people brought to Spanish America continued to rise, and by the late 1700s, the slave population was around 80,000 in the Caribbean islands and 271,000 throughout the rest of the colonies, including New Spain.[5]

As the British, French, and Spanish continued to claim significant territory in North America, a battle for supremacy gripped all three powers by the middle of what had already been a violent and bloody eighteenth century. At first this played out in the Great Lakes region and along the St. Lawrence River, between the British and the French and their Indian allies. The British had been eager to expand into the Ohio River valley, and an Ohio Company of Virginia and other, smaller companies had been formed. Land grants were then obtained for some of the territory between the Appalachian Mountains and the Mississippi River. The Native Americans stood firm in their claims to the land, while the French erected a number of strategic forts in the area, including Fort Duquesne where the Allegheny and Monongahela Rivers converge. The British rubbed up against the western edges of French territory, led by a young major, George Washington, on a mission resulting in a skirmish with French troops in a meadow in the Allegheny Mountains of western Pennsylvania in 1754. This proved to be the opening salvo in a conflict known as the French and Indian War, with Washington taking a defeat that summer at the makeshift Fort Necessity. Farther east, the British started to expel the French-speaking Acadians who lived in the prized farmland on the North Atlantic peninsula of Nova Scotia, which had been ceded to Britain under the 1713 Treaty of Utrecht; this expulsion further stoked French irritation.

In 1756 Britain and France declared war on each other, and the Seven Years' War began in Europe. It subsumed the French and Indian War and spread to all parts of the world, turning into a truly global conflict. Its theaters were found in places ranging from the Great Lakes to the Caribbean, and India to Senegal. In North America much of the fighting was between the British and French, but at its heart were concerns about the power balances within Europe.

The battle lines were drawn between Britain and Prussia on one side, with France, Austria, Russia, Sweden, and Spain, which entered in 1762, on the other. For much of the Seven Years' War, Spain wanted to avoid the conflict, but its relationship to France ultimately dragged it in. Although the Bourbon crowns of Spain and France had been separated under the treaty ending the War of the Spanish Succession, the two had a *pacte de famille* that reinforced their connections. In 1761 they signed a third pact (the previous two having been in 1733 and 1743) causing the British to assume that Spain was about to enter the war on the side of France. In June 1762 the British made a preemptive strike with a surprise attack on Havana, capturing it, and doing the same to the Spanish Pacific port of Manila. A few months later, in November, France and Spain signed the secret Treaty of Fontainebleau, which ceded New Orleans and France's huge Louisiana territory to Spain so that the British could not claim either should they win the war. For the Spanish, Louisiana could serve as an extra buffer to curb any desire of the British to expand west toward New Spain.[6]

When the war ended and the terms of the 1763 Treaty of Paris were negotiated, Britain emerged triumphant. In the Americas, the British received all of French Canada, the Great Lakes region east of the Mississippi, and the Caribbean islands of Grenada, St. Vincent, Dominica, and Tobago. France kept the tiny isles of St. Pierre and Miquelon in the Gulf of St. Lawrence, and the Caribbean colonies of Guadeloupe and Martinique. Spain retained Louisiana, but the real issue was the return of Havana. The Spanish considered Cuba crucial to Atlantic trade and defense, so they ceded Florida to the British in exchange.

The addition of Louisiana, however, gave Spain another eight hundred thousand square miles, and great expanses of it were simply unknown to the king or his officials. The Louisiana territory, starting with a dot in New Orleans, spreading like ink-spill on paper, was a place where three peoples collided: the Spanish; the British and other European settlers of the trans-Appalachia region; and Native Americans. Each of the three was aware of the risks and rewards that the other two posed.

Of most urgent concern to Madrid was the security of the northern frontier of New Spain, and so Cayetano María Pignatelli Rubí Corbera y San Climent, the Marqués de Rubí, was dispatched from Spain to inspect it. He spent two years, starting in March 1766, traveling thousands of miles through New Mexico and Texas, as well as parts of Nueva Vizcaya, Sonora, and Coahuila.[7] Although the Seven Years' War had not found its way that far west, there had been other conflicts. Rubí saw the devastation left by Indian raids, in particular those by the Comanche and Apache, who continued to dominate the area and resist Spanish influence.[8] Among the many suggestions Rubí included in his report, he put forward the idea that a line of presidios from Sonora to Texas, spaced about forty leagues (120 miles) apart, was needed. Existing ones could be closed or relocated, and each presidio should have at least fifty men. Officials studied his report and, despite his claim that other efficiencies would save 80,000 pesos, no line of presidios was forthcoming.[9]

This focus on defense was only one aspect of a long-running program of change throughout the empire, known as the "Bourbon reforms," the bulk of which took place under Carlos III, who came to the Spanish throne in 1759 and wanted to modernize his empire while also reinforcing his authority over it.[10] One of the leading reformers was José de Gálvez, who arrived in New Spain in 1765, around the same time Rubí was undertaking his tour. Gálvez started a six-year inspection of New Spain, in the role of *visitador general*. His task was to find ways to make the empire more efficient and modern—he was the first Spanish official to describe the American territories as "colonies"—as well as more profitable.[11] To this end he was involved in the creation of intendancies, or administrative districts, placing peninsular Spaniards in official posts to oversee matters such as tax collection, though by doing so he undermined local creole elites and caused a great deal of anger and disquiet. Gálvez also had his sights set on the colonization of what the Spanish now called upper, or Alta, California, which corresponds to today's state of California, north of New Spain's Baja (lower) California. As part of these measures, he opened the Pacific port of San Blas in 1768, in Mexico's Nayarit state, to use as a base.[12]

By 1775 Gálvez would rise to the post of secretary of the Indies, a position he kept until his death in 1787. In this role, he was able to continue the reorganization of New Spain, including putting the region that Rubí had inspected into a new administrative unit, the Internal Provinces (*Comandancia General de las Provincias Internas*), which was completed in 1776—just as the American Revolution was beginning three thousand miles away. This new administrative configuration put the territories of California, New Mexico, and Texas, as well as Nueva Vizcaya, Coahuila, and Sinaloa in northern New Spain, under a commandancy and captain-general, who reported to the viceroy. It was hoped this would better organize—and make more effective—the defense of this territory.[13]

There was also a push for more trade with Native Americans, with reformers noting the relative success English and French traders had enjoyed in commodities such as fur. The motivation was not solely economic—commercial ties could also allow for a greater degree of cooperation with groups that had long antagonized the Spanish at the frontier, such as the Apache. As one official wrote, they should aim to end the "frightening noise of the cannon and war, replacing them with the sweet ties of lucrative trade."[14] Commerce, however, had not quite overtaken Christianity, and Carlos III said the "conversion of the numerous nations of heathen Indians" remained a priority. He wrote in his 1776 instructions to the new commander of the Internal Provinces, Teodoro de Croix, that he wanted this enacted with "cajolery, good treatment, persuasion by missionaries, gifts, and the secure offers of my sovereign protection."[15]

Revenue was an ongoing concern across the less profitable colonies, and the crown was willing to experiment with *comercio libre*, or free trade. Here, Cuba offered a different model from northern New Spain: to raise the necessary money to improve defense, higher taxes had to be levied, but in exchange Cuba was granted permission in 1765 to trade with nine Spanish ports, something that had not been permitted before.[16] In the past, all trade and goods had to go through a few select main ports, like Veracruz in the Americas, or Seville in Spain. Allowing smaller ports to trade with Cuba proved successful. Sugar exports rose, helping to bring in an annual average royal revenue of 535,404 pesos between 1765 and 1775; in contrast, before the reforms, in 1762, the treasury in Cuba had only 178,000 pesos in income and received subsidies from New Spain. Encouraged by this success and influenced by new economic thinking at the time, in 1778 the crown rolled out its version of free trade, which, among other measures, entailed giving permission to ports across the empire to trade directly with a larger number of Spanish seaports.[17]

Spain was thus engaging with some of the new ideas about commerce and governance circulating around Enlightenment Europe, although this was not always straightforward. At times certain foreign books fell under the purview of the Inquisition, which had the power to censor them, especially if they were critical of the crown or the Church. Adam Smith's *Wealth of Nations*, for instance, was first published in 1776 but did not reach a Castilian-reading audience until it was translated in

1794. Many facets of Spanish cultural and intellectual life—including the Inquisition—had long been under attack, as intellectuals across Europe criticized the crown's policies, particularly in economics. Montesquieu in France voiced the common complaint about Spain's reliance on gold and silver, and its inability to foster agrarian development and commerce. If anything, this had become an economic Black Legend. Writing in his 1748 *The Spirit of the Laws*, Montesquieu noted that "the Spaniards considered these newly discovered countries [the Americas] as the subject of conquest; while others, more refined in their views, found them to be the proper subjects of commerce . . . hence several nations have conducted themselves with so much wisdom that they have given a kind of sovereignty to companies of merchants."[18] The agrarian ideals of the British also remained strong, with Smith noting in *The Wealth of Nations* that "there are no colonies of which the progress has been more rapid than that of English North America. Plenty of good land, and liberty to manage their own affairs their own way, seem to be the two great causes of the prosperity of all new colonies."[19]

For the French philosopher Abbé Raynal, Spain needed to strengthen its empire and to do so the Spanish should "not only admit strangers of their own persuasion, but encourage every sect without distinction to come and settle among them."[20] Catholicism still remained a powerful force in Spanish America, though it, too, had not escaped the reforming reach of Carlos III. In 1767 he had banished the Jesuit order from the entire Spanish realm. Although the Jesuits had long been a force for colonization, the king felt their power had grown too unwieldy. In North America, the Franciscans would take over what the Jesuits had been forced to relinquish.

Non-Catholics still faced barriers to living in Spanish possessions, but it was becoming obvious that any future success in North America depended on the inclusion of Protestants. However, Louisiana did receive a Catholic boost in the form of the Acadians, whom the British had hounded out of Nova Scotia. These former French colonists were welcomed in Louisiana and settled into a region later known as Acadiana, which runs along the lower half of the modern state, now known as Cajun country. Although they were Catholic, Spanish Louisiana would soon open its doors to Protestants, as Raynal had foreseen.

———⌒———

W<small>HILE</small> S<small>PAIN</small> <small>WAS</small> coming to terms with Louisiana, the British were working out what to do with Florida. After a century of raids and battles with the Spanish, the colony was at last theirs. They first decided to split their acquisition into East and West Florida along the Apalachicola River, which cuts across the panhandle and empties into the Gulf of Mexico. West Florida's northern boundary was at N 32°, corresponding with modern cities such as Jackson, Mississippi; and Montgomery, Alabama. Its western boundary was the Mississippi River, but it also included places that had been under French control and were ceded to the British, such as Mobile, Biloxi, and Baton Rouge, as well as the westernmost part of what had been Spanish Florida, with Pensacola being the largest settlement. By 1766, there were more than two thousand Europeans and around one thousand enslaved people in West Florida. Lured by generous land grants, the majority of settlers lived around Pensacola, replacing the Spanish who left.[21] In the Mobile area, some French people stayed on and swore loyalty to the British crown.[22] By 1774, some twenty-five hundred settlers and six hundred slaves were spread out in an area stretching from Baton Rouge to Pointe Coupée to Natchez.[23] Old forts were renamed or anglicized; Fort Condé in Mobile, for instance, became Fort Charlotte. The British also put their stamp on the colony's laws and slave codes, bringing them more in line with Georgia's and South Carolina's.[24]

When the West Florida governor George Johnstone arrived in the autumn of 1764 to take up his post, he was both alarmed at the extent of the power local Native Americans had and eager to capitalize on trade with them, thinking there now might be scope for the British to dominate Indian commerce in West Florida. In addition, Pensacola was near New Orleans and the wider Spanish Caribbean, including Havana and Veracruz, and Johnstone hoped this proximity would lead to more trade.[25] He petitioned for a relaxation of the Navigation Acts, protectionist measures that dated back more than a century and prohibited foreign boats from calling at British ports, but was not successful. The Royal Navy continued to enforce the legislation, seizing ships and stifling suspected contraband during this period, though some trade slipped through and Spanish silver managed to find its way into specie-starved British West Florida.[26]

Johnstone's hopes about relations with the Native Americans were similarly overoptimistic. He told the Choctaw and Chickasaw that if they wanted to trade, they needed to be prepared to yield land in return for goods. For their part, the Native Americans were accustomed to gift-giving and expected the British to abide by it. One Choctaw chief told the British, "We hope you will be as generous as the French were."[27] British traders in West Florida continued to point out that their Spanish competitors in Louisiana had few desirable manufactured goods and so would be poor trading partners, yet at the same time they did little to endear themselves to officials or Indians: by selling alcohol—which Johnstone decried as "the Primary Cause of all Mischief"—as well as harassing Indian women and manipulating prices, they provoked Indian attacks.[28]

Change also came to East Florida. On the eve of the Seven Years' War, St. Augustine had around 3,000 people, of whom 551 were in the military. There were around 400 people of color, slave and free; 246 Canary Islanders; 83 Indians; mestizos; and a few other Europeans.[29] Many of these residents were evacuated to Cuba after St. Augustine was handed over to the British. One anonymous author of a pamphlet was optimistic about the British prospects in Florida, writing in 1763 that "we may with great Probability say, that although the *Spaniards* have made but little Use of *Florida*, as having less Genius for Cultivation than ourselves, and not in want of Southern Land, yet we may fairly hope to avail ourselves from both its Soil and Situation."[30] Yet the British found themselves faced with the same question as the Spanish: how to attract settlers. Officials tried to entice South Carolina and Georgia planters, and a few answered the call, bringing hundreds of enslaved people who were soon put to work draining the swamps and chopping down the vast forests to create fields on the large tracts to be cultivated near the St. Marys and St. Johns Rivers, which would go on to yield rice, cotton, indigo, and sugar. The slave population rose to around 2,000 by 1775, with black people outnumbering whites by more than two to one. In less than a decade, the number of enslaved people rose to around 10,000.[31]

Florida also became a place of land speculation and unlikely ventures. In 1768 more than a thousand eager colonists arrived—though they were not English or Scottish, but Greeks and other Mediterraneans.[32] A Scottish doctor turned speculator named Andrew Turnbull had brought a group from what was the former Spanish, but now British-controlled, island of Minorca, in the Balearic Islands, to Florida as indentured laborers, claiming that people from the Mediterranean were more suited to the hot Florida climate.[33] These roughly fourteen hundred workers were to live in a settlement called New Smyrna, located about seventy-five miles down the coast from St. Augustine. In his early correspondence with British officials, Turnbull explained that his wife was Greek and that he wanted to settle "a Greek colony in that Province [Florida]."[34] He suggested it was possible to produce a range of products, from rice and indigo to olives, cotton, and silk. For good measure, he also said that "some Sugar canes brought from the Havannah [Havana] this Spring and planted last April by the governor are thriving fast. . . . The cotton plant is stronger than any I ever saw in Turkey."[35]

Whatever the intentions, the settlement was a disaster from the start. A band of three hundred rebels tried to commandeer a ship and flee to Cuba in 1768, after being there just two months. The remaining laborers were guarded by soldiers.[36] By 1769 about six hundred people had died of disease or the starvation that was used as a punishment.[37] Turnbull did, however, have some success with indigo, then a prized commodity. The Florida climate was ideal for it, and Turnbull pushed the workers with a determined relentlessness to harvest and process the crop, which he first exported in 1772.[38]

A new governor, Colonel Patrick Tonyn, arrived in 1774, and he and Turnbull took an immediate dislike to each other, not least because Turnbull's allies had put his name forward for governor.[39] The arrival of Tonyn was also the beginning of the end of the settlement, though the causes were not all political: a bad drought and soil depletion caused indigo output to drop. In 1776 Turnbull made a trip to England to attempt to have Tonyn removed from his post. The following year, while he was still away, the remaining settlers petitioned St. Augustine for sanctuary. They were released from their indentures and abandoned the site in 1777, before Turnbull's return.[40]

Elsewhere in East Florida, a new people were forming: the Seminoles. By now, many of the indigenous peoples of Florida and the Southeast had weathered serious challenges: European disease, Christian conversion, wars against other Native Americans and Europeans, and the loss of land. Different groups of Native Americans were at times forced to merge with other chiefdoms for their very survival. The Seminoles were one such group. The word "seminole" is a possible corruption of the Spanish word for runaway slave, *cimarrón*, and there were many runaways among the Seminoles. The Lower Creeks who had moved into Florida made up the main body of the Seminoles, taking over former lands of the Timucua and Apalachee, as they had died or moved away. The runaway Africans who joined them were not re-enslaved; rather, they lived in their own villages and paid tribute to the Creeks each year as well as providing military assistance.[41] At times throughout the period of British administration, members of the Creek nation traveled to Cuba to air their grievances and continue to trade. In one letter to the East Florida governor James Grant in 1769, Grant was told that two Creek men had "returned in April from the Havannah for which place they embarked in a Spanish Vessel at the Bay of Tampa in November. They were accompanied by several other Cowetas, they all received presents of Money, rum, ammunition and laced Cloaths from the Spanish Governors."[42] These became regular voyages, and by 1776 there had been at least nineteen trips by Creeks to Havana.[43]

THE SEVEN YEARS' War exacted a high social cost from all of the countries involved, as well as denting their treasuries. In an effort to raise revenue, Britian enacted a series of taxes that sparked protest and unrest in its North American colonies, including the Sugar Act of 1764, the Stamp Act of 1765, and then a series of bills known as the Townshend Acts of 1767, which levied duties on lead, glass, paper, paint, and tea. These were followed by public grumbling and a flurry of pamphlets pointing out the perceived unfairness of these measures. Refusal to comply and a general air of antagonism led to the increased presence of British troops in urban centers such as Boston, as well as a growing number of overt acts of defiance, among them the dumping of tea in Boston Harbor in 1773. By this point, a distinct "American" identity had formed in the British colonies, based on ideas concerning land, trade, and certain rights within the imperial system. Now this identity was being further molded by the colonists' growing anger.[44]

While much of this was taking place at the center of the British colonies, on the periphery a different story was unfolding. As Thomas Jefferson compiled his list of grievances to include in the 1776 Declaration of Independence, the residents of East and West Florida waited for news of developments, though no one from Florida would end up signing the declaration.[45] Though the opening shots of the American Revolution were in Massachusetts, West Florida would be a critical—and often overlooked—theater of the war. West Florida abutted Louisiana, putting the British and Spanish in close proximity, and many French people still lived in the territory, along with large Indian chiefdoms, including the Creek, Chickasaw, and Choctaw.[46] As the rebellion developed in 1776, the Spanish at first watched from afar, though not long afterward rebel leaders reached out to officials in Louisiana and Spain in the hope of loans or supplies to help fight British troops.

Benjamin Franklin, who had been sent to Paris to muster diplomatic support for the American cause, met the Spanish ambassador to France, Pedro Pablo Abarca de Bolea, Count of Aranda, on December 29, 1776. They spoke in secret because Spain, at the time, had not officially recognized the rebel colonists or their struggle for independence.[47] Aranda left the meeting with the realization that Spain needed to be on America's side. He could see that with all of the European immigration, a nation independent of Britain would be even stronger, writing in a later report to Madrid, "Spain shall find itself dealing with only one other power in all that terra firma of North America. And who is that power? One that is stable and territorial; that has already claimed the patrician name America with two and half million inhabitants."[48]

Franklin found Aranda "well dispos'd towards us."[49] Although Spain exercised caution at first, it soon began secretly channeling supplies and money that became crucial to the success of the Continental Army, utilizing merchant connections. Ships that left New England for Britain often called at Spanish ports, such as Bilbao and Cádiz, to purchase goods like cod or flour, so a commercial network was already in place. One firm, Joseph Gardoqui & Sons, would have a prominent part using those routes to funnel much-needed supplies.[50] While Spain did not want to be seen as supporting the rebel effort outright, Spanish financial support—which reached well into the millions of *reales*, though esti-mates vary as to how high—helped procure goods that included cannons, bullets, gunpowder, bombs, rifles, tents, and even lead for bullets, with supplies and money coming from Spain, New Spain, and the Caribbean. In just one instance, in 1777 Gardoqui & Sons sent on the *Rockingham* one thousand blankets, five thousand yards of material, and one hundred thousand musket flints.[51] Another letter, from October 1777, mentioned that "messrs. Gardoqui at Bilboa [Bilbao] have sent several Cargoes of Naval Stores, Cordage, Sailcloth, Anchors, &c."[52]

Around the same time, in 1777, Bernardo de Gálvez arrived in Louisiana to take over as governor. Gálvez came from a prominent family—his uncle was José de Gálvez, the reforming inspector of New Spain. He had a long career in the military, having served in Spain and New Spain. With the war already under way, Gálvez was soon involved in intrigues to help the U.S. forces against the British, aided in New Orleans by one of the key brokers between the Spanish and the Continental Army, the prominent Irish-born merchant Oliver Pollock.[53]

France entered the conflict, declaring war on Britain in 1778, and the following year, on June 21, 1779, Spain made an official declaration of war in support of France. The Spanish were less concerned about Brit-ain's colonial rebellion and rather hoped to use it as an opportunity to take back Gibraltar, a territory on the southern tip of the Iberian Peninsula that had been ceded to Britain under the Treaty of Utrecht in 1713.[54] Although the American Revolution is usually depicted as a war between Britain and its colonies, its scope was far larger. Many of the unresolved issues from the Seven Years' War were playing out in the thirteen colonies, and France and Spain could use the conflict in North America to challenge Britain's power in Europe.[55] No one was certain, however, that the Continental Army would win its war, or what would happen if it did, but France and Spain were willing to join the fight to further their own interests.

Gálvez had organized a West Florida campaign by August 1779, with royal support from Madrid and backup from the garrison in Havana. It included thirteen hundred men on the ground, composed of regular troops, local militiamen, free blacks, Acadians, and even British refugees who had left West Florida, as well as Houma, Choctaw, and Alabama people.[56] His men began to take small British outposts in West Florida, such as those in Manchac and Baton Rouge, in September, but the larger coastal forts—Mobile and Pensacola—were the real targets. In the meantime, U.S. leaders were pleased with Gálvez's assistance. Thomas Jefferson wrote to him in November 1779, saying, "The weight of your powerfull and wealthy Empire, has given us, all the certainty of a happy Issue to the present Contest, of which human Events will admit."[57]

By early 1780, Gálvez was ready to move on Mobile, the site of the star-shaped Fort Charlotte that overlooked the bay. Around 750 men, including regulars and militia members, volunteers, and slaves, left in January from New Orleans with plans to join a party from Havana. Their efforts to enter Mobile Bay were frustrated by bouts of stormy weather and they were forced to wait at a base near the Dog River, a few miles away. While they were there, reinforcements from Cuba arrived in mid-February, swelling troop numbers to well over 1,000. In the meantime, British regiments were marching overland from Pensacola to Mobile, avoiding Spanish ships, but they arrived too late. By March 13 the fort commander had surrendered after Spanish bombardment the day before had breached Fort Charlotte and the outnumbered British troops had used up their ammunition. Gálvez occupied the fort—soon to be renamed Fort Carlota—and the three hundred British troops retreated to Pensacola. Military leaders were buoyed by the news, and Gálvez's report detailing the operation was read to the Continental Congress on June 6.[58]

Gálvez's next target was Pensacola, an even larger prize. Capturing that port had a number of advantages, not least its position relative to New Orleans, Havana, and Veracruz. In 1772 the British built Fort George there, its earthen ramparts overlooking the city and its twenty cannons capable of firing on any ships coming into the harbor. The British, under the command of General John Campbell, were at the ready after the events in Mobile. Meanwhile, the Creek and Choctaw in West Florida exacted gifts, including goods such as rum, gunpowder, meat, and bread, from both sides and negotiated how much assistance they would give.

Gálvez made preparations for an attack in October 1780, but nature intervened once again and a hurricane scattered his fleet, forcing him to regroup. A few months later, he tried again, leaving Havana on February 13, 1781, for Pensacola with a fleet of twenty ships, including the sixty-one-gun flagship *San Ramón*, and around thirteen hundred troops.

General Campbell waited with his seventeen hundred troops, one thousand Native American allies, and three ships. On March 9 the Spanish were spotted, but Gálvez's fleet was having trouble entering the channel because of its shallowness. With mounting frustration, Gálvez took one of the smaller vessels, the *Galveztown*, and sailed into the bay on March 18, managing to dodge British fire. He was later followed by some of the fleet's frigates, and the town was soon under siege. Both sides were waiting for reinforcements, and the ships from Havana arrived in April before the British ones from Jamaica, swelling troop numbers to more than seven thousand. On May 8, a grenade destroyed a British powder magazine, causing a large explosion and ending the battle, with the official surrender on May 10, 1781, leaving the Spanish with seventy dead, and around one hundred British soldiers killed.[59] West Florida was once again in Spanish hands, and Fort George became Fort San Miguel.

The British surrendered to the Americans in October 1781, and peace negotiations began. Under the Treaty of Paris in 1783, Britain relinquished East Florida to Spain, and the boundary with the newly formed U.S. border was set at the St. Marys River. However, the question of West Florida—though it was already under Spanish control—was not so easy to resolve. Well before Gálvez's attacks in West Florida, there had been talks with Spain about U.S. access to the Mississippi River. Benjamin Franklin had broached the subject in the spring of 1777 in a letter to the Count of Aranda, saying that, should Spain help the Americans' cause, they would "assist in reducing to the Possession of Spain the Town and Harbour of Pensacola," though on the condition that "the Inhabitants of the United States shall have the free Navigation of the Missisipi [sic], and the Use of the Harbour of Pensacola."[60] Trade would put the new United States on the path to prosperity, and securing access to the Mississippi River was an early priority. Even while the war was raging, John Jay, then serving as minister to Spain, arrived in Cádiz in 1780 for a diplomatic mission that included concerns about the Mississippi. Jay met the first minister, José Moñino y Redondo, Count of Floridablanca, that May in Aranjuez, where the court was residing. Jay was eager to sign an alliance treaty.[61] He had been given instructions by the Continental Congress "to insist on the navigation of the Mississippi for the Citizens of the United States," but he could not secure a deal. Instead, Floridablanca hinted that if the United States wanted to have a good relationship with Spain, it would need to make sure Spanish navigation of the Mississippi River was not renounced.[62] Benjamin Franklin wrote to a frustrated Jay in October 1780, "If you are not so fortunate in Spain, continue however the even good temper you have hitherto manifested." He was optimistic, telling Jay, "Poor as we are, yet as I know we shall be rich, I would rather agree with them to buy at a great price the whole of their right on the Mississippi, than sell a drop of its waters. A neighbour might as well ask me to sell my street door."[63] However, with no sign of a change of heart over the matter, in February 1781 Congress ordered Jay to stop negotiations and "recede from the instructions above referred to, so far as they insist on the free navigation of that part of the river Mississippi, which lies below the thirty-first degree of north latitude."[64]

The issue would end up being resolved by the Treaty of Paris, which said in Article 8 that "the navigation of the river Mississippi, from its source to the ocean, shall forever remain free and open to the subjects of Great Britain and the citizens of the United States."[65] The peace deal also called for the boundary of the United States to be marked by a "line to be drawn along the middle of said river Mississippi until it shall intersect the northernmost part of the thirty-first degree of north latitude." However, there had also been secret dealings over this particular provision. British negotiators had made an offer, unbeknownst to Spain, that if West Florida were given back to Britain—a provision that some, including Jay, supported because they thought it would lead to access to the Mississippi River—then the boundary of West Florida would be set at N 32°. However, if West Florida was returned to Spain, Britain would support the line's placement at N 31°, giving the United States an extra strip of land. In late 1782, U.S. delegates wrote to Congress in secret over the issue of the West Florida border, but with Britain pressuring them to sign they proceeded with the treaty. Spain had little input in the deal because a treaty of alliance between the United States and Spain had never been achieved. In the end, the Spanish agreed to the Paris deal, which gave it back Florida and Minorca, but not the hoped-for Gibraltar.[66] Spanish ministers harbored some trepidation about what would follow, sentiments expressed by the Count of Aranda in a 1783 letter to Carlos III, which warned that the United States "will forget about the benefits it has received from both powers [France and Spain] and will think of nothing but its aggrandizement."[67]

Another immediate problem for Spain was the British loyalists—both free black and white—who now sought refuge in Florida, hoping to avoid retribution. Many did not want to pledge loyalty to the king of Spain, nor convert to Catholicism, but these were the conditions of staying; otherwise they had eighteen months to leave.[68] Vicente Manuel de Zéspedes arrived in St. Augustine in 1784 to take up the post of governor of both Floridas, and at this point some 3,400 white and 6,540 black people were leaving East Florida for other parts of the British empire.[69] In their place, though not in the same numbers, came some of the Florida families who had fled to Cuba in 1763.[70] In the years that followed, Spain clarified the land grants made to non-Spaniards so they would want to remain, and by 1790 settlers in East Florida were no longer required to convert to Catholicism and only had to swear an oath of allegiance. It was a pragmatic decision given Florida's circumstances, and it had an immediate effect, with around three hundred white planters coming into East Florida and bringing one thousand slaves with them. By 1804 the number of new Anglo settler families reached 750, with four thousand slaves.[71]

Despite allowing in enslaved people, Spain had continued to offer sanctuary for runaways. During the transition from British to Spanish rule, Zéspedes received the petitions of about 250 black people who wanted their freedom. The United States, however, was not as willing to tolerate this as the British had been, and, under pressure from Thomas Jefferson, the Spanish stopped offering refuge in 1790. The United States also demanded the return of all slaves who entered Florida after 1783, though Spain would only send back anyone who arrived in or after 1790.[72]

———

UNDER THE BRITISH, the Proclamation Line of 1763 had forbidden colonists to go past the Appalachian Mountains, though many people ignored the rule and started to farm or engage in land speculation in the Ohio valley.[73] Now, without British control, and with the Treaty

of Paris granting the United States land north of N 31° and west to the
Mississippi River, the region opened up. Legislation was passed to legit-
imize this expansion, including the Northwest Ordinance of 1787, which
paved the way for these lands to be territories first and states later on.
On paper, the ordinance said that Native Americans could not have their
land taken from them except in "just" wars, leaving a wide space for
interpretation, and for subsequent violent disagreements.[74]

In places far from the oversight of the nascent government on the
East Coast, the frontier developed its own rules. In 1784, a group of
men in the western fringes of North Carolina decided to break away
and form their own sovereign state. They represented the interests of
farmers and merchants of what was then considered the backcountry,
whose economic prospects were at stake. One of their main concerns
was over land use and development, issues to which they felt the politicians in the east of North Carolina gave little attention.[75] Debts had
already forced the state to sell off some of its eastern part to speculators.[76] Also of concern was the lack of organized protection from
Indian attacks. Some of the earlier settlers created the Watauga Association, which the state approved, to oversee the governance of the
region.[77] However, North Carolina's April 1784 Cession Act—the state's
agreement to hand over some of its land to Congress to pay its debt
from the Revolutionary War—fueled resentment among opponents
who thought the measure was misguided. On August 23, a group of
men held their first convention in Jonesborough, electing John Sevier
governor. A few months later, on December 14, they cast a vote among
themselves to leave North Carolina and create a new state, naming
it Franklin, in honor of Benjamin Franklin.[78] The territory, though in
North Carolina then, corresponded to the twelve easternmost counties
in modern Tennessee. Its makeshift capital was moved to a cabin in
Greeneville, also in Tennessee, in 1785.

The Franklinites won little support from the prominent politicians.
Jefferson expressed his "increased anxiety" about the situation, fearing
that other states, such as Virginia, would follow their example. Congress
rejected "Franklin's" petition for statehood.[79] While the Franklinites' supporters were plotting, in Spain Carlos III issued orders in June 1784 to
close the Spanish-controlled parts of the Mississippi to foreign river traffic,
sparking an explosion of anger from the United States, which argued that

its rights were protected by the 1783 treaty. This action and the establishment of Franklin had a brief, and potentially destabilizing, overlap.

Like the Creeks and Cherokee who were engaged in ongoing attacks along the Tennessee frontier, the Spanish also wanted to dam the stream of land-hungry arrivals from the east but instead would find themselves enmeshed in frontier politics.[80] Although Franklin was nestled in the valleys of the rolling green foothills of Appalachia, the fertile land had rivers that fed into the Mississippi, giving potential access to trading routes.

In 1786, James White, a former North Carolina congressman, called on the Spanish chargé d'affaires, Diego de Gardoqui—whose family firm had supplied the United States with goods and arms during the Revolutionary War—in New York City. The 1784 order closing the Mississippi was of great concern to everyone in the river valley, and so White proposed to Gardoqui that Spain open the river to trade with the southern territories, which would secede in order to protect their trade interests while also allowing themselves to "draw closer to His Majesty."[81] Gardoqui did not commit himself to White's plan, though he could see the idea's merits: the Franklinites wanted to trade, and the Spanish needed more loyal subjects in that region.[82]

By 1788, White planned to canvass influential Franklinites about supporting a sort of union between the state and Spain. Sevier also wrote to Gardoqui to outline his vision of the deal, which involved extending the settlements to the Tennessee River, with Spain helping to keep the peace with the Native Americans in order to allow for this expansion. In a second letter, Sevier claimed, "We are unanimously determined" to make the alliance, while reminding Gardoqui that "there will not be a more favorable time than the present" to put the plan into effect.[83] At this point, Franklin itself began to unravel under the weight of ongoing disagreements between bickering factions, as well as continued Indian attacks. To add to these matters, Sevier was arrested for treason by the state of North Carolina, though the charges were later dropped. By the end of 1788, panicked residents, who were unaware of the talks with Spain, asked North Carolina to intercede to protect them from the escalating Cherokee raids. Despite the efforts of White and others, talks with Spanish officials collapsed as well. Spain did not have enough confidence in the Franklinites, though White continued to press his case during the spring of 1789, to no avail.[84]

Franklin was not the only territory making overtures to the Spanish. The Kentucky territory that was then part of Virginia had also expressed a desire to be separate, though it had not yet drawn up a constitution. Brigadier General James Wilkinson traveled to New Orleans in 1787 to meet with Esteban Miró, then governor of Louisiana. Wilkinson had left the east after the end of the Revolutionary War and bought 12,550 acres in Kentucky, paid for in part with money from friends in Philadelphia who were hoping to profit through land speculation. He set up as a merchant in Lexington and soon began to work out how to get around the Spanish prohibition on the Mississippi, eager to sell tobacco to Mexico via Spanish New Orleans.[85] At this juncture the future of the United States was still fragile—in the same year Miró and Wilkinson met, the Constitutional Convention was taking place in Philadelphia, and the resulting document would not be promulgated until 1789. Who was part of the union and how that union would function were still very much up for discussion.[86]

Miró had a number of reservations about Wilkinson's plan, not least the number of Protestants this would involve.[87] However, he was willing to allow the Kentucky settlers in because he expected enough increased revenue from agricultural exports produced by these farmers to pay for the arrival of English-speaking Irish Catholic priests who could try to proselytize the Kentuckians.[88] The real issue at stake, however, involved tariffs and diplomacy. As had been the case with Franklin, if Kentucky joined Spain it would have access to the Mississippi and to Spain's large American market. This had the potential to anger the United States, not least because talks about the issue had been ongoing throughout this period and Spanish officials had to consider what the diplomatic repercussions of that might be.[89]

Wilkinson also seized the moment to pursue another opportunity. Although he was still a member of the military, he became in future years a paid informer—later known as agent 13—for the Spanish, involved in a number of intrigues, information about which would often be paid for in silver dollars.[90] In 1787, Wilkinson declared his loyalty to the Spanish crown and promised to bring more settlers to the region.[91]

Around this time, the Spanish also had to contend with ambitious settlers from Georgia who were moving into the lower reaches of the Mississippi, setting up in the Natchez territory, and going so far as to establish, with the approval of the state legislature in 1785, the "County of Bourbon." Its name was a rejoinder to Spanish claims as the annexed land was right at the thirty-first parallel, as stipulated by the Treaty of Paris, running from the Yazoo River to the Chattahoochee River.[92] Anglo settlers had already been creeping into the area for some time, and in 1781, during the Revolutionary War, Natchez was the site of a brief uprising that the Spanish quashed, after which some of the remaining Anglos pledged their loyalty to Spain. Initially, the settlers found it in their interest to express their loyalty to Spain and take advantage of a booming tobacco market, though this arrangement became more uncertain after the treaty of 1783.[93]

In the end, Spain approved a measure in December 1788 that would allow goods from Ohio and Kentucky to travel down the river, so long as the traders paid a 15 percent duty—defusing some of the tension though not providing the most satisfactory solution for the United States.[94]

At the same time, significant changes occurred in Madrid. Carlos III died in late 1788 and was succeeded by his son, Carlos IV, who was less interested in active governance. Alongside this, his ministers became enmeshed in the power struggles that emerged in the aftermath of the palace changes. In North America, the frontier breakaway groups and potential allies for Spain renegotiated their return to the U.S. fold. Kentucky became the fifteenth state to join the union, in 1792, followed by Tennessee in 1796, with the Franklinite leader John Sevier serving as its first governor.

———～———

THE UPPER LOUISIANA territory, which corresponds to modern Arkansas, Missouri, and points north all the way up to the Great Lakes, was, for the most part, a terra incognita to the Spanish who were supposed to administer it. The French had been the first Europeans to claim it, leaving a trail of small settlements. Cape Girardeau, today in the state of Missouri, was one such place. It was established on the banks of the Mississippi River around 1735 to ship furs, food, and other goods, and was one of a number of river communities. However, the Mississippi's many bends meant constant threats of flooding, which forced some of these small outposts to be shuffled up and down the river. The French continued to plant settlements along the Mississippi, with Ste. Genevieve established around 1750, and St. Louis, farther upstream, in 1764.[95] By the time of the Revolutionary War, Spain had sent officials there, but most of the settlers were not Spanish. They also had to make alliances with many of the Native Americans there; one 1769 report listed twenty-three chiefdoms to which the Spanish were giving gifts, including the Iowa, Little and Big Osage, and Peoria peoples.[96] Throughout the Revolutionary period and its aftermath, many Shawnee and Delaware people moved to Upper Louisiana to get away from the encroachment of U.S. settlers. The Spanish permitted them to stay to the south and west of Ste. Genevieve, and by the 1790s there were six villages with a Shawnee population of 1,200 and 600 Delaware, while farther south some Cherokees moved into Lower Louisiana.[97] A 1772 report on St. Louis and Ste. Genevieve showed that there were 399 whites and 198 slaves in St. Louis, while Ste. Genevieve had 404 whites and 287 slaves.[98]

In 1770, the then Louisiana governor, Alejandro O'Reilly, issued instructions stipulating that "the lieutenant-governor shall cause the Indians to know the greatness, clemency, and generosity of the King. He shall tell them that they will receive the same presents annually; that His Majesty desires their happiness."[99] In reality, Spain had little money to spend on this vast frontier. Indeed, O'Reilly's predecessor, Antonio de Ulloa, had tried to curb the gift-giving, with a special emphasis on banning the giving of guns, a ban that was not popular with Native American leaders.[100] Sometimes they acted on their irritation with the Spanish; for instance, in 1772 a band composed of Little Osages and Missouri people attacked some of the rudimentary forts the Spanish had placed along the Missouri River.[101] In this corner of its empire, administrators engaged in none of the mission-building or tribute-taking that had been the hallmark of Spanish rule elsewhere.[102] The potential for any sort of wealth was to be found in trade and farming—wheat, hemp, and flax were important crops. A letter to O'Reilly from one of his captains in 1769 noted that the "country is very fertile. It produces with great abundance whatever is planted. In my time there was a vast harvest of wheat and corn."[103]

Farther downriver, the search for profits would cause much consternation a decade later for Governor Miró. Spanish minister Gardoqui had made the acquaintance of another soldier turned speculator named George Morgan in Philadelphia. They agreed on a deal involving a land grant of fifteen million acres near where the Ohio River runs into the Mississippi. Morgan was quick to find eager farmers and settlers—not even waiting for royal assent, and passing around handbills promoting this "New Madrid."[104] Morgan also secured the right to appoint local officials, form a representative legislative assembly, and allow the construction of Protestant churches. Morgan arrived at the land in 1789 with some of the colonists, many of whom were German immigrants, and they began their work on the meandering west bank of the river, about forty-five miles south of its confluence with the Ohio.[105]

Although the Osages and Quapaw did not want to use this bit of land and allowed the arrival of these foreigners, Miró had numerous objections, not least Morgan's powers and his land speculation, which involved selling lots of 320 acres at a price of $48.[106] Miró wrote to protest against the extension of land given to Morgan "as it is contrary to the welfare of the state in general, and to the welfare of that province in particular."[107] Morgan's plans angered Miró, and he told Morgan that this was no way to treat land that "His Majesty conceded *gratis*."[108] The thorniest issue for Miró was that the deal had "no clause in it which expresses the least subordination to Spain."[109] Whispering into Miró's ear during this time was Wilkinson, who tried to turn the Spanish governor against this group of settlers, wanting to instill suspicions and doubts about Morgan. Because New Madrid was located in Spanish territory, Wilkinson realized that traders there would have an advantage over those in Kentucky, as they would not have to pay tariffs to ship their goods.[110]

Miró, however, had already accepted that the settlement was necessary, and so permitted the colonists to continue, though he demoted Morgan to vice-commandant of the district of New Madrid.[111] A small fortification was built in New Madrid in 1789; it was named Fort Celeste after Miró's wife, and its staff was to check any vessels coming down the river from U.S. territories and the papers of the people on them.[112]

By 1790 only about 300 people had moved from the United States to this area of Spanish Upper Louisiana. With such small numbers, New Madrid had not fared well. Flooding had hurt the livelihood of many colonists, and some, including Morgan, returned east.[113] An inventory from 1797 showed more cows (777) than humans (569 white, 46 slave).[114]

A British traveler, Francis Baily, described New Madrid in the late 1790s as being "situated on a level plain" with around three hundred houses "scattered about at unequal distances within a mile of the fort." He noted that settlers were given "great encouragement" by the land grants, and that many people from the United States now made up the majority of the population. He observed that "were it not for a few French and Spanish that are mixed with them, it might easily be mistaken for an American settlement."[115] Baily concluded, however, "I do not like New Madrid at all; I mean, if I had my choice of living in it."[116]

Despite being a tiny settlement on the fringes of the Spanish empire, New Madrid embodied the larger changes afoot in the Louisiana territory: the land speculation, the lack of interest in Spanish rule, the constant drive west. The town, as it found out during terrifying earthquakes in 1811–12, happened to be on a fault line. It was fitting somehow, as the old colonial order in North America had been thrown into disarray over the final decades of the eighteenth century, with the Spanish absorbing the aftershocks. Not only were two nations now abutting each other, but they had contrary political systems: on one hand, an empire still reliant on traditional ideas of monarchical rule; on the other, an experimental republic. However, there remained vast swaths of territory unknown to all these interlopers, and the Spanish were still trying to expand the farthest limits of their empire.

Chapter 6

Nootka Sound, Canada, ca. 1760s–1789

T HERE ARE STILL no roads to Nootka. Here, in what were the outer reaches of the territory claimed by Spain, unknown and unmapped, the quiet dark rivers of the sound remain the main arteries for travel, as they have been since the arrival of the Mowachaht people at least four thousand years ago. Today, small cargo vessels call at the many inlets along this part of the west coast of Vancouver Island, Canada, ferrying goods to and from the logging camps and salmon farms. Otherwise, the rolling limestone hills, carpeted with spruce and pine trees, appear much as they did when Captain James Cook sailed the *Resolution* into a cove along this coast in 1778, during his third voyage. It was a place he described as "so far advanced to the northward and eastward as to be far beyond the limits of European Geography." Cook felt he had reached "that void space in our maps, which is marked as a country unknown."[1]

Anchoring in the bay at the end of March 1778, Cook and his crew invited some of the locals on board, but they refused. He noticed that their weapons were made with copper and iron, which, he realized, "they could obtain only from the Russians, or from trade with the Hudson's Bay Company." They managed good relations and Cook stayed a few weeks to make repairs. He thought the Mowachaht behaved "apparently with much friendship," in part because they brought valuable seal and otter skins to trade for metal tools.[2] This place of refuge was known as Yuquot by the Mowachaht, but the British sailors called it Friendly Cove.

Cook was a late arrival in this corner of the world; the Spaniards had been sailing in nearby waters for some time. Spanish administrators had received reports as early as the 1740s about the activity of the Russians, who were inching over from their fur trading posts around the Aleutian Islands. Orders issued from Spain in 1761 called for a diplomat to make inquiries about "the discoveries of the Russians in their attempts of their navigation to California."[3] Russia in this period was growing in might, harboring its own imperial ambitions. As its fur trappers became more familiar with the coastline near Spanish possessions, it became clear that they could sail with ease into this territory and there would be no military garrison to stop them.[4]

By the time of the 1765 inspection tour of New Spain by José de Gálvez, there had been sufficient reports of activity to merit sending expeditions up the coast of Alta California, a trip of some three thousand miles from the port of San Blas. A few years later, the then viceroy of New Spain, Antonio María de Bucareli, agreed that these northernmost reaches needed further exploration. He sent Juan Pérez in 1774 on a mission, during which Pérez reached as far as N 55°, around Haida Gwaii island (the Queen Charlotte Islands), which lay to the north of Nootka Sound, though a storm prevented him from calling there.[5] In 1775, the Peruvian-born naval officer Juan Francisco Bodega y Quadra was dispatched to explore the northern limits of Alta California, as well as to keep hunting for the now long-sought route from the Pacific to the Atlantic. He returned with no passage and no reports of Russians. Bucareli was aware at this point that Cook was on his third voyage, though the British captain managed to call at Nootka undetected by the Spanish, who would have eagerly seized him.[6] Bodega y Quadra made one more trip to the Alaska region in 1779 before he was transferred to the Caribbean.

By 1786, there had been little action to rid the Spanish Pacific of Russia's presence. Two more vessels were dispatched in 1788 under the command of Esteban José Martínez and Gonzalo López de Haro, who found evidence of Russian activity around Nootka and heard of plans to build a garrison there.[7] They reported back to Manuel Antonio Flores, who had become viceroy of New Spain in 1787, and urged him to put a fort or settlement in Yuquot to make clear Spain's authority and have a base from which the stretch of coast down to San Francisco could be protected. In addition to the Russian threat, Flores was also concerned that traders from the United States might be seeking a Pacific port.[8]

He wrote to officials in Madrid, saying, "We should not be surprised if the English colonies of America, republican and independent, put into practice the design of discovering a safe port on the South Sea [Pacific], and try to sustain it by crossing the immense land of this continent above our possession of Texas, New Mexico, and the Californias."[9]

Two other factors were taking shape outside Flores's purview: in 1787, Russia's Catherine II canceled plans for a fort at Nootka, and in 1788 a British merchant named John Meares set up a fur trading post there.[10] While the Spanish officials may have wanted to ward off any further foreign incursion, the reality was that Nootka was more than two thousand miles from any major port in New Spain. California did not have a large enough Spanish population to draw a significant pool of settlers or soldiers to the north, but Madrid ordered officials in New Spain to put something there anyway.

Flores sent Martínez back to Nootka in February 1789, and he arrived by May, taking formal possession of the inlet and naming it San Lorenzo de Nuca. A few Franciscans went with him to convert people in Yuquot, with limited success. Also there in the sound to greet him were two vessels led by a trader from the United States, Robert Gray.[11] Martínez questioned Gray, who claimed he was on a Congress-backed mission to extend the New England fur trade to the Pacific. Soon afterward, another U.S. trader, John Kendrick, arrived in Nootka after a trip to the Queen Charlotte Islands, and told Martínez that he and his party were making repairs to their ships and would leave soon.[12] A British vessel, *Iphigenia*, was also in the sound, under the command of Captain William Douglas, who was working for the merchant John Meares. Upon learning this, Martínez began to interrogate Douglas, and later seized his ship and detained the crew.

Then, on June 24, another British schooner, the *North West America*, sailed into Nootka. Martínez took possession of it, though he allowed the *Iphigenia* to leave. A final ship, the *Argonaut*, arrived in July, and Martínez detained its captain, James Colnett, who claimed to be Meares's representative and on a mission to trade fur. Colnett argued that Nootka, by virtue of Cook's voyage, belonged to Britain. Martínez disputed this, not least because he had participated in the 1774 expedition of Juan Pérez.[13] A distressed Colnett, under guard by the Spanish, was later described in a report as being "so deranged, that he attempted frequently to destroy himself."[14] Colnett and the *Argonaut* were taken south to San Blas, as was another British ship that arrived later, the *Princess Royal*.[15]

Martínez received orders from New Spain by autumn 1789 to pack up the colony and leave, in part because there were not enough vessels to supply California and Nootka, and Flores had been satisfied that enough had now been done to ward off foreign interlopers. He also had no desire to pay for an actual garrison in such an outpost.[16] Martínez followed the orders but reiterated in the strongest terms that the British were a threat in Nootka.[17]

When news of the ships' capture reached Britain it stirred up public anti-Spanish feeling, and the animosity between a handful of British fur traders and Spanish soldiers soon captured national attention.[18] By early 1790 the British prime minister William Pitt the Younger realized he could use the issue to advance free trade in the Pacific, as well as stifle any attempts by Spain to advance its territorial claims.[19] Around the same time, Francisco de Eliza was sent to the colony to rebuild the small fort that Martínez had taken down and establish once again Spain's claim in the face of British hostility.[20]

John Meares presented a memorial to the House of Commons in London on May 13, 1790, reasserting Britain's right to be in Nootka, as well as recounting his own activities there. Meares said that "immediately" upon his arrival he "purchased from [Chief] Maquilla [Maquinna] . . . a spot of ground, whereon he [Meares] built a house for his occasional residence . . . and hoisted the British colours thereon."[21] He then went on to explain the presence of the U.S. ships in 1789, and the arrival of Martínez that May and his subsequent actions, which Meares deemed "unwarrantable and unjustifiable proceedings . . . in open violation of the treaty of peace subsisting between this country and the Court of Spain."[22] Britain demanded that Spain renounce its claim over Nootka or face the consequence: war.[23] The British had also started to ask U.S. diplomats for permission to cross the United States' North American territory should they want to make a retaliatory raid on the Spanish in Louisiana.[24]

While all this was taking place, the French Revolution had erupted in 1789, and amid the disruptions in Europe the task of ending the dispute fell to diplomats rather than soldiers. By October 1790, the first Nootka

Convention was hammered out between London and Madrid. It was a loss of face for Spain, which was forced to return the captured ships, pay compensation, and accept the restoration of British claims to territory in Nootka and the resumption of trade.[25] It was also a public concession of Spain's historic claims to the Pacific coastline.[26]

That document was the first of three, with the second reinforcing the payment of the first, and the third arranging the joint abandonment of Nootka. Before the last treaty was agreed on, however, there would be one more mission. It was part diplomatic, part scientific, and involved the return of Bodega y Quadra.[27] Known as the Expedition of the Limits of 1792, it was aimed to settle the question of territorial rights, but this time it was to be undertaken in conjunction with the British, who were represented by Captain George Vancouver. After leaving England in 1791, and sailing around the northwest waters, Vancouver arrived in August 1792, a few months after Bodega y Quadra. They did not know each other's language but one English midshipman spoke enough Spanish to translate.[28] They exchanged letters and dinners but never came to an agreement on what to do, except to turn the matter back over to their respective home countries and give the island the name Isla de Quadra y Vancouver, which appeared on maps until the 1820s.[29]

After this, the third and final convention, in 1794, stipulated that neither side could claim the island nor erect any sort of permanent settlement. The following year representatives from both sides went to Nootka to put the matter to rest. The British flag was raised and lowered, and the Spanish fort was destroyed. Both parties sailed away, leaving the fortunes of the island to the Mowachaht and the fur traders.[30]

The villagers soon dismantled what was left of the Spanish settlement, and all traces of it disappeared. The Spanish were reminded once again—as they had been in Santa Elena in the 1500s and along most of the Atlantic seaboard—that without a significant settler population it was almost impossible to keep control of territory in North America.[31] Little remains of this episode beyond a tiny marker that sits on a rocky outcrop near the Yuquot harbor, erected in 1903 to commemorate the meeting of Bodega y Quadra and Vancouver at the edge of their known world. It is now so weather-beaten by wind and rain that the words inscribed on it have almost completely worn away.

⌒

THE CONCERNS THE Spanish had about Nootka also stretched much farther south, though with the 1768 establishment of the San Blas base, ships could begin a more targeted campaign to establish fortifications at key points along the coast, and members of religious orders could be brought along so that missions would rise in tandem. California represented the final continental frontier. It still remained unknown to most Europeans, including the Spanish, though the legend of the warrior Queen Calafia persisted, as did the belief that California was an island. The fantasy was, for some time, a cartographic truth. Maps produced in the mid-seventeenth century, such as the 1650 effort by the Dutch mapmaker Joan Vinckeboons, depicted it as a long, thin, green wedge floating a few miles from the mainland, separate from the deserts and mountains across the bay.[32] One reason for these errors was that few Europeans had traversed the region, though the extensive journeys Father Eusebio Kino made in the 1680s and 1690s around the Baja Peninsula and Pimería Alta would help correct these misconceptions. Kino reasoned that there must be a land connection to California, on the basis of his observation that the Yuma people and other Native Americans possessed blue shells like the ones he had seen when he reached the Pacific in 1685, signifying travel and trade by foot.[33] His extensive notes resulted in a raft of new information, but another century passed before mapmakers absorbed it into their work.[34] Indeed, even as late as the mid-1800s, Japanese maps continued to portray California as an island.[35]

California also troubled Spanish administrators because it had no reliable connections to the other parts of the empire. The overland journey from New Spain was long and arduous and there was no main road to Alta California. Work on creating such a route began a decade before Captain Cook landed in Nootka Sound, and it would represent the final stage of Spain's concerted efforts at expansion in North America after more than two centuries in pursuit, over land and sea, of everything from the cities of Cíbola to a suitable place to plant crops. By this point, Spanish exploration and settlement were far more extensive than anything the French had managed; and the British settlers had lagged behind, rarely venturing farther than a three-week journey beyond the East Coast ports.[36] In the decades to come, the people of the new United States would be ready to push into the west, and Spain, without realizing it fully at the time, was now helping to open the way.

José de Gálvez—along with the governor of California, Gaspar de Portolá; and a Franciscan named Junípero Serra—started planning what they came to call the "sacred expedition" to connect the farthest reaches of California with the rest of the empire.[37] By this point, there were enough missions in Baja California to run the length of the peninsula, one after another, like a decade of rosary beads. Taking the missionizing effort into Alta California would be the Franciscans, who had replaced the Jesuits in Baja after the latter's 1767 expulsion. Serra, a diminutive priest who was just over five feet tall, came from the Spanish island of Mallorca (Majorca) and had already enjoyed a long career in the Americas. This included a period, along with former student and fellow missionary Francisco Palóu, in the Texas territory—a period which was cut short by a Lípan Apache attack on the San Sabá mission in 1758. The authorities considered the site too dangerous and they were ordered to leave.[38] Portolá, for his part, had a military background and had participated in the expulsion of the Jesuits by suppressing angry or violent local supporters of the priests.

Gálvez decided the best course of action would be to place soldiers at a presidio in Monterey, in the north of California, to ward off any potential Russian incursion. Portolá was put in overall command, and at a meeting in San Blas, it was decided that one group would go by sea and another by land, "so that both expeditions might unite at the same harbor of Monterey, and by means of the observations made by one and the other they might acquire for once and for all complete knowledge" of the routes to California.[39]

The first ship, the San Carlos, left La Paz, Baja, in January 1769 and storms drove it off course. It lumbered into San Diego at the end of April with much of the surviving crew suffering from scurvy. In the meantime, the other packet, the San Antonio, left in mid-February and arrived by April 11. A third vessel, the San José, was lost at sea.[40] Serra, meanwhile, had joined one of the overland parties, which were suffering their own hardships. The first group, which had around seventy soldiers and Indians, arrived in San Diego by May; the second party—which included Portolá and Serra, and initially about forty Indians—reached it in July. By the time all the members of the expedition were reunited, about half had died.[41]

On July 16, 1769, Serra placed a cross in the ground and dedicated San Diego de Alcalá, the first mission planted in Alta California. Meanwhile, Portolá made arrangements to continue to Monterey, five hundred miles to the north, taking Father Juan Crespí and a group of soldiers. They had only the report of the explorer Sebastián Vizcaíno, from more than a century earlier, to help them find the bay. So when they arrived overland at what they thought was the correct latitude, they could not see anything that matched Vizcaíno's description, in part because the original map had been rendered from the sea.[42] They continued north, reaching San Francisco Bay by November, before turning back to San Diego, where they were greeted by the news that, in their absence, the site had been attacked by a group of Kumeyaay in August, and Serra's assistant had been killed.[43] Meanwhile, the San Antonio had returned to Baja for supplies, but it took so long to return that the colony was now on the edge of collapse. Portolá was about to fold up the whole enterprise when the ship returned in March 1770, bringing much-needed reinforcements.[44]

Portolá soon sailed again in another attempt to locate Monterey. This time he was successful, and with the new supplies he was able to establish a settlement there in June 1770. Serra had traveled with him and later described the voyage, which lasted for more than a month, as "somewhat trying." A land expedition that had been sent out at the same time had already arrived.[45] Soon afterward, the priests and soldiers erected a cross and a chapel. They even suspended bells from the trees for the celebratory Mass, after which, according to Serra, "the officers proceeded to the act of taking formal possession . . . unfurling and waving once more the royal flag . . . all accompanied with cheers, ringing of bells, cannonades, etc."[46] Soon, Serra was able to add his second mission, San Carlos Borromeo de Carmelo, alongside the civil presidio. The Spanish explored to the north after this, but San Francisco would not have a settlement until after 1775, when the San Carlos sailed into the bay. The following year, work began on a presidio and the mission San Francisco de Asís. At the same time, three thousand miles to the east, rebel forces in the British colonies had declared their independence. California, at this point, was still a world unto itself.

The Native Americans that the Spanish encountered in California were as diverse as the landscape in which they lived and prospered. Small communities were scattered up and down the coast in villages with anywhere from tens to hundreds of people, places the Spanish called *rancherías*. The sea was an obvious source of food for the coastal communities, but inland the mild climate and fertile land provided edible plants, and abundant animals to hunt. Many of these groups moved around according to the season in order to make the best use of natural resources.[47]

There was great diversity—even among the seventeen thousand people in the San Francisco Bay Area alone and just within the Miwok language group there were subdivisions into Coast, Bay, Plains, and northern peoples, all of whom further divided into speakers of a number of languages, such as Unisumne, Huiluc, Chilamne, or Julpun.[48] Wider estimates of the language groups along all of Alta California claim that roughly ninety languages existed under the umbrella of seven broader linguistic families.[49] The peoples of California were known to use cardinal directions—northern, southern—to describe who they were, but this concept was probably not understood by the Spaniards.[50] Some of the names used for the Native American groups today were quite possibly Spanish interpretations, as misunderstanding was commonplace. Spanish words soon came to dominate, for example, describing people as Costanoan (sometimes Ohlone), which comes from the Castilian word *costeños* for people who live near the coast.[51] An accurate population figure is also complicated, but it is thought that some three hundred thousand Native Americans lived in Alta California at the time of the arrival of the Spanish.[52]

Farther to the south of San Francisco were the Chumash, whom the Spanish met during their first trek to Monterey in 1767 through what is now the Santa Clara valley. Father Crespí described in his diary coming upon a large village, where "we counted about thirty large, comfortable, and well-constructed houses," and he estimated that about four hundred people lived there, writing that they were "a large and healthy people, quick, industrious, and clever." The Spaniards traded beads with them in exchange for goods, including wooden plates, which "could not have been more elegant if they had been made on a potter's wheel."[53]

The missions, as had happened elsewhere in the Americas, would have a transformative and traumatic effect on the people of California, turning the Chutchui and Ohlone, the Oroysom and Salinan, among so many others, into Christians. In this process, their ways of life did not end entirely but were adapted to these new circumstances. The missions in California tried to tie Native Americans to the land, ending their seasonal movements and changing their relationship to the natural world. The friars baptized the native Californians and gave them Spanish names, which were recorded in a mission register.[54] The priests and officials likened them to children, and Native Americans were not considered *gente de razón*, or, literally "people of reason," a social category that signified someone who spoke Castilian and was Catholic and loyal to the Spanish crown.[55] It was a term that was meant to exclude Indians but was extended to mestizos, in part because most of the settlers who came to Alta California from New Spain and Baja during this time were varying degrees of mestizo, and in some cases of African origin as well. Twenty-six of the first forty-six settlers in the civilian pueblo Los Angeles, established in 1781, were either black or mulatto.[56] By 1790 such descriptions would change—even with regard to the same person. Manuel Camero, for example, was described as mulatto in 1781 but as mestizo by 1790. In 1781, José Navarro had been a mestizo, but by 1790 he was an *Español*.[57] Everyone who changed went a few shades lighter, and by 1790 Los Angeles had a population of seventy-three Spaniards, thirty-nine mestizos, twenty-two mulattoes, and seven Indians. This pattern of "whitening" was repeated throughout Alta California, in part because the necessities of frontier life wiped away many of the *casta* categories that dominated New Spain and replaced them with the local *Californio* identity of *sin* (without) *razón* or *de* (with) *razón*.[58] This allowed a degree of social mobility and gave some black and even indigenous people access to privileges that may have been granted only to lighter-skinned or Spanish immigrants elsewhere in New Spain or the wider empire.[59]

The Indians participated in mission life for a variety of reasons, some social and some economic. They could access European wares and tools and were introduced to farming and livestock, though the priests made them do much of the work. Animal husbandry changed the way that land was used—large areas were required for grazing—and the animals consumed what had previously been food for the Indians, who were then increasingly forced to rely on the missions.[60] Some Indians lived in the mission settlements and learned trades, such as how to handle livestock as a *vaquero*, or artisanal work.

The frontier missions in California, like those elsewhere in the Spanish empire, turned the religious orders into landowners and the indigenous people into their laborers. The missions were supposed to offer food, protection, and stability, though the arrival of the Spanish was part of what brought instability in the first place. Despite the conversions and changes, many of the California Indians retained their own beliefs within Catholicism; native symbols, for instance, were later found incorporated into mission decorations.[61]

The mission walls did not keep out the violence inflicted upon Native Americans by the Spanish, and priests complained about soldiers stationed at the presidios. One priest based in San Diego wrote to Serra in 1772, saying some of the troops from the presidio "deserve to be hanged on account of the continuous outrages which they are committing in seizing and raping the women."[62] These violations, coupled with other changes the Spanish were trying to impose, caused numerous rebellions. In 1775, some Kumeyaay people attacked the San Diego mission again.[63] An eyewitness report by Father Vicente Fuster described how, by his estimate, some six hundred people "pillaged the church of its precious articles, and after they set fire to it." Fuster recalled that he "saw on all sides around me so many arrows that you could not possibly count them."[64] He survived the attack, but the mission's other priest, Luis Jayme, was not so fortunate, and Fuster described the terrible moment when he found the body:

> He was disfigured from head to foot, and I could see that his death had been cruel beyond description . . . he was stripped completely of all his clothing, even to his undergarments around his middle. His chest and body were riddled through with countless jabs they had given him, and his face was one great bruise from the clubbing and stoning it had suffered.[65]

That mission, however, was rebuilt, in 1780. For his part, Serra accepted the many challenges and was known as well for his deep personal asceticism, including scourging himself and sleeping on a board.[66] He continued to be resilient in the face of not just Indian resistance but also difficulties with Spanish authorities. Disagreements between the Franciscans and colonial officials were constant, with the governor, Felipe de Neve, and Serra arguing over the treatment of Indians. Neve thought they were becoming too dependent on the missions and wanted them instead to have secular settlements and more civic integration. He pushed Serra to allow them to have certain official roles, such as *alcalde* or mayor; an angry Serra had little option but to comply.[67]

One non-Spanish visitor to California in these early years of settlement was Jean-François de Galaup, Count of Lapérouse, in 1786. The Frenchman had earlier warned the viceroy about the Russians in Nootka Sound and had been on a larger exploratory mission to search for the Northwest Passage, as well as to investigate the trade in the north Pacific.[68] He sailed into Monterey and spent time in California, where he observed the missions and their work with the Indians. It all left an unfavorable impression, and he noted that the Indians' "condition hardly differs from that of the negroes of those households in our colonies."[69] This feeling was further confirmed after his time at the San Carlos mission: "It hurts us to say but the resemblance [to the slave colony in Saint-Domingue] is so great that we have seen men and women loaded with irons, others in the *bloc*, and finally, the blows of the whip."[70] Floggings were common and violence was part of mission life.[71]

Rebellions continued as the missions grew. In 1776, the Ohlone people resisted mission encroachment until many of them were whipped, and in the same year Indians set the roof of San Luis Obispo on fire.[72] In 1785, a woman named Toypurina, who was not Christian, and Nicolas José, a convert, were convicted with two others of plotting an attack on the San Gabriel mission. Under interrogation, Toypurina told the Spanish officials that "she was angry with the priests and the others at the mission, because we were living on their land." She was first imprisoned, but later converted to Christianity and went to the mission of San Juan Bautista.[73] There was also the inevitable invisible enemy facing the Indians: disease, the spread of which was facilitated by the resettlement of Indians into smaller, settled spaces.[74]

Serra died in 1784 before he saw any serious epidemics take hold, and during his time in California he remained optimistic. At his death, nine missions and four presidios had been built.[75] By 1823 there would be twenty-one missions, almost all of them concerned with the conversion and subsequent labor of the Indians, while two towns—Los Angeles and San José de Guadalupe, founded on the southern edge of San Francisco Bay in 1777—were established and intended to have civilian settlements.[76]

Attempts to connect California to other parts of northern New Spain, such as New Mexico, also had been ongoing. In 1774, Viceroy Bucareli commissioned Juan Bautista de Anza, a soldier with a distinguished record, to establish and record that route. Anza left on January 8 from the small presidio in Tubac, in today's Arizona, located just north of the Tumacácori mission. He took thirty-five men and headed west, using existing Native American trails to forge a path through the desert and over the mountains. By March 22 they had reached Los Angeles, before heading up the coast to Monterey. Then the party retraced their steps back to their starting point, ensuring that the route was a certainty, not an accident.[77] After their return to Arizona, Anza was promoted to lieutenant colonel and led a group of 240 soldiers and settlers back to California, this time going north from Monterey all the way to San Francisco, arriving in June 1776.[78]

Elsewhere, two Franciscans—Francisco Atanasio Domínguez and Francisco Silvestre Vélez de Escalante—and a handful of men began a potentially epic journey from Santa Fe into the northwest. They left in July 1776, passing through parts of the Colorado Plateau and the Great Basin area of Utah before turning back, fearing for their survival, after two months of travel left them only a few hundred miles to the west of where they had started. They had completed a loop around the modern "four corners" region of the states of Colorado, Utah, Arizona, and New Mexico. A Spanish cartographer who lived in New Mexico, Bernardo Miera y Pacheco, was on that expedition, charged with mapping this difficult terrain. Part of the problem had been that there were no geographically accurate maps of the diverse and enormous lands between New Mexico and California; instead they had to depend on any Indian guides willing to help them. Although the expedition ended in failure, Miera managed to produce what was known as the "Geographic Map of the Newly Discovered Land to the North, Northwest, and West of

New Mexico"—a work of art in itself, depicting some 175,000 square miles and measuring two feet high by three feet wide—which became a valuable resource for future western exploration.[79]

In attempting to find new routes to California, the Spanish had constant encounters with Native Americans. Some of these were violent, such as the July 17, 1781, attack on a band of settlers on their way to California following Anza's path. It took place near the Colorado River, leaving around thirty soldiers and four Franciscans dead, and some of the women and children were abducted. Although Anza's route by this point had been in use for a little more than seven years, the massacre put a stop to any larger-scale overland movement of settlers.[80] By 1790, only 1,000 settlers were in California—up from 170 in 1774.[81] By comparison, in New Mexico in 1800 there were around 15,000 Spaniards.[82] These fringes of empire were tiny when set next to Mexico City or Lima, or even Philadelphia, which had a population of some 30,000 by 1776.

The Spanish continued searching for connecting routes within their North American territory. By the 1790s, parties were being sent from St. Louis in Spanish Upper Louisiana to color in the unknown hinterland on the map. They headed west along the Missouri River valley, with hopes that waterways would lead out to Alta California and function as a Northwest Passage of sorts. British trappers in Canada, French settlers in Missouri, or adventurous young men from the United States, at times backed by Spanish officials in Louisiana, set out in search of a practical continental water route between east and west, but it, too, proved elusive.[83] California would remain an island for a while longer.

Chapter 7

New Orleans, Louisiana, ca. 1790–1804

Dotted around New Orleans—the city considered to be the most "French" in the United States—are a number of tiled plaques on the side of buildings. They commemorate former street names, but they are Spanish, not French. A regal coat of arms sits to the left of the lettering on one of them, on chipped, uneven tiles. It reads: "When New Orleans was the Capital of the Spanish Province of Louisiana 1762–1803 / This square bore the name Plaza de Armas." Today, that plaza is called Jackson Square and is the heart of the Vieux Carré, or the French Quarter. Most of New Orleans's millions of tourists walk past these plaques without a second's curious hesitation. Yet the architectural footprint of the Spanish is far more evident than it may seem at first glance, not least because the Spanish were forced to rebuild the city twice.

Although the cities of the Spanish empire used straight lines and plazas to order space in the Americas, Spanish architects cannot take full credit for the gridded tranquillity of the oldest part of New Orleans. That original 1721 plan, drawn up by the French chief royal engineer Pierre le Blond de la Tour and his assistant Adrien de Pauger, envisaged a city bounded by three walls and streets laid out in a grid facing a bank of the Mississippi, with a central plaza placing the church at the heart of it. Work began while they were alive—Le Blond de la Tour died in 1724, and Pauger in 1726—though there were considerable delays owing to a hurricane in 1722.[1] New Orleans grew, but in 1788, by which time it was under Spanish rule, a fire started on Good Friday that devoured the city, consuming the many structures built from cypress wood. More than eight hundred buildings, including the main church, were destroyed. Spanish officials quickly tried to rebuild, though this was followed by another, less extensive fire in 1794.

The Spanish replaced the wooden buildings with grander edifices, befitting a city with a population then of around five thousand, leaving New Orleans with an urban environment that blended French and Spanish colonial styles. Civic leaders were at the center, while the slaves and free people of color were pushed to the fringes, a spatial arrangement connecting New Orleans to other parts of the Hispanic world, such as Havana.[2] The stone buildings that replaced the burned wooden ones included Spanish features, such as internal courtyards and balconies with ornamental iron railings.

Spain's time in charge of what had been French Louisiana was, in many respects, a tale of two colonies: the frontier of Upper Louisiana, a great expanse of land to the north and west of the northern part of the Mississippi River; and the world of New Orleans and Lower Louisiana, which was a part of the wider Gulf and Caribbean. Despite their differences, the two Louisianas would experience similar upheavals before the end of the eighteenth century.

THE EARLIEST YEARS of Spanish rule in New Orleans, beginning in 1763, had a turbulent start. When the first Spanish governor, Antonio de Ulloa, finally arrived in 1766, he faced the same problem his counterparts had in Florida—no money and no men—with the extra headache of a preexisting French political power structure. The captain-general of Cuba, Antonio María de Bucareli—who later became the viceroy of New Spain—reported in a 1767 letter to ministers in Spain that Ulloa had sent "two letters for me in which he made clear the sad situation he found himself in for lack of money, and asked me to send him quickly 40,000 to 50,000 pesos," which Bucareli was not able to do.[3] However, Ulloa was granted a budget of 250,000 pesos a year, at least on paper, starting in 1768, though much of this money depended on the silver being sent from New Spain.[4] As with the funding for Florida and the other less profitable colonies, this silver subsidy, known as the *situado*, had long been part of

Spanish imperial finance. The eighteenth century had been rocky finan-cially, as the constant rounds of warfare meant there were large spikes in the amount of silver being sent to these peripheral colonies to shore up defenses: in 1770–79 nearly 5 million pesos were exported, but by 1790–99, this figure would reach 9 million, representing about 40 percent of New Spain's silver production in this period.[5] Despite the sums involved and the urgency, payments could be delayed or lost, leaving many gover-nors, like Ulloa, to scrape through in the meantime.

Ulloa was a renowned scientist and intellectual, but he was a less able administrator, and he faced many challenges from the outset in Louisi-ana. At first, Ulloa and the French governor at the time of the handover, Charles-Philippe Aubry, tried to share power.[6] Ulloa struggled to assert his authority and by October 1786 the situation spiraled out of control as French colonists, including New Orleans merchants, had Ulloa arrested on charges of malfeasance, while they declared their ongoing loyalty to Louis XV. The French had a number of grievances, not least Ulloa's failed attempt to implement Spain's strict—and unpopular—trading laws, which included a crackdown on contraband and on smuggling. Local merchants were also frustrated that Spain produced few manufactured goods. Ulloa was given three days to leave, and he returned to Cuba, accompanied by his family, some officials, and a few soldiers.[7]

Spanish Louisiana was without a governor for many months, until Madrid sent one of its top military officers, Irish-born Alejandro O'Reilly, along with two thousand soldiers and twenty-one ships.[8] O'Reilly had an established career in the service of Spain before he arrived from Havana on the *Volante* on August 18, 1769, to cheers of *"Viva el Rey,"* while the artillery fired salutes.[9] He then raised the Spanish flag over the fleur-de-lis, a symbolic act that Ulloa had failed to perform.[10] After he executed five Frenchmen thought to be behind the earlier revolt, he earned the nickname "Bloody O'Reilly," but there would be no more rebellions on his watch. Spanish control was complete, for the time being.[11]

New Orleans, like many port cities of the era, was already earning a reputation for being raucous, and O'Reilly attempted to regulate the number of inns, billiard halls, and cabarets, "which many individuals have established with impunity and without permit," believing them to be "very dangerous to public order."[12] By early 1770 he had imple-mented a degree of what Spanish administrators often referred to as "tranquillity" through a number of such laws and reforms, something the governors after him would replicate. He put the administration of the territory under the control of the captain-general in Havana and shored up the military installations. In 1771, O'Reilly handed control to Luis Unzaga, who served until 1777, when he was replaced by Bernardo de Gálvez.

The development of Spanish New Orleans and Lower Louisiana happened against the backdrop of the aftermath of the Seven Years' War and the American Revolution. Its future would be shaped by more conflict: the French Revolution, the subsequent Revolutionary and Napoleonic Wars, and the mass slave rebellion in France's West Indian sugar colony, Saint-Domingue (today's Haiti). The three conflicts were connected, and Spain and Louisiana would be forced to respond to different aspects of them. For officials in Madrid, the most pressing concern was the fighting that erupted throughout Europe in the wake of the French Revolution. Closer to New Orleans, however, Lower Louisiana was threatened by the unrest taking place in the Caribbean.

Calls in France for liberty, equality, and fraternity traveled across the Atlantic, reverberating loudly in Saint-Domingue. That colony held some five hundred thousand enslaved people—many of them recent arrivals from Africa—thirty thousand free people of color, and thirty thousand whites. At first, the free people, many of whom were wealthy indigo or coffee planters, and even owners of their own slaves by this point, demanded the equality they were hearing about from France. They saw a chance to overthrow the discriminatory laws that had intensified over the years, for instance, placing restrictions on what sorts of clothing they could wear or which public places they could frequent.

Vincent Ogé, a member of the *gens de couleur* from Saint-Domingue, put his case for equality to the National Assembly in France in 1790, but his call went unanswered. He returned to the colony later that year and led a revolt before being captured and killed. At the same time, the white community was fracturing—the poor whites were leaning toward republicanism, while the wealthy sugar planters and the clergy remained supporters of the king. Into this already volatile mixture another combustible element was added: the hundreds of thousands of slaves who had been paying close attention to these events. In August 1791, they launched their own struggle for freedom, later known as the Haitian Revolution, which would last thirteen years.

Officials and slaveholders throughout the Caribbean became alarmed, as did the United States and the Spanish in Florida and Louisiana. For Spain, the threat had two faces: the prospect of freed slaves in the Americas and republicanism in Europe. The Spanish soon discovered a plot organized by Edmond-Charles Genêt, French ambassador to the United States during the Revolution, to attack Spain's colonies in the Americas, including Florida, though it did not come to fruition.[13] To add further concern, the National Assembly in France decided to recognize equal rights for free people of color in 1792, and this measure was followed by the abolition of slavery, declared by the French revolutionary commissioner in Saint-Domingue, Léger-Félicité Sonthonax, in August 1793. He hoped such a move might bring the uprising to an end, but although abolition was upheld by the National Assembly the following year, it did not smother the flames of the revolt on the island. By this point there were numerous factions, with black former slaves fighting free mulattoes, and royalists battling revolutionaries. There was an additional layer of complexity when the British sent in troops in 1793, hoping to use the upheaval to take the island from France, but they were driven out by 1798.

These events combined to provide a constant stream of anxiety in the minds of slave owners and colonial administrators throughout the region. The Spanish remained on high alert, and throughout their empire they tried to prohibit the circulation of incendiary material from Republican France, such as pamphlets or newspapers. Despite these efforts, the movement of information was difficult to control, especially in a port city like New Orleans, which was full of sailors and smugglers who could circulate illicit reading material and pass around the latest rumors. The then governor of Louisiana, Francisco Luis Héctor, Baron de Carondelet, issued propaganda critical of the Revolution in an effort to counter any positive reports from France.[14] Carondelet, who was French-born but married into a prominent Spanish family and served the Spanish crown, was in office from 1791 to 1797, through much of this period of uncertainty, and he implemented a range of policies in his efforts to keep the peace. Not all were popular—some of the French called Carondelet *cochon de lait* (suckling pig).[15] The white French in Louisiana were divided, too; some aligned with the Revolution, others remaining loyal to the monarchy or to Spain.[16] Likewise, people of color did not have a uniform stance. As in Saint-Domingue, there were social divisions, including slave, free, darker-skinned black (*moreno*), or lighter-skinned (*pardo*). Many people of color also were members of the *pardo* and *moreno* militias, a crucial part of the defense of Spanish Louisiana. Even before the slave rebellion in Saint-Domingue, Spanish administrators in Louisiana had taken care to keep firm control over people of color through legal means and manipulation, for instance, attempting to stop free people of color from fraternizing with slaves.[17]

Throughout the period of the Haitian Revolution, a number of restrictions were placed on the importation of enslaved people, including a ban on those from the French Caribbean. The entry of any people of color fleeing Saint-Domingue was also prohibited. Slavery in Louisiana was not on the same scale as in Saint-Domingue, though slave ships had been making regular arrivals by the 1770s, with some enslaved people ending up there after being re-exported via British colonies such as Jamaica.[18] From 1783 until 1789, at least sixty-two hundred slaves were brought to Louisiana; another seventeen hundred were brought from 1790 to 1796. With the addition of people born into enslavement, the total number of slaves reached around twenty thousand in 1788 in an overall population of around forty-two thousand.[19]

Slaves in Louisiana, as elsewhere in the Spanish empire, could exercise the right to buy their freedom, known as *coartación*. This was a long-standing legal provision that allowed enslaved people to negotiate a price and pay their masters for manumission. In New Orleans, there were just under one hundred free people of color in 1771, but this number had reached nine hundred freed people by 1785, against a larger city population of around forty-four hundred whites and ninety-five hundred slaves.[20]

For those still enslaved, the Spanish, like the French, implemented slave codes in Louisiana to govern behavior. In general, these codes outlined provisions such as religious instruction for slaves, what sort of punishment was allowed, and how to deal with captured runaways, though many of these rules were often ignored. France's *Code Noir* was first issued in 1685, and a version for Louisiana was enacted in 1724. Spain's laws for the treatment of enslaved people stretched back to the thirteenth century's *Las Siete Partidas*, with its roots in Roman law. In

1784, the crown issued the *Código negro carolino*, an attempt to copy the French code and foster the growth of slavery and agriculture in Santo Domingo, the poorer Spanish neighbor of Saint-Domingue. This was later followed by the 1789 instructions *Codigo negro español*, and the social control placed upon slaves and free people of color grew in the 1790s as it became clear that other parts of Spain's Caribbean empire could profit from the events in Saint-Domingue. The years of fighting had seen many planters flee and cane fields destroyed. Cuba and Puerto Rico, and to a lesser degree Louisiana, were in a position to turn their economies to sugar, taking over where Saint-Domingue had left off. Cuba, especially, would emerge as the sugar powerhouse of the Caribbean.

The treatment of slaves and free people of color was also subject to local rules and ordinances. For instance, in the beginning of Spanish rule in Louisiana, Ulloa had implemented measures such as a curfew, permission for slaves to be whipped, and not allowing the slaves of different masters to assemble together.[21] At the same time, however, he gave his own chaplain permission to marry a white man and an enslaved woman—the French laws had prohibited marrying across these lines—causing a scandal in French planter society.[22] The white French worried that the Spanish were too permissive and that their approach would undermine the whole slavery regime.[23] Despite these concerns, concubinage continued in New Orleans, while the population of free people of color grew. By the 1780s, the then governor, Esteban Miró (1785–91), instituted ordinances to curb the social powers of this growing community. He made a number of other edicts directed at people of color, turning his attention to concubinage. He targeted women he described as concubines, requiring them to dress in less elegant garb. Expensive hats and heavily coiffured hair were prohibited, to be replaced by a *tignon*, a hair wrap worn by slaves, in an attempt to keep these women in the confines of their social category.[24] Miró criticized the "idleness of the free negro and quadroon [women]," claiming that "they subsist from the product of their licentious life without abstaining from carnal pleasures," and calling for them to "go back to work."[25]

Despite the many restrictions placed on people of color in Louisiana, one tradition was not infringed upon: the Sunday afternoon assembling of enslaved people after the morning market in New Orleans, to drum and dance at a site on the edge of the city later known as Congo Square.

Slaves were meant to be given the Sabbath off, and many in the city would gather for these "dances, or amusements." This continued through the Spanish period, with the stipulation from officials that "they shall always cease before night" lest the slaves entertain more subversive notions.[26]

Although the Haitian Revolution remains the best-known and largest slave uprising, it was not the only one in the 1790s. Indeed, in 1795 alone, the Dutch faced an uprising in Curaçao, and the British a revolt in Dominica, in addition to the ongoing conflict, known as the Maroon Wars, against the descendants of runaway slaves who lived in the hills of Jamaica. Revolution, rebellion, and the corresponding hopes and anxieties found their way to Louisiana, too. North of Baton Rouge is an area called Pointe Coupée, where by 1788 enslaved outnumbered free almost three times over, 1,492 to 512—numbers that grew by 1795 to 2,000 whites and 7,000 enslaved people. Two plots were uncovered, in 1791 and 1795, with the latter also including white participants, to the consternation of the Spanish officials. The alleged ringleaders were rounded up and tried, with around 25 black people sentenced to be hanged, another 30 or so people sent to hard labor at a Spanish presidio, and others banished from Louisiana. Four of the people who were hanged were then decapitated, their heads put on posts along the main road at Pointe Coupée to serve as a warning; another two severed heads went to New Orleans, and six others were scattered around other Louisiana outposts.[27] In the following year, 1796, Governor Carondelet attempted to ban all entry of enslaved people to Louisiana, while also trying to convince owners that they needed to treat their slaves better in order to prevent any further conspiracies. Despite the ban, slave smuggling persisted, and the next governor, Manuel Gayoso de Lemos, rescinded the order in 1799.[28]

———

THE ISSUE OF West Florida's unresolved status also resurfaced during the tumult of the 1790s. Now back under Spanish control after the 1783 Treaty of Paris, the colony still had a small population.[29] The United States persisted in its demands about the disputed Florida boundary, and in 1795 the first minister of Spain, Manuel de Godoy—who had replaced Floridablanca—yielded to them. Distracted by Spain's involvement in the French Revolutionary Wars in Europe, and desiring a good relationship with the United States while simultaneously displaying little interest in Louisiana, in October 1795 he signed the Treaty of San Lorenzo, also known as Pinckney's Treaty in the United States after the negotiator Thomas Pinckney.[30] This treaty granted the United States everything it wanted, including confirmation of the West Florida boundary at N 31°, navigation and trade rights for U.S. ships on the Mississippi, a joint U.S.-Spanish effort to prevent cross-border Indian attacks, and sharing trade with Native Americans rather than competing over it.[31] Upon hearing its terms, James Madison received the initial impression that, as he told Thomas Jefferson, it "adjusts both the boundary and the navigation in a very satisfactory manner."[32] By 1798, the United States had created its Mississippi Territory, which reached along the thirty-first parallel from that river to the Chattahoochee River, today part of the border between Alabama and Georgia.[33]

This drive for expansion was not a confident one, however, as U.S. leaders considered each move west in these earliest years of nationhood to be a potential snag that could unravel the delicate fabric of the republic.[34] Once Congress ratified Pinckney's Treaty, Madison tempered his earlier enthusiasm, calling the deal "a bitter pill to some," in part because it was "inviting additional emigrations to the Western Country."[35] They had cause for concern, as breakaway schemes like Franklin in 1784 had shown the extent of the fragility at the edges of the nation. Also unsettling were the ongoing hostilities with the Native Americans, which Secretary of War Henry Knox blamed on the "desires of too many frontier white people, to seize, by force or fraud upon the neighboring Indian lands." Knox found the settlers' treatment of Native Americans worrying, saying, "Our modes of population have been more destructive to the Indian natives than the conduct of the conquerors of Mexico and Peru."[36] Yet Spain and the United States were on the brink of a land deal that would overshadow the 1795 agreement and transform the fortunes of both nations.

By 1800, Napoleon Bonaparte had consolidated power in France and turned to his still rebelling colony, Saint-Domingue, eager to return it to being the wealthy, sugar-producing, slave-owning "pearl of the Antilles."

Bonaparte now redoubled his efforts, which included reinstating slavery in 1802 and sending his brother-in-law, Charles Leclerc, with ten thousand troops to take back the colony. Almost the entire expedition was killed, if not by the renewed and invigorated effort against the French led by former slave Jean-Jacques Dessalines, then by yellow fever. Leclerc succumbed to the disease and was replaced by Donatien-Marie-Joseph de Vimeur, Vicomte de Rochambeau, a general whose father had led French troops during the American Revolution. Rochambeau and his men were no match for the former slaves. He capitulated in 1803. The toll on France was high; an estimated fifty thousand soldiers died over the course of the conflict.

Bonaparte had also run up a great deal of debt fighting in that war and in Europe. While the conflict in Saint-Domingue was in its final throes, Bonaparte and Spain opened negotiations over Louisiana. Spanish ministers thought returning Louisiana to France could help them better protect the much more valuable New Spain.[37] They were growing increasingly concerned that the United States would push through Louisiana into Texas, and then to their silver mines. The French, on the other hand, would be far less likely to pursue this course of action and could help keep U.S. settlers out of the west. Bonaparte, however, had something else in mind when he signed the secret Third Treaty of San Ildefonso in 1800. The deal returned control of Louisiana to France under the requirement that it not be sold to a third party, a stipulation Bonaparte quickly ignored. He sold the Louisiana territory to the United States in 1803 for $15 million (about $250–$300 million today), a bargain that would double the size of the young nation.

When the negotiations began, Jefferson and his ministers harbored the more modest hope of obtaining New Orleans and West Florida, though this soon grew to include lands that extended to the Río Grande.[38] By 1803 Republicans and Federalists were questioning the wisdom of the much larger deal now on offer, both feeling that such an extensive acquisition came with many risks.[39] Jefferson also had to do a delicate political dance around the fact that this purchase was not in line with the Constitution. The negotiators had not been authorized to buy so much land, and Jefferson's own interpretation of the government's powers within the Constitution prohibited such a purchase as well, meaning the government would need an amendment in order to have the power to acquire such an enormous addition.[40] Its passage could take months and there simply was not time to wait for Congress, so Jefferson went ahead, realizing that the opportunity was too good to let slip through his fingers.[41] As he later wrote to Madison: "The less we say about the constitutional difficulties respecting Louisiana, the better."[42] Although Jefferson signed the deal, he did not receive everything he had hoped for: Florida remained Spain's. Spanish minister Pedro Cevallos wrote to the Louisiana governor Marqués de Casa Calvo, who had been given the task of overseeing the transition, that the United States had Florida in its sights, wrongly believing it should be part of the Louisiana deal. Louisiana was ceded to Spain, argued Cevallos, but Florida was "founded on the right of conquest."[43]

The Spanish were outraged by Bonaparte's double-dealing and tried to nullify the purchase, while attempting to claw back parts of Arkansas and Missouri using some of their maps as evidence; this too failed, however. They continued to fear for New Spain, knowing that Jefferson had become inquisitive about it. He solicited information from the visiting naturalist Alexander von Humboldt, who had traveled to New Spain and who was well positioned to answer the president's questions on the extent of "ore production . . . especially [in] those [territories] to be ceded in the event that the mouth of the Rio Bravo del Norte [Río Grande] becomes the boundary of Louisiana."[44] During the boundary negotiations with Spain, Jefferson continued to argue that the territory ceded by France stretched all the way to the Río Grande to the west and into much of West Florida to the east, a claim Spain dismissed.[45] In 1804, Jefferson sent Meriwether Lewis and William Clark to survey the Louisiana territory, and they began their epic march west. The spy James Wilkinson reappeared at this juncture to tip off the Spanish and try to goad them into intercepting Lewis, but holding back the mission of the U.S. explorers would only have delayed what was clearly becoming the inevitable.[46]

Chapter 8

Sabine River,
ca. 1804–23

THE SABINE RIVER flows down a narrow basin from its headwaters in northeast Texas, to where three creeks converge east of Dallas, stretching southeast before turning due south, covering around three hundred miles. Its name is thought to come from a Spanish word, *sabina*, after the cypress trees that line its banks. Today the southern part of the river meanders past the heavy machinery, tankers, and cranes of the Texas oil industry as it makes its way to Sabine Lake, near Port Arthur, before draining into the Gulf. It is not the most majestic waterway, but it has a cartographic importance: it is part of, at the thirty-second parallel, the state line between modern Texas and Louisiana, and in the early nineteenth century it was supposed to divide the United States from New Spain.

After the Louisiana Purchase, the area around the river was intended to serve as a "neutral strip" to buffer disputes between Spain and the United States over the latter's claims to land as far west as the Río Grande. The Sabine River formed the western boundary of this zone, while the eastern limits were marked by two waterways: the Arroyo Hondo (or Río Hondo) near Natchitoches to the north; and the Calcasieu River to the south, running for about two hundred miles through bayous and into Lake Charles, going from there into the Gulf of Mexico. The Caddo people had long lived in the area, but this agreement transformed it into a legal buffer zone, attracting thieves, slave-smugglers, and other outlaws into its swampy hiding places.[1]

This western hinterland was the ideal setting for perhaps the most infamous land scheme of its time. It, once again, involved the duplicitous James Wilkinson. By 1804 he and the former vice president Aaron Burr had discussed occupying the territory between the United States and New Spain. Burr, who had served under Jefferson during the latter's first term in office (1801–5), was soon tangled up in this Anglo-Spanish intrigue. The plotters wanted a military operation, but Wilkinson was still in the army and so could not have his fingerprints on any such plan. At the same time, Wilkinson was negotiating with Spain on behalf of the U.S. government to come to a diplomatic arrangement over the Sabine boundary.

Rumors soon swelled into a storm of misinformation. The plans involved—depending on who was explaining them—raising an army of volunteers, claiming a part of the Spanish territory and separating it from the United States with New Orleans as the capital, and then using this new colony as a springboard for attacks on New Spain. For good measure, some said the whole scheme was intended to undermine the unity of the United States. The plot reached the point where men were at the ready, including volunteers from the Tennessee militia, but the Spanish caught wind of this and prepared their troops.[2] Before bullets could fly, Wilkinson instead double-crossed Burr and told Jefferson about his involvement in the scheme; this led to Burr's arrest and subsequent trial. At once Wilkinson tried to make himself look like a hero to both sides; indeed he even tried—and failed—to exact a special payment from the viceroy of New Spain for stopping the chaos that he himself had created.[3]

The U.S. government struggled to control plotters and schemers like Wilkinson, and these adventurers were becoming a growing problem.[4] Similar activity was taking place as well in West Florida, where the Kemper brothers tried to use the abutting boundaries to their advantage. In 1804, the three men, Reuben, Samuel, and Nathan, declared a "West Florida Republic," with the aim of securing U.S. intervention and annexation. The strategy involved making raids between U.S. and Spanish territory, which had the counterproductive effect of irritating other Anglos, and causing the Kempers to lose what little support they had. Spain's West Florida troops were able to stifle them and restore order.[5] Some in Washington thought these sorts of disturbances would end if the United States simply controlled these territories, and in March 1806, Congress gave Secretary of State James Madison permission to spend up to $5 million on an offer to Spain for Florida and Texas, though nothing came of it.[6]

Instead, Spanish Florida was dealt a blow in 1807 with Jefferson's Embargo Act, a controversial piece of legislation aimed at Britain and France—who were again at war and both of whom wanted exclusive trading rights with the United States. The act prevented any foreign vessels—including Spain's—from entering U.S. ports. Spanish officials were quick to demand an exemption, a request Madison denied. At the same time, U.S. ships sailed into Lake Pontchartrain, north of New Orleans, effectively placing the West Florida territory under a blockade. The U.S. policy backfired, however, as merchants began smuggling goods throughout the Mississippi valley and along the coast of Spanish East Florida. By late 1808, the act was repealed.[7]

TRADE DISPUTES WITH the United States would soon fade into the background, however, as Spain faced its biggest challenge yet, this time from Napoleon Bonaparte. By May 1808, Carlos IV had abdicated and his heir, Fernando VII, had been persuaded to go into exile in France by Bonaparte, who had his troops in Spain at the ready. Bonaparte then put his own brother, Joseph, on the Spanish throne. The outrage in Spain was immediate, and the uprisings that started in Madrid spread throughout the country and crossed the ocean.

Initially, the public in Spanish America expressed loyalty to Fernando VII, in part because the colonies were considered—and they considered themselves—to be constituent kingdoms of Spain, and so this was seen as a shared problem.[8] Without Fernando VII at the helm, sovereignty would have to reside temporarily with the people, an idea rooted in medieval Spanish political tradition.[9] In order to put this into practice, the initial step in Spain and the Americas involved setting up a number of provincial councils, or *juntas*, around which national sovereignty and resistance to France could be organized.[10] In Spain, the smaller regional juntas answered to a central junta, or *junta suprema central*, first based in Aranjuez, a town about thirty-five miles south of Madrid and home to one of the royal palaces. The central junta was soon pushed south by the fighting, to Seville and finally Cádiz, where British ships aided Spain by patrolling the coast.

In the Americas juntas began to appear, and, as in Spain, they articulated a fierce loyalty to Fernando VII, though it was also clear that the opportunity now presented itself to air some long-standing grievances. At the heart of the complaints throughout the Americas was the fact that many of the reforms enacted under Carlos III had caused friction between the local-born creoles and the peninsular Spaniards (*peninsulares*, or *gachupines* in New Spain) who had been sent to the colonies to govern. The majority of governors, viceroys, judges, bishops, and other officials were from Spain, yet by this point across Spanish America there was a large, established, and often wealthy population of creoles, many of whom were increasingly irritated by their place in colonial society. Here, too, an "American" identity was forming and drawing from both its European and its indigenous antecedents, a "creole patriotism" that had grown hostile to Spanish administrators.[11]

Creoles across the empire called for more political power, economic opportunity, and autonomy at a local level, but not independence—at least not yet. The local and regional nature of the complaints across such a vast and diverse geography made it practically impossible for the kingdoms of Spanish America to come to any larger agreement, barring their shared loyalty to Fernando VII. It was a situation quite distinct from that of the thirteen British colonies, whose anger was directed at the king and which had a clearer sense of common goals. In Spanish America, tensions were not between the monarch and his subjects but between the monarch's administrators and the people they were meant to oversee in his name.

In such circumstances, the old order could not hold. In New Spain, the viceroy at the time, José de Iturrigaray, favored a creole junta with temporary autonomy that would function with him in charge while serving the interests of wealthy creole land- and mine owners. However, a group of Spaniards mounted a coup d'état in 1808 and he was replaced by Pedro de Garibay, who represented the sovereignty of the central junta in Spain.[12] This move was not popular with the wider public, who now felt that these *gachupines* had little basis for their authority.

Meanwhile, in Spain, the central junta in 1809 issued a decree for the American territories to elect delegates to join it. Despite their belief that they were equal parts of the crown, the kingdoms of the Americas would now see the true imbalance of power. They considered their juntas equal to those in Spain, but when they were invited to send delegates, only one person was allotted from each of the four viceroyalties and five others were chosen from the independent captaincies-general, a total of nine seats to Spain's thirty-six.[13]*

Before that process could go very far, another call was issued after the central junta merged with the Regency Council, which was acting on behalf of Fernando VII, to send representatives to a national assembly, the *Cortes*, which was to be held in Cádiz. It would have its first session in September 1810, and this issue of proportion reappeared as delegates were being organized. In terms of population—10.5 million in Spain against some 13 million to 15 million in Spanish America—as well as wealth, the colonies had more, yet the Spanish took more seats in the Cortes.[14] People in Spain were fearful of being outvoted by the overseas delegates, though, at the same time, they extended the invitation to send representatives beyond the viceroyalties and independent captaincies-general. Because of the difficulties in actually getting to Spain, many of the deputies for the Americas ended up being chosen from creoles who happened to be in Cádiz at the time, a procedure people in the colonies branded illegitimate and unrepresentative. A group of 177 electors from the Americas met to choose these proxy—and in theory, temporary—delegates, known as *suplentes*. Just one delegate from the Americas made it over before the opening: Puerto Rico's Ramón Power.[15] When the Cortes finally convened on September 24, 1810, there were 104 deputies, with 27 representing the Americas and 2 for the Philippines, all of whom, barring Power, were *suplentes*. The others had yet to arrive, and in the end, of the 300 deputies there, some 65 represented Spanish America.[16]

Spanish authority continued to crumble throughout this process, and as the cracks deepened into chasms, new ideas and leaders emerged. In New Spain, a middle-class creole priest, Father Miguel Hidalgo y Costilla, tolled a church bell on the morning of Sunday, September 16, 1810, in the town of Dolores, about two hundred miles north of the

---

* By 1808, there were four viceroyalties—New Spain, Peru, New Granada, and Río de la Plata—and the independent captaincies-general were Guatemala, Cuba, Puerto Rico, Chile, Venezuela, and the Philippines.

capital in the Bajío region. He was calling the faithful not to Mass, but to a rebellion, a moment known as the *Grito de Dolores*, or the cry of Dolores. Hidalgo had been plotting with other members of the middle class—landowners with medium-sized holdings, army officers, and the clergy—who were frustrated by the instability in Spain, the inability of *gachupines* to initiate reform, and the fact that too much trade remained in the hands of Spanish and European merchants.[17] Hidalgo and some of the other creoles organized a revolutionary junta, which supported Fernando VII, but when they were uncovered, they decided to take more drastic action.

Hidalgo sensed the opportunity for a wider-reaching change, and it was not only the middle classes who enlisted in his fight; he attracted people from many backgrounds: mestizos, mulattoes, Indians, laborers, and artisans, among others.[18] The demographic reality was that the Spanish were far outnumbered; by 1800 there were about 6 million people in New Spain. Of that population about 1.1 million or 18 percent were white creoles, while there were only 15,000 Spaniards from the peninsula. Indians made up about 60 percent of the population, and *castas*, including mestizo, mulatto, and black people, constituted the remaining 22 percent.[19]

Taking up arms in the name of the king and marching under the banner of the Virgin of Guadalupe with cries of "Death to the *gachupines*," Hidalgo and tens of thousands of followers fought their way south to Mexico City.[20] Yet they had not picked up many creole supporters. Instead, many creoles at this juncture saw themselves as distinct from the *castas* and Indians and, in fact, feared that racial violence might be directed at them. This concern was not unique to New Spain, and as factions formed throughout Latin America, ideas about race became another factor in an increasingly complex period.

Hidalgo's march was stopped by the military. He managed to escape for a short while before being captured, imprisoned, and shot in July 1811. Earlier in that same month, Simón Bolívar had issued a declaration of independence in Venezuela.[21] France's occupation of Spain exposed Spain's many weaknesses, despite the efforts of the juntas to preserve some sort of national sovereignty. Uncertainty reigned in this period on both sides of the Atlantic. The Spanish were trying to hold their own nation together while also attempting to highlight Spain's place in the

Americas by appealing to their "brothers" across the Atlantic through their shared language and religion as a justification for a continued connection, while burying the claims of past injustices.[22]

Leaders in the United States were paying close attention to the unheralded events across the hemisphere. President Madison told Congress in his annual message of November 1811 that the events of the "great communities which occupy the southern portion of our own hemisphere and extend into our neighborhood" elicited in the United States "an obligation to take a deep interest in their destinies."[23] Jefferson, however, expressed a less optimistic sentiment about the people of Spanish America, believing "the degrading ignorance into which their priests and kings have sunk them" rendered the people "disqualified . . . from the maintenance or even knowledge of their rights."[24] The instability, however, might settle the Florida matter for good, as Jefferson explained in 1809 in a letter to Madison, and it also raised the enticing possibility of obtaining Cuba: "Napoleon will certainly give his consent without difficulty to our receiving the Floridas, & with some difficulty, Cuba."[25] The growing profitability of the sugar island of Cuba, with its proximity to the United States, made it attractive to Jefferson and others as a natural addition to the slaveholding South. Indeed, even some New England investors already held stakes in Cuban plantations.[26]

However, Cuba, along with the fellow Spanish island of Puerto Rico, was not following the same path as the rest of Spanish America. While attempts were made to set up a junta, the island remained a strong military garrison.[27] In addition, the planters and merchants who saw what had happened in Haiti feared that a similar slave rebellion would erupt should colonial authority be eroded during a struggle for independence. In fact, Cuba was forced to confront one consequence of the revolution in Haiti: refugees. When Saint-Domingue was ablaze during that revolution, thousands of people fled to Cuba. Many set up coffee plantations in the east, around Santiago, thinking they would one day return to their homes, but the establishment of the black republic of Haiti in 1804 changed their plans and they remained in Cuba. However, when the news of a Bonaparte on the Spanish throne reached Cuban royalists, they quickly set up a junta to expel these so-called French. Around ten thousand people were deported but, not wishing to go to Haiti, many arrived instead in New Orleans throughout 1809–10, hoping to connect with the existing French-speaking community there.[28]

The Floridas also took a path different from that of their fellow Spanish American territories. In 1809, Carlos de Hault de Lassus was appointed governor of the Baton Rouge district of West Florida, though his unpopularity soon led to irritation and unrest. In 1810, a group of residents wanted to form a Spanish-style junta, which de Lassus permitted, in part to keep relations peaceful. Delegates from all parts of West Florida attended, some of whom were open about their wish to join the United States, while others wanted to ally with the British or simply remain under Spanish rule.[29] The group met a number of times in July and August 1810, finally arousing Spanish suspicions. Vincent Folch, the West Florida governor based in Pensacola, threatened to break up the meetings, and rumors circulated that troops were being sent.[30] In response, a group of the delegates attacked the small, crumbling fort in Baton Rouge, issuing a declaration of independence in late September, and raising a flag, a single white star on a blue background representing the Republic of West Florida.[31]

News of this "republic" reached Washington, and President James Madison wrote to Jefferson on October 19, 1810, saying, "The Crisis in W. Florida, as you will see, has come home to our feelings and our interests," before warning that "it presents at the same time serious questions, as to the Authority of the Executive, and the adequacy of the existing laws of the U.S. for territorial administration." His concerns, however, did not preclude the U.S. annexation of part of West Florida—the area between the Mississippi and Perdido Rivers—in late October. Madison believed this to be part of the Louisiana Purchase territory anyway, and now felt that "the Country to the Perdido [River], being our own, may be fairly taken possession of, if it can be done without violence."[32] On December 10, U.S. troops took formal control of the Baton Rouge area of West Florida.[33]

East Florida would not escape confrontation either. President Madison sent General George Mathews, a former governor of Georgia; and John McKee, a former agent to the Choctaw Indians, to rally support among Anglos for the colony's break from Spain.[34] By this point, the Embargo

Act of 1807 had turned the northern part of the Spanish territory into a hotbed of illicit commerce, including trading in slaves, while in that same year Congress had also passed legislation prohibiting the importation of enslaved people to the United States.

Mathews had tried earlier, in September 1810, to reopen negotiations with the West Florida governor Vicente Folch about transferring that part of Florida. After those failed, Mathews went to East Florida to have a similar conversation with its governor, Enrique White, but the refusal was so clear that the men did not even meet in person. Defeated for the moment, Mathews returned to Washington, D.C.[35] The question of Florida did not fade, and in fact rumors that the British might acquire the territory caused some alarm. To prevent this from happening, Congress passed a No Transfer Resolution in January 1811, which was designed to ward off any potential handover of Spanish-American territory to a European power, but was crafted with Britain in mind.[36]

After the rebellion in Baton Rouge during the final months of 1810, Folch had a change of heart and was reported to be considering some sort of alliance with the United States, in part because he feared future uprisings. He was willing to cede control of Mobile and Pensacola in exchange for help in securing the rest of West Florida.[37] By the time Mathews and McKee returned to the Gulf in March 1811 to negotiate with him, Folch reneged on the idea after receiving orders from Havana to carry on defending West Florida without U.S. assistance.[38]

Mathews stayed in West Florida for a while, but upon hearing news of the death of Governor White in East Florida, he arrived at the St. Marys River border with Georgia in early June 1811.[39] By August, he had started to build up alliances with people who were willing to overthrow the Spanish, a plot that would take some months to organize. While Mathews tried to arrange soldiers and arms, news of the scheme became a source of concern for the Spanish and of consternation for British consuls in nearby Georgia, who did not welcome this meddling.[40]

Mathews was able to round up enough "Patriots"—this conflict was later known as the Patriot War—to lead an attack on Fernandina, a town on the eastern side of Amelia Island, with ports that faced the St. Marys River. Mathews and his men marched into Fernandina on March 12, 1812, declaring East Florida independent. A few days later, and with the backing of U.S. gunboats, the whole of Amelia Island was ceded, and the Spanish garrison on Fernandina surrendered by March 25.[41]

From there, Matthews and his men wanted to march on St. Augustine. When news reached the new East Florida governor, Juan José de Estrada, he alerted his Indian allies and black militiamen.[42] These groups had good reason to assist the Spanish—they knew U.S. control meant a loss of land and liberties. The Patriots arrived in April and St. Augustine was soon under siege, while protests from angry Spanish diplomats caused President Madison to disavow the whole affair. He wrote in an April 1812 letter to Thomas Jefferson that Mathews "has been playing a tragi-comedy" and was annoyed that " his extravagances place us in the most distressing dilemma."[43] Mathews was recalled from Florida and died in August 1812 on his way to Washington, D.C.

The next East Florida governor, Sebastián Kindelán, was sent in May from Cuba along with reinforcements, believing the entire incident to be an act of aggression.[44] Then, in the middle of this dispute, Britain and the United States officially went to war on June 18, 1812. Despite the skirmishes taking place in Florida, this was not the conflict's focus. Rather, the War of 1812 had grown out of an unresolved antagonism over naval matters and issues relating to Canada. Most of the land battles against the British took place near Canada's border.

In Florida, the Patriot War segued into that larger conflict—at this point Britain and Spain were also allies—and the possibility began to present itself of a permanent Florida settlement that would favor the United States, though this was stymied in 1813 as Congress rejected measures for a military seizure of East Florida. Guerrilla attacks and skirmishes continued, this time with heavier involvement of the Seminoles on the side of the Spanish, until a final ambush dealt the last blow for the Patriots in 1814. The Spanish, once again on their guard against the United States, completed Fort San Carlos in Fernandina, a final attempt at protecting East Florida.

Farther west, in New Spain, the revolutionary momentum that had started under Father Hidalgo continued under the leadership of another priest, José María Morelos, and spread to many corners, including the northern frontier. Although the combined populations of Texas, New Mexico, and Baja and Alta California totaled less than 10 percent of the population of New Spain, the region became caught up in the struggle.[45] By January 1811, San Antonio had aligned itself with the revolutionaries, and further plans were sketched out to rally additional troops from Coahuila, Nuevo León, and Nuevo Santander, as well as U.S. volunteers.[46]

Spanish authorities uncovered this plot and some of the leaders were killed, though one organizer, José Bernardo Gutiérrez de Lara, who had been appointed a plenipotentiary for the group, managed to escape and leave for the United States in August 1811. It was a dangerous and deadly expedition—Gutiérrez lost most of his party after they were attacked by royalist troops while crossing the neutral strip. Despite this setback, he made his way across the United States, arriving in Washington, D.C., by December.[47] Once there, he met with the secretary of war, William Eustis, who told him that "it would be easy to send an army to the banks of the Río Grande under the pretext that they were going to take possession of the lands which France sold them," but Gutiérrez was uncomfortable with such a plan and wanted any aid to be "given in such a way as would benefit both."[48] While in Washington, he also briefly met President Madison before having talks with Secretary of State James Monroe, who said Gutiérrez would need to return to New Spain to obtain the correct paperwork for buying arms and "to report the friendly disposition of this country to favor the Republic of Mexico."[49]

On his return to Texas, Gutiérrez stopped in New Orleans, where he made contact with the U.S. agent William Shaler and a former U.S. Army officer, Augustus Magee, who helped him recruit around one hundred willing Anglo adventurers to attack the royalists in Texas.[50] They captured Nacogdoches on August 12, 1812, and headed toward the Gulf, taking the presidio at La Bahía del Espíritu Santo, near Goliad, in November. The months that followed saw heavy attacks from royalists; Magee was killed and replaced by Samuel Kemper, one of the brothers who had been involved in the 1804 West Florida plot and who now assumed command of the U.S volunteers.[51] By late March 1813, Gutiérrez and his "Republican Army of the North" marched into San Antonio de Béxar, imploring residents to embrace the Anglo soldiers fighting alongside them who, he claimed, were "free descendants of the men who fought for the independence of the United States."[52]

A few days later, on the night of April 3, 1813, the revolutionary leaders slit the throats of seventeen royalist prisoners.[53] The executions unnerved many of the U.S. volunteers, but for the time being Gutiérrez remained in charge. Three days later, he and his men issued a declaration of independence, calling for Texas to be a state that could "take advantage of the opportune occasion that presents itself of Working for the regeneration of the Mexican *Pueblo*, separating ourselves from the weight of all Foreign domination."[54] However, in the middle of this, Gutiérrez was ousted and replaced by the revolutionary Cuban-born exile José Álvarez de Toledo in August, in part over the loss of confidence by Anglo troops after the earlier killings. Gutiérrez left for Louisiana by July, and in doing so was spared the bloodshed that was to come.[55]

Spanish royalist forces, under the leadership of José Joaquín de Arredondo, struck back at this group of rebel *Tejanos* (Mexican Texans), Anglos, and Indians. He marched eighteen hundred troops into Texas on August 18, 1813, and the Battle of Medina began about six miles from San Antonio, with Arredondo reducing the fourteen hundred rebel troops to about one hundred. From there, the soldiers entered the town itself, killing Tejanos who had not fled, searching for rebels, beating some residents, and putting others in work gangs, while also taking the property of suspected insurgents.[56] The devastation stifled any further rebellions in Texas for the time being, and as the Spanish brigadier general in charge of the operation, Arredondo remained commandant-general of the Eastern Internal Provinces until 1821.

B y 1810 the Cortes in Spain was in session, and the liberal reformers among the delegates seized the opportunity to create a constitution for Spain, an unprecedented move. The March 1812 *Constitución política de la Monarquía Española* made profound changes in the relationship between the monarch and his subjects. It curbed royal powers and placed sovereignty with the people, bolstering the role of an elected Cortes and promising a fairer share of representation to the Americas.* It also extended the vote to all men—including Indians and mestizos—in the

---

* The final delegate from the Americas, Pedro Bautista Pino, who represented New Mexico, arrived that summer after the constitution had been issued.

Americas, without any property or literacy requirements, with the very notable exception of free black people.[57] This exclusion was in part due to prejudice—black people had been pushed to the lower rungs of the social order throughout most of Spanish America—but it also resulted because the deputies thought that by leaving black voters out, it would give Spain and the Americas a more or less equal franchise, though the numbers cited in the debate varied wildly, with one deputy claiming there were ten million people who could be considered black across Spanish America, and others saying there were as few as forty thousand in Peru and other parts of South America.[58]

There were many other provisions in the constitution, including abolishing the Inquisition and granting more press freedom. Significantly, however, it did not end the slave trade or the practice of slavery, in part because of pressure from Cuban delegates.[59] Overall, this constitution opened the way for greater and more direct political participation for people in Spanish America, but it was not enough to hold the empire together.

The Peninsular War in Spain, which also involved the Portuguese and British, ended in 1814 with the French driven out and Fernando VII restored to the throne. Despite all hopes and expectations to the contrary, he tore up the constitution, rejecting it completely. He instead reasserted his absolute authority, angering many in the Americas. This would stoke the fires in South America, as each former colony began to peel away from this point on: Mexico and Venezuela had been or soon would be joined by New Granada, Ecuador, Peru, and Río de la Plata (Argentina). Fernando VII dispatched 10,500 men from Spain to end these rebellions.[60] Much remained at stake, not least the mines. Mexico's silver production alone reached a value of 27 million pesos in 1804—up from 5 million pesos in 1702—and accounted for 67 percent of all the silver produced in the Americas.[61] Fernando VII was determined to return to the pre-1808 world, though his American colonies no longer shared that desire; his attitude illustrated by a tone-deaf proclamation from 1814, lambasting them: "Do not be ungrateful to your parents; such ingratitude is a scandalous monstrosity."[62] As anger and hostility toward the Spanish Americans set in, it became clear that the colonies were gearing up for a fight. One Spanish official, in a report from 1814, could scarcely contain his scorn, describing the independence leaders as "monsters," and complaining that "it was not enough for them to ravage, burn and drown in blood the unhappy country in which they were born."[63] The Council of the Indies met in 1814 to discuss the matter, declaring that a "club of villains" was to blame for the problem, while another report claimed that the majority of the population in the Americas did not support emancipation.[64] Such assertions could not be immediately proved, and it would take another decade of fighting for the situation to come to a clear resolution.

WHILE SPAIN'S TROOPS were battling to regain control of parts of its empire, the War of 1812 in the Florida borderlands took on a new and bloody dimension. On August 30, 1813, a group of some seven hundred Creeks attacked Fort Mims, a fortified outpost on a plantation about forty-five miles north of Mobile, in protest at growing U.S. encroachment on their land. Led by Red Eagle, whose father was a Scottish trader and whose mother was a Creek, the Indians killed around 250 people within the fort and set it on fire.[65] The attackers were known as the Red Sticks, after the clubs they painted red and used in war.[66]

The U.S. retribution was swift, and led by General Andrew Jackson, who was authorized to raise five thousand men. However, the operation was complicated because a Creek civil war had started some months before.[67] On one side were the Red Sticks and on the other were members of the Creek confederation who did not want to go to war against the United States and put their allegiance with Jackson after he pledged to protect them.[68] The Red Sticks allied with the British, some of whom were agitating in the Florida and Georgia borderlands.[69]

Fighting continued throughout 1813 in Alabama and in parts of Georgia, and Jackson received reinforcements in early 1814. On March 27 he landed a decisive blow on the Red Sticks when he and between two thousand and three thousand troops, aided by Cherokee allies, marched to Horseshoe Bend on the Tallapoosa River, in central Alabama, to attack the Red Sticks who had barricaded themselves there. Jackson's men broke through their defenses and after a day of fighting some nine hundred Red Sticks were dead, added to the thousand already killed in 1813.[70]

The Creeks later signed a treaty ceding millions of acres in Georgia and Alabama to the United States, making this a turning point not only in U.S.-Indian relations but also in western expansion.

Throughout the Red Stick War, Jackson kept Florida in his sights, in part because he wanted to stop the British from landing around Pensacola and to drive out the troops who were already there. In addition, he suspected that the Spanish were aiding British efforts against the United States, as well as harboring Red Sticks. However, the then secretary of war, John Armstrong, had sent instructions to Jackson to hold fire on Pensacola and proceed with caution in order not to damage relations with Spain. Armstrong agreed that "if they admit, feed, arm and cooperate with the British and hostile Indians, we must strike on the broad principle of self-preservation," yet he also told Jackson that "under other & different circumstances, we must forbear." The letter was dated in July 1814, but Jackson did not receive it until January 1815, by which time he had already taken matters into his own hands.[71]

Jackson had returned to the Alabama area to negotiate the peace treaty with the Creeks in the summer of 1814, and once that was finished he wrote a menacing letter to the governor of West Florida, making claims that enemies of the United States "have sought and obtained an asylum from justice within the territory of Spain."[72] Governor Mateo González Manrique, in his reply, claimed that Jackson's allegations were without foundation and that "it is evident that no act direct, or indirect has emanated from this Government, from which disagreeable consequences can result." González Manrique pointed out that while the United States was fighting the Creeks, there were "many others whom the American Government protects, and maintains, in committing hostilities, in fomenting the revolution, and in lighting up the flames of discord in the internal provinces of the Kingdom of Mexico."[73]

By August 1814, Jackson's exasperation was palpable, and he moved from Fort Jackson to the fort in nearby Mobile, which U.S. troops had captured from the Spanish in 1813. Jackson wrote to Armstrong, asking "how long will the government of the United States tamely submit to disgrace and open insult from Spain."[74] Over the months that followed, Jackson plotted his long-desired attack on Pensacola, finally marching into the town on November 6, 1814, with forty-one hundred soldiers and Indian allies, and seizing the Spanish forts.[75] He wasted no time in making demands on González Manrique, including possession of "the [fort] Barrancas and other fortifications, with all the munitions of War." Alongside this was the threat that "if not delivered peaceably, let the blood of your subjects be upon your own head. I will not hold myself responsible for the conduct of my enraged soldiers and warriors. . . . I give you one hour for deliberation."[76] González Manrique made a cool reply, telling Jackson that his demands were "in no way acceptable" before asking him to "abstain from similar messages" because the answer would be the same. As far as the Spanish governor was concerned, Jackson would be "responsible for the blood that is spilled."[77] The next day Jackson attacked Pensacola, and the Spanish capitulated. The following morning the British, who were using Fort Barrancas, blew it up and fled to their squadron anchored in the Gulf of Mexico. With the British and their Indian allies run out of town, Jackson's mission came to a temporary end.[78] He left for Mobile a few days later, and from there went to New Orleans, where the British fleet was thought to be landing. Jackson was in the city in time to defend it and defeat the British in the Battle of New Orleans on January 8, 1815—two weeks after the Treaty of Ghent that ended the War of 1812 had been signed in Europe.

With the British gone and the war over, Jackson's gaze on Florida intensified. He was determined to run the Spanish out and defeat their Seminole allies. There had already been retaliatory U.S. attacks against the Seminoles in 1812–13, during the Mathews rebellion in East Florida, and ongoing skirmishes followed.[79] One of Jackson's immediate concerns was the free black settlement known as Negro Fort—also known as Prospect Bluff—located deep in the forest on the edge of East Florida, with the Apalachicola River running alongside it. Occupied mostly by free people of color and some Native Americans, it had a relatively sizable population of 2,810, supported by the fort that the British had built during the war a few years earlier.[80] Negro Fort was in Spanish territory, but Jackson claimed that the settlement's occupants—and their alleged ammunition—presented a threat to the state of Georgia, as well as to any boats moving along the Apalachicola River. He wrote to the governor of West Florida in April 1816 with complaints that "secret practises to inveigle Negroes from the frontier citizens of Georgia as well as from the Cherokee and Creek nations of Indians are still continued by this Banditti and the Hostile Creeks," a situation that could "interrupt that

good understanding that so happily exists between our governments."
Jackson also sought clarification over who built the fort, and whether
the 250 people who lived within it were subjects of the king, though he
made his own intentions clear. If these people were "not put down by
the Spanish Authority," he wrote, "[it] will compel us in self Defence
to destroy them."[81]

The then governor, Mauricio de Zuñiga, appeared to agree with
Jackson's assessment in his reply, saying that his "sentiments coincide
entirely with yours on the . . . necessity of dislodging the Negroes from
said fort." He claimed it was not built by the Spanish government and
that the people living there were "by me considered in light of Insurgents or Rebels against the authority not only of that of H.C.M. [His
Catholic Majesty] but also of the proprietors from whose Service they
have withdrawn." The problem, Zuñiga claimed, was that he could
not act without orders from his superior, who he was confident would
sanction taking action, but in the meantime Zuñiga asked Jackson that
"neither the Government of the U.S. nor Yr. Exy. will take any step to
the prejudice of the sovereignty of the King."[82] The pace of Spanish
bureaucracy, however, exhausted Jackson's patience. He instructed his
men to destroy the fort, and a small base was set up nearby from which
they could launch attacks.

By June 1816, Jackson had received reports that "about 20 Choctaws, a
number of Seminoles and a great number of runaway negroes . . . have
abandoned the Fort on account of scarcity of provisions and have gone
to Savannah (alias St. Josephs) River in East Florida, whither they will no
doubt all retire in case of an attack by land, as they have a Schooner and
several large Boats to make good their retreat. . . . From this spot they
can easily annoy our Settlements on Flint River and the whole Georgia
Frontier."[83] Drastic action was now needed, and on the morning of July
27, 1816, ships were dispatched down the Apalachicola River, with a navy
gunboat making a direct hit on a gunpowder magazine left over from
the war. The resulting blast killed 270 people and demolished the Negro
Fort settlement in one fatal shot.

From there, U.S troops were authorized in 1817 to go to war against
the Seminoles in retaliation for earlier attacks, as well as to recapture any
runaway slaves they were harboring. Jackson, himself a slave owner, over-
saw a series of battles known as the First Seminole War (1817–18), which

forced the Seminoles south, out of the panhandle and border region with Georgia. For Jackson, the Indians in Florida needed to be destroyed and the runaway slaves returned to their owners, and he refused to let the issue of Spanish sovereignty stand in his way. A man of the frontier, Jackson was comfortable pushing boundaries, political and physical.

While the attacks against the Seminoles were taking place, the Amelia Island question resurfaced. Even after Spanish rule was restored, the island continued to be a base for smuggling and privateering. In 1817 it was again the target of a breakaway expedition, this one led by Gregor MacGregor, a Scot who had been a soldier in the British army before enlisting in the fight for Venezuelan independence in 1811.[84] After initial success there, he fell out with Simón Bolívar and turned his attention to Spanish Florida, where Amelia Island lured him with the promise of lucrative privateering. He organized funds, borrowed a schooner, and rounded up men—many of them rebel agents from South America— willing to help him attack.[85] On June 29, 1817, MacGregor approached Fort San Carlos and demanded its surrender. Believing themselves to be outnumbered, the Spanish officers agreed. MacGregor declared the island's independence and ran up his flag, a green cross on a white background.[86]

He sent the Spanish troops to St. Augustine and asked the residents who had fled upon hearing of the impending attack to return, assuring them that their property would be safe.[87] He and French privateer Louis Aury, who joined him that September, turned to smuggling, which included enslaved humans, some of whom had been taken from Spanish ships and brought to the island.[88] Before long power struggles overwhelmed profits, as Aury, MacGregor, and the other eager privateers fought among themselves. The dividing line was one of color, with Aury's backers including former slaves from Haiti and free black people from around the Caribbean, while MacGregor and his supporters were a mostly white faction from the United States.[89] The United States took advantage of the chaos to send in troops, which arrived in December 1817, taking control of the island with the justification that the rebels were illegally smuggling slaves and Spain was not doing anything to stop it.[90]

The enraged Spanish minister, Luis de Onís, wrote to Secretary of State John Quincy Adams to "strongly protest, in the name of the King, my master, against the occupation of Amelia Island . . . one of the possessions of the Spanish monarchy on this continent."[91] Although Onís considered it "a violent invasion of the dominions of Spain, at the time of a profound peace," the occupation attracted support in the United States, including some among southern newspapers unnerved by the presence of Aury's black privateers and potential insurgents so near Georgia.[92] The U.S. troops stayed put, and Adams wrote to Onís defending the measure, saying, "You well know, that if Spain could have kept, or recovered the possession of it [Amelia Island] from the trifling force by which it was occupied, the American government would have been spared the necessity of the measure which was taken . . . but Spain cannot expect that the United States should employ their forces for the defence of her territories."[93]

Jackson, meanwhile, continued to claim that Native Americans in Florida were posing a threat to U.S. territory, and on that basis he attacked the San Marcos de Apalache fort, located between the St. Marks and Wakulla Rivers, in April 1818. He wrote to the Spanish officer in charge, Francisco Caso y Luengo, of "a savage foe, who, combined with a lawless band of negro brigands have for some time past been carrying on a cruel and unprovoked war against the citizens of the United States." He justified the occupation by saying he wanted "to prevent the recurrence of so gross a violation of neutrality, and to exclude our savage enemies from so strong a hold as St. Mark's."[94] A short time later, on May 24, 1818, Jackson rode once more into Pensacola, which had reverted to Spanish rule after his previous incursion. Despite continued instructions to tread with caution, he seized the town and its forts with minimal resistance.[95] Jackson later explained to his superiors that this was not prompted by "a wish to extend the territorial limits of the United States" but rather that the Seminole people had "for more than two years past, visited our frontier settlement with all the horrors of savage massacre—helpless women have been butchered and the cradle stained with the blood of innocence," before alleging that the Spanish were arming them, or at the very least not blocking their access to weapons. "The immutable law of self-defense therefore compelled the American government to take possession of such parts of the Floridas, in which the Spanish authority could not be maintained," he concluded.[96] A few days later he wrote to his wife, Rachel, declaring that by taking the forts he had "destroyed the babylon of the South, the hot bed of Indian war & depredations on our frontier."[97]

When news of these events in West Florida reached Florida's east coast, Spain's Luis de Onís was quick to protest, and President Monroe wrote to Jackson over the taking of Pensacola, saying it could produce "unfavorable consequences." Monroe—whose administration had been distressed by Jackson's actions—told the general that he had been "transcending the limit" of his orders. However, Monroe claimed the United States was "justified in ordering their troops into Florida in pursuit of their [Seminole] enemy," but that was not an act of hostility toward Spain. The seizure of Pensacola, however, "would assume another character"—that of war, one initiated without the approval of Congress.[98]

Jackson defended his actions, telling Monroe that "it will afford me pleasure to aid the Government in procuring any testimony that may be necessary to prove the hostility of the officers of Spain, to the United States."[99] Congress investigated his actions in January 1819, including the question of whether he had instigated an unauthorized war. After a debate that lasted nearly a month, a House proposal to condemn the Pensacola expedition as unconstitutional netted 70 votes in favor, and 100 against, vindicating Jackson and clearing the way for his political ascent.[100]

Part of Monroe's frustration with Jackson was that he didn't want the invasion of Pensacola to spoil what was so tantalizingly close, as he explained in his earlier letter:

> The events which have occurr'd in both the Floridas, shew the incompetency of Spain to maintain her authority in either, & the progress of the revolution in So[uth] America, will require all her forces there. There is much reason to presume, that this act, will furnish a strong induc'ment to Spain, to cede the territory, provided we do not wound, too deeply, her pride, by holding it.[101]

Monroe was correct: the Florida situation had reached a turning point. Spain had to cut its losses, and Florida had always been on the fringes of the empire it was now failing to preserve. The United States was also concerned that a weakened Spain would leave open a back door for potential enemies to enter the United States, something that had been made clear with the British during the War of 1812.[102] Negotiations began for the transfer of both Floridas to the United States, finally putting to rest a boundary dispute that had lasted decades.

Spain was not pleased with the circumstances, as a letter from Onís to Secretary of State John Quincy Adams in December 1818 made clear; Onís complained that Jackson "fell upon Florida as a haughty invader and conqueror, regardless of the laws of humanity and the feelings of nature."[103] Despite the many difficulties that led to this point—raids, independence attacks, the invasion of Pensacola—the two sides managed an agreement. The 1819 Adams-Onís Treaty, also called the Transcontinental Treaty, was signed on February 22, 1819. Its key provisions were the cession of East and West Florida to the United States, with the new boundary being the Sabine River. From the river's mouth in the Gulf of Mexico, the line moved north to N 32°, where the Sabine intersected with the Red River; from there, the line moved steplike in a northwest direction to the Arkansas River, going on to reach a final boundary of N 42°, with the westernmost limit being the Pacific. In exchange, the United States renounced claims to or any designs on territory southwest of the Sabine River, while also promising $5 million in compensation to Spanish subjects in Florida, though that would come later and, for many of the families in Florida at the time of the handover, not until after a long legal fight.[104]

Congress ratified the treaty in 1819, on the heels of the 1818 Anglo-American Convention, which established a boundary between the United States and Canada along N 49° as far west as the Rocky Mountains, freeing the Oregon territory beyond that for joint occupation. A pathway to the Pacific was opening up. Spain, meanwhile, did not ratify the agreement until 1821, the same year that Andrew Jackson became military governor of the Florida territory. The following year, 1822, the U.S. Army sent Lieutenant Colonel Zachary Taylor to mark the western edge of the treaty boundary, building Fort Jesup on the Louisiana side of the river. Another twenty-three years passed before Florida achieved U.S. statehood, but its more than three hundred years as a Spanish colony had come to a decisive end.

THE YEARS THAT followed the return of Fernando VII were fraught, as he struggled to keep his kingdom intact, at home and overseas. By 1820,

Spain was in the throes of a constitutional second act, triggered by a mutiny in Cádiz of troops about to be sent to the Río de la Plata in Argentina to fight against revolutionaries. The soldiers turned on the king and demanded that he accept the 1812 constitution. Rebellions in support of this move erupted throughout Spanish cities.[105] The king capitulated, and the period that followed, known as the *Trienio Liberal*, saw a restoration of the constitution. The liberals in power tried to reach out to the warring parts of the Americas and call for conciliation, but by 1820 it was too late.[106]

The *Trienio Liberal* was brought to an end with a French invasion of Spain in 1823, backed by the Holy Alliance of Austria, Prussia, and Russia. Their aim was to restore Fernando VII's full authority, which they did. In the Americas, however, a crushing defeat of royalists at the December 9, 1824, Battle of Ayacucho in Peru more or less brought an end to the wars of independence, with Spain defeated. Spanish America became a continent of republics, with the creation of Mexico, Gran Colombia (Venezuela, Colombia, and Ecuador after 1830), Peru, Chile, the United Provinces of Central America (Guatemala, Honduras, El Salvador, Costa Rica, and Nicaragua after 1840), Bolivia, and the United Provinces of Río de la Plata (Argentina). A reluctant Spain, however, would take years to recognize their independence.

The transformation of their hemispheric neighbors from colonies to nations captivated the U.S. public, echoing their own experience and lending some universalism to their republican ideals. This interest manifested itself in a number of ways, from breathless newspaper coverage to a spate of babies named after the Venezuelan independence leader Simón Bolívar.[107] Wars so close to the United States had been good for business, too, and merchants sold arms to rebels and, occasionally, royalists. Estimates put the number of firearms sent to rebels during the final decade of fighting at 150,000 or more—a somewhat ironic payback for Spain's help during the American Revolution.[108] The United States began to grant recognition to these emerging nations. However, some of places closest to the United States did not attract the same enthusiasm, because they had followed a somewhat different path. Cuba and Puerto Rico were still loyal to Spain and remained colonies, and Santo Domingo was under Haitian rule by 1822, Although the United States opened diplomatic relations with Mexico in 1822, many were discomfited when it opted to become an empire, rather than a republic.[109]

A DECADE AFTER HIDALGO'S *Grito de Dolores*, the creole elites who had balked at his movement had found the ideal moment to implement their vision. The transition from viceroyalty to independent nation was a profound rupture, as would be the transition from a worldview defined by the existence of a divinely appointed king and the Catholic Church to that of an independent republic. After a decade of upheaval and war, it would take some trial—and error—to work out how power was to be exercised in Mexico and how former subjects would transform themselves into citizens.

In 1820, the wealthy landowner and former royalist army commander Agustín de Iturbide reached out to Vicente Guerrero, a prominent rebel general in the south of Mexico, persuading him to put aside their differences and find a way forward. The result, in the following February, was the Plan of Iguala, which based itself on three concepts: independence, religion, and union. Although Guerrero favored total independence, the plan retained a connection to the peninsula. It called for the creation of an autonomous monarchy in the form of a "regency" in the name of the king, with Fernando VII or another Bourbon at the head, but also called for an assembly and a written constitution.[110]

It also, crucially, protected the existing privileges of the military and the Church, winning the backing of those sections of society. The plan also opened all public offices to people of any background, attempting to put an end to racial distinctions while still more or less protecting the existing social hierarchies. The plan proved popular with the public and was ratified eight months later by the Treaty of Córdoba, which recognized Mexico as a "sovereign and independent nation."[111] The last Spanish viceroy, Juan O'Donojú, felt he had no option but to sign the document that August, and it was followed by a Declaration of Independence of the Mexican Empire on September 28, 1821. In theory, this political configuration would require the approval of the Cortes and the appointment of a royal to be at the head of this new monarchy.[112] However, the crown and government stayed quiet, with no explanation given to the Cortes. Once the legislative body found out about events in Mexico, it decided, after a two-week debate, to send commissioners to Mexico to reject the Treaty of Córdoba.[113] With no royal willing to head the proposed constitutional monarchy, the Mexican Congress approved the coronation of Iturbide as emperor, and he was crowned Agustín I in July 1822. His empire, however, soon fell apart, as factions—including the wider public, the Spanish officials now out of office, and the Catholic Church—became dissatisfied. These problems were compounded by a faltering and war-torn economy and provoked as well by Agustín I's dissolution of the Congress at the end of October 1822. He abdicated in March 1823 and was executed the following year. A few months earlier, in December 1822, Antonio López de Santa Anna, a commander at Veracruz and an early supporter of Agustín I, had issued his Plan of Veracruz in opposition to the emperor, outlining a federal vision for Mexico. This was followed by the Plan of Casa Mata, calling for the restoration of Congress.[114] A constitution was approved in 1824 that reflected these changes—in place of a king or emperor of the United States of Mexico (Estados Unidos Mexicanos), a president would lead the country and he would be held to account by a strong legislature in a federal system with regions divided into states and territories.[115]

Political culture remained fragmented, however, with federalist against centralist, liberal against conservative, and even some lingering monarchists against republicans. Many of the men involved in political life also became associated with certain Masonic lodge orders that were powerful during the 1820s, with their memberships consisting of landowners, military officers, intellectuals, and other prominent people. Their divisions roughly mirrored the wider political ones. The Scottish Rite members, or *escoceses*, tended to be the Conservatives, who were in favor of centralist government, pro-Church, and pro-Spanish. The Rite of York, or *yorkinos*, represented the Liberals, who desired a federal government, and also wanted to reduce or eliminate the power of the clerics and of the remaining Spanish. At a time of such significant transition, beliefs and membership were subject to change, but for the moment, the distinct divisions of opinion on how best to proceed as a nation remained.

⌒

IN THE UNITED States, the addition of new territory continued to present challenges to its union, though by 1820 a number of states had been carved out: Ohio, Louisiana, Indiana, Mississippi, Illinois, and Alabama. Missouri petitioned in 1819 to join as well, and at this juncture expansion hit a bump. Two New York congressmen, James Tallmadge and John W. Taylor, raised their concerns about the admission of another slaveholding state. Louisiana, which had joined in 1812, included slaves, and there remained thousands of acres of Louisiana Purchase lands that were still unorganized. At the same time, a bloc of southern legislators in Congress had been keeping an eye on the admission of Maine, which was also taking place, fearful that the balance of slave and free states would be tipped in the opposite direction.[116]

No one expected either of the admissions to be blocked, but Tallmadge put forward a resolution to the Missouri enabling bill in February 1819 that would have banned the further introduction of slaves there and freed, after they reached the age of twenty-five, the ones born there. The bill was killed and any resolution of the matter would have to wait until the following Congress, giving plenty of time for it to build into a full political drama.

After the drawing up of House and Senate bills when Congress resumed, and with much diplomacy on the part of President Monroe and the Kentucky statesman Henry Clay, a compromise was reached: Missouri could enter as a slave state, which it did in August 1821, but any new state formed north of 36°30′ could not be slaveholding. Maine joined the union as a free state in 1820. The balance, fragile as it was, remained even at twelve slave states, twelve free. The Missouri problem may have been solved, but there were still thousands of acres of territory ahead. Southern planters would also begin to take a closer look south, eyeing the Hispanic frontier.

By 1823 the United States was a nation transformed. Over the previous two decades it had acquired the vast lands of Louisiana and the strategic Florida territory, fought back against British incursion in the War of 1812, and weathered the heated Missouri debates. Along the way, it had become a more confident and stable nation.[117] In addition, European powers were no longer the proximate or physical threat they had been. Although Britain still had a large and powerful empire, in North America it was relegated to the extremes: Canada to the north, and the West Indies to the south, where its colonies were joined by those of France and Spain.

The creation of the Latin American republics was also a radical change in the political landscape of the Americas, even if early leadership struggles in some of the countries were a source of concern to the United States. There were worries that their instability could result in the return of European colonial powers in uncomfortable proximity. Some people were unnerved to see the Holy Alliance's 1823 intervention in Spain and feared that these nations might entertain ideas about sending troops to Latin America as well or try to take control of nearby Cuba, a worry that was shared by Great Britain, which claimed to oppose any such intervention.[118]

This was the general climate in 1823 when President James Monroe set out what would be called his "doctrine" during his seventh annual message to Congress. He told the assembled legislators that "the American continents, by the free and independent condition which they have assumed and maintain, are henceforth not to be considered as subjects for future colonization by any European powers."[119] It was a sentiment that immediately took root and would continue to grow in scope over the decades to come.[120]

A WHITE OBELISK SITS in St. Augustine's main square, its thin pillar tapering to a point that reaches up to the trees that shade it. It is one of the few tangible remains of this turbulent period in Florida. It owes its existence to a Cortes decree of 1812 that each of the empire's cities must change the name of its main plaza to Plaza de la Constitución to honor the newly created document. Officials in St. Augustine were happy to oblige: the square was renamed and the monument erected in 1813. However, when news arrived in 1814 that the king had returned, all such celebrations of the constitution were ordered to be destroyed. This time, St. Augustinians were less eager to comply, and now the monument is thought to be the sole 1812 memorial of this type left in Spanish America.

Traveling north along the coast to Amelia Island, Fernandina's Plaza San Carlos retains little evidence of the chaotic final years under Spanish rule, except a browning patch of grass where a historical marker is planted. The remains of the fort, which overlooked the Amelia River, eroded after it was abandoned in the 1820s, and a lone antique cannon faces out to the water. Both markers are physical reminders of Spain's long-running Florida problem. While it could be argued that Jackson and some of the more enterprising adventurers had been aggressors, Spain had also failed to anticipate or meet many of the challenges posed by the creation and rise of the United States, and this failure forced it to pay a heavy price.

Although the Spanish presence was retreating from the map of the Americas, its shadow lingered. Many people in the United States shared Thomas Jefferson's concerns about the larger changes in Spain's former empire, unconvinced that people there could govern themselves. Jefferson wrote in a letter to the Prussian naturalist Alexander von Humboldt, who in 1803–4 had traveled through parts of Latin America, including New Spain and Cuba, that "they will throw off their European dependence I have no doubt." What was less certain to him was what sort of system of governance would replace it. The Black Legend of Spanish cupidity and cruelty in the Americas had not yet been laid to rest in the late eighteenth and early nineteenth centuries. In the 1770s, well before he started formulating the ideas about the "American" identity that he would expand on in his *Letters from an American Farmer* in 1782, the French writer Hector de St. John de Crèvecoeur highlighted the differences in the two abutting empires in "A Sketch of the Contrast Between the Spanish and the English Colonies." Much of the tract focuses on the Spaniards' Catholicism, claiming, "Their [Spaniards'] immense religious system has no greater effect toward the amelioration of society than the simpler ones of these climes. . . . Here [in the United States], religion required of the husbandman but little or nothing; there, it absorbs and consumes the best wealth of society by the pomp their church requires."[121] Jefferson echoed this sentiment in a remark to Humboldt: "History, I believe, furnishes no example of a priest-ridden people maintaining a free civil government."

Jefferson's pessimistic prediction was that "the different casts of their inhabitants, their mutual hatreds and jealousies, their profound ignorance and bigotry, will be played off by cunning leaders," though he did admit that much of his knowledge was secondhand. Unlike Humboldt, Jefferson never ventured so far south, admitting that the scientist's writings were useful for these purposes: "In truth we have little knowledge of them to be depended on, but through you."[122] Jefferson may have had little experience of New Spain, but in the years that elapsed after his letter to Humboldt, many more people had become familiar with what was now Mexico, especially its northern territory, as adventurers, smugglers, and mercenaries traversed the Sabine River boundary.

Chapter 9

San Antonio de Béxar, Texas, ca. 1820–48

In April 1828, the Mexican lieutenant José María Sánchez y Tapia arrived at a village near the Río de los Brazos de Dios. He was on a mission with a small team led by independence hero General Manuel de Mier y Terán and sent by Mexican officials to survey the boundary that had been agreed to a decade earlier in the Adams-Onís Treaty. Along the way, they were to study and take note of the natural resources of the remote region, as well as inspect some of the settlements populated by immigrants from the United States.

They left Mexico City in November 1827 and arrived in San Felipe de Austin, about fifty miles west of modern Houston, on April 27, 1828, having stopped in Laredo and San Antonio de Béxar along the way. Sánchez had not been impressed with Texas. In San Felipe de Austin, he wrote in his diary, the forty or so wooden houses "lie in an irregular and desultory manner," and added that only around ten of the two hundred people were Mexican.[1] He also noted that "they treat with considerable harshness" their black slaves.[2] Sánchez was suspicious of the Anglos and sensed that these towns were not as simple or tranquil as they might appear. "In my judgment," he wrote, "the spark that will start the conflagration that will deprive us of Tejas, will start from this colony [San Felipe de Austin]."[3] Mier y Terán shared Sánchez's concerns and outlined them in even starker terms, writing to President Guadalupe Victoria from Nacogdoches in June 1828 that Texas "could throw the whole nation into revolution."[4]

It was not only Mexicans taking note of these frontier settlements. The French writer Alexis de Tocqueville mentioned Texas in his now classic *Democracy in America*, observing that "each day, little by little, inhabitants of the United States are introducing themselves into Texas," but if Mexico was not alert to the pace of immigration "soon Mexicans, so to speak, will not be found in it." Published in 1835, Tocqueville's book was based on his time in the United States five years earlier, and his observations were prescient. "The limits separating these two races [Spanish and Anglo] have been fixed by a treaty," he wrote. "But however favorable this treaty should be to the Anglo-Americans, I do not doubt that they will soon come to infringe it."[5]

After Mexico had secured its independence in 1821, some people in the United States sensed opportunity in Texas, which abutted Louisiana. While 9.6 million people lived in the United States and 6.2 million in Mexico, Texas was remote from the population centers of both. It was fourteen hundred miles from Washington, D.C., and almost one thousand miles from Mexico City, and so had a low degree of official oversight. By 1823, 3,000 Anglo squatters were already in Texas, though much of the region remained exhausted and impoverished because of the struggle for independence.[6] In addition, the region had a large and diverse population of Native Americans, including the Caddo, Wichita, and Lipan Apache, as well as the powerful Comanche, all of whom at various points had been involved in raids and conflicts with the Mexicans.[7] The ongoing violence had proved an effective deterrent to extensive settlement in Texas, and some Mexican officials, distracted by their own independence struggle, did not realize that people from the United States were arriving.[8]

Indeed, the Anglos had not waited long. In 1819, around the time the Adams-Onís Treaty was being finalized, a group of men from Natchez, Mississippi, led by James Long, decided to invade Texas, with the aim of "liberating" it, using Nacogdoches as a base. The Spanish—still fighting against Mexican independence—worried that this presaged a larger U.S.-backed invasion, and troops were dispatched. When Spanish soldiers arrived in the Nacogdoches area, they found at least thirty farms growing cotton, but without the necessary permission. Long and his men fled, and the Spanish troops torched all the homes they could find, though this would prove only a temporary deterrent.[9] By the early 1820s some 167,000 settlers were inching toward the border, setting up in Louisiana and Arkansas, but with their eyes on Texas, while only 2,500 Mexicans (Tejanos) lived there.[10] Planters along the Mississippi River and the Gulf of Mexico could see the potential in cotton, with the fertile land of coastal East Texas having the right conditions for the crop.

One person willing to take his chances in Texas was Moses Austin. He had been born in Connecticut but made his fortune mining lead in Spanish Louisiana. He was experienced in dealing with Spain, having at an earlier point sworn his loyalty to the Spanish crown. Louisiana's change from Spanish to U.S. control, coupled with the national financial crisis of 1819 that cost him his fortune, pushed him back into Spanish arms. He had heard that land in Texas was cheap, and he arrived in San Antonio in 1820.[11] He tried to meet with Antonio Martínez, the last Spanish governor of Texas, who told him to leave. Unwanted freebooters, like the party that had tried to invade in 1819, had become a threat and an irritant to Spanish officials trying to keep control of New Spain.

Austin, however, managed to wangle one more audience with the governor after running into a well-connected Dutch acquaintance who organized the meeting. He presented his colonization plan, which involved bringing in three hundred settlers.[12] This time Martínez took more interest because Austin offered an attractive alternative in the long-running struggle to subdue the Native Americans and fortify the frontier. By early 1821, New Spain changed its policy regarding U.S. settlers, but Austin died that June.

Moses's son, Stephen, decided to continue his father's work, though it was a turbulent time in Texas: in 1821 Mexico had declared its independence, which the United States recognized the following year. Austin managed to secure the necessary permissions for the scheme to continue, and by 1824 a settlement on the Brazos River, or the Río de los Brazos de Dios as it was also known, was in place. It was called San Felipe de Austin and located about 150 miles east of the older town of San Antonio de Béxar. Austin had inherited his father's *empresario* agreement, giving him the right to parcel out large tracts of land—which were cheap and could amount to thousands of acres—as well as to exact a payment from the settlers for his services.[13] The area around the Brazos River seemed ideal. The soil was good and the river could transport crops down to the Gulf. Most of his "old three hundred"—the first group of settlers—arrived by 1824, spreading out in the area between the Brazos and Colorado Rivers.*

Soon, other would-be settlers started traveling to Mexico City to obtain similar contracts. Among them was the spy James Wilkinson, still straddling the Anglo and Hispanic worlds, making plans, and plotting intrigues.[14]** A U.S. map from this period shows colored blocks of pink, yellow, green, and blue in Tejas, labeled "Austin's colony," or "John Cameron's Grant," or "Austin & Williams Grant."[15]

Although the Anglos did not have to become Mexican citizens, they did have to take an oath of loyalty and profess that they would convert to Catholicism. This initial period of settlement was marked by a degree of social and cultural mixing, and there were even incentives for this, such as giving an Anglo man extra land if he married a Mexican woman.[16] Some Tejanos welcomed the new arrivals, and before long there were strategic marriages, business deals, or both between prominent Anglo and Tejano families. English-speakers began to learn Spanish, and Spanish-speakers to learn English. Among the former was Jim Bowie, the famed frontiersman, who married Úrsula Veramendi, the daughter of the vice governor of the state of Coahuila y Tejas, in 1831.[17] The following year, a report signed by leading Tejanos in San Antonio de Béxar praised the Anglos for "having made great improvements."[18]

The Anglos mostly stayed in their new settlements, while Tejanos continued to live in older towns, such as San Antonio de Béxar.[19] As the numbers of Anglos rose—reaching seven thousand people by 1830—the assimilation tapered off. [20] By 1835, one guide for would-be immigrants described the Tejano population as being "completely Spanish, the hospitable inhabitants freely indulging themselves in habits of indolence and ease, in smoking, music, dancing, horse-racing, and other sports." The Anglo community, however, were the bearers of the "activity, industry, and frugality of the American population."[21]

---

* This Colorado River runs only through Texas and is not to be confused with the other Colorado River, which flows from Colorado to the Gulf of California.

** He was not successful this time. Mexico was his final venture, and he died in Mexico City in 1825.

Most of the Anglos were there to grow cotton. The rise of the British textile mills had spurred demand for the sturdy fibers of this lucrative plant, and the Gulf region of Texas, with its warm climate and plentiful water supply necessary to grow the crop, was ideal. The question of who would do the work—enslaved Africans—had not been up for discussion initially because under Spanish rule slavery was legal. However, there was no guarantee that this would continue under independent Mexico.[22]

The United States began to push harder for more territory near the Gulf, sending Joel R. Poinsett to negotiate the boundary between the United States and Mexico. Poinsett was the first to be appointed to the role of U.S. minister to Mexico, a post he held from 1825 to 1829.* With the arrival of Mexican independence in 1821, some hoped that the Adams-Onís treaty would be rendered void, as it had been negotiated by the Spanish, not Mexicans.[23] The United States wanted its boundary to be the Río Grande, not the Sabine River, but despite the willingness of the United States to pay for it, Mexico refused any offers. In addition, Poinsett soon made powerful enemies because of his association with the *yorkino* Masonic lodges and Liberal politicians, and he was recalled to the United States. Treaty negotiations dragged on for a couple of years more, and by 1831 Mexico ratified the Treaty of Limits, which confirmed the 1819 boundary, giving both sides an agreement but not pleasing either.

⁂

During this time, California remained so remote and unconnected that a year passed before the news of Mexico's 1821 Declaration of Independence arrived. Officials in Monterey swore their loyalty to Mexico in 1822, though with the enactment of Mexico's 1824 constitution, problems arose.[24] The document categorized California as a territory rather than a state, as it also did to New Mexico. Alongside this, ongoing animosities intensified as the priests struggled to comply with the more secular aims of the constitution.[25] The mission Franciscans continued to be loyal

---

* He also brought back with him a bright red plant that flowers in the winter, the traditional Christmas flora known in the United States as the poinsettia.

to the Spanish crown, unlike the republican Mexicans, while other residents were vocal in their dislike of the new administrative regime, wanting less meddling and oversight.[26]

More than two thousand miles of land separated Monterey and Mexico City. To the *Californios*, or Spanish Californians, their fellow Mexicans were almost like foreigners, though they themselves hardly constituted the majority in what they considered their land.[27] As late as 1830, California was estimated to have around ten thousand Mexicans, against a Native American population of ninety-eight thousand. Concern about Indian uprisings was constant, especially after a number of serious incidents, including the 1824 Chumash rebellion, involving attacks on the missions of La Purísima, Santa Inés, and Santa Bárbara.[28] This was followed by an uprising among the Miwok in the San Joaquín valley, which continued to simmer even after an immediate punitive expedition.[29]

The Mexican government landed a further blow in 1833 with the Secularization Act, accelerating the distribution of mission land to settlers and assimilated Indians, and carried out in California under the watch of its governor, General José María Figueroa.[30] To settle the contentious issue of dividing the land, he stipulated that half of the mission properties should go to Indians, but after his death in 1835 his plan was ignored, and little land passed into Native American hands, going instead to elite Californios who became large landholders, adding to their ranchos.[31]

The growing irritation with Mexican rule motivated one group of disgruntled Californios, led by Juan Bautista Alvarado—and backed by some enthusiastic volunteers from Tennessee—to declare California an independent state on November 7, 1836. At the heart of the grievances was an ongoing dissatisfaction with the military governors being sent to Alta California, aggravating earlier clashes, in 1831, between Californio ranchers and Mexican officials. Although independence was not forthcoming, the territory was upgraded to a department and Alvarado was appointed governor.[32] It is around this time that a clearer Californio identity begins to emerge, one set apart from Mexicanness.

Although the European population of California remained small, trade was turning it into a cosmopolitan place, as ships from New England and Asia called at its ports, eager for cattle hides from its ranchos. Russians, too, had continued their drive along the coast, setting up a colony about one hundred miles north of San Francisco, funded by the

Russian-American Company and thought to be built with the help of the Alutiiq people in 1812. Eager U.S. ship captains found it profitable to join the Russians on some of their fur-trapping expeditions, and Native Americans, as well as people from other parts of Mexico, also came in search of work.[33]

In 1835, a young seaman named Richard Henry Dana arrived in California. He was no ordinary sailor, having been born to a distinguished Massachusetts family. An illness interrupted his studies at Harvard, and as part of his recovery he decided to join the crew of the merchant brig *Pilgrim* in 1834. After rounding Cape Horn, they made their way to the California coast. Even then, he was one of few people from the East who had gone to California. As they approached, he thought it looked "very disagreeable," though he soon changed his mind. Before long he was taking a great interest in California and its people, though his observations were not always complimentary. His New England heritage was evident in his complaints about the local economy; Californians were "an idle, thriftless people" and "things sell . . . at an advance for nearly three hundred percent upon the Boston prices."[34]

He had a particular fascination with the appearance of the people he met, describing how the "'gente de razón,' or aristocracy, wear cloaks of black or dark blue broadcloth, with as much velvet trimmings as may be, and from this they go down to the blanket of the Indian."[35] He also noted their skin color, observing that "those with pure Spanish blood, never having intermarried with the aborigines, have clear brunette complexions . . . there are but a few of these families in California," and adding that from there "they go down by regular shades, growing more and more dark and muddy."[36]

The California that Dana observed was changing, and he remarked on the number of British or U.S. traders he saw in Monterey who had married into Californio families and "acquired considerable property," often running shops.[37] Outsiders were attracted by the "five hundred miles of sea-coast, with several good harbours; with fine forests in the north; the waters filled with fish, and the plains covered with thousands of herds of cattle; blessed with a climate, than which there can be no better in the world."[38] To Dana, though, such riches were lost on the Californios: "In hands of an enterprising people, what a country this might be!"[39] He returned to Massachusetts in 1836 and published the diary, which became a huge hit and turned the public gaze west, to this little-known Pacific frontier.

———~———

LIKE THE COTTON growing along the Gulf, by the mid-1830s the practice of slavery had also taken root in Texas, though Mexico had embraced abolition. As early as 1810, Padre Hidalgo had proclaimed the emancipation of slaves, and this was echoed in 1821 by Iturbide, who freed anyone who fought for the republican cause. As part of Spain's empire, Mexico had an estimated two hundred thousand enslaved Africans brought during the entire colonial period. However, much of the labor throughout New Spain was undertaken by Indians and was waged. In addition, the overall economy was not as geared toward export monocrop commodities like sugar, tobacco, or cotton as were economies in the Caribbean and the southern United States. By the 1820s, most Africans and their descendants in Mexico had merged into the wider, and free, *casta* society, leaving slave numbers low by the time of independence.[40]

Now Mexican leaders wanted to put into law a ban on slavery, though Anglo settlers in Texas made clear they would fiercely oppose this.[41] The constitution of 1824, however, would make this difficult for the Anglos, because under it Texas was coupled into a state with Coahuila (Coahuila y Tejas), limiting the level of representation Texians—as the Anglos then called themselves—would receive. On a map, this state had a sledgehammer shape, with Texas being the squarish head, and the north-south axis of Coahuila being the handle, but the larger share of the population lived in that latter part.[42]

In June 1824, the Republic of Mexico received official recognition from pro-abolitionist Britain—though at this juncture Britain had not actually abolished the practice of using enslaved people in its own colonies; it had ended only the trade in slaves. A short time later, on July 13, Mexico outlawed the slave trade.[43] The Anglo settlers in Texas mostly ignored the decree, but tempers flared.[44] One Anglo *empresario*, Haden Edwards, and his brother, Benjamin, went as far as establishing a breakaway state in December 1826. Allied with Cherokee people who had moved to the

Nacogdoches area, a number of squatters joined the Edwards brothers, who tried to arrest Mexican officials and declare their independence. Haden even designed a flag and wrote a declaration of independence. He marched into Nacogdoches proclaiming the existence of the Republic of Fredonia, with one part for the "Red People" and another for the "White People."[45]

The Edwardses were taken seriously enough that a joint Anglo and Mexican diplomatic mission was sent in January 1827, though it failed to defuse the situation. A report described the plotters as "vagabonds and fugitives from justice" who had "so shamefully debased the American character." Stephen Austin and other *empresarios* were worried that their own reputation, as immigrants from the United States, would be besmirched.[46] To avoid this, they allied with the Mexican troops who planned to attack the Fredonia colony. This threw the Edwards brothers' plans into disarray and left them fleeing across the Sabine River into Louisiana.

Around the same time, Coahuila y Tejas began to wrestle over the contents of the state's own 1827 constitution. Local legislators wanted to abolish slavery but conceded to pressure from Austin and others. The result was a compromise: no one could be born into slavery in Coahuila y Tejas from the date of the promulgation of the constitution, and after the first six months no further importation of enslaved people was allowed. In the place of importation came bondage agreements, which promised freedom but only after an impossible amount of debt had been cleared, more or less ensuring enslavement. The contracts were enough to maintain the status quo on a local level, but national politics soon intervened.[47]

Texas, while a concern, had been just one of Mexico's many problems; a far more pressing issue was Spain. It continued to send troops and launch attacks, desperate to regain New Spain. A last-gasp effort was made in 1829, with an invasion at the Gulf port of Tampico, where General Santa Anna, aided by General Mier y Terán, led his men to a resounding victory, driving the Spanish out and confirming that the long-running struggle for independence was over. Spain, however, would not grant official recognition to Mexico until 1836. In the meantime, Santa Anna became a national hero.

As Mexican forces were driving the Spanish from Tampico, farther north along the Gulf the Anglo cotton farmers were enjoying a boom, annually exporting between 350,000 and 450,000 pounds of the crop, which represented a doubling of production from only a few years earlier.[48] Around the same time, in September 1829, the Mexican government abolished slavery and granted freedom to existing slaves. The following year, the federal government passed laws to stop the arrival of further immigrants from the United States, though other settlers, such as Germans and the Irish, were permitted, and even encouraged with cash advances.[49] The government also pushed for more Mexican immigration to these outlying areas, while calling for the "prevention of further introduction of slaves."[50] This fueled more animosity between the slaveholders and the Mexican authorities but did little to stop more Anglos from arriving. The military in the north was not strong enough to monitor or to stop them, and so the Anglo population doubled between 1830 and 1834, despite the restrictions.[51] In 1832, the state of Coahuila y Tejas set a ten-year limit on labor contracts in another attempt to end slavery.[52] However, ships from Cuba and other points in the West Indies continued to arrive in Galveston Bay with slaves, while other schemes tried to entice free blacks from the Caribbean to come as laborers, after which they would be more or less enslaved.[53]

The Mexican government added more fuel to an already volatile situation by trying to collect tariffs along the border, leading to a clash in 1831 at a fort in Anahuac, which bridged Lake Anahuac and Trinity Bay, north of Galveston. The federal soldiers there annoyed residents with their quibbling over land titles, and then enraged the Anglos when they tried to collect taxes. The result was a short-lived fight put down by the soldiers, but the key issues remained unresolved and so armed skirmishes continued throughout 1832. The Anglos managed to avoid an all-out war by issuing the June 13, 1832, Turtle Bayou Resolutions, in which they claimed they were attacking not Mexico but rather the hated centralist troops of President Anastasio Bustamante, who had come to power in 1830 and whose government had made "repeated violations of the constitution." Instead, they cast their allegiance with Federalists and with "the firm manly resistance, which is made by the highly talented and distinguished Cheiftan [sic]—General Santa Anna, to the numberless encroachments and infractions, which have been made by the present administration, upon the Constitution and laws of our adopted and beloved country."[54] The Anglos wanted the 1824 constitution to be fully respected and believed Santa Anna did, too, which is why they backed the Federalists.

Concerns lingered in the Anglo colonies and in October 1832 some residents organized a convention, held in San Felipe de Austin, to outline their grievances. They met again the following year, in April 1833, and among the delegates was the former Tennessee congressman and governor Sam Houston, who had become involved with land speculation in Texas after quitting the governorship of Tennessee in 1829. He had resurfaced in Nacogdoches in 1832, when he joined the heated discussions about Texas.

These conventions made clear that Anglo farmers felt their needs were at odds with those of the rest of the state and the nation, especially concerning slavery. Talk turned to the idea of petitioning for Texas to split from Coahuila, a move that few Mexican leaders of any political persuasion were willing to countenance. Tejanos, who numbered only around four thousand, were not so eager for this separation, either, but the idea of statehood inspired the Anglos to envisage their own Texas constitution.[55]

Santa Anna finally took the presidency in 1833 after launching a revolt against Bustamante the previous year, around the same time as the disturbances in Anahuac.[56] His mission to restore the Federalist order complete, Santa Anna moved to his estate in Veracruz, leaving the business of governance in the hands of his vice president, Valentín Gómez Farías. In Santa Anna's absence, Gómez Farías passed a number of liberal reforms aimed at the Church, the bureaucracy, and the military, successfully angering all of them.

In the meantime, Stephen Austin had made his way to the capital to meet Santa Anna on November 5, 1833, to make the case for statehood. The government turned down the request but did once again permit him to allow the entry of U.S. immigrants.[57] The local officials in Coahuila y Tejas were now on high alert. Although the state had an overall population of 86,887 in 1833, with the majority in Coahuila, many of the officials were concerned that the 30,000 Anglos in Tejas would try to leave anyway.[58] A security report from January 1834 mentioned that "prohibited meetings" had taken place, and added that Austin's "abnormalities should not go unpunished."[59] Indeed, he was apprehended in the state's capital, Saltillo, on his way back to Texas that same January, after which he was returned to Mexico City and imprisoned on charges of inciting a revolt.[60]

Elsewhere in the Mexican capital, the earlier reforms had left the Mexican Congress embroiled in a number of disputes, leading to the creation of the Plan of Cuernavaca in an effort to end the disagreements. Santa Anna was granted powers to enact the plan's measures, but he took them a step further, shutting down Congress and dismissing the vice president, declaring that he was using emergency powers. After Mexico's new Congress met in early 1835, he once again returned to Veracruz.[61] By April he was in Zacatecas, suppressing a revolt against the now more centralist government, before going once again to his hacienda. That summer, politicians debated the future of the 1824 constitution: its federalism was causing too many problems. So in October 1835, it was abolished and a constituent congress called to draw up a new, more centralist constitution with a more powerful national government that, it was hoped, could hold the country together.[62]

Texian anxiety was palpable. The 1824 constitution and the federal system it underpinned were no more. Lacking any faith that what might replace it would serve their interests, Anglos demanded its return.[63] They were, however, increasingly isolated: not only were they alone in their stance on slavery; few of the newer settlers had learned Spanish or acculturated in other ways, and this made it all the more difficult for Anglos to understand the political machinations taking place or to build alliances with Tejanos.

The summer of 1835 was marked by unrest and skirmishes. A handful of men attacked Anahuac in June, forcing the surrender of the Mexican troops. Although the Anglos agreed to withdraw to keep the peace, the Mexican authorities took this as a worrying sign. Writing from Matamoros, some five hundred miles south of Nacogdoches, General Martín Perfecto de Cos told officials that "the neglect that has been until now of the policing of Texas, has necessarily produced the introduction of many men who are without patriotism, morality, nor the means to survive, risking nothing in a continuous revolution in igniting discord."[64]

At the same time, the Anglo community was not yet strategically united. Some Anglos, like the military leader at San Antonio de Béxar, Francis W. Johnson, believed the constitution of 1824 should be defended but that this should not lead to a breakaway movement. Because of this, Johnson thought efforts should be made to include Tejanos and "all friends to freedom, of whatever name or nation." Others wanted total independence, arguing that Mexicans and Anglos in Texas "can never be one and the same people."[65]

In August 1835, residents in San Jacinto, a settlement near where Buffalo Bayou runs into Galveston Bay, held a meeting to discuss the news that "the federal republican government of Mexico has been violently occupied" and that "the late President of the republic, General Santa Ana [sic], has been invested with extraordinary dictorial [sic] powers." Even more worrying to them was the rumor that the militia had been disbanded and some Mexican states invaded, and that "a similar invasion is contemplated, and in preparation, to be made upon Texas."[66] The San Jacinto group decided it was within its rights to reject this government and call for an assembly of Anglo delegates within Texas to "confer on the state of public affairs: to devise and carry into execution such measures, as may be necessary, to preserve good order, and the due administration of the laws."[67] One group in Nacogdoches took a more conciliatory tone, resolving that "the Emigrants from the United States of the North now in Texas are indebted to the Mexican Republic and people our deepest sence [sic] of gratitude for there [sic] liberalities exercised toward us in giving us such excellent houses" and expressed instead a desire to be "at peace with all men."[68]

It was finally decided that a "consultation" on the matter would be held in mid-October. By this point, Austin was back in Texas, and he and the other Anglos were ready to take more unified action.[69] The conflict over state power had come much closer to home as well, as there had been a revolt in Monclova, a city in Coahuila jostling with Saltillo to be the capital.[70] While Mexican officials were distracted, Texian plots intensified. Austin, whose earlier sympathies with Mexico had all but drained away, wrote to his cousin in August that "the situation in Texas is daily becoming more and more interesting," predicting that "the best interests of the United States require that Texas should be effectually, and fully, Americanized—that is—settled by a population that will harmonize with their neigbours on the East, in language, political principles, common origin, sympathy, and even interest." One of those interests was slavery, and here Austin made his position clear: "Texas must be a slave country. It is no longer a matter of doubt."[71]

The acrimony worsened into the autumn: on October 2, 1835, a dispute over a cannon led Texian settlers in the town of Gonzalez to taunt Mexican troops with cries of "Come and take it." A week later, on October 9, some of the settlers seized control of La Bahía presidio just outside Goliad, then one of the most populated towns in Texas. Soon afterward, Austin wrote to fellow Texian David G. Burnet, "I hope to see Texas forever free from Mexican domination of any kind. It is yet too soon to say this publically—but that is the point we shall aim at. . . . But we must arrive at it by steps."[72]

As October filled up with battles, the consultation was pushed back to November, when fifty-eight of a total of ninety-eight delegates were able to attend the two-week session in San Felipe. The delegates debated their options: fight to reinstate the 1824 constitution or make a break for independence. The result, for the moment, was a compromise of limited action and unclear direction, though they did manage to establish a provisional government.[73]

As reports of these developments in Texas reached the East Coast cities of the United States, an enraged Mexican chargé d'affaires at the legation in Philadelphia, Joaquín María del Castillo y Lanzas, wrote to the U.S. secretary of state, John Forsyth. In his missive, he hit out at the Texians, arguing that it came as no surprise "that mere adventurers, who have nothing to lose, that fugitives from justice, and others who may gain without risking any thing, that those who delight in revolutions, either from temperament, or from character, or from the desire of rendering themselves conspicuous, should promote political convulsions."[74] A government circular from 1835 lamented the "ungrateful Colonists of Texas [who] mock the laws of the Mexican nation despite the generous welcome she gave them."[75]

While the majority of the people who wanted to form a state were Anglo, some Mexicans supported them, even from farther afield. One of Santa Anna's former brigadier-generals, José Antonio Mexía (also Mejía), who also spent time in the Mexican legation in the United States, set off from New Orleans with plans to attack the Gulf port city of Tampico in a show of support for the Texians, though he believed the Anglos were still fighting on the side of the Federalists rather than going after their own independence.[76] He departed on November 6, 1835, but his ship ran aground near Tampico on November 14. Santa Anna's troops easily defeated the attack the following day. Within Texas, some Tejanos were starting to side with the Anglos, including the provisional mayor of San Antonio de Béxar, Juan Nepomuceno Seguín, who signed up for Austin's militia.[77]

In December, some members of the consultation went on a mission to the United States to raise money, stopping in New Orleans, Louisville, Nashville, and Cincinnati. They drummed up support for their troops but faced a significant obstacle in enlisting volunteers. The United States and Mexico were at peace, and a law of 1818 made it illegal for U.S. citizens to organize or support an attack on a peaceful nation from the United States.[78] Mexico and the United States tacitly agreed that the Texians in any case had forfeited their allegiance to the United States and were Mexican citizens, rendering the conflict a civil war, meaning that a volunteer on the side of Tejas also had to, in theory, expatriate himself, which many of them did.[79]

By early 1836 loyalty to Mexico was increasingly hard to find among the Anglos, and slogans such as "Liberty or death" were being used by some of the Texians, evoking the earlier American Revolution. Alongside this, municipal committees of safety and correspondence, similar to the ones used during the Revolutionary War, had been organized into militias.[80] One February 1836 broadside declared that the "sons of the brave patriots of '76 are invincible in the cause of freedom and the rights of man."[81] Alongside these sentiments were more racialized ones, with Sam Houston proclaiming in January 1836 that the "vigor of the descendants of the north [will never] mix with the phlegm of the indolent Mexicans."[82]

Santa Anna decided that he would have to deal with the insurgents himself. He issued a proclamation calling for Mexicans to "combat with that mob of ungrateful adventurers."[83] He began his march north, picking up troops along the way in San Luis Potosí before arriving in San Antonio de Béxar in the afternoon of February 23, 1836, with around six thousand soldiers.[84] Although the Texians' numbers were shored up by U.S. recruits, there were too few of them to protect the gains they had made in San Antonio de Béxar, which they had taken in early December 1835, after forcing a surrender from the garrison there. The town was now under Anglo militia occupation, but many of the Texan Bexareños did not want to join the Anglos or the centralists.[85]

Though the Texians knew Santa Anna was on his way, the Mexican leader's entrance into San Antonio de Béxar caught the town off guard. Texian scouts managed to spot Santa Anna before he could lead an attack, giving the militia time to retreat to the Alamo, a garrison housed in the former Spanish mission San Antonio de Valero.

Nothing about the Alamo itself would indicate the outsize place that it would later occupy in U.S. history. At that time it was a small fortification, of a size and bearing that reflected its position in the frontier. Its purpose had fluctuated over the preceding decades; it was abandoned for the first time in 1793 and brought back to use in 1802 when a Spanish cavalry unit moved in. The troops were members of La Segunda Compañía Volante de San Carlos de Alamo de Parras, and soon the mission-turned-presidio was nicknamed the Alamo in honor of their hometown, Alamo de Parras, Coahuila.[86] It was left vacant once again around 1810 and remained so until Mexican troops made it a fort in 1821. Its condition reflected this periodic use, and parts of it had crumbled away or were in need of reinforcements—there was not even a roof over the chapel. It was all the Texians had, however, and they had earlier set to work making it stronger after taking control of San Antonio, reinforcing the walls, digging trenches, and repositioning cannons, now put to use shooting at Mexican troops.

After Santa Anna's arrival, the Texian colonel William Barret Travis sent for reinforcements, writing to the garrison at Goliad on February 23, "We have one hundred and forty-six men, who are determined never to retreat."[87] In the end, only thirty-two extra men arrived.[88] Santa Anna, for his part, had little interest in a battle in San Antonio; his true aim was to reach the Sabine River area and Houston's troops.[89] However, the following day, the Mexicans set up a makeshift battery, and in the week that followed, 15 of their troops and the 146 Texians exchanged fire. The Texians remained barricaded in the Alamo, and by March 4, Santa Anna felt forced to take more drastic action. He called a meeting that night to draw up plans for an assault that would wipe out the rebels.

In later explaining his decisions, Santa Anna—who was somewhat prone to exaggeration—wrote, "Before undertaking the assault . . . I still wanted to try a generous measure, characteristic of Mexican kindness, and I offered life to the defendants who would surrender their arms." The Texians refused any offer.[90] At the same time, the men inside the

Alamo were struggling, and some wanted to surrender, as food and ammunition were running low.[91]

In the cool, dark hours of the morning of March 6, the Mexican troops crept from their camp across the Medina River to the Alamo, and four columns of troops surrounded it.[92] With cries of *"¡Viva Mexico!"* the battle began at around five a.m. The Texians fired cannons at the oncoming Mexicans, but they managed to reach the walls and, using ladders, climb over. The fighting moved into closer—and bloodier—quarters inside the Alamo. Some of the Texians retreated into the chapel, the door to which the Mexican troops then broke down, leaving the men cornered. Other Texians tried to surrender or flee, but in the end there was no escape.[93] Almost everyone inside—including Travis, Bowie, and Davy Crockett—died in the space of a few hours.[94] There were, however, some survivors. A handful of Anglo and Tejano women and children hiding in the Alamo were discovered, as were some slaves. Santa Anna later released them all.[95]

Another survivor was Juan Seguín, whose life had been spared when he was sent out earlier as a courier with a message. He returned on March 6 to find the fort fallen.[96] In the days that followed, Santa Anna ordered the dead Anglos to be burned and the Mexicans buried, though owing to a shortage of graveyard spaces, their bodies were dumped in the river.[97] Most of the Tejanos in San Antonio fled the city or stayed out of the conflict, but a handful—between five and ten; no exact number is known—died fighting the Mexicans in the Alamo.

Santa Anna lost at least seventy men—though some estimates go far higher, to more than one thousand—and another three hundred were injured.[98] The Mexican press had a mixed reaction to what happened at the Alamo, depending on whether a newspaper supported Santa Anna or not. The Mexico City paper *La Lima de Vulcano* praised the country's "invincible liberator," believing that "Mexico has been vindicated."[99] Many of the newspapers thought this would bring the insurrection in Texas to an end, though the more critical press began to question the necessity of the battle in the first place. *La Luna*, a newspaper in Toluca, argued that the Alamo "has not been a real gain, a true triumph of the nation."[100]

While the siege of the Alamo was taking place, a group of Texians and Tejanos who had gathered on March 1 in Washington-on-the-Brazos, a small town upriver from San Felipe de Austin, adopted a declaration of independence on March 2, followed by the promulgation of a Constitution of the Republic of Texas on March 17. This document outlined a government not dissimilar from the United States' in structure, with a separate legislature, executive, and judiciary. Slavery was protected, with a provision that "congress shall pass no laws to prohibit emigrants from bringing their slaves into the republic with them . . . nor shall congress have the power to emancipate slaves," and no free person of color "either in whole or part, shall be permitted to reside permanently in the republic, without the consent of congress."

Regarding Tejanos, the constitution stipulated that all persons—with the exception of "Africans, the descendants of Africans, and Indians"—should be considered citizens of the republic and entitled to all the privileges of such.[101] The equality outlined on paper would not match the reality, as the conflict had brought to the fore much discussion of Anglo-Tejano differences, an example of which was found in an earlier address made by George Childress, Texian supporter and one of the authors of the republic's constitution. Speaking at a public meeting in Nashville, which was reported that February in the *Telegraph and Texas Register*, he asked his audience to "contemplate the national character of the Mexicans," whom he described as "a cowardly, treacherous, semi-civilized people, without enterprize [*sic*], workmanship or discipline." The Anglos, to Childress, were the opposite, being "brave, hardy, enterprising."[102] A front-page article in the following week's edition of the newspaper painted Mexicans as "a people one half of whom are the most depraved of different races of Indians, different in color, pursuits and character; and all of whom are divided by the insurmountable barrier which nature and refined taste have thrown between us—a people whose inert and idle habits, general ignorance and superstition, prevents the possibility of our ever mingling in the same harmonious family."[103] Despite such a hostile rhetorical climate, the prominent Tejano Lorenzo de Zavala, who would later be named vice president of the republic, and José Francisco Ruíz ended up being signatories to the declaration of independence and constitution.[104]

The fighting continued into late March, after Colonel James Walker Fannin and 350 men who had been captured in earlier battles were imprisoned at the presidio in Goliad. To Santa Anna, these "foreigners taken with arms in their hands, making war upon the nation" were little more than land pirates, and so should be executed.[105] Their resulting deaths on March 27, known as the "Goliad massacre," sparked public anger and rallied further support in Texas and the United States for the cause of independence.

On April 15, Austin wrote a letter to President Andrew Jackson and Congress, explaining that Santa Anna "has succeeded in uniting the whole of the mexicans against Texas by making it a national war against heritics [sic]." He asked if the United States was really able to "turn a deaf ear to the appeals of your fellow citizens in favor of *their* and *your* country men and friends, who are massacred, butchered, outraged in Texas at your very doors?" Austin wanted reinforcements and called for the conflict to be a "national war," utilizing the sympathy and support of the public for "a war in which every free american, who is not a fanatic abolitionist . . . is deeply, warmly, ardently interested."[106]

Some people in the United States were interested in the events in Texas and had been involved well before Austin wrote his letter asking for help. A letter from the Mexican chargé d'affaires, José María Ortiz Monasterio, complained that the "colonists of Texas have since obtained, and continue to obtain daily from New Orleans succours of every kind, in provisions, arms, ammunition, money and even in soldiers, who are openly enlisted in that city."[107] Companies like the Galveston Bay and Texas Land Company and other speculators and profiteers were backing Texan independence, while around 200 initial volunteers arrived in the autumn of 1835 to join the Texians.[108] Over the course of the rebellion, some 3,600 men fought for Texas, including 1,000 volunteers from the United States and 138 Tejanos.[109]

President Jackson, however, had to stand in favor of supporting existing treaties with Mexico. He noted on the back of Austin's letter that the "Texians before they took the step to declare themselves Independent, which has aroused and united all mexico against them ought to have pondered well, it was a rash and premature act, our neutrality must be faithfully maintained."[110]

Santa Anna rode into San Felipe de Austin on April 7, 1836, hunting Sam Houston. He believed the Texians would retreat if his troops crossed the Brazos, and as Santa Anna searched for a suitable crossing point, news reached the nearby town of Harrisburg, which the residents fled before setting it alight. Santa Anna kept on Houston's trail, catching up to him on April 20, 1836, where the Buffalo Bayou and San Jacinto River converge. After the Alamo, Santa Anna had divided up his men into columns, leaving one in San Antonio and sending one to Goliad. By this point Santa Anna's column had around 750 troops, with reinforcements consisting of 400 more arriving the following morning, while Houston had around 800. He set up camp near the bayou and waited, while his men tried to reinforce their position.[111] Then on the afternoon of April 21 came the unexpected cries of "Remember the Alamo!" just as the Mexican troops had settled in for a rest.[112] Houston and his men routed the Mexicans in a surprise attack at the Battle of San Jacinto. Around half of the Mexican troops were killed during this "Yorktown of Texas," and the others were taken prisoner, including Santa Anna. He had managed to escape and spent one night in a barn, though he was later picked up by Texian troops who did not recognize him, taking him to Houston's camp where the cries of "El presidente" from the other prisoners gave his identity away.[113]

Santa Anna signed two treaties with the Texians, one public and one private. The public one promised an end to hostilities and the evacuation of troops south of the Río Grande, while the private deal involved a promise for the recognition of Texan independence, something that was not forthcoming. In exchange, Santa Anna was released some months later, though he was first taken to Washington, where he met President Jackson in January 1837. No official record remains of the conversation the men had over dinner, except for one attendee's later report that Santa Anna had indicated that the issue of official recognition would have to be overseen by Mexico's Congress.[114]

The victory in San Jacinto was enthusiastically received across the United States. One Pennsylvania newspaper was breathless over the victory of the "gallant little army," extolling the virtues of the troops while overlooking the contribution of Tejanos, saying the force was "composed of men from the United States, with probably a proportion from Great Britain—the Anglo-Saxon blood, which ever maintains its superiority, as well in the field as in the pursuits of a peaceful life," concluding that "they well deserve the immortality they have achieved."[115]

By the end of 1836, Houston was installed as president of the republic and Austin had died. In April 1837 the ashes of the soldiers who were killed at the Alamo received an interment, presided over by Juan Seguín. In his speech, he praised the men and the "remains which we have the honor of carrying on our shoulders," before telling the assembled crowd: "I invite you to declare to the entire world, 'Texas shall be free and independent or we shall perish in glorious combat.'"[116] Seguín was also honored for his actions in 1838 when the settlement of Walnut Springs, around forty miles east of San Antonio de Béxar, renamed itself Seguin. Santa Anna, meanwhile, languished during these years in defeat and humiliation, and General Anastasio Bustamante became president again.

The next hurdle for Texas was annexation to the United States, which, after the problems of the Missouri Compromise, would take almost a decade. Texas was unwavering on the issue of slavery. Following independence from Mexico, the slave population within Texas, now unencumbered by any prohibition, rose from around 3,700 in 1837 to 24,400 by 1845.[117]

The years that followed Texas's independence were difficult for the Tejanos, many of whom had been reluctant to join the Texians' fight. Even for those like Juan Seguín who had aided the Anglos, the future was far from certain. Some Mexicans could see what lay ahead. One diplomat, Manuel Eduardo de Gorostiza, wrote from Washington, D.C., in the summer of 1836 that "the primary object of the plot, is to take possession of the entire coast of Texas, unite it with the United States, to make from Texas four or five States with slavery."[118] Tejanos would lose some of their land as this goal was achieved; Anglo claims to their property and threats of personal violence in the aftermath of independence drove many Tejanos to live elsewhere in Mexico.[119]

———

Wɪᴛʜɪɴ ᴛʜᴇ Uɴɪᴛᴇᴅ States, the 1820s and 1830s had also been a time of great political change, as embodied in the rise of Andrew Jackson. He symbolized the direction the United States was turning: westward. Jackson, born into a poor family on the western edges of the Carolina territory in 1767, was created by the frontier, and in many ways would be defined by it. He became a wealthy lawyer, land speculator, and slave owner in Tennessee. Admiration for Jackson was not limited to the

United States. In 1830, Lorenzo de Zavala—who five years later would become embroiled in the Texian struggle—left Mexico for New Orleans to embark on a tour of the United States. His political life, like his travels, took him to points far and wide. He had been one of the main architects of the 1824 Mexican constitution and served in various government posts, though he was forced out by the centralists, and that led him to his arrival in New Orleans. From there he went through Louisiana and up the Mississippi River to Louisville and Cincinnati, then spent time in New York, New England, and Canada.[120]

His 1830 book detailing his time in the United States remains one of the earliest known accounts of U.S.-Mexican relations, written to "give a more useful lesson in politics to my fellow citizens than the knowledge of the manners, customs, habits, and government of the United States, whose institutions they have copied so servilely."[121] Zavala remained impressed with the country throughout his journey, giving extensive descriptions of the national political and economic situation.[122]* He was also an admirer of President Jackson. He arrived in Cincinnati in time to see the crowds cheer the president during a visit, noting the freedom from pomp and ceremony and describing "a numerous crowd of people running along the banks of the river to receive and see their first citizen . . . there was music with banners, flags, shouts and cries of joy. Everything was natural and spontaneous." The next day the two men had a meeting in what struck Zavala as a "modestly furnished house" with around thirty men, who "by their dress seemed to be workmen or craftsmen," causing him to write in admiration of "the simplest court in the world."[123]

With the return of Federalists in Mexico, Zavala was able to resume his political career and in 1833 he was sent to Paris as Mexico's first minister to France. The news of Santa Anna's centralist reforms alarmed him. He resigned from his post and moved to Texas, where he owned land.[124] From there he entered the complicated world of Anglo Texian politics, transforming himself from a Mexican Federalist to a supporter of Texan independence, helping to draft the constitution at Washington-on-the-Brazos, ensuring it was in both English and Spanish. He was then

---

* His book was published in Paris in 1834, but the work did not appear in Mexico until 1846.

appointed the Republic of Texas's first vice president, but he resigned after a month, tired of Anglo suspicions of his alleged intentions to return Texas to Mexican rule. Soon afterward, he contracted pneumonia and died in November 1836 in Texas.[125]

In the conclusion to his book, Zavala lavished lyrical praise on U.S. democracy, while bemoaning the military and ecclesiastical culture he believed held Mexico back, making a final prognostication in the last line that "the American system will obtain a complete though bloody victory" in his homeland.[126] He lived long enough to see the first signs of this, in Texas, but died before he could watch his prediction come true.

TEXANS VOTED IN 1836 in favor of becoming a state, and the following year a resolution was introduced in the U.S. Senate. President Jackson had a long history with Sam Houston and no doubt he favored Texas's joining the union, but he was able only to grant diplomatic recognition. Jackson knew it was too dangerous to offer annexation because Texas would enter as a slave state, unsettling the slave-free balance and angering abolitionists at home and abroad, especially in Britain.[127] This did not cause him to lose interest in the issue, and he continued to wield his influence in favor of Texas's annexation on his successors.

Opinion on Texas was divided. The Rhode Island legislature, for instance, believed that the inclusion of Texas "would load the nation with debt and taxes" and, even worse, propagate "slavery, and promot[e] the raising of slaves within its own bosom—the very bosom of freedom—to be exported and sold in those unhallowed regions."[128] In Tennessee, sentiments were markedly different. Its legislators said they "believe[d] that the gallant and chivalrous bravery of Texans in their struggle for liberty and free Government, is an assurance of their worth, and sufficient evidence of their qualification to entitle them to brotherhood and citizenship with us."[129]

The question of Texas's future was not just a domestic one. The British, who had signed antislavery treaties with Mexico, were concerned about this new republic, yet at the same time they were eager to buy its cotton. Houston began a campaign in 1837 for Britain to grant official recognition to Texas, but as part of the deal the British wanted Texas to sign an anti–slave trade agreement, which included the right of British ships to search for illicit slaves on Texan vessels, a proposal that met with little enthusiasm.[130] While these negotiations were being conducted, some enslaved people in Texas continually tried to take advantage of their proximity to Mexico, running away to freedom when they could. They were sometimes aided by Tejanos, to the annoyance of Anglo owners, though other Tejanos were slave owners themselves.[131]

Throughout this period, Mexico never granted Texas official recognition. The republic continued to receive more arrivals, while the Tejanos were pushed toward the margins of this now Anglo-dominated place. When Santa Anna returned to power in October 1841, he began to harbor ambitions to recapture Texas.[132] Mexican troops raided Texas at intervals throughout 1842, and in September San Antonio was briefly taken twice, though both times the Mexicans retreated. This caused the Texans to organize a punitive expedition into Mexico that autumn, including one mission of 320 men to Santa Fe, which ended in their immediate surrender and imprisonment.[133] Another mission culminated with a group of some 300 men, in defiance of their orders, crossing the Río Grande and attacking Mexican troops in the town of Mier. This also ended in defeat, and the men were sent to prison or executed, with 76 released a couple of years later.[134]

Santa Anna eventually gave up his fight, realizing that any further hostilities toward Texas might result in provoking the United States.[135] The official mood in Washington about annexation of Texas was changing, and it looked as if an end to its political limbo might be in sight. John Tyler, a Whig who had come to the presidency following the death of President William Henry Harrison in 1841, after one month in office, had few allies and saw annexation as a possible vote-winner.[136] In March 1844, Tyler tapped John C. Calhoun, a former vice president, to be secretary of state. Calhoun's predecessor, Abel Upshur, had been working on secret negotiations with Texas before his death in an accident on the USS *Princeton*.[137] The result was a Treaty of Annexation, signed between the United States and the Republic of Texas on April 12, 1844, which—if ratified— would allow Texas to be "incorporated into the Union of the United States."[138] In Mexico, Santa Anna tried to win congressional approval that summer for a thirty-thousand-strong army to launch a decisive attack to take back Texas, but his demands were repeatedly denied by a Mexican legislature on the verge of an internal political crisis.[139]

As a South Carolina slaveholder, Calhoun saw the advantages of adding Texas to the union, tipping the balance in favor of slave states; he and other southerners were also eager to curb British antislavery pressure on Texas, and he denounced such pressure in his infamous "Pakenham letter."[140] Britain's minister to Mexico, Richard Pakenham, promoted abolition, and Calhoun wrote to him around the time the treaty was signed, demanding not only that Texas be annexed to the United States to protect the South but also that the extension of slavery was "essential to the peace, safety, and prosperity of states in the union in which it exists."[141] The letter found its way into the press, and debate about Texas became more fevered. Fellow southerner Henry Clay came out in opposition, in a letter that also saw publication, arguing that "if the Government of the United States were to acquire Texas, it would acquire along with it all the encumbrances which Texas is under, and among them the actual or suspended war between Mexico and Texas. Of that consequence there cannot be a doubt. Annexation and war with Mexico are identical."[142] The annexation debate continued into the election year 1844, after the Senate failed to ratify the treaty in June, with a vote of 16 for and 35 against.[143]

In the 1844 presidential election, James Knox Polk, a protégé of Jackson's with a low profile, won through a combination of the Democratic Party machine and a resonant message. The Texas question had grown into a national preoccupation, and now chained to this territory was the idea of westward expansion. Bringing in Texas would benefit the whole nation and keep the South happy. Polk had faced fierce competition for his office from Henry Clay, by this point one of the most famous statesmen in the nation. Clay—who had tried to win the presidency twice before—held firm to his anti-annexation stance, despite being a slaveholder. Polk, bolstered by southern support, won with 170 electoral college votes to Clay's 105, although he had only a tiny lead of 38,000 in the popular vote.[144]

Texas had not been the only issue: Polk's gaze reached all the way to the Pacific. Also taking place was a long-running diplomatic squabble with Britain over a square of territory between Canada and California. Many people wanted the U.S. boundary to be farther north at N 54°40", a designation so important that one of Polk's most effective slogans was "Fifty-four forty or fight!"* Before tackling the northern dispute, the focus returned to resolving the Texas question. On February 27, 1845, a few days before Polk took office, a joint resolution, which needed only a majority and not a two-thirds vote, was pushed through both houses of Congress to admit Texas, and it received its formal statehood ten months later.[145] In his March 1845 inaugural address, Polk dived headlong into the incorporation of Texas, echoing incorrect prior claims that it had been part of the Louisiana territory, and saying that "Texas was once a part of our country—was unwisely ceded away to a foreign power—is now independent" before explaining that it now had "an undoubted right . . . to merge [its] sovereignty as a separate and independent state in ours."[146]

He went on to outline a future of U.S. expansion. "Foreign powers do not seem to appreciate the true character of our Government. Our Union is a confederation of independent States, whose policy is peace with each other and all the world," he told the assembled audience. "To enlarge its limits is to extend the dominions of peace over additional territories and increasing millions. The world has nothing to fear from military ambition in our Government."[147] A few months later, the journalist John Louis O'Sullivan, in an unsigned article in the July/August 1845 issue of *United States Democratic Review*, coined the term "manifest destiny," explaining how the United States had permission "to overspread the continent allotted by Providence," and expand to the west. He was writing in relation to the annexation of Texas, which he supported, as well as the long-running Oregon question, but he also included in his western future California, where the "Anglo-Saxon foot is already on its borders."[148]

This "overspread" came one step closer in 1845. General Zachary Taylor had been ordered in late spring to station four thousand troops in Corpus Christi, Texas, near the Nueces River. On the diplomatic front, Polk dispatched John Slidell, a Louisiana politician, to negotiate with Mexico over the ongoing issue of U.S. citizens' claims for compensation arising from Mexican raids, hoping to get in exchange a recognition that the long-disputed Texas boundary was the Río Grande and not the

---

* Though in the end there was a compromise and it was set at N 49°.

Nueces River. In addition there had been claims that the Texas territory included Santa Fe—claims also angrily contested by Mexico. Slidell was given additional instructions to offer up to $25 million for New Mexico and California.[149] Mexico refused to consider it, and, with frustrations rising, Clay's 1844 warning—that the annexation of Texas would lead to war with Mexico—seemed prophetic.[150]

Such pessimistic views could be found in Mexico as well. A front-page editorial across all five columns of a February 1846 edition of the Mexico City newspaper *El Tiempo* said the United States had capitalized on infighting among Mexican politicians, lamenting that this internal focus came at a high price: "Texas has been lost: California is going to be lost: the frontier departments will be lost as well."[151]

Taylor had spent the rest of 1845 around the Nueces River in Corpus Christi, where he set up camp. In January 1846, after Mexico rejected the U.S. deal, orders were sent to move the troops to the north bank of the Río Grande, where they put a fortification across from the Mexican town of Matamoros (near today's Brownsville, Texas). Mexico considered this a provocation.[152] Taylor and his men waited for the Mexicans to attack; Polk hoped this would make the whole enterprise more acceptable to the public.

The Mexican general Mariano Arista arrived on his side of the Río Grande on April 24, 1846, and ordered some of his troops across the river. The following day, Mexican soldiers attacked a scouting party, killing eleven U.S. troops. Mexico had acted first.[153] Less than two weeks later, the United States and Mexico had their first significant battle, on May 8, 1846, in a field of prickly cordgrass at Palo Alto, about five miles from Taylor's fort. The two thousand U.S. troops defeated Mexico's six thousand, led by General Arista. After losing about two hundred men, Arista retreated five miles south to Resaca de la Palma, using the brush in a dried riverbed for cover. The following day, Taylor launched another attack on the Mexicans, this time killing twelve hundred men and forcing the remaining ones across the Río Grande to Matamoros. He followed them across the river, and by May 18 the town of Matamoros was under U.S. occupation.[154]

Between the opening shots at Palo Alto and the occupation of Matamoros, Polk went before Congress, explaining, in a May 11 speech, that "Mexico has passed the boundary of the United States, has invaded our territory and shed American blood upon the American soil." The annexation of Texas, he claimed, was behind the hostilities, and now "under these circumstances it was plainly our duty to extend our protection over her citizens and soil."[155] By May 13 Congress gave him the declaration of war he sought. Polk had been canny in putting forward the war bill, crafting it so that it sounded as if a war, started by Mexico, was already under way and so that the legislation authorized funding for troops. This left any opposition in a bind: vote against supporting the troops, an unpopular move; or vote for an unwanted war? Some politicians saw the game Polk was playing. A Kentucky Whig representative, Garrett Davis, declared on the floor that had the bill been written honestly, it would admit "this war was begun by the president."[156] The bill passed the Senate, 42 to 2.

Polk's motives came under further scrutiny when, on August 8, he asked Congress for $2 million to pay Mexico for the land he expected to gain when the war was over. A first-term Democratic congressman from Pennsylvania, David Wilmot, moved an amendment to an appropriation bill that called for the banning of slavery in any new resulting territory. It set out that "as an express and fundamental condition to the acquisition of any territory from the Republic of Mexico by the United States . . . neither slavery nor involuntary servitude shall ever exist in any part of said territory." Wilmot's maneuver also spoke to the growing Free-Soil movement, which had at its heart the idea that slavery undermined and devalued the labor of white people, and so any new state should be a free one. As Wilmot put it, he desired to preserve "for free white labour a fair country . . . where the sons of toil, of my own race and own color, can live without the disgrace which association with Negro slavery brings upon free labor."[157]

The proviso passed the House and was tabled in the Senate. Voting was along regional—slaveholding—and not party lines, with most southerners, both Whig and Democrat, in the House voting against the amendment and those in the Senate in favor of tabling it.[158] This reopened another round of debate over slave and free states, and Congress and the nation now stared straight at a question that would dominate the next two decades.[159]

Whatever the reasons proffered for war, the public had great initial enthusiasm for the conflict. Tens of thousands of men rushed to enlist from the east and west, with some seventy thousand of the seventy-eight thousand who fought in the Mexican-American War being volunteers.[160] They were marched across the north of Mexico, some toward Monterrey and Saltillo, some to New Mexico and California, and still others were sent on an expedition to Veracruz.[161] Battle news was followed with great interest on both sides, and U.S. papers or articles were read in Mexico, too.[162] Beyond the headlines, the war had tapped a rich seam in the public imagination. A flurry of cheap "novelette" books, as they were called then, were printed with tantalizing titles such as *The Mexican Spy: Or the Bride of Buena Vista* and *The Prisoner of Perote: A Tale of American Valor*. The seemingly exotic backdrop of Mexico, coupled with the patriotic fervor around the conflict, proved to be a popular combination.[163] Soldiers found inspiration by reading Massachusetts writer William Hickling Prescott's *History of the Conquest of Mexico*. Published in 1843, the weighty tome was a best-seller, and its detailed and romanticized account of the Spanish conquest of Tenochtitlán helped fuel the imagination of eager volunteers who believed they were following in the footsteps of Cortés.[164] Such a consequence horrified Prescott, and he later described the war as a "mad ambition for conquest" on the part of the United States.[165]

In northern Mexico, U.S. soldiers under the leadership of Stephen Watts Kearny marched into Santa Fe on August 18, 1846, and captured the city before heading west.[166] The occupation lasted until January 1847, when a fierce revolt in Taos pitted New Mexicans against the regime of the territorial governor, Charles Bent. The U.S. troops managed to take back the territory and the plot's organizers were later tried and hanged.[167]

In California, before news of the war even arrived, there had already been a pro-U.S. uprising. On June 14, 1846, a group of settlers descended on the town of Sonoma, raising a flag emblazoned with a star and a grizzly bear. They captured the small barracks and imprisoned the Mexican general Mariano Vallejo. This rebellion was thought to have been encouraged by the adventurer John C. Frémont, though he claimed to have been on a scientific expedition north of Sonoma at the time and did not take part.[168] Known as the "Bear Flag" party, the group declared California a republic, and Frémont became the group's leader a short time later. Soon afterward, they were subsumed into the larger California Battalion, which included the frontiersman Kit Carson. By July, a U.S. Navy ship arrived, sending men ashore and raising the U.S. flag in

Monterey on July 7, and by August U.S. forces had taken San Diego, Santa Barbara, and Los Angeles, though that was not the end of the fighting.[169]

When Kearny arrived near San Diego on December 6 with around 120 men, he met with a surprise: a column of Californios, led by Andrés Pico, the brother of the Mexican governor, at the Battle of San Pasqual, where more than twenty U.S. soldiers were killed. The Californios managed to retake San Diego, as well as Los Angeles and Santa Barbara.[170] By January 1847, however, the U.S. troops, in conjunction with Frémont and his men, fought back and forced them to surrender. On March 1, 1847, Kearny issued a proclamation that "hereby absolves all the inhabitants of California from any further allegiance to the Republic of Mexico, and will consider them as citizens of the United States."[171]

As U.S. troops prevailed, Santa Anna was in Mexico planning his return to the front. He was now fifty-two years old and had seen decades of political and military battle. He had lost his left leg during a war with France in 1838, and even buried it—much to the disgust of his enemies—with full military honors.[172] He had returned as president again after that conflict and, following a number of vacillations in office, found himself out of power and forced into exile in Cuba. By August 1846, however, he was again in Veracruz and was organizing troops—something Polk later claimed he allowed to happen because Santa Anna's return would distract and weaken Mexico, supporting rumors at the time that a secret deal between the two had been negotiated.[173]

Among Mexico's enlistees was a brigade called the San Patricios, or St. Patrick's Battalion, composed of Irish and other immigrant troops who had deserted the U.S. Army and joined forces with Mexico, fed up with anti-Catholic prejudice in the United States.[174] Juan Seguín, the Tejano who helped secure Texan independence, also returned to battle, but this time on the side of Mexico. Living between two worlds, he felt he had little option but to change sides. After Texas had been established as a republic, he became the only Tejano and native Spanish-speaking member of its senate. Like many of the Anglos, he also started speculating in land, but he was left with debts and enemies. He left in 1840 to assist the Federalist Mexican general Antonio Canales, but his return to Mexico came at a high political price: once he was back in Texas, whispers arose that he had betrayed Texan plots to the Mexicans. This compelled him to return to Mexico, where he took part in the Anglo-Mexican skirmishes of 1842.[175]

Not everyone in the United States had been enveloped in a patriotic haze, and opponents of "Mr. Polk's War" existed inside Washington and outside, not least among abolitionists who harbored deep fears about where the conflict would lead. Others were concerned about the political implications of this aggressive behavior. A July 1846 article in the *American Review* argued that the war "has been brought about in the determined pursuit of one principal object, and one only: that object was the acquisition of more territory," explaining that the fifteen hundred miles of desired land had "several of the richest mines in all Mexico. . . . And if Upper California, with Monterey, and the fine harbor of San Francisco, could be clutched at the same time, no doubt the President has thought that his administration would be signalized as among the most glorious in the annals of the aggrandized republic."[176]

Public opinion in the United States started to turn in 1847 as reports emerged of atrocities inflicted by soldiers on Mexican civilians. Morale was dropping. One colonel, John Hardin, wrote in a letter, "Although I was for annexing all this part of Mexico to the United States before I came here, yet I now doubt whether it is worth it."[177] He died at Buena Vista on February 23, 1847. That battle, which took place just south of Saltillo, in Coahuila, was particularly brutal, with both sides suffering significant losses in the freezing cold and rain. Mexican forces killed or injured seven hundred U.S. soldiers, while thirty-five hundred of their own were killed or wounded, or went missing.[178] Among the U.S. dead in Buena Vista was Henry Clay's son, and as the body count rose, public support plummeted. Santa Anna was putting up a fight, though he sustained huge losses, too, with around fifteen thousand of his men killed by March 1847.[179] He later remarked that Polk and his allies were mistaken if they thought he would betray Mexico, saying he "would rather be burnt on a pyre and that my ashes were spread in such a way that not one atom was left."[180]

The climax of the war came when General Winfield Scott planned an invasion of Mexico by water. Like Hernando Cortés, he sailed into Veracruz in March and his soldiers started by penetrating the walls of the city, bombing the residents, who refused to surrender, and using some 463,000 pounds of shot and shell in the process.[181] Hoping to justify his actions, Scott published a proclamation addressed to the "wise nation of Mexico," explaining that, despite the invasion, "the Americans are not your enemies" but rather "friends of the peaceful inhabitants of this land which we occupy." He even went so far as to explain that "an American who raped a Mexican woman has been hanged. Isn't this an indication of good faith and vigorous discipline?"[182] He ended the awkward pronouncement by saying that the war would finish soon and Americans would be "counting themselves very happy to leave Mexico and return to their homeland."[183]

The violence of the siege elicited condemnation in the United States though Mexicans in the capital were gripped by their own civil crisis and were not prepared for what was to come. While Santa Anna was taken by surprise by the Veracruz landing, in Mexico City there was a storm brewing between two political factions, with the moderates, or *moderados*, trying to overthrow the radical, or *puro*, government of Valentín Gómez Farías, in part because he was going to appropriate Church property to pay for the war: this intention had angered the *moderados*, who counted senior clergymen among their ranks. For almost two weeks at the end of February and the beginning of March 1847, these two groups battled on the capital's streets, and Gómez Farías even sent in regular troops to fight against the *moderado* militia. This conflict became known as the Revolt of the Polkos. The origins of the name are unclear: it may have been a derisive reference to the *moderados'* wealth, alluding to the fashionable polka dance, or it could have its origins in those who favored the actions of U.S. president Polk.[184] In the end Santa Anna was forced to replace Gómez Farías that April with a *moderado*, Pedro María de Anaya. One Mexican officer, Manuel Balbontín, reflected decades later on the advantage that the unrest had given the United States, writing that Mexico's "civil war was a powerful help to the invaders . . . the national resistance did not present the greatest energy."[185]

A brief armistice between the two sides was negotiated in August but it soon broke down after Mexico rejected a U.S. plan under which the United States would gain Texas, New Mexico, all of California, and part of Sonora in exchange for cash and the waiving of any reparations payment.[186] The U.S. campaign resumed in September, culminating in the Battle of Chapultepec, at the hilltop castle in the capital that was being used as a military academy. Troops stormed the building on September 13, 1847, and the U.S. flag was flying over it a couple of days later. The United States had not only humiliated Mexico at the frontier but pierced its ancient Mexica heart. Even the historian William Prescott, no fan of the war, was swept up by its conclusion, writing to one colonel that the victory was "as brilliant as that of the great *conquistador* himself."[187] Scott even invited Prescott in July 1848 to write the history of the "Second Mexican War," but the author declined.[188]

Others remained less impressed by these events. At the Concord Lyceum in January 1848 Henry David Thoreau gave a lecture—later published as part of his essay "Civil Disobedience"—in which he pointed at the "present Mexican war" as indicative of the worst type of governance, "the working of comparatively a few individuals using the standing government as their tool."[189]

In Washington, war fever raged as some cabinet members tried to convince Polk to take all of Mexico, or at least everything north of N 26°.[190] Most of the ardent supporters of this All-Mexico Movement were Democrats, though some prominent slave owners, such as John C. Calhoun, resisted such annexation in part because they didn't think slavery could be extended, but also because they did not believe millions of Mexicans could be absorbed into the United States.[191]

Throughout this period, ideas about Anglo-Saxon superiority crystallized, bolstered by a racialized field of scientific inquiry that would end up placing Anglos at the top of the evolutionary pile but also building on the foundation of prejudices laid by Anglos in Texas. Whiteness in the United States became bound up with the idea of manifest destiny and the providence that the Anglo-Protestants were somehow chosen to spread themselves across the continent. Victory against Mexico was but one more step along that road.[192] Accordingly, the long-running anti-Mexican rhetoric intensified. The *American Review*, a Whig publication, parodied this point of view in one article, saying that the pro-war contingent had been inspired by the idea that "Mexico was poor, distracted, in anarchy, and almost in ruins—what could she do . . . to impede the march of our greatness? We are Anglo-Saxon Americans; it was our 'destiny' to possess and to rule this continent. . . . We were a chosen people, and this was our allotted inheritance, and we must drive out all other nations before us."[193]

Humor cut close to the truth when, in December 1847, Congress started to debate the "all-Mexico" idea. Polk, however, was looking west, not south—his eyes were on California, which he wanted to obtain by treaty as soon as possible.[194] Other politicians, including Clay, thought the United States should end the whole disgraceful episode and withdraw with no land at all. John C. Calhoun continued to warn that taking the entire nation meant the United States might "find ourselves . . . with eight or nine millions of Mexicans, without a government, on our hands, not knowing what to do with them."[195] He elaborated his concerns to the Senate, saying:

> To incorporate Mexico, would be the first departure of the kind; for more than half of its population are pure Indians, and by far the larger portion of the residue mixed blood. I protest against the incorporation of such a people. Ours is the Government of the white man. The great misfortune of what was formerly Spanish America, is to be traced to the fatal error of placing the coloured race on an equality with the white.[196]

The newspapers chimed in as well—Calhoun had noted that "you can hardly read a newspaper without finding it filled with speculation upon this subject"—with some arguing that it would be of great benefit to Mexico if it became part of the United States.[197] Many Whigs opposed "all-Mexico" on the grounds not that Mexico was a sovereign nation but rather that Mexican culture rendered the people too "inferior" to be part of the United States, along with the subtext that the Mexicans could potentially make common cause with the Irish and other Catholics.[198]

Not everyone shared these views, however. An 1847 pamphlet, *Peace with Mexico*, by the Swiss-born former politician Albert Gallatin, rebuked such notions, writing:

> It is said, that the people of the United States have an hereditary superiority of race over the Mexicans, which gives them the right to subjugate and keep in bondage the inferior nation. This, it is also alleged, will be the means of enlightening the degraded Mexicans, of improving their social states, and of ultimately increasing the happiness of the masses. Is it compatible with the principle of Democracy, which

rejects every hereditary claim of individuals, to admit an hereditary
superiority of races? . . . Can you for a moment suppose, that a very
doubtful descent from men, who lived one thousand years ago, has
transmitted to you a superiority over your fellow-men?[199]

Gallatin had a long memory, arriving in the United States when it was
still fighting for its independence, and later serving as the fourth secretary of the treasury, in Congress, and as a diplomat. He published the
tract shortly before his death in 1849, decrying the annexation of Texas,
castigating the United States for not being a model to other nations,
and lamenting that "nothing can be more injurious, more lamentable,
more scandalous, than the war between the two adjacent republics of
North America."[200]

As senators continued to debate the taking of Mexico, the U.S. emissary
Nicholas Trist was negotiating with the provisional Mexican president,
Manuel de la Peña y Peña. Trist was doing this despite being recalled,
in part because Polk did not trust him to execute orders and felt Trist
may even have been conspiring against him.[201] However, he managed
to produce a deal with Mexico, with the initial agreement negotiated
at a villa in Guadalupe Hidalgo, near the spiritual home of the national
symbol, the Virgin of Guadalupe. The February 2, 1848, treaty involved
Mexico recognizing the Río Grande border in Texas and giving the
United States Alta California and New Mexico in exchange for $15 million.
Peña y Peña reluctantly agreed to it, fearful that further negotiation,
delay, or refusal would lead to the loss of even more land.[202] After the
two parties concurred, they went to Mass at the basilica there.[203] Polk
had turned the deal down at first, and then reconsidered, realizing that
he could placate the anti-expansionist Whigs by showing that he paid
for the territory.[204]

   The war and its aftermath caused political problems for Mexico, too.
Liberals wanted to keep fighting and not sign the treaty. Peña y Peña
was forced to point out that "whoever wants to describe the Treaty of
Guadalupe Hidalgo as dishonorable by the extension of the ceded territory will never resolve how to end this disgraceful war."[205] After heated
debate, the chamber of deputies voted 51 to 35 to accept the treaty, while
the Mexican senate passed it 32 to 4.[206]

In Washington, a young first-term Illinois congressman, Abraham Lincoln, criticized the government over the whole debacle in December 1847. In what became known as the "spot resolutions," Lincoln demanded to know if the "particular spot on which the blood of our citizens was so shed was or was not at that time our own soil," a question to which he was given no answer. Two months later, the Treaty of Guadalupe Hidalgo was signed, ceding 51 percent of Mexico's territory to the United States, with the Río Grande set as the border. Besides California, Texas, and New Mexico, the 525,000 square miles would later become part or all of the states of Arizona, Colorado, Nevada, Utah, and Wyoming.

It was a bitter episode for Mexico. As the Mexican officer Manuel Balbontín later reflected, the problems facing the nation were many, but it was not aided by a "misunderstood national pride and an inconsiderate contempt for our neighbors."[207] A Mexican history of the conflict published soon afterward concurred but laid much of the blame on "the spirit of aggrandizement of the United States of the North, having used its power to conquer us."[208]

A year later, in his December 1848 annual message, Polk told Congress that "we may congratulate ourselves that we are the most favored people on the face of the earth," adding that "the United States are now estimated to be nearly as large as the whole of Europe."[209] He went on to reveal even better news regarding California: there were gold mines in this new territory, and one "is believed to be among the most productive in the world."[210] By the time Spaniards colonized and then lost California, the early conquistadores' dreams of the Seven Cities of Cíbola had long since faded, but its wealth had been sitting in the ground all along.

———

IN THE GROUNDS of the Tennessee State Capitol in Nashville, there is a modest tomb sheltered by a small roof supported by four Doric pillars and ringed by flowers, accessible to any inquisitive passerby. On one side, the tomb of James K. Polk and his wife, Sarah, bears an inscription that "by his public policy he defined, established and extended the boundaries of his Country." It was moved there in 1901 from the city cemetery, and while this seems like an idyllic resting spot, it is eclipsed by another nearby monument, one to Andrew Jackson, who sits tall upon a rearing iron horse. The entire site is on a hill, so Jackson—waving his hat in triumph—can see the city of Nashville, and by extension the South and the nation, below. Polk's tomb is off to the side, under the shade of two trees.

Despite adding millions of acres to the United States and in the process working himself to an early death in 1849, Polk remains an unpopular—or, worse, forgotten—president. His war was overshadowed by the civil conflict to come, and his mentor, Jackson, had died in 1845. This period is often cast as the warm-up to, or sometimes the cause of, the Civil War that started in 1861. Indeed, many of the military leaders in the Mexican-American War would participate, including Scott, Ulysses S. Grant, Robert E. Lee, and Jefferson Davis.[211] Grant, reflecting on the Mexican war in his memoirs, called it "one of the most unjust ever waged by a stronger nation against a weaker nation."[212] The two conflicts between Mexico and the United States defined the first half of the nineteenth century and finally set a physical boundary between the two republics, but also established cultural and emotional divisions.

In the wake of the violence that washed over the borderlands, a scattering of heroes and monuments remains. Of all of these, the Alamo continues to loom far larger in myth than the diminutive structure itself. Its legend was planted at the time, with letters like the one William Barret Travis wrote while in the fort, addressed to "the People of Texas and all Americans in the world." In the brief missive he merged the Texian struggle with the future of the United States, calling on those who read it "in the name of Liberty, of patriotism and every thing dear to the American character, to come to our aid." He also established the heroic status of those involved in the battle, ending the letter, "I am determined . . . to die like a soldier who never forgets what is due his own honor and that of his country. Victory or death."[213] At the Alamo, which remains the "shrine of Texas liberty" and where the heroism of the defeated is much discussed, the slavery that underpinned these events receives scarcely a mention.

Despite the fact that San Jacinto was the site of a Texan victory, it receives far fewer visitors. The road that leads there from Houston is dotted with oil refineries and lined with train tracks, though the large obelisk marking the battlefield is set in an oasis of green space facing a rectangular pool, and resembles the Washington Monument. Con-struction on the memorial started in 1936, on the centenary of Texan independence, and it opened three years later. An engraving on one side of the plinth describes San Jacinto as "one of the decisive battles of the world." In an even more remote site, on the Brazos River, Stephen Aus-tin, seated on a marble base, looks out over the settlement he founded, where the episode began. San Felipe remains small, with a population of around 760.

Much smaller still is a memorial to Juan Seguín. After the war, he returned to Texas and its turbulent politics. He published a memoir in 1858 defending his actions and trying to clear his name, reminding readers: "I embraced the cause of Texas at the sound of the first can-non. . . . I now find myself exposed to the attacks of scribblers and personal enemies."[214] He stayed in Texas for many years before moving to Nuevo Laredo, Mexico, where one of his sons lived. A 1887 inter-view with him in the *Clarksville Standard* described the then eighty-year-old as looking young enough to "easily pass now for a man of sixty," except for his white hair, with a "countenance indicating firmness and gentleness of heart."[215] He died a few years later, in 1890. His remains were returned to Texas and reinterred with honors on July 4, 1976, in Seguin, where his headstone describes him as a "Texas patriot." A painting of Seguín, dated around 1838, hangs in Washington, D.C., at the National Portrait Gallery, where the accompanying tag describes him as the only survivor of the Alamo and a "hero of the Texas War of Independence" before explaining his change in fortunes and his return to Mexico "where the government forced him to fight on its side" in the Mexican-American War.

Heroes were not restricted to the United States. Inside the rambling Chapultepec Castle in Mexico City is a room devoted to the events of 1846–48, complete with depictions and explanations of the battle there. Among those memorialized are Colonel Felipe Santiago Xicoténcatl, who died defending the castle's entrance, while inside were six young men, all cadets at the military school. They ranged in age from just out of childhood—Francisco Márquez (thirteen) and Vicente Suárez (fifteen)—to young adulthood: Fernando Montes de Oca (eighteen), Juan de la Barrera (nineteen), Agustín Melgar (eighteen), and Juan Escutia (twenty). These young heroes, *los niños héroes*, died with valor when the U.S. troops stormed the castle. According to one legend, Escutia did not want the flag to fall into U.S. hands, so he wrapped himself in it and jumped off the side of the hill to certain death. In the room, commemorative portraits of the young men in their uniforms, with solemn faces and knowing eyes, are arranged along two sides with the flag of the Battalion of San Blas centered behind them. Outside the building, and at the bottom of the hill, sits an obelisk, erected in 1884, with the date of the battle and their names carved in the marble, with the castle hovering high above. Elsewhere in Chapultepec Park is a much grander twentieth-century memorial, ordered after the centenary of their death and completed in 1952. Six thin, white columns, arranged in a semicircle, reach into the air, while a statue of a woman in the center depicts her standing next to one young man and holding another, who is limp in her arms. The words "A los defensores de la patria (To the defenders of the country), 1846–1847," are inscribed underneath.[216]

Chapter 10

Mesilla, New Mexico, ca. 1850–77

THE MESILLA THAT German artist Carl Schuchard depicted in 1854 seemed like a forlorn place. His lithograph, published in 1856, shows a tiny hamlet positioned on a plain in southern New Mexico in front of the distant white-capped Organ Mountains, under a blue-gray sky. The scene is one of winter cold, with the trees bare and the ground yellowed. In Schuchard's portrayal, the village had around thirty small adobe dwellings, most with straw roofs, and no plaza or church in sight. Two women bundled against the winter huddled in the left corner of the work, while in the center, on a main street devoid of a general store or saloon, was a lone Mexican man, identifiable by his sombrero. Schuchard's other lithographs told a similar story—abandoned missions, such as that of San José de Tumacácori, or silent villages, like the former Spanish presidio of Tubac, where all that remained was a scattering of buildings and no sign of human habitation.

Schuchard was part of an 1854 survey for the Texas Western Railroad Company, from San Antonio to San Diego along the thirty-second parallel and winding into and out of northern Mexico. The survey's aim was to examine the feasibility of laying tracks through the region, and his resulting images gave the impression that there was little in this desolate landscape to prevent trains from barreling through. The Mesilla that Schuchard drew appeared to be a poor village struggling to thrive, yet the numbers tell a different story: its population reached an estimated two thousand the year before the surveyors arrived.[1]

Mesilla's past and future were inseparable from the Treaty of Guadalupe Hidalgo of 1848, when, for a brief time it was the center of the larger territorial adjustments taking place. The treaty had left many people upset and perplexed, and many Mexicans did not want to live in the United States. "Mexicans were reduced to the humiliating state of being strangers in their own land," was the feeling General José Mariano Salas expressed around this time, and thousands agreed. There is a saying in parts of the West that "we didn't cross the border, the border crossed us," and so some people elected instead to recross the border.

Under the terms of the treaty, Mexicans had a year to decide whether they wanted to keep their Mexican citizenship or automatically become U.S. citizens. Overall, around 150,000 decided to stay, but thousands left, a migration that had in fact started even before the war.[2] As early as the end of the Texas rebellion in 1836, local campaigns had driven out Mexican families in places such as Goliad.[3] Reports reached the Mexican consulate that people living near the town were being warned off by a U.S. general, who told the Tejanos to leave, unless they wanted to be "put to the knife." Around 100 families fled, arriving in New Orleans in July 1836.[4] After 1848, this type of behavior started to spill into the other territories ceded after the war, though it was less pronounced in New Mexico, owing in part to the smaller Anglo population. Of the 60,000 people in New Mexico around the time of the transfer, around 90 percent were Mexican, 5 percent Native American, and 5 percent Anglos and European immigrants.[5]

Some New Mexicans living near the Río Grande wanted to stay in Mexico, and so, using the boundaries stipulated in the treaty, they established a small town on what was now the Mexican side of the river and called it Mesilla. A few hundred people turned into a few thousand as the town grew, with its residents believing they were in Mexico—but they were about to have the map pulled out from underneath them.

The U.S.-Mexico border is not a straight line but rather a story of two halves. The first part of the boundary is Mexico's eastern edge with the United States, outlined by the Río Grande. The river then turns north at El Paso, reaching modern Colorado. Article V of the Guadalupe Hidalgo Treaty stipulated that to the west, the boundary would run along "the western line of New Mexico, until it intersects the first branch of the

River Gila" and from there follow the Gila until it joins the Colorado River, and then run along the division between Baja and Alta California. This was all based on the 1847 *Map of the United Mexican States, as Organized and Defined by Various Acts of Congress of Said Republic, and Constructed According to the Best Authorities*, by J. Disturnell. Although Disturnell's map was recently published, much of its data came from an 1822 map by Henry S. Tanner in Philadelphia, or even older sources. In addition, Disturnell was more a publisher than a cartographer, producing the map in response to public interest in the Mexican-American War, eventually releasing seven editions of it in 1847.[6] On the ground, no one was sure where the United States ended and Mexico began.

The surveyors of the Joint United States and Mexican Boundary Commission soon discovered mapping errors as they began their trek to draw a dividing line in 1849. These men had been charged with surveying and marking the border in line with the treaty, but heat, hostility from some Native Americans, logistical obstacles, and financial shortfalls made it impossible to demarcate the border in one trip. Progress was also slowed by the discovery of cartographic discrepancies. The Río Grande was more to the east than depicted on the Disturnell map, and, even worse, El Paso, the surveyors calculated, was off by 34 miles to the south and 130 miles to the west.[7] Fixing this problem meant either ceding land to the United States, which would anger Mexicans, or following the treaty and what the existing map showed, which would leave the Mesilla valley in Mexico. Surveyors met in the middle in an agreement called the Bartlett-García Conde Compromise in 1850, making calculations based on a point on the Río Grande that allowed Mexico to keep a bit of land to the north and the United States to gain some to the west.[8] The commission finished in 1855—almost seven years later—after surveying 1,952 miles, and authoritative maps soon followed.[9]

Mesilla, for the moment, remained in Mexico, but the situation could not continue for long, because the flat Mesilla valley, created by the flood plain of the Río Grande, was an ideal place to lay train tracks. Pressure to expand the railways was mounting, fueled by the discovery of gold in California and the pressing need for quick transcontinental travel. In addition, there was a great deal of interest in copper and silver mining around the Santa Rita Mountains, also in Mexico. President Franklin

Pierce dispatched James Gadsden to negotiate with Mexico over the valley a short time later.

Gadsden was an early railroad baron who had connections across the southern United States, from California to Florida. He had served in the military under Andrew Jackson, fighting the Seminoles in Florida, and was charged with building what became Fort Gadsden on the site of the destroyed Negro Fort. After leaving the military, he moved to South Carolina and became involved with railways. Gadsden's dream involved running his lines to California on a southern route to San Diego, linking the slaveholding South to the new territories. Gadsden and his allies, including future Confederate president Jefferson Davis, made their case to President Franklin Pierce, who became convinced of the merits of the scheme, not least because it had the potential to appease southern states.[10]

Gadsden arrived in Mexico in 1853 with authorization to spend $50 million, and he made an offer for parts of the northern Mexican states of Chihuahua and Sonora, and most or all of Tamaulipas, Coahuila, Nuevo León, and Baja. Already bruised and frustrated, Mexican officials refused the plans.[11] In any case, such a large addition would have further exacerbated the concerns of abolitionists in the United States. The United States and Mexico agreed instead on a payment of $10 million for a strip of land south of the Gila River and west of the Río Grande—the southern part of modern Arizona and New Mexico—of around thirty thousand square miles. Signing the December 30, 1853, deal for Mexico was Santa Anna, who was back from exile and enjoying another of his nine political lives as president. He was in need of money—the war had been expensive and Mexico was in debt—and willing to negotiate over a more realistic offer. He also wanted to avoid another conflict with the United States.[12]

Although Santa Anna ceded little in the Gadsden Purchase, many Mexicans were outraged. Not only did Mexico lose even more land, but as part of the deal the United States no longer had to help prevent Indian raids in the territory, an important issue where Apache attacks were still common. Indeed, many of the Native Americans in the former Mexican lands had not acknowledged that country's authority and were unlikely to do so for the United States.[13] This new border cut through the lands of many nations, including the Tohono O'odham. Some had met and extended hospitality to the earlier group of surveyors as they were working their way west, while other groups paid them little mind, but all of the Native Americans in the borderlands would at some point be forced to confront the line drawn by these interlopers.[14]

The purchase included Mesilla, which saw the border move across it, tipping it into U.S. control. On November 16, 1854, troops raised the U.S. flag over Mesilla Plaza.[15] Today it is a suburb to the southwest of Las Cruces, but it retains its village feel. A small bandstand in the main square has the flags of both nations painted on it, with an *M* above and a "54" below. On the other side of the structure is the city seal illustrated with a cross and mallet, and its motto "A Dios rogando y con el mazo dando": Pray to God and strike with your mallet, or, as the saying in English goes: Heaven helps those who help themselves.

⌣

IF DETERMINING THE actual boundary line was the first matter of concern after Guadalupe Hidalgo, the second was to determine who owned the land in the parts ceded to the United States. The Mexicans had built upon the Spanish precedent of land grants, but the majority of these were around the settled areas of California, Texas, and New Mexico, although some stretched into places that would become Colorado, Utah, and Nevada. While the treaty stipulated that such grants would be respected, potential Anglo settlers had their suspicions—and hopes—that they might not be. Thousands of acres had not been surveyed and the U.S. government now needed to determine which lands were public. Nowhere was this land question more pressing than in gold rush California.

The lure of riches pulled in people not only from the eastern United States but from all over the world. Even before the famed "forty-niners," many Mexicans, Peruvians, and Chileans, who had experience in Latin American mines, arrived in California. They were joined by fortune hunters from Europe and East Asia. As the waves of people rushed into California, their force transformed the landscape. Military or mission outposts such as San Francisco became urban centers, as saloons, shops, bordellos, and boardinghouses mushroomed.

The competition to find the mother lode was fierce, and U.S. miners were quick to complain about the foreign prospectors. By 1850, California introduced a tax that required any miner who was not a U.S. citizen to pay a license fee of $20 a month. This led to immediate protests, and it was rewritten the following year, this time exempting white Europeans but not Mexicans or other Latin Americans. Instead, they were objects of assaults and even lynchings in the aftermath of what was known as the "Great Greaser Extermination Meeting" held in the summer of 1850 by Anglos in Sonora. As a result, the number of Hispanic miners dropped from fifteen thousand in 1849 to around five thousand by the end of the following year.[16] The Native American population fared badly as well, plummeting to thirty thousand by the 1870s.[17] Many California Indians were pushed off their land by speculators or prospectors, or exploited as workers in the mines. Legislation was aimed at their displacement—Indians who were "loitering" could be pressed into a work gang for months at a time.[18] At the same time, some five hundred thousand migrants flooded into California between 1848 and 1870, most of them white settlers from elsewhere in the United States, especially the Northeast and Midwest.[19]

Amid the spectacular growth and radical transformation of California, the question of statehood quickly arose. By 1849 all of the necessary articles were in place, including a governor and legislature. A constitution had been drawn up, which made the crucial stipulation that the state would be free and prohibit slavery. When California brought all of this to the attention of Washington for confirmation, it provoked a political crisis. Another bargain was struck, once more brokered by Henry Clay, and known as the Compromise of 1850. This was a series of measures that allowed California to join the union as a free state but created territorial governments in Utah and New Mexico, which at this point included Arizona, with no mention of slavery. The other parts of the compromise abolished the slave trade in the District of Columbia, although slavery itself was still permitted in the capital. To appease southerners, the controversial Fugitive Slave Act was passed, requiring free citizens in any part of the country to aid in the recovery of runaway slaves. After these deals were made, California joined the union on September 9, 1850.

Gold was not the sole interest in California: fortunes were being made in land speculation as well. Henry Cerruti arrived in Monterey on January

27, 1847, as a surgeon with the U.S. military, when the territory was still on the brink of many of these changes. Even then, Cerruti was able to observe that "shortly after the Treaty of Guadalupe Hidalgo was signed, their [Californios'] herds and lands increased in value one hundred fold. . . . Unaccustomed to the sharp trading of the newcomers they were soon relieved of their lands by selling them very cheap."[20] He was not surprised to find that the Californios were now a "hostile people, contented and happy previous to the advent of the Anglo Saxon ruling territory."[21]

California, at the time of the 1848 treaty, had more than ten million acres under Spanish or Mexican land grants.[22] Two issues now loomed: the validity of these grants, and the arrival of squatters. The military governor Stephen Watts Kearny pledged that under U.S. administration the Californios' rights and property would be protected. Despite being "now but one people," many Californios and foreigners who had earlier been granted land remained wary.[23] Letters expressing concern soon landed on the desk of Kearny and his successor, Richard Barnes Mason.[24] Pierre Sainsevain, a Frenchman who owned land around Santa Cruz, soon saw the arrival of squatters on his property. Mason heard Sainsevain's complaints, agreeing that "those persons who have no claim to land adjoining this Frenchman should not be permitted to intrude within the claimed boundaries."[25] The sentiment might have been reassuring, but there was little Mason could do to enforce it. Thousands of these "squatter" migrants who arrived in California brought with them the belief that they were entitled to land now that it was part of the United States. In addition, many were supporters of Free-Soil sentiments and considered the earlier Mexican system as semifeudal and, correspondingly, of Indians and Mexicans as unfree, nonwhite labor.[26] The squatters looked to the legal system to support their views, arguing that the Mexican land distribution system was a relic of an older order that gave power to the wealthy through the concentration of landowning. One prospector wrote in 1850 that the recognition of the Mexican grants would place "the multitude at the mercy of the few, engrafting in fact the peon system of Mexico or the feudal tenure of Europe upon our republican institutions in California . . . a state of things to which our Anglo-Saxon race are strangers."[27] It was an argument the courts had agreed with, in part because of the Preemption Act of 1841, which, in theory, allowed squatters to buy the land they had been working from the federal government at the minimum price. However, the existing land grants in California meant that the land was not yet public and could not be sold.

At first, some squatters staked out land for gold prospecting, while others chose to farm, drawing from the earlier precedent of "improving" the land and thus having a right to it.[28] Growing demand meant that land speculation in itself could be lucrative, aided by an overall lack of reliable surveys. The squatters erected fences, built makeshift dwellings, and tried to establish their right to the land through filing preemption claims.[29] In doing so, they stoked the growing anger of the Californios whose land they occupied. Their behavior also provoked other Anglo settlers and, at times, the government, both of whom often disapproved of the squatters' methods.[30] At various points throughout the 1850s and into the early 1860s violent clashes erupted between squatters and the authorities, as in 1850 in Sacramento, and in 1861 in San Jose.[31]

In 1851 Congress passed the California Land Act, turning the question—and, in theory, any unclaimed land—over to the state. A Board of Land Commissioners was established, in front of which people would have to produce the required paperwork to prove the validity of their grant, be it from Spain or Mexico. Similar processes had been employed in settling land grant questions in other former Spanish territories, such as Louisiana and Florida.[32] In California, people had two years to produce their claim, or the property would become public.[33] The board had some eight hundred grants to wade through, and there was also an appeals process, which reached all the way to the U.S. Supreme Court.[34] It was a confusing and distressing process, not least because of legal and language barriers. Defending a claim could take years, and doing so left very few people with their full initial holdings.[35] Lawyers were expensive and many poorer grant holders—especially within the Native American communities—had little choice but to sell all their land just to pay their legal fees. Even wealthier landowners could not escape losing some property.

By 1854, the courts had ruled that land grants in California were different from those in Spanish territories east of the Mississippi, and this precedent was made concrete in the U.S. Supreme Court decision that

December involving the large grant of John C. Frémont. He had bought the tract, Las Mariposas, from Juan Alvarado in 1847, as the Treaty of Guadalupe Hidalgo was awaiting ratification. It had been a Mexican grant area but its boundaries were never precisely surveyed. The terms of Alvarado's Mexican grant meant he was supposed to live on and work the land, and not sell it, though he ignored these provisions. When Frémont went in front of the land commission in 1852, his case prompted a number of legal questions about Mexican law, customs, and actual use of the land. In the end, the Supreme Court came down on the side of Frémont, ruling that his 44,787-acre grant was valid, and in doing so protected the interests of other large landholders, preventing their territory from being ceded to the public domain and into the hands of squatters.[36]

The land commission continued to process the more than eight hundred claims brought in front of it into the 1870s. In the end, around six hundred grants were confirmed, covering more than eight million acres.[37] Some 47 percent of the claimants were Anglo—and yet only 17.7 percent were original Anglo grantees, meaning the grants had often already passed from Californio to Anglo hands before being confirmed by the board.[38] To Pablo de la Guerra, a politician and judge, the matter had long been clear, and it was about more than land. Californios had become "foreigners in their own country."[39]

CALIFORNIOS, AS WELL as other Mexicans who were now American, spent much of the late nineteenth century trying to understand what a future in the United States might hold. One such Californio was Francisco P. Ramírez, who edited *El Clamor Público*, a Los Angeles–based publication that was the first Spanish-language newspaper to appear in California after the U.S. occupation. His editorials highlighted the injustices that were becoming part of everyday life for Mexican Californians. "Since the year of 1849," he wrote in 1855, "a certain animosity (so contrary to a magnanimous and free people) has existed between the Mexicans and Americans, to such an extent that the Americans have wished with all their heart that all the Mexicans put together had no more than one head to cut off (to do away with them all at once)."[40]

Ramírez was only eighteen years old when he began publishing the weekly paper in the summer of 1855, but he already had some experience with newspapers. He was a true Californio—his grandparents had settled around the Santa Barbara mission in the late eighteenth century, later moving to Los Angeles, where Ramírez was born in 1837, the fourth of thirteen children. Although his mother was from the prominent Ávila family in the city, he did not have much in the way of formal education, but he had learned English and French. By 1851 Ramírez was working as a compositor at the *Los Angeles Star* before moving to San Francisco in 1853 to work on the *Catholic Standard*, one of sixteen papers in the city at the time. The following year he returned to Los Angeles and was appointed editor of a Spanish-language page in the *Los Angeles Star*, transforming it into a popular section.[41]

He would witness the metamorphosis of the village of Los Angeles into a bustling city. In 1850, it had a population of only sixteen hundred, but by the early decades of the next century it soared to over a million.[42] He experienced the arrival of not just Anglos but people from all over the world, and saw at first hand the difficulties of the transition to U.S. statehood, as Californios attempted to realign their social and political status.

Inspired by *El Clamor Público* (The Public Outcry) of Madrid, Spain, he chose this name for his four-page publication.[43] One particular complication from the start was that Californios—his intended audience—were not a uniform group. The wealthy landowners and the poorest workers did not necessarily share his politics, and there was also the small middle class of merchants and farmers, of which Ramírez was a part. These groups all faced the discrimination directed against them at times, but the wealthier and more powerful Californios had a better chance of insulating themselves from the worst abuses.

In the same vein, the Anglo newcomers did not agree on the national issues of the day, including slavery. Although California was a free state, it had lured many people from the southern slaveholding areas, some of whom had arrived before statehood. They formed alliances with prominent Californios, drawn together by shared interests in landownership and in maintaining a certain social order.[44] These men were Democrats, and their faction was known as the "Chivalry." The Democrats had gained power in California, and in addition to the Chivalry, they had some initial success in courting the support of the squatters in the early 1850s.[45]

In addition to politics, with many of the southerners continuing to advocate the spread of slavery into the West, their Californio allies also took part in lynchings and other vigilante activity.[46] It was an alliance Ramírez loathed. He was very clear in his opposition to slavery and the hypocrisy that underpinned it, writing in one 1855 editorial that "very little is known here in California of the strange amalgam that appears in the United States for the liberty of individuals and associates, and the slavery of the black race. . . . Here in America, among a people so proud of their government, they do not care much for moral delicacy."[47] Ramírez may have seen enslaved people himself, given that around one thousand were brought by white owners from the South to California around the time of the gold rush.[48] Some of the slaves were used in mining, or hired out, with some owners claiming they were "servants."[49] The state even passed its own 1852 Fugitive Slave Act, under which all runaway slaves would be sent back to their masters, crushing any hope that this westernmost state could be a place of freedom. It also allowed owners in California to continue to keep hold of their slaves, or legally remove them from the state.[50]

Although Ramírez was from a privileged background, he struggled with the elite Californios, especially those who aligned with the pro-slavery Democrats. His liberal opinions on issues such as slavery often angered or offended more conservative readers.[51] In addition to national issues, Ramírez covered topics that he felt should be important to the Californio community, including the death of many Mexicans at the hands of vigilante mobs, the ongoing land issue, and the growing awareness of their social persecution. He directed his ire at measures like the 1855 Vagrancy Act, better known as the "Greaser" Act, because it targeted Mexicans as well as Native Americans. Under this statute, anyone found "loitering" risked arrest and possible forced labor. Writing about the act, he said such laws "have no equal in the annals of any civilized nation," lamenting that the legislation "has served to widen the barrier that has existed for some time between foreigners and natives."[52]

Law and order issues affected the poorest Mexicans, but Ramírez failed to attract them as readers, in part because many were illiterate, and his paper folded in December 1859. In his final editorial Ramírez wrote, with palpable disappointment, that his purpose had been "the defense of the moral and material interests of Southern California; and speaking without reservation and with sincerity, my object was almost only to dedicate myself to the service of my native California compatriots, and generally of all Hispanic Americans."[53]*

———— ~ ————

In Texas, the land issue had an extra level of complication. The original draft of the Treaty of Guadalupe Hidalgo had included Article X, which protected existing land grants, including Texas. James Polk, who was still president, demanded that the article be deleted before the treaty could be ratified. Sam Houston, then a senator for Texas, moved that the Senate debate the matter in secret, and there is no account of what was said in the chamber.[54] The then secretary of state, James Buchanan, insisted that "if the grantees of lands in Texas, under the Mexican government, possess valid titles, they can maintain their claims before our courts of justice."[55] Mexican officials wanted clarification on the matter. This led to the creation of the Protocol of Querétaro, which stipulated that the United States had no intention of annulling any land grants made by Mexico in the ceded territories. The second article of the protocol said that legitimate titles "existing in the ceded territories, are those which were legitimate titles under the Mexican law in California and New Mexico up to the 13th of May 1846, and in Texas up to the 2d March 1836."[56] Polk had not been happy with this result, and he did not present the protocol along with the treaty when it went before the Senate for ratification.

For many Tejanos, the matter was not clarified until the 1856 Supreme Court case *McKinney v. Saviego*, which ruled that the 1848 Treaty of Guadalupe Hidalgo did not apply to Texas, making the Querétaro agreement invalid. This meant that Texas was seen as separate from the Mexican cession, in part because in 1836 it had declared its independence—which

---

* Ramírez continued to be involved in politics and journalism for much of his life, until he was accused of bank fraud many years later, at which point he left for Ensenada, a small town in Baja California about two hundred miles south of Los Angeles, and lived there until his death in 1908.

Mexico never recognized—and in 1845 it was admitted as a state. The state's constitution had not allowed "aliens," including any Tejanos who left during the rebellion, to hold property.[57] Mexican governments and legal experts ended up fighting this interpretation of the law well into the twentieth century. Some of the wealthy ranching families in south Texas managed to hang on to their land through a combination of money, political influence, and intermarriages, though less fortunate Tejanos were left with nothing.[58]

This land question arose in a time of growing animosity. Anglos continued to cast Mexicans as decadent, conservative, oppressed by tradition, mixed-blood "degenerates," lazy, and dirty, with the added irritation of not speaking English. One account of a journey through Texas published in 1879 in *Harper's New Monthly* described coming upon the "Mexican or 'greaser' element" in San Antonio, whom the author portrays as being "not inclined to assimilate their customs and modes to those of whites, but persist in sombreros, slashed breeches, and ornamental buttons *ad infinitum.*"[59] Such stereotypes were also put to use in challenging the legitimacy of Mexican-American citizenship. Although the Treaty of Guadalupe Hidalgo stipulated that citizenship be transferred to all people in the new territories, its application would not be so straightforward. Under Mexican law, mestizos and Indians were citizens. This did not mean they escaped social and economic prejudice, but they were entitled to Mexican citizenship.[60] In the United States, however, full citizenship was reserved for free white people. A problem officials now faced was that there was no legal racial vocabulary for Mexicans. They were neither "black" nor "white." Native Americans in this period were considered to be part of another "nation" and were excluded, though underpinning this were racialized ideas as well.

The California constitution of 1849, for instance, stipulated that "every White male citizen of the United States, and every White male citizen of Mexico, who shall have elected to become a citizen of the United States . . . shall be entitled to vote at all elections which are now or hereafter may be authorized by law." The forty-eight delegates in charge of drawing up the constitution at the 1849 convention had an average residency in California of two years, and only eight were Californios. Their definition of "white" remained ambiguous, though the document's exclusion of black or Indian people was clear.[61] The problem came in judging the mestizo population, who constituted the majority of Mexican Californians. No one knew what a "white Mexican" was, and no law specified how that was to be determined.[62] In some areas this left mestizos claiming their "Spanish" heritage in order to be granted whiteness, while Indians often claimed to be mestizo so they could claim citizenship.[63]

Ideas about whiteness were also supported by racial pseudoscience, fueled by the growing social Darwinism of the nineteenth century. Nativist vitriol directed at immigrants intensified in the 1840s and 1850s, triggered in part by the arrival of some three million Europeans in the United States between 1845 and 1854.[64] Groups like the Know-Nothings espoused anti-immigrant and often anti-Catholic sentiments, which would also feed into ideas about Hispanics. Their Catholicism was considered suspect and at odds with the Protestant Anglo-Saxon culture that dominated political and cultural life east of the Mississippi River.[65] Whereas whiteness was linked to "civilization" and productivity, brown Mexicans were always cast as "lazy" and backward. In addition, Anglos were threatened by the fact that Mexican-Americans and Indians often lived within their own communities, and by concerns that black people might "mix" with these groups in the West.[66]

The New Mexico territory initially extended full rights to the Pueblo Indians, under the terms of the 1848 treaty. This was gradually stripped away over the subsequent years, as more Anglos arrived in the region and there were legal challenges over the Pueblos' status, culminating in an 1876 Supreme Court decision that overturned their right to citizenship.[67] Once Arizona became a territory separate from New Mexico in 1863, it, too, passed laws similar to California's, limiting the political participation of Mexicans and Native Americans.[68] Likewise, Texas granted citizenship to "white" Mexicans, forcing any Mexican arriving in Texas after 1845 to somehow prove his of her "whiteness."[69]

The flip side of racial division was the question of assimilation. Californios, New Mexicans, and Tejanos were forced in many ways to adapt to these changes, not least by speaking English and coming to terms with life in the United States. What was often a painful transformation appeared to some outsiders as a natural progression rather than a necessary suppression. One such observer was J. H. Watts, an Anglo who left for New Mexico in 1857, when he was eighteen. His father, John Sebrie Watts, had served as a judge there from 1851 until 1854. To the younger Watts, it appeared that New Mexico had experienced profound changes in a short time, in part due to the Anglos and German immigrants who had moved there. In little more than twenty years, he said, the atmosphere had changed radically:

> The feeling against the American population was very strong when I went there. It is not so now. The Mexicans have become thorough Americans now. They say that we are a superior race, and that they have to conform to our manners & customs, & they are satisfied that the American government is better for them than any Mexican government would be . . . the generation which has now come up is Americanized, & speaks English rather fluently, especially the half breeds.[70]

Yet such assimilation was often not enough. It took the ruling in *In re Rodriguez* in Texas in 1897 to reaffirm the right of all Mexicans in Texas to be full citizens. The case had been brought in 1896—the same year that segregation in *Plessy v. Ferguson* was upheld by the Supreme Court—by Ricardo Rodríguez, who was born in Mexico.[71] He wanted U.S. citizenship, which would allow him to vote, but was denied it on the grounds that he was an "Indian" and thus not eligible. The argument against him invoked rulings supporting the claim that the Fourteenth Amendment, which granted citizenship to anyone born or naturalized in the United States, applied only to black and white people, and, based on his physical appearance, under which "he may be classed with copper-colored or red men," Rodríguez was neither. Nor did he appear to be a true Indian, according to the judge, because "he knows nothing of the Aztecs or Toltecs."[72] The ruling, rather than contesting this interpretation of race or ethnicity, instead turned to the Treaty of Guadalupe Hidalgo. If Mexicans in the ceded territory had been "whitened" to be made into citizens in the aftermath of 1848, then the same right could be extended toward Mexican immigrants. While the ruling went some way toward securing the right to naturalize, it only further muddied the question of whiteness.[73]

These legal and cultural ambiguities meant that the former Mexicans were granted U.S.—that is, federal—citizenship, but this did not necessarily mean they would be granted full rights in states such as Texas or California, or equal access to public services.[74] For instance, in 1855 the state legislature in California appropriated school funds in proportion to the number of white children. Three years later, a series of bills segregated schools, with Anglo children put in separate facilities from black, Hispanic, Indian, and Chinese children. This culminated in the California School Law (1870), which was aimed at the growing Chinese community but affected all nonwhite children.[75] It would take decades and many more court battles to desegregate California's schools.

These states also failed to protect their residents from harm. Mexican Texans or Californians were often forced to reckon with vigilante justice, with little interference from people who were supposed to defend them. In Texas, Mexicans confronted increasing hostility from Anglos, including seizure of their property. People who were unwilling to bow to demands could find a violent resolution awaiting them.[76] From 1848 until 1928 at least 597 known lynchings of Mexicans occurred—though estimates range into the thousands—and people lived in fear of mob violence.[77] These killings also occurred in places where there was little oversight by law enforcement or, indeed, active collusion.[78] This was not unique to Texas, though it had the highest number of such killings in this period, with 232, to California's 143 and New Mexico's 87. The others were spread around neighboring states and territories.[79]

One of the most infamous mob killings took place in California, its victim a woman known as Juana Loaiza and also called Juanita, though later identified as Josefa Segovia. She was living with her partner, though it is not clear if they were married, in Downieville, California, a settlement in the northern gold rush territory. This was a tough place for anyone, man or woman. In 1850 the ratio was around twelve men to each woman, and these mining camps could be places of rough-and-tumble frontier living.[80] Some women were wives of the miners, others cooks or housekeepers, and some engaged in prostitution, though the threat of sexual violence stalked all women there.[81] Segovia had outraged the community by killing an Anglo miner with a knife after he tried to attack her at home. A vigilante committee ignored claims that she was pregnant and that she was defending her honor, and she was sentenced to death by hanging in July 1851. According to one account, she "walked alone with her head held high" to the gallows where she proceeded to put the noose on herself, saying, *"Adiós, señores"* to the assembled crowd.[82]

Retribution for these abuses could be swift and just as fierce. One Mexican who fought back in Texas was the "Red Robber of the Río Grande," Juan Nepomuceno Cortina Goseacochea, also known as Cheno Cortina or Juan Cortina. He was born in Camargo, Tamaulipas, in 1824, but his family later moved to Matamoros. He fought against the United States at the battles of Palo Alto and Resaca de Palma during the Mexican-American War. Before 1848, Cortina's family owned a sizable amount of land, including his ranch, San José. The war's aftermath changed Cortina's world, and he angrily pointed out, "I never signed the Treaty of Guadalupe Hidalgo."[83]

Land was at the heart of Cortina's grievances, both with the treaty and with the Anglos who arrived in the Río Grande valley, but the treatment of Tejanos also enraged him. His family had ended up, like many others, in complicated and costly land dealings. In Brownsville, established just after the end of the Mexican-American War, a group of speculators tried to lure Tejanos into their plans to create a Río Grande Territory separate from Texas. The scheme was soon tangled in controversy and collapsed, but not before many Tejanos had signed away their land.[84]

At the same time, there was a lot of agitation over trade. The high Mexican tariffs had led to a rise in smuggling, and to calls for a small free trade zone, which was set up in 1858. It stretched from the mouth of the Río Grande westward into cities in Tamaulipas, including Matamoros and Reynosa, going about twelve miles into the interior.[85] On the U.S side, Brownsville became a center of this trade, and the town began to boom, with its population already hitting three thousand only a few years after its founding in 1848. Alongside this grew a political machine, one that used Tejanos for their votes but for the most part kept them out of office. As an 1856 issue of the newspaper *American Flag* put it: "An hour before the election they are fast friends, 'Mexicans, my very good friends'—and an hour after the election they were a 'crowd of greasers.'"[86]

Cortina watched these changes with increasing ire, as Brownsville attracted more outsiders ready to buy up land and discriminate against Tejanos. His temper snapped on a hot July day in 1859, after he saw the town's marshal beat a Mexican man who had worked for Cortina's mother. Cortina killed the officer after he refused to release the worker. Then, on September 28, Cortina and around seventy Tejano men thundered into Brownsville on their horses in the early hours of the morning, with cries of *"¡Viva México!"* and *"¡Mueran los gringos!"* (Death to the gringos!). Their anger over bitter land disputes and other abuses fueled the attack on their long-standing Anglo enemies.[87] A number of battles followed, later called the Cortina Wars, which lasted for a decade. Cortina and his *cortinista* followers took on the U.S. Army, the Texas Rangers, militias, and later even Confederate soldiers.[88] He also continued to raid cattle along the border and was arrested in Mexico in 1875 and again in 1877, when he was taken to the capital, found guilty, and sentenced to be executed, though a last-minute presidential reprieve saved him, and he died instead of natural causes at the age of seventy, in 1894.[89]

THE WEST REMAINED a political preoccupation throughout the 1850s, as people began to migrate to these new territories, which had yet to be organized into states. A number of bills concerning homesteading were put forward and in 1853, the Democratic senator Stephen Douglas proposed legislation that would become the Kansas-Nebraska Act. Under the prevailing idea of "popular sovereignty," settlers in these two territories would be allowed to decide for themselves whether to allow slavery. This part of the territory was north of the line established by the Missouri Compromise, which would be violated by a vote in favor of slavery. The 1854 bill split the Whig Party, with southern members voting for it, and northerners against, leaving the party in tatters. Southerners ended up joining the Democratic Party, and northern Whigs signed up for the new Republican Party.[90]

Around the same time, some adventurous—if not foolhardy—men had been looking much farther south for new areas to expand slavery into. They were known as filibusters, an adaptation of the Dutch word *vrijbuiter*, or pirate, and as *filibusteros* in Spanish.* These men were land pirates, launching expeditions in search of territory. They acted without any official sanction—as many of the Anglo "adventurers" had done in Texas in the 1830s—and, depending on the mission and the result, a blind eye was often turned to their exploits.

In 1851, a Venezuelan-born general, Narciso López, led an expedition from the United States to free Cuba from Spanish rule. Although most of Latin America was long independent by that point, this sugar island was not. It had continued to cling to Spain, in part out of fear of a slave rebellion. As the decades of the nineteenth century wore on, however, irritation with the colonial regime grew; many Cubans left the island and, from abroad, began to make plans for independence. Some wanted Cuba to be an independent republic; others wanted it to be annexed to the United States. The latter group enjoyed the support of southern slaveholders.

The U.S. government was also interested in the island; successive presidents had made offers to buy it, but Spain refused—Cuba's sugar exports were too valuable to forgo. In fact, Spain had been refusing for quite some time. As early as 1810, the envoy William Shaler was sent to "feel the pulse of Cuba" concerning the "incorporation of that island with the United States," though nothing came of the visit.[91] Later, Polk tried to buy the island for $100 million in 1848. Spain rejected the offer, but the idea that Cuba was a natural fit for the United States persisted. One senator, Mississippi's Albert Gallatin Brown, reflected the general sentiment of the slaveholding south: "I want Cuba, and I know that sooner or later we must have it. I want Tamaulipas, Potosí, and one or two other Mexican states; and I want them all for the same reason—for the planting and spreading of slavery."[92]

Men like López were willing to take matters into their own hands, but filibustering was a risky enterprise, in part because these were men the government could not—or did not want to—control, though sometimes it had to intervene. In López's case, when President Zachary Taylor heard of the initial scheme, he had the filibuster's ships seized in 1849.[93] The following year, López managed his first expedition in May, landing in the town of Cárdenas, where he raised the flag of free Cuba and

---

* This use of filibuster is not to be confused with the contemporary U.S. term, that is, a legislative tactic used to stall proceedings.

declared the town liberated. He and around six hundred men moved east toward Havana, with the town of Matanzas in their sights, as it was one of the hubs of the sugar industry. He was met with far less enthusiasm there, in part because the slave owners did not want a political rebellion to trigger a potentially more dangerous one by the slaves. Sensing the reluctance, López retreated to Key West, Florida.

Despite the initial failure, López was greeted as a hero by the southern slave owners, and he counted on politicians like John A. Quitman, a governor of Mississippi and veteran of the Mexican-American War, for support.[94] News of López's exploits spread from New Orleans around the country. The front page of the New Orleans Daily Crescent carried the headline: "Important from Cuba: The Invasion! Landing of Gen. Lopez."[95] López tried again the following year, landing just outside Havana. He had hoped to rally people upon his arrival but instead the expedition went quite wrong—he was captured and executed.

A couple of years later, in 1853, President Franklin Pierce offered $130 million in another unsuccessful attempt to buy the island. The following year a communiqué between U.S. diplomats was leaked from a conference in Ostend, Belgium, saying the United States "ought, if practicable, to purchase Cuba with as little delay as possible."[96] The island had become "an unceasing danger, and a permanent cause of anxiety and alarm" because Spain failed, in the eyes of the United States, to exercise sufficient control over it. Both the island and the United States were slaveholding societies, and this fed the diplomats' unease. The memo also echoed the fear that any sort of independence movement might lead to "a second St. Domingo [Haiti], with all its attendant horrors to the white race, and suffer the flames to extend to our own neighboring shores." The communiqué's final line noted that "we have already witnessed the happy results for both countries which followed a similar arrangement in regard to Florida."[97] The leak caused outrage in Cuba and Spain, and a diplomatic row for the United States.

One of the people in New Orleans who had been paying close attention to events in Cuba was a young newspaper editor named William Walker. Around the time of López's expeditions, Walker quit his job and headed west to try his hand at filibustering, later earning himself the nickname "gray-eyed man of destiny." His first targets were the Mexican territories of Baja and Sonora. On November 3, 1853, he and some forty-five men landed in La Paz, Baja, where he declared himself president of Lower California, abolishing duties and establishing the territory under the legal code of Louisiana, which would permit slavery.[98] He justified his actions by claiming that "the moral and social ties which bound it to Mexico, have been even weaker and more dissolute than the physical" and that to "develop of the resources of Lower California . . . it was necessary to make it Independent."[99]

The Mexican chargé d'affaires in the United States, Juan Nepomuceno Almonte, wrote to the U.S. secretary of state, William Marcy, expressing his outrage at these "scandalous proceedings." Almonte reminded Marcy that President Pierce had pledged in his most recent annual message to Congress that "he would use all the means at his command in order vigorously to repress any attempts that might be made within the territory of the United States for the purpose of arming illegal expeditions against the territory of friendly nations." He asked Marcy to "have the kindness to inform him, whether any measures have been adopted, on the part of the American government, for preventing the repetition and continuance of the piratical depredations, which have already begun to take place upon Mexican territory."[100]

The answer appeared to be negative, as Walker's scheme survived a few months longer, despite his trouble in controlling his ragtag band of soldiers. Mexican troops forced them back to the United States by the spring of 1854 and afterward Walker was tried for violating U.S. neutrality laws, though his acquittal was rushed through by slavery sympathizers. A small slap on the wrist did little to dampen his enthusiasm for filibustering, and he decided to go farther south. By 1855, Walker was inviting fellow filibusters and potential settlers to come to Nicaragua, luring "persons of thrift and industry" with promises of land grants and no duties on imported goods. After arriving in the Central American nation and becoming embroiled in local politics, Walker declared himself president, but his scheme soon collapsed and in 1860 he was shot dead in Honduras.

Still, the quest for northern Mexico continued. In 1857, President James Buchanan offered $15 million for parts of Chihuahua and Sonora, claiming that these more naturally belonged with the land already taken; they also contained mines and the course of the Colorado River, which flows into the Gulf of California. The offer was refused, and Mexico struggled to fortify its border with enough soldiers to effectively patrol it, while also trying to encourage more settlers to move there in order to create a stronger buffer against the United States.[101]

The attempts to obtain Cuba and parts of Mexico had been humiliating failures. Animosity between slave and free states finally exploded when shots were fired at Fort Sumter, South Carolina, on April 12, 1861. The Civil War was not limited to the eastern United States: Mexican-Americans in the West would find themselves drawn into this conflict, as would Californios. Some Hispanic soldiers sided with the Union and organized themselves into Company C of the First Battalion of Native Cavalry, which patrolled the Arizona and New Mexico territories, and the California Battalion of the Second Massachusetts Cavalry ended up in the heart of battle, fighting in Virginia.[102]

Slaveholding Texas, however, seceded from the Union on February 1, 1861. It was well positioned to trade with Mexicans along the border for arms and contraband goods; and the lands of northern Mexico could, in theory, later be taken in order to make real the ongoing fantasy of a southern slaveholding empire.[103] By the summer of 1861, the Confederacy's Lieutenant Colonel John R. Baylor had marched troops from El Paso up the Río Grande and into New Mexico, and on August 1, Mesilla found itself the capital of the Confederate territory of Arizona, formed of the half of New Mexico that lay south of the thirty-fourth parallel.[104]

A few years earlier, in 1859, the New Mexico territorial legislature had promulgated a slave code which included in its provisions that slaves were property and allowed for runaways to be captured. The measure was taken even though the black population was very small, hovering around one hundred, and mostly free. It may instead have been the several hundred Indians, some of whom had been captured and sold from other nomadic chiefdoms in the West, whom the legislature had in mind. These Indians, while officially free, labored under a system of debt peonage, which left them bonded to their owners in slave-like conditions.

However, there were no doubt larger political considerations—New Mexico's desired statehood—that factored into the creation of the code. It provided a way for New Mexican politicians to try to appeal to the existing racial order, presenting themselves as "white," through the code's measures, such as its prohibiting black people from marrying or even testifying against a "white" person in New Mexico.[105] Before the outbreak of war, the passage of the code attracted the support of southern congressmen, who in turn pledged to help New Mexico become a state.[106] Two years later, and with the Confederates now in New Mexico, the territory's legislature did an about-face, revoking the slave code and making clear its support of the Union in December 1861.[107]

The Confederacy was eyeing a further southwest extension, in part to secure supply routes from the West and in part to capture valuable goldfields; in response, the governor organized the Unionist First New Mexico Volunteers Infantry Regiment, and New Mexicans were quick to join, under the command of Kit Carson.[108]

On February 21, 1862, blue and gray met at the Battle of Valverde, with many losses on both sides. By March, the Confederates had taken Albuquerque and Santa Fe.[109] North and South soon met again at Glorieta Pass, from March 26 to 28, in one of the most significant battles of the western theater. Around twelve hundred Confederates were forced to retreat by thirteen hundred Union troops. The Union's success was in part due to a raid, led by Lieutenant Colonel Manuel Chavez, to set fire to a train of supply wagons. The Confederacy ended its occupation of New Mexico, and its ambition for western expansion.[110]

Tejanos and Mexicans in Texas were wary of the conflict, though some Hispanic people ultimately did end up with the Confederacy—an estimated 2,550 Tejanos fought on that side, while 958 joined the Union.[111] All over the West, including California, the Arizona territory, and the New Mexico territory, soldiers enlisted, and Hispanic names were found in regiments as near as Louisiana and as far away as Vermont.[112] Whichever side they were on, the estimated Hispanic soldier population of 10,000 to 20,000 faced ongoing Anglo suspicion, especially in the Southwest, of being disloyal or treasonous.

WHILE THE UNITED States was distracted by its Civil War, European powers returned to the Americas. Spain reannexed the Dominican Republic in 1861, after the island had suffered a number of internal conflicts, occupying it until 1865.[113] Around the same time, another

European intervention took place in Mexico, though this involved not its former colonial ruler, Spain, but rather the French. The Republic of Mexico owed millions in unpaid loans. Its woeful finances began with independence, as mining and agricultural output plummeted amid the years of warfare. It took decades—and lots of money from Britain and France—to regain a financial footing.[114] The Mexican-American War did little to remedy matters, and there had been more political changes in the decades that followed, including another civil conflict, known as the Reform War (1858–60), triggered by a series of new laws that stripped away ecclesiastical powers and confiscated Church property, causing resentments that were exacerbated by a new constitution in 1857 that did not make Catholicism the national religion.

The Conservatives, whose membership comprised the clergy, the military, and the wealthy, were quick to voice their opposition. The liberal president Ignacio Comonfort, who was elected in the summer of 1857 after serving as interim president since 1855, ended up dismissing Mexico's Congress by December. Soon afterward, a Conservative general, Félix María Zuloaga, sent Comonfort into exile and assumed the presidency. According to the constitution, however, the president of the supreme court—at that moment Benito Juárez—was the rightful successor. Now Juárez and his Liberal backers would have to fight for the presidency, and by 1858, the Reform War had begun.[115]

In the United States, an article in the *Democratic Review* commented on this crisis, blaming Mexico's problems not on religion or governance but on race: "She [Mexico] started with every chance in her favor except one—*her people were not white men—they were not Caucasians*. . . . There were a bad mixture of Spaniards, Indians, and negroes. . . . *Such men did not know how to be free:* they have not learned the lesson to this day." The piece further argued that "Mexico cannot govern herself . . . the time has come when it is as imperatively our duty—made so by Providence—to take control of Mexico."[116] Such words were rhetorical bluster, as there was little popular support, except among a few southern slaveholders, for any such involvement with Mexico. Yet articles such as this indicated a lingering contempt for Mexico.

The Reform War ended in 1860, with Juárez as president, but he faced numerous challenges. External pressure was now mounting from foreign lenders. Juárez, however, did not have the money to make debt repayments. Britain, France, and Spain wanted to seize the port of Vera-cruz so that they could continue to collect customs revenue. Rumors of an impending invasion of Mexico were moving through Europe, even prompting Karl Marx to thunder in a November 1861 *New York Daily Tribune* article that such an intervention would be "one of the most monstrous enterprises ever chronicled in the annals of international history."[117]

In the end France acted alone. Louis-Napoleon Bonaparte, as Emperor Napoleon III, saw a much bigger opportunity than simple debt collec-tion and a way for France to spread its influence in the Americas.[118] His plan involved placing a puppet monarch in charge of Mexico, and he found in the Austrian Habsburg Archduke Ferdinand Maximilian Joseph a naive and pliable candidate. This was not as far-fetched as it may now seem—some Conservatives within Mexico had been discussing, if not explicitly advocating, the return to monarchy since the 1840s.[119] They saw constitutional monarchy as a way to restore order after what they considered to be the failure of republican Liberal rule, as well as a means to protect their privileges and restore the Church's position. It was a vision of a return to a hierarchical, Catholic Mexico.

Around the same time, France, under Napoleon III, had been casting itself as part—and protector—of *l'Amérique latine*, a broad "Latin" Amer-ica that was composed of a "Latin race." This expression had already been in use, but the French adopted it with enthusiasm.[120] For France, the "Latin" connection was the common origin of the languages of France, Spain, and Portugal, and their Catholicism, which was considered to be as much a culturally unifying force as Protestantism was for the Anglo-Saxon world.[121] France's global ambitions had been reignited in this period, and they reached far beyond this "Latin" sphere, into places like Southeast Asia (French Indochina). In the Americas, the situation in Mexico provided a favorable opportunity to add to France's handful of Caribbean islands.

In 1862, Napoleon III sent around thirty thousand soldiers to Mexico to place the Austrian on its throne.[122] Juárez was not going to let this happen without a fight, and Mexico won a key victory in Puebla, on May 5, 1862, which was later commemorated by the holiday Cinco de Mayo. The French continued their advance and by June 1864 the Austrian had become Maximilian I, the emperor of Mexico, placed upon the "cactus throne." Angry about this turn of events in Mexico, the U.S. president Abraham Lincoln recalled the Union's minister there and refused to recognize the French-backed regime, while also sending more troops to Texas.[123]

The Confederates, however, welcomed the French arrivals. They held a series of talks that would have given them recognition by France in exchange for support in keeping Maximilian in power. One French pamphlet, written by Michel Chevalier, a leading proponent of France's "Latin" ideology, claimed that the purpose of the war had been "to aid the Mexicans in establishing, according to their own free will and choice, a government which may have some chance of stability."[124] Alongside this, France wanted to "oppose the absorption of Southern America by Northern America," as well as "oppose the degradation of the Latin race." Thus, to Chevalier, it was "the interests which compel France to sympathize with the Confederate States which have led our banners up to the walls of Mexico."[125]

With the Union victory in 1865, hundreds of Confederate soldiers left the South and headed to Mexico. One letter from Sterling Price—a general who had also fought in the Mexican-American War—spoke of the "greatest kindness" of the emperor in receiving him. Maximilian issued a decree that September allowing the ex-soldiers to settle around Veracruz, where five hundred thousand acres would be given over for the development of Confederate colonies.[126] Price settled in a place they named Cordova, some seventy miles from Veracruz, with the intention of planting coffee. He presented a glowing picture of his new life "in the best climate in the world," explaining that land cost only one dollar an acre and that he and other Confederates "are in high spirits and expect to make fortunes raising coffee."[127] It was an optimistic picture of a hard life; these settlements remained basic, and years passed before coffee beans could be harvested.[128]

Mexican public hostility toward the Austrian interloper had not dimmed, and he had a poor understanding of the country he was meant to govern. Maximilian sometimes backed liberal policies—such as not returning confiscated lands to the Catholic Church—to the consternation of the Conservatives who brought him to power.[129] Guerrilla warfare was continuous, aided by the covert sale of arms and ammunition from the United

States to Juárez and the Liberals.[130] A frustrated Napoleon III decided to pull his troops out of Mexico, taking nine thousand in the autumn of 1866 and the rest over the course of the following year. Facing the removal of the forces that propped up his regime, Maximilian considered abdication but decided to fight Juárez, backed by Mexican royalists who were outnumbered. Maximilian was captured and imprisoned by May 1867. He was tried for treason and executed by firing squad on June 19.[131]

Juárez returned to power and the Confederates in Mexico realized they had once again chosen the wrong side. Those who stayed in Mexico risked incurring the wrath of Juárez and attacks by his supporters, who wanted to rid the country of meddling foreigners. Many experienced raids or harassment from their angry Mexican neighbors. Most decided to leave, though a handful took their chances and stayed on.[132]

For the United States, the Maximilian episode compounded many negative ideas about Mexican politics. For many U.S. politicians, Mexico represented the antithesis of a functioning nation. By 1876, however, some people began to fear that the United States could suffer decades of similar turbulence, and this manifested itself in the brief "Mexicanization" panic. This was a shorthand and pejorative way of expressing the fear that the Civil War had weakened the nation to the point where it, like Mexico, might lurch from one internal conflict to the next.[133] The term also implied endless local corruption at the ballot box.[134] That year's November presidential election between the Republican Rutherford B. Hayes and the Democrat Samuel Tilden was disputed, and Hayes wasn't declared the winner until the following March. The presidential ballot had become mired in Reconstruction politics, with claims that black Republican voters in the South had been intimidated at the voting booth.

A December 1876 edition of the *Nation* called Mexicanization "a disease of which frequent fights over presidencies and chief-justiceships are but symptoms in its last and most aggravated stage."[135] Such problems were not limited to Mexico, the article argued: "Among the ways in which these habits are destroyed or the growth of them prevented is the practice of treating the political party opposed to your own as a band of criminals or conspirators against the government. This practice has been cultivated in France ever since 1790; it is firmly rooted in Mexican politics."[136]

Within the word "Mexicanization" was an implication that the forms of democracy in Mexico were somehow the result of an "inferior" people attempting to use an Anglo-Saxon model and failing—the concern now was that democracy in the United States was following suit.[137] The *Nation* piece went on to argue that the Reconstruction South "is Mexicanized . . . in the present dispute over the Presidency there are actually signs, not only that we have not cured the South, but that, by nursing and manipulating the South, we have ourselves caught the contagion."[138]

———

Two pieces of legislation that passed at the outset of the Civil War would have a significant influence once it was over. In May 1862, Abraham Lincoln signed the Homestead Act, which granted 160 acres to settlers who were prepared to work the land for five years. After the war, Union veterans could deduct the time of their service from the five-year period; this provision gave them an extra incentive to move and spurred a population boom in the West.[139]

The second important bill was the Pacific Railroad Act, passed in the same year, creating the Union Pacific Railroad Company to lay track west from Omaha, Nebraska, in order to connect with a line that the Central Pacific Railroad had built between Utah and Sacramento, California; such transcontinental transport was an important symbol at a time of disunity. Fifteen years later, the Southern Pacific completed a bridge over the Colorado River at Yuma, Arizona, a crucial step in its growing network connecting California with Texas and New Orleans.[140]

The trains proved an important catalyst in western development by fostering trade and making travel easier. Crossing the country before the era of transcontinental trains could be an endurance test. Willa Cather captured the epic nature of such journeys in her 1927 novel *Death Comes for the Archbishop*, set in the mid-nineteenth century just after the Mexican-American War. Undertaking the journey from Cincinnati, Ohio, to his post in New Mexico, Bishop Jean Marie Latour had no idea how to make it: "No one in Cincinnati could tell him how to get to New Mexico—no one had ever been there. Since young Father Latour's arrival in America, a railroad had been built from New York to Cincinnati; but there it ended. New Mexico lay in the middle of a dark continent." In the end, it took him almost a year, traveling on steamers via New

Orleans and Galveston.[141] Such arduous journeys would no longer be necessary. With the ease of rail transport, people from the East began to explore the West. It was now the future, the war-torn South the past. The essence of this western enthusiasm even found its way into everyday objects. The glassmakers Gillinder & Sons produced a range of pressed dishes decorated with motifs from the West, including such items as a marmalade jar with a kneeling Native American providing the handle, and other dishes adorned with images of buffalo and prairies.

People were also lured beyond the Mississippi River by economic prospects, including work in mining or on the railroads. Metal extraction remained a booming business as silver mines joined those of gold and copper.[142] Nevada, with its silver lode, had become a state in 1864.[143] Related to these economic developments was the invention of barbed wire, which would be in widespread use by the end of the century, allowing landowners and ranchers to demarcate and lay claim to boundaries with more certainty. Land could be marked, cattle better contained, property divided.

The trains began to run north and south, too. By late 1882, the Arizona and New Mexico Railway connected with the Sonora Railway, becoming the first line to cross the border with Mexico.[144] The shipping of goods and the movement of people became easier, and this led to economic expansion on both sides of the border. The trains transformed their surroundings, with all the tunneling, blasting, and clearing they required. They had a similar impact on the people, as towns sprang up and work moved away from ranching.

Alongside this, throughout the later decades of the nineteenth century battles broke out against Native Americans, who were trying to protect their lands from further incursion. This was the era of the Apache Wars and Geronimo, who became famous for his attacks on U.S. and Mexican forces. In 1876, the Native American victory at the Battle of Little Bighorn in the Great Plains acted as an impetus for the United States in its efforts to push Indians on to reservations, taking their land as more tracks were laid, mines dug, and buildings constructed throughout the West.

Some of the new towns that followed in the trains' paths straddled the U.S.-Mexico border, which was resurveyed starting in 1882. This time the old markers, which were often just piles of stones that had been ignored or dislodged, were replaced by new, standardized stone or iron columns that were at least six feet tall, set at roughly five-mile intervals. However, these border towns could prove tricky to mark. In Nogales, split between Sonora and the Arizona territory, the marker had to be put right outside a saloon on the U.S. side.[145]

By around 1910, Nogales had a population of 3,514. Other, similar bifurcated cities would spring up along the tracks, though not always sharing a name, such as Douglas, Arizona; and Agua Prieta, Sonora. These places needed to have company offices for the trains and customs houses for goods. The shared economic needs and commercial interests, coupled with the movement of people, turned these pairs of discrete towns on maps into "binational" cities on the ground.[146]

Another significant piece of legislation for the West was the 1877 Desert Land Act, which built on the land distribution of the Homestead Act, parceling public lands into private ownership on the condition that they were irrigated and cultivated. It also allowed claimants to have up to 320 acres instead of the earlier 160 acres. At the same time, questions about landownership in the former Mexican territories of the United States continued to present problems, and by the end of the century, with a rising Anglo population, New Mexico was in need of arbitration. By 1891, the U.S. government had been forced to set up a Court of Private Land Claims to adjudicate these battles. As with Texas and California, the fights often involved multiple layers of law—proving first the Spanish grant, then the legitimacy of the subsequent Mexican authorization. Even with intact paperwork, families often lost thousands of acres.[147] One troubling aspect in New Mexico was how communal land grants had been used and later divided, which caused legal and political problems that spilled into the twentieth century. In the end, only about 6 percent of the total land area of around 35 million acres sought by the claimants was confirmed.[148]

Land speculators and lawyers—both Anglo and Hispanic—were well positioned to profit from the failure of so many grants. In New Mexico, these elites came together in what was called the Santa Fe Ring, which was linked with political and financial corruption—a charge that would also hinder New Mexico's future attempts at statehood.[149] The men in this loose association—their name was coined by their adversaries—often made their money from land speculation, which led to involvement in lucrative investments in railroads and mines throughout the latter half of the nineteenth century, though many of them denied there was any such "ring."[150]

One infamous example involved the Maxwell land grant—the vast territory acquired by Lucien Maxwell through his gradual acquisition of the Beaubien-Miranda land grant, which covered part of today's northern New Mexico and extended into southern Colorado. It was originally given to Carlos Beaubien and Guadalupe Miranda. After the Mexican-American War, Maxwell, who had married Beaubien's daughter, Luz, acquired that part of the granted lands and later bought Miranda's share.[151] Gold was discovered in nearby Baldy Mountain in 1866, and Maxwell was soon overrun with prospectors and squatters. By 1869, he was ready to sell, and he did so the following year to a group of investors, who decided to keep the grant's name. The Maxwell Land Grant and Railway Company had British backers but also connections to the Santa Fe Ring, including the leading politician Stephen Elkins.[152]

Congress had confirmed the grant in 1869, but not the size of the land, and an attempt that year to undertake a survey was stopped. The secretary of the interior ruled that the original grant could not be larger than 97,000 acres, basing this figure on a Mexican decree of 1824 that limited a grant to eleven leagues, with one league being equal to 4,428 acres. Given that there were two original grantees—Beaubien and Miranda—the allowable grant now was twenty-two leagues, totaling just over 97,000 acres. The Maxwell Land Grant and Railway Company, however, had based the purchase on the claim that the actual size was 2 million acres. This had enabled it to issue millions of dollars' worth of stock to cover the costs of investing in mining and ranching plans.[153] The company was now in disarray, and many of the people who had long lived there continued to press their claims. Such was the growing violence that U.S. troops had to be sent to intervene in what was later known as the Colfax County War.

The Maxwell company struggled on, but by 1876 it was purchased on foreclosure and then sold to Dutch investors who also kept the name, settled the backlog of unpaid taxes, and hoped to profit on renewed railroad interest.[154] In the meantime, the legal question of the size of the grant worked its way up to the Supreme Court in 1887. This time, thanks to earlier legal rulings, Congress no longer had to abide by the eleven-leagues rule and instead could issue a new grant. In the end, this

incarnation of the Maxwell company was given 1,714,764 acres, a deci-
sion that angered many of the smaller claimants living in the territory.[155]
The long-running debacle also attracted the attention of the national
press, and the episode reinforced the view of lawmakers and judges in
Washington that the honesty of politicians and business leaders in New
Mexico was dubious at best, undermining any plans for statehood.[156]

In the spirit of resistance that Juan Cortina had wielded in 1850s Texas,
similar attempts were made in 1880s New Mexico to frustrate, anger,
and punish Anglos who were seen to have cheated people out of their
land. The best-known group, *Las Gorras Blancas* (the White Masks or
White Caps), sabotaged ranches and railway lines where disputed lands
had been seized. They cut barbed wire, drove off cattle, and destroyed
bridges. From these acts, they moved into organized politics, setting up
El Partido del Pueblo Unido.[157] In 1890, they issued a manifesto that aimed
to protect the rights of the poor, warning that they wanted "no more
land thieves, or any obstructionists who might want to interfere. We
are watching you."[158]

———

AMID ALL EARLIER talk of Mexicanization, whiteness, and land, a different
vision of the West was starting to take shape by the late 1880s. The
history of California, in particular, took on a heavy air of romanticization
after only a generation of statehood, with the tales of striking gold on
one hand and crumbling mission churches needing to be "saved" on the
other.

The dilapidated condition of the churches was no fiction. An 1852
surveyor's report noted that at the mission of San Luis Rey, about forty
miles north of San Diego, "the gardens and orchard here once being
extensive . . . are fast going to ruin. Some half a dozen soldiers are stationed there to protect the grounds and buildings from further depredations until the title to the property shall be definitely settled."[159] Many
continued to fall into disrepair. Immediately after the Civil War ended,
the U.S. government returned the missions to the Catholic Church—the
Mexican government had secularized the missions and taken their lands
in the 1830s—but some parishes did not have the funds for their upkeep.

The missions' decline was an echo of the altered fortunes of Californios and Indians, for whom statehood represented a permanent destruction of their way of life. For millions of people, however, the addition of California excited their imaginations. Indeed, some of the individuals who would become the state's most ardent proponents were not Californios but Anglos from the East. They were active participants in what they claimed was "discovering"—but was closer to creating—a "Spanish" past, replete with gentlemanly *dons* and benevolent mission friars, a story at odds with the realities of the actual Spanish past, Mexican rule, and subsequent U.S. conquest.

By the 1870s and 1880s, California had turned from an imagined land into a touristic reality. Trains facilitated easy travel there and the climate was touted as health-giving. Publications played up to this image, even in their titles: one of them was the magazine *The Land of Sunshine,* edited by Charles Lummis. The Massachusetts-born Lummis was one of many Anglos from the East who went westward, in his case attracting national attention by walking from Cincinnati to Los Angeles for a job, an experience he later wrote about in *A Tramp Across the Continent.* He worked as a journalist and was an enthusiastic promoter of California. Lummis published a number of books about the West and its people, including *The Spanish Pioneers and the California Missions,* in which he wrote:

> It is pretty hard to read romance into the Puritans . . . whereas the whole Mission Era, both in its activity and its perennial influence, is saturated with romance—the thousands of place-names, the hundreds of Spanish fiestas, the innumerable Spanish songs, the remnants of the old Spanish *ranchos,* homes of incomparable hospitality and grace—for the Spanish Pastoral Era in California was notably the happiest and most charming life ever lived in this country.[160]

Another outsider, Hubert Howe Bancroft, agreed with this assessment of California's past and, like Lummis, managed to profit from it. Bancroft was born in Ohio and worked in New York as a bookseller before leaving for California in 1852 and settling in San Francisco.[161] He started a bookstore in 1856 and collected rare histories of California before turning his hand to producing them.[162] The result was a thirty-nine-volume history on the West and Mexico, with seven volumes devoted to California. He took credit, but the books were, in fact, the work of a staff of some six hundred people.[163] Bancroft sold the histories through subscription and they were popular, though at one point he managed to anger his core audience, falling out with the Society of California Pioneers. That organization struck him off its list of honorary members because of "certain misrepresentations in his books," not least his labeling John Frémont a "filibuster" in one volume, and his commenting elsewhere with some understatement that perhaps there had been some unfair treatment of Mexicans. The society went so far as to issue a pamphlet to counter what it called a "monstrous series of libels."[164]

The professionalization of historical writing was then in its earliest days; only in 1881 was the first professorial chair in U.S. history appointed. For Bancroft, history was a passion, but it was also a business. He later sold his voluminous private collection of papers and books to the University of California Library, which used these as the foundation of its Bancroft Library.

However, he did take a genuine interest in his adopted state, including its surviving Californio community, sending his employees to collect oral histories from Californios as they recalled their families' stories under Mexican and even Spanish rule. One prominent Californio mentioned in an anecdote in *California Pastoral* was María Amparo Ruiz, the "charming Californian" who married U.S. captain Henry S. Burton. When a competing suitor heard about their engagement, he pointed out to the priest that they could not be married because she was a Catholic and he was Protestant. Despite this, "the Loreto girl married the Yankee captain."[165] The Loreto girl—a reference to Ruiz de Burton's birthplace in Baja—would end up in publishing, too, but to tell a less happy tale.

Ruiz de Burton was angered by the treatment Californios faced, writing to a friend in 1859 that "they [the U.S.] broke their faith so solemnly pledged at Guadalupe Hidalgo. . . . How shameful this, in the conquering, the prosperous, the mighty nation! Better to crush us at once and not trick us out of our lands."[166] That same year, she and her family moved to the East Coast, living much of the time near Washington, D.C. After her husband died in 1869, she returned to California to find that the land they had bought years earlier was under dispute. While fighting to save it, she wrote her first novel, *Who Would Have Thought It?* This was published in 1872, making Ruiz de Burton one of the earliest Mexican-American female authors to write in English. Set in New England, the novel took aim at many of the hypocrisies that she witnessed while in the East. Her second work, *The Squatter and the Don*, published in 1885, hit much closer to home. This novel, set in the 1870s and '80s, tells the story of the relationship between a Californio family, the Alamars, and a squatter family, the Darrells.

Ruiz de Burton used the novel to counter the stereotypes of Californios and highlight the indignities that her people bore at the hands of state and local government, mostly focusing on the elite Californios who were facing the loss of their land. In the first chapter, the squatter William Darrell points out to his wife, "We aren't squatters. We are 'settlers.' We take up land that belongs to us, American citizens, by paying the government price for it."[167] To Mariano Alamar, the Californio *ranchero* with tens of thousands of acres, the situation was less clear-cut:

> By those laws any man can come to my land, for instance, and plant ten acres of grain, without any bench, and then catch my cattle which, seeing the green grass without a fence, will go to eat it. He then puts them in a "corral" and makes me pay damages.[168]

Ruiz de Burton used the two families' experiences to show a wider public the transformation that was taking place in California. Her novel failed to become a bestseller, perhaps overshadowed by another book about California that was published the year before, in 1884. *Ramona*, by Helen Hunt Jackson, was not only a hit, it was a cultural phenomenon. Such was its popularity that even future Cuban independence leader José Martí translated it into Spanish in 1887, writing in the introduction that "with more fire and knowledge, [Jackson] has written perhaps in Ramona, our novel," linking it to the wider story of the Spanish and indigenous people in the Americas.[169]

Unlike Ruiz de Burton, Jackson was not a California native, and visited the state only twice. Instead, like Lummis, she was born in Massachusetts and later became a prominent campaigner for Native American rights in the West.[170] While in California in 1882, she saw the missions that would inspire her novel and that at this point were in terrible condition. Some were in such a dire state after having had been used as saloons, while others had lost their stones and tiles and animals grazed where there had once been a floor.[171]

The missions provided the physical and moral landscape for Jackson's novel, which tells a story that, while different, overlaps Ruiz de Burton's. The title character, Ramona, the daughter of a Scottish man and an Indian woman, was taken in upon her father's death by a prominent California family, placing her both inside and outside elite society. She falls in love with one of the Indian laborers at the ranch, Alessandro. This angers the coldhearted widow Señora Moreno, who raised her, but she elopes with Alessandro anyway and assumes the life of a California Indian. Their struggle to survive in the years that follow is put in the context of the collapse of the mission system, one that Jackson presented as a world of gentle priests and peaceful villages torn apart by the arrival of the Anglos. When Alessandro's people, the Temecula, are driven off their mission land, their way of life is upended. He and Ramona go in search of security but are unable to find it among other displaced Indians, enduring a series of misfortunes. Years later, Señora Moreno's son, Felipe, sets out to find Ramona. In his search, he visits many of the missions:

> He would leave no stone unturned; no Indian village unsearched; no Indian unquestioned. San Juan Bautista came first; then Soledad; San Antonio, San Miguel, San Luis Obispo, Santa Inez; and that brought him to Santa Barbara. He had spent two months on the journey. At each of these places he had found Indians; miserable, half-starved creatures, most of them. Felipe's heart ached, and he was hot with shame, at their condition. The ruins of the old Mission buildings were sad to see, but the human ruins were sadder.[172]

Felipe finds Ramona, though not before Alessandro has been shot by an Anglo. She and Felipe decide to marry at the end of the novel, and they also agree to move to Mexico, where Felipe hopes they "might live among men of his own race and degree, and of congenial beliefs and occupations."[173]

Although intended to bring attention to the plight of the Indians, Jackson's depiction of the mission churches is what enraptured readers. Tourists began poking around the ruins, and soon campaigns were under way to save them. Lummis joined the effort, setting up the Landmarks Club in 1895. To Lummis, the missions were physical evidence that the Spanish were the "first colonizers" and represented "an outpost of civilization in the wilderness."[174] To many people in the late nineteenth century, the churches were the remains of an acceptable, civilized, and civilizing past, with a noble lineage involving Spaniards—not mestizo Mexicans and not Native Americans. In some ways this myth de-Mexicanized the elite Californios and bestowed on them a Spanishness which also coincided with the legal realities of needing to be a "white" Mexican in order to become a full citizen. It also set apart the Native Americans, pushing aside the mestizo reality of California and the harshness of the mission system. Jackson's work spawned the "mission myth," painting California's past as a thriving center of Spanish culture.[175] The work of Ruiz de Burton, however, was too full of contemporary realities to be transformed into a similarly romantic tale.

Around the same time, across the country in Washington, D.C., in 1859 the Italian-born artist Constantino Brumidi began sketches for a painted frieze of American history intended to decorate the Rotunda dome in the Capitol building. Once he set to work after the Civil War, there was not enough money to pay for an actual frieze, so instead he painted the surface using grisaille to make it look as if it were carved.[176] Sitting fifty-eight feet above the floor, measuring around three hundred feet in circumference, and just over eight feet high, the work that Brumidi finally started in 1878 in the Rotunda dome displays a panorama of U.S. history. Montgomery C. Meigs, the engineer in charge of building at the Capitol at the time, wanted the decorative theme to show an onward march of American history, explaining that it would illustrate "the gradual progress of the continent from the depths of barbarism to the heights of civilization; the rude and barbarous civilization of some of the Ante-Columbian tribes; the contests of the Aztecs with their less civilized predecessors; their own conquest by the Spanish race . . . the gradual advance of the white, and retreat of the red races, our own revolutionary and other struggles."[177]

The frieze was designed to sit below the dome's windows and above its doorways, under the fresco of George Washington hovering in the center of its ceiling.[178] The work begins with the allegorical figures of

Liberty, America, and History, followed by Columbus making his landing, over the western entrance to the Rotunda. The next panel is *Cortez and Montezuma at Mexican Temple*, where an apprehensive Cortés, with only a couple of guards alongside him, meets the Mexica leader Moteuczoma, who has a retinue of seven men and women, standing with his right hand on his heart and his left hand out, palm open, to welcome the men. The backdrop is the palace, and all the Mexica are in elaborate clothing and headdresses.

From there, the work moves toward the east and includes an image of the Mexican-American War over the southern entrance, showing General Winfield Scott entering Mexico City, though this part—indeed the majority of the frieze—was undertaken by another Italian artist, Filippo Costaggini, after Brumidi's death in 1880.[179] This section suggests none of the earlier hesitation of Cortés and his men. The U.S. troops outnumber the Mexicans twelve to four. Scott's men are in uniform, dignified and orderly, while the four Mexicans are in traditional dress, holding sombreros and wearing sarapes, rather than in the military uniform they would have worn at the time, with the leader—whose beard and wavy hair bear little resemblance to Santa Anna—bowing, his hand outstretched. Behind the Mexicans are aloe plants and palm trees, while Scott's men are framed by a sturdy oak. The subjugation was complete.*

IN JULY 1893, at the American Historical Association's meeting in Chicago, the historian Frederick Jackson Turner delivered a paper that would go far beyond the conference hall. In what became the essay "The Significance of the Frontier in American History," Turner argued that the conquest of the West gave the United States its unique "American" identity, saying: "The peculiarity of American institutions is, the fact that they have been compelled to adapt themselves to the changes of an expanding people." Those changes were involved in "winning a

---

* Despite Costaggini's contribution, there was still a thirty-one-foot gap in need of completion, which was eventually done by artist Allyn Cox in 1953. Cox added scenes from the end of the Civil War, a gun crew in the Spanish-American-Cuban War, and the birth of aviation.

wilderness, and in developing at each area of progress out of the primitive economic and political conditions of the frontier into the complexity of city life."[180] This "Turner thesis" was an idea that found a favorable place in the public consciousness, and though historians initially accepted it as well, they have subsequently wrestled with his assessment.

To Turner, the frontier was the "meeting point between savagery and civilization," and what marked it was not a physical boundary but "free land," which enabled successive waves of people to settle it. He presented a strange story, one not identifiable if viewed from the Tejano or Californio—to say nothing of the Native American—perspective. Nowhere in his article did he mention one of the most important factors to have allowed this "colonization of the Great West": the gain of millions of acres after the Mexican-American War. In his account of the battle to civilize, not a single mention of the Spanish or even the Mexican past appears. There are no mission churches, no presidios, and no ranchos. The relationship between Hispanics and Native Americans before the Anglos or Europeans crossed the Mississippi is wiped away as well, and nothing is made of the active and preexisting hubs of civilization, as represented by everything from a Pueblo village to a mission church in California. Instead, he championed a taming of a uniformly hostile wilderness and Indian "savagery," only after which the institutions of American life and its economy could take root.

The people who achieved this were Americans of a "composite nationality"—English, Scots-Irish, and Germans who, in "the crucible of the frontier," were "fused into a mixed race, English in neither nationality nor characteristics." Nowhere to be found were the people who already lived on the frontier. Turner, by design or oversight, wrote the Hispanic past out of U.S. history in one of the most influential essays of the time.

Whatever the means, and whoever was involved, there was no denying the outcome. By the time Turner put pen to paper, the United States reached from the bustling cities of the Eastern Seaboard over the Mississippi and past the farms that were strung through the prairies of the Great Plains, traversing rivers and mountains, ending in the golden promise of California. Although it had involved two wars and countless local acts of violence directed against Mexicans and Native Americans over the better part of the century, the United States now stretched from coast to coast.

Chapter 11

Ybor City, Florida,
ca. 1870–98

Near the southern tip of the island of Manhattan, a brownstone church sits on James Street. Now dwarfed by tall glass buildings, its elegant Greek revival pillars speak of a different time in the city. Tacked to the shuttered main doors in 2014 was a crumpled piece of paper, with photos of Pope John Paul II on the left and one of a dark-haired man with glasses on the right, with the text between them reading: "Pray for us and save our church + *ora por nosotros salva nuestra iglesia* Padre Félix Varela y Santo Juan Pablo II." Nearly two hundred years after his arrival in New York City, the memory of Varela remains alive.

A Cuban priest, Padre Félix Varela was a spiritual and intellectual leader who helped establish this parish and church in 1827. A plaque on the front of the church commemorates the two-hundredth anniversary of his birth, praising his time as a priest and educator as well as his work as a "defender of human and civil rights in Cuba and in the United States," and his bespectacled, serious gaze adorned a commemorative U.S. postage stamp in 1997. The priest served both his religious community and a wider one in 1824 by establishing *El habanero*, a newspaper directed at Cuban exiles that was also smuggled back to the island, as well as contributing a steady stream of writing about religious and political matters. He also translated works from English into Spanish, including Thomas Jefferson's *Manual of Parliamentary Practice*.[1]

Varela was part of an earlier group of Cubans who sought opportunities or refuge in the United States, a few thousand people scattered in cities like New York and Philadelphia. Although he was a priest, by the early 1820s in Cuba, Varela's interests had begun to encompass politics. In 1822–23, during the *Trienio Liberal*, he served as one of Cuba's representatives to the Spanish Cortes and spoke of political independence and the need to abolish slavery. When Fernando VII resumed his full powers in 1823, Varela was condemned to death and so fled to the United States. He had spent part of his childhood in St. Augustine, when it was still in Spanish Florida, though this time he went farther north, to Philadelphia, where he started his newspaper and tried to gain an ecclesiastical posting. By 1825 he was in New York ministering to Irish immigrants on the Lower East Side of Manhattan.

In Varela's time, political change for Cuba was still a way off, though the example of the other former Spanish colonies turning into republics was an inspiration. There had been attempts at independence in Cuba, but the authorities suppressed them with a fierce brutality. The continued fear of triggering "another Haiti" was a powerful incentive. Some frustrated Cubans began to look at possibilities away from the island, and Varela became a beacon to other exiles.

Varela never saw Cuba again, staying in New York and retiring in 1853 to St. Augustine, Florida, where a statue of him graces the churchyard of the city's cathedral. Nor did he live long enough to see Cuba make its first large-scale attempt at independence: the Ten Years' War, which began in 1868, more than a decade after his death. It was ignited with the *Grito de Yara* (cry of Yara), when Carlos Manuel de Céspedes led a small army, which included slaves freed from his own plantation, to fight against Spain.

By this point, U.S. interest in Cuba—which still allowed slavery—had cooled after the United States' own Civil War. Attempts to buy the island stopped for the moment, and any enthusiasm that the Cubans in New York and elsewhere on the East Coast had throughout the 1850s for annexation plans was supplanted by a growing desire for independence.[2] However, once the Ten Years' War began, many people in Washington believed the Cubans, like the Mexicans, were not capable of self-governance. President Ulysses S. Grant told Congress in his 1875 annual message that there was no end in sight for the "ruinous conflict" in Cuba. To Grant, it was not apparent that a "civil organization exists which may be recognized as an independent government capable of performing its international obligations." This being the case, recognition of Cuban independence was, in his opinion, "impracticable and indefensible."³ Later, Grant offered to mediate a peace deal between the colony and Spain. Others in Washington continued to hope that Spain would relent and put the island up for sale.⁴

The desire for independence was not limited to Cuba. The fellow Spanish colony of Puerto Rico harbored similar dreams. In the small village of Lares, surrounded by the lush green of the Cordillera Central mountains, around one thousand feet about sea level and seventy miles to the west of San Juan, a rebellion broke out in the same year as Cuba's. In fact, Puerto Rico shouted first. Known as the *Grito de Lares*, this revolt took place on September 23, 1868. Organized by Ramón Emeterio Betances, it directed much of its frustration at the economic injustices that persisted under colonial rule, targeting the Spanish merchants in the coffee-growing region, as well as officials.⁵ It was put down by the authorities soon afterward, and no further war followed.

Betances already had a record with the Spanish and went into exile. He, too, headed for New York and spent time with other exiles. The Cubans and Puerto Ricans could make common cause there, though many Puerto Ricans favored reform rather than entering what they could see was becoming a long-running conflict in Cuba.⁶ While Betances planned, moderate Puerto Rican delegates—much to his annoyance—sought to air their grievances to the Cortes in Spain, leaving in 1871. They did, however, manage to secure the abolition of slavery, which had been one of Betances's aims, by 1873.⁷ He was still in exile and did not live to see the island's independence, though by the time of his death in France in September 1898, he would have lived just long enough to see Puerto Rico transferred from one colonial power to another.

TEN YEARS OF civil conflict left Cuba battered, and the exodus of Cubans to the United States grew throughout the 1870s. Some people left for political reasons, but many others for financial ones—the economy was in tatters. By 1878, both sides were exhausted, and negotiations began to bring the conflict to a close, resulting in the Pact of Zanjón. It brought the war to an end, but not before some 50,000 Cubans and between

150,000 and 200,000 Spaniards had been killed.[8] In an effort to prevent another uprising the colonial authorities made certain concessions, one of the most significant being the abolition of slavery, though it was to be done in gradual phases, with the practice finally ending in 1886. For some Cubans, however, this was not enough. Now only independence would do, and many regrouped in the relative safety of the United States to determine how to achieve it. Varela's writings remained influential during this time, and a later independence leader, José Martí, said the priest "taught us how to think." As Cubans began to plan what would come next, the exile community grew, though this time, instead of New York, its hub would be a little industrial suburb on the edge of Tampa, Florida.

A small neighborhood of cigar factories and workers' cottages might seem an incongruous place to launch a liberation struggle, but for the nascent Cuban community Ybor City would become one of the central organizing points of the junta to free the island. The neighborhood's evolution into the "cradle of Cuban liberty" was not what Vicente Martínez Ybor had in mind when he decided to relocate his cigar factory to a tract of sandy land to the west of the small town of Tampa in 1885. Ybor was a Spaniard from Valencia who, like many of his contemporaries from the peninsula, worked in Cuba. He, however, decided to leave the island for the United States, where the economy was better and where he could escape high tariffs.[9]

In 1869 Ybor moved his factory to Key West, which was fast becoming home to a growing exile population, providing a ready labor force to produce his Príncipe de Gales cigars. Ybor wanted to continue to use Cuban cigar makers, as they were famed for their skill, and many were happy to have an excuse to leave war-torn Cuba. From there he moved to Tampa, which had a good port. This was crucial to his success, as he needed access to Cuban tobacco as well as the ability to ship his cigars. He bought his plot of land on the edge of town in 1885, and the Ybor City suburb that bore his name grew and soon became part of Tampa, in 1887.

During these later decades of the nineteenth century at least one hundred thousand Cubans left the island for the United States, Europe, and Latin American countries.[10] The wealthiest emigrants went to Europe, the middle-class professionals to the large cities of the U.S. East Coast, and workers to Florida.[11] Some sixteen thousand Cubans came to the United States between 1886 and 1890 alone.[12] For centuries, Spain had tried—and for the most part failed—to increase the settlement of Florida. Now, long after Spanish control of Florida had evaporated, it was turning into one of the largest magnets for people living in the remnants of Spain's empire.

Although stable, life for workers in Ybor City was not easy. The tidy fronts of the small wooden workers' houses often belied the number living behind them, as many as four or five families crammed within their walls. Cubans were also not the sole group of immigrants; Italians and other Europeans were coming to the city to work, too, and there was also a significant Jewish population.*

The poet and political exile José Martí entered this world in 1891. He had been invited to Tampa by some of the Cuban leaders in the city and traveled down from New York, arriving in Florida on November 25; some fifty people braved a downpour to meet him at the train station. Martí was well-known—he had devoted most of his life to the struggle for independence, having been forced into exile at the age of seventeen, and his works of poetry and political essays also brought him wide recognition.

The years before his trip to Tampa had been eventful. He returned to Cuba in 1877 for a short visit, using a false name, and soon afterward left for Mexico. Once Cuba's war was over, he went back to the island and was there during a revolt called the Little War (Guerra Chiquita) in the summer of 1879. This conflict lasted for just over a year, but during this time Martí was forced into exile again. He traveled to New York in 1880 and connected with the exile community there, writing for newspapers and journals. The 1891 trip to Tampa, however, was his first to Florida.

The evening after his arrival, he spoke at the Liceo Cubano club, housed in a former cigar factory, and there he enshrined himself in Cuban history with a passionate speech declaring: "For suffering Cuba, the first word. Cuba must be considered an altar for the offering of our lives, not a pedestal for lifting us above it."[13] The audience embraced his words and he had clearly stoked the passion of this Florida community.

---

* Tampa today remains the only place in the United States to have a trilingual newspaper, *La Gaceta*, published in English, Spanish, and Italian.

He then drafted what were called the Tampa Resolutions, which aimed to unify the various patriotic societies, laying the foundation for what later became the Cuban Revolutionary Party (Partido Revolucionario Cubano) in 1892. By the end of his busy trip, which lasted only four days, he was escorted to the train station by most of the town: four thousand people saw him off to the Florida Keys with shouts of *"¡Viva Martí!"*[14]

Martí's desire to unite Cubans was significant because the groups of exiles around the country had different visions of what Cuba should do and be, fragmentations that had developed during the Ten Years' War. Martí was not at first popular with everyone, but part of his genius was the ability to bring Cubans together. From there, this unified group would go on to establish societies and raise money to aid the cause of a free Cuba, *Cuba libre*, with the cigar workers themselves often making a regular contribution of a day's pay.[15]

At one point Florida had more than one hundred cigar factories, and in Tampa the population reached about sixteen thousand by the turn of the century.[16] As Ybor City continued to expand, thousands of households in the United States became familiar with the cigar boxes produced in this town, decorated with lavish floral motifs, regal symbols, or romanticized scenes from literature or history—for instance those of the Treaty Bond brand were illustrated with a picture of Thomas Jefferson, Napoleon Bonaparte, and a scroll representing the Louisiana Purchase.

Although hierarchies and discrimination had long existed in Cuba on the basis of skin color, with darker-skinned people on the lower rungs of the socioeconomic ladder and lighter-skinned people among the elite, Cubans in the United States were often not prepared for the level of segregation they encountered in the Jim Crow South. Some Cubans discovered they had been classified as "black" and so were forced to endure the treatment that accompanied this. By the end of the century, the 1896 Supreme Court ruling in the case of Homer Plessy, a Louisiana creole who sat in a white railway car and was arrested because he was one-eighth black, established the legal precedent of "separate but equal." Black Cubans were not exempt. In Florida, many of them found themselves living in places apart from lighter-skinned Cubans, and they were also forced to socialize in different worlds. By 1890, some sixteen hundred people in Tampa were deemed "black," a number that included African-Americans.

The whiter Cubans were considered "foreign-born" and grouped with the Italian and other Mediterranean immigrants in the city.[17]

The question of color in Florida was complicated by the fact that the rebels during the Ten Years' War had made clear slavery would have no part in a free Cuba. That war and the subsequent reorganization by exiles in Florida had united people from the island across class and color lines. The promise of independence and equality was extended to Afro-Cubans, as embodied by Antonio Maceo, a black general and hero of the Ten Years' War who would return during the Cuban War of Independence in 1895. For Martí and others, the inclusion of Afro-Cubans was a crucial part of a free Cuba and vital for the future of the nation. In an 1891 article, "Our America," Martí made his views on this clear: "there is no racial hatred, because there are no races. . . . Anyone who promotes and disseminates opposition or hatred among races sins against humanity."[18]

While Cubans were seeking better economic opportunities in Florida or New York, U.S. capital had been flowing into Cuban sugar—by this point for decades, with significant activity starting again after the end of the U.S. Civil War, spurred on in part by technological developments in sugar refining.[19] Although the Ten Years' War caused some disruption, it was clear that a free Cuba could be a very profitable one. The U.S. backers began to show their support for *Cuba libre* by joining the Cuban American League, set up by the New York businessman William O. McDowell in 1892.[20] Spain's finances had long been devastated by conflict, and the Spanish had little to spend on rebuilding Cuba after the war. Planters in Cuba thus took credit from U.S. banks, or investors bought plantations from planters who were unable to recover from the drop in sugar prices at the beginning of the 1880s.[21] This was further aided by the 1890 McKinley Tariff, which removed the duty on raw sugar imported to the United States, giving Cuban producers extra impetus to rebuild their plantations, often with foreign help.[22] Soon, family estates were being taken over by U.S. banks, though at the same time many planters were trying to obtain U.S. citizenship in order to protect their interests.[23] The commercial ties between the United States and Cuba began to tighten.[24]

The United States and Cuba were also becoming linked by something that aroused a bit more passion than talk of tariffs: baseball. The brothers

Nemesio and Ernesto Guilló, who had studied in Alabama, are credited with being the first to bring the game to the island, establishing the Havana Baseball Club in 1868. The first game between two provincial teams took place in 1874, and by 1878 the Cuban League of Professional Baseball was up and running.[25] The enthusiasm was based on more than just a love of playing or watching the sport. For Cubans, an important aspect of the game was the team itself, a symbol for building a new nation, as contrasted against the individual performance of Spanish bull-fighting. Baseball also represented the progress and "modernity" of U.S. culture for a war-torn country still under colonial rule at the end of the nineteenth century.[26] Indeed, the authorities even banned a team from calling itself Yara in 1876 because the name evoked the *Grito de Yara* that had started the war.[27]

The sport boomed in popularity as clubs sprang up all over the island. Local teams also played games against people from the United States who were working or living on the island.[28] In Havana, newspapers were dedicated to the sport, including the weekly *Base-Ball*, which was started in 1881 and printed scores, gossip, and even poems. Cuban players were quick to establish a reputation and travel to play in the United States; in 1871, Esteban "Steve" Bellán was considered to be the first Hispanic player in the United States. He played at Fordham University (then known as St. John's College), and then as a member of the Troy Haymakers, and later on for the New York Mutuals, one of the founding teams of the National League. Cubans also helped spread the sport around Latin America, taking it to the Dominican Republic and to Puerto Rico.[29] In 1903 the *Puerto Rico Herald* reported: "Four years ago Puerto Ricans had never heard of baseball: it is now becoming the insular game. A league has been established at San Juan, and the regular Wednesday and Saturday games between the four teams composing it attract large crowds. . . . Enthusiasm among the spectators runs high."[30]

Away from the island, Cubans developed a reputation as talented baseball players and, in the decades to come, would have a great impact on the game in the United States. In one odd—though perhaps not isolated—case, African-Americans were told to impersonate them. In 1885, the managers of the Argyle Hotel on Long Island wanted its black waiters to play baseball for the amusement of the white patrons, though they worried that it might make the guests uncomfortable to see black men outside their usual roles at the hotel. Instead, the men were to be called the "Cuban Giants" and were given instructions to "speak heavily accented gibberish that sounded like Spanish." The ruse worked—the guests loved it and the team was so popular that it ended up touring and becoming semiprofessional.[31]

———

In 1894, the United States introduced the Wilson-Gorman Tariff Act, imposing a 40 percent duty on imported sugar to help domestic production and wrecking any trade advantage Cuba enjoyed. Sugar exports collapsed, the cost of imports rose, and frustration with Spanish trade policies reached a boil.[32] At the same time, Cubans in exile and on the island were now ready to try again for independence. In 1895, under the organization of Martí, the War of Independence started, and uprisings took place throughout the island. Martí had convinced two heroes of the previous war, Máximo Gómez and Antonio Maceo, to lead once more. Martí returned to Cuba, and he died in battle that May. Maceo was killed the following December. Despite losing two leaders, the rebellion continued, and now, unlike during the Ten Years' War, the United States watched with great interest, with significant sections of public opinion supporting the Cubans in their struggle. The powerful newspaper proprietors William Randolph Hearst and Joseph Pulitzer started competing campaigns backing the liberation of Cuba in their respective papers, the *New York Journal* and the *New York World*. Tales of violence at the hands of the unpopular and repressive Spanish governor of Cuba, Valeriano Weyler, helped arouse sympathy for Cubans. African-American newspapers covered events on the island, too, watching a war that not only involved black people but, in the case of Maceo, was being led by them.[33] The position of black people on the island was also of great interest, with one journalist in the *Colored American* answering his question "Will Cuba be a Negro Republic?" in the affirmative, on the basis that "the greater portion of the insurgents are Negroes and they are politically ambitious."[34] Some politicians and officials in the United States might have thought this, too, watching the events unfold with wariness about the role of black people in the conflict.[35]

More directly for the United States, the business interests of some of its citizens were being destroyed—one of the revolutionary tactics was to burn sugarcane fields.[36] By 1898, after three years of war on the island, coupled with the change in sugar tariffs, New York merchants complained that they were losing $100 million a year in lost or disrupted trade with Cuba.[37] Businesses in cities such as Boston, Philadelphia, and Baltimore began to lobby William McKinley, who became U.S. president in 1897, to find a way to end the costly conflict. In a letter that year, they pointed to their "large interests in Cuba, either as property holders or holders of mortgages," before asking him—"in order to prevent further losses"—to find a way of brokering a peace deal.[38]

Certain factions in Washington began to express a desire for much more than a deal. Republican senator Henry Cabot Lodge of Massachusetts—who would go on to be one of the leading advocates of war against Spain—had written in 1895 that "we desire no extension to the south," yet proceeded to list the actions in that region that would benefit the United States, including building a canal across Nicaragua. His vision included having "among those islands at least one strong naval station, and when the Nicaragua canal is built, the island of Cuba, still sparsely settled and of almost unbounded fertility, will become to us a necessity."[39]

Other groups opposed involvement in Cuban affairs; their position was articulated by an antiwar press, citing practical concerns, including the perceived strength of the Spanish navy, the dangers posed to troops by tropical diseases, and the potential economic cost.[40] Some antiwar newspapers were also concerned about the future of Cuba's large black population. The New York Herald explained in one article that "Cuba libre means another Black Republic. . . . We don't want one so near. Hayti [sic] is already too close."[41]

In a bid to avert a war but solve the crisis, President McKinley made one final attempt in January 1898 to buy Cuba for $300 million, which Spain refused.[42] Around the same time rumors reached Washington that four German warships in the Caribbean might be there to take Cuba as part of a secret deal with Spain.[43] Public and political opinion about how to proceed was still divided when President McKinley sent the battleship USS Maine from Key West to Havana on January 24, 1898, in what was presented as a peaceful visit, though Hearst's New York Journal exclaimed, "Our Flag in Havana at Last" in the next day's edition.[44]

On February 15 an onboard explosion killed 266 of the ship's officers and crew. The source of the blast was never identified, but Hearst's *Journal* was quick to blame Spain, despite the lack of evidence, its headline shouting: "Destruction of the Warship Maine Was the Work of an Enemy."[45] A somewhat more circumspect *New York Times* reported, "Only Theory as to the Cause of the Disaster."[46] Some naval experts at the time explained that it was quite probably an accident, in part because the vessel's coal bunker was near where the gunpowder was stored. However, in late March an official U.S. inquiry concluded that while an exact cause could not be found, it most likely was the fault of a Spanish mine outside the ship.[47] Whatever the reason, the destruction of the *Maine* was now a useful casus belli. The United States gave Spain one last ultimatum to leave Cuba, which was refused.

President McKinley explained to Congress a short time later that he was now willing to take action because of the "intimate connection of the Cuban question with the state of our own Union."[48] Part of his concern was the potential damage to U.S. citizens' property and he said the "prospect of such a protraction and conclusion of the present strife is a contingency hardly to be contemplated with equanimity by the civilized world, and least of all by the United States."[49] There was no mention of a *Cuba libre* in his call to war, and this gave Cubans reason to fear the creeping hand of U.S. imperialism.[50] On the contrary, President McKinley said he did not think it "would be wise or prudent for this government to recognize at the present time the independence of the so-called Cuban Republic. Such recognition is not necessary in order to enable the United States to intervene."[51]

By April 19, Congress had passed the joint resolution for war against Spain. However, before it was passed a crucial amendment had been added. This was proposed by the Republican senator Henry Moore Teller of Colorado, who wanted to ensure that the United States would only help Cuba free itself from Spain, and not try to acquire it; or, in the words of his amendment, that the United States would "leave the government and control of the island to its people."[52] Given that his state was a beet sugar producer, Teller may have had Colorado's economic interests in mind as well.[53] Cubans, for their part, had long been concerned about U.S. intervention. José Martí's vision had rejected any annexation or alliance with the United States. As Martí asked in an 1889 letter, once the United States is in Cuba, who will drive them out?"[54] The Teller amendment helped assuage this concern, but Cuban fears were not fully extinguished.

The United States declared war on Spain on April 25, and its opening attack followed less than a week later, though not in Cuba but in the Philippines, which also had remained under Spanish rule. The United States attacked in the Battle of Manila Bay on May 1, using ships already in the Pacific, and sank the Spanish squadron. By early July, a joint resolution had passed Congress for the annexation of the Hawaiian Islands because of their strategic importance and use as a naval base.

In Cuba, Theodore Roosevelt arrived with his "Rough Riders," the 1st United States Volunteer Cavalry Regiment, scoring a key victory at the Battle of San Juan Hill on July 1. Spain surrendered to the United States before the end of the month, in a ceremony that took place in Santiago.[55] Cubans were not allowed to attend or to celebrate their own victory, nor did any Cuban sign the Treaty of Paris that ended the war. All of this reignited the anxiety about the United States' intentions.[56] For the independence leader Calixto García, such actions had left Cuba "in a tremendous haze, with the bleakest of futures."[57] Each side now watched the other—the Cubans to see if the United States would keep its promise to leave the island free, and the United States to see if Cuba "behaved" well enough to deserve it.[58]

Puerto Rico would also be swept up in the war: U.S. ships bombarded San Juan in May, but the army did not land until a couple of months later. In June, Philip Hanna, who had been the last U.S. consul to Spanish Puerto Rico, wrote to the assistant secretary of state, John Bassett Moore, to warn that "in case the United States takes possession of Puerto Rico," it was crucial that the United States prove "Americans are better than Spaniards, that American government is far above Spanish, and that the United States is indeed their friend come to give them a taste of the benefits of liberty."[59]

Around three thousand troops that had been fighting in Cuba were sent to Puerto Rico in July, landing near the southern town of Guánica on the twenty-fifth. They moved inland, stopping at the city of Ponce, where a proclamation declared that the purpose of their invasion was to bring a "banner of freedom." Puerto Rico was soon under U.S.

control. By August 12, the entire "splendid little war," as Secretary of State John Hay was said to have called it, came to an end. The humiliation for Spain was complete. Its once vast empire whittled away by independence movements and now by war with the United States, it was left with only a few small protectorates in North and West Africa. A new era beckoned for everyone involved, not least the United States. Hearst's *New York Journal* beamed: "War Officially Ended. Business Boom Begins."[60]

Despite growing national unease at this sort of imperial behavior, the arch-expansionist Indiana senator Albert Beveridge saw little problem in taking control of these territories, arguing in his "March of the Flag" speech in September 1898 that "the rule of liberty that all just government derives its authority from the consent of the governed, applies only to those who are capable of self-government. We govern the Indians without their consent, we govern our territories without their consent, we govern our children without their consent. How do they know that our government would be without their consent? . . . Do not the blazing fires of joy and the ringing bells of gladness in Porto Rico prove the welcome of our flag?"[61]

By the end of the year, the Treaty of Paris was signed, under which the United States agreed to pay $20 million for the Philippines, and also gained Puerto Rico and the Micronesian island of Guam. Well before this was signed, Beveridge's glee was already evident:

> Hawaii is ours; Porto Rico is to be ours; at the prayer of the people Cuba will finally be ours; in the islands of the east, even to the gates of Asia, coaling stations are to be ours; at the very least the flag of a liberal government is to float over the Philippines, and it will be the stars and stripes of glory.[62]

A couple of years later, in 1900, W. E. B. Du Bois would see U.S. imperialism somewhat differently, asking in one essay, "What is to be our attitude towards these new lands and toward the masses of dark men and women who inhabit them?" referring to Puerto Rico, Cuba, Hawaii, and the Philippines. He called for black Americans to "guard and guide them with our vote," reminding his readers that "we must remember that the twentieth century will find nearly twenty million

Nogales, Arizona c. 1934 with the rooftops that say 'Mexico'
and 'U.S.A.' showing where the border is.

Monument erected in 1925 on Parris Island,
South Carolina, to commemorate the arrival of
the French Huguenots in 1562.

An engraving by Theodor de Bry (c. 1591) of Timucua people in Florida cultivating a field and planting crops. The image was based on earlier paintings by Jacques Le Moyne, who had been a member of the 1564 French expedition.

Timucua youths in Florida play ball games, practice shooting arrows, and run races in this engraving from Theodor de Bry (c. 1591) based on earlier works by Jacques Le Moyne, who was in Florida in 1564.

An engraving of Hernando Cortés
(date unknown).

Church of St Stephen (San Estevan del Rey)
on the Acoma Pueblo around 1902.

Inscription made by Juan de Oñate during his travels around North America,
on a rock outcrop near the modern Arizona-New Mexico state line. It reads:
'The Adelantado Don Juan de Oñate passed by here from the discovery
of the South Sea, on the 16th day of April 1606 [1605].'

Aerial view of Castillo de San Marcos fort,
which dates back to 1672, in Saint Augustine, Florida.

A 1791 engraving of Anglo-Spanish hostilities, entitled
'The Spanish Insult to the British Flag at Nootka Sound,' by Robert Dodd.

Portrait of Father Miguel Hidalgo in a Mexican broadside published in Mexico City, c. 1890–1913.

The 18th-century San Xavier del Bac mission in 2015.

An engraving of San Xavier del Bac, near Tucson, Arizona in the U.S. Pacific Railroad Expedition and Survey report (c. 1855).

The San José de Tumacácori mission (c. 1753), near Tubac, Arizona, in 2015. Today it is a National Historic Park.

The Alamo (San Antonio de Valero), in 2015.

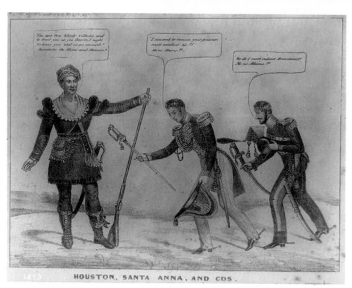

HOUSTON, SANTA ANNA, AND COS.

An engraving published in New York by Henry R. Robinson depicting the surrender of Mexican president Antonio López de Santa Anna and General Martin Perfecto de Cos to Texian leader Samuel Houston after the Battle of San Jacinto in late April 1836. Houston, holding a musket on the left, says 'You are two bloody villians, and to treat you as you deserve, I ought to have you shot as an example! Remember the Alamo and Fannin!' while Santa Anna (center), bows and offers his sword to Houston, saying, 'I consent to remain your prisoner, most excellent sir!! Me no Alamo!!' Cos follows suit, saying 'So do I most valiant Americano!! Me no Alamo!!'

Carl Schuchard's 'Town and Valley of Mesilla New-Mexico' was produced as part of a 1854 railway survey between San Antonio to San Diego.

The 12th edition of the 1847 J. Disturnell map that was at the root of many boundary problems after the Mexican-American war.

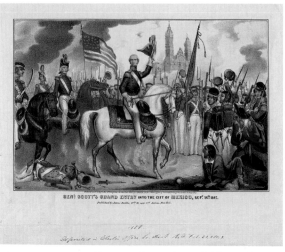

An 1848 engraving showing General Winfield Scott's 1847
entry into Mexico City during the Mexican-American War.

The U.S. army entering Mexico during the Mexican-American War as
depicted on the frieze (c. 1880s) of the Capitol rotunda in Washington, D.C.

An 1847 lithograph entitled 'Battle of Buena Vista,'
which was fought on February 22–23, 1847,
by famed print-makers Currier & Ives.

A dish in the 'Westward Ho!'
pattern produced by
James Gillinder & Sons, c. 1880.

A border marker dating back to the
International Boundary Commission
survey of the 1890s,
near Douglas, Arizona.

A park in Ybor City, outside of Tampa, Florida, continues to honour 19th-century
Cuban leader José Martí.

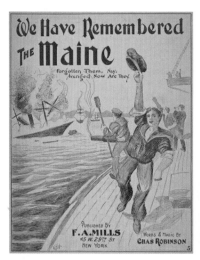

Patriotic sheet music from
the Spanish-American-Cuban war, 1898.

Red Cross nurses at a bazaar held
at a girls' charity school in
San Juan, Puerto Rico, c. 1920.

A print by J.S. Pughe, published in a 1899 edition of *Puck* magazine,
depicting Cuba as a woman, appealing to Uncle Sam for continued help.
The caption reads: 'Cuba – If you leave me to myself it will mean the old troubles.
With your help I can have peace and prosperity. Do not desert me!'

The California Mission of San Juan Capistrano around 1918, before its restoration.

San Juan Capistrano in 2015.

A postcard of 'Ramona's Marriage place'—alluding to the heroine of the popular eponymous novel—in San Diego c. 1900–1902.

An anonymous photo with the title 'Americans and Insurectos at Rio Grande' was thought to be taken around 1911, at the beginning of the Mexican Revolution.

Mexican Revolutionary General Francisco 'Pancho' Villa, pictured on a horse, thought to be taken sometime between 1908 and 1919.

Mexican Revolutionary leader Emiliano Zapata, pictured in 1911.

Columbus, New Mexico, in the aftermath of Pancho Villa's 1916 raid.

Roberto Berdecio, an assoicate of Mexican muralist David Alfaro Siqueiros, stands in front of the artist's controversial 'América Tropical,' which was unveiled in Los Angeles in 1932 and soon whitewashed over.

'América Tropical' in 2015, after a long-running restoration effort.

Seven young men who were arrested during the 'zoot suit' riots
in June 1942 wait in a Los Angeles courtroom.

A mural at the Chamizal National Memorial, in El Paso, Texas, in 2015.

The border fence in southern Arizona in December 2016.

Participants in the All Souls
Procession in Tucson, Arizona,
in November 2014.

of brown and black people under the protection of the American flag, a third of the nation."[63]

Throughout talks on the treaty and its subsequent ratification, the anti-imperialist movement became more outspoken, arguing that the United States should not take any territories in the aftermath of the war.[64] The gradual nature of U.S. territorial expansion—even though that, too, had involved a war in 1846—was perceived to be different from taking overseas colonies, separate from the North American landmass.[65] Although many were pleased to see Spain driven out of the hemisphere, in its place the United States had picked up another eleven million people scattered across the globe.[66] This was disquieting to many, with some concerned about these new subjects' not being "white." Soon organizations like the Anti-Imperialist League began to hold meetings and criticize the direction of the United States. Heated debates also followed in Congress.

One of the most prominent anti-imperialists to emerge was William Jennings Bryan, a three-time Democratic candidate for president, whose firm stance on this issue became a key component of his presidential bid in 1900. His platform decried the unfairness of Puerto Ricans' receiving "a government without their consent," while also demanding that the promise of Cuban freedom be delivered.[67] Popular as these sentiments might have been, Bryan's stance on another issue of the day—"free silver," an economy policy that would have allowed for the unlimited coinage of silver—overshadowed his campaign and ultimately may have cost him a victory.[68]

While the United States was having an internal debate about its place in the world, Cubans were forced to accept the immediate reality of a U.S. military occupation. "[This] cannot be our ultimate fate," declared General Máximo Gómez in 1899, "after years of struggle."[69] The talk in Washington turned to "stability," as well as the "pacification" included in one of the clauses of the earlier joint resolution, which stipulated that the United States would not "exercise sovereignty, jurisdiction, or control over said island except for pacification thereof." It was an ambiguous— and to Cubans, menacing—phrase, one indicating that intervention would be the result if Cuba did not act in favor of U.S. interests.[70]

Underneath this talk was a subtext of race: that the island's large Afro-Cuban population had been mentioned more than once in the same breath as Haiti indicated some of the accepted ideas about the ability of Cubans to self-govern, with one U.S. official quipping that universal suffrage on the island would be counterproductive and that "we might just as well retire and let it drift to Hayti No. 2."[71] The occupying government attempted to institute what were more or less Jim Crow policies, with literacy and property requirements that excluded two-thirds of Cuban men, many of them black, from voting—a move that met with angry reaction and protests.[72]

In the end, Cuba would have its independence in 1902, though not without the United States erecting a few more barriers along the way, the largest of which took the form of the 1901 Platt Amendment. This legislation reflected the ongoing U.S. distrust of Cubans and set out a number of new demands as part of a larger bill to end the military occupation of the island. It was crafted to leave U.S. interests protected and U.S. influence undiminished. One key stipulation obliged Cuba to lease land to the United States for a naval station; today Guantánamo Bay remains a base for the U.S. Navy. The amendment also allowed the United States to exercise its "right to intervene for the preservation of Cuban independence," which was vague enough for a wide degree of interpretation.[73] The reaction in Cuba was immediate, and anti-U.S. demonstrations erupted across the island. Cuban leaders were forced to accept the amendment in the end, believing that otherwise the United States would never leave.

The long dream of owning or annexing Cuba outright may have come to an end, but the United States had no intention of leaving the island in peace.[74] It was back only a few years later, putting its right of intervention to use in 1906, after the collapse of the presidency of Tomás Estrada Palma. The United States sent the secretary of war and future president William Howard Taft for a few weeks before he was replaced as provisional governor by Charles Mangoon, who stayed until 1909.

In addition to political uncertainties, the island's economy suffered tremendous swings in its fortunes. In 1903 the United States and Cuba also agreed to a trade reciprocity deal that gave a 20 percent reduction in tariffs on Cuban goods and a similar concession on certain goods that the United States sent to the island. While it was useful in bringing a wider range of imports to Cuba—everything from steel products to cotton goods and luxuries like perfume—the treaty also increased

Cuba's reliance on its much larger trading partner and encouraged sugar production at the expense of the island's agricultural and economic diversification.[75]

To offset the financial pain that some landowners were experiencing, U.S. officials at first implemented a number of measures, such as delayed debt collection, abolition of certain duties and taxes, and a moratorium on plantation foreclosure.[76] These provided some relief, but at the same time it was clear there were bargains to be had.[77] By 1905, around $50 million in land purchases had been made, with some thirteen thousand U.S. investors owning titles.[78] Between 1903 and 1919, some forty-four thousand people from the United States emigrated to Cuba, by then an island of 1.5 million people.[79] By 1920, North American sugar interests were producing 63 percent of the total crop.[80]

For Puerto Rico, the outlook was bleaker than Cuba's, despite former U.S. consul Hanna's cheerful assertion that Puerto Ricans should be congratulated "at their good fortune in becoming a part of the territory of the great United States."[81] Puerto Rico faced a fate much different from its island neighbor's. To begin with, the timing was unfortunate: it was ceded to the United States only a short while after it had finally managed a deal with Spain in 1897 that granted it more powers of self-government, including setting its own tariffs, creating a currency, and establishing a legislature. The prominent journalist and politician Luis Muñoz Rivera had been elected head of the new body that spring, only months before U.S. troops came ashore. In addition, a year after the war ended, the island was slammed by one of the worst hurricanes in its history, San Ciriaco, which made landfall in the south of the island on August 8, 1899.[82]

When the United States took charge, all the reforms that had been enacted before the invasion were wiped away and replaced with the Foraker Act of 1900, also known as the Organic Act. It established a government for the island with a governor and a council appointed by the U.S. president, although Puerto Ricans could vote for the members of the legislative chamber and a resident commissioner who was a nonvoting representative to Washington.[83] Added soon after this was the 1902 Official Languages Act, which made English an equal official language to Spanish, to be used in government and in the schools, despite the fact that most people, including civil servants and teachers, did not speak it. Language issues and the lack of cultural understanding angered and frustrated Puerto Ricans both at home and abroad. An article in the *Puerto Rico Herald* —edited at the time by Luis Muñoz Rivera—thundered from its offices in New York that "it is absolutely necessary that the Governor of Puerto Rico should be thoroughly acquainted with the language spoken in the island."[84] Indeed, the U.S. paperwork from the Foraker Act onward misspelled the name of the island "Porto Rico," an error that would require thirty-two years of campaigning to correct.[85]

The United States sent a succession of unpopular governors to Puerto Rico, starting with Charles Herbert Allen. During the one year he was in office he managed to earn the suspicion and hostility of people on the island by buying up land that would later be the basis for a powerful sugar syndicate. Allen would go on in 1913 to be president of the American Sugar Refining Company, a firm better known as Domino Sugar.

In 1902, Allen contributed a chapter to a book, *Opportunities in the Colonies and Cuba*, about what awaited potential investors in Puerto Rico. He praised the soil for still being fertile even though "portions of it were under tillage long before the Pilgrims waded ashore at Plymouth." Yet much was being used for pastures, which Allen thought "under proper conditions could be devoted to the cultivation of sugar cane"—a topic about which he had learned a great deal.[86]

In the book, he divided the 950,000 Puerto Ricans on the island into "whites," "negroes," and "mestizos," and claimed that Puerto Rico had "a larger percentage of white inhabitants than is found in any other island in the West Indies."[87] He found the people to have a "distinct individuality," though predicted that with the "thrift and industry which follows the Anglo-Saxon, in time this very individuality will disappear."[88] Allen also envisioned an island that could support industry or be ideal for a second home, as it had "little to be vainly looked for by the continental resident seeking a winter residence."[89]

Despite its many natural resources, the island economy lagged, as a 1903 headline in the *New York Times* made clear: "Porto Rico Not Prospering Under United States Rules." The unsigned piece pointed a finger at the United States for not doing more to buy Puerto Rican coffee and other products, yet it made the improbable claim that "thus far Porto Rico has been blessed with honest American officials."[90] Blaming the "shiftless native labor," the article boasted that "an American can do ten times as much work as a Porto Rican, and do it better at that." The myth of the lazy Hispanic continued to stalk the former Spanish territory.

Puerto Ricans were working hard, on and off the island. Many landless or peasant agricultural workers—known on the island as *jíbaros*—had left to labor in the fields of a fellow territory, Hawaii. Small farmers devastated by the 1899 hurricane felt they had few other options, not least because a coffee crop takes about five years to yield a harvest. By 1901, more than fifty-two hundred Puerto Ricans had arrived in Hawaii, desperate enough to take their chances to work in fields thousands of miles away.[91] In the meantime, U.S. interests continued to pour money into Puerto Rican sugar operations, taking control of or buying out other growers, until five major corporations dominated sugar on the island.[92]

The Mexicans in Texas or New Mexico had citizenship, or at least the right to obtain it, conferred on them. By contrast, the situation in Puerto Rico was unclear. In the 1901 *Downes v. Bidwell* case, the Supreme Court ruled that the Constitution did not have the same application on the island as it did on the mainland. As a result, Justice Edward White introduced the doctrine of territorial nonincorporation; in domestic terms, Puerto Ricans were foreign; in international terms they belonged to United States.[93]

This principle was difficult to translate into practice, and a high-profile case the following year tested the limits of nonincorporation for Puerto Ricans. The legal battle began when a young Puerto Rican woman named Isabel González tried to enter the mainland United States in 1902. She was a single mother traveling without her child but also pregnant. Her intention was to follow her fiancé to Staten Island, where he was working, and marry him. Her brother lived there along with other relatives. Put into the same category of "alien" as other foreigners, Puerto Ricans in 1902 had to enter via Ellis Island, which at that time was under the commissionership of William Williams. He was an advocate of strict enforcement, and the rate of people turned away had doubled in his first year.[94] Of special interest to him were the people thought likely to need recourse to public funds, or, as it was put in the case of González, "likely to become a public charge."[95] Under this regime, unmarried mothers or women who were pregnant were taken for further questioning, while single women had to be collected by a family member. Once González's pregnancy was revealed, she was pulled aside, although family members were present to meet her. Officials asked whether her relatives were "able, willing and legally bound" to give her support.[96]

Her family explained to officials that she was a widow about to remarry.[97] However, her fiancé was not there in person because he was at work, and this aroused further suspicion. The final blow came when her brother, Luis, assured the officials that her family would make sure Isabel and her fiancé married, leaving the impression that the fiancé was being forced to wed Isabel.[98] After that, she was denied entry. She turned to the well-known Puerto Rican lawyer Domingo Collazo to take up the case. This soon turned into a larger battle that was about more than just her right to entry—it was about the status of all Puerto Ricans. In fact, while she was awaiting the trial on bond she married her fiancé, and that would have changed her eligibility, but she hid this fact because she knew what was at stake.[99]

The case reached the Supreme Court by 1903, and after two months of hearings and deliberations it issued a unanimous ruling that the word "alien" could not be used in relation to Puerto Ricans. It did not make them full citizens, but it meant they could have more freedom to travel and live on the mainland.[100] Isabel González, for her part, was not pleased, and criticized the decision for not addressing the real issue of true citizenship. It did, however, open the way for more people to head north. After the 1904 ruling in *Gonzales v. Williams*—the court misspelled her name—more Puerto Ricans began to pack their bags for El Norte.[101]

On the island, divisions persisted about the direction of its future. Some wanted independence, but others, like Luis Muñoz Rivera, who was resident commissioner from 1911 to 1916, advocated a sort of self-governing in-between status. This was, in part because although he and his party, the Unión de Puerto Rico (Unionist Party), preferred statehood, they believed the U.S. Congress would not pursue it. At the same time, Muñoz Rivera considered full independence by this point a "purely abstract ideal."[102] Instead, Puerto Rico came a step closer to this desired autonomy in March 1917 with the Jones-Shafroth Act, though Muñoz Rivera died in late 1916, before its passage. This legislation created an elected bicameral legislature for the island, giving Puerto Ricans a greater degree of local democracy. It also made them U.S. citizens, partially incorporating them into the wider nation while also reminding them of the limits of self-rule on the island.[103]

A crucial element of Jones-Shafroth was the opening of the U.S. military to Puerto Ricans. As the First World War began in Europe, the United States realized it needed to shore up its influence in its own backyard. Rumors that Germany had an increasing interest in the Caribbean unnerved Washington; and not coincidentally, in 1917 the United States also purchased the Danish West Indian islands of St. Croix, St. John, and St. Thomas, today's U.S. Virgin Islands.

On May 18, 1917, Congress passed the Selective Service Act, which meant all men between ages eighteen and thirty-two had to register for military service. At the request of the Puerto Rican legislature, Congress extended the draft to include Puerto Rico.[104] On the first day, 104,550 Puerto Rican men signed up; the number later reached 236,853, with 17,885 called into service.[105] A Puerto Rican regiment was sent to Panama, while other soldiers joined black regiments.[106]

A few years after the First World War ended, E. Montgomery Reily arrived as governor of Puerto Rico, in 1921. He had no previous experience in governance and diplomacy, and his background was as an assistant postmaster and businessman in Kansas City. He had become involved in local and then national Republican politics, helping to build support for the successful presidential bid by Warren Harding, who in turn appointed Reily to the governorship.

Among all the unpopular governors sent to the island, he may well have been the most despised. He was so ill-prepared for his post that President Harding had to edit Reily's inaugural address. It was delivered on July 10, 1921, and, despite the blue pencil marks of the president, Reily managed to offend his audience, saying that "there is no sympathy or possible hope in the United States for independence" for the island.[107] His overall plan was to "Americanize" it. He later complained to Harding in a letter that "after my inaugural address was made, I received a number of letters threatening my life."[108] During his two years in office, sugar prices collapsed. Puerto Ricans in New York also joined in the chorus against him.[109] With the situation deteriorating, Reily wrote to the president in March 1922, telling him that everything was "tranquil and peaceful" except for the fact that his enemies on the island had "appointed a Grand

Jury about three weeks ago to investigate everything my administration accomplished. It is nothing but a political Grand Jury."[110] Reily tendered his resignation in February 1923.

The combination of ongoing economic struggles and the stream of incompetent governors continued to cause problems in Puerto Rico throughout the 1920s and 1930s. While this turned some people into more ardent supporters of independence, thousands more decided to leave Puerto Rico and take their chances on the mainland.[111]

After the end of the Spanish-American-Cuban War, the United States reached even farther south, to the Isthmus of Panama, which was then part of Colombia. The dream of connecting the Atlantic and Pacific, like that of finding the fabled Northwest Passage, had persisted for centuries, but now engineering could make the connection a cartographic reality. The former French diplomat Ferdinand de Lesseps, who been the force behind the construction of the Suez Canal, which opened in 1869, set up a private company to do the same in the Americas, paying Colombia for a concession to the land. Construction began in 1880 through the dense jungle that blankets the isthmus. Thousands of workers died from malaria and other tropical diseases, and Lesseps ran out of money before quitting in 1889.

Other plans for a canal through Nicaragua came to nothing, and by 1902, the United States wanted to pick up where the French had left off. However, the Colombian Congress was not pleased with the terms of the Hay-Herrán Treaty that U.S. and Colombian ministers had drawn up: $10 million for a ninety-nine-year lease and an annual payment of $250,000. The Colombian politicians knew the canal would be worth more and Colombia's Congress refused to ratify the treaty. The United States was forced to find another way. It enticed separatists to foment a "revolution" to break away from Colombia, establish a new nation, and permit the construction of the canal. By 1903, with the backing of U.S. gunships, the Republic of Panama was proclaimed, and by 1914 the canal was open.[112]

The year after the creation of Panama, President Theodore Roosevelt outlined in his annual address to Congress of 1904 what became known as the Roosevelt Corollary. No longer satisfied with the strictures of the Monroe Doctrine of more than eighty years before, Roosevelt's described this new vision as the United States' desire "to see the neighboring countries stable, orderly, and prosperous. Any country whose people conduct themselves well can count upon our hearty friendship."[113] Yet those who fell out of line might "ultimately require intervention by some civilized nation, and in the Western Hemisphere the adherence of the United States to the Monroe Doctrine may force the United States, however reluctantly, in flagrant cases of such wrongdoing or impotence, to the exercise of an international police power."[114] Roosevelt cited as examples the recent events in Cuba and Panama where "we have acted in our own interest as well as in the interest of humanity at large."[115]

WHILE EVENTS IN Cuba, Puerto Rico, and Panama had been taking place, in the West the territories of Arizona and New Mexico continued in their dogged pursuit of statehood, now more than fifty years after the Mexican-American War. Although the people who lived there were U.S. citizens, their continued status as residents of territories meant they could not vote for their own governor, nor did they have national representation, and so they could not share in the same rights and privileges as citizens in established states.[116] In the years since the end of the conflict in 1848, fifteen new states had joined the union. The only territories in the continental United States that remained at the turn of the century were New Mexico, Arizona, Oklahoma, and what was known as Indian territory. The last two would become combined into the state of Oklahoma in 1907.[117]

New Mexico's failure to obtain statehood had not been for lack of trying. Numerous attempts had been made over the years, led for the most part by local elites, both Anglo and *Nuevomexicano*, who stood to profit from the changed status.[118] In 1874 the congressional delegate for New Mexico, the businessman and Santa Fe Ring member Stephen Elkins, received a note congratulating him on his attempts to have the territory admitted as a state, saying: "More rapid growth and development will follow the organization of a state government . . . emigration will increase, old mines will be worked, new ones opened, railroads completed, and a resort for health and pleasure opened to the people of other states."[119] Such optimism was misplaced when Congress rejected the bid for statehood. Elkins and the Santa Fe Ring were in part the reason this process had taken so long, as they tainted the territory by incurring charges of corruption and mismanagement. Elkins later left the territory for West Virginia, where he finished his political career as a senator for that state.

Hopeful New Mexicans continued to push on. An 1881 pamphlet published by the Territorial Bureau of Immigration voiced optimism: "What can be had in new Mexico to-day in the way of mining property for a trifle, will, in a few years, command thousands."[120] Indeed, the territory had been growing throughout this time: the population was about 150,000, with Santa Fe being the largest town at 7,000 inhabitants. Of this population, around 20,000 were Native Americans, and the majority of the remaining people were, as the pamphlet explained, "native whites, often called for convenience 'Mexicans.'"[121] They were also known as *nativos*, U.S. citizens but of Mexican descent. The press and politicians often described New Mexican *nativos* as not "ready" for the responsibilities of statehood, prompting supporters to rise to the territory's defense. The Colorado state senator Casimiro Barela made a speech in 1889 laying out the reasons that his birthplace, New Mexico, should have statehood:

> I am aware that the enemies of the admission of New Mexico claim that its native population is not yet qualified to assume the burden, the duties and the obligations of citizenship; they assert that the Mexican population is ignorant and can be easily controlled by talented but desperate American adventurers who have infested the territory, and who aim to use the Mexican population as the implements of their corrupt schemes. I repel the charge with earnest scorn.[122]

Alongside this was the implication that New Mexicans were unfit for statehood because they were, in the racial terms of the time, mixed. Out of these charges emerged one line of defense espoused by pro-statehood Anglo and Hispanic leaders: that New Mexicans were of "Spanish"— that is, European—blood. This led to a historical pronouncements and a blurred fantasy past—not unlike that of the Californios—bolstered by Anglo defenders, such as LeBaron Bradford Prince, a judge who also served as a territorial governor. Prince claimed that while there were many Pueblo villages in New Mexico, "no marriage or similar connections take place between the races." Prince, who was born in New York and moved to New Mexico in 1878, was a tireless champion of statehood and later wrote books about New Mexico's history, but during the statehood debate he helped lay a foundation for a "Spanish American" identity. These New Mexicans were, as he put it, "fit representatives of the land of the Cid, and successors of the historic discoverers and conquerors of the soil." Given the belief in Washington that a racially "mixed" population was unfit to govern, there was a certain logic in denying that there had ever been mixing between Spaniards and Indians or black people, even if it was at odds with reality. Prince instead argued that *Nuevomexicanos* were "racially distinct from the mestizos and 'lower' classes."[123]

This idea backfired somewhat when the Spanish-American-Cuban War of 1898 brought to New Mexico's door charges that, as Spanish-speaking people in the Southwest, New Mexicans were supporting Spain in secret—a rumor that the territorial governor Miguel Otero, who served from 1897 until 1906, was quick to counter.[124] When the conflict started, he recalled in his memoir, "our people were ready to do their share of the fighting, and more—even though many of them were proud of their Spanish blood."[125] After the explosion on the *Maine* Otero was contacted by the newspaper *New York World* for comment, and he used the opportunity to remind readers that "a large majority of her [New Mexico's] soldiers are Spanish-speaking and are as loyal to this country as any New England troops."[126] More than four hundred men joined up and rode into battle with Theodore Roosevelt, making Otero proud that "in proportion to her population, New Mexico had furnished more volunteers for the war, per capita, than any other state or territory."[127]

After the contribution of the New Mexicans in that war, some of New Mexico's politicians once more pressed their case for statehood to President Roosevelt, who had succeded to the presidency after McKinley was assassinated in September 1901.[128] Otero had not started out as a supporter of statehood, on the basis that New Mexico did not have the money to pay the expenses of being a state, but the economy had expanded through the 1890s and he changed his mind, making a hopeful prediction in 1902 that he would not be able to finish his second term in office because New Mexico would become a state within those four years.[129]

Otero and fellow proponents of statehood assumed the attempt in 1902–03 would be successful, as it had plenty of congressional support. A bill put forward by the Massachusetts congressman William Knox to allow New Mexico, Arizona, and Oklahoma to begin the statehood process passed the House—but the bill also had a very committed foe. Senator Albert Beveridge, the Republican who spoke with such determination about the forward march of the U.S. flag, was also the chairman of the Senate Committee on Territories, and his own view was that New Mexico had a "savage and an alien population."[130]

In the late autumn of 1902, a Senate committee arrived to inspect these territories. According to Otero, they never stood a chance, in part because L. G. Rothschild, known as "the Baron," was accompanying the senators—Rothschild was from Indianapolis, and Beveridge represented Indiana. During the trip, Rothschild acted as the "outside man," by undertaking reconnaissance in the worst parts of town. Otero harbored little hope that any positive aspect of New Mexico would be acknowledged. He said Rothschild "visited the saloons and the dance hall district. . . . He would photograph a lewd, dirty prostitute or a drunken scoundrel stretched out in some alley. . . . These exhibits were to be used to convince eastern people that such were the general conditions of society in New Mexico."[131] The negative campaign worked. The bill was killed. President Roosevelt later told Otero: "If I were in your place I would remain a territory as long as the United States government will pay your running expenses."[132]

Three areas of concern emerged from this second attempt at statehood. The first was that not enough people in the territory spoke English. Otero argued that the committee members had misrepresented this in their report by choosing witnesses who had poor English in order to bolster the idea that too much Spanish was still being used.[133] Arizona faced similar criticism, as around a quarter of its 123,000 people did not speak English.[134] Yet in the years between the two statehood attempts, efforts to use English had grown. In 1890, for instance, students in 143 of the 342 public schools in New Mexico were taught only in English. There was an increase in English-language newspapers as well, and the territory's Spanish-speakers were on their way to becoming bilingual, though the same could not be said about the Anglo population.[135]

The second issue was the long-running idea that nearly two hundred thousand New Mexicans in the territory lacked the education and ability to govern themselves, a discussion that intersected with racial ideas and was furthered and fostered by the campaign against the Knox Bill. The final concern, also of long standing, was related to the political balance of the West. This issue had been brewing since the end of the Civil War, with Democrats and Republicans vying for voters in new states. An earlier chairman of the congressional Committee on Territories, Orville Platt—the same politician who crafted the 1901 amendment relating to Cuba and the United States—had written to Stephen Elkins in 1889 to say that "the only way to make a Republican State of it [New Mexico] is to postpone the question of admission until Republican judges, governor, and other officers, have been in the Territory long enough, so that the Mexican population can realize that it is a Republican administration we are to live under."[136]

The Republicans continued to seek political control of New Mexico and Arizona. After killing off the statehood bill, Beveridge changed his approach and proposed instead to admit New Mexico and Arizona as one state. Of interest to Beveridge was the fact that Arizona's voters opted for Republicans, so merging the two might tip the balance in his party's favor. In addition, mixing the Anglo minority in New Mexico and the majority in Arizona would consolidate Anglo dominance overall.[137] President Roosevelt even mentioned the plan in his annual message to Congress in 1905, recommending that "New Mexico and Arizona be admitted as one state. . . . Nothing has taken up more time in Congress during the past few years than the question as to Statehood to be granted to the four Territories above mentioned [New Mexico, Arizona, Oklahoma, and Indian territory]."[138]

A split vote in Arizona and New Mexico in 1906 quashed that idea, with Arizonans rejecting it 16,265 to 3,141, in part because Anglos were fearful of the influx of a large Spanish-speaking population. By 1900 Arizona had a population of 122,000, but only about 20 percent were of Mexican descent, down from 45 percent in 1870. Mining and railroad jobs had attracted white settlers from across the country, as well as Mexico-born immigrants, who, at 14,172, accounted for more than half the Hispanic population in Arizona. However, these migrants could not vote. That left around 10,000 Hispanic U.S. citizens in Arizona, of whom only a few thousand would be eligible voters. In addition some mestizo voters, despite being U.S. citizens, were denied the opportunity to cast their ballots if they appeared too "Indian." This left Hispanic citizens in Arizona with little political clout.[139]

New Mexicans, on the other hand, backed the measure, 26,195 to 14,735. In New Mexico, the *nativo* population was estimated to be around 90,000 out of a total of 195,000 in the territory, most of whom were born in the United States. Because they had been classified as "white"—as were 180,207 people in New Mexico—most Hispanic men were eligible to vote. The *nativos* promoted a pluralist idea and vision for the territory; they used the term to continue to emphasize their long lineage in the region and to imply that they shared a European heritage with Anglos due to their "pure" Spanish roots.[140] Many *nativos* were middle-class and bilingual, and worked as doctors, journalists, and lawyers. At the same time, however, Spanish-language newspapers promoted the continued speaking of Spanish in the face of long-running criticism from Washington and elsewhere in the United States. As one newspaper put it in 1911: "We need to learn the language of our country . . . but we don't need to, with such motive, deny our origin, our race, our language."[141] Many of these contradictions were encapsulated by the emergence of the identifier *hispano-americano*, which was understood in the context of the New Mexican fight for statehood to highlight a person's Spanish origins, while at the same time disavowing a more recent Mexican—and probably indigenous—past.[142]

When William Howard Taft entered the White House in 1909, political momentum to resolve the statehood issue was renewed. He visited Albuquerque in October of that year as part of a longer trip to El Paso, where he met the Mexican president Porfirio Díaz. While in New Mexico, he told assembled local politicians and leaders, after a spirited discussion: "I am not contending against your coming in. I am only contending that you should come in sane."[143]

The way forward was becoming clearer, and the failure of the single-state plan had shown the necessity of allowing two separate states, leading to the 1910 Enabling Act, which empowered Arizona and New Mexico to draft their respective constitutions. New Mexico's reflected its more pluralistic view, safeguarding political rights for Hispanic people, ensuring equal access to education, and even stipulating that public documents should be in English and Spanish. Arizona's document took a more exclusionary route, for example limiting certain jobs to U.S. citizens or English-speakers, and not providing for official papers to be translated into English.[144] Once the constitutions were hammered out, congressional approval followed.[145] On January 6, 1912, more than half a century after the Mexican-American War, New Mexico joined the union, and Arizona followed on February 14 in the same year.[146]

Chapter 12

Del Rio, Texas, ca. 1910–40

At FIRST GLANCE, the sepia-tinted photograph appears to show a normal Sunday outing from around the turn of the century: men in suits and bowler hats, women in long dresses using parasols to shield their skin from the burning rays of the sun. The people are dispersed along the riverbank, most of them looking across, to the south. Yet this is no ordinary scene. It is a picture of "Americans and inssurectos [*sic*] at Río Grande," as its handwritten caption indicates. Across the river from the well-dressed Texans, lining the opposite bank are Mexican men, wearing sombreros and ammunition belts, the light casting their reflection in the water, while behind them, beyond a narrow stretch of flat land, are large hills.[1] The image, thought to have been taken sometime around 1911 near the El Paso–Juárez border, is not a battle shot. On both sides, people are milling about, watching and waiting. The Anglos were not armed— they were there for amusement. The ongoing unrest in Mexico was common knowledge along the border, and when these Mexicans, often depicted as fearsome *bandidos*, showed up, people wanted to watch. This could be a dangerous form of entertainment: four spectators were killed by stray bullets during a battle near Juárez in 1911.[2] However risky it was, spectators were watching live history, as the Mexican Revolution unfolded in front of their eyes.

The drama at the border and beyond would last for more than a decade and shape the future of Mexico, as well as its relationship with the United States. The Mexican Revolution was the culmination of many different strands of discontent within Mexico, offering competing visions of what the country could be.[3] It was a liberating, confusing, violent, and often terrifying time for Mexicans, with fear reaching into the borderlands. The emerging mass media of photography and newsreels meant that events during the revolution were recorded and circulated, taking the conflict well beyond the confines of Mexico.[4]

The roots of the revolution lay in the regime of Porfirio Díaz, known as the *Porfiriato*. Díaz had been in power since 1876, except for an interregnum when army general Manuel González, his ally, was president from 1880 to 1884; and the *Porfiriato* period was marked by peace, political stability, and economic growth—but it came with dictatorship as its price. It was a time of men in silk top hats and women in elegant dresses at one end of the social spectrum, and of landless, impoverished peasants at the other. It was Mexico's version of the Gilded Age, guided by an administration in thrall to French positivist ideas of the importance of quantifiable progress—no matter how pseudoscientific the instruments for measuring it were—giving rise to the nickname *Científicos* (scientists) for government ministers. Foreign investment was welcomed, railways crossed the land, and mines and factories sprang up, while the poorest—who were often indigenous—were pushed aside and languished in poverty. In the capital and regional cities, urban professional and middle classes wanted to see political reforms, in part to widen their own limited access to governmental roles.[5]

By the early 1900s, the multiple reelections of Díaz and the heavy hand of his regime had become a source of discontent for many Mexicans. This was underscored by unresolved issues concerning land. Under Díaz, land policy had its roots the 1856 Ley Lerdo (or Lerdo Law, named after the finance minister at the time), which had involved the forced sale of Church land and communal peasant holdings. It was a move that benefited urban professionals, regional elites, and smaller private landowners who were in a position to buy up these assets but angered the Church and peasant communities.[6] Intermittent rebellions took place from that point through the 1870s. Díaz had, at the start of his presidency, given the appearance of favoring village communities over the landed elite, but that ended up being not quite the case. His drive to modernize meant bringing railroads to Mexico, which entailed buying up land, including that held by villages, sparking further regional insurrections that were suppressed in the 1880s.[7]

With trains to take products farther from the field, markets opened up for agriculture and large landholders; increasingly, foreign investors, including those from the United States, Canada, Britain, France, and Germany, looked to further develop the railway infrastructure and the land. In the northern border area alone, between 1877 and 1910 the number of small ranches (ranchos) increased five times over, and there was a doubling of the larger haciendas.[8] A labor shortage in the north meant that workers from elsewhere needed to be enticed to these estates. At times, wage advances were offered as an incentive, resulting in a system that left some laborers constantly indebted to their employers.[9]

Over the course of the *Porfiriato*, community landholdings dropped to 2 percent of national land, down from 25 percent. Foreigners held 90 percent of the incorporated value of Mexican industry and 150 million acres of land. Of that, U.S. investors were the owners of 70 percent of the industrial wealth and 130 million acres of land.[10] "Poor Mexico," Díaz was said to have remarked, "so far from God, so close to the United States."[11]

As dissent grew, Mexicans persecuted by the Díaz regime sometimes crossed into the United States, for instance, the vocal brothers Ricardo and Enrique Flores Magón, who had been imprisoned in Mexico for what they published in their newspaper *Regeneración*. They fled to San Antonio in 1904, and later to St. Louis, then Los Angeles where they continued to speak out against Díaz. They also established the Partido Liberal Mexicano (Mexican Liberal Party), calling for freedom of speech, better working conditions, and agrarian reform.[12] Their radical ideas managed to attract the attention of U.S. authorities, landing them in prison—where they could be closely watched—on dubious charges such as the violation of neutrality laws.[13]

Another voice joining the growing opposition was that of Francisco Madero, who captured the Mexican public's attention in 1908 after publishing a critique of Díaz's policies, *The Presidential Succession in 1910*. Madero was a wealthy scion of a landowning family in Coahuila, and his book reflected much of the anger about political corruption, calling, for instance, for the implementation of a rule allowing a president to serve only one term. The tract spoke to segments of the public who were fed up with Díaz and his cronies, and momentum gathered behind Madero, especially across the north of the country, propelling him toward a run for the presidency. All of these murmurings of discontent were taking place at the time of the hundredth anniversary of Padre Hidalgo's famous *Grito de Dolores*. Díaz had planned lavish celebrations to mark the centenary on September 16, 1910, and was determined that voices of dissent would not interrupt the festivities or impede his reelection later that year.

Díaz had Madero arrested ahead of the election on false sedition charges, rendering him ineligible to run. He was released on bail that October, after Díaz had again secured the presidency. Madero fled to Texas where he drafted and released his Plan de San Luís Potosí, in which he declared that after the result of the last election, it would be "treason to the people" if he did not "compel General Díaz by force of arms, to respect the national will" and step down.[14] By November 20, 1910, armed uprisings started. At first, Díaz dismissed the violence as banditry, but it was soon clear, as the jails filled with political prisoners, that something much larger was afoot.[15] At this early juncture, the United States was officially disinclined to become involved with what it regarded as an internal issue, so long as its interests remained unharmed.[16]

By early 1911, more revolts broke out, including one in Morelos, a state to the south of the capital. Leading the fighters was Emiliano Zapata, who grew up in Anenecuilco, a village in that state, in a landowning family. Like many in these rural regions, Zapata became concerned, and then mobilized, over the preservation of local lands, especially as sugar interests dominated Morelos.[17] His desire to defend the poorest farmers—coupled with photographs of his unwavering gaze and enormous mustache—later transformed him into a national figure who became known well beyond Mexico. Also riding into battle in 1911 was Francisco "Pancho" Villa, who would enjoy wide renown as he allowed newsreel cameras to follow his exploits. His chubby, often smiling face; large sombrero; and bandoliers slung across his chest would make him instantly recognizable. Villa was from humble origins in Durango and had joined the revolution under the leadership of Pascual Orozco, who was organizing forces in Chihuahua.[18] The rebels soon moved in on Ciudad Juárez, across from El Paso, and this now signaled to an ailing Díaz the scale of the revolt. Almost every state was embroiled in some sort of upheaval, causing U.S. president Taft to send troops to reinforce the border in March.[19]

Madero, by this point, had enough support to put him in a position to insist on a deal. Talks at first focused on a demand for Díaz's resignation, which was rejected, and so fighting resumed, with at least twenty-five thousand revolutionaries taking up arms.[20] On May 10, 1911, Orozco's troops defeated federal forces and took Juárez, a strategic move, as the city had access to the railways and proximity to willing arms smugglers across the border.[21]

The shouts against the president grew louder, as the public flooded into Zócalo, the main square in Mexico City—despite the fact that troops were firing on them—to demand again that Díaz step down. He relented, offering his resignation on May 25, and a few hours later he left for exile in France.[22] Elections were scheduled for October, and Madero won. Now that he was in power, however, he faced a new challenge. Significant differences existed between him and the hastily organized outfits that had come to his aid. In these conditions, Madero soon misstepped, angering allies by allowing some government and military officials from the previous regime to keep their roles.[23] Madero also enraged Zapata by refusing to order an immediate return of village lands, and he even appeared to be privatizing holdings in some areas. In response, on November 25 Zapata issued his Plan de Ayala, which called for, among other things, the overthrow of Madero. He also incensed Orozco by not giving him a significant political post.[24] Before long, Orozco also proclaimed himself against the new regime, in spring 1912, as other regional commanders joined in the rebellion against Madero.

The United States continued to watch with concern, both at the border and farther south, not least because Zapata and his Zapatistas were raiding U.S. investors' large landholdings. Many Americans living in Mexico were running back north. At one point, President Taft sent the USS *Buford* to evacuate U.S. citizens from the Pacific coast. He also put an embargo on selling weapons to Mexico.[25]

Throughout that year a number of revolts occurred around the country, as did crippling strikes as unions called for better working conditions. Two more key players emerged on Madero's side: Álvaro Obregón, who had pushed rebels under Orozco out of Sonora; and General Victoriano Huerta, a leftover from the Díaz regime.[26] Huerta would prove to be a dangerous ally. He orchestrated behind the scenes—with the involvement of the U.S. ambassador Henry Lane Wilson—Madero's eventual assassination on February 22, 1913, along with that of his vice president, José María Pino Suárez, which ended a particularly violent episode known as the *Decena Trágica* (Tragic Ten Days).[27]

What had been unleashed in 1910 now had very different dimensions. Representing the old order, Huerta—now installed as president—faced a large rebellion across the northern states, where Villa returned to action after Huerta had the antagonistic governor of Chihuahua, Abraham González, killed. Now the rebels were calling for a return to a constitutional government based on the Plan de Guadalupe, written by Venustiano Carranza, a former supporter of Madero and governor of Coahuila. These "Constitutionalists" decided that Carranza would be their "first chief," until Huerta could be thrown out of office and the constitution restored.[28]

The north of Mexico was a key area—Villa and Obregón led divisions there, and Constitutionalist troops were positioned across states that bordered the United States, as well as in their provisional government headquarters in Hermosillo, Sonora.[29] In particular, Villa's División del Norte continued to attract willing fighters from many walks of life, including miners, farmers, and *vaqueros*. For a short while, U.S. interests even favored him to be the future president of Mexico.[30] So magnetic was the pull around Villa that the writer Ambrose Bierce, seventy-one years old at the time, traveled to Mexico to join his troops. Bierce's last known letter was sent from Chihuahua in 1913, and he was never heard from again. Not everyone was seduced by the legend, least of all press baron William Randolph Hearst, who owned land in Chihuahua. Villa and his men attacked Hearst's Babicora Ranch in late 1915, taking sixty thousand head of cattle and chasing the ranch manager all the way to Texas.[31] The coverage of Villa in Hearst's newspapers painted a far from flattering portrait, as might be expected.

Throughout this period, often called the "brown scare," concern grew about the number of Mexicans seeking refuge in the United States. Some of these refugees were monitored by agents, were arrested, or faced physical violence.[32] The revolution was spilling across the border; not only were people traversing it, but so were guns, ammunition, drugs, cattle, and stolen goods. The U.S. guards were on the lookout for all manner of suspects, from contrabandists to political radicals, though innocent people were apprehended, too.[33] Many Mexicans in the United States and Mexican-Americans had their own reservations about the United States' involvement in this conflict. In 1913, New Mexico senator Albert B. Fall received a copy of an open letter addressed to him by Pedro Portillo, a local man angered that the senator was "fathering a bill in Congress that if passed will allow the exportation of guns and ammunition to both government and rebels in Mexico." For Portillo, the hypocrisy was clear because "at the same time you and other senators are raising cane [Cain] because the Mexican government has not been able to protect the life and property of Americans in some isolated places."[34] Fall—who was later implicated for secretly leasing oil reserve lands in the Teapot Dome Scandal—had been sent the letter by a friend who wanted to alert him that it was being distributed "through the mail to the Spanish Americans." In replying to this friend, an unconcerned Fall noted that the letter "simply caused amusement," explaining:

> Portillo like a great many others, seems to imagine that Mexico con-
> ferred a great favor upon us by allowing us to invest one and a half
> billions of dollars in the commercial conquest and actual civilization
> in that country until we own practically twice as much of Mexico as
> do the Mexicans themselves, and at the same time he thinks that we
> should display our gratitude to them by allowing them to destroy
> with impunity all this property.[35]

As the conflict near the border intensified, Villa continued to reassure U.S. representatives in Mexico that their interests were not in danger, though his confiscation of hacienda land that had belonged to Huerta's supporters in the north gave them some cause for concern.[36] Senator Thomas Catron of New Mexico received a telegram in April 1914 from a contact in El Paso who heard that Villa was on his way to the city and that he had seven thousand men within thirty miles of Juárez.[37] Catron fired off a letter to William Jennings Bryan, now serving as secretary of state, asking him to "take the necessary steps to secure the safety of persons and property in El Paso."[38] Army units from San Francisco and Kansas left soon afterward to fortify the border.

By this point, Woodrow Wilson had become president of the United States. He was reluctant to recognize Huerta's government until there were fresh elections and ran out of patience by the time they were finally held in October 1913 and immediately criticized as being fraudulent. Huerta remained in power, despite Wilson's demand that he resign.[39] By February 1914 Wilson lifted the arms embargo, allowing ammunition to reach Villa and Carranza.[40] Then, in April, after receiving reports of the arrest of U.S. sailors in the Mexican port of Tampico and news of a German ship bound for Veracruz loaded with arms for Huerta's troops, Wilson decided to act. On April 21, the U.S. president sent in the Navy, and fifteen ships bombarded Veracruz, leaving hundreds dead, most of them innocent civilians. Afterward thirty-five hundred U.S. troops went ashore to occupy the city.[41] The return of the United States to Mexican soil—especially to the same city assaulted in the Mexican-American War—was greeted with a unanimous cry of outrage.[42] Even Carranza declared the intervention to be a violation of national sovereignty.[43] There were protests and attacks on U.S. civilians, which worsened relations between Wilson and the Constitutionalists. By November, the United States pulled out.[44]

Villa had, in the first half of 1914, managed to strike a number of blows against Huerta's troops, including a key victory at Zacatecas in June. As the Constitutionalists successfully pushed south, Huerta lost ground, and by mid-July 1914, he capitulated and resigned, going into exile. On August 20, Carranza entered the capital, where Obregón had brought some six thousand troops five days earlier. From there, Carranza established his government, though this did not end the fighting.[45]

New factions were emerging, and they would lead to more violence. In very general terms, Carranza and Obregón represented the interests of some regional elites, the middle classes, merchants, and other professionals, while Villa and Zapata claimed the support of the working class, including the miners and vaqueros, as well as the poorer agricultural workers, smallholders, and peasants. Both sides also had the support of women who accompanied their husbands to battle, went in support roles such as nurses, or took up arms themselves as *soldaderas*.

Carranza, Obregón, Villa, and Zapata disagreed about a number of issues, most of all land.[46] Although Villa redistributed some of the lands he had confiscated in the north, land reform was not a defining issue for him, as it was for Zapata. The rifts among the four men continued to grow, and so, to quell the animosity, a convention was called, with delegates to be sent from the Constitutionalists, Villa's División del Norte, and the Zapatistas. They convened at Aguascalientes, about three hundred miles northwest of the capital, on October 10, 1914. By this point, only a handful of the hundred or so delegates still supported Carranza, but they continued to be committed Constitutionalists and so were slow to encourage a Villa-Zapata alliance. The delegates did, however, commit to adopting parts of Zapata's Plan de Ayala, promising to put agrarian reform in any future constitution.[47] By the end of the convention, the delegates voted Carranza out and put General Eulalio Gutiérrez in his place. Carranza refused to step down, and so Gutiérrez put Villa in charge of leading the attack on him, and Zapata also followed suit. Carranza retreated to Veracruz, while a tenuous "Conventionalist" alliance of Villa and Zapata, with Gutiérrez as an interim president, was formed.[48] Soon after the convention, Villa and Zapata had a meeting in Xochimilco, just south of the capital, in early December, discussing their shared hatred of Carranza and the petit bourgeois he represented. A couple of days later, they paraded their armies into Mexico City.[49] Despite the seemingly united start, the two men soon discovered their divisions. During his campaign to drive Carranza's troops out of Puebla, Zapata was annoyed that the artillery Villa had promised him was late in arriving, and this was only around a week after their meeting.[50] A short time later, in December 1914, Carranza decided to declare that, among other reforms, he would return land to dispossessed people and villages. While Carranza was trying to broaden his support, Gutiérrez decided to flee the capital and the interim presidency in 1915, leaving the Conventionalists under Villa and Zapata facing an uncertain future.[51]

Meanwhile, hostilities in Mexico toward non-Mexicans continued to rise. In 1915, foreign landowners in Sonora were told to show their land titles. One businessman, L. W. Mix, owner of the Arcadia Hotel in Hermosillo, sent a letter to the U.S. consulate in Nogales, Mexico, to find out if he had to comply. He was fearful that he would lose everything, especially if he did not have the necessary papers. "Conditions in Mexico are, in my opinion, growing worse," he wrote. "Also at various times during the recent anarchy and revolution, which has ruined Sonora, public records of all kinds, have been maliciously and wantonly destroyed."[52]

The poet Langston Hughes recalled how his father lived in Mexico during this period, working for a New York–based electric-light company in the Toluca area, to the west of Mexico City. Unlike other Americans, he had an unexpected advantage. "Because he was brown, the Mexicans could not tell at sight that he was a Yankee," Hughes recalled in his memoir *The Big Sea*. "and even after they knew it, they did not believe he was like the white Yankees." Hughes's father managed to stay when other foreigners fled, as "the followers of Zapata and Villa did not run him away as they did the whites."[53]

Mexicans living near the border, meanwhile, suffered no matter what side they supported. Estimates put the overall death toll somewhere between 350,000 and one million.[54] Food shortages were common, as Amparo F. De Valencia recalled: "Sometimes one ate and sometimes one didn't. What good was money? Everyone suffered because one couldn't buy anything."[55] Aurora Mendoza was forced to go to El Paso because the ongoing violence cost her family their livelihood. "The federalists and the revolutionaries came and took whatever they wanted from our ranch," she recalled. "Many times they came and we didn't know what side they were on."[56]

By early 1915, revolution had crept into Texas in the guise of the Plan de San Diego. This plot was hatched in a prison in Monterrey, Mexico, but named after the Texas town of twenty-five hundred people where the manifesto, signed by nine men, was promulgated on January 6, 1915.[57] Police in nearby McAllen, Texas, found a copy of the manifesto in a pocket of one of the organizers, Basilio Ramos, having arrested him on a tip.[58]

The plan's objective was for Mexicans and Tejanos to stage a rebellion against Anglo rule on February 20 with a "Liberating army for Races and Peoples," which included Hispanics, African-Americans, and even Japanese. It proclaimed independence from "Yankee tyranny which has held us in iniquitous slavery since remote times."[59] They wanted to take back territory of which "the Republic of Mexico was robbed in a most perfidious manner by North American imperialism" in Texas, New Mexico, Arizona, California, and even Colorado.[60] Other parts of the plan included killing all Anglo men over the age of sixteen, giving black people their own republic, and returning some ancestral territory to Native Americans.

Agustín Garza commanded the liberating army, and bands of men, ranging in number from twenty-five to more than one hundred, attacked property, infrastructure such as railway lines, and livestock throughout the summer of 1915.[61] Retaliation in the Río Grande valley at the hands of the Texas Rangers was ferocious. Although the plan may have attracted as many as three thousand supporters, the Rangers' hunt for perpetrators resulted in the deaths of many innocent Mexicans and Tejanos wrongly charged with involvement. The Rangers explained the violence away in terms of self-defense in the face of racial warfare. Lynchings and executions became common and, in addition, rumors spread that the Germans and Japanese were arming the insurgents.[62] According to some estimates, around three hundred people were killed, though others place the number of dead in the thousands.[63]

Some historians have argued that the Plan de San Diego was a plot by Carranza who, depending on the interpretation, was funding these *sediciosos* to exact revenge for the Mexican-American War, foment a race and class war, or push President Wilson into recognizing his claim to the Mexican presidency, with the last being the most probable.[64] Even if there were national or larger geopolitical forces behind it, much of the plan's language was based on local grievances, and the fighting was mostly between Tejanos and Mexicans against the Texas Rangers.

By October 1915, Carranza received the recognition he wanted from the United States. As he dealt with a series of crippling strikes in the main cities, including the capital, Obregón was leading Constitutionalist troops into victories against Villa during 1915.[65] In November, Villa tried to mount another round of attacks, at Agua Prieta, just south of the border at Douglas, Arizona. The Constitutionalists were able defeat him, this time in part because the United States allowed Mexican reinforcements to enter via Texas and Arizona.[66]

A firm alliance between Villa and Zapata had never materialized, for a number of reasons. Some of the difficulty was structural, in that Zapata stuck to the south, and the area around Morelos, while Villa's base was in the north. Part of Villa's strategy was to raise a large army, while Zapata relied on guerrilla tactics. Their views on land distribution varied, but both men were grounded in the rural fight and the power of the regions, as opposed to the capital.[67] By 1916, they were turning in their own respective directions. For Villa, this meant going even farther north.

Wilson's recognition of Carranza had been a blow to Villa, who began to make more raids in the Río Grande valley.[68] Villa also reneged on his promises to leave U.S. interests alone. In January 1916, Villa's men stopped a train near Santa Ysabel, Chihuahua, that had U.S. mining engineers on board: at least sixteen men were taken off the train and murdered.[69]

Not long afterward, on a February morning in 1916, Lucy Read heard pounding at the front door of her home, also in Chihuahua. Her family "awoke to the sound of shattering window glass . . . and the angry voices of Villa and his men." Her British father was away on business in Sonora. "Villa reached out to me and pulled my hair," she said. "I recall his very words: 'Now *güerita* [fair one], you will never see your gringo daddy anymore.'" Villa's men searched the house and ransacked it before leaving. Read and her family fled to El Paso for safety.[70]

Villa made his way north, toward the border, riding into Columbus, New Mexico, on March 9, with five hundred men. A number of different explanations have been offered for this bold move: he and his men were in search of food and supplies; they wanted to punish arms dealers who had swindled them; they wanted to send a clear signal about Wilson backing the Constitutionalists; or, more ambitiously, Villa was hoping to needle the United States into another invasion of Mexico, in part to enhance his own image.[71]

Mary Means Scott was a child at the time of Villa's raid. She recalled that people in Columbus were familiar with the sound of the gunshots of Villa and his men in the distance but did not expect the attack on her town. "By daylight, the shooting became sporadic and finally ceased," she later wrote. "We stood at the window facing the center of town, aghast at the spectacular and horrifying sight." Buildings were on fire, and some of Villa's men lay dead in the street.[72]

Whatever Villa's aim, he succeeded in rousing the U.S. Army; around half the United States' mobile armed forces were already stationed near the border.[73] Wilson sent General John Pershing with around ten thousand troops on a "Punitive Expedition" to wipe out Villa, or at least break up his troops.[74] Scott recalled how relieved they were upon hearing the news, and how she and her family were "proud of him and our army."[75]

A report by a member of the 13th Cavalry on that expedition recounted their march into Mexico, when the "spirits of the men were excellent, all of them being anxious to get after Mexicans again on account of the Columbus raid." Along the way, they spotted the body of a dead U.S. citizen, according to the report "said to have been wantonly killed by Villa's Band," which made the men all the more eager to "avenge Villa's wanton killing of Americans."[76] Carranza's forces also engaged in the fight against Villa, and in the end some 350 *villistas* were killed or wounded in the aftermath of the Columbus raid.[77] The U.S Army came close to capturing Villa in Chihuahua, but he eluded them while the *villistas* fought back.

Having failed to capture Villa, and with war raging in Europe, the United States withdrew by early 1917. Zapata, meanwhile, had continued battling in the south, a fight that had mostly become guerrilla warfare.[78] Around the same time, in January 1917, a telegram was intercepted by the British. In it, Germany's foreign secretary, Arthur Zimmermann, instructed the German minister in Mexico to propose an alliance offering to help the country regain some of the territory lost to the United States if it aided Germany. The telegram specified "an understanding on our part that Mexico is to reconquer the lost territory in Texas, New Mexico, and Arizona."[79] This helped spur the United States—which had been trying to stay out of the conflict in Europe—to enter the First World War in April 1917. The episode also raised suspicions about Mexico, which declared its neutrality, and by extension that of Mexicans in the United States. All of this served to undermine an already shaky confidence in Carranza.[80]

Carranza was also trying to bring together a new constitution, and he gathered delegates in the city of Querétaro, in central Mexico, in December 1916 to produce one, which they did by the end of January 1917. Attempting to curb regional power, this constitution—still in use today—put the unity of the federal nation at its core, along with a strong presidency. In addition, the constitution pushed the anticlericalism of the 1857 constitution even further, with religious education outlawed, among other measures. The document's Article 123 established a number of labor laws considered to be among the most progressive in the world at the time, including the right of workers to organize and strike, as well as improvements to working conditions such as limits on hours and days worked in a week. Another key article, number 27, returned land, water, and any mineral wealth to the state. Villages were to see land that had been taken from them during the years under the *Porfiriato* returned in what was known as the *ejido* (community land) system. In addition, in the future only Mexican citizens or companies could own land or gain mining concessions, though the constitution granted "the same right to foreigners" so long as they did not "invoke the protection of their governments," should any dispute rise. The United States was quick to criticize this particular provision, demanding the repeal of Article 27 a few years later.[81]

Although the shape of Mexico's future was becoming clearer, Carranza still had to contend with his detractors. First was Zapata, who met his end on April 12, 1919, in an assassination plot organized by one of Carranza's generals. It was clear to many that the murder was really Carranza's doing, and his support faltered.[82] The angry Zapatistas then entered into a deal with Obregón, who by this juncture had indicated that he wanted to run for president. Carranza responded by backing Ignacio Bonillas, who at the time was ambassador to the United States. Obregón and his allies in Sonora issued the Plan de Agua Prieta in 1920, denouncing Carranza as a dictator. Their revolt attracted enough followers and posed a sufficient threat to persuade Carranza to retreat again to Veracruz, but while passing through the state of Puebla by train, his party was pursued by rebels, and forced to flee on foot after the train tracks were sabotaged. They sought refuge in a tiny village, and the next day Carranza was killed by assassins.[83] An interim president was appointed until an election could be held, which Obregón won, taking office in December 1920.

Villa, meanwhile, was willing to negotiate a peace deal with the new regime, disbanding his *villistas* in exchange for his land in Durango, which was technically under government possession. Although Villa was now out of political life, he was not out of sight. On July 20, 1923, he, too, was gunned down, joining Zapata, Carranza, and Madero in the ranks of assassinated Mexican leaders, while the public pointed fingers at the president.[84]

North of the border was not left unscathed by these years. In addition to the fighting over the Plan de San Diego, there were other instances where both sides were quick to pull the trigger. The Arizona border city of Nogales endured a number of small battles, with a final one in 1918 that erupted after a Mexican man refused to stop for U.S. customs agents. They fired on him, and Mexican troops shot at the U.S. soldiers, leaving a dozen people dead. Later, the United States claimed the man was a smuggler or spy. Residents on both sides were growing exasperated. A plan had existed for some time to erect a six-foot wire fence, at the instigation of the municipal leader of Nogales, who ended up being killed in the battle. Afterward, it was carried out by U.S. officials, who also supported a plan to reduce crossings to two designated points. At the time, the fence was considered to be not antagonistic but rather a cooperative measure that local administrators in both countries supported.[85]

The violence along the Texas border did not relent, either, with the Rangers continuing in their conflict with Mexicans and Tejanos. Ranger numbers experienced a dramatic rise in this period, from 26 in 1915 to 1,350 by 1918, due in part to the fighting during the Plan de San Diego. There was limited oversight in screening the applicants and so some Rangers had quite free rein in choosing which laws to enforce, a practice that often got out of hand.[86]

In late January 1918, a band of Rangers rode into the west Texas village of Porvenir, not far from the Río Grande. They were on a mission to find out who was behind raids on a nearby ranch that had resulted in a number of Anglo and Mexican deaths. They believed the answer might be found in the village where, they claimed, the residents were acting on behalf of Mexican ranchers who lived across the river. They arrested 15 men in the early hours of the morning, marched them to a nearby bluff, and executed them on the spot. The rest of the village, around 140 people, fled to Mexico. Five Rangers were later fired, but no one faced criminal indictments.[87] The episode capped off a period known as the *Hora de Sangre* (the hour or time of blood), the name that Mexicans and Tejanos gave to the violent years between the Plan de San Diego and the executions in Porvenir.[88] Most of these lynchings did not receive proper investigations, nor did the perpetrators face harsh, if any, punishment. In 1919, José T. Canales, a member of the Texas house of representatives, called for an investigation of the Rangers. While his attempts to pass legislation that would curb their excesses failed, his efforts brought public attention to some of the abuses the Rangers committed.[89] In addition, Mexicans in Texas also had to contend with the Ku Klux Klan, which would raid labor camps, drag people from their tents, and assault them. The Klansmen did not limit their activities to Texas, and there were reports of KKK violence as far west as San Diego.[90]

Without justice, and often without newspaper coverage, murders, executions, and lynchings slipped from the collective Anglo memory, the violence blurring behind sayings associated with the "Wild" West, such as "Shoot first, ask questions later." For Mexican-Americans and Tejanos, however, these stories never died, preserved in mournful *corridos* (ballads) or family stories, outside mainstream culture.[91]

THROUGHOUT THIS PERIOD, another sort of revolution was taking place in the United States, but it was a quiet, more surreptitious one, though it would reshape the way the land was used and the lives of the people who worked on it. Prior to the Mexican Revolution, few Mexicans came to the United States with the intention of settling. Men, and sometimes entire families, moved in pursuit of employment but with the intent of working for a few years on projects such as the railroads. Others found jobs with large landholders, who often had thousands of head of cattle. They needed able horsemen to move the herds, so they often employed Mexican vaqueros.* These large ranches, however, were part of a land-scape that was in transition. Mines had already been dug into the earth and railway tracks laid across the land, but in the twentieth century, water would dominate. Developments in hydrological technology meant that rain or even snow—in the form of melted ice flowing into the rivers—could be brought to the desert. A flurry of state and federal legislation allotted funding for infrastructure projects to facilitate what amounted to an environmental recasting of the West.

California was at the heart of this massive irrigation program, draw-ing the waters of the Sacramento, San Joaquin, and Colorado Rivers to convert the arid ground. The lowlands area of the Salton Sink in the

---

* Many of the terms related to ranching have their roots in Spanish: *vaquero* (cowboy), *lazo* (lasso), and *ranchero* (rancher), to name but a few contributions, and of course rodeo, from *rodear*, to surround.

southwest of the state was, by 1901, rebranded with the evocative and grand title Imperial Valley.[92] The tangle of pipes, canals, and aqueducts also gave cities like Los Angeles the capacity for growth.[93] This was not, however, limited to California—access to water was also crucial in New Mexico and Texas, and those states also launched irrigation schemes, for instance, using water from the Pecos River, which runs west of the Río Grande and south into Texas.[94]

As with the battle over land grants and mining rights, water, too, became a point of contention, with small farmers losing out to larger interests.[95] The scale of these irrigation schemes—or "reclamation" projects, as they were called at the time—was great enough to warrant the establishment of the federal Bureau of Reclamation in 1902; the Reclamation Act was passed in the same year, forcing landowners to pay in part for the irrigation projects from which they would be benefiting. The agency was also involved in the construction of dams throughout the West, with Roosevelt Dam on the Salt River in Arizona being its first major project.[96] When that was completed in 1911, the result was the largest artificial lake in the world at the time, taking up sixteen thousand acres.[97]

These projects changed the desert to meet growing human needs, part of a seemingly unstoppable march to a modern life where nature could be tamed at will. Endless brown scrub became verdant fields, allowing this part of the West to share in the Jeffersonian dream of a smallholder democracy. California's Imperial Valley was likened to the Nile valley, with all the attendant biblical metaphors, as this land was made fertile.[98] Soon, however, the rise and power of large landowners cast a shadow over this vision. New problems were created as old ones were solved; for instance, in Arizona and New Mexico, people on Indian lands faced poor harvests and starvation because the river water was siphoned off for irrigation, and what remained could no longer deliver what communities needed for survival.[99] In Texas, the ranches, and the social and economic ecosystems they supported, gave way as agriculture took over the Río Grande valley.[100]

As rivers ebbed and flowed, and were dammed and released, so, too, went the movement of people. The rise of intensive agriculture demanded seasonal workers who were paid as little as possible, and a number of groups—from Native Americans to Chinese immigrants to Southern and Eastern Europeans to Filipinos and Japanese—filled that role with varying degrees of success. However, mounting anxiety about foreigners and nativist demands to limit immigration led to restrictions being placed on certain groups. Japanese farmworkers, for instance, had organized in the 1890s to demand better wages, and as a result they were branded as troublesome, and their legally permitted numbers were reduced.[101]

The Chinese, too, faced prejudice. Sinophobia had long existed in the West, becoming widespread after large numbers of Chinese immigrants arrived in California in the wake of the gold rush. Many prospered and over time they were blamed for taking jobs or depressing wages, as well as for social ills, such as running illicit gambling and opium operations. The growing racism directed at the Chinese culminated in the 1882 Chinese Exclusion Act, the first significant law directed at immigrants in the United States. It banned the immigration of laborers from China for a decade, and the prohibition was later extended. However, Chinese people could and did continue to go to Mexico in this period, and many then simply crossed the border into the United States. There was little to stop them, at first. In the 1890s, few border guards patrolled in Texas, Arizona, New Mexico, or California. By 1904, however, the number of Chinese crossing the Río Grande was deemed significant enough for immigration inspectors to be sent to border towns; they were known as the Mounted Guard of Chinese Inspectors.[102]

In addition to people moving illegally, authorities expressed concern about goods not being properly taxed. Commerce was one engine that drove the busy pace of border crossings, and customs collection became important on both sides of the line, as each government realized it could profit from people being eager to go back and forth. In 1858, Mexico had established a *zona libre* along the border of Tamaulipas state, and in 1884 this was extended along the entire frontier. Goods could be imported without duties, but exportation was not exempt, causing a number of problems and leading to Mexico's terminating the zone in 1905 and replacing it with specific tax exemptions on certain items.[103] Around the same time, the U.S. and Mexican governments also decided to establish ports of entry. As a result, smuggling proliferated.[104] Dutiable goods, such as cigars and spirits, were often carried across out of the sight of customs officials, or with bribed complicity.

Smuggled articles often included harder substances too. Until 1914, when the Harrison Narcotics Act placed a tax on the importation, production, and manufacture of opium and coca, these drugs were not illegal.[105] The tax pushed the buying and selling of these substances underground, though their actual use remained legal. It was a lucrative trade: by 1924, a $35 ounce of morphine sourced in Mexico could be sold in Los Angeles for $100.[106]

The growing border towns soon became targets of moral reformers in the United States. Campaigners against alcohol, narcotics, gambling, and prostitution had made great strides within the United States, culminating in the prohibition of alcohol in 1920, but this stopped at the border. For people who lived on the southern frontier, a drink was never far away. This fact rankled morality campaigners, but it was a boon for Mexican officials. Mexico decided to tax these vices and so raise revenue from the people from the United States who were now forced to head south for a tipple. Tijuana was perhaps the most famous vice district of this time, growing from an outpost of around four hundred people to a thriving gambling mecca, where casinos, boxing, and horse-racing, coupled with a steady stream of alcohol, provided popular— and profitable—entertainment for U.S. visitors. The town was scarcely recognizable as the small village it had been. In 1928 the grand Agua Caliente hotel and casino opened, its $10 million price tag paid for by U.S. investors. Visitors could drink cocktails in its gilt Gold Bar, go for a swim, play golf, or enjoy a bet at the hotel's dog or horse tracks. The city attracted movie stars from Los Angeles, such as Clark Gable; and mobsters from farther afield, such as Al Capone. Although Tijuana was perhaps the grandest border city of the period, other towns on the southern side of the divide followed its lead and profited from it.[107]

However, many Mexicans living along the border and its surroundings were upset at the reputation these towns brought the country as a whole, not least because, for the most part, U.S. visitors were doing all of the misbehaving yet claiming such behavior was "Mexican" and that border towns were "lawless." The casinos were U.S.-owned, and almost all the money spent in these border-town dens of iniquity belonged to people who were not Mexican, leading to growing resentment of this "Americanization."[108]

In response to a corresponding rise in smuggling, the United States and Mexico stepped up their patrols of the region. Some of the border crossings on the U.S. side began to shut at night to stop wayward activities—legal or not. In 1924 the government pressed for a nine p.m.

closing at the Tijuana and Mexicali crossings, which was later brought forward to six p.m.[109] Such restrictions were not popular with consumers or merchants on either side of the border. By the 1930s, however, with the repeal of prohibition, almost all of the crossings returned to opening twenty-four hours a day.[110]

———◦———

ALTHOUGH THE UNITED States had felt it necessary to intervene at certain points in the Mexican Revolution, such as after the Punitive Expedition in response to Villa's Columbus raid, the border was not the most pressing issue of the time. Immigration from elsewhere occupied public discussion to a much greater extent, given that from 1880 until the 1920s, around twenty-four million people had come to the United States, many of them from Southern and Eastern Europe, provoking nativist pressure to limit the numbers of migrants.[111] The United States Immigration Commission, known as the Dillingham Commission, met from 1907 to 1911, and its recommendations filtered into legislation that was rolled out in subsequent years. Mexicans, however, were not a target or a priority. Instead, the 1917 Immigration Act focused on Chinese and Japanese people, barring people from a wide swath of Asia, as well as immigrants from Southern Europe, and all manner of others, including "all idiots . . . persons with chronic alcoholism; paupers; professional beggars . . . polygamists . . . anarchists, or persons who believe in or advocate the overthrow by force or violence of the Government of the United States."[112] It was also illegal to contract labor or transport aliens to work without the necessary permission, and barriers to immigration now included literacy tests, a costly $8-a-head tax, and health inspections.

Although the number of Mexican workers in the United States between 1900 and 1910 was not well documented at the time, early estimates put it at around fifty thousand.[113] Once the head tax and literacy tests were implemented, documented immigration dropped 40 percent, in part because some people started crossing surreptitiously to avoid the taxes and tests.[114] However, the growers in California's Imperial Valley needed workers, and so after the 1917 act, they, along with railways and mining interests, lobbied the U.S. government to exempt Mexicans from the restrictions, which it did. For many, Mexicans were different from other immigrants, in that they were neighbors crossing by land, coming to work in a place that not so long before had been part of Mexico.[115]

The exemption to the 1917 act allowed Mexicans to continue to cross the border and work in agriculture, mining, railroads, construction, and factories. The United States' involvement in the First World War also meant there were extra jobs to fill.[116] Undocumented people continued to slip across the Río Grande rather than enter through the checkpoints in the border towns; this suited some employers because of the many rules governing the exemption, including the retention of 25 cents a day of a worker's wage to ensure there was enough money for his fare back to Mexico once his contract expired. It was often easier for everyone concerned to find a way around the regulations.[117] The term "wetbacks" came into use to describe the people who crossed the river—a slur, like the earlier "greaser," that would become racist shorthand for Mexicans living in the United States.

Another image was also developing, of Mexicans as having a timeless rural, agrarian nature, making them ideally suited to be seasonal field hands for low wages—an idea that persists to the present day. A 1930 article in *Nation's Business*, the magazine of the Chamber of Commerce of the United States, claimed, "Apparently the Mexicans are especially well adapted to the common labor tasks required in the Southwest; they are fond of outdoor life and rural occupations . . . they easily enter a nomadic mode of living which permits them to meet the seasonal, migratory demands of southwest agriculture, and they remain in farm occupations more loyally than other groups, the growers say."[118]

Mexican immigration rose throughout the 1920s, in part because of the displacement caused by the revolution, coupled with the fact that many industries in Mexico, such as mining, had been damaged or disrupted by the fighting. Prospects in the United States, for the moment, appeared brighter. Alongside this, however, discrimination against Mexicans grew, fed by the pseudoscientific discourse that positioned them as inferior to Anglos, "dirty," and unable to assimilate to U.S. life. Some of this reflected the economic anxieties of the border region in the 1920s: in Texas, large landowners—regardless of their racial ideas—wanted cheap Mexican labor while smaller farmers and business owners, fearing for their livelihood, wanted Mexicans deported and the border strictly monitored.[119]

The next significant change in immigration law was the 1924 Johnson-Reed Act, which placed quotas on "undesirable" groups while making exceptions for Mexicans and people from "contiguous countries," including Canada, Cuba, Haiti, and the Dominican Republic. For everyone else—though this did not include people from what was called the "Asiatic Barred Zone"—the annual quota was set at 2 percent of the number of people of that nationality already residing in the United States as reported in the 1890 census, with a minimum quota of one hundred people.

In 1924, the government also set aside $1 million to establish a Border Patrol. Small outposts soon dotted the U.S-Mexican frontier, as the initial 472 inspectors started work, a handful of whom were sent to the Canadian border.[120] One of the first posts on the southern border was in Del Rio, Texas, where two men were put in 1924. They were mounted on horses, receiving extra pay if they brought their own steeds, though patrol cars were introduced by 1926. The men in Del Rio were responsible for covering about two hundred miles of the Río Grande area, most of which was ranches and farmland.

One of the initial Del Rio Border Patrol guards recalled his early days: "No one knew what we were supposed to do to or how we were supposed to do it. . . . So we just walked around and looked wise."[121] They soon figured it out; the Del Rio sector reported that in 1925 its officers— by then there were eight—had questioned or investigated 32,516 people in an area that had a population in 1930 of just 25,528, of whom 14,559 were Mexican. To reach such figures, they massaged their numbers through such techniques as counting the total number of passengers in a train or car as being "interrogated" as they cast a wide net of surveillance.[122]

By 1929 at least six men with Spanish surnames were on the Border Patrol roster. While the Anglo officers were often from working-class backgrounds, the Mexican-American members tended to be from the middle and even upper classes of their community. Because of their status, they had what one historian termed "uncertain access" to a sort of official whiteness, which allowed them to take up roles in bodies like the Border Patrol, policing their own people.[123]

SOME MEXICANS FOUND relief from the pressures of the border in other parts of the United States. In New Orleans, Mexicans were able to claim a degree of "whiteness" in a way that was not possible in the Southwest.[124] With its access to the Gulf ports of Mexico and its long history of connection through trade, the city had offered an alternative for people looking to leave revolutionary Mexico. By the 1920s, Mexicans were the largest group of Latin Americans in New Orleans, though they would later be eclipsed by Cubans.[125] Mexicans of all classes came to the Gulf region, and while the middle class settled in New Orleans, workers were lured to the cotton fields of the Mississippi delta, where they were paid more than they would have been in Texas or California.[126] Mexicans in the Gulf and delta region were able, unlike African-Americans, to send their children to white schools and to marry whites with little interference from the law.[127]

Florida, however, continued to present problems for other Spanish-speaking people. The Afro-Cubans in Tampa were under increasing pressure from Jim Crow laws by the turn of the century, and the larger Cuban community was driven further apart because of these laws. Not long after their arrival in the late nineteenth century, Cubans in Tampa had organized mutual-aid societies, such as El Círculo Cubano and the Centro Español. Through membership dues, these organizations provided a number of social services, such as paying for medical care, funeral costs, and other necessities, as well as staging activities such as dances and drama performances. By the early 1900s, the local authorities in Florida decided that dark-skinned Cubans—anyone who looked "black"—had to form their own distinct social organizations. They were forced to leave groups like El Club Nacional Cubano, which had been concerned with independence and, until that point, was open to members of all hues. Dark-skinned Afro-Cubans were no longer permitted by the rules of Jim Crow Florida to access "white" mutual-aid societies, so they had to set up their own, which they did in Tampa in 1904: the Sociedad La Unión Martí-Maceo, which merged two other Afro-Cuban groups. Membership photos from the early 1900s show men of varying shades of skin tone, continuing to blur a color line that white Florida wanted to imagine was distinct.

The anger in the Cuban community lasted far after this segregation was first enforced. A writer working on a Works Progress Administration (WPA) guide to Tampa in the 1930s noted: "Since negroes in Cuba are accorded social and economic equality with whites, Cuban negroes in Florida are naturally dissatisfied with the inferior position which they must accept when they come to live here."[128] Being lighter-skinned, however, was no guarantee of easy assimilation. Another WPA report described Ybor City as "a Latin community where a large number of the inhabitants have not become American citizens." The anonymous writer observed: "The government . . . has done very little toward making the Cuban people . . . feel that they are Americans. Even many of the second and third generations of the Cubans, although born in the United States, and by right of the constitution, Americans, are not considered as Americans by many of the English-speaking Americans."[129] Through their enforced segregation, Cubans were experiencing a different type of "Americanization."

Evelio Grillo, an Afro-Cuban who grew up in the Ybor City of this time, said that in Florida "black Cubans went to a neighborhood . . . inhabited by black Americans and a scattering of poor whites" while lighter-skinned Cubans "had a much wider range of choices."[130] His parents worked in a cigar factory where "black Cubans and white Cubans worked side by side," but this intermingling did not extend outside the workplace.[131] "I don't remember playing with a single white Cuban child," he recalled.[132]

The issue of whiteness dragged on through the 1920s, while the United States grappled with immigration. Who was deemed "white"—and therefore a U.S. citizen—was still unresolved. People from India and Japan were still considered not quite "Caucasian," as described by the Supreme Court, yet they were not black. They were "nonwhite."[133] On the back of this, renewed efforts by nativist groups, judges, and politicians challenged naturalization of Mexicans on the grounds that they were also in this nonwhite category, implying that Mexicans should be denied citizenship.[134]

OBSERVING THE MANY changes to south Texas in the 1920s and '30s was
a young Mexican-American woman named Jovita González. She had
been born in 1904, in Roma, Texas, a border town, though her family
later moved to San Antonio. Her father's family was Mexican, and her
mother's included Tejano landowners reaching back at least five generations.[135] At a time when most women did not pursue higher education,
González earned a degree in Spanish from Our Lady of the Lake College
in 1927 and went on to complete a master's degree in history at the
University of Texas at Austin three years later.

Of special interest to her was local folklore, and with the encouragement of academic mentors she gathered up Texan histories and stories.
González became the president of the Texas Folklore Society in 1930,
when it was dominated by Anglos in full thrall to the romanticized
versions of the state's history, as embodied in the works of one mentor,
the writer J. Frank Dobie. González, however, published work that was
unearthed from the soil of the present rather than spun out of the mists
of time, and received a Rockefeller grant for her efforts.[136]

In her master's thesis, *Social Life in Cameron, Starr, and Zapata Counties*,
she described a place where "Anglo-Americans . . . look down upon the
Mexicans of the border counties as interlopers, undesirable aliens, and
a menace to the community."[137] Her work attempted to document these
communities, as well as to restore their place within Texas, pointing out
that "the majority of these so-called undesirable aliens have been in the
state long before Texas was Texas."[138] González's pioneering work was
unsparing about what she observed, such as the growing segregation,
under which Tejanos "resent the fact that in some of the Valley towns,
Mexicans are not admitted at cafes, picture shows, hotels, and bathing
beaches." She conducted fieldwork, speaking to residents of the border
counties. One interviewee in Edinburg, Hidalgo County, summed up
the complexity of Anglo-Mexican relations:

> We were wholly unprepared, politically, educationally, and socially
> when the avalanche of Americans fell upon us. . . . And it is our place
> and our duty now to learn American ways, to send our children to

American schools, to learn the English language, not that we are ashamed of our Mexican descent, but because these things will enable us to demand our rights and to improve ourselves. . . . Americans are egoists, and provincial, they overestimate their power and doing so are unwilling to see any other way but their own. It is to our advantage then, to educate ourselves in American institutions, to learn the English language and to exercise our rights as citizens.[139]

Around the time González was putting together the history of her region, the wider public's strange love affair with "Spanish" culture intensified. Not long before, a frustrated Spanish journalist named Julián Juderías popularized the term "Black Legend" (*leyenda negra*) in a 1914 book, which finally gave form to the nebulous prejudice that Spaniards in Europe and, by extension, Hispanics in the Americas had been shrouded by for more than four hundred years. To him, this legend was "not a thing of the past, but something that influences the present."[140] He wrote that the legend continued to suggest an "inquisitorial, ignorant, fanatical" Spain that was "an enemy of progress."[141]

Prejudicial ideas die a slow death, and as they die they can give life to other complex notions that are likewise untethered from historical realities. In the United States, the imagined "Spanish" culture that emerged in California around the 1880s began to move east. What evolved was a vision of a "de-Mexicanized" and pseudo-Spanish people that Anglos now wanted to "discover," served up with a large dollop of nostalgia. This recasting of the past created an image of a people who were absorbed through conquest but whose "culture" rendered them "other." By creating and promoting the Southwest on the basis of this mythical past, the Anglo world was able to control the image of Hispanics in the region, reducing their experience to a form of tourist spectacle. Yet real Mexicans were still in this landscape, relegated to the fields and other labors.[142] Their everyday experiences, as well as those of Mexican-Americans, were being written out of history, the prejudices and discriminations replaced by an imagined heritage. These extremes—romantic and exclusionary— developed in the context of rising immigration, nativist agitation, lynchings, and continued discrimination.

One Tejana, Adina de Zavala, found herself at this intersection when she decided to become involved with the preservation of the Alamo.

Although the state was steeped in its legend by the late nineteenth century, the Alamo had suffered the fate of other missions, falling into
disrepair, because for many years the U.S. government expected local
preservationists to raise their own funding for cultural and historical
sites.[143] Such was the case for the Alamo. Today, the Alamo is one of
the most visited sites in Texas, but for a long while it was used to store
grain as part of a U.S. quartermaster depot, and for several other purposes, until the state bought the lease in 1883 and the entire property
in 1904 at the urging of the Daughters of the Republic of Texas.[144] That
organization was then given custody of the site, and its restoration was
completed through the efforts of two women: Zavala—whose grandfather, Lorenzo, was the first vice president of Texas and helped craft its
constitution—and the wealthy Texan Anglo Clara Driscoll, who had the
means to help fund its purchase.[145] The women had differing views on
how the site should be restored, a disagreement so intense that it was
later referred to as "the second battle of the Alamo."[146]

For Zavala, the Alamo could honor the men who fought there in 1836
and at the same time be returned as much as possible to what it had been
like as a Spanish mission, including the restoration of the convent that
had been next to the church. For Driscoll, the ruin of the convent should
be torn down as it only distracted from the chapel, which, in her mind,
ought be the main focus because that was where the heroes of the Alamo
died.[147] This led to years of heated disagreement; Zavala at one point
barricaded herself inside the Alamo site in 1908. A court order in 1910
established the legitimacy of Driscoll to manage the Alamo, though this
did not affect Zavala's willingness to continue her battle. Their division
represented the quite divergent views of Texans. Driscoll's vision was
of an Alamo that represented victory by Anglo-Americans and pride in
their accomplishment. Zavala, on the other hand, drew from ideas that
reached back to the Spanish period, as evidenced by her interest in the
convent, and into a longer, more layered, and more entangled history.
Remembering the Alamo, it turned out, would be much more difficult
than it sounded.

Driscoll's vision ultimately won out and the site of heroic commemoration was renovated and expanded by 1936, in time for the Texas centennial, celebrating the state's independence from Mexico. That would
be the year, according to the retailer Stanley Marcus, of Neiman-Marcus,

that "the rest of America discovered Texas."[148] Indeed the famed department store was involved in the celebrations, and many Texas businesses hoped it would draw the nation's attention to the state. In Texas, unlike California, however, the rosy glow of the past was cast not on the state's Spanish roots but on its Anglo ones.

In California, the Spanish craze continued to spread, aided by the creation of an entire architectural style, known as Spanish Revival, which emerged around the 1920s.[149] Newly built towns, such as San Clemente, which billed itself as the "Spanish Village by the Sea," looked postcard perfect, with their white houses with red-tiled roofs. That such a trend emerged in the interwar period was, to some observers, a form of cultural respite from the challenges of modern life, not least war, technological changes, and shifting social demographics, including the rise of immigration and the growth of urban living.[150] Evoking a mythical "Spanish past" may have been a reassuring distraction from contemporary concerns, but not everyone was buying it. The prominent Californian journalist Carey McWilliams wrote in a 1946 essay that what was really driving what he called the "fantasy heritage" was the arrival of so many outsiders from elsewhere in the United States who needed a "mythology" in order to give themselves "a sense of continuity in a region long characterized by rapid social dislocations."[151]

Californio families were cast as living museum pieces in this fading past, though they were really split between a heritage that on one hand romanticized the story of their "Spanish" predecessors and on the other forced them to confront a world that increasingly called them Mexicans.[152] However, they were able to carve out enough social space to claim this Spanish past and the implied whiteness for themselves, while the more recent immigrants were branded "lower-class" stock and "Mexican."[153] Californios continued into the twentieth century to be active in this recasting of their past, with many helping to create and promote local pageants and parades that highlighted the "Spanish" nature of the state. These fiestas served to invent traditions; perhaps the best-known surviving festival is Santa Barbara's Old Spanish Days, which began in 1924. The initial fiesta involved parades, rodeos, musical events, and "traditional" Spanish dancing. Participants wore costumes that depicted them as Spaniards, Chumash Indians, or Mexicans. Posters from the earliest days of the festival and even from more recent times are illustrated with women wearing the flamenco dresses of southern Spain, while men were sometimes in embroidered Mexican *charro* suits, playing guitars or on horseback. Often the Santa Barbara mission church was used as a peaceful background. Although newly created, the event was meant to evoke a sense of tradition.

The enthusiasm for all things Spanish could be found throughout the state. In San Diego, it was embodied in the restoration of the Casa de Estudillo in the Old Town part of the city, which tried to cash in on the *Ramona* myth, as this building was supposed to be the inspiration for the house where the popular novel's heroine marries. The Old Town was restored and its hilltop presidio was rebuilt in 1929.

Even earlier, in 1915, San Diego wanted to hold an exposition in honor of the opening of the Panama Canal, but San Francisco was hosting the Panama-Pacific International Exposition in the same year. Undeterred, San Diego set to work on its ambitious celebration, renaming its City Park after Vasco Núñez de Balboa, the first European to cross the Isthmus of Panama. The project was plagued with internal squabbles and a change of architects. New Yorker Bertram Grosvenor Goodhue was appointed, and he wanted to put Spanish Baroque in place of the Native American, Mission, and Pueblo styles that the local committee was more eager to use. Goodhue was already known for his "Spanish churrigue-resque" work, with its elaborate ornamentation, which won out in the end.[154] The park today is a nearly overwhelming mix of styles, showing influences all the way from Moorish to Mexican Baroque, with wide walkways, fountains, and gardens evoking the sense of a world lost to time. The San Francisco exhibition, on the other hand, used temporary structures.[155]

The growing interest in the Spanish past was not limited to the West. In the 1920s, a movement arose to bring a network of roads together into the Old Spanish Trail, mostly what became U.S. Highways 90 and 80 running from Jacksonville, Florida, to San Diego. At the time, no major road connected the southern parts of East and West. Today, that road intersects with what is considered to be the "real" old Spanish trail in Arizona and New Mexico—mule tracks used for herding cattle, smuggling, or gold prospecting.

The idea for the Old Spanish Trail highway was first expressed in 1915, and the project's managing director, Harral Ayres, claimed it was born from the enthusiasm of some four hundred people. He wrote, "Somehow it seemed as though the spirit of the *padres* and the *conquistadores* flamed again in the soul of these Anglo-Saxon pioneers. . . . We who have watched these modern men from Florida to California rise to the demands of this southern highway construction are proud that the soul of the crusaders is not dead."[156] By October 7, 1929, these motoring enthusiasts gathered for a banquet in San Antonio to celebrate the trail's completion—groups from across the country had raised money to pay for some roads and bridges. Ayres was also shrewd enough to request federal funds from the War Department to improve the road between Pensacola and New Orleans by framing the lack of a connected highway along the borderlands as a national defense issue.[157] Today a large concrete sphere, which has a plaque on the front commemorating its dedication in 1928, is the mile zero marker for the Old Spanish Trail, sitting under the shade of a large tree on the grounds of the visitor center in St. Augustine, while its corresponding end point waits more than two thousand miles away in San Diego.

The road had a powerful pull, not just for motorists but also for the cities along the route, such as Albuquerque. New Mexico, like other parts of the West, had seen the arrival of tourists, as well as people looking for a healthier climate, appearing by the trainload. This had already bolstered tourism and efforts to sell Spanish, Mexican, and Native American handicrafts.[158] The rise of the automobile would bring even more of the adventurous, the curious, and the health-minded. While the Old Spanish Trail passed south of Albuquerque, Route 66, which linked Chicago to California, went right through it. By the 1930s, outsiders began to buy up the single-story adobe and wooden homes in the village and convert them to shops, selling arts and crafts.[159]

Like the other cities founded by the Spanish, Alburquerque had a plaza. Known as La Plaza Vieja, it sits in front of an eighteenth-century church, San Felipe de Neri. In the 1880s, the town had been divided into Old and New parts, with the latter a couple of miles away, home to most of the Anglo and European settlers who, along the way, managed to drop the first "r" out of the town's spelling, rendering it Albuquerque.[160]

When the tourists started to arrive, Anglos in the city began to demand that Albuquerque be "improved," worried that a placid and "dirty" Old Town, mostly populated by Hispanic *Nuevomexicanos*, would not appeal to tourists. To its residents, it was a close-knit and lively home, but the pastures around La Plaza Vieja were soon swallowed up as land was used for housing. The Old Town was subsumed into the larger city, its authentic past replaced by a commercial present trading on the old days.[161] The Hispanic legacy in New Mexico now had to be packaged up and made desirable to tourists.

The southeastern United States also joined in the rediscovery of its Spanish roots. Hernando de Soto received a hero's commemoration during the quadricentennial celebrations of his landing and exploration of North America in 1935. Congress set up a De Soto Expedition Commission to plan the events and mark out his actual route, though in the end it decided to participate only in 1939's Pan American Exposition in Tampa.[162] On May 30, 1939, in the sleepy Florida town of Bradenton, the National Society of the Colonial Dames of America erected a slab of carved rock, not unlike a rough-hewn gravestone, as the De Soto Trail Monument, which was donated to the National Park Service in 1948. Since there is no evidence that De Soto actually landed here, the marker is vague, saying it "commemorates the 400th anniversary of his arrival on the shores of Florida."

De Soto loomed large in those years. The first De Soto sedan rolled off Chrysler's assembly lines in 1929, and models—often with a conquistador as a hood ornament or incorporated into the logo—remained in production until 1960. Motorists, it implied, were modern conquistadores who could discover their own new lands. At the same time, the mighty conquerors had been reduced to consumable kitsch.

During the WPA period in the 1930s artwork on public buildings—influenced by the Mexican mural movement that started a decade earlier—included depictions of de Soto or was often based on the broader theme of "discovery."[163] Admiration of the conquistadores in this period reflected not only their use as symbols of conquest but also the comfortable dominance of the Anglo world over the Hispanic. The Spaniards' association with Catholicism and even the atrocities they committed melted away, leaving instead men who seemed to be little more than figures from an adventure story.

Against this larger cultural backdrop, the historian Herbert Eugene Bolton wrote a number of pioneering works about the borderlands, volumes that covered the earliest period of Spanish exploration in the Southwest as well as Florida. Bolton himself was a man of the frontier, born in 1870 and raised for the most part in rural Wisconsin. He studied for part of his PhD under Frederick Jackson Turner, whose writings no doubt influenced him on some level.[164] Bolton's work took him to Austin, Texas, which inspired him to focus on the Southwest. He then joined the University of California at Berkeley in 1911 and never left, cultivating a steady stream of graduate students who focused on borderlands history, at a time when the Spanish language was also starting to be taught in public schools in the United States. (The number of public school students learning Spanish rose from 5,000 in 1910 to 263,000 by 1922.)[165]

One of Bolton's most enduring contributions to the field was his transcription and translation of borderlands documents from archives in Spain and Mexico. However, his best-known work, *The Spanish Borderlands: A Chronicle of Old Florida and the Southwest*, gave him the greatest set of problems, and his struggle with the book—first published in 1921—illustrates the challenges in bringing the Hispanic history of the United States to a broader audience, even at a time when there was interest. *Spanish Borderlands* was meant to be part of the Chronicles of America series published by Yale University Press, but when Bolton submitted his manuscript, his editor rejected it and three further drafts. At issue was Bolton's interpretation; his editor wanted him to take a more Anglocentric stance and explain how Protestantism and the spread of Anglo culture triumphed over and drove out Catholic Spanish culture, but Bolton refused.[166] His editor insisted on hiring a ghostwriter to help push the dominant Anglo narrative into the work. In the end, Bolton prevailed, and he even made a point of illustrating how Spanish culture had persisted, especially in the Southwest:

Even in the old borderlands north of the Rio Grande, the imprint of Spain's sway is still deep and clear. Scores of rivers and mountains and hundreds of towns and cities in the United States still bear the names of saints dear to the Spanish pioneers. Southwestern Indians yet speak Spanish in preference to English. Scores of the towns have Spanish quarters, where the life of the old days still goes on and where the soft Castilian tongue is still spoken.[167]

Bolton's interest in the borderlands later broadened into an even larger vision, which he spoke about in his 1932 address to the American Historical Association. He called this the "Epic of Greater America," and it conceived of the development of the Western Hemisphere in a more holistic way, rather than focusing solely on the story of the United States. Bolton believed that the history of the United States could be better understood in a transnational context and that "the study of thirteen English colonies and the United States in isolation has obscured many of the larger factors in their development, and helped to raise up a nation of chauvinists."[168]

Many historians at the time found his comments controversial, though the following year U.S. president Franklin D. Roosevelt would take a similarly hemispheric approach in his attempt to foster, in theory, better relations with Latin America through his Good Neighbor Policy. This was an attempt to focus more on trade and less on military interventions in Latin America, a point he spelled out in his inaugural address of March 4, 1933, saying he wanted to dedicate the United States to "the policy of the good neighbor—the neighbor who resolutely respects himself and, because he does so, respects the rights of others."[169]

THE FIRST TWO decades of the twentieth century were a time of large and intimately connected realignments for both Mexico and the United States, in the context of a world profoundly shaken up by the conflict in Europe. Amid all the memorable events, the everyday lives of millions of people were swept up in the momentum produced by the wars, revolutions, and economic meltdowns. Anita Brenner was caught in such waves, moving back and forth across the border, and far and wide away from it.

She was born in 1905 in Aguascalientes, in central Mexico, to an Eastern European Jewish family. Her father, Isidore, had left Riga, in Latvia, and tried his luck in Chicago in the 1880s, before moving on to Mexico, ending up in Aguascalientes, which had railroad and mining work. The residents of the town were already an international mix, with people from the United States, France, and Germany lured by job prospects. Isidore started as a waiter at a local restaurant and over time worked his way up into landholding prosperity. Like millions of other people in Mexico, he saw this tranquillity ruptured by the coming of the Mexican Revolution.

The revolution was a defining period in Anita Brenner's life, for logistical, emotional, and artistic reasons. Her family left Aguascalientes a number of times during the conflict—first fleeing in 1912; returning and leaving again in 1914; and then departing for the last time in 1916, settling in San Antonio, Texas.[170] Such was the hostility against the United States that on one of their crossings the family were forced to wave a German flag in an attempt to identify themselves as anything but American.[171]

After the fighting ended, Anita continued to return to Mexico, alternating those trips with studying in Texas and, later, attending Columbia University in New York. In Mexico, she found herself surrounded by people who would become key members in the flourishing artistic circles that arose during and after the revolution. Photos of Brenner at this time show a young woman with short, cropped hair and an intense gaze—a photographer's muse and a friend of people like the muralists Diego Rivera and his wife, the artist Frida Kahlo. She also enjoyed the company of other foreign artists lured to Mexico, such as the Italian-American photographer Tina Modotti. Many of the Mexican artists she socialized with were connected to left-wing movements and causes, ranging from Communist Party members to those offering refuge to Stalin's enemy Leon Trotsky, who was later murdered in Mexico. Her life and work began to overlap, and in 1929 she published Idols Behind Altars, which introduced an English-speaking world to Mexican art. The following year she was granted a Guggenheim Fellowship to continue her writing.

More than two decades later, she returned to those formative revolutionary years, publishing The Wind That Swept Mexico in 1943. It is an unusual history, a work of two halves: one written, one visual. About one hundred pages are devoted to her words and the remaining two hundred pages are a pictorial history. It starts with a portrait of Porfirio Díaz, wearing a jacket bejeweled with military medals, his mustache obscuring his mouth, his eyes calmly looking back at the camera. The photos that follow attempt to document those years—the smug *Cientif-icos*, the barefoot children, the workers on strike, the dead bodies in the street, Zapata's glowering visage and Villa's cheeky grin, Pershing on his horse—with the final image being one of a young man in a white shirt and straw sombrero, his concern about the future palpable, with the caption asking, "And the boys who had grown up with the idea that the revolution would somehow make their future. Would they lose it all . . . ?" For Brenner, the revolution in Mexico was "not a finished story."[172] Neither was the relationship between Mexico and its powerful neighbor, something Brenner lived, summing it up by writing, "Being an American brought up in Mexico gives one an obsession to reconcile two ways of life, two almost opposed points of view, and two sets of emotions and interests."[173]

Chapter 13

New York,
ca. 1920s–'60s

THE POPULARITY OF "Spanish" culture also took hold in New York City.
Although the city had a growing population of Cubans and Puerto
Ricans, immigrants from Spain lived there as well. Had any of them
journeyed to north Manhattan in 1927, they could have seen El Cid, the
famed eleventh-century slayer of Moors, sitting astride his steed, with
a spear held over his head, his horse prancing on a plinth in front of an
imposing Beaux-Arts building in Washington Heights. El Cid's exploits
were memorialized in a twelfth-century poem, and for centuries he had
been a symbol of Spain, so he was seen as a fitting figure to welcome
visitors to the Hispanic Society of America, which had opened nearly
two decades earlier, born from the passion, and deep pockets, of Archer
Milton Huntington, the son of a railway tycoon.

Huntington founded the society in 1904 after accompanying his father
to Mexico, where they dined at Chapultepec Castle with president Porfirio Díaz. Huntington later recalled that the trip was "a sort of strange
awakening . . . Mexico was a revelation."[1] Although this was his introduction to the larger Hispanic world, Spain, not Mexico, enthralled him for
the rest of his life. In 1909, just after the society's opening, Huntington
organized a retrospective of the contemporary Valencian painter Joaquín
Sorolla y Bastida. It was a hit with the public and triggered a fashion
for Spanish art among the wealthy, who found themselves fighting each
other to buy works not only by Sorolla, but also by artists such as El
Greco and Goya.[2]

Huntington continued to acquire books, manuscripts, artwork, and photographs related to Spain, and the society published monographs about Spanish culture. The museum remains a repository of treasures— from medieval icons to paintings from Spain's golden age to an entire room lined with panels painted by Sorolla. In that salon, each panel depicts crowds of people in traditional dress in the various regions of Spain. Sorolla's Basques, Catalans, and Galicians have an air of time-lessness—it could be a scene from three hundred years ago, or one of twenty-first-century people donning their folk costumes for a fiesta. Sorolla worked on the panels until his death in 1923, and the room was opened to the public in 1926.

New York City at this time had a small but thriving community of Span-ish immigrants who, like the Italians and Greeks, had left the poverty and lack of opportunity in Europe for the United States. In Spain, the nineteenth century had been marked by a series of civil wars, and the influx of Spanish immigrants to New York was part of a longer and larger process of people from the Iberian Peninsula resettling in the Americas; from 1880 until 1930 more people from Spain crossed the Atlantic than had done so between 1492 and 1880.[3] In New York, this immigration cut across all classes, from Spanish workers seeking a well-paid factory job to educated elites seeking to practice law or medicine. They lived in the city during the peak of the "Spanish craze" that emerged in the eastern United States. As with the nineteenth-century enthusiasm for the mission churches of California, this, too, was a time of great interest in anything Spanish, as witnessed by Huntington's successful Sorolla exhibition.[4]

A *New York Times* article in 1924 profiled the Spanish-speaking com-munity in the city, describing it as "like Spain itself, with rivalries of old provinces still lingering. . . . Here are not Chelsea nor old Peter Stuyvesant's farm, but Estremadura and Leon." The piece also went on to note the other, non-peninsular Spanish-speakers in the city, as "Argentina lies next to Castile and Uruguay is near by, with Cuba in the offing."[5] The article claimed there were about thirty thousand such Spanish-speakers, half from Spain, a fifth from Mexico, and the rest from the Caribbean and Central and South America, all "scattered over Manhattan and Brooklyn."[6]

The number of Spaniards would be curtailed by the 1924 Immigration Act. Because quotas for visas were now based on the population at the time of the 1890 census, the Spanish were left with a minuscule quota of 131.[7] Enough people, however, had already arrived from Spain for there to be a Little Spain neighborhood in Lower Manhattan, on the northwest edge of Greenwich Village, near the docks, with Fourteenth Street acting as a main thoroughfare, and adjacent streets lined with shops selling goods from Spain.[8]

Many people joined social clubs that represented their regions of origin, which included the Basque country, Catalonia, and Galicia, while others were members of broad-based groups that promoted a type of Hispanic unity. Efforts at forging *Hispanidad*—the idea that there was a shared culture, heritage, and language between Spain and Latin America—had predated Spain's loss of its empire, but the effort was renewed in the early twentieth century. Promoters of a "pan-Hispanic" identity thought it could counter the growing global influence of English-speaking U.S. culture.[9] For instance, the Unión Ibero-Americana, a body that promoted good relations between Spain and Latin America, was able to use the success of the Columbus Day celebration—with the Admiral already appropriated by Italian-Americans—to lay the groundwork for the *Día de la Raza* (day of the race), instituted on October 12, 1918, to celebrate Hispanidad.[10] The idea was successful enough to survive in the Spanish-speaking world to the present day, although, like Columbus Day in the United States, the Día de la Raza in many Latin American countries has attracted increasing criticism.

In June 1929, the Spanish poet Federico García Lorca arrived in New York to study at Columbia University. He was already well-known within Spain, but in the United States he had no reputation, except among the Spanish in the city, whom he came to know the minute he stepped off the ship. Upon his arrival, he found that "a group of Spaniards was there waiting for us."[11] It was not just any group; among the coterie were artists and writers, publishers and politicians, including Federico de Onís, a descendant of the foreign minister who signed the treaty ceding Florida to the United States.[12]

While his diary reveals many social occasions and parties, his poems speak of a lonely city. In the poem "Dawn" he wrote:

Dawn in New York has
four columns of mire
and a hurricane of black pigeons
splashing in the putrid waters.[13]

He later explained at a lecture that he thought Wall Street, with its "rivers of gold," was terrifying and had a "total absence of the spirit." He found the people who worked there dispiriting because they believed "it is their duty to keep that huge machine running, day and night, forever." Lorca put this down to "a Protestant morality that I, as a (thank God) typical Spaniard, found unnerving."[14] His letters to his family, however, tell of a different New York, a much more cheerful one with a large community of Spaniards and high-profile Hispanophiles. Lorca noted with surprise in one letter that "there are over six hundred students of Spanish language and literature [at Columbia]."[15] He returned to Spain in 1930 and six years later he was assassinated by nationalist forces, an early victim during the Spanish Civil War, which lasted from 1936 until 1939. By this point, the enthusiasm that fueled the "Spanish craze" had come to an end, dampened by the rise of fascism in Spain and the resulting conflict there. However, some Americans took a great interest in that war, going as far as volunteering to fight on the side of republican Spain. Ernest Hemingway memorialized this in his 1940 novel *For Whom the Bell Tolls*. Many Spaniards left the peninsula during this violent time, going into exile. However, the Spanish population of New York, limited by the tiny U.S. immigration quota, could not absorb them, and thousands instead went to Latin America.

───────

ALTHOUGH THE NUMBER of arrivals from Spain was dropping, other Spanish-speakers were making their way to the city, Puerto Ricans in particular. In 1920 there were 7,364 Puerto Ricans in New York, 2,572 Mexicans, and 8,722 Cubans and other West Indians.[16] Many people from the Hispanic Caribbean found employment at the docks or on construction sites, and in hotels and restaurants, as well as in the uptown cigar-making operations in the city at this time. Others started their own businesses, including bodegas, bars, and cafés, building on the foundation earlier Puerto Rican and Cuban exiles had laid.[17] Cubans in New York opened mutual-aid societies similar to those in Tampa. Institutions like El Club Cubano Inter-Americano were cultural as well as social centers, welcoming people from other Spanish-speaking nations. That club's founding charter declared its intent to "maintain the fraternity that should exist between the Cuban colony and the rest of the Latin-American countries."[18]

By 1930, the Puerto Rican population in New York had boomed to 44,908, now constituting around 40 percent of the Spanish-speaking community. While Cubans, Dominicans, and other West Indians had a combined population of 23,000 by 1940, the Puerto Rican community was more than twice as large at 61,500. By 1954, one in every twenty New Yorkers was Puerto Rican. This number continued to rise, soaring to 612,574 by 1960.[19] Puerto Rico's División de Educación a la Comunidad, a government agency on the island, printed pamphlets warning of the risks—as well as describing the rewards—of heading north. Readers of the 1954 leaflet *Emigración* were told that Puerto Ricans were considered "a problem" in New York and that they should look to other parts of the United States for work. The booklet also urged cultural assimilation, which was the official policy of the Migration Division of Puerto Rico's offices in New York and Chicago.[20] One illustration showed men disembarking from an airplane with the tagline: "Do Puerto Ricans know the country where they are emigrating? New York is not the only city."[21] Behind the scenes, however, Governor Luis Muñoz Marín and officials in Washington were promoting migration to the mainland, seeing it as a way to prevent social unrest, such as strikes, on the island.[22]

The influx of Puerto Ricans had an enormous impact on the city, as their community spread out beyond East Harlem—often called El Barrio—into Brooklyn and the Bronx.[23] The earliest years were a struggle for many, and housing was a particular problem, as immigrants from the Caribbean were pushed into tenement housing, which was often substandard and unhealthy.[24] These parts of the city were often seen as no-go areas for outsiders. A report in *Civil Rights Digest* in the late 1960s described the area starting at East Ninety-Sixth Street, by then also known as "Spanish" Harlem, as being "like an invisible Berlin Wall between affluent Manhattanites and East Harlem puertorriqueños and Harlem blacks."[25] In these parts of New York, apartments were "poorly ventilated . . . the smell of the sweat and refuse of generations is stifling. Most of the dwellings are privately owned (few by Puerto Ricans themselves), and in the final stages of dilapidation; most of the buildings, which house many times the occupants they were meant to house, were built before the First World War."[26]

Not everyone settled in the city; some headed to suburbs or smaller towns, a world that Judith Ortiz Cofer evoked in her novel *The Line of the Sun*. One character described life in an apartment block called *El Building*, in Paterson, New Jersey, as a place where "the adults conducted their lives in two worlds in blithe acceptance of cultural schizophrenia." Describing the residents of *El Building*, Ortiz Cofer wrote: "Fortified in their illusion that all could be kept the same within the family as it had been on the Island, women decorated their apartments with every artifact that enhanced the fantasy. Religious objects imported from the Island were favorite wall hangings. . . . Mary could always be found smiling serenely from walls."[27]

Immigrants often bear the blame for bringing disease or crime to an area, and it was no different for those from the Hispanic Caribbean. In one case, a *World-Telegram* article in October 1947 quoted New York's deputy health commissioner, who claimed Puerto Ricans brought tuberculosis, among other illnesses. Rafael Angel Marín, a doctor and activist, was quick to respond that "the half truths, the errors and misrepresentation . . . are not only a gratuitous injury to Puerto Ricans . . . but . . . an insult to scientific accuracy." He was angered by the claim that one in ten Puerto Ricans had TB, pointing out that no reliable statistics existed.[28]

New York offered some respite from the strict Jim Crow laws of the Deep South, though people from the Spanish-speaking islands all eventually became familiar with U.S.-style prejudice, often finding their "race" redefined upon their arrival.[29] In a 1934 article in the newspaper *Alma Boricua* (Puerto Rican Soul, or Soul of Puerto Rico), Bernardo Vega argued that "the principal characteristic that distinguished us from the [Anglo-] Saxon Americans was our racial tolerance," warning Puerto Ricans that if they were not careful, they would be "on the verge of poisoning ourselves with the filth of the racial hatred of the US."[30]

Cubans and Puerto Ricans in New York were joined during this period by people from a third Spanish-speaking island in the Caribbean: the Dominican Republic. It, too, had fallen into the sphere of U.S. influence and interference. At the same time that U.S. troops had been in Mexico hunting down Pancho Villa in 1916, another branch of the military was occupying the Dominican Republic. The United States had earlier taken over the island's custom house in 1905, claiming it would help to bring the island's debt under control. A decade later, with entry into the First World War looming, President Woodrow Wilson was fearful of potential German influence in the Dominican Republic, as well as its ongoing political instability. Pressure was put on Dominican president Juan Isidro Jimenes (sometimes spelled Jiménez) to give U.S. officials governmental posts, as well as access to the island's finances, but he refused. Around the same time, political infighting was weakening Jimenes's control of the situation, and in May 1916, the first contingent of marines arrived. Martial law was declared, and a military government was established. Troops also began working on infrastructure projects and building up the Dominican Guardia Nacional. The United States thought that bolstering the Dominican national guard would help solve some of the island's problems. Marines occupied the Dominican Republic until 1924, though control of the custom house did not revert back to the island until 1940.

In the years after the marine withdrawals, a young member of the national guard, Rafael Leónidas Trujillo Molina, rose through the ranks with such speed that he was able to take control of the presidency—and the military—by 1930. He would stay in power for the next thirty-one years, until he was assassinated. Those three decades were a time of terror for many Dominicans, and some people were forced into exile. The novelist Julia Alvarez, who was born in the United States to Dominican parents who fled the regime, reflected this fear in her novel *How the Garcia Girls Lost Their Accents*. The father of the main characters is unable to let go of his anxiety: "Now in America he was safe, a success even. . . . But in his dreams, he went back to those awful days and long nights, and his wife's screams confirmed his secret fear: they had not gotten away after all; the SIM [Servicio de Inteligencia Militar] had come for them at last."[31]

Out of the diverse communities living alongside each other in New York would grow one of the city's most important contributions to the culture of the United States and the world: music. The islands had musical traditions that had long merged popular Spanish and African forms, among them Cuban *son* and Puerto Rican *bomba*. Once these sounds moved north, they came under the influence of other musical forms, including African-American music, first overlapping in early twentieth-century New Orleans, whose rich Spanish, French, and African traditions gave rise to the "Latin Tinge" and would eventually influence the development of jazz in that city and beyond.[32]

Some music historians trace the modern Latin sound to New York, after the return from the First World War of the African-American "Harlem Hellfighters," the 369th Infantry Regiment, which included Puerto Rican soldiers who had played in military bands.[33] In the decades that followed, performers like Rafael Hernández—who had served in that regiment—and his Trio Borinquen began to appear. Their 1929 "Lamento Borincano" became an unofficial anthem for Puerto Ricans living away from the island, with its lines "Borinquén, the land of Eden / the one that when sung by the great Gautier / he called the Pearl of the Seas / now that you are dying with your sorrows / let me sing to you also."[34]

Cuban music also made up part of the city's—and eventually, the nation's—soundscape. At this time, tourists were going to Havana in their thousands, and popular culture became enamored of Cuba throughout the decades that followed. Through films with titles like *Week-End in Havana* and *Holiday in Havana*, Cuba—or, at least an imagined approximation of it—became accessible to a wider audience, as did its music.[35] The first Cuban song to become a hit in the United States was "El Manisero" ("The Peanut Seller"), in 1930.[36] Soon the ballrooms of New York were playing their own versions of this song, and before long the country was in the grip of a *rumba* (sometimes, *rhumba*) fever, for both the music and the dance steps.

Rumba music has at its structural core the *clave*, a pattern of five beats usually played on *claves*, a pair of wooden sticks; at its historical core, rumba was part of Afro-Cuban culture, coming from slaves in sugar plantations and free people of color in the cities, as part of a tradition in which people gathered to sing and dance, and was also connected to Cuba's vibrant culture of Catholic processions.[37] Anglo musicians learned the style and some of them even tried to pass themselves off as Cubans, such as Don Carlos and His Rumba Band, whose earlier incarnation had been Lou Gold and His Orchestra.[38]

Alongside this, demand increased for actual Cuban musicians and their music. In 1946 the Cuban Desi Arnaz scored a hit with his rendition of "Babalú," before becoming a household name a few years later in the TV show *I Love Lucy*. Despite the musical successes, in general race continued to stalk musicians from the Hispanic Caribbean, with lighter-skinned Puerto Ricans and Cubans playing to all-white downtown crowds in New York, many times as the "relief" bands for bigger orchestras at clubs or upscale hotels, while Afro-Caribbean musicians were often limited to playing in Harlem and elsewhere uptown.[39]

Following on the heels of the rumba came the even more popular *mambo*, again a style drawing from Cuba's African roots, with the term possibly being of Congolese origin. Its use of Cuban percussion, such as the conga drum, reflected its history, but its development was also influenced by the proximity of Cuban musicians and composers to popular U.S. big band jazz.[40] This mixture of influences was exemplified by Pérez Prado, who moved from Cuba to Mexico, where he recorded "Qué rico el mambo" in 1949, the energy of its full brass horns and drums propelling it into a hit, first in Latin America and soon afterward in the United States, helping to spark a mambo craze across the country.[41] Places like New York's Palladium Ballroom at Broadway and Fifty-Third featured the mambo throughout the early 1950s, hosting the big bands of rising stars like the percussionist and bandleader Ernesto "Tito" Puente.[42] The music industry was trying to cash in on this trend anywhere it could, creating what have become known as "latunes"—basically, songs with Latin rhythms but lyrics in English. In the rumba era, among the songs that qualified for the category was Cole Porter's "Night and Day."[43] By the time of the mambo, however, songwriters were churning out "mamboids"—compositions that more or less just mentioned the mambo rather than copying its musical style, such as "Mambo Italiano," "Papa Loves Mambo," and even "Mardi Gras Mambo."[44] As fevered as the mambo was, by the mid-1950s it gave way to the smoother cha-cha (or cha-cha-chá), another Cuban style that found its way north. It was slower than the mambo, and its dance steps were an "one-two-cha-cha-chá."[45]

While the various types of Cuban music enjoyed some success, Puerto Rican styles, including the danza, the bomba, and the countryside sounds of *música jíbara*, did not gain as large a public following as Cuba's, though they were influential components of the music coming out of the Latin scene in New York. In the later part of the 1960s, another musical form was on the rise: the Latin boogaloo, mixing elements of African-American and Puerto Rican traditions. The song "Bang Bang," released in 1967 by the Joe Cuba Sextet, was a nationwide hit and introduced the public to this latest musical genre.[46] It is around this point that salsa, a sound that blended these influences, also began to gain ground. Salsa would take over Latin American music, becoming popular throughout the world and tying together many of the strains of Latin music in New York.[47] When asked about what constituted salsa, bandleader and composer Tito Puente, who played across a wide range of styles, was said to have replied: "I'm a musician, not a cook."[48]

ON THE CORNER of Calle de la Cruz and Calle Sol in San Juan, Puerto Rico, is a rose-colored building with white trim that bears a small golden plaque near one of its windows. This elegant building, with its carved wooden balconies on the second floor, was once the headquarters of the Nationalist Party of Puerto Rico (Partido Nacionalista de Puerto Rico) and the residence of Pedro Albizu Campos, who led the party. The marker, featuring a black-and-white picture of Albizu holding his fist in the air, says, "During the revolutionary acts of 1950, in defense of our right to independence, this building was shot at for two days by the island police and the National Guard."

As a leader and politician, Albizu Campos occupies a complicated place in Puerto Rico's history, and his party has been described as everything from "patriotic to criminal, self-sacrificing to demented, proto-socialist to fascist."[49] He rose out of poverty to study at the University of Vermont before earning an undergraduate degree in 1916 at Harvard, where he would go on to law school. His studies were interrupted when he volunteered for the U.S. military during the First World War and was assigned to an all-black regiment, owing to the skin color he inherited from his mother. It was a formative experience because he discovered at first hand the prejudices and discriminations of the mainland. After the war, he finished his law degree, returned to Puerto Rico, and was soon active in the island's politics, joining the nascent Nationalist Party in 1924; by 1930 he was its leader. Part of his motivation in advocating nationhood was the realization, after his time in the United States, that dark-skinned Puerto Ricans had no hope of equality under U.S. rule.[50] The party wanted independence, state ownership of utilities, and land reforms limiting private-sector ownership to three hundred acres.[51] Albizu Campos's aims were not merely economic and political. He also had a vision of a Puerto Rican *raza*, a form of Hispanism that was a cultural rejection of Americanization.[52] To Albizu Campos, the Puerto Rican republic was born in 1868, during the revolt in Lares when rebels tried to throw off Spanish rule. In a 1936 speech, he called Puerto Rico an "island property" of the United States, saying, "We stand today, docile and defenseless, because, since 1868, our political and economic power has been systematically stripped away by the United States for its own political and economic gain." He was angered by the United States' "imposing its own culture and language" and argued that Puerto Ricans "must be a free nation in order to survive as a people."[53] His vision embraced the Spanish language and also Catholicism, which he considered part of the expression of Puerto Rican nationhood.

During the Great Depression, Puerto Rico had suffered.[54] The sugar industry had been hit hard, and cane cutters saw their wages drop or lost their jobs. Puerto Ricans were heading north in droves. Although the United States tried to cobble together some relief measures for the island, sugar workers began striking for better pay. At least eighty-five strikes occurred in the second half of 1933, not only among cane cutters but also among people who worked in tobacco, at the docks, or in the needlework industry.[55] The sugar workers returned in 1934 with an even larger strike that disrupted the harvest.

In 1935, President Roosevelt extended a version of the New Deal to the island, establishing the Puerto Rico Reconstruction Administration (PRRA). Cement and glass factories were built, and a number of public health measures were attempted, such as slum clearance. In all, some $58 million was spent by 1938.[56] The PRRA also sought to put more sugar production back in the hands of Puerto Ricans through the establishment of cooperative mills, and to enforce the provision in the Jones-Shafroth Act that limited corporate landownership to five hundred acres. This move upset large U.S. sugar interests, though it pleased growers on the island. One frustrated Puerto Rican wrote to Charles West, acting secretary of the interior, in 1936 to complain: "I have not yet met one of them [Americans living on the island] who does not defend the monopoly of our profitable agricultural lands by the Sugar Centrals. Not one of them has taken the side of the Puerto Rican."[57]

As PRRA policies were being implemented, relations between the authorities and the nationalists took a violent turn. In October 1935, four nationalists were killed after an altercation between demonstrators and police at the University of Puerto Rico–Río Piedras. A few months later, on February 23, 1936, two Nationalist Party members killed the police commissioner, Elisha Francis Riggs. They were later shot at police headquarters, and many Puerto Ricans believed they had been summarily executed—a belief that sparked public anger. The authorities arrested Albizu Campos and other prominent nationalists in 1936, locking them up in the imposing Princesa prison, built by the Spanish a century before on the Bay of San Juan. The men were charged with sedition and conspiracy to overthrow the U.S. government on the island, but their first trial—in which seven of the jurors were Puerto Rican and five American—ended in a hung jury. They were retried, this time with a jury of ten Americans and two Puerto Ricans, and found guilty in a 10 to 2 vote.[58] Albizu Campos and six others were moved to a federal penitentiary in Atlanta.

That summer, the island's governor, Blanton Winship, wrote to Harold L. Ickes, secretary of the interior, about these tumultuous events. Of particular irritation to Winship were the repeated calls for the direct election of a Puerto Rican governor, which he sarcastically described as "only natural" because he did not expect the Puerto Rican political class to "admit that it could not furnish the brains, character and other equipment necessary for carrying on the government of the territory it inhabits." In addition, the growing nationalist agitation was "particularly evident," said Winship, since the rise of Albizu Campos. To his mind, the nationalist leader's purpose was "to break down the American government established here."[59]

Later that year, Millard Tydings, chair of the Senate Committee on Interior and Insular Affairs, put forward a bill in support of Puerto Rico's independence, though it was no victory for the nationalists. The bill offered the island a vote on independence, but if independence was chosen, the United States would offer no transitional assistance, and would impose high tariffs that were to rise over the first four years.[60] It also would give individual Puerto Ricans only six months to decide if they wanted to retain their U.S. citizenship, which had the potential to be a serious dilemma for the hundreds of thousands of Puerto Ricans living on the mainland. In addition, the immigration quota would be set at five hundred people a year.[61] Its punitive message was clear, the subtext being that Puerto Rico could not survive without the United States. Tydings had made his political point and withdrew the bill.

Then, on March 21, 1937— Palm Sunday—the violence worsened. The Nationalist Party had announced that it would hold a parade of its cadet corps in the southern town of Ponce that Sunday and applied for a permit, which was granted the night before, but on the basis that it would not be any sort of military parade. After the request was made, a number of police were sent into Ponce.[62] Before the parade was due to start, the mayor of the town revoked the permit on the grounds that it was a religious holiday, while the nationalists argued that their cadets would cause no disruptions.[63]

While discussions were taking place about how to proceed, spectators began to arrive in the town center, with family members of the cadets gathering to watch the procession. At around three p.m., the eighty or so cadets started to line up, and a band struck up the island anthem "La Borinqueña." A shot rang out and chaos ensued. A photographer captured the moment, in a picture showing one policeman firing his gun at civilians on the curb, though his face could not be identified. Other accounts claimed a civilian fired first, though the man who was said to have done so was killed in the subsequent volley of bullets. Later, no weapon was found on him.[64] In the end, nineteen people died that afternoon, and around 150 were wounded, in what was called the Ponce Massacre.

Whether or not that photo captured the actual first shot or a subsequent one, rumors and accusations flew, and in an attempt to get to the truth for the distressed people of Ponce and across the island, a commission was formed to investigate the shooting. It was led by Arthur Garfield Hays of the American Civil Liberties Union, who was joined by seven Puerto Ricans, though no one from the Nationalist Party took part and there were no representatives of the colonial authorities, who were uncooperative with regard to the entire undertaking.

In his report to the Department of the Interior on March 23, Governor Winship said the parade was not of the cadets but of the "Liberating Army" of the party and that the chief of police had decided it should not go ahead. He reported that at 3:30 p.m., after the anthem was played, they began to march and the police chief told them the parade was prohibited. At this point, "two shots were fired by the Nationalists," with the bullets striking policemen to the left and right of the chief. In Winship's account, this was followed by an exchange of fire with "Nationalists firing from the street, and from the roofs and balconies."[65]

The director of the U.S. Division of Territories and Island Possessions wrote to Governor Winship to convey the outrage expressed in the letters he was receiving from Puerto Ricans, including claims that the nationalists who were killed had no weapons on them; that the police fired into the crowd, killing innocent women and children; and that had the parade been allowed to go ahead in the first place, there would not have been any bloodshed.[66] A classified report from the commander of the "Borinqueneers" Sixty-Fifth Infantry Regiment in Puerto Rico included the "Nationalist Version" of events, in which "they claim that the shooting was initiated 'on the part of the police exclusively,' and 'the police shot down the Nationalists like rats.'"[67]

The commission's findings challenged many of Winship's claims. Its report said, for instance, that "photographs taken at the time show not a single nationalist with any weapon of any kind," and that the cadets were "hemmed on all sides by heavily armed police."[68] It concluded its findings with the observation that "the people of Ponce have given this tragedy the only possible descriptive title: This was the Ponce Massacre— and the more so because it occurred in a time of peace."[69]

Winship continued as governor, though the anger directed at him infused public life. In spite of the heated climate, he decided to hold a military parade on July 25, 1938, to celebrate the fortieth anniversary of the U.S. landing in Puerto Rico. In order to drive home the point about U.S. rule, he opted to hold it in Ponce. The soldiers had scarcely taken a step when the nationalist Ángel Esteban Antongiorgi tried to assassinate Winship but instead killed a national guard colonel who had leaped in front of the governor. Antongiorgi was shot dead on the spot by police.

President Roosevelt decided to replace Winship with Admiral William D. Leahy, whom he named as governor on May 12, 1939.[70] The day before the announcement about Leahy, Vito Marcantonio, a New York congressman whose district included East Harlem, had called for Winship to be removed from the post. Marcantonio had many Puerto Rican constituents and over the course of his political career would introduce five bills for independence for the island.

His May 11 speech referred to the ongoing efforts of Winship and others to avoid implementing the 25-cents-an-hour minimum wage stipulated under the U.S. Fair Labor Standards Act of 1938. Marcantonio denounced the "slave wages" paid to Puerto Ricans, especially those in the sugar industry, insisting, "Everybody knows it can pay 25 cents per hour to its workers and should." He blamed wages staying at 12.5 cents an hour on Winship because "the Governor on many, many occasions . . . advised them [the sugar industry] not to worry about the law."[71]

A few months later, after Winship's departure, Marcantonio made his "Five Years of Tyranny in Puerto Rico" speech to the House of Representatives in Washington, describing Winship's term as a time when "Citizens were terrorized. . . . American workers were persecuted and shot down whenever they sought to exercise their right to strike or organize. . . . The insular police was militarized. . . . Winship drank cocktails and danced in the Governor's palace while the police ruthlessly killed and persecuted Puerto Rican citizens."[72]

Leahy may have been a change, but he still represented U.S. rule. Many of the same problems remained, and colonial policies were not working.[73] At the same time, another political leader was emerging: Luís Muñoz Marín. He was the son of Luis Muñoz Rivera, the island's former resident commissioner to the U.S. Congress. Muñoz Marín had spent many of his formative years in the United States, studying at Georgetown University before dropping out in 1915. By 1920 he had started to take an interest in politics, moving back and forth between the United States and the island over the next few years, before finally settling back in Puerto Rico in 1931.[74] A year later he won a seat in the island's senate as a member of the Partido Liberal (Liberal Party).

Muñoz Marín later broke away from the Partido Liberal, and in 1938 he and his supporters set up the Partido Popular Democrático (Popular Democratic Party), which was initially still in favor of independence.[75] In the November 1940 election, the party took enough seats to make him president of the senate. Later that month, Muñoz Marín wrote to congratulate President Roosevelt on his own recent reelection and to discuss in emollient tones "a real opportunity for establishing a relationship of true understanding." In the letter, he explained to the president that his primary issue was not independent status but rather to see that "economically and administratively our purposes are parallel to those of the New Deal." Muñoz Marín signed off the letter pledging his "full cooperation to the end that, with your help, the endeavor and the results should be in harmony with that reality."[76] This was illustrative of Muñoz Marín's shift toward greater autonomy in lieu of independence, a move informed in part by the island's growing economic dependence on the United States.[77] Other theories attribute his change of heart to the U.S. intelligence on him detailing opium usage, leaving him little option but to be compliant.[78] His party continued to make gains in elections, pledging changes to land use and the economy and winning support among the rural and often impoverished *jíbaro* communities throughout the island.

The U.S. officials remained wary of nationalists well into the next decade. Leahy wrote in 1940 that there were on the island "a considerable number of disaffected individuals who would undoubtedly, in the case of war, engage in actual subversive activities and would form a very troublesome 5th column." According to Leahy, these people were even receiving funds "through the Republic of Santo Domingo and probably Natzi [sic] sources," which is why military intelligence and the FBI were keeping watch on them.[79] The FBI also monitored Puerto Ricans in the United States, with one report noting that there was a "close relationship between the [Nationalist] party and the American Communist organization, particularly in New York."[80]

Leahy was not in the post long, and in 1941 Rexford Tugwell—one of the members of the "Brain Trust," advisers to FDR—was appointed governor. More sympathetic to Puerto Rico's plight, he expressed his deep dismay at the state of the island, despite the efforts of the New Deal, later writing in his book *The Stricken Land*, "This is what colonialism was and did: it distorted all ordinary processes of the mind, made beggars of honest men, sycophants of cynics, American-haters of those who ought to have been working beside us for world-betterment." However, the relief effort angered him most. He pointed a finger at Congress, blaming it for making the island "beg for [help], hard, and in the most revolting ways." To Tugwell, this was "the real crime of America in the Caribbean, making of Puerto Ricans something less than the men they were born to be."[81] Congress continued to debate the Puerto Rico question. In 1945, Senator Tydings introduced another bill calling for a plebiscite on the status issue, this time with different economic guarantees, but it was later vetoed.[82]

In the meantime, Albizu Campos had grown ill in prison in Atlanta. There had been many calls for his release, from activists in the United States and abroad. Even Tugwell supported it. In 1943, he wrote to Secretary of the Interior Harold Ickes that he "hoped he [Albizu Campos] will be pardoned and come back to Puerto Rico." Tugwell believed it was important to demonstrate that Americans were "a people who do not often deprive anyone of the freedom to speak; and especially that we do not fear the advocacy of independence for Puerto Rico." He also believed that Albizu Campos would now "find that many of his Independista friends here are ready to acknowledge the wisdom of our gradual and rational approach."[83] In the end, Albizu Campos was transferred to a hospital in New York City for treatment and stayed there until 1947. The FBI file on him, however, expressed doubts about his illness. A letter in 1943 from the FBI director J. Edgar Hoover to the White House adviser Harry L. Hopkins remarked that "thus far the doctors at that institution have been unable to find any significant physical disabilities."[84] A few months later, another letter from Hoover to Hopkins noted that Albizu Campos "is reported to be using his private room in the Columbus Hospital as the headquarters of the Nationalist Party of Puerto Rico in New York City and it has been said that he receives many notable visitors and holds meetings in this room, which, according to reliable sources, is paid for by the Communist Party, U.S.A."[85] Albizu Campos would never be free from the scrutiny of the security service, but in 1947 he was released from the hospital, his imprisonment over—for the time being.

After the end of the Second World War, there had been a shift in focus on the island toward advocating the stimulation of private investment from the United States, especially for industrialization. Legislation was passed to allow tax breaks on some manufactured goods, ushering in an era known as Operación Manos a la Obra or Operation Bootstrap, with the emphasis now being on economic output.[86] Manufacturers started to take advantage of available subsidies; other industries, like tourism, also began to attract investment from the United States, and hotels began to go up along the glistening seafront. Wages from manufacturing were good at first, more than doubling between 1953 and 1963, from $18 a week for men to $44, and from $12 to $37 for women.[87] It was a promising start, but it soon faltered. While Operation Bootstrap allowed workers on the island to move away from sugar, the overall gains made by industrialization did not outstrip the losses from abandoning agriculture, not least because industrialization made the island even more dependent on U.S. markets.[88] The economic boom in the postwar United States meant that it was still often more profitable to work on the mainland, and many Puerto Ricans continued emigrating north.

In addition to economic expansion during the 1940s, the United States enlarged its military presence on the island. At the start of the Second World War, the U.S. government expropriated two-thirds of the land on Vieques, an islet off the east coast, on which to build a naval base. Prior to this, Vieques had been used for growing sugar, and much of the land was already in the hands of corporations or wealthy individuals. The landless workers switched over to construction and, with the world war raging, the island became part of larger regional efforts to secure the Caribbean against any German influence or invasion.[89] In the end, plans for the base were scaled back as the United States turned to the Pacific, and by 1943 Vieques was put on maintenance status, halting the economic boost it had provided.[90] By 1947 the plan for the base had changed: it would be used for training and as a fuel depot. Despite this, the navy wanted more land, and the issue of what to do with the families living on Vieques became a heated political question. The United States relented over plans for evictions, and instead the island government would build housing on the small part of Vieques that remained habitable while the base was developed into a site for bomb testing and ammunition storage.[91]

Albizu Campos returned to Puerto Rico in December 1947. In celebration, some university students raised the Puerto Rican flag on the day of his arrival; they were expelled.[92] Much had happened since he had been away. In 1946, the United States appointed the island's first Puerto Rican governor, Jesús Piñero. Alongside this, legislation passed that paved the way for Puerto Ricans to vote for their own governor. This effort was led by Muñoz Marín, convincing both his party of the need to change direction and the United States of the legitimacy of such plans—something the government approved in part because the United States, after the Second World War, wanted to be seen to promote democratic values.[93]

In June 1948, after the return of Albizu Campos, the Puerto Rican legislature—under the control of Muñoz Marín and his party—passed the Gag Law (known as *la mordaza*), which made it illegal to show support for independence—legislation directed at the nationalists.[94] A few months later, in November, the island voted in Muñoz Marín as its first elected governor, as his party took 61.2 percent of the vote. His heavy brow and tidy mustache would be the face of Puerto Rican politics for decades to come.

The question of status continued to be unresolved, and Muñoz Marín was now in favor of a plan to give the island its own constitution.[95] The 1950 Public Law 600—which would allow the island to draw up such a document, as states in the United States had done—was signed into law by President Harry S. Truman in 1950 but needed to be approved by a referendum. For the nationalists, the constitution was no substitute for independence.[96] As debates about the legislation began, high-profile arrests of some leading nationalists again led to bloodshed, and on October 30, 1950, some party activists launched an armed insurrection.[97] It started in the southern town of Peñuelas, spreading to at least seven more cities on the island.[98] The objective was to cause a political crisis, embarrass the United States, and derail the referendum vote.[99] Police stations were attacked, as was the governor's mansion in San Juan, with Muñoz Marín the intended target. Albizu Campos remained in his home, also the party's headquarters, which came under siege by police, who fired at the building while others who were in there with Albizu Campos retaliated. Elsewhere on the island, the nationalists were outnumbered and the revolts were quickly put down.[100]

The attacks had not quite finished, however. On November 1, 1950, the nationalists Griselio Torresola and Oscar Collazo had an even larger target in their sights: President Harry S. Truman. The two men had traveled to Washington from New York and tried to shoot their way into Blair House, where Truman was staying during a White House renovation. The plan, as described by the *New York Times*, "was framed in such ignorance as to suggest insanity."[101] Police shot and killed Torresola, and Collazo was sentenced to death, though Truman commuted this to life in prison. By November 2, the island's newspapers, which had been full of grisly pictures of the corpses of those who were killed, now had pictures of Albizu Campos being led away by island authorities. He had surrendered after sustained attacks by the police and national guard. In the aftermath of the uprising, one thousand people were apprehended.[102]

In the end, the referendum took place in June 1951, and Public Law 600 passed with 76.5 percent in favor, though around 35 percent of registered voters did not turn out.[103] A constitution was drafted and another vote in March 1952 approved it, with 374,649 in favor and 82,923 against. From there it went to the U.S. Senate for confirmation. The Estado Libre Asociado (Associated Free State), or Commonwealth, was proclaimed on July 25, 1952—fifty-four years to the day after U.S. troops landed on the island.[104]

Albizu Campos had been sent to jail after the 1950 attempted assassination of Truman, but Governor Muñoz Marín gave him a conditional pardon in 1953. He would not stay free for long. On the afternoon of March 1, 1954, four Puerto Rican nationalists brought guns into the U.S. House of Representatives and opened fire, shouting "¡Viva Puerto Rico libre!" No one was killed, but five representatives were wounded. According to one account, the shooters "shouted for the freedom of their homeland as they fired murderously although at random from a spectators' gallery."[105] Three assailants—Lolita Lebrón, Rafael Cancel Miranda, and Andrés Figueroa Cordero—were caught by police, with Lebrón "still clutching the Puerto Rican flag."[106] Police later discovered a letter in her purse, explaining, "My life I give for the freedom of my country. This is a cry for victory in our struggle for independence."[107] The fourth member of the group, Irving Flores Rodríguez, fled the scene but was later found along with the gun he used.

The photos of the three with police outside the Capitol show a defiant Lebrón, her hair styled away from her face, her gaze determined, and her appearance as polished as a movie star's. She glared into the camera while two officers each took an arm to restrain her. In the image, as Lebrón's granddaughter Irene Vilar, would later observe, "the very details of her outfit can be seen: starched shirt and jacket, silver earrings, black patent-leather high-heeled shoes. All this given a glaring majesty by the language of the press."[108]

Dolores "Lolita" Lebrón was born in Lares, the town where the first independence struggle began. Like many Puerto Ricans, she left the island—in her case, in 1941—to work in New York, which she did for a while as a seamstress.[109] She returned in 1948 but, as Vilar wrote, "she came back a militant. New York had transformed her."[110] Lebrón remained steadfast during her trial, explaining to prosecutors, "I didn't come here to kill but to die."[111] She was given a fifty-six-year sentence, serving it at a women's prison in Alderson, West Virginia.

After the shooting in Congress, Albizu's pardon was revoked and he returned to prison in the spring of 1954. He spent most of the rest of his life incarcerated, suffering a stroke and claiming for years that he was the victim of radiation experiments that burned his skin.[112] He was pardoned again in 1964 because of his poor health and died the following year, his dream of an independent Puerto Rico unrealized.

With Muñoz Marín in power until 1964, the island settled into its commonwealth status, though another plebiscite was held in 1967 on the issue. Around 60 percent opted for the commonwealth model; 39 percent for statehood; and 1 percent for independence, though nationalists had boycotted the referendum.[113] More people from the mainland began to visit the island, and its tourism industry grew. The journalist Hunter S. Thompson moved to Puerto Rico early in his career, in 1960, and stayed a few months working on English-language publications. His novel *The Rum Diary* exhibits little admiration for what the United States wrought on the island:

> There was a strange and unreal air about the whole world I'd come into. It was amusing and vaguely depressing at the same time. Here I was, living in a luxury hotel, racing around a half-Latin city in a toy car that looked like a cockroach and sounded like a jet fighter, sneaking down alleys and humping on the beach, scavenging for food in shark-infested waters, hounded by mobs yelling in a foreign tongue—and the whole thing was taking place in quaint old Spanish Puerto Rico, where everybody spent American dollars and drove American cars and sat around roulette wheels pretending they were in Casablanca. One part of the city looked like Tampa and the other part looked like a medieval asylum.[114]

In 1979, President Jimmy Carter pardoned Lebrón, Cancel Miranda, and Flores Rodríguez,, as well as Collazo, who had been involved in the 1950 attack on Blair House. The sentence of the fourth member of the group that attacked Congress, Figueroa Cordero, had been commuted in 1977 because of his failing health. It later emerged that Lebrón had turned down earlier offers of parole because she would have been required to promise not to engage in "subversive activities." The release of Lebrón and the others was not universally popular, and the island's governor at the time, Carlos Romero Barceló, objected to it. One angry resident, Frederick Kidder, who had lived on the island for thirty-five years, wrote against their release, arguing that they had not paid their debt to society because "they do not recognize either society or the debt."[115] The government, however, believed that the "world around them has changed substantially," that it was a matter of "humanitarian judgment" because they were serving much longer terms than called for by the guidelines of the time, and that they "would pose no substantial risk of . . . becoming the rallying point for terrorist groups."[116]

As Lebrón left the prison, she called out to some of the inmates, "I'll never forget you, fight oppression and break the prisons," before facing the reporters waiting outside the gates.[117] From there, she was reunited with the others in New York City. All four received a warm welcome as some four hundred people—many shouting, "¡Viva Puerto Rico libre!"— greeted them at the airport.[118] They went on to the United Nations and spoke at a press conference. Holding a dozen red roses that she said were from "the Puerto Rican people," Lebrón took questions from journalists, including one about recent bombings by an underground group, the Fuerzas Armadas de Liberación Nacional (Armed Forces of National Liberation, FALN), which had been demanding the release of her and the others. She told the press: "I am a revolutionary. . . . I cannot disavow people who stand for liberation, and if they use bombs, what can we do, we are going forward. I hate bombs but we might have to use them."[119] The four left for San Juan, where around five thousand people gathered to greet their arrival, with the crowds chanting, "Lolita Lebrón—an example of courage."[120]

Members of FALN would go on to claim responsibility for some seventy bombings in U.S. cities from 1974 to 1983, killing five, injuring dozens, and causing millions of dollars worth of property damage. One of their most notorious attacks was the 1975 bombing at Fraunces Tavern in New York City which left four people dead. In connection with these events, Oscar López Rivera was arrested, but the charge was for "seditious conspiracy," or attempting to overthrow the U.S. government. López Rivera was born in Puerto Rico and moved to Chicago at fourteen. He was later drafted and served in the Vietnam War, earning a Bronze Star. Upon his return, he became involved in Puerto Rican activism in Chicago, eventually joining FALN.

In 1981, he began his seventy-year sentence, but he was not alone in his imprisonment—other members of FALN had also been arrested, with eleven later being freed from prison in exchange for renouncing violence, in a 1999 clemency deal under President Bill Clinton. López Rivera, however, turned down an offer at this time, in part because the negotiations included only some of the group's imprisoned members. He would have to wait until 2017, when his sentence was commuted by President Barack Obama—controversially, because while some people consider López Rivera a freedom fighter, others call him a terrorist.

López Rivera told the *Guardian* in an interview before his release that in its heyday FALN focused on structural targets, not people. "We called it 'armed propaganda'—using targets to draw attention to our struggle." He defended the group as "adhering to international law that says that colonialism is a crime against humanity and that colonial people have a right to achieve self-determination by any means, including force," but said the days of attacks were long over. "I don't think I could be a threat," he said. "We have transcended violence."[121]

However, FALN was not the only clandestine group on the island. Throughout the 1980s the Boricua Popular Army, or Los Macheteros (the machete wielders, or cane cutters), was also dedicated to the island's independence struggle. Founded in 1976, the group claimed responsibility for a number of bombings on the island, including some at military installations. The Macheteros drew wider public attention with their 1983 heist, in which $7.2 million was taken from a Wells Fargo depot in West Hartford, Connecticut. In connection with this, one of the group's leaders, Filiberto Ojeda Ríos—who had also been involved with FALN—was arrested but managed to jump bail ahead of his trial in 1990. He lived as a fugitive until 2005, when FBI agents tracked him down at his home in Hormigueros, in the west of Puerto Rico, where he died after a standoff and shoot-out. His death took place on September 23, the same day as the *Grito de Lares* independence uprising in 1868, prompting angry demonstrations by supporters who considered him a hero and those upset by the FBI's tactics and timing.[122] The Macheteros are thought to still be active, and to be operating cells in the United States.

Chapter 14

Los Angeles, California, ca. 1920s–'70s

W HEN THE EAGER California conservationist Christine Sterling decided to explore the oldest part of the city of Los Angeles in the mid-1920s, she was disappointed to find the Mexican neighborhood of El Pueblo "forsaken and forgotten."[1] She was hoping to see obvious traces of the Spanish past, but there was nothing that matched her expectations. That is not to say this part of the growing city was empty—the main plaza itself had long been a place for political exiles from Mexico and Mexican-Americans to meet and debate, and over time it was used by socialists and communists, among others.[2] The Mexican community that was based there had spread into neighborhoods to the east of the city, leaving El Pueblo with a growing reputation for crime, but it was still home to Mexicans, as well as other immigrants including Italians and Chinese. By 1926, however, the neighborhood was slated to be razed and the site used for a train station.[3]

Sterling, unlike some earlier California boosters, was actually from the state, having been born in Oakland. She and her husband, a lawyer for the film industry, also fell under the sway of the Southern California myth. They were lured there—as she described it—by "the attractive literature" that was sent out to entice visitors. "The booklets and folders I read . . . were painted in colors of Spanish-Mexican romance . . . with old Missions, rambling adobes—the strumming of guitars and the click of castanets."[4] She fell in love with Los Angeles and became concerned about the future of El Pueblo. Of special interest to her was the Avila

Adobe, built around 1818, the oldest known house in the city, which she found "down a dirty alley," where the abode had a "condemned" sign on its door, though she thought the building was "dignified even in its decay."[5] Once the home of the mayor of Los Angeles, it had been used as a military headquarters in 1847 when U.S. troops occupied the state, housing John C. Frémont and Kit Carson. In later years it was a restaurant and hotel.[6] Sterling wrote in her diary that this adobe deserved to join other landmarks, noting that "the homes of Washington, Lincoln, and Jefferson have become truly American Shrines. This old adobe belongs to the history of Los Angeles."[7]

Her aim, however, was not just to preserve the area around Olvera Street, which was one of El Pueblo's main thoroughfares, but also to re-create a "Mexican" village. In this sense, she at least acknowledged the city's Mexican heritage—there had been some debate among city councillors over whether the town should be "Spanish" or even "Latin American," but in the end "Mexican" won out as perhaps the most authentic.[8] She joined forces with Harry Chandler, the publisher of the *Los Angeles Times*, who supported a different location for the planned train station. With the newspaper's backing, her campaign came to the public's attention and was successful, although Sterling faced a great deal of antagonism from some quarters of the Anglo community, with one opponent taking her fight to the California supreme court. Sterling managed to overcome this, and convinced the city council that El Pueblo would be a profitable tourist draw. By 1930, she unveiled El Pueblo's site, centered on Olvera Street: "A Mexican Street of Yesterday in a City of Today."[9] She wrote at the time that it opened with a "blaze of glory," and she was pleased that it held "all the charm and beauty which I dreamed for it." This was, to her mind, because of the Mexican people in whose hearts, she believed, "is spun the gold of Romance and Contentment."[10] It was an immediate success.

For Sterling to make this Mexican village, she had to drive away one of its most authentic groups: the city's tamale vendors, who had been hawking the traditional corn snack since the 1880s. By the 1920s, they had become mobile food vendors offering a range of foods to the growing Mexican-American community. Instead, Sterling pushed for Olvera Street to have a sit-down restaurant, and the tamale vendors soon disappeared.

As an editorial in the *Los Angeles Times* noted: "They were born of the pueblo—they perish in the metropolis."[11]

The centerpiece to celebrate the completion of El Pueblo was to be a large mural. In 1932—the year the city hosted the Olympic Games—a leading Mexican muralist, David Alfaro Siqueiros, was invited to paint a large work on a wall in Olvera Street. He was living in the United States in exile at the time, and the commission was highly anticipated by the city's cultural and artistic community. The resulting work, *América Tropical*, was unveiled on October 9, 1932. The city's artists and intellectuals came out that rainy evening to view the work at its opening. When Sterling saw the mural in its full glory, she was horrified. At the center of the work, a dark-skinned man was stretched out on a cross, his limp head resting on his extended left arm. Below, his legs were forced wide apart in a V shape, bound to a parallel piece of wood. Above him sat a bald eagle, though it waited with the demeanor of a vulture. The rest of the scene included pre-Columbian statues, jungles, and on the far right of the work, revolutionaries with their guns, crouching and ready for battle. Onlookers gasped in surprise when the mural was revealed, reported the *Los Angeles Times* art critic Arthur Millier, who was at the opening. In his review of the mural, he pointed out: "In the midst of our popular conception of Mexico as a land of eternal dancing, gayety, and light-headedness, this stern, strong tragic work unrolls its painted cement surface."[12] Sterling, for her part, found it "anti-American."[13]

The mural was painted over, and "whitewashed" out of the city's history by 1938. Siqueiros later wrote that the central image was intended to be a "violent symbol of the Indian peon of feudal America doubly crucified by that nation's exploitative classes, and in turn, by imperialism. It is the living symbol of the destruction of past national American cultures by the invaders of yesterday and today."[14]

By the 1970s, however, the whitewashing had started to fade, and local artists and preservationists took a renewed interest in the mural, trying to protect what was left of *América Tropical*.[15] Today there is a small museum explaining the work's trajectory in El Pueblo, where Christine Sterling's legacy remains. Tourists continue to mill around a large Mexican-style craft market stuffed with piñatas and pottery, walk over to the main plaza, or visit La Placita, the Our Lady of the Angels

Church built by Franciscans, trying to get a glimpse of this re-created "timeless" Mexican world in the heart of one of the nation's most modern cities.[16]

The treatment of Siqueiros was part of larger dynamics in Los Angeles, the one city in the United States where fantasy could live side by side with reality. By the 1930s, Hollywood was booming, and it fell in love with all things Mexican, a fashion that reached its peak during the Great Depression.[17] Even the *New York Times* reported in 1933 on the "enormous vogue of things Mexican."[18] The daring romantic heroes of the Mexican Revolution, such as Pancho Villa, had captured the public imagination, and Mexico's proximity played a part in the culture's popularization as well. Angelenos had been going down to Tijuana and other border towns during prohibition, experiencing a form of Mexican culture at first hand.

Mexico, too, was having its own "golden age" of cinema, which started in the 1930s, putting Mexican actors and actresses—including stars like Dolores del Río, who worked in both countries—on Hollywood's radar. Indeed, she starred in a film adaptation of the novel *Ramona*—one of three made in as many decades. The first had been a silent version made in 1910, starring Mary Pickford and given the subtitle "A Story of the White Man's Injustice to the Indians." It was directed by D. W. Griffith, who would make the controversial movie *The Birth of a Nation* five years later. The 1928 version that starred del Río was also silent, but the final 1936 *Ramona* had color and sound and featured Loretta Young in the lead role. As moving pictures began to incorporate sound, Mexican composers like Juan García Esquivel and Johnny Richards (Juan Manuel Cascales) were influential in creating Hollywood's sonic style.

Around the same time, another dashing Californio won the public's affection: Zorro. The masked crusader first leaped off the page in the 1919 story *The Mark of Zorro: The Curse of Capistrano*. Like Ramona, Zorro was not the product of a Californio; rather, his creator was an Illinois-born pulp fiction writer, Johnston McCulley. The story—and the many Zorro tales that followed it—focused on the exploits of the wealthy landowner Don Diego Vega, who by night is the masked vigilante Zorro, the Spanish word for fox. He acts in the name of justice, claiming to have "robbed none except officials who have stolen from the missions and the poor, and punished none except brutes who mistreat natives."[19] The series was set roughly between the 1820s, around the time of Mexican independence, and the arrival of the United States in 1848, among the missions of Southern California and the pueblo of Los Angeles. It reflected the influence of the mission myth, describing the tensions between the authorities and the priests at a time when "there was little peace between the robed Franciscans who followed in the footsteps of the sainted Junípero Serra . . . and those who followed the politicians and had high places in the army."[20] Zorro was a hit and was soon scooped up by Hollywood, with Douglas Fairbanks starring in *The Mark of Zorro* in 1920, and Tyrone Power in a 1940 remake.*

The Mexican vogue applied not only to popular culture such as films but across the spectrum of the arts. The composer Aaron Copland, for instance, had been inspired by Mexico, writing *El Salón México* after visits there to see his friend, the fellow composer Carlos Chávez. Like many Mexicans during this period, Chávez had spent time in the United States, living for a few years in the late 1920s in New York. He had come to public attention after the debut of his 1921 ballet based on pre-Columbian themes, *El fuego nuevo* (The New Fire).[21]

While in the United States, Chávez also met photographer Paul Strand, who would make the reverse journey into 1930s Mexico. Strand captured the reality of peasant life throughout his travels in the country, showing the beauty and hardship of the more remote areas. His images from this period show a stern, resilient Mexico: straw-hatted farmers exhausted after a day in the fields, women tending their babies, solemn statues of Mary in the many churches he visited, and the dusty streets of quiet villages. Strand would stay in Mexico for a few years in the 1930s, aided by Chávez, who had become head of the National Conservatory of Music and of the government's Department of Fine Arts. Later, in 1936, Strand made a film about a fishing community for the culture ministry, *Redes* (called *The Waves* in English), now considered a classic of Mexican cinema.[22] Strand, like other foreign photographers before him, captured Mexico at a time of great change, and in 1940, after returning to the United States, he exhibited and published a portfolio of that work.[23]

---

* Television executives turned Zorro's exploits into a series in 1958, and the character's Hollywood appeal continued for the rest of the century and beyond, with 1998's *The Mask of Zorro*, starring Spaniard Antonio Banderas, who also reappeared in 2005's *The Legend of Zorro*.

The Mexican attempt to merge the present and past to resolve the question of national identity could perhaps be seen with the most clarity in the work of muralists of the 1920s and 1930s, such as Siqueiros, José Clemente Orozco, and their famed contemporary, Diego Rivera. Their forms and themes came out of concerns of the time. Murals were thought to be a more democratic medium for communicating with the public. In addition, the idea of *mestizaje* had been popularized after the Revolution, with the Mexican mestizo being a symbol of modernized Mexican politics. The mestizo was meant to represent the "ideal" mixed citizen, though later reassessments have highlighted the inherent discrimination of *mestizaje*. While appearing inclusive at one level, it excludes on another level people who were not considered "mixed," especially blacks, Asians, and indigenous Mexicans.[24]

At the time, however, *mestizaje* manifested itself in murals, which sought to celebrate the new, postrevolutionary Mexico, and to look forward. Rivera's work blended the present, past, and future, combining symbols of the Mexica people with more recent national heroes, workers, peasants, and revolutionaries.[25] He attracted commissions in the United States but controversy as well. His 1933 mural *Man at the Crossroads* was intended for Rockefeller Center in New York, but after Rivera, a supporter of communism, included a depiction of Lenin and refused to paint over him, he was forced to stop work on the project and it was later destroyed. Rivera had saved the design, however, and the following year he returned to the project, painting on the walls of the Museo del Palacio de Bellas Artes in Mexico City, where this work can be seen today, with a new title: *Man, Controller of the Universe*. An unmissable Lenin is featured to the left of the central image of a worker, while farther left Leon Trotsky holds a banner calling for workers of the world to unite, with Karl Marx and Friedrich Engels looking on.

Although Hollywood may have been undergoing an affair with all things Mexican on-screen, the mood was somewhat different on the street. Between 1920 and 1930, the Mexican and Mexican-American population in the United States doubled to around 1.4 million, as recorded in the 1930 census, with the vast majority living in Texas, New Mexico, Arizona, California, and Colorado.[26] Much of this immigration soon ground to a halt with the start of the Great Depression, in part because

Mexicans were blamed for rising unemployment but also because workers had started to organize and relations were turning sour. At the turn of the twentieth century, many labor bosses considered Mexicans to be strike-breaking outsiders, but now, faced with increasing prejudice and economic disadvantage, some Mexican workers attempted to set up trade unions in the 1920s and into the 1930s. The Confederación de Uniones Obreras Mexicanas (Confederation of Mexican Workers' Unions) was established in 1927, and the Mexican Mutual Aid Society of Imperial Valley in 1928. The latter started demanding better pay and conditions, and its cantaloupe workers went on strike later that year.[27] Local police were quick to level charges of communism, and arrests were made.[28] In 1930, the Mexican Mutual Aid Society led eight thousand out on strike—in addition to Mexicans, they included Japanese, Chinese, Filipino, and Sikh workers—and this strike, too, was followed by roundups and arrests.[29] In 1933, a number of strikes occurred in California, including one in October of cotton workers in which three men were killed and nine were injured. As that standoff wore on, workers' families were evicted from their homes. They returned to the fields by the end of the month.[30] The strikes died down after another violent suppression, this time in San Francisco in 1934, when the National Guard was brought in.[31] They continued to take place, however, and were not limited to California. In Texas, for instance, Emma Tenayuca led more than ten thousand pecan shellers in San Antonio out on a strike over low wages and poor conditions in 1938.[32] The growing national hostility to communism made union activity difficult for many workers, including Mexicans; every strike had the potential to turn into a witch hunt.

Matters were not helped by the progressive policies enacted in Mexico under President Lázaro Cárdenas, who took office in 1934. After the end of the revolution, investment from the United States in Mexico had continued despite initial concerns about the 1917 constitution's Article 27, regarding state ownership of the land. Direct U.S. investment was higher by 1929 than it had been before the conflict started in 1910.[33] With the arrival of Cárdenas, however, that relationship would experience some significant changes. In 1935, Cárdenas closed brothels and declared gambling illegal, shutting down the casinos in Tijuana that had lured so many Southern Californians to the border—two of those casinos were partly owned by former president Abelardo Rodríguez.[34] His real focus, however, was on land, the redistribution of which had slowed down since the revolution, and he wanted to build up the communal *ejido* farms. By 1940 he had redistributed some eighteen million hectares, taking the number of *ejidos* from 15 percent of cultivated land to 47 percent.[35] In other sectors of the economy, Cárdenas faced ongoing strikes, including one by oil workers in 1937. They wanted better wages, and an arbitration board found that they should be paid more. The British and U.S. oil companies that owned most of the firms took the matter to the Mexican supreme court. When it, too, ruled in the workers' favor, the foreign companies tried to defy the decision. Cárdenas decided to expropriate the oil industry in 1938, a move that delighted sectors of the public, but caused a diplomatic row with Britain. With the Second World War looming, President Roosevelt did not make overt threats toward Mexico, but he supported U.S. oil firms' ongoing demands for compensation from the Mexican government. Private U.S. investors became uneasy and some began to divest themselves of their interests in the country.[36]

The 1930s would be a brutal decade for Mexicans and Mexican-Americans within the United States. Worsening job prospects and growing hostility meant fewer Mexicans were crossing legally, and the recorded numbers fell from 61,622 in 1928 to 2,058 in 1932.[37] Throughout the decade, the tide of migrants turned, repelled in part by discrimination and given an extra impetus in some places by rumors of imminent deportation. In Los Angeles, officials conducted raids in Mexican neighborhoods—including El Pueblo on February 26, 1931—further raising fears and sending a strong message to the Mexican community.[38] It worked: in 1931, some 40,000 Mexicans left California, and that year more people were sent out of the United States than had entered.[39] The Immigration Service continued to operate sweeps and roundups of Mexicans at places all over the country, including cities such as New York, Chicago, and Detroit.[40]

The Mexican government also became involved, offering free transportation from the border inland and waiving duties on U.S. goods brought back to Mexico by the deportees. The result was the repatriation, voluntary or by force, of at least four hundred thousand Mexicans in the 1930s, though some calculations suggest that more than one million returned. Underneath that figure is a more surprising statistic: up to 60 percent of these people were born in the United States and were thus full citizens.

It was a traumatic time for many of these deportees, especially those who had never lived in Mexico before and felt themselves to be—and indeed often were—American.[41]

For those remaining in the United States, discrimination continued. The situation was so serious that in the early 1940s the Mexican ambassador Francisco Castillo Nájera was forced to write about incidents on a regular basis to the secretary of state, Cordell Hull. One letter cited complaints from people in Azusa (then Azuza), California, where "discrimination has been shown against Mexicans by the owners of the theater and pool of the town in question." Mexicans were not allowed to use either. The Mexican consulate's attempts to stop this were fruitless, and Nájera described the reasons set out by the mayor as not "sufficient to justify humiliating treatment for Mexicans." Local discrimination was now an international issue.[42] In denying the charges of racism leveled against the state, the governor of California, Culbert L. Olson, wrote to the U.S. secretary of state, Sumner Welles, in 1941, claiming, "I safely say there does not exist any sentiment of racial prejudice against the Mexican population of California as such." He went on to assert that the "very large Mexican population" in Southern California "has received equal consideration" with regard to state policy and the law.[43]

With the onset of the Second World War, good relations between the United States and its southern neighbor took on a new level of importance, in geopolitics and economics, as there was an immediate need for workers. Relations and security along the border were deemed crucial as well. Some people feared that without the help of Mexicans, Axis troops would be able to land in Mexico and attack the United States from the south.[44] Some border communities went out of their way to demonstrate their patriotism or support for the United States in this period. For instance, in Sonoran border towns there were celebrations on the Fourth of July.[45]

Although hundreds of thousands of Mexican-Americans were volunteering for the war, anti-Mexican rancor continued to flare. Los Angeles was the starting point of a series of attacks that would spread throughout other big cities in 1943; their targets were Mexicans or Mexican-Americans who were members of a youthful subculture: the *pachucos*. These California teenagers had their own language, *Caló*, which drew from Spanish and English, and angered adults and officials who used both languages;

they were stumped by its vocabulary.[46] In the same way that *Caló* was considered to be slang, the pachucos were likewise considered to be thugs. Anglos and even middle-class Mexican-Americans often described the boys and young men as gang members, and if that indeed was the case, then they would be branded "criminals" whether or not they had ever been arrested. Some of the young men were Mexican, but many were Mexican-American U.S. citizens.[47]

The pachucos came to public attention in 1942, when members of the 38th Street gang were put on trial for the murder of José Díaz, whose body was found in an abandoned quarry. In the hunt for suspects, some six hundred Mexican-Americans had been rounded up and questioned.[48] During the trial in what became known as the Sleepy Lagoon case, an overexcited press referred to the men as "baby gangsters." In the end, twenty-two men—all but one of Mexican origin—were indicted. Five were charged with assault, and twelve convicted of first- or second-degree murder and imprisoned. A Sleepy Lagoon Defense Committee was formed for their appeal and by 1944 the convictions were reversed and the cases were dismissed, owing to lack of evidence.

Pachucos, male and female, now in the public spotlight, faced criticism over their sartorial signature: the zoot suit, which incorporated high-waisted trousers that flared out around the knee before tapering down to the ankle, accompanied by a broad-shouldered jacket, and topped with a wide-brimmed hat. Female zoot-suiters wore a similar oversize jacket, but with a short skirt and heavy makeup.[49] This was, in many ways, simply the vanity of youth and the rebellion of adolescence, but a significant segment of the Anglo community did not find this peacockery pretty, chastising pachucos for using excessive fabric during a time of shortages and rationing.[50]

On the evening of June 3, 1943, a fight broke out between some sailors and young Mexican-Americans. The genesis of the disagreement is disputed, but there was no mistaking what began the following night, as some two hundred sailors and marines hailed a flotilla of taxis and set off in search of pachucos.[51] Known as the Zoot Suit Riots, the ensuing brawls between the servicemen and the Mexicans lasted for more than a week. Men in zoot suits were the targets, though others who looked "Mexican," and even black men in regular clothing, were beaten up, as enraged sailors jumped out of the cabs and grabbed men on the street or even yanked them off buses. Those wearing the suits were often stripped of them in public, and left almost naked, lying on the street. The police did little to quell the fracases, which caused fear and panic throughout the city, especially in Mexican neighborhoods, leaving hundreds battered and humiliated.[52] Vicente Morales had been enjoying music by the Lionel Hampton Band at the Orpheum Theatre on June 7 when a group of white sailors began shoving and insulting him. Morales recalled that "about eight sailors got me outside of the theater and they started beating me up. It happened so fast, I passed out. I woke up with a cracked rib, a broken nose, black and blue all over."[53]

The Mexican consul in Los Angeles alerted the ambassador in Washington and a minister in Mexico City about the riots. Likewise, the American consul in Monterrey, Henry S. Waterman, hurried to effect damage control after the editor of El Porvenir ran a story with the headline "Attack Against Mexicans in Los Angeles by Sailors and Soldiers." Waterman later told the secretary of state that he had tried to explain to the editor that the targeted young men were "usually hangers-on at dance halls, pool rooms and worse, and were usually considered ne'er-do-wells," insisting that the suits "were worn by many of the shiftless young men, without regard to racial origins." In Los Angeles, Waterman claimed, some of the zoot-suiters just happened to be of Mexican origin.[54] Waterman blamed the Associated Press for "having sent out such a distorted account of the riots, making them appear as a racial riot."[55]

The Mexican and Spanish-language press in the United States covered the riots as well. Some reports were unsympathetic to the victims, with old class and color prejudices on display.[56] La Prensa more or less blamed the young men, claiming that the pachucos were "a real affront to our country."[57] Another paper, El Nacional in Mexico City, wrote that the "sowers of hate will not destroy the Good Neighborliness, nor divert either of the two countries in their common effort against the Axis."[58] Not everyone in Mexico was convinced by the official U.S. interpretation of the riots, and students at the National Autonomous University of Mexico held a demonstration to protest the poor response by Mexico's government. A flyer was distributed that blamed the riots on "Hearst interests, the Ku Klux Klan, United States imperialists, Fifth Columnists of all kinds, and those interested in bringing about a victory for Hitler."[59] Other U.S. authorities, in wartime mode, claimed the riots must have been provoked by a "foreign" agent and used them as a pretext to target communists, who in turn blamed the fascists.[60] Similar riots erupted across the country, as zoot-suiters were attacked as far away as Philadelphia and New York. No servicemen were charged for the attacks in Los Angeles, but around five hundred Hispanic men who had been assaulted were rounded up and faced charges such as vagrancy. California journalist Carey McWilliams later noted that the riots "left a residue of resentment and hatred in the minds and hearts of thousands of young Mexican-Americans."[61]

LIKE CUBANS AND Puerto Ricans in New York and Florida, Mexicans living in the United States around the turn of the century also formed social and mutual-aid societies, called *mutulistas*.[62] Groups such as the Arizona-based Alianza Hispano-Americana (La Alianza) spread throughout the Southwest. By the 1930s, in addition to offering their members practical services, such as health care, these organizations also started to take up civil rights struggles, while at the same time often espousing loyalty to the very nation that was discriminating against them. For instance, the League of United Latin American Citizens (LULAC), which was founded in 1929 and led by Bernardo (Ben) Garza, pledged to be loyal to the United States and encouraged members to learn English.[63] Membership in LULAC was at first restricted to U.S. citizens, as its leaders felt that including too many immigrants might undermine their efforts to secure gains for the entire community.[64] This "Mexican-American generation," as they were later called, placed great value on their U.S. citizenship and in general played down their "Mexicanness," willing to become active in politics with the expectation that they would have access to more extensive rights and economic opportunities than their parents did.[65]

Military service had been seen as another way to express this growing civic engagement. In the Second World War, some five hundred thousand people of Hispanic origin served in the U.S. military, although records often did not categorize them as such.[66] Most such soldiers were placed in white units, but because some military units were based on a geographical area, there were also Hispanic units, such as the Puerto Rican Sixty-Fifth Infantry Regiment.[67] Mexican-Americans composed the largest group of recruits, followed by Puerto Ricans.[68] Mexican nationals who lived in the United States were also drafted into the U.S. Army, with some fifteen thousand serving during the war. Some people crossed the border knowing they would be drafted, though a few ran the other way when they found out they were not exempt from military service.[69] The Selective Service Act of 1940 had required all male foreign nationals to register, though those from neutral countries could, theoretically, be exempted from service.[70] Some confusion developed over the issue of nationality, but the Mexican government clarified that, since Mexico was an ally, its citizens were free to enlist in the U.S. Army, and the two nations signed a military agreement in 1943.[71] Once the war was over, Mexican nationals who had served were allowed to be naturalized as U.S. citizens—but they had to prove they had entered the United States legally. Without documentation, they would be denied citizenship and associated veterans' benefits, though the draft boards often failed to explain this.[72]

Fighting in the war led to an increased feeling among Hispanic people of being stakeholders in U.S. society. After returning from the war, the soldiers wanted a share of the prosperity, and a stronger push for equality and civil rights began. One such serviceman was Hector García, who was born in Mexico in 1913 but whose family fled during the revolution. García was, in many ways, the face of middle-class Mexican-Americans. His family crossed over at Matamoros and later settled in Mercedes, Texas. As an officer in the Army Medical Corps, he served tours in North Africa and Europe, where he met his future wife, Wanda Fusillo, in Italy. He had also studied medicine and trained to be a physician. Upon his return to the United States, he set up a practice in Corpus Christi in 1946.[73] Like many other Hispanic veterans, García was disappointed by the prejudice he had encountered in the army. He also noticed that other former Hispanic servicemen were not taking full advantage of their military benefits, including those in the GI Bill, and that some were not receiving them at all.[74] This motivated García to organize other ex-servicemen, and the result was the American GI Forum (AGIF), with García as its first president. It, too, embraced a language of patriotism, as its name attests.[75]

The organization came to national attention with the case of Private Felix Z. Longoria, who had been killed in the Philippines. His body had been sent back to Three Rivers, Texas, where the Anglo-owned Rice Funeral Home—the only one in the small town—refused to bury him because he was "Mexican." The AGIF mobilized the public, organizing a rally of one thousand people in Corpus Christi. García lobbied then senator Lyndon B. Johnson, who arranged for a burial with full military honors in Arlington National Cemetery in 1949.[76]

The question of legal whiteness continued to plague Mexican-Americans, despite the efforts of organizations like LULAC to ensure that Mexicans were officially considered "white."[77] Nativist groups called on the government to make "Mexican" a category, which it did in the 1930 census, although this classification was removed a decade later. In the end, the 1940 Nationality Act extended citizenship to "descendants of races indigenous to the Western Hemisphere," but the ruling did little to change wider public opinion about the "whiteness" or otherwise of Mexicans and other Hispanic people.[78]

Many Mexicans and Mexican-Americans in the Southwest were also forced to confront Jaime (sometimes Juan) Crow. Texas was a place, as one commentator described it, where "Jim Crow wears a sombrero."[79] Through a number of informal means, the southern system of discrimination seeped into the Southwest. There might have been nothing on the law books, but certain conventions led to rampant discrimination. The Mexican-American author and campaigner Alonso Perales kept a running list in the 1940s of places in Texas that denied service to Mexicans. One entry, about Midland, gives some indication of what Mexicans faced:

> Mexicans are segregated and obligated to use a balcony in the section reserved for Negroes at the Yucca, Ritz and Rex Theaters. Mexicans are denied service in restaurants. At the Ritz Café there is a sign which reads: "No Mexicans Admitted Here." Five American soldiers of Mexican descent were denied service at said café due to their Mexican origin. The local police are very unjust with persons of Mexican extraction. . . . Mexicans are segregated at all the elementary schools. Persons of Mexican descent are not permitted to enter the Catholic Church during the hour of religious services for Anglo-Americans.[80]

A steady stream of complaints about this sort of treatment also emanated from the Mexican government. The charges made against towns in the Southwest were serious enough for U.S. authorities to commission a confidential report on Texas and New Mexico, undertaken by the American consul general William P. Blocker in 1942. Blocker traveled to various cities and towns and concluded that "there is a certain amount of truth to the protests made by the Mexican Consuls in regard to the prohibiting of certain classes or groups of people from acquiring lands or homes in given localities." According to Blocker, smaller towns had more discrimination but believed "these problems have been fairly well adjusted in large cities."[81]

He also acknowledged the role of civil rights groups but thought their battles came from positions of weakness. He wrote that the Latin American "does not feel himself to be an equal to a north American, he either feels himself superior or inferior—the latter prevailing," which underscored the "activities of the so-called welfare societies, such as the Lulacs and the League of Loyal Americans." Blocker, using many of the tropes of the time, felt Hispanics exhibited "a battle of temperament between the Indian blood mixed with the Moor and the Castilian, a combination of which is conceded by eminent psychologists as mistaking kindness for weakness and in some cases, courtesy for timidity. These people are exceedingly individualistic and emotional, coupled with having plenty of sensitivity."[82] His recommendations at the end of the report included trying to change Anglo attitudes in smaller towns through programs of talks and lectures; demanding that law enforcement treat Mexicans with more respect; and using civic organizations such as Rotary Clubs to help forge improved links between communities.[83]

At one point, the Mexican government became so frustrated that in June 1943 it enacted a temporary ban on Mexicans going to work in Texas.[84] These workers, along with LULAC and similar organizations, were trying to pressure the state into legislating for better treatment of Mexicans. A month earlier, the Texas legislature had passed a resolution, "Caucasian Race—Equal Privileges," which entitled "all persons of the Caucasian Race" equal access to all public places. It made a point of saying that "our neighbors to the South" were Caucasians and as such should not be victims of discrimination, especially at a time when they were working together with the United States to fight Nazism.[85] Mexico did not feel that the legislation had any teeth and so instead pushed forward with its ban. The Texas farmers quickly reacted, needing people to work in their fields. A bill was introduced in 1945 to resolve the matter, stipulating equal access to goods and services for Mexicans, as well as a fine of up to $500 for any violation of this rule, though by the time the bill passed, it had been watered down in the Texas senate so as to offer little, if any, protection from discrimination.[86]

The situation barely improved after the war. In Corpus Christi, Hector García received notes from fellow citizens about their everyday experiences of prejudice. One, from Rosie Escobar in 1951, recounted how she went to eat at a restaurant she had previously visited in Big Spring, Texas, but this time the waiter presented her with a card that said, "We reserve the right to refuse service to anyone." She tried a different place and was given another card, this time in inept Spanish, that told her, "Nosotros no podemos sirvir a gente de color o Mexicanos en al Barra." Escobar told García that after the refusals "I really had a red color on my face . . . here at this city of Big Spring is lots of Discrimination for our Latin-American People." He told her to send the cards to him, to add to his growing dossier.[87]

Following the deportations of the 1930s, the California growers' lobby and other farmers' groups had to clamor for Mexican labor again by the start of the Second World War. There were sharp demands for food, and the war had reduced the number of men available to work. The response was the establishment in 1942 of the *bracero* program (from *brazos*, the Spanish word for arms).[88] It was intended to grant seasonal visas and streamline the processing of migrant workers. By 1943, seventy-six thousand braceros toiled in fields throughout the United States, and by 1945 the number had risen to three hundred thousand.[89]

Some Mexicans found the conditions of the visa troublesome and just crossed the border without papers, as workers had done in the 1920s. After the war, however, the government tightened up its immigration laws. The 1952 McCarran-Walter Act made it a crime to bring in or harbor an undocumented worker; in part this was intended to keep out suspected communists—this being the height of the "red scare"—or anyone else involved in subversive activity.[90] The anti-immigration chorus grew louder at this time as well. Mexican workers continued to arrive, however.

After Cárdenas's presidency ended in 1940 the country's economy moved away from land distribution and the *ejido* system, so while the cities and urban classes prospered, rural communities fell behind. Between 1940 and 1960, the number of landless people who had worked in agriculture rose by 60 percent; this forced many to seek bracero contracts, or simply to cross the border and take their chances.[91]

The bracero program and the issue of illegal migrants was also a major concern for groups like LULAC and AGIF. To them, the question of documentation was a crucial one; undocumented workers threatened to roll back the hard-won gains of those with the proper papers and Mexican-Americans.[92] Middle-class community leaders like Hector García believed their position was in the best interests of the wider community, including the undocumented workers, who they felt were too often exploited.[93] García and Senator Lyndon Johnson were in regular correspondence about the issue. In one letter explaining to García the measures being taken in Washington, Johnson said, "If our relations with Mexico are to continue on the friendly basis of the past, some suitable solution to the wetback labor problem is going to have to be worked out," before asking García for his suggestions on the matter.[94]

In 1953, García's AGIF published a report titled "What Price Wetbacks?" It argued that Mexican migrants were "a threat to our health, our economy, our American way of life."[95] The report argued further that the poor living standards suffered by Mexicans under the migration system left everyone worse off, claiming: "These are the wetbacks—sad-eyed and sick, desperate beings unaware that their illegal entry and existence bring with them to the areas they infest soaring statistics on syphilis, tuberculosis, infantile diarrhea and other diseases, along with a host of crime and other socio-economic problems."[96] The report outraged some members of the Mexican-American community, in part because it seemed to reaffirm every stereotype about Mexicans while revealing internal class divisions. However, García and the AGIF continued to campaign for a repeal of the bracero program.[97]

The year after García's report, an answer to this question emerged: Operation Wetback.[98] It was led by Joseph Swing, who was commissioner of immigration after a long career in the military that included being part of the Punitive Expedition against Pancho Villa in 1916. The deportation operation claimed great success despite corresponding public criticism of its rough tactics. More than 1,000 people were arrested daily, and it was claimed that more than a million people were sent to Mexico by 1955. However, the bracero program was still in place. In the same period, the number of legal bracero contracts continued to rise, more than doubling from 201,280 in 1953 to 447,535 by 1959, with around 150,000 to 200,000 braceros working in California's Central Valley alone.[99] Often workers without papers ended up being legalized through what was called "drying out the wetbacks." This involved illegal farmworkers being taken to the border, given papers, and returned to work. Sometimes a worker needed only to set one foot across the border to make the "reentry" legal.[100] In the end, the power of the growers' lobby contributed to the longevity of the bracero program, which had been due to end in 1947 but lasted until 1964.

The following year, the Hart-Celler Act of 1965 introduced another overhaul of the immigration system, repealing the national-origins quotas and allowing 290,000 visas a year, with up to 20,000 per country in the Eastern Hemisphere (Europe, Asia, and Africa), for a maximum total of 170,000, while the entire Western Hemisphere was allotted 120,000 overall. At first there were no specific country quotas, and at this time Mexicans and Canadians accounted for up to two-thirds of immigrants to the United States. Overall, visas were to be prioritized for current citizens' or residents' family members, or for immigrants who had desirable professional skills.[101] Just over a decade later, in 1976, an amendment was introduced to establish country quotas of 20,000 for the nations of the Western Hemisphere; it hit Mexicans the hardest, as they were the largest group of immigrants.[102] In that same year, 781,000 Mexicans were apprehended as "illegal" after the quota changes, in addition to the closing of a loophole that had previously allowed undocumented Mexicans to regularize their papers if they gave birth to children in the United States. The exceptions that had long existed for Mexico were now firmly at an end.[103]

As sports arenas go, Dodger Stadium is in a league of its own. It seems to hover above the ground, ringed by mountains, and its smooth, modern design made it a classic of contemporary architecture from the moment it opened in 1962. Before the construction of this sporting icon, the area northeast of downtown Los Angeles where it was located had been known as Chavez Ravine, home to more than a thousand mostly Hispanic working-class families. A small panel inside the stadium notes the date—September 17, 1959—when ground was broken, after which more than eight million cubic yards of earth were moved.

The area was named for the councilman Julian Chavez, who served the city from 1850 to 1875. In 1912–13, the land had been sold and houses built across what had been three parts—Palo Verde, La Loma, and Bishop—all of which Chavez Ravine now comprised. It was a neighborly, close-knit community but not a wealthy one. Its residents had to petition the city council for improvements, such as streetlights and paved roads.[104] Using this poverty as a rationale, in 1949 the city council decided by a unanimous vote to relocate all the people living there to a public housing project as part of a wider urban renewal scheme. Such a move would have turned many homeowners into renters, an unpopular prospect among the residents, who did not want to lose their homes.[105] At this point, Chavez Ravine had a population of around thirty-seven hundred people, of whom roughly two-thirds were Mexican or Mexican-American.[106]

Plans were designed for Elysian Park Heights, a development of 3,364 housing units in tower blocks for seventeen thousand people on 278 acres, with schools, a community hall, and shops.[107] The high-rises did little to sway the residents of Chavez Ravine, who did not want to give up their small plots of land to live in apartments. Throughout this period, residents of Chavez Ravine were forced to defend their position, with women in many of these families taking special pains to point out that their husbands, brothers, and sons had served in the Second World War and the conflict in Korea; these were families of veterans.[108] Agnes Cerda, who had two soldier sons, told one of the hearings about Chavez Ravine's future: "Take our homes away from us and you are taking away our incentive to be good American citizens. . . . Would you put your mother out of your home and give it to the Housing Authority? You would not."[109] After much debate, the plan was canceled in 1953.

Despite the failure of the plan, the city acquired Chavez Ravine in 1955, under Ordinance 105,801, approved by Mayor Norris Poulson, which authorized the purchase of the 185-acre Chavez Ravine site from the federal government for $1.3 million, with the proviso that it was to be used for "public purposes only."[110] By this time, many of the residents had left, and the plan at one point was to turn the area into a city park, including an eighteen-hole golf course. Instead, baseball solved the city's conundrum. Los Angeles offered Walter O'Malley, the owner of the Brooklyn Dodgers, the 185 acres, plus $2 million to clear it and another 115 acres of land in the area, if he would move his team across the country from Brooklyn. O'Malley agreed, and the Dodgers became the first major-league team on the West Coast, followed immediately by the New York Giants, who moved to San Francisco.[111] Once O'Malley's deal became publicized, residents and concerned Angelenos started a "Save Chavez Ravine for the People" movement, but the citywide voter referendum to approve the contract passed 351,638 to 325,898 in June 1958.[112]

The following May, forced evictions began, including that of Manuel and Avrana Aréchiga, who had been fighting in court to keep their home of thirty-six years.[113] When the construction crew and police arrived, the Aréchiga family, consisting of four adults and three children, barricaded themselves in their home. In response, deputies broke down the doors, and, less than ten minutes after they were dragged out, two bulldozers leveled their home.[114] Another resident, Aurora Vargas, vowed, "They'll have to carry me out," which they did on May 8. The Aréchigas took their battle to the courtroom, this time to obtain what they considered to be fair compensation: $17,500 against the $10,050 they had been offered, as well as $150 a month until the payment was made. After years in court, the family accepted the lower offer.[115]

The Dodgers would go on to fill that stadium time and again with fans, many of whom by the 1960s had seen the game of baseball itself experiencing profound changes, starting with the then Brooklyn Dodgers' decision to overturn the sport's color line by hiring Jackie Robinson in 1947. This brought about the end of the Negro leagues and opened the door for darker-skinned Cuban, Dominican, and Puerto Rican players to join Robinson in the majors.

While the game had been segregated in the United States from its inception, it had not been in Cuba. Segregation did exist in the amateur leagues, which were usually affiliated with private social clubs that often excluded Afro-Cubans. However, the professional leagues had no color bar, and black and white players from Cuba and, later on, the United States could train and play through the winter months on the island. In 1908, the first professional team, the Cincinnati Reds, played against the Cuban All-Stars.[116] The talent of Cuban players was obvious: Cristóbal Torriente managed, in one 1920 matchup, to outslug the Yankees' Babe Ruth three home runs to none.[117] Ruth was not gracious in defeat, saying, "Them greasers are punk ballplayers. Only a few of them are any good."[118] The pitcher José Méndez—known as the Black Diamond—later managed to strike out Ruth three times during the winter of 1921–22 with his impressive fastball.[119]

Yet in the United States prior to 1947 anyone with black skin could play only in the Negro leagues. Rodolfo Fernández, who played in the Negro leagues in the 1930s, as well as on Cuban teams, recalled life on the road in the United States: "Sometimes we couldn't find a place to sleep, so we would sleep on the bus." The struggle was worth it to Fernández, who said: "I was proud though, because when we would play in the United States, people would point us out as Cubans. This was because the Cubans had something that other people thought was special."[120] Many talented Hispanic players went to the Negro leagues, such as the Puerto Rican Francisco "Pancho" Coimbre, who played for the New York Cubans in the 1940s; and the Cuban Bernard Fernández, who pitched for the New York Black Yankees. Afro-Caribbean players were deeply involved in both suffering under segregation and later navigating the changes as the game became integrated.[121]

Lighter-skinned Cubans had a better chance, though team owners often had to prove their players' "whiteness" through sworn affidavits and other evidence shown to officials and journalists.[122] A few players, like Adolfo "Dolf" Luque, managed to join the majors; Luque spent most of his career with the Cincinnati Reds, with one newspaper describing him as "very light-skinned" and looking "more like an Italian than a full-blooded Cuban."[123] His pale complexion and blue eyes were not sufficient, however, to shield him from racial taunts from the crowds.[124] Most Hispanic players, like Martín Dihigo—nicknamed "El Maestro"— played in the Negro leagues, as well as in Cuba and elsewhere in Latin

America, but never had a chance in the majors, barred by the color of their skin. Dihigo retired before the integration of the game but was later inducted into the U.S. Baseball Hall of Fame, as well as halls of fame in Cuba, Mexico, and Venezuela.[125]

The post-segregation era of baseball would see many great Hispanic players reach the major leagues, including the "Cuban Comet" Orestes "Minnie" Miñoso, who joined the Cleveland Indians in 1948, debuting the following year, before becoming the first black player for the Chicago White Sox in 1951. Before this he, too, had played in the Negro leagues. Perhaps the most famous Hispanic player was Puerto Rico's Roberto Clemente, who debuted for the Pittsburgh Pirates in 1955; sadly, his brilliant career was cut short when he died in a plane crash in 1972 while helping deliver supplies to earthquake-ravaged Nicaragua.

Miñoso and other Afro-Latino players found in their early years in the majors that they were caught in a strange bind: besides not being white, they were also not black enough to achieve the level of popularity in the black community that African-American players had.[126] Hispanic players more generally found themselves objects of ridicule at the hands of sportswriters who belittled their Spanish-accented English or repeatedly described them as "hot-blooded." They also faced residual prejudice from white teammates and opponents; for example, Miñoso was one of the players most often hit by pitches, and despite being the first Afro-Latino star, he still awaits a place in the Hall of Fame.[127]

Great players have also come from Mexico, where a baseball league dates back to the 1920s. Fernando Valenzuela Anguamea, who had a stunning decade pitching for the Los Angeles Dodgers from 1980 to 1990, inspired "Fernandomania" in the city. Cubans also continue to arrive, though they have to defect from Cuba first, as Yoenis Céspedes and José Abreu have done. Dominicans have been an increasing force in the major leagues, contributing many of the game's best players. One of the most recent inductees to the Baseball Hall of Fame was Pedro Martínez, his 2015 election making him only the second player from the Dominican Republic to receive the honor, the first being the Giants pitcher Juan Marichal, in 1983. Overall, the number of Hispanic players of all hues and nationalities continues to rise steadily, and they now make up 27 percent of major-league players.[128]

THE FAILED HOUSING scheme for Chavez Ravine was one example of the postwar enthusiasm for "urban renewal" in the 1950s and 1960s. The aim of renewal was to clear slums and put in their place high-density public housing. The Housing Act of 1949 set out ambitious plans for 810,000 units of public housing in six years. It was followed by the Housing Act of 1954, and federal funding was given to almost one thousand urban renewal projects in total between 1949 and 1964.[129] In some places, entire communities were uprooted, as in parts of the Upper West Side neighborhood of New York City, made famous by the film *West Side Story*, with its warring teenage gangs the Sharks (Puerto Ricans) and the Jets (Polish-Americans). The Upper West Side stretches roughly from 59th Street to 110th, along Central Park. Although an expensive area of New York City today, for part of its history it was home to poorer immigrant communities, like the ones in *West Side Story.* In the early 1960s, buildings in part of the area were razed to make way for the Lincoln Center performing arts complex, which sits between West 62nd and 65th Streets.

Urban renewal was not confined to big cities. Smaller towns in the West also had problems with inadequate housing. Even in the 1930s, officials said Hispanic and black neighborhoods in Phoenix were as bad as any "tenement districts of New York," and many people lived in shacks without running water.[130] Phoenix constructed 604 units of public housing in response by 1941.[131] Another report described San Antonio as having "one of the most extensive slums" in the entire nation, with twelve thousand Mexicans or Mexican-Americans living in a one-mile patch.[132] These were not urban apartments or tenements but wooden shacks, some of which had been horse stalls.[133] Between 1949 and 1958, the city built 3,600 units of public housing.[134] At the same time in Dallas, Albuquerque, and Phoenix, fierce opposition to public housing projects arose, though other forms of "urban renewal"—which often led to the displacement and resettlement of established communities—continued in the decades that followed.[135]

Poverty was not the only barrier to home ownership. Often Hispanics were barred from owning or even renting in certain parts of cities, or, in

more extreme cases, they were excluded from an entire town. Peppered
throughout the United States were what were known as "sundown"
towns—shorthand for the sentiment "Don't let the sun set on you here"—
with the intention of keeping the population white. Local ordinances
permitted discrimination against potential black residents, and at times
this extended to Hispanics, Jews, Chinese, and Native Americans.[136] In
the case of Mexicans, one such example was South Pasadena, California,
a "sundown suburb" that permitted Native Americans but tried to keep
out Mexicans and Chinese people. It was accidentally integrated when
Manuel Servin, a professor at the University of Southern California, was
allowed to buy a historic home there because residents thought he was
Native American when he was actually Mexican.[137]

Other types of housing discrimination were often more straightforward. The "declaration of restrictions" for a new housing estate in
1950s Phoenix stipulated, "None of the lots numbered One (1) to Thirteen
(13) inclusive; Fifteen to Seventy (15 to 70) inclusive, shall ever be sold,
leased, rented to or occupied by any person who is, or whose spouse is,
or who is a descendant of or whose spouse is a descendant of a Mexican,
Japanese, Chinese, Mexican-Indian, American-Indian, Korean, Malay, Filipino, Negro or Hindu, or any person of any race other than the White
or Caucasian Race."[138] Such stipulations were far from uncommon.

The Sunbelt areas of the Southwest had experienced rapid population growth during and after the war. Tucson, for example, which had
35,000 people in 1940, became a city of 213,000 by 1960.[139] In such places,
attempts were made to keep Mexican-Americans from buying homes
in certain exclusive neighborhoods. Middle-class Mexican-Americans
found themselves at times being forced to distance themselves from
working-class Hispanics because the term "Mexican" was becoming
associated with a lower social class.[140] The historian David Gutiérrez
remembered these types of tension spilling into his personal life in East
Los Angeles. "Even as a child," he wrote, "I was struck by what often
seemed to me to be almost comical love/hate relationships between U.S.-
born Mexican-Americans and more recent immigrants from Mexico."
In his own family, the "wetbacks" were a target of reproach because
"the mass immigration of so-called backward, un-Americanized illegal
aliens reinforced the negative stereotypes Anglo Americans held about
all Mexicans."[141]

The Fair Housing Act of 1968 would attempt to end the practices that led to these divisions by prohibiting "discrimination in the sale, rental and financing of dwellings based on race, color, religion, sex or national origin." By this point, however, many cities were already entrenched in segregation, and those invisible lines continue making silent divisions to the present day. Places like Los Angeles, New York, Chicago, and Miami have all historically been home to Hispanic neighborhoods (barrios), and studies show that this general trend has continued, with at least nine million Hispanic people in 2000 living in metropolitan areas where they still experience a high degree of segregation.[142]

The inequalities that Hispanic people faced in finding a home were paired with similar discrepancies in finding schools for their children. Throughout the 1920s and 1930s, Mexican and Mexican-American children often attended segregated facilities; some 90 percent of schools in Texas and 85 percent of those in California were separate.[143] At a time when thousands of people were trying to assimilate to life in the United States, schools and the wider culture were reinforcing the idea that Mexicans were distinct and "inferior."[144] In 1935, some children of Mexican descent were even segregated by laws passed by the California legislature on the grounds that they were "Indian."[145] Overall, school officials often justified segregated schools by pointing to children of migrant workers, saying they had different needs from other children; or these officials argued that local schools simply represented the demographic makeup of neighborhoods which were themselves often segregated. Some school districts used English-language provisions to section off Mexican children; the practice led to majority-Mexican schools. Many of these schools also offered different courses for Mexican children, placing them on more vocational tracks and giving them little access to more academic subjects.[146]

A 1940 study by the pioneering education researcher George I. Sánchez noted that in the 1937–38 school year, New Mexico spent $51 per pupil annually on average, but the counties with the highest percentage of Spanish-speaking students spent less than $35 per pupil. The effects of this funding shortfall were compounded by a curriculum based on the assumption that the children would come from English-speaking homes "that reflect American cultural standards." The lack of funding and the cultural presumptions led Sánchez to describe New Mexicans as being the "stepchildren of a nation."[147] He exhorted readers to remember that in recalling the "heroic past" of the "American of Spanish descent . . . it should not be overlooked that today he faces perplexing problems and issues for which no solution has yet been found."[148]

Hispanic civil rights groups began to involve themselves in the school-house struggle, and a number of legal cases forced changes in the 1930s. The ruling in the 1931 case *Roberto Alvarez v. Lemon Grove School District* found in favor of the Mexican students in this California locality on the basis that they would not Americanize if they did not have access to Anglo institutions.[149] After the war, and buoyed by the growth of Mexican-American civil rights groups, legal challenges mounted amid acute awareness that Mexican and Mexican-American children were being forced to accept second-rate services.[150]

The parents of Sylvia Mendez took their frustrations with this to court in 1945. They wanted to send their daughter to a mostly Anglo school in the Westminster School District in Orange County, California. It was closer to the Mendezes' home and young Sylvia wanted to go there, too, lured by the beautiful playground—there were no swings at her school, which had a majority of Mexican children.[151] Her parents, Gonzalo and Felicitas, along with other families who wanted their children to be allowed to attend majority-white schools, brought a class-action lawsuit against four school districts in a case known as *Mendez v. Westminster.* They won in 1947 after the case went to the Ninth Circuit Court of Appeals. At the core of the argument was the fact that the Mexicans had been segregated on the basis of their appearance, and, because no federal law declared that Mexicans were Indian, the precedents set by earlier rulings or legislation, such as the 1935 law in California, did not apply. The 1848 Treaty of Guadalupe Hidalgo and its promise of equal rights was also invoked.[152] The ruling was one of several in the 1940s and early 1950s that would lead to a reassessment of what constituted segregation, who was being segregated, and the concept of "separate but equal," opening the way for the landmark *Brown v. Board of Education* ruling in 1954 that would start the process of school desegregation for African-Americans.

In an interview with National Public Radio on the sixtieth anniversary of the *Brown* ruling, Sylvia Mendez said: "I went to court every single day not knowing what they were fighting for. I just thought my parents wanted us to go to the nice-looking school." She realized later that they desired something far larger than her access to the better playground. Yet today, some 50 percent of Hispanic children in California attend schools, often in poorer areas, where the student body is less than 10 percent white.[153] "We are more segregated in school today than we were in 1947," Mendez said. "What we have now is *de facto* segregation."

Around the same time as the *Mendez* case, LULAC and AGIF were supporting a similar one in Texas, *Delgado et al. v. Bastrop Independent School District*. Lawyers for this 1948 case argued that the principle "separate but equal" in the 1896 Supreme Court ruling in *Plessy v. Ferguson* did not apply to Hispanic children because they were "Caucasian," and the plaintiffs won. In 1954, the Supreme Court ruled in *Hernández v. Texas* that Mexicans were not considered another race but were "other white."[154]

Schools in Arizona faced similar legal challenges. One high-profile case occurred in the farming town of Tolleson, where the Alianza Hispano-Americana demanded better educational services. The Anglo children had modern facilities, and Mexicans dilapidated ones. The suit attempting to correct this came to trial in 1951 as *Gonzales v. Sheely*, in which it was argued that Mexican-American children were being denied their constitutional right under the Fourteenth Amendment. The school district claimed that children who could not speak English were holding everyone else back, although the courts had earlier dismissed language as a basis for segregation. The ruling went against the school district, and the case became another that paved the way for *Brown*.[155]

Despite the many legal challenges to school systems in the Southwest, problems related to segregation and inequality continued after the *Brown* ruling. In New York, Puerto Rican students were crammed into schools with limited resources, and by the 1960s, the students in El Barrio were going to school in shifts and had few bilingual teachers.[156] In Texas, similar grievances culminated in *Cisneros v. Corpus Christi Independent School District*, which was filed in 1968. This case originated when José Cisneros, a steelworker in Corpus Christi, heard his children complain about the poor facilities at their school. He met with school officials to discuss having parts of the building repaired but realized the problems were more than just superficial, for the students did not have the same curriculum options as those at Anglo schools. He contacted Hector García, and Cisneros's union, the United Steelworkers of America, also became involved, offering to pay the legal fees.[157]

The case focused on the long-term and systematic discrimination that Mexican-Americans faced in Texas. The numbers told their own story. Total high school enrollment was 56 percent Anglo and 39 percent Mexican-American, yet the pool of thirteen hundred Mexican-American and two hundred African-American students attended schools that were less than 10 percent Anglo, while Anglo students attended high school with 90 percent white classmates.[158] The composition of the schools reflected the social geography of the town, with Anglos and Mexicans clustered in different parts of the city. The federal judge Woodrow Seals found there was a de jure segregated system in the town, but that was not the end of the matter. The question of how to desegregate the schools turned into a legal battle of its own, stretching well into the 1970s. By 1973, the Supreme Court upheld a 1971 district court decision that Mexican-Americans were a definable minority and that the schools were to be desegregated.

A 1977 report from the Texas State Advisory Committee to the United States Commission on Civil Rights, of which García was a member, listed as its top finding "that despite almost 10 years of protracted litigation and court orders mandating desegregation, the Corpus Christi Independent School District continues to maintain a segregated school system."[159] Indeed, the working title of the report was subtitled "A Decade of Strife," though that was toned down in the final version to "School Desegregation in Corpus Christi: Eight Years After *Cisneros*."[160]

Another area of concern for activists was access to voting. To prevent Mexican-Americans from casting ballots, some places had long had Jim Crow–type barriers such as the poll tax in Texas, which was not ruled unconstitutional until 1966.[161] Correspondingly, Hispanic representation across the Southwest was minimal, although John F. Kennedy's election in 1960 mobilized Hispanic voters. Excited about the prospect of Kennedy's presidency, Hector García became involved in the *Viva Kennedy* clubs set up by Mexican-Americans for the 1960 campaign to bolster national support among Hispanic voters. A membership card from the campaign features a blue-and-white illustration of JFK wearing a sombrero with "Viva" written on the front, while sitting on a Democratic donkey. García was instrumental in organizing the Hispanic community; Kennedy won 91 percent of the Mexican-American vote in Texas and 70 percent in

New Mexico.[162] Afterward, President Kennedy appointed García as a representative for the signing of a trade deal with the Federation of the West Indies in 1961.[163] Soon after that, Hispanic politicians such as Texas's Henry B. González started winning seats in Congress. Kennedy also appointed a Mexican-American, Reynaldo Garza, to a federal judgeship in the Southern District of Texas.[164]

When Lyndon Johnson assumed the presidency after Kennedy's assassination, he already had a relationship with the Mexican-American community in Texas, but it had been a tricky balance to maintain. As a senator, he helped constituents but then would play down any involvement with the Hispanic community if attacked for his sympathies. This on-off relationship would continue into the White House, though over time he became more supportive. He told a press conference in 1966, in answer to a question about whether Mexican-Americas should receive more national attention: "I think they should have more attention . . . I think that they are entitled to more consideration in government employment than they have received. I think they have been discriminated against in housing, in education, in jobs. I don't think we can be very proud of our record in that field."[165]

While García and many other activists in Mexican-American communities made great gains in the 1950s and early 1960s, by the end of the latter decade a new generation was on the rise, and moving in a very different direction. Perhaps the best-known figure of this period was César Chávez, who brought the appalling conditions of migrant farmworkers to national attention. He knew their struggle well. Chávez grew up poor in Arizona; though his family had land, they lost it after suffering financial difficulties and not being able to pay their taxes.[166] The family headed west in the 1930s during the depths of the Great Depression to look for work. Chávez was twelve when he became a migrant worker, in insecure employment, on poor wages, and living in tents and shacks.[167] He enlisted in the navy in 1946 and was honorably discharged a couple of years later, returning to work in the fields around Delano, California. He married and began a family in 1949 and soon became involved with the Community Service Organization, a civil rights group focused on helping Mexican-Americans.

By the 1960s, the large-scale strikes of the 1930s had dwindled, but the work remained difficult and underpaid. Chávez saw the need to organize unions in the fields. He, along with Dolores Huerta, founded the National Farm Workers Association in 1962; it merged with the Agricultural Workers Organizing Committee to become the United Farm Workers in 1966. He fought for fair wages and better working conditions in an industry where the lives of the workers were often as harsh as they had been in the 1930s.

Chávez was a proponent of nonviolent means, though confrontation had long been the hallmark of suppression of agricultural unions in California and Texas.[168] One of his best-known campaigns involved the Delano grape strike and boycott, a series of protests and strikes starting in 1965 and involving Hispanic and Filipino grape-pickers. As part of this, Chávez led farmworkers on a march for more than 250 miles from Delano to the California state capital, Sacramento, under a banner with an image of Our Lady of Guadalupe, imploring consumers to boycott any grapes that did not have a union sticker on them. By 1970, the boycott had paid off and grape-growers allowed union contracts for their workers. Chávez said in a 1984 speech, "The union's survival, its very existence, sent out a signal to all Hispanics that we were fighting for our dignity."[169]

As the 1960s progressed, some Mexican activists began to reject earlier ideas about assimilation or claims to "whiteness," pushing instead for a different vision. In 1969, Rodolfo "Corky" Gonzales, who ran the group Crusade for Justice, gave a name to this spirit of activism, addressing the young Mexican-Americans at a conference he organized as "Chicanos."[170] At the time, that word had a negative connotation associated with poorer Mexicans, dating back decades. Gonzales reclaimed it and turned it into a linguistic symbol of not only the treatment of Mexican-Americans but also their unwillingness to accept Anglo norms.[171] The Chicano movement—also known as El Movimiento or, for some, La Reconquista—pushed for rights and equality in work, politics, and social services, with a corresponding aim to raise awareness and the status of Chicanos.[172]

At Gonzales's landmark Chicano National Liberation Youth Conference, he and the participants adopted El plan espiritual de Aztlán (The Spiritual Plan of Aztlán), based on the mythical starting point of Mexica cosmology. Indeed, the Disturnell map of 1847 actually showed Aztlán, described as "Antigua Residencia de los Aztecas"—the ancient home of the Aztecs—in modern southeast Utah, near the Colorado River.[173]

Gonazales's vision involved the creation of a Chicano homeland in the Southwest, on the lands lost to the United States in 1848 and to the Europeans before that. He wanted Chicanos to pursue "social, economic, cultural, and political independence," which should be the "only road to total liberation from oppression, exploitation, and racism."[174] Aztlán was to be a place for "bronze people" and their Chicano nation.[175] The Chicana activist Enriqueta Vasquez wrote in the New Mexican newspaper *El Grito del Norte,* around this time, that with Aztlán "we have the answer to the call of the spirit. We know that we will not let our culture die. . . . The Plan de Aztlán is very clear and very strong. You are either for your brothers or you are not. You either live in the spirit of Aztlán or you do not."[176]

Chicano activism also challenged prevailing ideas about "Spanish" culture. The historian John Nieto-Phillips has written about his own experiences of being bound in that particular cultural knot. As a child he would be taken to his mother's village near Bernalillo, New Mexico, to participate in the Matachines dance on the Day of San Lorenzo, commemorating the moment in 1693 when the Spaniards made peace with the Pueblos. Nieto-Phillips recalled how this story was enshrined in family lore and how "for years to come I wanted to erase such stories from my memory . . . they also caused me a great deal of anguish." Part of this distress came from his mother's insistence that her New Mexican family was "Spanish." To the young Nieto-Phillips, "most of our neighbors [in Pomona, California] were from Mexico and I couldn't possibly go around our neighborhoods proclaiming *we* are Spanish and not Mexican—as if we were somehow better than them."[177] He was further confused by the fact that part of his family tree included Pueblo Indians, which made him wonder "how could we be Spanish and Indian at the same time, but not Mexican?"[178] These contradictions left him feeling "trapped by our supposed 'Spanish' heritage."[179]

The Chicano generation rejected the "Spanish myth" and instead looked to indigenous culture in the Southwest and Mexico, often criticizing Mexican-Americans who claimed whiteness at the expense of their Indian roots.[180] The question of identity, however, would not be easily resolved, in part because of the diversity of backgrounds and experiences that coexisted under the umbrella of Latino and Mexican. Chicano activists were not a static group, and there were differing aims and rifts within activist circles. For the author Gregory Rodriguez, "the Chicano portrayal of Mexican-Americans as a unified, downtrodden people preternaturally loyal to their ancestral culture was astonishingly similar to the way Anglo racists had been characterizing Mexican Americans for more than a hundred years."[181]

In Texas, activism entered politics, as Raza Unida was established as an alternative to the traditional parties.[182] By 1971 it had been established in New Mexico. The party there focused on issues such as police brutality, labor, and education. It did not have much success putting its members into elected office, though it was able to push its concerns onto the agendas of the main parties.[183]

Also in New Mexico, another activist group formed in 1963, focusing on land issues. Called La Alianza Federal de Mercedes (Federal Alliance of Land Grants), and known as La Alianza, the group was led by Reies López Tijerina, a charismatic Pentecostal minister later known as "King Tiger," who was born in Texas but whose work took him to Arizona and New Mexico. His obsession was land: he wanted the group to "organize and acquaint the heirs of all the Spanish Land Grants covered by the Guadalupe Hidalgo Treaty."[184] In effect, he wanted his followers to demand back the land lost to Anglos in the years that followed the Mexican-American War.

López Tijerina had been living in a community with a dozen or so families in a place he called the Valley of Peace, in Arizona, but fled to New Mexico in 1957 after being accused of attempting a jailbreak to free his brother. There he learned about the land grants and developed a passion to have them returned to New Mexicans. López Tijerina had many run-ins with state authorities and, as with other activist leaders of the time, the Federal Bureau of Investigation maintained a large file on him. He was aware of the surveillance, at one point sending his brother to the Albuquerque FBI office to invite agents to the Alianza convention in 1964. The FBI noted: "Mr. Tijerina . . . was thanked for his courtesy in coming to the FBI and he was told that an Agent of the FBI could not attend the convention."[185]

As well as working on the land grants, the group tried to influence education and social policies. One of its pamphlets noted that, for Chicanos, "education the American way means being taught how to become jani-tors, garbagemen, dishwashers and migrants." It called for Chicanos to "have their language, customs, thinking and way of life taught to their children so that they will understand their own history, not Puritan or Manifest Destiny history."[186]

One of the most significant locations in their land struggle was about two hours north of Santa Fe, in Tierra Amarilla, a site of more than half a million acres. Under an 1832 grant, it belonged to Manuel Martínez, with some parts reserved for common use. In 1860 his brother Francisco received U.S. confirmation of the grant, though this time it was listed as wholly private, with no mention of the communal land. So in 1881, when the Martínez family sold the land to the speculator Thomas Catron, he then went to court to obtain the hundred or so titles Martínez had given to settlers.[187] By 1889, these families had lost their holdings, and Catron was on his way to becoming one of the largest landholders in the United States.[188] Although the land was gone, the memory of the loss remained. López Tijerina was so committed to fighting to return the land that he even traveled to the Spanish colonial archives in Seville, Spain, in 1966, to research the legal basis for the grants.[189]

However, clashes with the courts and the federal government con-tinued to dog him, culminating in a raid on the Río Arriba courthouse on June 5, 1967, in Tierra Amarilla. Activists were there looking for the district attorney in the belief that some of their members were being detained. In the melee that ensued, two police officers were shot and wounded, and a reporter and deputy sheriff were taken hostage. The governor sent in 350 National Guard troops. López Tijerina fled the scene. He was arrested and imprisoned, but later released in 1971.[190]

Such activism was not limited to the Southwest or the preserve of Mexican-American groups, and in the 1960s Puerto Rican activism gained ground. One of its highest-profile groups was the Young Lords, who were nationalists in favor of the island's independence but who also tried to make alliances with African-Americans within the United States, in part because they lived together in cities like New York and felt they had a common cause.[191] One of the founding members of the Young Lords, Pablo "Yoruba" Guzmán, recalled that many Puerto Ricans in New York "felt that the potential for revolution had always been there for Puerto Rican people." Guzmán was born in East Harlem to a Cuban father and a Puerto Rican mother, and he grew up in the South Bronx. Living alongside black Americans who were having their own struggle did not necessarily form the basis for an alliance, however. "We found that on a grassroots level a high degree of racism existed between Puerto Ricans and blacks, and between light-skinned and dark-skinned Puerto Ricans. We had to deal with the racism because it blocked any kind of growth for our people."[192] The organization was pulled in many directions, and across other urban centers beyond New York, a process which led to the gradual disintegration of some branches in the late 1970s and early 1980s.

A CENTURY AFTER THE Treaty of Guadalupe Hidalgo, the Río Grande was still not abiding by it. A problem with rivers is that they will not hold fast to the paths charted by cartographers. They are given to changing course, as was the case for a tiny strip of land in the river, between El Paso and Ciudad Juárez. Known as Chamizal, this small but shifting bit of earth caused big problems from the moment surveyors fixed the river's boundaries in 1852. By the 1860s, the Río Grande started to drift south; adding to the complications, this part of the river was also prone to flooding. By the 1890s, part of Chamizal seemed to be north of the Río Grande, and the question of landownership became a sticking point, because in theory it belonged to a Mexican farmer, Pedro García. While the Mexican and U.S. authorities tried to figure out what to do, droughts in 1895–96 left the river in that area dry. When it did rain the following year, both El Paso and Ciudad Juárez flooded, in part because of the sand deposits that had built up but also because of erosion along the riverbed near El Paso.[193]

As a result, a flood-control measure to straighten the channel was introduced, and this created Cordova Island, measuring about four hundred acres in size. It was on the U.S. side of the border, but ownership was still open to interpretation.[194] Agreements and disagreements came and went at regular intervals until the 1960s. President Kennedy and Mexican president Adolfo López Mateos were finally able to work out a deal that involved relocating part of the river to be as close as possible to where it was in 1864. After that was completed the United States would receive the northern part of the island, just under two hundred acres, with the rest going to Mexico. A treaty was concluded on July 18, 1963, sealing the deal.[195] The following year, President Johnson ratified it, and infrastructure work began on the project, the cost of which ran in excess of $40 million. By 1967, Johnson and Mexican president Gustavo Díaz Ordaz were at last able to celebrate the opening of the concrete river channel designed to move the river and end the dispute.

Today, just on the edge of El Paso, those acres are part of the Chamizal National Memorial, where flags of both nations wave, and where visitors can see the Bridge of the Americas that links the U.S. city with Ciudad Juárez, one of the four crossings between the two cities. The visitor center is covered in a large mural, depicting scenes from life in the United States—including portraits of Presidents Kennedy and Obama—as well as in Mexico, with couples dancing in folk costumes, while in the far corner of the work are a mission church, a friar, and conquistadores. Even though the river in this troublesome spot was tamed after nearly a century, the need to define the border and decide who was allowed to be on which side of it would only become stronger.

Chapter 15

Miami, Florida, ca. 1960–80

Amid the blocks of offices in downtown Miami sits an unusual structure, its elaborate ornamentation setting it apart from the sleek minimalism of the surrounding buildings. It looks like an artifact from another time and place, with its long yellow tower and multitiered top perched on a small base, like a steeple that has misplaced its church. That may well have been the original intention, as this edifice was inspired by the Giralda bell tower that sits next to the cathedral in Seville, Spain. That tower dates from the 1100s and is an example of *mudéjar* architecture, the merging of European and Islamic designs from the period when southern Spain was still under Muslim rule. The one in Miami—now known as the Freedom Tower—was built in 1925 and is a relic of that fascination with the Spanish past almost a century ago. It was part of a larger architectural engagement with the colonial style, influenced by the fashions of the time as well as the city's proximity to Cuba.[1]

The Freedom Tower has changed uses many times. Originally built to house the *Miami News*, which stayed there until 1957, today it is part of Miami Dade College. In between, it served as a reception center for Cubans, from 1962 to 1974, and so was dubbed the "Ellis Island of the South." Rather than an immigration processing point, it was an assistance center to help Cubans fleeing the revolution to secure housing, find out about their resettlement options, and obtain other services.

The building was then bought and sold and fell into a state of neglect until it was restored in the 1980s. During this process, local artists painted a mural on the mezzanine level that re-created an original and decayed tapestry from the 1920s. Known as the *New World Mural*, this forty-foot work of art depicts the arrival of Ponce de León, with a map of the Americas to the left and the rest of the world to the right. Galleons and mermaids adorn the bottom of the scene, while Ponce shares his perch in the middle with a Tequesta chief. At either edge are four rectangular paintings of identical size showing scenes of Native Americans on the right side and Europeans on the left. The brochure handed out by the college calls it "a beautiful symbol of the meeting of the Old World and New World," that "serves as an iconic visual reference of Miami's history." Today the tower hosts two permanent exhibitions, the Cuban Exile Experience and Cuban Diaspora Cultural Legacy Gallery. Old and new, real and imagined, converge in Miami. What is considered by many to be the modern capital of Latin America was never a city in the Spanish empire. Instead, it was developed by the tycoon Henry Flagler in 1896.

Although Flagler could not have foreseen it, Miami would become a sort of border town of its own, with the Florida Straits, rather than the desert, providing the boundary. The mix of people living in the city today includes Cubans, Haitians, Venezuelans, and others from across the hemisphere. Although Tampa had been home to Cuba's earlier generation of émigrés, Miami would far eclipse it.

In Flagler's time, however, Miami was still a hot, sandy outpost bordered by swamps, near the southern end of the state. He had become a fan of Florida in the 1870s, his businessman's eye seeing its potential for tourism. Because of his railroad connections, backed by his oil fortune, Flagler was able to create the Florida East Coast Railway system, laying track that reached Biscayne Bay by 1896. Along the way, he opened the opulent Hotel Ponce de León in St. Augustine, an overwhelming Spanish Revival monolith, with elegant palm trees and lavish fountains outside, and Tiffany glass and elaborate murals within. Its size was such that today it is home to the campus of Flagler College.

Flagler's Florida, however, was still an underpopulated novelty. Even when the Ponce de León hotel opened, the real metropolis was farther to the south, in Havana. The Cuban capital was one of the largest, grandest, and most powerful cities in the Caribbean, if not the Americas. Separated by less than one hundred miles of the Florida Straits, Miami and Havana could not have been more different at the turn of the century, one a sandy village, the other an urban center with an almost four-hundred-year history. Although Florida's time as an eighteenth-century buffer between Spanish and Anglo worlds was long over, it was developing into a different, modern type of frontier with its own border culture, with Havana and Miami pulled into the same orbit, their people moving back and forth across the Florida Straits.[2]

As the Miami of the 1920s began to boom, it attempted to import some of the charm of Havana; new neighborhoods used Spanish street names, and houses and buildings were constructed from materials imported from Cuba, including old floor and roof tiles, wooden doors, and other weathered objects.[3] Travel between the two cities was regular, and it was possible to sail on a day trip from Miami to Havana.[4] Air travel soon made the journey even quicker. Still, Miami's population was not large—around 6,000 Cubans were thought to live in Miami in the 1930s, amid a larger population of about 110,000.[5] There were business connections, the shopping was good, and Spanish was widely spoken.[6] Middle-class Cubans could afford to go to Miami for a holiday—even Fidel Castro and his first wife, Mirta Díaz-Balart, spent some of their honeymoon in the city.[7]

Through the 1940s, Cubans kept arriving, and not always for vacations. Cuba had been under the rule of Fulgencio Batista, after a military coup in 1933, though he did not become president until 1940. At first, this new regime enacted a number of popular policies, including abrogating the hated 1903 Platt Amendment (though the United States kept its base in Guantánamo Bay), reforming land use, and giving women the right to vote. However, by the mid-1930s the island also experienced strikes and political unrest, and in 1940 a new constitution was drawn up. Batista won the election that year, and served a four-year term. In 1952, he prepared to run again, but decided to seize power before the elections were held.

The later years of Batista represent Cuba at its most infamous—the nightclubs, the casinos, the zenith of corruption, not least deals with Mafia bosses like Meyer Lansky who opened large, glamorous casino hotels, making Havana a sort of Las Vegas–by–the–Sea. Visitors from the United States continued their love affair with the city, lured by the climate and the illicit fun it offered, something that people from an earlier generation had discovered during the prohibition era.

The influx of fun-seeking Yankees did not please everyone. Although some Cubans had made handsome profits from sugar during the Second World War, a yawning gap between rich and poor existed and was growing wider. Stability was fragile. Then, on July 26, 1953, a young lawyer named Fidel Castro, leading a force of some 150 rebels, launched an attack on the Moncada Barracks in the southern city of Santiago. It was the start of in the Cuban Revolution, and over the following years large swaths of the public turned on Batista and his regime. Many Cubans had grown weary of the situation on the island—and for critics of the regime it had become dangerous—so people turned toward to Miami. The Cuban community there had by this point reached about 20,000; overall, the number of Cuban immigrants coming to the United States in 1956–58 averaged 13,422 per year, though some moved north to New York or west to Los Angeles.[8] Castro and his followers would be triumphant with their revolution less than six years after his attack in Santiago, and Batista fled the island on New Year's Day 1959. Miami would never be the same.

Amid the turmoil in Cuba, Miami seemed a safe harbor, and thousands arrived in the months following the revolution, hoping to return to the island when things settled down. The arrival of Cubans coincided with a time of growth in the city—the population of the Greater Miami area, just under 500,000 in 1950, had reached 935,000 by 1960, at which point Cubans and other Spanish-speaking people were still only about 5 percent of the population.[9]

Many who left Cuba were wealthy, people who had wielded power during the Batista years, such as judges or prominent business owners. Often they were light-skinned, but like the Cubans who emigrated before them to Ybor City in the late nineteenth century, they were entering the South of Jim Crow. In part because they were identified as Spanish-speakers, they ended up occupying a space in Miami somewhere between black and white. Unlike their Spanish-speaking counterparts in places like Texas, Cubans in Miami could, for the most part, swim, eat, and take public transportation in the same places as the white community.[10]

The defeat of the CIA-backed Cubans who attacked the island in the Bay of Pigs incident in April 1961, followed by the missile crisis in October 1962, put Cuba in the middle of the Cold War and signaled that there might be no going back to the island. Some two hundred thousand Cubans had arrived in the United States between 1960 and 1962 alone, and usually at the high cost of having to leave behind all of their possessions as well as their homes.[11] Among them were a number of unaccompanied children whose passage had been arranged through Operation Peter Pan, organized by the Catholic Welfare Bureau in the United States. By the end of 1962, some fourteen thousand young people had arrived to face an uncertain future. Many were later reunited with their parents or joined relatives already established in the United States, while others lived with host families.

Some Cubans, however, decided to return, though the numbers were far smaller. The Communist newspaper *Noticias de Hoy* claimed in 1961 that the United States was keeping Cuban "patriots"—some of whom had already been residents in the United States—against their will, "practically incarcerated."[12] A short time later, it reported that forty-four people had returned to Cuba on board the *Covadonga*. One passenger, Juan Socorro Peña, said he left after being in the United States for more than a decade, telling *Noticias de Hoy*: "I've wasted 11 years in the United States. . . . I worked in New York as a boss in a cement factory, but I gave up my residency, with my wife and son, because there you cannot live peacefully. They harass the good Cubans, who they mistreat every time they have the chance. . . . We will work in Cuba and defend the Revolution."[13]

Some people in Miami's Anglo community expressed a desire to see Cubans there do the same. Jack Kofoed, a columnist for the *Miami Herald*, described the city in October 1965 as being "up to our armpits with Cuban refugees." While some had become "good, solid members" of the community, "others have been a drag, and a number have added to the criminal problem."[14] That November, Kofoed further bemoaned activities he described as "quite normal to Cubans," which included "playing TVs and radios at the highest possible pitch at all hours of the night . . . talking loudly . . . bad driving . . . crowding of three or four families in a one-family house."[15]

However Anglo Miamians felt about the new arrivals, Cubans were actors in a much larger Cold War drama, one that was taking place uncomfortably close to the United States, and so they were afforded special privileges, not least the 1966 Cuban Adjustment Act. This allowed any Cuban who had been in the United States for a year to become a permanent resident. Then, they would be eligible for an expedited pathway to U.S. citizenship. In addition, between 1961 and 1971 the U.S. government spent $730 million on its Cuban Refugee Program, facilitating resettlement by providing services like transportation or help in finding employment. Other policies and plans were established on a local level to aid the new arrivals, including classes in English.[16]

Although many immigrants lost everything they had in Cuba, some still had social capital and access to finance, and before long Cuban-owned businesses served the thriving community, with an army of Cuban doctors and lawyers making up a vital sector of the Miami economy. Newspapers, television channels, and radio stations in Spanish were set up as well. The Cubans were fast becoming one of the city's main economic engines.

Into the late 1960s and early 1970s, some Cubans were still not reconciled to the revolution, and Miami and other parts of the United States suffered a series of bombings, the blame for which was put on anti-Castro extremists. Two of the most infamous groups were Omega 7 and Alpha 66, which made a number of attacks against individuals or groups thought to be willing to have a dialogue with the Castro regime. They threatened to assassinate anyone who traveled to Cuba and targeted foreign governments or organizations that maintained diplomatic links with the island. Another group, Cuban Power, ran an extensive bombing campaign, with targets across the United States; it was blamed for the 1968 bombing one of Mexico's tourism offices in Chicago.[17]

In this same period, there were also many airplane hijackings involving Cuba. Initially, in the early 1960s, Cubans hijacked planes demanding to be taken to the United States. Not long afterward, planes were seized by passengers and taken in the opposite direction, sometimes for political reasons, as when Antulio Ramírez Ortiz demanded that the pilots of National Airlines Flight 337 from Miami to Key West on May 1, 1961, divert to Cuba.[18] Ramírez Ortiz claimed he had been offered $100,000 by the Dominican Republic's Rafael Trujillo to kill Castro, and now wanted to warn the Cuban leader.[19] In 1969, Tyrone and Linda Austin forced an Eastern flight from New York to Miami to take them to Cuba, shouting, "Black power, Havana" during the hijacking.[20]

Eventually Castro shifted from welcoming hijackers—and charging the airlines considerable sums to retrieve their planes—to interrogating the hijackers, worried that they were CIA operatives.[21] The volume of hijackings was such that for a while, all cockpits had charts of the Caribbean Sea with instructions on how to land at José Martí International Airport, no matter what the intended destination was. In addition, the pilots were given cards in Spanish with phrases like "Aircraft has mechanical problems" in case they needed to communicate with hijackers who did not speak English.[22]

By the 1980s, the number of Cuban-born people in the United States reached around 700,000, though not all were in Miami.[23] In this decade, the nature of Cuban emigration also began to change when the *Marielitos*—people who left from the port of Mariel—arrived. These were not members of the elite but poorer Cubans. Among them were people who had been released from prison and other "undesirables" whom Castro announced he would not try to stop. More than 120,000 Cubans arrived in Miami between May and October 1980, as a nonstop flotilla brought people to Florida. These Cubans faced more prejudice, both from within the community and from outside, than those who had come in the 1960s. One stereotype of the *Marielito* Cuban is Tony Montana, the fictional character played by Al Pacino in the 1983 film *Scarface*. Montana arrived during the boatlift, entered the drug trade, made a fortune, and lost it. The film depicted a seedy Miami of shootouts, nightclubs, piles of cocaine, and Cuban criminals: a far cry from the images of wealthy Cubans elegantly disembarking from TWA planes in the 1960s.

By the end of the 1980s, the number of Cubans in Miami reached more than one million. By this point, however, many had become U.S. citizens and so had voting power. This was soon reflected in the political makeup of Miami, as Cubans took posts in a number of public offices within the city, as well as in Washington; the first Cuban elected to Congress, in 1989, was the Republican Ileana Ros-Lehtinen, who retired in 2018.[24]

Cubans were not alone in the migration of the 1980s. By this point, thousands of people were coming from all over Latin America, often from countries that had been destabilized by U.S. policy or CIA-backed interventions. The United States had been covertly involved in conflicts since the start of the Cold War; its operations included the toppling of the regime in Guatemala in 1954; the coup against President Salvador Allende in Chile in 1973; training and funding the Contras to fight a civil war against the ruling Sandinista National Liberation Front (FSLN), which had overthrown the Somoza dictatorship in Nicaragua in 1979; and backing government forces in El Salvador's civil war. Millions of people were displaced by these and other conflicts, though they did not qualify as refugees under the terms of the Refugee Act of 1980.[25] Undeterred, tens of thousands of people arrived throughout the 1980s and 1990s. The 2000 census counted 129,000 Central Americans in the Miami area alone.[26] The same census calculated that there were more than 1.2 million Salvadorans, Guatemalans, and Nicaraguans in the United States, most of whom were first-generation immigrants.[27]

At the same time, Mexicans were coming north, trying to escape the dire straits of the economy in this period. Despite strong growth through the 1960s in Mexico, the economy suffered, as did many others, in the 1970s oil crisis triggered by OPEC (Organization of Petroleum Exporting Countries). Although Mexico was an oil-producing nation, it felt the impact of the overall global slowdown. Mexicans began to see high inflation, a devalued peso, and a decline in real wages. All this was coupled with ongoing political violence, as seen in October 1968, less than a fortnight before the Olympic Games were to begin, when Mexican troops opened fire on protesting students in Tlatelolco Plaza—the exact death toll remains unknown.

In 1982, Mexico, owing billions, defaulted on loans given by foreign banks. The default led to an 85 percent devaluation of the peso relative to the dollar. This series of events triggered what has been called the *década perdida*, or lost decade.[28] Mexicans began to look north again, and by the 1980s and early 1990s, the number of "alien apprehensions" rose significantly, reaching more than one million a year, a 50 percent increase over the volume in the 1970s.[29] Overall, the Hispanic population more than tripled in the 1980s and 1990s, going from 4.2 million in 1980 to just over 14 million by 2000. Of those, the number of undocumented people entering was estimated at 2 million for 1980–89 and around 5 million from 1990 to 1999, though around 20 percent of those people were not from Mexico or Central America.[30]

Within the United States, calls for immigration reform grew louder, and the result was the Immigration Reform and Control Act, signed by President Ronald Reagan in 1986. This legislation granted amnesty to anyone who was undocumented and who had been in the United States since 1982. Some three million people qualified to have their status legalized. In return, security on the border was increased and more responsibility was placed on employers, who had to prove their workers had the correct papers. Despite this adjustment, in the 1990s some states started to propose or pass their own legislation that was considered hostile to immigrants, such as 1994's divisive Proposition 187 in California. This bill called for taking away all public support—including access to schools—for undocumented people, the sole exception being emergency medical services. It became so controversial that the incoming president of Mexico at the time, Ernesto Zedillo, denounced it.[31] It passed 59 percent to 41 percent, though it was never implemented, as legal challenges were quick to follow.

Further significant changes were introduced under Bill Clinton throughout the 1990s, including the Personal Responsibility and Work Opportunity Reconciliation Act of 1996, which cut off almost all welfare benefits for people who were not U.S. citizens or who were undocumented. The law stopped access to food stamps and left it to the states to decide if these people could have recourse to any sort of temporary assistance, as well as access to Medicare.[32]

Reforms to Cuban immigration were also introduced. With the collapse of the Soviet Union in 1989, the enormous sugar subsidy that Cuba received from Russia dried up, and the years after the fall of the Berlin Wall were known in Cuba as the *período especial* (special period), when severe shortages of everything afflicted the island. People were desperate to leave, and they crossed the Florida Straits on whatever they could find, from dangerous *balsas* (rafts) to hijacked boats. The United States introduced a new visa system to control the number of arrivals. A processing station was set up just outside Cuba's territorial waters, where Cubans were intercepted in Operation Sea Signal and taken to the U.S. base at Guantánamo Bay to have their papers examined. Before long, the United States was overwhelmed and forced to come to a new agreement with Cuba: the United States would grant twenty thousand visas a year to Cubans if the island's government would do more to stop people from leaving.[33] Included in the 1994–95 reforms was the creation of the "wet foot, dry foot" policy, by which any Cuban caught at sea was returned to the island, but those who reached the United States were allowed to stay. In 1996, Congress passed the Helms-Burton Act after Cuba's military shot down two civilian aircraft flown by members of a Cuban exile group. The legislation was meant to discourage international investment in Cuba, curb travel to the island, and tighten the existing embargo. The Castro regime continued to survive, however, despite the decades of U.S. effort to undermine or destroy it.

Although thousands of people from Latin American came to live in Miami throughout the 1980s and 1990s, no one group has superseded the Cubans' influence on the city, as Calle Ocho in Miami's Little Havana testifies. A stroll around the neighborhood reveals a persistent patriotism, and a not insignificant number of markers and monuments: one to the exiles who died at the Bay of Pigs in 1961; a statue of Nestor A. Izquierdo, an anticommunist Cuban who died in a plane crash in 1979. The indestructible José Martí also has a presence. Under a large, leafy tree sits a beige stone slab with a raised map of Cuba on it, on which are his words: "La patria es agonía y deber." The homeland is agony and duty.

The journalist Joan Didion observed in her 1987 book *Miami* that for "Anglos who did not perceive themselves as economically or socially threatened by Cubans, there remained considerable uneasiness on the matter of language" in the city, in part because at some level not speaking English could "undermine [the Anglos'] conviction that assimilation was an ideal universally shared by those who were to be assimilated."[34] Local resident Milton Weiss, in a 1990 letter to the *Miami Herald*, complained of always being asked for directions in Spanish on the street in Miami. Despite speaking the language and being married to a non-Cuban Hispanic woman, he wrote, "If I wanted to live in a Latin country, I would have moved to one. Instead, one has moved here." He pointed out in the letter that this was the reason for Anglo flight from Miami, remarking, "Many non-Hispanics feel threatened by these developments. The threat is not physical: it's sociocultural, psychological."[35]

These feelings were not exclusive to Miami, nor were they new. The presence of Spanish-speakers who were unwilling to give up their language has long elicited a range of emotions, ranging from indifference to outright hostility. For Mexicans, Cubans, and others, their language was often under attack, leaving many puzzled about what the nature of U.S. assimilation was supposed to entail. The response by Spanish-speaking communities has varied over time as well; in the 1950s some parents in Texas, for instance, spoke English at home so their children would learn, but by the more activist 1970s there was renewed interest and pride in speaking Spanish.

Schools were an obvious battleground for this. Many Hispanic people who grew up in the United States in the 1940s and 1950s can recall being punished for speaking Spanish at school. The chicana writer Gloria Anzaldúa remembered being rapped with "three licks on the knuckles with a sharp ruler" for speaking Spanish at recess, and being "sent to the corner of the classroom for 'talking back' to the Anglo teacher when all I was trying to do was tell her how to pronounce my name."[36]

Decades later, in 1998, Californian voters considered Proposition 227, which had the state's bilingual education program in its sights. The Bilingual Education Act had been introduced in 1968, with the aim of using federal funding in schools for language help; this included all immigrant children, not just the Spanish-speaking ones, assisting more than one million children in kindergarten through the fifth grade who were not proficient in English. Proposition 227 provided for replacing the existing long-term program with a one-year immersion program for such students. The proposition, which passed by 61 percent to 39 percent, split the Hispanic community, as some felt that students needed to learn English quickly to thrive in California.[37] Arizona passed similar legislation in 2000, intensifying language immersion in its schools.

In 2013, the Tucson Unified School District in Arizona voted to rescind an unpopular ban that it had imposed the year before on seven books, including such titles as *Occupied America: A History of Chicanos* by Rodolfo Acuña and *Chicano! The History of the Mexican American Civil Rights Movement* by Arturo Rosales.[38] The school district had already come to national attention for its part in banning Mexican-American studies in 2010, with the passage of Arizona House Bill 2281, legislation that has been challenged in court on First Amendment grounds; its enforcement was blocked by a district judge in 2017.

School textbooks have also prompted controversy. Texas has exercised increasing influence by virtue of the fact that it has more pupils than any other state except California. Because Texas orders so many books, publishers have adopted Texan standards and then sold these texts in the rest of the country. A powerful conservative faction on the Texas board of education voted in 2010 to make significant and controversial changes to the state's history curriculum. One board member defended the decision, saying, "History has already been skewed. Academia is skewed too far to the left." At issue was the inclusion of concepts well outside mainstream historical thinking, such as calling into question the founders' intention to separate church and state. Efforts to include the Hispanic contribution or focus on the long struggle for equality for Mexican-Americans in the state and country were rebuffed. Hispanic board members were left frustrated, with one saying the board was empowered to "just pretend this is a white America and Hispanics don't exist."[39] In 2015, activists scored a victory of sorts by pressuring the Texas board of education to include Mexican-Americans in the curriculum, though the resulting textbook, *The Mexican American Heritage*, was derided before it even went to press. A review of a sample of the book in 2016 described it as "racist, revisionist and in some parts just blatantly false," claiming that, among other errors, it conflated U.S.-born chicano with recent immigrants; played down Hispanic land claims in the Southwest; and described Mexican-Americans as lazy.[40]

One critical factor in the persistence of Spanish has been its constant reinvigoration by the steady arrival of new immigrants; by contrast, other language groups, such as Germans or Italians, saw their numbers decline. According to census data, the overall number of Spanish-speakers rose throughout the period 1980 to 2000, with an increase of 60 percent to just over twenty-eight million by 2000.[41] During the 1990s, the number of people in California who spoke a language other than English at home rose from 31 percent to 39 percent, making it the state with the largest percentage of people who did not speak English, with Spanish being the most prevalent language spoken at home other than English.[42]

In Miami, one effort to promote English was the government-funded sitcom *¿Qué Pasa, U.S.A.?* aired on Miami's WPBT in 1977. The show, based on the fictional Cuban Peña family who lived in Little Havana, was in both English and Spanish, with the aim of helping people improve their English. It ran for only four seasons but was enormously popular.[43]

Less fondly remembered is the campaign launched the following year, in 1978, by Miami resident Emmy Shafer. Frustrated because public employees in the city did not speak a level of English that she deemed acceptable, she wanted to put an end to the city's bilingualism. A survivor of a Nazi concentration camp, she explained her position: she had to learn English and did not understand why other refugees were not made to do the same. She launched a petition that garnered twenty-six thousand signatures. In November 1980, an "anti-bilingual" referendum to make English the official language for government business was put on the election ballot. The vote, which took place soon after the arrival of tens of thousands of people during the Mariel boatlift, passed with 59 percent in favor. The resulting ordinance was repealed in 1993.[44] However, in 1988, the Florida constitution was amended to make English the official language.

Similar battles erupted around the country. In Arizona, a 1987 petition to make that state's constitution include English as the official language became Proposition 106, which passed by fewer than twelve thousand votes, a margin of 1 percent. However, its victory was met by a lengthy court battle, in part because it stipulated that state employees, government agencies, and even elected officials could use only English. In 1998, the Arizona supreme court ruled that what had become Article 28 in the state's constitution violated the First Amendment rights of elected officials and public employees, and limited non-English-speakers' access to the Equal Protection Clause of the Fourteenth Amendment. The ruling forced proponents of Article 28 to amend it to make English the state's official language but not prohibit government employees from speaking other languages.[45]

As English-only laws continued to spread, individuals, activists, and immigration rights groups mounted legal challenges. The *Alexander v. Sandoval* case, involving a class-action suit over Alabama making English the official language, reached the U.S. Supreme Court in 2001; in a 5 to 4 decision, it upheld Alabama's English-only law.[46] English as an official language has now been adopted by thirty-two states.

Throughout the changes of the 1980s and 1990s, another development was quietly taking place: the invention of the "Hispanic." The diverse Spanish-speaking groups still had an uneasy solidarity, in part because of geography: the East held largely Puerto Ricans, Dominicans, and Cubans, and the West had Mexicans and people from Central America. Their historical relationships to the United States had been both similar and varied. Puerto Ricans were living with the island's commonwealth status; Cubans had a long history of U.S. interference; and Mexicans had to contend with the legacy of 1848. Some mutual suspicion also divided the groups. Puerto Ricans, for instance, thought the demographic clout of Mexican-Americans meant that more resources would be diverted to the Southwest rather than the Northeast.[47] Government agencies were struggling as well. "Mexican" had been taken off the census by 1940, and by the 1960s legal interpretation positioned Mexicans as "white."[48] By the 1970s, when concern grew that the needs of the Spanish-speaking population in the United States were not being met, there was no way to compile social data based on the census. The 1970 census had asked Hispanic people to identify their origins or descent among the following options: Mexican, Puerto Rican, Cuban, Central or South American; other Spanish; or none of these.[49] This still left many dissatisfied because it felt too limited.

One of the people behind the search for better terminology was Grace Flores-Hughes, a Mexican-American from Texas who worked in the Office for Spanish Surnamed Americans, part of the Department of Health, Education, and Welfare (HEW). Flores-Hughes grew up in Taft, Texas, in a Mexican-American family, before moving to Washington, D.C., to work in a variety of civil service positions.[50] In 1973, Flores-Hughes recalled in her memoir, a meeting of government officials and community leaders was convened to discuss the educational status of Hispanic people and Native Americans, but it soon fell apart because "all the attendees could talk about was the terms used in the report to refer to their respective populations." One of the many complaints was that not all the Hispanics present wanted to be called chicano or Mexicans. The meeting was stopped, and a committee was set up to determine what racial and ethnic terms should be employed by the federal government.[51]

Heated debate followed within the committee over terms such as "Spanish-speaking" and "Hispanic." At one point they settled on recommending "Latino" but, according to Flores-Hughes, some people felt it "was masculine in nature and would include peoples of Italy and other Europeans with Latin roots."[52] In the end, Flores-Hughes backed "Hispanic" because it was the term "that best identified those persons with Spanish surnames that claimed their origin was Spanish." She brought others around to her way of thinking, and in 1975 Hispanic was implemented into federal language.[53]

Its adoption and usage, however, spread well beyond HEW, and it was criticized by people who preferred Latino, or others who thought they needed no label at all.[54] In 1977, the Office of Management and Budget issued its Statistical Policy Directive No 15, which forced federal agencies to collect data based on four racial categories: black, white, American Indian/Alaskan, and Asian/Pacific Islander. It placed Hispanic/Latino as an "ethnic" category, rather than a racial one, meaning a person could be Hispanic and of any race.[55] After this, in 1980 "Hispanic" appeared on the census, where it has remained.[56] In 2010, a specific question on the census asked if a person is "of Hispanic, Latino, or Spanish origin." For those answering in the affirmative, the form gave four "yes" options: Mexican, Mexican-American, Chicano; Puerto Rican; Cuban; or "another Hispanic, Latino, or Spanish origin" with instructions to write in a box below, for example, "Argentinian, Colombian, Dominican, Nicaraguan, Salvadoran, Spaniard, and so on." After that came a question for all individuals, asking for their race, allowing them to choose from white, black, American Indian/Alaska Native, Asian, Native Hawaiian/Pacific Islanders, or some other race. Out of the 47.4 million people who identified themselves as Hispanic, around one-third (15.8 million) chose "some other race" and wrote in either Mexican, Mexican-American, Hispanic, Hispano/a, Latin American, or Latino/a, eschewing traditional census racial categories like black or white.[57] That the census form decoupled a "Hispanic" identity from race seems to reinforce the idea that Hispanic people can be categorized as black, white, or Native American, while the responses of the people who wrote in their race indicate that there remains no consensus over the meaning of Hispanic.[58] In March 2018, the Census Bureau announced that the 2020 census would ask respondents whether they are U.S. citizens, a question that has not been included since 1950. One outcome of this may well be that undocumented people steer clear of the census forms, but the ramifications of such a move—census statistics are used to help formulate federal funding—could be serious for many parts of the United States, not least areas with large Hispanic communities.[59]

The sociologist G. Cristina Mora has argued in her work *Making Hispanics* that the rise of this "panethnic" idea of the Hispanic "did not have to happen"; the term gained wide usage because "government officials, activists, and media executives never precisely defined who Hispanics actually were."[60] Two factors made this identity stick: the large Spanish-speaking community not only within the United States but also throughout the hemisphere; and the fast-rising consumer society, in which eager marketing executives saw the lucrative potential in a broadly defined Hispanic group. Today, the Hispanic community has been estimated to have an annual purchasing power of around $1 trillion.[61]

Although previous generations of immigrants had forced their children to "become American" by learning English and assimilating, by the 1980s Univision—a Spanish-language TV channel—and magazines, advertisements, and products started targeting this community in Spanish. Such mass media could at once cater to their desires as consumers, while also redefining the boundaries between Hispanics and "Americans." Paradoxically, however, their separation as consumers served to reinforce ideas that Hispanic people were, indeed, a different culture with their own traditions and speaking their own language.

Miami-based Univision developed strategies to foster a Hispanic community in order to facilitate selling national advertising, so that businesses could aim their products at Cubans in Miami and Mexican-Americans in Los Angeles. Univision portrayed an "ideal Hispanic," putting people on the air who had dark eyes and light but olive skin. This effort also extended to the type of Spanish that was spoken, stripping out regional and national expressions and instead making sure everyone spoke a more universal version.[62]

Some marketing firms learned to exploit the differences that exist between Spanish-speaking people, as exemplified by the various campaigns for Café Bustelo coffee. Marketers discovered that Mexicans and Central Americans preferred instant coffee instead of espresso, so they tailored ads for people in those markets. The company also monitored how people's tastes changed when they moved—for instance, Mexicans in Miami who started to prefer espresso coffee.[63]

"Hispanicness" is also sold to the Anglo community, in particular with food. In much of the United States there is no "Hispanic" food, only Mexican. Its style is drawn from northern Mexico or the borderlands. Now "Tex-Mex" means Mexican, much as Sicilian cuisine came to represent "Italian" cooking, and many Mexican cookbooks published in the

United States with recipes purporting to be "authentic" are written by Anglos, a tradition stretching back to nineteenth-century California.[64] As part of a fund-raiser for the mission churches, the Landmarks Club published a cookbook in 1903 with an introductory essay on "Spanish-American Cookery" by the California booster Charles Lummis.[65]

Although the U.S. versions may differ from what is served south of the border, tacos and burritos and other Mexican foods have become staples of American cuisine. Small towns across the country have at least one Mexican restaurant, and there is the ubiquitous—though dubious in its authenticity—Taco Bell, which in recent years has seen increased competition from other chains such as Chipotle. Foods like corn chips and salsa are popular snacks, and grocery store aisles are stocked with plenty of refried beans, jalapeño peppers, and hot sauces, all of which can be washed down with imported Mexican beers and, of course, tequila. So associated is Mexican food with "Hispanicness" in the United States, that there have no doubt been tourists in Puerto Rico and Cuba puzzled by the lack of tacos on the islands. Indeed, the food of the Hispanic Caribbean has fared less well, though its rums remain popular. Outside places with large Puerto Rican, Dominican, or Cuban populations, there is little culinary reach, except perhaps for the "Cuban" sandwich, popularized, of course, in Florida, but it is far more difficult to find good *tostones* (fried plantains) than tacos.

One of the most obvious points where food commercialization and culture overlap is in the annual Cinco de Mayo celebrations. The commemoration of one victorious battle in 1862 against France in a war that Mexico lost is not, perhaps, the most obvious occasion for a cheerful fiesta, but it has become just that, despite the fact that it is not much celebrated in Mexico. The holiday took root among Mexicans in the United States in the aftermath of the U.S. Civil War and the French occupation of Mexico, as an expression of solidarity founded on both nations having overcome their respective struggles. Its celebration continued among Mexican communities in places like California through the nineteenth century and was refreshed by immigrants in the 1900s. In the first part of the twentieth century, the date continued to be used to reaffirm good U.S.-Mexican relations. For instance, in 1942 in Los Angeles, the mayor held a Cinco de Mayo celebration that some five thousand people, including the Mexican consul, attended. In the 1970s, it became more politicized, when students at the University of California, Irvine used the commemoration as a basis for holding a five-day conference on the state of chicanos in California. Cinco de Mayo's more recent incarnation took shape in the 1980s, with alcohol and food companies sponsoring fiestas and encouraging people to celebrate Mexico's battle by having a margarita and some nachos.[66]

FROM THE RISE of rumba fever and the beginning of the Mexican vogue in the 1930s, there has always been a degree of Hispanic influence in wider U.S. popular culture, though it remains uneven and to some degree depends on not alienating non-Spanish-speakers. An early model of this was the popular TV show *I Love Lucy*. This 1950s classic comedy about Lucy and Ricky Ricardo was in many ways ahead of its time, depicting on television a marriage of a Cuban and an Anglo, something that could have been controversial but instead proved an enormous success, due in no small part to Lucille Ball's expert comic timing but also to the likability of Desi Arnaz, who was already well known as a musician.

Desiderio Alberto Arnaz y de Acha III was from a privileged Cuban family who fled during the Batista dictatorship, and his fame on the show came before the rise of the Cuban Revolution. Despite his accented English, Arnaz was light-skinned enough for the marriage to be acceptable to the social mores of 1950s television. The Spanish inflection of his English could be played for laughs, as in one episode where Lucy teased him, saying she could understand him now because "I've learned to listen with an accent."

Later shows developed during the 1970s also had crossover appeal, for example *Chico and the Man*, which ran on NBC from 1974 to 1978. Set in a Mexican neighborhood in Los Angeles, it reflected the changing attitudes about Hispanics and often used barbed comedy to address racism and discrimination. The show focused on the relationship between Chico and Ed, an Anglo garage-owner and Chico's boss. Chico, however, was played not by a Mexican-American but by Freddie Prinze, whose father was German and mother was Puerto Rican and who grew up in New York.

The 2000s saw the arrival of the show *Ugly Betty*, starring America Ferrera as the title character, a plain young woman who managed to land a job on a fashion magazine. The show, which ran from 2006 to 2010, was an adaptation of a Colombian *telenovela*, *Yo soy Betty, la fea*. Hispanic characters also have appeared in other shows; an example is Gabrielle Solis, one of the residents of Wisteria Lane in *Desperate Housewives* (2004–12), played by Eva Longoria.

Overall, however, Hispanic people remain underrepresented in mainstream U.S. media. One recent study, *The Latino Disconnect: Latinos in the Age of Media Mergers*, commissioned by the National Association of Latino Independent Producers, Columbia University, and the National Hispanic Foundation for the Arts found in a review of TV and films that even "when Latinos are visible, they tend to be portrayed through decades-old stereotypes as criminals, law enforcers, cheap labor, and hypersexualized beings."[67] The report noted that, overall, large media mergers are leaving Hispanic consumers worse off and with less diverse offerings; even though Hispanic audiences are "watchful of their image" and quick to speak up against discriminatory content, "Latino participation in mainstream English-language media is stunningly low." Another study by the University of Southern California found that out of 3,932 speaking characters in top-grossing films between 2007 and 2013, only 4.9 percent were Latino—this despite the fact that the community is thought to buy 25 percent of all film tickets.[68]

The crossover factor has also had an influence in music. The Cuban sound carried on into the 1980s, with Gloria Estefan dominating the music coming out of Miami in that decade, scoring a number of hits with songs like "Rhythm Is Gonna Get You" and "Get on Your Feet." Meanwhile, in Texas, Selena Quintanilla-Pérez brought Tejano music out of the Mexican-American neighborhoods of south Texas and into the mainstream in the 1990s, winning numerous Latin Grammys and enjoying success in the English-language market as her albums went gold. She, like many Mexican-Americans, grew up speaking English and listening to U.S. pop music as well, but her musician father taught her to sing in Spanish to broaden her appeal. Tragically, her career was cut short when the president of her fan club, Yolanda Saldívar, shot her in 1995. Twenty years on, a museum dedicated to Quintanilla-Perez's life and work in Corpus Christi, Texas, continues to attract devoted fans. A biopic about her, starring Jennifer Lopez in her breakout role, was made in 1997. Lopez, an actress and singer from New York born to Puerto Rican parents, has gone on to become a superstar in both English and Spanish. The 1990s and 2000s saw the rise of many other pop singers willing to record in both languages, and winning legions of fans in both worlds, including superstars like the Colombian Shakira, and the Puerto Rican Ricky Martin, and Marc Anthony, born in New York City to Puerto Rican parents.

In a shared Anglo-Hispanic popular culture, who or what is "Hispanic" remains unresolved. A commoditized Hispanic culture can only give a veneer of cohesion: pop stars and actors still have to perform in English to reach a national audience. Food culture, meanwhile, has become so ingrained in the national culinary fabric that the memory of how it got here—and how it connects to contemporary issues—has faded. Commercialization can spread culture but can also weaken it, rendering it disposable. A love of tacos and JLo songs does not go very far in resolving the ongoing debate about Hispanics, Mexicans, undocumented migrants, and who is allowed to be an American.

Chapter 16

Tucson, Arizona,
ca. 1994–2018

"W HEN MEXICO SENDS its people, they're not sending their best. . . . They're sending people that have lots of problems, and they're bringing those problems with [*sic*] us. They're bringing drugs. They're bringing crime. They're rapists. And some, I assume, are good people."[1] With this speech, the property tycoon Donald Trump announced his candidacy for president of the United States in June 2015. As his campaign gathered pace, one of his most popular pledges was a plan to build a "beautiful" wall along the border. This promise, alongside further assurances that he would deport illegal immigrants, was coupled with the campaign slogan "Make America great again"—countered by a few quick wits who produced hats with the slogan "Make America Mexico again."

Throughout the campaign Trump put forward policies that would adversely affect Hispanic people living in the United States and made negative references to them, using the phrase "bad hombres" in the third presidential debate, something no other candidate has ever done. At other times he would deliberately embrace his idea of Hispanic culture, posting on Twitter a picture of himself eating from a taco bowl on Cinco de Mayo with the line "I love Hispanics!" At one point, Trump even traveled to Mexico to meet with the president, Enrique Peña Nieto, and the two held an awkward press conference that skirted the issues, not least Trump's demands that Mexico pay for his proposed wall. For the Mexican president, already struggling with low approval ratings, the move did not play well to a nation worried about the implications of a

Trump presidency for their families and friends across the border. A few hours later, Trump was back in the United States, at a rally in Phoenix, where he said: "We will build a great wall along the southern border and Mexico will pay for the wall. One hundred percent."[2]

Although the Hispanic vote has long been seen as important to the Democratic Party, its presidential nominee, Hillary Clinton, did not choose a Hispanic running mate; she did, however, find one who speaks Spanish. Tim Kaine, a senator from and former governor of Virginia, had spent time working with missionaries in Honduras, where he learned the language. In addition, Kaine is a Catholic, no small matter for some Hispanic voters. On the eve of the election, many observers thought the Republican candidate's rhetoric would spur a record number of Hispanic voters and secure Clinton's victory, but such hopes were misplaced.

The overall number of eligible Hispanic voters in 2016 was twenty-seven million, up from twenty-three million in 2012, and the total Hispanic share of the vote grew from 10 percent in 2012 to 11 percent in 2016. Clinton took about 66 percent of the Hispanic vote, and Trump 29 percent, while in the previous election Hispanics gave Barack Obama 71 percent of their vote and gave 27 percent to Mitt Romney. Both figures represented significant Republican declines since George W. Bush polled 40 percent of the Hispanic vote in 2004 and 35 percent in 2000.[3]

Overall, Hispanics' participation in U.S. politics is rising, owing to their growing numbers and to changes in the law. The Voting Rights Act of 1965 was extended ten years later to protect what were referred to as "language minorities"—groups that had struggled to cast a vote despite having the legal right to, facing discrimination or threats that blocked them from the polls. The legislative alteration also helped open the way for more active Hispanic involvement at all levels of politics. The Southwest Voter Registration Education Project, for instance, claims that it has helped register 2.5 million voters since it was founded in 1974.[4] Now there are fears that some voting rights could be rolled back after the Supreme Court struck down part of the original 1965 voting rights legislation in 2013, opening the way for states to impose their own restrictions, including controversial demands for photo IDs such as driving licenses. Not everyone who is eligible to vote has a photo ID and, as with the literacy tests of the past, critics of such measures claim they could disproportionally affect Hispanic voters.

Progress for Hispanics in public life has been uneven. While there have been some high-profile gains, such as appointment to the Supreme Court in 2009 of Sonia Sotomayor, who was born in New York to Puerto Rican parents, the judiciary, Congress, and state and local politics do not have representation proportional to the size of the Hispanic community. For instance, a report in the *Austin American-Statesman* found that 1.3 million Hispanics in Texas—more than 10 percent of the overall Hispanic population—live in cities or counties with no Hispanic representation on the city or council commissions. Statewide, about 10 percent of mayors and county judges are Hispanic, although Hispanic people make up about 38 percent of the population of Texas.[5]

Another study, by the California Latino Legislative Caucus and affiliated groups, found in 2015 that at 38.6 percent, "Latinos represent the most populous ethnic group" in California, but they made up only 19.6 percent of its registered voters. Latino political representation remains low as well, with the state assembly being 23.8 percent Latino and the state's city councils 14.6 percent.[6] There are some exceptions, such as Santa Ana in Orange County, California, which has a city council made up entirely of Hispanic officeholders, in a town where the population is 78 percent Hispanic.[7]

Nationally, the 2016 election saw the first Hispanic woman to reach the Senate, Nevada Democrat Catherine Cortez Masto, while the 115th Congress (January 2017–January 2019) can count a record forty-five Hispanic members: thirty-one Democrats and fourteen Republicans. They are 8.4 percent of Congress, though their numbers remain some way off the 17 percent of Hispanics nationally.[8]

However active the Hispanic community was in the 2016 election and political life, what all Hispanic people—documented or not, U.S. citizens or not— face now is a climate of increasing hostility within the debate on immigration. Nativist ideas of the United States as a white, English-speaking country have resurfaced, as have economic anxieties, specifically that cheaper labor in Mexico is undercutting U.S. jobs, while fears about *narco* drug gangs permeate border communities and beyond. Trump's wall has become a powerful symbol of an answer to these problems, whatever the demographic or economic reality that underpins it. In that sense, there are echoes of the mass deportations of Mexicans in the 1930s, but the context is markedly different, not only because of the diversity of people from Central and South America who have emigrated to the United States—this issue now goes far beyond the United States and Mexico—but also because of the changes wrought by increased economic globalization and the rise of China's industrial powerhouse.

One particular irritant to Trump and many other people in the United States has been the North American Free Trade Agreement. Grumbling and at times strong disagreement over trade have long been a hallmark of U.S.-Mexican economic relations, which have not always run smoothly. The later decades of the twentieth century saw various experiments in trade, including the further cutting back of restrictions, in a border region that was familiar with pressures to lower tariffs, and the development of free trade zones long before the implementation of NAFTA in 1994.

The *maquiladoras* (factories) that are now strung along the border had their start with the Border Industrialization Program of 1965, coming fast on the heels of the end of the bracero scheme. These plants imported, duty-free, materials that needed assembling, processing, or finishing into a final product, which was then shipped out of Mexico. The tariff on the product reflected the value of the labor, not the total value of the materials, and U.S firms were quick to utilize this scheme.[9] The Mexican government at the time also thought that by putting these plants—and jobs—along the border, it could stop people from leaving the country. Well before NAFTA was signed, around 550,000 Mexicans were working in some two thousand *maquiladoras*. Besides an economic change, there was a significant gender shift, as many of the employees were women, who were deemed to be less likely to unionize.[10]

Under President Carlos Salinas de Gortari, who came to power in 1988, Mexico had also experienced further economic reforms. Salinas lifted the conditions placed on foreign investment that had earlier been written into the 1917 constitution's controversial Article 27, while also privatizing land held by the communal *ejidos* and selling off many of the state's public services.[11] By 1990, leaders in Mexico, the United States, and Canada agreed that a larger trade deal could benefit all three nations. There was an implication as well that such an arrangement could offer more domestic opportunities so Mexican citizens would stay home. That same year, the number of Mexican-Americans in the United States was around fifteen million, and the number of undocumented workers was between two million and three million.[12]

As NAFTA came into force on January 1, 1994, a group of people in the state of Chiapas, Mexico, started a rebellion named in honor of the revolutionary leader Emiliano Zapata. The Zapatista National Liberation Army (Ejército Zapatista de Liberación Nacional, EZLN), led by the balaclava-wearing, pipe-smoking Subcomandante Marcos, denounced NAFTA and pressed its case for land reform and indigenous rights.[13] Marcos and the other Zapatistas feared that the reforms in the plan would affect the poor, mostly indigenous, farmers in the region. Marcos also wanted a fuller political inclusion of people who had continued to be marginalized—fellow citizens whose land and livelihoods were now at further risk as the country was opened to more foreign investment.

A trade deal as large as NAFTA had both positive and negative outcomes for the economies involved, though there have been some clear impacts on certain groups.[14] For instance, NAFTA has been tough for Mexican farmers. Under NAFTA, U.S. farmers, who receive government subsidies, were able to undercut Mexicans by selling meat and grain below market price, including the staple commodity maize. This led to subsidized U.S. corn flooding the Mexican market, driving farmers to look for work elsewhere, including in the United States. Between 1993 and 2008, the number of Mexicans employed in agriculture dropped from 8.1 million to 5.8 million, leaving far more unemployed than could be absorbed by the factories along the border.[15]

Throughout the 1990s, the way of life of many people changed beyond recognition, in rural hamlets and in the growing cities of the border. Women's unpaid work was critical to households, but now many women were leaving home for jobs in factories, uprooting whole communities.[16] As people moved north within Mexico, many decided to cross the border—legally or otherwise. The number of Mexican-born residents in the United States hit 12.6 million in 2009, up from 4.5 million in 1990.[17] Many of these immigrants had good incentives to go across, not least because jobs in Mexico often paid less for a day's work than what a U.S. worker could make in an hour. The industrial zones in Mexico had also become blighted by pollution, poverty, and violence: at least 370 female workers have been murdered around Ciudad Juárez and elsewhere along the border in the state of Chihuahua since 1993.

Mexicans remain ambivalent about the positive impact of NAFTA, not least because 50 percent of the population lives below the poverty line, a figure that is more or less unchanged since the deal went into effect. A poll in 2016 found that only 20 percent of Mexicans felt that NAFTA had benefited them.[18] A 2014 report from the Washington, D.C.–based Center for Economic and Policy Research documented that, twenty years on, the deal had indeed done little, on balance, to help Mexico, at least compared with the economies in the rest of Latin America. It explained that if NAFTA had worked as designed, and restored Mexican economic growth rates to pre-1980s levels, it "would be a relatively high income country, with income per person significantly higher than that of Portugal or Greece." Instead, Mexico ranked eighteenth out of twenty Latin American nations for growth of real GDP (gross domestic product) per person.[19]

The United States has also had its problems with NAFTA. Many people blame NAFTA for the decline of manufacturing and unskilled labor jobs in the United States, a constant theme during the 2016 presidential election campaign. However, a report by the Peterson Institute for International Economics found that overall the United States had gained from the deal because for every 100 jobs U.S. firms created in Mexico for manufacturing, they created 250 at their operations in the United States.[20] In addition, U.S. unemployment has remained low in general since the enactment of NAFTA, though income inequality has worsened in both countries. Trump has pledged to renegotiate NAFTA or leave it altogether. The United States' trade with Mexico and Canada is worth $1 trillion annually, or about 30 percent of total U.S. trade in 2016, and its leaving the agreement could send shock waves through the economies of all three members.[21]

Related to the shifts brought about by NAFTA, perhaps no issue has been debated in the United States in recent years with such ferocity as that of immigration and the question of what to do about undocumented or unauthorized migrants. Attempts at immigration reform continued into the 1990s, with the Illegal Immigration Reform and Immigrant Responsibility Act in 1996, which gave more funding to the Border Patrol and pressured employers to comply with the law by not hiring undocumented workers. At the end of 2005, a bill passed the House of Representatives that proposed measures to curb the number of migrants; the most controversial of these measures was to make it a felony to be in the United States illegally. In addition, anyone who hired or assisted an undocumented worker could face the same charge.[22]

As the Senate met to discuss this bill, and other reforms on the table, lawmakers were taken by surprise by a wave of marches and protests that started in March 2006 in support of Hispanic immigrants, documented or not. Tens of thousands of people came together in Chicago, Milwaukee, New York, and Phoenix, and the marchers in Los Angeles were estimated to have numbered almost 1 million.[23] The marches continued into April 2006, with some occurring in smaller cities, like Nashville, Tennessee, that had not had traditional associations with Hispanic populations. Then, on April 9–10, simultaneous rallies took place across the country, with a total estimated turnout of 1.3 million to 1.7 million.[24] This culminated in another round on May 1, a day celebrated in other nations as a workers' day, and this time many people went on strike. For the political establishment, it was an eye-opener. For many Anglos, it was the first time they had a sense of just how widespread Hispanic communities were across the nation. The bill was shelved. However, the anger from the Hispanic community and from supporters of immigration would lead to a backlash soon enough, as the tone of the debate about illegal immigration grew even shriller in the aftermath.

The administration of George W. Bush made a final attempt to resolve some of the issues surrounding immigration in the Secure Borders, Economic Opportunity and Immigration Reform Act of 2007. This plan stalled, in part owing to provisions that could have allowed a pathway to citizenship for some undocumented workers. The Republican-controlled Senate voted to end debate on it, and it died in Congress.

Immigration remained an issue during the presidency of Barack Obama after he took office in 2008. Under his administration, deportations began to rise, reaching more than two million by 2015, this time in the context of policies that would make it almost impossible for a deportee to return to the United States. This made the most impact on people who had recently crossed over, as two-thirds of the people picked up were within 100 miles of the border. In the past, many of these apprehensions would have been considered "voluntary returns" and not counted as formal deportations or removals, but this system changed during the later part of George W Bush's term. The change in classification—from return to removal—was intended to discourage people from making repeated attempts to enter the United States: having formal charges on their records would be a deterrent.[25]

In November 2014, Obama passed a number of executive orders aimed at immigration, including the expansion of the number of people eligible for the 2012 Deferred Action for Childhood Arrivals (DACA) program, so that it would include anyone who had entered the United States before the age of sixteen and had lived in the country since January 1, 2010. He also introduced the Deferred Action for Parents of Americans and Lawful Permanent Residents (DAPA) program, covering qualifying parents who had lived in the United States from January 1, 2010. Meanwhile, repeated attempts to pass a version of the Development, Relief and Education for Alien Minors (DREAM) Act, which would give people who came over as undocumented minors a pathway to permanent residency, continued to fail. DACA, therefore was intended to provide temporary permission to work, to have access to a driver's license, and to attend college and pay in-state tuition fees.

A few months earlier, in the summer of 2014, the Obama administration had faced a perfect storm, of drugs, gangs, and immigration along the southern border. Women and children fled Guatemala, Honduras, and El Salvador to escape the mounting violence perpetrated by the *narcotraficantes* in these countries where governments were too weak or corrupt to protect the public. Mexico, too, had spent much of the 1990s battling the rise of the drug cartels and continued to do so through the 2000s. The center of the drug world had shifted north from Colombia over those years, heading toward the border, in part because the main market for illegal drugs remains the United States. Guatemala, El Salvador, and Honduras have been racked by gang violence related to the cartels. Anxious to make sure their children were safe, many parents had a coyote (smuggler) take them across the border. Some teenage boys were sent on their own by their families to get them away from the gangs, whose power in some places is so strong that they can recruit or strong-arm members straight from the school classroom.

The particular surge in the summer of 2014 was fueled in part by a rumor, which started in Central America, that women and children who made it across the border would be allowed to stay, something U.S.

officials took pains to correct. The confusion lay in people's thinking that being allowed to stay with relatives rather than in a detention facility meant they could remain in the United States. Federal law mandated that there must be attempts to find and send children to relatives living in the United States while the children awaited immigration hearings, but they still faced the prospect of deportation.[26] Nevertheless, tens of thousands of people arrived that summer and temporary accommodation had to be set up for them.[27] Warehouses, military bases, and other makeshift spaces along the border filled up in those summer months. According to U.S. Customs and Border Protection statistics, in the fiscal year ending in 2013, 5,990 "unaccompanied alien children" arrived from El Salvador; 8,068 from Guatemala; and 6,747 from Honduras. The numbers for the end of 2014 had more than doubled to 16,404; 17,057; and 18,244, respectively.[28]

Vice President Joe Biden met with the presidents of Guatemala and El Salvador and high-ranking Honduran and Mexican officials in 2014, pressuring them to address the root causes of this wave of immigration, though part of the problem originated in the United States.[29] A United Nations report noted that the presence of one of the biggest street gangs in El Salvador, Mara Salvatrucha (MS-13), "is almost certainly a result of the wave of criminal deportations . . . after 1996."[30] The gangs were born on the streets of Los Angeles, formed by young people who had left—or whose parents had fled—El Salvador in the 1980s. Some of them ended up in prison and were later deported to El Salvador, where they could reestablish their gangs. Their involvement in the global drug trade means they have evolved to be more a military force than a street gang, now spreading terror and violence, driving more people to make the dangerous crossing into the United States.

Within the United States, the media raged with a polarized debate on whether the children involved should be considered "refugees," and public sympathy was mixed. An editorial in the New York Times summed up the hysteria:

In Congress, which gave up on creating an orderly immigration system, Republicans are watching President Obama struggle to get a handle on the problem, and trying very hard not to help. Their reaction is one part panic, two parts glee. Representative Phil Gingrey of Georgia is warn-

ing the Centers for Disease Control and Prevention about migrants carrying the Ebola virus. For Representative Louie Gohmert of Texas, it's
H1N1 flu virus. Senator Ted Cruz of Texas is using the crisis to demand
an end to President Obama's program deferring deportations of young
people known as Dreamers. There is no time like a crisis to blow up
earlier efforts to fix the system's failures.[31]

Refugees continued to flow north, and from October 2015 to May 2016,
around 120,700 people from Guatemala, Honduras, and El Salvador were
stopped at the Mexican border. Figures from the U.S. Border Patrol put
total apprehensions for the fiscal year (FY) 2016 (October 2015–September
2016) at 408,870, with just under 60,000 being unaccompanied children,
for the most part from Central America.[32] Thousands more were turned
back before they could even attempt to cross, as Mexican officials stepped
up their vigilance, encouraged in part by U.S. pressure and extra funding;
in 2016, Mexico deported around 177,000 Central Americans. In FY 2017,
the numbers dropped by more than 20 percent, with total apprehensions
of 310,531 and 41,435 apprehensions of unaccompanied children.[33] However, earlier in 2017 the Mexican government—now antagonized by the
Trump administration over the border wall—said it would not cooperate
with any plans to deport apprehended non-Mexicans to Mexico.[34]

Another related issue that emerged during the Obama years and the
run-up to the 2016 presidential election was that of the so-called anchor
babies, a loaded term used to describe children born to foreigners in the
United States; these children are entitled to citizenship. According to the
Pew Research Center, three hundred thousand children a year are born
to unauthorized immigrants. A common misconception is that giving
birth to a baby in the United States entitles an undocumented parent to
remain in the country, but it does not. The question of what happens
to children when a parent is deported has taken on a new urgency since
Trump came to office, and in 2017 it was a problem faced by an estimated
five million children, who have at least one undocumented parent.[35]

The Department of Homeland Security received guidance in 2017
allowing it to prioritize the deportation of unauthorized immigrants
who have a record of criminal convictions, no matter how minor, or are
suspected of a crime.[36] At the same time, some six hundred thousand
people in 2017 were awaiting their immigration hearings, with the legal

system struggling with the case backlog.[37] Then, in September 2017, the Trump administration announced that DACA would be stopped, though renewals were permitted to continue while legal and legislative issues were resolved, leaving around eight hundred thousand young people—the majority of whom were from Mexico but who also included people from other parts of Latin America—facing a very uncertain future. In addition, some 2,500 Nicaraguans and 200,000 Salvadorans with Temporary Protected Status (TPS) were informed that they would have to leave the United States by 2019. TPS was created in 1990 to help foreigners fleeing from war or natural disasters, providing legal status to affected people even if they had made an unlawful entry. In late 2017 Trump announced that TPS for these two groups would no longer be renewed. The Salvadorans who qualified for TPS arrived in 2001, after two earthquakes devastated their country, and were the largest group in the program. After living in the United States for nearly two decades, many of the people with TPS have a cause for great concern about what lies ahead.

By the spring of 2018, the Trump administration had put into effect a "zero-tolerance" policy to deter migrants or refugees entering at the border, which meant adults would face criminal charges and any children traveling with them would be placed in a separate holding facility, leading to an estimated 2,300 children being separated from their parent or guardian. This drew heavy criticism from across the political spectrum, and by June the president signed an executive order declaring that families must be kept together while awaiting trial. The following month, a federal court ordered that any separated children must be reunited by the end of July, though it was clear that this deadline would not be met, in part because of the numbers involved and problems the different agencies were having in matching information in order to reunite families. This particular moment came at a time of heated debate about immigration, and the question of how to reform the system—especially given that opinions remain deeply divided—will continue to challenge policy-makers on all sides.[38]

Mexicans remain the largest group of Hispanic people in the United States, making up some 64 percent of the Hispanic population, and correspondingly making up a large segment of unauthorized immigrants.[39] Overall, according to the Pew Research Center, the number of unauthorized immigrants in the United States in 2015 was 11 million, which is about 3.5 percent of the nation's total population. This number has remained steady since 2009 and represents a decline from a peak of 12.2 million in 2007.[40] Underneath these figures, some significant changes are occurring. The number of people arriving from China and India is beginning to overtake the number from Mexico, especially in states farther away from the border, such as Ohio and New York. According to a 2016 *Wall Street Journal* analysis, around 136,000 people immigrated from India and 128,000 from China in 2014, while only 123,000 came from Mexico; a further 82,000 arrived from other Central American countries.[41] In the same year, thirty-one states saw the arrival of more Chinese than Mexican people in 2014, and twenty-five states had more Indian immigrants than Mexican. Although many of these newer migrants are highly skilled and brought in on work visas, not all are, and not everyone is legal. Asians have become the second-largest group of undocumented immigrants, but at around 13 percent of all undocumented people in the United States, they are still quite a way behind people from Mexico and Central America, who between them make up about 71 percent.[42] Mexicans have actually seen an overall net fall in migration. Net migration from Mexico has actually fallen below zero, according to a 2015 Pew study, with a net loss of some 140,000 between 2009 and 2014. In those years, around 1 million Mexicans left the United States to return to Mexico, while another 870,000 Mexicans came to the United States.[43]

In 2015, the overall Hispanic population—including recent immigrants and U.S. citizens—reached a new high, at fifty-seven million people, and accounted for 54 percent of total U.S. population growth from 2000 to 2014.[44] Hispanic people are also living in more diverse regions, with 2014 data pointing out that half of the counties in the United States had at least one thousand Hispanics: the place with the fastest-growing Hispanic population growth from 2007 to 2014 was Williams County, North Dakota, with an increase of 367 percent.[45]

MEXICO'S HISTORY WITH illegal substances goes back many decades, but the rise in the twenty-first century of narco crime has been without precedent. No part of Mexico remains untouched, and the associated violence—wars between cartels, or shoot-outs between narcos and the police and military—has cost, according to some estimates, at least eighty thousand lives, with tens of thousands more people disappearing as well. Journalists have paid a high price, as those trying to report on the cartels or corruption in their own towns end up silenced by a gun.[46]

One indirect solution to part of the problem may lie in the growing number of U.S. states willing to legalize marijuana. The Border Patrol's seizure of that drug in FY 2016 was the lowest it has been in a decade, at just under 1.3 million pounds.[47] Legal growers in states like Colorado are forcing the price down while keeping the quality high. In fact, in 2015 the Drug Enforcement Agency reported some evidence that marijuana from the United States was being smuggled into Mexico.[48] Now the more lucrative substances for the cartels are methamphetamine and heroin. Demand for the latter is fueled by prescription opioid abuse; no longer able to obtain legal opioids, many users have turned to heroin, and in parts of the United States the number of overdoses has skyrocketed.

The cartels' access to arms—often smuggled from the United States— allows them to win the battle against police and the Mexican military. Corruption infiltrates the system at the highest levels. The United States has poured more than $2.5 billion into the Merida Initiative since its inception in 2008, aiming to target organized crime, establish anticorruption programs, build up the police, and reform the judiciary.[49] The violence has infiltrated the lives of millions of people along the border and well beyond, as a network of distributors moves Mexican drugs throughout the United States, from Alaska to Atlanta. Even the music of the *frontera* has been infused by the cartels, as *narcocorridos*—a variation of the *corrido* ballad—provide a sound track for the stories of communities struggling with violence and loss.

There is also another sort of drug trafficking taking place along the border. The expense of pharmaceuticals in the United States draws people across, where they can buy the same drugs in cheaper forms produced in Mexico at what seem like endless blocks of pharmacies in most border towns. These pharmacies are a crucial part of local economies. At the entrance to the pedestrian crossing at the Progreso–Nuevo

Progreso International Bridge, a sign in English reads: "Thank God for America & for Our Winter Texans. Welcome Home."

Well before Donald Trump's insistence on building a wall at the Mexican border, many efforts had been made to tighten control along the frontier. The number of agents was increased along sections of the border near El Paso under Operation Hold the Line in 1993, and in Operation Gatekeeper the following year in San Diego, both heavily trafficked sectors. Some fencing was put up in this period, but the push for an even more fortified border came after the September 11, 2001, terror attacks. The U.S. government began to spend billions shoring up the border region, fearing that its porousness could lead potential terrorists to come in from the south. The Department of Homeland Security was created and the Immigration and Naturalization Service was put under its command and reorganized into new departments, including U.S. Immigration and Customs Enforcement (ICE) and U.S. Customs and Border Protection (CBP), under which the Border Patrol operates.

The Intelligence Reform and Terrorism Prevention Act of 2004 provided ten thousand more agents for the Border Patrol, pushing the total number employed to some twenty thousand in 2016. In addition, unofficial border agents arrived around 2004, in the form of a vigilante group known as the Minutemen Project, which would patrol parts of the border looking for the Mexican it calls "José Sanchez"—a catchall applied to people who made the illegal crossing.[50] At first the group of mostly white, working-class, ex-military men attracted visits from the American Civil Liberties Union to make sure no Mexicans were being harmed, and the Minutemen remained controversial, with some people praising them as patriots and others condemning them as racists.[51] One member explained that he joined because, "What's happening is nothing less than an invasion. We have already lost California."[52] In the end, the group splintered and membership declined, particularly after one prominent member, Shawna Forde, was sentenced for murder, while the group's cofounder, Chris Simcox, was imprisoned for child sex abuse.

In 2005, the Secure Border Initiative was introduced; its aim was to create a "wall" of surveillance between the United States and Mexico with high-tech monitoring equipment. The aircraft manufacturer Boeing won a bid to work on the project and was given a $1 billion contract.[53] Technology such as radar, drones, infrared detectors, and sophisticated cameras does not come cheap, and the program's costs rose so much that it had to be suspended.[54] The changes in this period also attracted criticism for the "militarization" of the border. This was further extended by the Secure Fence Act of 2006, which funded additional fencing. By 2011, about 650 miles had been completed, at a cost of around $3.4 billion.[55] A bipartisan bill in the Senate in 2013—the Border Security, Economic Opportunity, and Immigration Modernization Bill—sought to further increase spending on the border, as well as provide pathways to citizenship for undocumented people. It passed the Senate but died in the Republican-controlled House of Representatives. The next phase of border security may be Trump's promised wall, though its political support, design, construction, and funding remain, for the moment, under heated discussion.

On a cool evening in Tucson in 2014, visions of the dead paraded through the city's downtown streets during the annual All Souls Procession, held around the time of the Mexican Day of the Dead (día de los muertos). Faces glowed with white paint, disguised as elaborate Mexican death masks; some paraders donned full costumes, looking like smartly dressed Victorian skeletons though the genesis of this skeletal imagery goes back much earlier, to the pre-Columbian commemorations of the dead.

Others in the procession took a simpler approach, wearing everyday clothes, with no makeup, each holding a stick to which an empty plastic water jug was tied with a string. Each jug had a small light inside, giving off a dim glow. The jugs swung in the desert night air, an eerie and powerful symbol of the thousands of people who have died near Tucson trying to cross the border through the Sonoran Desert. Water could have saved their lives. These gallon jugs are among the common artifacts found throughout southern Arizona, left behind by people trying to enter the United States, along with knapsacks, clothing, and children's toys.

This gathering has become a city tradition, falling on the first Sunday after the Day of the Dead, on November 2. The whole evening is somber—there is no alcohol sold, and the mood is quiet and respectful. People walk the parade route carrying pictures of loved ones, often mounted on placards and decorated with flowers and tinsel. Participants and observers can also write down names of people who have died, which are put into a giant urn at the end of the night. This is hoisted onto a platform by a crane and set ablaze.

The procession was the idea of two local artists who were inspired by the Mexican tradition, and they began it in the 1990s as a way of coming to terms with their own losses. Today it is an event that involves an estimated one hundred thousand people.[56] Mexican-Americans did not take part at first, but more have started to join in, bringing the communities together in a town that has long been segregated, and which continues to face many problems because it is on the front line of the immigration debate. As a handwritten sign two young men carried in the procession said: "If you use/steal our culture and would still deport us, you're honoring *no one.*"

In Arizona alone, the border fencing stretched 180 miles by 2010, impelling people to find another way across, one that has caused a lot of problems for the state.[57] The routes through the Sonoran Desert into Arizona are fraught with dangers, not least the extreme temperatures and the ease with which a person can become disoriented and lost amid the sagebrush. According to data collected by the local charity Humane Borders, there were 3,002 deaths from October 1, 1999, through July 31, 2016, in southern Arizona, with dehydration being a main cause. The charity's maps plot the deaths in the area, and the dots around Tucson look like red blood cells clustered under a microscope.[58]

Everyone in Tucson seems to have a story—from a friend of a friend, or from someone who owns land to the south—of helping people across, or finding old clothes and shoes, dropped knapsacks, toothbrushes. The artist Valarie James, who lives in the Tucson area, began to collect such objects, using them in her work, including a collaborative creation of three life-size sculptures—*Las Madres*, or The Mothers—to honor those who had died in the desert. She told the *Wall Street Journal*, "For those of us who live close to the border, the humanitarian crisis is not an abstraction."[59] Some landowners and residents in Arizona now want the wall Trump promised so that it will put an end to the grisly encounters in their fields.

The Tucson area is one of the busiest corridors of undocumented immigration traffic, though it has begun to slow. Customs and Border Protection apprehended 70,074 people in Arizona in FY 2015, a significant decline from the 613,346 in 2000.[60] Likewise, there has been a more than 50 percent reduction in the number of undocumented people living in the state between 2007 and 2014, from 500,000 to around 244,000, in an overall population of nearly 7 million.[61]

In 2010, Arizona's legislative efforts to curb undocumented migrants came to national attention, owing to state senate bill SB 1070.[62] This bill in the state legislature proposed allowing police to check a person's immigration status if there was "reasonable suspicion" that he or she might be illegal, and this could be done during routine policing, such as a simple traffic stop for a minor violation. Before it could go into effect, President Obama's Department of Justice filed an injunction against Arizona on the grounds that the legislation was unconstitutional, and a nationwide controversy followed. The bill also required immigrants to carry their documents or face a misdemeanor charge; and it gave law enforcement the ability to make arrests without a warrant if there was "probable cause" that the person could be removed from the United States.

To opponents, the legislation looked like a bill to sanction racial profiling. SB 1070 inspired a group of rappers to produce "Back to Arizona," an updated version of Public Enemy's "By the Time I Get to Arizona," which was itself written in response to Arizona's 1990 opposition to a state holiday to honor Dr. Martin Luther King Jr. After the 1993 Super Bowl was pulled from Tempe, a vote was taken again, and the holiday was reinstated. Similar economic boycotts took place over SB 1070, with conference bookings dropping by 30 percent.[63]

The state launched an appeal, but the injunction was upheld by the Ninth Circuit Court of Appeals in April 2011. It reached the Supreme Court the following year. In its June 2012 decision, the Court upheld section 2B, which required "law enforcement officers to determine immigration status during a lawful stop." The three other contested sections—making it a crime not to carry alien registration papers; forbidding an unauthorized immigrant to solicit or undertake work; and allowing an arrest without a warrant for anyone suspected of being undocumented—were struck down. Still, other states followed suit, with attempts at or passage of similar legislation in Alabama, Georgia, Indiana, South Carolina, and Utah.

Arizona is also home to Joe Arpaio, the sheriff of Maricopa County, who came to national prominence for his own controversial methods in dealing with detainees and prisoners. Although voters in the 2016 election decided to end his twenty-four-year reign, denying him a seventh term, he was back in the public spotlight in August 2017 after receiving a presidential pardon. Arpaio and the Maricopa Country Sheriff's Office had been charged with routinely violating the rights of Hispanic people by detaining them on the basis of racial profiling. In 2011 he was ordered to stop such behavior, and in July 2017, after much legal wrangling, he was found guilty of criminal contempt of court for defying that order. The pardon was a controversial move for Trump and immediately met with criticism from Hispanic and immigration rights groups.[64]

A 2009 *New Yorker* profile of Arpaio highlighted many of the reasons he has been embraced by opponents of immigration.[65] In response to prison overcrowding, he set up army surplus tents and surrounded them with barbed wire until his tent city held twenty-five hundred inmates. He banned cigarettes, coffee, hot food, even salt and pepper, spending 30 cents per meal on the inmates. Most television was banned, and he put the prisoners to work in chain gangs. He also tried to humiliate them by making them wear pink garments, including underclothes.

Many of those in his custody had not been charged with a crime; indeed, most were undocumented people rounded up by the police. Arpaio charged illegal immigrants as "coconspirators" in their own human trafficking, making their transgression a class 4 felony—and rendering them ineligible to post bond.[66] Yet what Arpaio saved in salt and pepper was far outstripped by the cost of lawsuits. Inmates, and families of inmates who died in custody, have gone to court in droves, and by the time of his run for reelection in 2016, the county had paid out nearly $80 million in legal costs.[67]

THE FIRST TWO decades of the twenty-first century have also been eventful for Cubans and Puerto Ricans. Relations between the United States and Cuba were rocky throughout the 2000s, starting with the fight over Elián González. In November 1999, the five-year-old boy was found floating in an inner tube off the coast of Florida. His mother and others who had tried to leave Cuba on a raft had drowned. He was turned over to relatives in Miami, but the Cuban government requested that the boy be taken back to Cuba where his father lived. The Immigration and Naturalization Services ruled that his father be given custody of the boy. This decision was met by protests and lawsuits, and by January 2000 it had been turned over to the attorney general, Janet Reno, all the while growing into a national issue.

Elián's father, Juan Miguel González, arrived in the United States that April, but the boy's Miami family continued to fight in the courts. The situation reached a climax on the morning of April 22 when federal agents burst into the home of his relatives in Miami and seized the boy. A photographer captured the moment when an armed INS agent holding a machine gun in his right arm reached out with his left to grab the terrified boy being hidden by one of his relatives in a closet. The shocking and dramatic image was transmitted around the world. The boy was taken back to Cuba—though not before another two months of lawsuits and paperwork—and greeted as a hero. He has lived on the island ever since. The episode was another low point in the relationship between the United States and Cuba, but in 2014 entirely new prospects appeared on the horizon.

That December the Obama administration announced its plans to normalize relations with Cuba, a deal agreed on with the Cuban president Raúl Castro and brokered by Pope Francis. There would be a release of political prisoners and a loosening of U.S. restrictions on travel and banking transactions, allowing more tourists and more money into the island. However, a total end to the embargo would require a vote from Congress. Within a few months, rumors began to circulate within Cuba that Cubans would soon lose their privileged immigration status enshrined in the Cuban Adjustment Act, leading thousands to rush to reach the United States. Some Cubans with the money to leave by air were flying to Ecuador, which did not require a visa for them to enter, and then traveling by land through Central America to cross on foot at the Mexican border, hoping to get into the United States under the "dry foot" proviso of the existing legislation. In the last three months of 2015, around 12,100 Cubans entered via Texas border crossings alone, and a total of 43,159 arrived via all ports of entry in the whole year.[68] Indeed, as feared, before he left office in January 2017, President Obama announced the end of "wet foot, dry foot," as part of the normalization of relations. This left thousands of Cubans who were trying to get into the United States overland stranded at the border or elsewhere in Latin America.

This was followed by Trump's rolling back the Obama deal by the summer of 2017 and bringing back restrictions on travel and some trade, on the basis that the United States had a bad deal with Cuba and political reform there had not gone far enough. Some in the Cuban-American community think no relationship between the two nations should exist while Cuba remains communist. However, with Raúl Castro handing over the presidency to Miguel Díaz-Canel in April 2018, coupled with the death of Fidel in November 2016, the island has entered a post-Castro age, at least officially, though it remains unclear what it will take for the two nations to rekindle their relations.

PUERTO RICO HAS also had a rough ride with the United States in recent decades, suffering a debt crisis; mass depopulation; and Maria, a devastating category 4 hurricane that slammed into the island in September 2017.

At the root of the financial problems was Section 936, an exemption status created by the U.S. government in 1976 that allowed U.S. companies to operate in Puerto Rico tax-free. Pharmaceutical companies were among the firms that moved in, and economic growth followed, with some one hundred thousand people working in the pharmaceutical sector by the 1990s.[69] Firms like Johnson & Johnson were estimated to have saved $1 billion in taxes between 1980 and 1990, while also providing the island with jobs.[70] However, Congress decided that such a large corporate welfare scheme was too costly and in 1996 resolved to phase out Section 936 over the following decade. By 2006, much of the industry had departed along with it. The island scrambled to create a loophole that would persuade some businesses to stay, which took the form of allowing U.S. firms to create subsidiaries that would not pay tax on their revenue, so long as the money was held offshore.[71]

To compound these problems, a debt crisis began to form in 2012. This would inflict more damage on Puerto Rico's already fragile economy; by 2014, credit rating agencies had downgraded the island's debt to junk status.[72] Part of the reason Puerto Rico found itself in this mess is that its bonds are "triple-exempt," meaning bondholders do not pay city, island, or federal tax on the interest; this made them a popular investment. When the economy faltered after 2006, the island government continued to issue bonds to cover budget shortfalls, and when those bonds—which were considered "safe" investments for many Puerto Ricans and their pension funds—were downgraded, hedge funds swooped in to provide loans to the indebted island, worsening its plight.

Because of its commonwealth status, the island is not allowed to declare bankruptcy, unlike a U.S. state. As of 2017, Puerto Rico had $123 billion in debt and no way to pay it, lurching toward a default. One article in the *New York Times* in August 2016 branded it a "failed state" within the United States.[73] The U.S. government established a seven-member "federal control board," under the Puerto Rico Oversight, Management, and Economic Stability Act (PROMESA) passed in 2016 to restructure the island's finances. In May 2017, Puerto Rico went to federal court to attempt to obtain some bankruptcy relief, as the lawsuits from creditors continued to mount.[74]

Referendums on the island's status continued to point in different directions. A plebiscite in 1993 gave a narrow victory, at 48.6 percent, to continuing as an Estado Libre Asociado (Commonwealth), while statehood garnered a close 46.3 percent.[75] Another, in 1998, had a more complicated result. It offered: territorial free associated state (commonwealth status), free association, statehood, independence, or "none of the above," and angry voters gave that last option 50.3 percent of the vote, with statehood gaining 46.5 percent. The next vote, in 2012, came in two parts. The first asked if the island should continue with the existing commonwealth status, to which 970,910 voters, or around 54 percent, said "no." Voters were then asked a second question on the future options: statehood, "sovereign free association," or independence. Statehood won, supported by more than 61 percent of people who cast a vote on the second question.

In the 2016 elections, the pro-statehood politician Ricardo Rosselló, of the New Progressive Party, won the governorship of the island. He took office in the face of a population crisis: the island had lost about 9 percent of its residents since 2000, around 334,000 people, with three-quarters of that exodus taking place after 2010.[76] Instead of New York, Florida, especially the Orlando area, has become home for many of these people, pushing the Puerto Rican population in the state past the one million mark.[77] Rosselló held another plebiscite on the island's status in June 2017; the results came back with 97 percent (518,199 votes) in favor of statehood, though turnout was only 23 percent, compared with the usual 60 to 70 percent, in part because of a boycott by the other parties.[78]

Then, a few months later, the island was thrown into chaos by the 150-mile-per-hour winds of Hurricane María, which made landfall on September 20. The island lost all power, homes were destroyed, crops were wiped out. Official figures claim 64 people were killed, but an investigation by the *New York Times* calculated the number to be around 1,052, in part because people died after the storm owing to factors like the lack of electricity and the scarcity of medical provisions.[79]

The Trump administration was criticized by many—including people on the island—for being too slow in its response. The image of inefficiency was compounded by a picture of Trump tossing rolls of paper towels to people at a shelter in San Juan when he made a visit to see the devastation in early October 2017. Puerto Rico also found its initial relief efforts hamstrung by the Jones Act of 1920, which required that trade between all U.S. ports had to be in ships built, owned, and operated by Americans, a legislative hangover from a time when the country wanted to encourage shipbuilding. The law stayed on the books and disproportionately affected Puerto Rico compared with other U.S. ports. In the aftermath of the hurricane, it was temporarily waived to allow shipments of food, water, medicine, and other supplies to arrive.

As the relief effort got under way, it emerged that only around 54 percent of people in the United States even realized Puerto Rico was a U.S. colony and that its 3.4 million people are U.S. citizens, which made the disaster a domestic, not a foreign, one.[80] In the aftermath of the storm, thousands of Puerto Ricans used their citizenship to move to, or at least take respite in, the mainland United States. Many observers now expect the fall in the island's population that was already under way to accelerate.

Months after the event, Puerto Rico continued to suffer blackouts, with just under half of the island without electricity and its infrastructure

still deeply damaged. However, in December 2017, lawmakers decided
to allow a further financial blow to the island with a Republican tax
plan that would bring to an end breaks for U.S. subsidiaries remaining there. The new rules would force any U.S. subsidiary to be treated
like a foreign company, and so be subject to paying tax on any income
generated from offshore assets, compounding the island's problems.[81]

Puerto Rico may be facing its biggest test since the combination of
the 1898 Spanish-American War and the 1899 San Ciriaco hurricane, and
it will take years for the island to recover. There are no signs in Washington of any interest in extending statehood to the island, and so it will
struggle on as a territory, trying to rebuild its devastated infrastructure
and solve its debt crisis.

THE LEGACY OF the Hispanic past has made itself felt in the troubled
present. As the United States grapples with immigration, NAFTA, relations with Cuba, and the reconstruction of Puerto Rico, uncertainty
hangs in the air for everyone involved. Time pushes forward, though,
and down on the border, on the U.S. side of the existing wall, cell phone
users receive texts saying, "Welcome to MEXICO." It is a useful reminder
that borders remain elusive, and even if they can be drawn on a map,
they are changeable. Controlling the fickle waters of the Río Grande
proved tricky in the past, but changes in engineering reined it in; likewise,
mobile phones and the internet now make it easier to bridge divides,
connecting people whether or not they physically cross.

It is the imagined walls or boundaries that are more difficult to tra-
verse. The U.S. border will always loom large in the public imagination
as long as it remains a symbol of a United States that wants to distance
itself from its neighbors. More than that, beyond the wall is the zone
of the other, the boundary of the unknown, the place of lawlessness
so enshrined by lore and Hollywood legend. Perhaps that is the reason
that one of the few films to capture the nuance and complexity of this
tangled relationship is set in a border town. John Sayles's *Lone Star* (1996)
allows family secrets to overlap with local history. While he is trying
to solve a murder, Sam Deeds, the sheriff of fictional Frontera, Texas,

rekindles his romance with his former high school girlfriend, Pilar, now a history teacher in the town. Deeds later discovers that his father had a long-running affair with Pilar's mother, Mercedes Cruz, a Mexican businesswoman. Throughout the film, Cruz claims she is "Spanish" and laments the arrival of undocumented immigrants from the other side of the border who don't speak English, but whom she hires to work in her restaurant.

Decades earlier, both parents—their affair then unknown—had been opposed to Deeds and Pilar's dating when they were teenagers. The final scene reveals why: Deeds and Pilar were half siblings, sharing, as it transpires, the same father. Deeds and Cruz decide to continue their relationship anyway. Pilar says, "All that other stuff, all that history—the hell with it, right?" She continues, in the final line of the film: "Forget the Alamo."

Epilogue
Dalton, Georgia, 2014

I RETURNED TO MY old high school in October 2014 for my twentieth class reunion. The parking lot of Dalton High was full of new Mustang and classic Mercedes convertibles festooned with ribbons and balloons, under a clear blue sky and late-autumn Georgia sun. These chariots awaited the homecoming princesses, who would soon be waving to onlookers. A veritable tradition by the standards of such a young nation.

Sometimes a visit to an old school can render it smaller than it loomed in a youthful imagination, but this time it was far bigger. The school had doubled in size, from fewer than 1,000 students when I was there to 1,875. Some of the same lockers still lined the hallways; the gym, the indoor pool, the athletics track, and the off-site football field had all changed little in twenty years—logos and references to the mascot of the school team, the Catamounts, were dotted around the building as they had always been before football games—but the main building included a large new wing, with more classrooms and lecture halls. The classroom where I studied Georgia history was now a room for Junior ROTC cadets. The school gave, as good ones always do give, a sense of continuity and progress. The biggest change is that the student body is now 69 percent Hispanic. Around 80 percent receive free or reduced-cost lunches, indicating that many students are from low-income families, and around 17 percent are English-language learners, meaning they are not yet proficient in English.

The town became caught up in larger national events in 2014 when undocumented Central American minors began flocking to the U.S.

border, and some of them were sent to Dalton, where they had family connections. The result was the Newcomer Academy, a small school designed to help them. Beth Jordan is a teacher of English-learners in Dalton and also a graduate of the high school, and she remembers the influx from 2014. "That was a crazy situation for us. At one point I had sixty-something students in my class. I put thirty in one room and thirty in another and just ran back and forth." The school hired more staff to deal with the students, many of whom "had never been to school. They couldn't read—they didn't know their letters, their colors, their numbers."[1]

Jordan said the school district has about 150 English-learners at the high school level. Most of them are Hispanic, although some are from countries such as China. The Hispanic children come from Mexico, as well as Honduras, Guatemala, El Salvador, and even Cuba and Puerto Rico. "We're a border city," Jordan said, remarking that Dalton schools have more in common with those in Texas or Arizona than with other schools in Georgia.

Jennifer Phinney, another Dalton High School graduate, is now a director of school support for Dalton Public Schools. "I graduated in 1986 and then I started teaching there in 1991 and it was very much the same high school I had left . . . it was very white and very privileged," she said. Then, in the late 1990s, the change was sudden. "In three years [1996–1999] we went to 50 percent Hispanic. It was a very rapid shift."[2]

A local lawyer and former U.S. Congressman, Erwin Mitchell, set up an exchange program in 1997, with the support of Shaw Industries, one of Dalton's major employers. The Georgia Project sent teachers from Dalton to the University of Monterrey, in Mexico, and vice versa for a decade.[3] It helped the two groups of teachers to learn and understand more about each other, and prepared the town's education facilities for the changes ahead.

Dalton has maintained a population of around 33,000, but now about half the town is Hispanic, an explosive growth since 1990, when the Hispanic population was only 1,400.[4] In the whole of Whitfield County, Georgia, the Hispanic population went from 2,321 out of a total of 72,462 in 1990 to 34,518 out of 103,542 people in 2014, a rise from 3 percent of the county's population to 33 percent.[5]

Not everyone works in the carpet industry that has long dominated the town's economy; some people are seasonal agricultural workers, picking apple crops in nearby Ellijay, for instance. As families have taken root and prospered, many have moved into white-collar jobs; indeed some of the Hispanic pupils who arrived in the late 1990s are now teachers in the Dalton school system.

Immigrants from Guatemala and other Central American countries have joined the mix, and their arrival has brought a unique set of challenges for Esther Familia-Cabrera, a Puerto Rican who moved from New York City in 2010 to help Dalton coordinate community health care workers, known as *promotoras de salud*. She has a passion for the job, which, while similar to what she was doing in New York, has its unique aspects. "Language is a huge barrier," she said. Many of the recent immigrants are from rural areas, not cities, and speak only indigenous languages.

Many of the Hispanic people in Dalton and the region are also undocumented immigrants, so Familia-Cabrera and her staff have to find ways to reach these "invisibles," as she calls them.[6] Here, Dalton faces challenges similar to those of much larger cities. The biggest challenge is integration: "They feel segregated and they feel 'Why should I adapt, if I don't belong here, I'm not accepted here? I'm going back to Mexico at some point because I'm never going to be American.' " The second generation is stuck between the two worlds, she feels, with young people being told, "You're not Mexican enough" by their families and, "You're too Mexican—you need to be more American" by the outside world.

———

Luis Viamonte, a physician in Dalton, was born into a family of doctors in Cuba but left when he was seventeen, in 1961, as part of Operation Peter Pan, which ended the following October. "The story in Cuba was, in 1960, that they [the revolutionaries] were going to take the children away from the parents and educate them. And they had started that," he recalled. "The other rumor was that at the age of eighteen I was going to have to serve in Castro's military. Most of my friends were leaving. I only had four friends left in the class." Soon he was on his way to Miami, where an aunt and uncle lived. "They [the Cuban government] allowed you $5," he said. "So I got $5 and one suitcase, one blanket, one pair of shoes, and one change of clothes." From there, Viamonte, like many Cubans, waited to return to the island but soon realized he would not be going back. He followed the family tradition and studied medicine at Emory University in Atlanta, where he met his wife. After stints in Dallas and San Diego, they moved to Georgia, where they have lived since the 1970s. He said that his patients, and most people in Dalton, have little or no idea of his connection to Cuba. In fact, for a long time he accepted, and even encouraged, the mispronunciation of his own name, the more Southern *Lew-is*. "I have an accent but they think it's some kind of weird Southern accent," he said. "I'm amazed how many out there have no idea I was born in Cuba."

Dalton, Georgia—like so many American communities—connects in differing ways to the variety and diversity of experiences within Latin America: third-generation Mexican-Americans teaching in the schools; first-generation Guatemalans speaking neither Spanish nor English; a Cuban doctor who thrived in the United States after the revolution; and a Nuyorican who decided to try out southern living. In this quiet mountain town, and across the United States, the Hispanic past continues to live in the present.

THE HISTORIAN SAMUEL Huntington argued in the early 2000s that the arrival of Hispanics in large numbers was a direct threat to the United States, a view that continues to resonate for many. He wrote that "America was created by 17th- and 18th-century settlers who were overwhelmingly white, British, and Protestant. Their values, institutions, and culture provided the foundation for and shaped the development of the United States in the following centuries."[7] Such a view is misguided, not least because it appears to draw from only one part of the country. The United States' values, institutions, and culture were not formed just in New England, or in a vacuum. To a considerable degree they were shaped by interaction with the Spanish, Mexican, and other Hispanic people in North America, as well as with wider Latin America. Some of this interaction was oppositional—Spanish Catholic as opposed to British Protestant, for instance—yet on the other hand, Spain came to the aid of the fledgling United States during the Revolutionary War. The West that Spain lost when its empire crumbled became the future for the United States. Westward expansion remains part of the national psyche; the search for new horizons began on the same landmass. The United States learned what it meant to be a regional power and, soon afterward, a global one, first taking Native American lands, then 51 percent of Mexico in 1848, before going on to acquire Puerto Rico in 1898, all of which contributed to the might it had to engage in later military operations around the world.

Much of what happened in the nineteenth-century West became shrouded in the nostalgia of conquest, turning an often violent and unjust process into a fantasy world reflected by images throughout popular culture: gracious Spanish señoritas, rough-and-ready cowboys, and loyal Indians, but no land-grabbing or lynchings.

The reality of that time was far more troubled and complex. The addition of people who had lived in part of New Spain presented a number of serious problems, including how they could fit into the larger panorama of the United States. Some felt they had no option but to invoke the chimera of "whiteness"; others could not escape their brown skin, yet they were not "black"; still others were considered "Indian," and not European, despite being a bit of both. The idea of race could be stretched only so far, and its shortcomings were evident in attempts to place Hispanic people in the black-white dichotomy that had evolved during and after the era of slavery in the United States. More than a century on, the consequences of such racialized thinking have become painfully clear.

To be "American" continues, in some quarters, to signify whiteness, Protestantism, and the English language. In the aftermath of the 2016 election, the writer Toni Morrison observed: "Unlike any nation in Europe, the United States holds whiteness as the unifying force. Here, for many people, the definition of 'Americanness' is color."[8] The struggle of Hispanic people against such discrimination and the gains they made have also become part of the American story. Hispanics in the nineteenth century fought for their land, their rights, and their place in

the United States. By the twentieth, they were fighting for the United
States as soldiers, and later for equal access to all the opportunities the
nation had to offer them as citizens. Hispanics, however, unlike some
other immigrant groups, have continued to arrive over the decades,
and where they are living is changing: Los Angeles and Miami may
continue to top the list, but places like Dalton, Georgia, are no longer
exceptions.[9]

Some of the charges leveled against Hispanic culture seem to echo
the anti-Catholic Black Legend about the cruel conquistador. Samuel Huntington also invoked it, as he saw immigrants as people with
"dual nationalities and dual loyalties" due to their Spanish language
and Catholic religion.[10] The theorist of decoloniality Walter Mignolo
challenged Huntington's ideas, saying, "Five hundred years after the
expulsion of the Moors from the Iberian Peninsula and five hundred
years after the invasion and invention of America, Samuel Huntington
identified the Moors as enemies of Western civilization and Hispanics
(that is Latinos and Latinas) as a challenge to Anglo identity in the
United States," adding that the "specter of the Black Legend is still
alive and well, contributing to diminishing Spaniards in Europe, mar-
ginalizing 'Latins' in South America, and criminalizing Latinos and
Latinas in the United States."[11]

Indeed, the loyalties Huntington worried about are not inflexible.
People can speak Spanish and be Catholic and still enjoy aspects of U.S.
culture, not least apple pie and baseball. By the same token, Anglo Protestant Americans can enjoy eating tacos and listening to Cuban music and
not disavow their background and religion. The cultural combinations
that are possible in the modern United States are endless. The question
the United States faces at the moment is how—or if—these two visions
will be reconciled: will it be by assimilation, or variation, or, eschewing
such binaries, some sort of combination?

One of the consolations of history is that although events themselves
cannot be undone, the way they are thought about can be revisited and,
if needed, revised. This has happened—and continues—with regard to
the reality and the legacy of slavery in the United States. Such reassessments are also necessarily taking place about the Hispanic past. Hispanic

people were part of the past of the United States, and they will be part of tomorrow, too.

⁓

From the vista of Mexico City, the heart of the Spanish empire for three hundred years, *El Norte* was a poor and barren place, while the capital was rich in history, ranging from its ancient Mexica temples to lavish Catholic Baroque churches. The mythic north was little more than a myth for many years—Cíbola was never found.

Mexico remains immersed in a dense history, with all corners containing ruins, churches, missions, and other remnants of its turbulent past. Many of its most important traditions, such as the Day of the Dead, a love of large and symbolic murals, and the devotion to the Virgin of Guadalupe, have their roots in pre-Columbian practices, but the colonial past is ever-present. In the middle of Mexico City, on the wide, tree-lined Paseo De Reforma, there is a statue of Christopher Columbus, gesturing toward the horizon. The statue and the plinth have at times been splattered by red paint, giving the appearance of a chest wound. The authorities are forever cleaning up, but Columbus is defaced time and again.

Mexico has, in some ways, a pragmatic approach to its history, as three of its museums illustrate. The Museum of the Viceroyalty (Museo Nacional del Virreinato) in Tepotzotlán, near Mexico City, is dedicated to artifacts from the colonial era. A small building in central Mexico City—Museo de las Constituciones—is devoted to Mexico's three constitutions and the struggle to create, reform, and preserve them. The National Museum of Interventions (Museo Nacional de las Intervenciones), housed in a seventeenth-century monastery, is nothing if not honest about the many foreign invasions, including those by the United States, that the Mexican republic has endured and, indeed, overcome.

History in the United States often seems, by comparison, a mere adolescent, subject to moodiness and outbursts, taking constructive criticism personally. In the Edna Ferber novel *Giant*, about the fortunes of a Texas ranching family, the East Coast heroine Leslie Lynnton (later brought to life in the movie version by Elizabeth Taylor) asks Bick Benedict (played by Rock Hudson), the Texas rancher she would go on to marry: "We really stole Texas, didn't we?"

Ferber wrote:

> He jumped as if he touched a live wire. His eyes were agate. He wait-
> ed a moment before he trusted himself to speak. "I don't understand
> the joke," he finally said through stiff lips. He thought how many men
> had been killed in Texas for saying so much less than this thing that
> had been said to him.
>
> "I'm not joking, Mr Benedict. It's right there in the history books,
> isn't it? This Mr. Austin moved down there with two or three hundred
> families from the East, it says, and the Mexicans were polite and said
> they could settle and homestead if they wanted to, under the rule of
> Mexico. And the next thing you know they're claiming they want to
> free themselves from Mexico and they fight and take it. Really! How
> impolite."

Although Bick is angered by her words—"if she had been a man he would have hit her, he told himself"—they end up falling in love and Leslie goes with him to Texas.[12]

History remains full of sore spots, and one that lingers is the question of where the story of Hispanic people fits in the national narrative. There have been efforts at inclusion. National Hispanic Heritage Month, which runs from September 15 to October 15 every year, aims to celebrate "the histories, cultures and contributions of American citizens whose ancestors came from Spain, Mexico, the Caribbean, and Central and South America." Still, though, there remain many cultural and historical blind spots. In 2014, Bernardo de Gálvez, who helped the Continental Army during the Revolutionary War, was granted honorary U.S. citizenship by the House Judiciary Committee even though, as a news report noted, "some of its members said they had never heard of him." The effort was led by Jeff Miller, a former U.S. representative from Florida, whose constituency included Pensacola, the town Gálvez took from the British in 1781. A bust of the Spaniard overlooks the town from Fort George, with the words "Yo Solo" (I alone) commemorating his entry into the bay and larger contribution to the American Revolution. At the time John Conyers, representative from Michigan, told the media: "I would be less than candid if I say this is a familiar name in American history."[13]

The research for this project took me into Mexico and across the border and the borderlands, from Florida to California, up the West Coast to Canada, and into other states, including New York, Tennessee, and Alabama. Spanish place-names rolled past, along with the miles: St. Augustine, San Antonio, Los Angeles, sharing the map with towns named for Native American, French, and British locations. Some I found while pounding the pavement, for instance looking up one day in New York City to see that East 116th Street is also named Luis Muñoz Marín Boulevard.

I traveled along El Camino Real de los Tejas highway, calling in at mission churches up and down the spine of California; reading plinths and pillars everywhere from the St. Johns River in Jacksonville to the main square in Sonoma, California; and taking photographs of every kitschy neon hotel sign with a conquistador that I saw. I drove to Hidalgo, Texas, to see if something there honors Mexico's Padre Hidalgo, and indeed found a statue in the middle of that tiny town, which sits just across the Río Grande from Reynosa, Mexico. While in Puerto Palomas, Mexico, I couldn't fail to notice a 2001 monument to Pancho Villa, who crossed the border there on his raid into New Mexico. In a small plaza in that Chihuahua town, tucked just off the main street that runs between the two nations, Villa continues to ride along the border atop a galloping horse, a twin to the likeness in Tucson.

How a statue of Villa ended up in Tucson is a reminder of the power of these symbols.[14] In 1981, this controversial monument was given to the city, intended by Mexican officials and members of the journalists' association Agrupación Nacional Periodista to be a gift of friendship and a sign of the shared struggle for justice on both sides of the border. Not everyone saw it that way. Many Tucson residents were horrified at a monument honoring a man who raided the United States and killed some of its citizens, and lawsuits to stop its installation soon followed. In the end, however, supporters of the fourteen-foot statue persevered, and around six hundred people gathered to watch its unveiling at Veinte de Agosto Park, a small patch of grass in downtown Tucson ringed by busy roads, near La Placita, one of the city's traditional plazas.

The statue's sculptor, Julián Martínez, was then commissioned in 1987 to produce a fifteen-foot equestrian statue of Father Eusebio Kino, considered by many to be the founder of Arizona. The priest was a true symbol of the struggle for justice, his supporters claimed, and he was also the patron saint of the modern Sunbelt because, in their eyes, he had imposed order through Christianity and developed the vast plains with ranching and agriculture. Today the Kino statue inhabits a patch of dusty earth on a corner of Kino Parkway. He sits up straight in his saddle, though his horse looks weary, with its head low, but determined to finish the journey. A portly Villa, by contrast, is depicted atop a much livelier steed, one that looks as if it was about to leap off the plinth and head for Mexico. For the historian Geraldo Cadava, who has studied the statues and their multiple meanings, both Villa and Kino evoke the tensions over how people in Tucson think about their history, but they have their place, he argues, as "giant weights that hold together seemingly fractured geographies and communities."[15]

The real and imagined Hispanic past of the United States can be found in so many places: along the sea, on both sides of the border, in a forgotten corner of a military base, or in the middle of Manhattan. Of course, some of the cultural memory is reductive and even a bit silly, for instance the Fountain of Youth site in St. Augustine. There are also the newer, hybrid traditions, embodied, for instance, in the young ladies known as the "Marthas" of Laredo, Texas, the most Hispanic city in the United States. These are the privileged young women who are presented at the annual Society of Martha Washington Colonial Pageant and Ball. The event is in honor of George Washington's birthday on February 22, even though he died before Texas was ever a gleam in an expansionist's eye. The young women don elaborate and expensive dresses, which can often take months to make, for their social debut. Is this the merging of cultures, or an expression of U.S. cultural hegemony? A double-consciousness more in line with a colonial past, or the expression of a multicultural present?

One of my final stops was at the Capitol Visitor Center in Washington, D.C. In the main hall are two statues, almost directly across from each other, separated only by the snaking queue of tourists waiting to buy tickets. One is Po'pay, the Pueblo Revolt leader, carved out of white marble.

He looks off into the distance, holding a knotted rope of the sort used to pass secret messages, a potent symbol of the 1680 uprising. On the other side of the ticket hall, cast in bronze, Father Eusebio Kino appears once more, this time holding his right hand up, as if bestowing a blessing on the visitors. Near his foot is a small cactus, emblematic of his work in the desert. These two men are contributions from their respective states, New Mexico and Arizona. Each of the fifty states has contributed two figures of historical significance to the National Statuary Hall, though some of these sculptures have been placed in the Visitor Center. Among those inside the Statuary Hall is California's Junípero Serra. These are complicated choices. Po'pay represents the spirit of resistance to European incursion, while Kino and Serra are reminders of the legacy of colonization and the connection to Europe, in recent times a point of contention. In 2015, Serra was controversially canonized, with his detractors claiming that he represented the oppression and destruction of Native American culture. As discussions continue over the removal of Confederate monuments placed throughout the South during the Jim Crow era—an issue that became a flash point in the summer of 2017—it is worth reflecting on how the Hispanic past is commemorated as well. What do the representations of Villa, or Hidalgo, or Kino say about the parts of this history that are allowed to be incorporated into the larger national narrative?

In the summer of 2016, news came from Parris Island, South Carolina, of a significant discovery. Archaeologists using technology that can measure changes in magnetic fields were at last able to pinpoint the site of San Marcos, one of the seventeenth-century forts built by the Spanish at the Santa Elena site. The autumn before, in late 2015, researchers at the University of West Florida unearthed sixteenth-century ceramic shards, nails, and other remains from the short-lived Spanish settlement put on Pensacola Bay by Tristán de Luna in 1559.[16] All around these sites, submerged in the peninsular waters of Florida, lie Spanish shipwrecks, awaiting discovery. The landscape contains what the eye sometimes cannot see.

The long and complex history of the Spanish and Hispanics is inescapably entwined with that of the United States; it is not a separate history of outsiders or interlopers, but one that is central to how the United States has and will continue to develop. The United States is part of the *Americas* and likewise the people of the Americas are part of the United States.

Time Line
of Key Events

1492–1600

1492—Christopher Columbus lands in Hispaniola, claims the island for the monarchs of Castile and Aragon.

1494—The Treaty of Tordesillas divides the Americas between Spanish and Portuguese spheres of influence.

1508—Juan Ponce de León claims the island of Puerto Rico for Spain.

1511—Diego Velázquez de Cuéllar leads an expedition to Cuba.

1513—Juan Ponce de León lands in Florida while searching for the island of Bimini.

1519—Hernán Cortés sets off for Mexico. Álvarez de Píneda sails along the Gulf coast of Florida, Alabama, and Mississippi.

1521—The Mexica empire falls to Spain, becoming New Spain (Nueva España). Ponce de León returns to Florida, but is injured in a battle and dies in Cuba. Pedro de Quejo lands in Winyah Bay (near Myrtle Beach, South Carolina).

1525—Pedro de Quejo reconnoiters the Atlantic coast as far north as Cape Fear, North Carolina, also naming the Punta de Santa Elena (today's Parris Island, South Carolina).

1526—Lucas Vázquez de Ayllón attempts to take settlers to Winyah Bay, but instead ends up farther south, somewhere around Sapelo Sound in Georgia, establishing the first Spanish settlement in North America, San Miguel de Gualdape.

1528—Pánfilo de Narváez makes a failed attempt to colonize Florida, landing around Tampa.

1532—Spain launches a campaign to control the Inca empire and Peru, extending its reach into South America.

1533—Fortún Jiménez crosses the Gulf of California, reaching the Baja Peninsula.

1535—Hernando Cortés sails to Baja California in search of pearls.

1536—Álvar Núñez Cabeza de Vaca and three other survivors from the disastrous Narváez expedition resurface in northern New Spain.

1539—Hernando de Soto lands in Florida. Francisco de Ulloa further explores the Gulf of California. Fray Marcos de Niza goes to the frontier of New Spain and claims to have seen the fabled Seven Cities of Cíbola.

1540—On the basis of Fray Marco de Niza's report, Francisco Vázquez de Coronado sets off for the cities of Cíbola, but fails to find them.

1542—Juan Rodríguez Cabrillo makes a reconnaissance of California's coastline. De Soto dies somewhere around modern Arkansas or Louisiana.

1559—Tristán de Luna y Arellano's Florida expedition lands near Pensacola, Florida.

1562—French Huguenots sail into the St. Johns River, near modern Jacksonville, Florida, before going north to Port Royale, South Carolina, establishing their Charlesfort settlement, which they abandoned the following year.

1564—The French return to the St. Johns River in Florida, this time establishing Fort Caroline on a bluff overlooking the river.

1565—Pedro Menéndez de Avilés establishes the first permanent settlement in Florida, in St. Augustine, on the Atlantic coast, and proceeds to drive the French out of Fort Caroline. In the Pacific, the Spanish add the Philippines to their empire.

1566—Fort San Felipe founded by the Spanish near the old Charlesfort site in Santa Elena. Juan Pardo goes on an expedition into the interior, through parts of modern North Carolina.

1567—Pardo makes a second inland trip, returning in the spring of 1568 having possibly reached modern Tennessee.

1568—Dominique de Gourgues arrives from France to avenge the deaths of his follow Frenchmen, attacking and killing Spanish troops at San Mateo (the former Fort Caroline) before returning to France.

1577—Pedro Menéndez Marquez is ordered to fortify Santa Elena; this leads to the construction of Fort San Marcos.

1579—Francis Drake arrives in northern California, naming it Nova Albion (New England).

1586—Francis Drake attacks St. Augustine.

1587—Santa Elena is abandoned and its residents are moved to St. Augustine.

1597—There is an uprising led by the Guale, also known as Juanillo's Revolt, against the Spanish missions.

1598—Juan de Oñate leaves for New Mexico to establish a Spanish settlement.

1600–1700

1602—Sebastián Vizcaino manages to reach Cape Mendocino, California, naming Monterey and San Diego along the way.

1607—English settlers establish the Virginia Colony.

1609—Francisco Fernández de Écija explores the coast of the Carolinas, reaching Chesapeake Bay, in a search for signs of English activity.

1610—Santa Fe (Nuevo Mexico) founded.

1620—The *Mayflower* lands, and its Pilgrim settlers establish Plymouth Colony.

1670—The English settlement of Charles Town (today's Charleston, South Carolina) is established.

1680—The Pueblo Revolt against the Spanish begins, as Native Americans drive out Spanish settlers from many of the pueblos, leaving some five hundred dead and forcing them south of the Río Grande, to El Paso.

1682—René-Robert Cavelier, Sieur de La Salle, travels down the Mississippi River and claims the area for France, calling it La Louisiane in honor of Louis XIV.

1683—The Jesuits, led by Eusebio Kino, begin to explore Baja California, later building missions there.

1700–1800

1701—Europe becomes engulfed in the War of the Spanish Succession, and the conflict reaches North America the following year in Queen Anne's War.

1706—Alburquerque (Nuevo Mexico) founded.

1714—War of the Spanish Succession ends, and the British are ceded much of French Canada; they also win the slave *asiento,* a lucrative contract permitting them the right to supply Spanish America with African slaves.

1718—A military presidio, San Antonio de Béxar, is built in southern Texas. It is followed by the construction of the mission San Antonio de Valero, later known as the Alamo. In Louisiana, La Nouvelle-Orléans (New Orleans) is founded.

1721—The Spanish continue to fortify Texas, adding the presidio of Nuestra Señora de la Bahía de Espíritu Santo de Zúñiga on the Gulf coast, though it is later moved.

1732—British settlers are granted a charter to put a debtor colony between the Savannah and Altamaha Rivers, creating Georgia.

1754—The French and Indian War begins in the upper Ohio River Valley, and this conflict later segues into the Seven Years' War that erupts in Europe in 1756.

1762—The French sign a secret treaty ceding the Louisiana territory to Spain, in order to keep it out of British hands.

1763—Under the terms of the Treaty of Paris, which ends the Seven Years' War, Britain is given Spanish Florida in exchange for returning Havana, which it occupied in 1762, to Spain. The British divide Florida into East and West. The

Spanish retain the Louisiana territory, while France loses its Canadian regions and some Caribbean islands.

1767—Spain's Carlos III banishes the Jesuit order from the entire Spanish realm.

1769—The "Sacred Expedition" to California begins, and San Diego de Alcalá is founded.

1774—Juan Pérez reaches as far as N 55°, around the Haida Gwaii island (Queen Charlotte Islands). Juan Baustista de Anza starts his journey overland from New Mexico to California.

1775—The American Revolution begins. Juan Francisco Bodega y Quadra is dispatched to explore the northernmost reaches of Spain's Alta California; he makes another trip in 1779.

1776—Benjamin Franklin holds secret talks with the Count of Aranda, the Spanish ambassador to France, in hopes of securing support.

1777—Bernado de Gálvez arrives as governor of Louisiana.

1778—Captain James Cook sails into Nootka Bay.

1779—Spain enters the American Revolution, following France's decision to back the rebels in 1778. Gálvez organizes his West Florida Campaign.

1781—Gálvez takes Pensacola from the British. The town of Los Angeles in Alta California is founded.

1783—The Treaty of Paris brings the conflict between Britain and its thirteen colonies, France, and Spain to an end. Florida returns to Spanish control.

1790—Competing claims to Nootka Sound by the British and Spanish renew hostilities between the two nations. Spain agrees to the first of three conventions ceding it to British claims.

1800–1900

1803—The United States buys the Louisiana territory from France, which had signed a treaty to take it back from Spain.

1808—Napoleon Bonaparte invades Spain and places his brother on the Spanish throne.

1810—The short-lived Republic of West Florida is declared in September, with U.S. troops taking control of part of the area by December. In New Spain, Padre Miguel Hidalgo issues his *grito,* or cry, of Dolores, rebelling against Spanish officials.

1812—Independence of East Florida is declared in March, but unravels after a failed attack on St. Augustine. War of 1812 begins over British and U.S. disputed land in Canada. Spain issues a constitution.

1814—Peninsular War in Spain ends and Fernando VII is restored to the throne, where he rejects the reforms in the 1812 constitution. In the United States, Andrew Jackson attacks Pensacola, temporarily taking it from the Spanish.

1818—Andrew Jackson takes Pensacola again, this time permanently.

1819—The Adams-Onís Treaty is signed, ceding both East and West Florida to the United States.

1821—Mexico issues its Declaration of Independence.

1822—Agustín de Iturbide becomes Mexico's emperor, Agustín I. The United States recognizes Mexico's independence.

1823—Anglo settlers, led by Stephen Austin, begin to arrive in East Texas.

1824—The Mexican empire is replaced by a republic with a president, and a constitution is drawn up. Mexico also bans the slave trade. In California, the Chumash revolt, attacking three missions.

1826—The Edwards brothers try to declare independence from Mexico and briefly establish the Republic of Fredonia near Nacogdoches, Texas.

1829—Spain loses a battle in Tampico in an attempt to retake Mexico. Later that year slavery is abolished in Mexico.

1830—The Mexican government passes legislation to curb immigration from the United States.

1836—Anglo settlers in Texas declare their independence from Mexico on March 2. Mexican troops, led by Antonio López de Santa Anna, rout rebelling Anglos at the Battle of the Alamo on March 6. The Anglos manage to win the Battle of San Jacinto on April 21, securing Texan independence, which Mexico refuses to recognize.

1845—Texas is admitted to the union as a slave state.

1846—The Mexican-American War begins.

1848—The Treaty of Guadalupe Hidalgo is signed, bringing the Mexican-American War to an end. The United States is ceded Mexico's Alta California and New Mexico territories—51 percent of its land. That territory today comprises California, New Mexico, Arizona, Utah, Nevada, and part of Wyoming and Colorado.

1849—Joint United States and Mexican Boundary Commission surveys the border, a project that lasts nearly seven years. The gold rush in California begins.

1850–51—Narciso López makes two failed efforts, with the backing of slaveholding southerners, to free Cuba from Spanish rule.

1853—Mexico agrees to the Gadsden Purchase and the United States pays $10 million for the Mesilla valley, a strip of land south of the Gila River—today's southern Arizona and New Mexico. President Franklin Pierce offers Spain $130 million for Cuba. The U.S. filibuster William Walker lands in Baja and declares himself president of Lower California.

1861—The U.S. Civil War begins. Texas joins the Confederacy, and a Confederate territory of Arizona is established.

1862—Battle of Glorieta Pass on March 26–28 leads to the Confederates being driven out of New Mexico. France sends troops to Mexico.

1864—Austrian archduke Ferdinand Maximilian Joseph becomes Mexico's Maximilian I.

1865—The U.S. Civil War ends.

1867—Maximilian I is executed and Benito Juárez returns to power in Mexico.

1868—The Ten Years' War begins in Cuba, while Puerto Rico's attempt at a rebellion, the *Grito de Lares*, is suppressed.

1873—Slavery is abolished in Puerto Rico.

1878—The pact of Zanjón ends Cuba's Ten Years' War, but leaves the Spanish in power.

1886—Slavery ends in Cuba.

1895—The Cuban War of Independence begins.

1898—The USS *Maine* explodes in Havana's harbor on February 15 and Spanish-American-Cuban War is declared by April and is over by the summer. Cuba is placed under temporary U.S. administration, but Puerto Rico and the Philippines are put under full U.S. rule.

1900–2000s

1910—Francisco Madero issues his Plan de San Luis Postosi in Mexico, calling for the end of the existing regime and triggering a series of uprisings and political transformations over the next decade, known as the Mexican Revolution.

1911—Porfirio Díaz is forced from office, and Francisco Madero elected president.

1912—The states of New Mexico and Arizona join the United States.

1914—First World War begins. The Panama Canal opens.

1916—Francisco "Pancho" Villa and his men raid Columbus, New Mexico, and U.S. troops are sent on a Punitive Expedition against him.

1917—Jones-Shafroth Act grants Puerto Ricans U.S. citizenship. The United States enters First World War. The Immigration Act of 1917 is issued. Mexico draws up a new constitution.

1919—Johnston McCulley publishes his first *Zorro* story.

1924—The Johnson-Reed Act puts immigration quotas in place, and also establishes the Border Patrol.

1931—Some 40,000 Mexicans leave California as immigration raids are made across larger U.S. cities. By the end of the decade some 400,000 Mexicans leave the United States.

1936—Puerto Rican independence leader Pedro Albizu Campos is imprisoned after two members of his Nationalist Party assassinate the police commissioner in response to the killing of party members in 1935.

1937—Members of Puerto Rico's Nationalist Party and island police exchange fire in what becomes known as the Ponce Massacre, leaving twenty dead.

1938—Lázaro Cárdenas expropriates the oil industry in Mexico, after a series of crippling strikes.

1939—The Second World War begins in Europe.

1940—Luis Muñoz Marín, leader of Puerto Rico's Popular Democratic Party, is elected president of the Puerto Rican senate.

1941—The United States enters the Second World War.

1942—The Bracero program begins, granting seasonal visas for Mexican workers to come to the United States

1943—The zoot suit riots take place in Los Angeles. Anita Brenner publishes *The Wind That Swept Mexico*.

1945—Second World War ends. In California, Mexican parents go to court to fight school segregation in what would be landmark *Mendez v. Westminster* case.

1946—The United States passes legislation allowing Puerto Ricans to vote for their own governor.

1948—Luis Muñoz Marín is elected governor of Puerto Rico.

1950—There is an armed uprising in Puerto Rico in October as the island nears a referendum to approve a constitution, stifling the independence movement. On November 1, two nationalists in the United States make a failed attempt to assassinate President Harry Truman. Nationalist leader Albizu Campos is arrested again.

1951—Puerto Rico votes in favor of Public Law 600, paving the way for a constitution.

1952—Puerto Rico becomes a Commonwealth, or Estado Libre Asociado, of the United States. The Immigration and Nationalization Act (also known as the McCarran-Walter Act) passes, upholding the quotas of the Immigration Act of 1924 and also introducing preferences for skilled workers and family reunification.

1953—Fidel Castro launches an attack on the Moncada Barracks in Santiago, Cuba.

1959—The Cuban Revolution, under the leadership of Fidel Castro, takes power. President Fulgencio Batista flees the island.

1961—Cuban forces defeat CIA-backed exiles' attack on the island at the Bay of Pigs.

1962—Cuba, the Soviet Union, and the United States face off in the Cuban missile crisis. César Chavez and Dolores Huerta set up the National Farm Workers Association, the forerunner of United Farm Workers.

1963—Mexico and the United States sign a treaty settling the long-running dispute over the Chamizal strip of land in the Río Grande.

1964—The *bracero* visa program for Mexican workers ends.

1965—The Hart-Celler Act overhauls the immigration system, with 120,000 visas now allotted for the entire Western Hemisphere. A decade later this is amended to give each nation a quota of 20,000.

1980—Fidel Castro lifts restrictions on emigration, and the United States sees the arrival of more than 100,000 Cubans in what was called the Mariel boatlift.

1986—The Immigration Reform and Control Act legalizes the status of undocumented people who had been in the United States since 1982.

1994—North American Free Trade Agreement (NAFTA) comes into force. A rebellion over land use starts in the Mexican state of Chiapas, led by a group calling themselves the Zapatistas.

1996—The Illegal Immigration Reform and Immigrant Responsibility Act gives more funding to the Border Patrol.

2005—The Secure Border Initiative aims to use surveillance and monitoring technology to further fortify the U.S.-Mexico frontier.

2006—The Secure Fence Act leads to about 650 miles of fencing along the U.S.-Mexican border. A wave of marches and rallies takes place in support of Hispanic immigrants and against proposed legislation that included provisions to make it a felony to be in the United States illegally, causing the bill to be shelved.

2012—The Deferred Action for Childhood Arrivals (DACA) program is established, delaying deportation for some undocumented people who came to the United States as children.

2014—The United States and Cuba announced a normalization of relations, including the release of political prisoners and the loosening of travel restrictions.

2016—Donald Trump is elected U.S. president, promising to build a wall on the border with Mexico.

2017—Before leaving office, Barack Obama ends the Cuban Adjustment Act, which had given preferential treatment to Cubans, as part of ongoing opening of relations with Cuba. In the summer, Donald Trump rolls back the Obama deal. In September, a category 4 hurricane, Maria, slams into Puerto Rico, devastating the island.

Acknowledgments

W RITING AND RESEARCHING this book involved a tremendous voyage through the present as much as the past, and I am very thankful to have had so many people supporting me along the way. I would first like to thank the team at Grove Atlantic, not least my editor, George Gibson, whose insightful comments and suggestions added a great deal to this book; as well as his predecessor Jamison Stolz and publisher Morgan Entrekin, who were enthusiastic about the idea from the start. My gratitude also goes to Emily Burns and Julia Berner-Tobin for all their help and patience. Many thanks, too, to my agent, Bill Hamilton, for his ongoing support.

Special thanks go to my very generous friends who took time to read earlier chapters, or, indeed, entire drafts. Thank you to Andrea Acle-Kreysing, Juan Cobo Betancourt, Teresa Cribelli, J. Michael Francis, and Juan José Ponce-Vázquez. Also, a big thank you to Rory Foster for helping me keep my comma usage, and my facts, straight. Any subsequent errors, despite their efforts, are my own.

I was also fortunate to have the opportunity to work out some of my ideas through presenting seminar papers, and would like to thank Eduardo Posada-Carbó at the Latin American Centre at the University of Oxford and Kate Quinn, Gad Heuman, and Steve Cushion at the UCL Institute of the Americas Caribbean seminar for their interest in this project. A book like this could not exist without the work of so many others, and I am profoundly grateful that there is such a rich and diverse historiography from which to draw.

★　★　★

The travel for this book was extensive. Starting in Tennessee and Georgia, I'd like to thank my family, especially my mom and dad, whose homes were the hubs for my travel, as well as my brothers and extended family. In Georgia, thanks also go to Benjamin Carr, Hollie Cope, Beth and Nick Gadd, and Crystal and Teague Paulk-Buchanan. Special thanks are due to the Dalton High School class of 1994. My classmates threw a great twentieth reunion, and some even helped me contact the necessary people for my research. A special thank-you goes to the generosity of the Viamonte family.

Over the course of my travels, I stopped at a lot of U.S. national parks, where I was impressed and touched by the obvious enthusiasm of the staff. The parks were one of the real joys of this trip, and the National Park Service employees deserve a great deal of gratitude for the work they do.

In South Carolina, Eric and Charlotte Rayburn were, as always, exemplary hosts. In Florida, David and Rebecca Ferguson's generosity allowed me to explore Pensacola, and Michael Deibert helped me make sense of Miami. The staffs at the St. Augustine Historical Society, the University of South Florida, and the University of West Florida were generous with their time. Farther north, in New York City, thanks go to Jennifer and Dana Burleson, Christine de la Garza, and Reynaldo Ortiz-Minaya. The Hunter College Centro de Estudios Puertorriqueños and the New York Public Library's Schomburg Center for Research in Black Culture continue to be wonderful places to work.

Heading west, I found it a delight to make numerous trips to Arizona, and thanks go to Carol Brochin, Kira Dixon-Weinstein, Ceci Garcia, Valarie James, and Lauren Raine. In Texas, it was lovely to have Ernesto J. Cavazos and Kristal Gaston meet me while I was making my way around the exceptionally helpful special collections at the University of Houston, Rice University, Texas A&M Corpus Christi, and the wonderful Dolph Briscoe Center for American History at the University of Texas at Austin. Thanks are also due to Tony and Carla Hughes for their hospitality in Harlingen. In New Mexico, a very big thank-you goes to Joseph Martin for my tour of Acoma Sky City. Thanks, too, go to the University of New Mexico Center for Southwestern Research and Special Collections in Albuquerque, and the New Mexico State University Special Collection in Las Cruces.

On the West Coast, the Bancroft Library at the University of California Berkeley was a rich repository, and it was also a delight for me to talk history with Elena Schneider while I was in town. Farther up the coast, special thanks go to Renee Koplan for my memorable stay in Lopez Island, Washington. A big thank-you as well to Julie Schimunek and the crew of the MV Uchuck III for helping me reach Nootka Sound.

A few thousand miles away in Cuba, Jorge Renato Ibarra Guitart was once again a great help, as was Angelina Rojas Blaquier. It was always a pleasure to stay with Armando and Betty Gutiérrez at my Cuban home away from home. At the Instituto de Historia de Cuba, thanks go to René González Barrios and Yoel Cordoví Núñez, with a special thank-you to Belkis Quesada Guerra. In Puerto Rico, thanks go to Héctor Feliciano and María Concepción for their hospitality.

In Mexico City, many thanks are due to Lourdes Aguirre for her generosity in showing us so many of Mexico's fabulous historical sites. Thanks also to Anne Staples, Ryan Jordan, Ricardo Fagoaga, and Isabel Povea Moreno. It was an added treat to cross paths with Iris Montero while we were both visiting the capital.

My friends in the U.K. and Europe have been listening to me talk about this book for years, and for that alone they deserve a shout-out: thanks go to David Batty, Mark Berry, Victoria Burgher, Lucas Cavazos, Chloe Stockford, Yvonne Singh, Tiffany Ferris and Chris Hall, Vicky Frost and Anthony Pickles, Lisa and Simon Hill, Mariama Ifode-Blease and Oliver Blease, Diana Siclovan and Josh Newton, Anne-Isabelle Richard and Alexandre Afonso.

More gratitude than I could fit on these pages is due to my husband, Chris Stanford, whose patience, humor, and generosity have helped me navigate the sometimes rocky logistical and emotional terrain of researching and writing a book like this. Finally, I must thank my dear friend and brother, Matthew Cavazos, who introduced me to the world of the border with his tales of growing up in Texas. Little did he know, a few years later he would be my guide through El Norte. This book is for him.

Selected Bibliography

I have included here more recent books or classic texts in English that might be of interest to the nonspecialist reader. For a full list of primary and secondary sources consulted in English and Spanish, see carriegibson.co.uk.

Acuña, Rodolfo. *Occupied America: A History of Chicanos.* 3rd ed. New York: Harper & Row, 1988.

Anderson, Benedict. *Imagined Communities: Reflections on the Origin and Spread of Nationalism.* Rev. ed. London: Verso Books, 1991.

Anzaldúa, Gloria. *Borderlands/La Frontera: The New Mesitza.* 4th ed. San Francisco: Aunt Lute Books, 2012.

Arellano, Gustavo. *Taco USA: How Mexican Food Conquered America.* New York: Scribner, 2012.

Aron, Stephen. *American Confluence: The Missouri Frontier from Borderland to Border State.* Bloomington: Indiana University Press, 2006.

Ayala, César J. *American Sugar Kingdom: The Plantation Economy of the Spanish Caribbean, 1898–1934.* Chapel Hill: University of North Carolina Press, 1999.

———, and Rafael Bernabe. *Puerto Rico in the American Century: A History Since 1898.* Chapel Hill: University of North Carolina Press, 2007.

Balderrama, Francisco E., and Raymond Rodríguez. *Decade of Betrayal: Mexican Repatriation in the 1930s.* Albuquerque: University of New Mexico Press, 1995.

Balsera, Viviana Díaz, and Rachel A. May, eds. *La Florida: Five Hundred Years of Hispanic Presence.* Gainesville: University Press of Florida, 2014.

Beltrán, Cristina. *The Trouble with Unity: Latino Politics and the Creation of Identity.* Oxford: Oxford University Press, 2010.

Brading, D. A. *The First America: The Spanish Monarchy, Creole Patriots, and the Liberal State, 1492–1867.* Cambridge: Cambridge University Press, 1991.

Brenner, Anita. *The Wind That Swept Mexico: The History of the Mexican Revolution, 1910–1942.* Photography assembled by George R. Leighton. Austin: University of Texas Press, 1971.

Brioso, César. *Havana Hardball: Spring Training, Jackie Robinson, and the Cuban League.* Gainesville: University Press of Florida, 2015.

Cadava, Geraldo L. *Standing on Common Ground: The Making of a Sunbelt Borderland.* Cambridge, Mass.: Harvard University Press, 2013. Kindle e-book.

Calloway, Colin G. *One Vast Winter Count: The Native American West Before Lewis and Clark.* Lincoln: University of Nebraska Press, 2003.

Carrigan, William D., and Clive Webb. *Forgotten Dead: Mob Violence Against Mexicans in the United States, 1848–1928.* Oxford: Oxford University Press, 2013.

Clayton, Lawrence A. *Bartolomé de las Casas: A Biography.* Cambridge: Cambridge University Press, 2012.

Clendinnen, Inga. *Ambivalent Conquests: Maya and Spaniard in Yucatan, 1517–1570.* Cambridge: Cambridge University Press, 1987.

Cohen, Deborah. *Braceros: Migrant Citizens and Transnational Subjects in the Postwar United States and Mexico.* Chapel Hill: University of North Carolina Press, 2011.

Coronado, Raúl. *A World Not to Come: A History of Latino Writing and Print Culture.* Cambridge, Mass.: Harvard University Press, 2013.

Deibert, Michael. *In the Shadow of Saint Death: The Gulf Cartel and the Price of America's Drug War in Mexico.* Guilford, Conn.: Lyons Press, 2014.

de la Teja, Jesús F., and Ross Frank, eds. *Choice, Persuasion, and Coercion: Social Control on Spain's North American Frontiers.* Albuquerque: University of New Mexico Press, 2005.

Delpar, Helen. *The Enormous Vogue of Things Mexican: Cultural Relations Between the United States and Mexico, 1920–1935.* Tuscaloosa: University of Alabama Press, 1992.

Dunkel, Tom. *Color Blind: The Forgotten Team That Broke Baseball's Color Line.* New York: Atlantic Monthly Press, 2013.

DuVal, Kathleen. *Independence Lost: Lives on the Edge of the American Revolution.* New York: Random House, 2015. Kindle e-book.

Elliott, J. H. *Empires of the Atlantic World: Britain and Spain in America, 1492–1830.* New Haven, Conn.: Yale University Press, 2006.

Fernández-Armesto, Felipe. *Our America: A Hispanic History of the United States.* New York: W. W. Norton, 2014.

Ferrer, Ada. *Insurgent Cuba: Race, Nation, and Revolution, 1868–1898.* Chapel Hill: University of North Carolina Press, 1999.

Fitz, Caitlin. *Our Sister Republics: The United States in an Age of American Revolutions.* New York: Liveright, 2016.

Flores, Juan. *Salsa Rising: New York Latin Music of the Sixties Generation.* Oxford: Oxford University Press, 2016.

Flores, Richard R. *Remembering the Alamo: Memory, Modernity and the Master Symbol.* Austin: University of Texas Press, 2002.

Foley, Neil. *Mexicans in the Making of America.* Cambridge, Mass.: Belknap Press of Harvard University Press, 2014.

Fowler, Will. *Santa Anna of Mexico.* Lincoln: University of Nebraska Press, 2007.

Gallay, Alan, ed. *Indian Slavery in Colonial America.* Lincoln: University of Nebraska Press, 2009.

Glasser, Ruth. *My Music Is My Flag: Puerto Rican Musicians and Their New York Communities, 1917–1940.* Berkeley: University of California Press, 1995.

Gómez, Laura E. *Manifest Destinies: The Making of the Mexican American Race.* New York: New York University Press, 2007.

Gonzalez, Juan. *Harvest of Empire: A History of Latinos in America.* Rev. ed. New York: Penguin Books, 2011.

Gonzales-Berry, Erlinda, and David Maciel, eds. *The Contested Homeland: A Chicano History of New Mexico.* Albuquerque: University of New Mexico Press, 2000.

Grady, Timothy Paul. *Anglo-Spanish Rivalry in Colonial South-East America, 1650–1725.* London: Pickering & Chatto, 2010.

Gray, Paul Bryan. *A Clamor for Equality: Emergence and Exile of Californio Activist Francisco P. Ramírez.* Lubbock: Texas Tech University Press, 2012.

Grillo, Evelio. *Black Cuban, Black American: A Memoir.* Houston: Arte Público Press, 2000.

Greenberg, Amy S. *A Wicked War: Polk, Clay, Lincoln, and the 1846 U.S. Invasion of Mexico.* New York: Alfred A. Knopf, 2012.

Gutiérrez, Ramón A. *When Jesus Came, the Corn Mothers Went Away: Marriage, Sexuality, and Power in New Mexico, 1500–1846.* Stanford, Calif.: Stanford University Press, 1991.

Hahn, Steven. *A Nation Without Borders: The United States and Its World in An Age of Civil Wars, 1830–1910.* New York: Penguin, 2016.

Hann, John H. *A History of the Timucua Indians and Missions.* Gainesville: University Press of Florida, 1996.

Henderson, Timothy J. *Beyond Borders: A History of Mexican Migration to the United States.* Malden, Mass.: Wiley-Blackwell, 2011.

Hernández, José Angel. *Mexican American Colonization During the Nineteenth Century: A History of the U.S.-Mexico Borderlands.* Cambridge: Cambridge University Press, 2012.

Hernández, Kelly Lytle. *Migra! A History of the U.S. Border Patrol.* Berkeley: University of California Press, 2010.

Hilfrich, Fabian. *Debating American Exceptionalism: Empire and Democracy in the Wake of the Spanish-American War.* New York: Palgrave Macmillan, 2012.

Hoerder, Dirk, and Nora Faires, eds. *Migrants and Migration in Modern North America: Cross-Border Lives, Labor Markets, and Politics.* Durham, N.C.: Duke University Press, 2011.

Holtby, David V. *Forty-Seventh Star: New Mexico's Struggle for Statehood.* Norman: University of Oklahoma Press, 2012.

Horne, Gerald. *Race to Revolution: The United States and Cuba During Slavery and Jim Crow.* New York: Monthly Review Press, 2014.

Israel, J. I. *Race, Class, and Politics in Colonial Mexico, 1610–1670.* London: Oxford University Press, 1975.

Joseph, Gilbert M., and Jürgen Buchenau. *Mexico's Once and Future Revolution: Social Upheaval and the Challenge of Rule Since the Late Nineteenth Century.* Durham, N.C.: Duke University Press, 2013.

Landers, Jane. *Black Society in Spanish Florida.* Urbana: University of Illinois Press, 1999.

Kagan, Richard L., ed. *Spain in America: The Origins of Hispanism in the United States.* Urbana: University of Illinois Press, 2002.

Kanellos, Nicolás, ed. *Herencia: The Anthology of Hispanic Literature of the United States.* Oxford: Oxford University Press, 2002.

Keller, Renata. *Mexico's Cold War: Cuba, the United States, and the Legacy of the Mexican Revolution.* New York: Cambridge University Press, 2015.

Kinzer, Stephen. *The True Flag: Theodore Roosevelt, Mark Twain, and the Birth of American Empire.* New York: Henry Holt, 2017. Kindle e-book.

Knight, Alan. *The Mexican Revolution.* 2 vols. Cambridge: Cambridge University Press, 1986.

Kropp, Phoebe S. *California Vieja: Culture and Memory in a Modern American Place.* Berkeley: University of California Press, 2006.

Malavet, Pedro A. *America's Colony: The Political and Cultural Conflict Between the United States and Puerto Rico.* New York: New York University Press, 2004.

Martínez, María Elena. *Genealogical Fictions: Limpieza de Sangre, Religion, and Gender in Colonial Mexico.* Stanford, Calif.: Stanford University Press, 2008.

Martinez HoSang, Daniel, Oneka LaBennett, and Laura Pulido, eds. *Racial Formation in the Twenty-First Century.* Berkeley: University of California Press, 2012.

May, Robert E. *The Southern Dream of a Caribbean Empire, 1854–1861.* 2nd pbk. ed. Gainesville: University Press of Florida, 2002.

McCoy, Alfred W., and Francisco A. Scarano, eds. *The Colonial Crucible: Empire in the Making of the Modern American State.* Madison: University of Wisconsin Press, 2009.

McMichael, Andrew. *Atlantic Loyalties: Americans in Spanish West Florida, 1785–1810.* Athens: University of Georgia Press, 2008.

McWilliams, Carey. *North from Mexico: The Spanish-Speaking People of the United States.* Updated by Matt S. Meier. New York: Praeger, 1990.

Milanich, Jerald T. *Laboring in the Fields of the Lord: Spanish Missions and Southeastern Indians.* Gainesville: University Press of Florida, 2006.

Monroy, Douglas. *The Borders Within: Encounters Between Mexico and the U.S.* Tucson: University of Arizona Press, 2008.

Montejano, David. *Anglos and Mexicans in the Making of Texas, 1836–1986.* Austin: University of Texas Press, 1987.

Mora, G. Cristina. *Making Hispanics: How Activists, Bureaucrats, and Media Constructed a New American.* Chicago: University of Chicago Press, 2014.

Narrett, David. *Adventurism and Empire: The Struggle for Mastery in the Louisiana-Florida Borderlands, 1762–1803.* Chapel Hill: University of North Carolina Press, 2014.

Ngai, Mae M. *Impossible Subjects: Illegal Aliens and the Making of Modern America.* Princeton, N.J.: Princeton University Press, 2004.

Nieto-Phillips, John M. *The Language of Blood: The Making of Spanish-American Identity in New Mexico, 1880s–1930s.* Albuquerque: University of New Mexico Press, 2004.

Noel, Linda C. *Debating American Identity: Southwestern Statehood and Mexican Immigration.* Tucson: University of Arizona Press, 2014.

Omi, Michael, and Howard Winant. *Racial Formation in the United States.* 3rd ed. New York: Routledge/Taylor and Francis Group, 2015.

Painter, Nell Irvin. *The History of White People.* New York: W. W. Norton, 2010. Kindle e-book.

Paz, Octavio. *The Labyrinth of Solitude and Other Writings.* Translated by Lysander Kemp, Yara Milos, and Rachel Phillips Belash. New York: Grove Press, 1985.

Pérez, Louis A., Jr. *Cuba and the United States: Ties of Singular Intimacy*. 2nd ed. Athens: University of Georgia Press, 1997.

———. *Cuba Between Empires, 1878–1902*. Pittsburgh: University of Pittsburgh Press, 1983.

Pérez Firmat, Gustavo. *The Havana Habit*. New Haven, Conn.: Yale University Press, 2010.

Picó, Fernando. *History of Puerto Rico: A Panorama of Its People*. Princeton, NJ: Markus Wiener Publishers, 2006.

Remeseira, Claudio Iván, ed. *Hispanic New York: A Sourcebook*. New York: Columbia University Press, 2010.

Restall, Matthew. *Seven Myths of the Spanish Conquest*. New York: Oxford University Press, 2003.

Rodriguez, Gregory. *Mongrels, Bastards, Orphans, and Vagabonds: Mexican Immigration and the Future of Race in America*. New York: Pantheon Books, 2007.

Rodriguez, Richard. *Brown: The Last Discovery of America*. New York: Viking, 2002.

Rosales, F. Arturo. *Chicano! The History of the Mexican American Civil Rights Movement*. 2nd rev. ed. Houston: Arte Público Press, 1997.

Sánchez, George J. *Becoming Mexican American: Ethnicity, Culture, and Identity in Chicano Los Angeles, 1900–1945*. New York: Oxford University Press, 1993.

Sánchez, Joseph P., Robert L. Spude, and Art Gómez. *New Mexico: A History*. Norman: University of Oklahoma Press, 2013.

Santiago, Roberto, ed. *Boricuas: Influential Puerto Rican Writings—An Anthology*. New York: One World, 1995.

Saunt, Claudio. *West of the Revolution: An Uncommon History of 1776*. New York: W. W. Norton, 2014.

———. *A New Order of Things: Property, Power, and the Transformation of the Creek Indians, 1733–1816*. Cambridge: Cambridge University Press, 1999.

Schmidt-Nowara, Christopher, and John M. Nieto-Phillips, eds. *Interpreting Spanish Colonialism: Empires, Nations, and Legends*. Albuquerque: University of New Mexico Press, 2005.

Schoultz, Lars. *Beneath the United States: A History of U.S. Policy Toward Latin America*. Cambridge Mass.: Harvard University Press, 1998.

Schrank, Sarah. *Art and the City: Civic Imagination and Cultural Authority in Los Angeles*. Philadelphia: University of Pennsylvania Press, 2009.

Sheridan, Thomas E. *Arizona: A History*. Rev. ed. Tucson: University of Arizona Press, 2012.

Stagg, J. C. A. *Borderlines in Borderlands: James Madison and the Spanish-American Frontier, 1776–1821*. New Haven, Conn.: Yale University Press, 2009.

Starr, Kevin. *California: A History*. New York: Modern Library, 2005.

St. John, Rachel. *Line in the Sand: A History of the Western U.S.-Mexico Border*. Princeton, N.J.: Princeton University Press, 2011.

Suarez, Ray. *Latino Americans: The 500-Year Legacy That Shaped a Nation*. New York: Celebra, 2013.

Thomas, Evan. *The War Lovers: Roosevelt, Lodge, Hearst, and the Rush to Empire, 1898*. New York: Little, Brown, 2010.

Thomas, Hugh. *Conquest: Montezuma, Cortés, and the Fall of Old Mexico*. New York: Simon and Schuster, 1993.

Thompson, Jerry. *Cortina: Defending the Mexican Name in Texas*. College Station: Texas A & M University Press, 2007.

Truett, Samuel. *Fugitive Landscapes: The Forgotten History of the U.S.-Mexico Borderlands*. New Haven, Conn.: Yale University Press, 2006.

Tutino, John. *From Insurrection to Revolution in Mexico: Social Bases of Agrarian Violence, 1750–1940*. Princeton, N.J.: Princeton University Press, 1986.

Vargas, Zaragosa. *Crucible of Struggle: A History of Mexican Americans from Colonial Times to the Present Era*. New York: Oxford University Press, 2010.

Weber, David J. *Bárbaros: Spaniards and Their Savages in the Age of Enlightenment*. New Haven, Conn.: Yale University Press, 2005.

———, ed. *Foreigners in Their Native Land: Historical Roots of the Mexican Americans*. 30th anniversary pbk. ed. Albuquerque: University of New Mexico Press, 2003.

———. *The Spanish Frontier in North America*. New Haven, Conn.: Yale University Press, 1992.

Womack, John, Jr. *Zapata and the Mexican Revolution*. Harmondsworth, U.K.: Penguin, 1972.

Worth, John E., ed. and trans. *Discovering Florida: First-Contact Narratives from Spanish Expeditions Along the Lower Gulf Coast*. Gainesville: University Press of Florida, 2014.

Notes

Author's Note

1 "Walt Whitman to the Tertio-Millennial Anniversary Association," Santa Fe, New Mexico, July 20, 1883, in Ted Genoways (ed.), *The Correspondence* (Iowa City: University of Iowa Press, 2004). Available at Walt Whitman Archive, http://whitmanarchive.org/biography/correspondence/tei/med.00660.html (accessed November 7, 2016).

Introduction: Nogales, Arizona

1 Rachel St. John, *Line in the Sand: A History of the Western U.S.-Mexico Border* (Princeton, N.J.: Princeton University Press, 2011), p. 95.
2 Juan Poblete, "Americanism/o: Intercultural Border Zones in Postsocial Times," in Marisa Belausteguigoitia, Ben. Sifuentes-Jáuregui, and Yolanda Martínez-San Miguel (eds.), *Critical Terms in Caribbean and Latin American Thought: Historical and Institutional Trajectories* (London: Palgrave Macmillan, 2016), p. 47.
3 Octavio Paz, "Mexico and the United States," in Rachel Philips Belash, Yara Milos, and Lysander Kemp (trans.), *The Labyrinth of Solitude and Other Writings* (New York: Grove Press, 1985), p. 357.
4 Gloria Anzaldúa, *Borderlands/La Frontera: The New Mestiza* (San Francisco: Aunt Lute Books, 2012), p. 25.
5 José Luis Abellán, *La idea de América: Origen y evolución* (Madrid: Iberoamericana, 2009), p. 25.
6 Felipe Fernández-Armesto, *Our America: A Hispanic History of the United States* (New York: W. W. Norton, 2014), Kindle Edition, p. 330.
7 G. Cristina Mora, *Making Hispanics: How Activists, Bureaucrats, and Media Constructed a New American* (Chicago: University of Chicago Press, 2014), p. 169.
8 Jens Manuel Krogstad and Mark Hugo Lopez, "Use of Spanish Declines Among Latinos in Major U.S. Metros," Pew Research Center FactTank, October 31, 2017,

http://www.pewresearch.org/fact-tank/2017/10/31/use-of-spanish-declines-among
-latinos-in-major-u-s-metros/ (accessed March 22, 2018).

9 Michel-Rolph Trouillot, *Silencing the Past: Power and the Production of History* (Boston: Beacon Press, 1995), p. xxiii.

10 On the development of race and social control, see, for instance, Patrick Wolfe, "Land, Labor, and Difference: Elementary Structures of Race," *American Historical Review* 106, no. 3 (2001): 866–905.

11 Nell Irvin Painter, *The History of White People* (New York: W. W. Norton, 2010), loc. 88, Kindle.

12 Michael Omi and Howard Winant, *Racial Formation in the United States* (London: Routledge, 2014), pp. 105–11.

13 On Mexico, see, for instance, Mónica G. Moreno Figueroa and Emiko Saldívar Tanaka, "Comics, Dolls and the Disavowal of Racism: Learning from Mexican Mestizaje," in Encarnación Gutiérrez Rodríguez and Shirley Anne Tate (eds.), *Creolizing Europe: Legacies and Transformations* (Liverpool: Liverpool University Press, 2015); on the Dominican Republic, see David John Howard, *Coloring the Nation: Race and Ethnicity in the Dominican Republic* (Boulder, Colo.: L. Rienner, 2001).

14 Richard Rodriguez, *Brown: The Last Discovery of America* (New York: Penguin, 2002), pp. xi–xii.

15 Alan Gallay, *The Indian Slave Trade: The Rise of the English Empire in the American South, 1670–1717* (New Haven, Conn.: Yale University Press, 2002), p. 9.

16 George J. Sánchez, *Becoming Mexican American: Ethnicity, Culture, and Identity in Chicano Los Angeles, 1900–45* (Oxford: Oxford University Press, 1993), p. 1.

17 Carey McWilliams and Matt S. Meier (ed.), *North from Mexico: The Spanish-Speaking People of the United States* (New York: Praeger, 1990), p. 8.

18 Mae N. Ngai, *Impossible Subjects: Illegal Aliens and the Making of Modern America* (Princeton, N.J.: Princeton University Press, 2004), p. 2.

19 Quoted in Simon Schama, *The American Future: A History* (New York: Ecco, 2009), p. 240.

20 Gordon S. Wood, *The Purpose of the Past: Reflections on the Uses of History* (New York: Penguin, 2009), p. 244.

21 Quoted in Schama, *The American Future*, p. 242. For more on the creation and imagining of national identity, see the classic Benedict Anderson, *Imagined Communities: Reflections on the Origin and Spread of Nationalism* (New York: Verso Books, 1991).

22 J. Hector St. John de Crèvecoeur, *Letters from an American Farmer and Sketches of Eighteenth-Century America* (New York: Penguin Classics, 1981), pp. 68, 70.

23 Eliga Gould, "Entangled Histories, Entangled Worlds: The English-Speaking Atlantic as a Spanish Periphery," *American Historical Review* 112, no. 3 (2007): 764–786.

24 For more on Columbus and the early settlement of the Caribbean, with references and suggestions for further reading, see the first two chapters of Carrie Gibson, *Empire's Crossroads: A History of the Caribbean from Columbus to the Present Day* (New York: Grove Press, 2014).

25 Patricia Seed, "Exploration and Conquest," in Thomas H. Holloway (ed.), *A Companion to Latin American History* (Oxford: Blackwell, 2008), pp. 73–74.

26 Edwin Williamson, *The Penguin History of Latin America* (London: Penguin, 1992), pp. 80–81.

27 Quoted in David J. Weber, *The Spanish Frontier in North America: The Brief Edition* (New Haven, Conn.: Yale University Press, 2009), p. 21.

28 "Inter Caetera, 1493," in J. H. Parry and Robert G. Keith (eds.), *New Iberian World: A Documentary History of the Discovery and Settlement of Latin America to the Early 17th Century*, vol. 1 (New York: Times Books: Hector & Rose, 1984), pp. 272–73.

29 Colin M. MacLachlan, *Imperialism and the Origins of Mexican Culture* (Cambridge, Mass.: Harvard University Press, 2015), p. 181.

30 Columbus had a long-standing relationship with the Franciscans. See Julia McClure, *The Franciscan Invention of the New World* (London: Palgrave Macmillan, 2017), pp. 96–97.

31 On this theme, see, for instance, M. J. Rodríguez-Salgado, "Christians, Civilised and Spanish: Multiple Identities in Sixteenth-Century Spain," *Transactions of the Royal Historical Society* 8 (1998): 233–51.

32 John Huxtable Elliott, *Empires of the Atlantic World: Britain and Spain in America, 1492–1830* (New Haven, Conn.: Yale University Press, 2006), p. 9.

33 Felipe Fernández-Armesto, *Amerigo: The Man Who Gave His Name to America* (London: Weidenfeld & Nicolson, 2006), p. 120.

34 Apparently, Martin Waldseemüller later changed his mind about Amerigo Vespucci and stopped putting his name on maps, but by then the use of "America" had taken root. Ibid., pp. 187–91; C. R. Johnson, "Renaissance German Cosmographers and the Naming of America," *Past & Present* 191, no. 1 (2006): 3–45.

Chapter 1: Santa Elena, South Carolina

1 Robert S. Weddle, *Spanish Sea: The Gulf of Mexico in North American Discovery, 1500–1685* (College Station: Texas A&M University Press, 1985), p. 40.

2 Fernando Picó, *History of Puerto Rico: A Panorama of Its People* (Princeton, N.J.: Markus Wiener, 2006), pp. 36–37.

3 Ibid.

4 John E. Worth (ed.), *Discovering Florida: First Contact Narratives from Spanish Expeditions Along the Lower Gulf Coast* (Gainesville: University Press of Florida, 2014), p. 8.

5 Picó, *History of Puerto Rico*, p. 38.

6 Worth, *Discovering Florida*, p. 9; Margaret F. Pickett and Dwayne W. Pickett, *The European Struggle to Settle North America: Colonizing Attempts by England, France and Spain, 1521–1608* (Jefferson, N.C.: McFarland, 2011), p. 17.

7 Jerald T. Milanich, *Laboring in the Fields of the Lord: Spanish Missions and Southeastern Indians* (Gainesville: University Press of Florida, 2006), p. 59.

8 Worth, *Discovering Florida*, p. 16; Milanich, *Laboring in the Fields of the Lord*, p. 55.

9 Worth, *Discovering Florida*, p. 14.

10 Jerald T. Milanich, "Charting Juan Ponce de León's 1513 Voyage to Florida: The Calusa Indians amid Latitude of Controversy," in Viviana Díaz Balsera and Rachel May (eds.), *La Florida: Five Hundred Years of Hispanic Presence* (Gainesville:

University Press of Florida, 2014), p. 54. See this chapter for a detailed discussion of Ponce's possible landing sites.

11 Milanich, *Laboring in the Fields of the Lord*, p. 57.

12 Worth, *Discovering Florida*, p. 17.

13 T. D. Allman, *Finding Florida: The True History of the Sunshine State* (New York: Atlantic Monthly Press, 2013), p. 7.

14 There is some uncertainty about whether Cortés left in 1504 or 1506, with more recent works coming down on the side of the later date. See Elliott, *Empires of the Atlantic World*, p. 7; Hugh Thomas, *Conquest: Cortes, Montezuma, and the Fall of Old Mexico* (New York: Simon and Schuster, 1995), p. 117; Anthony Pagden (ed.), *Hernan Cortes: Letters from Mexico* (New Haven, Conn.: Yale University Press, 1986), p. xiv.

15 He may have also named the island Juana in honor of Prince John (Juan), but it remains unclear. For more on Columbus's names for the islands, see Evelina Gužauskytė, *Christopher Columbus's Naming in the Diarios of the Four Voyages (1492–1504): A Discourse of Negotiation* (Toronto: University of Toronto Press, 2014).

16 John Frederick Schwaller and Helen Nader, *The First Letter from New Spain: The Lost Petition of Cortés and His Company, June 20, 1519* (Austin: University of Texas Press, 2014), p. 13; Thomas, *Conquest*, pp. 76, 133–34.

17 An online version of these laws can be found at http://faculty.smu.edu/bakewell/bakewell/texts/burgoslaws.html.

18 Anthony Pagden, "Introduction," in Bartolomé de Las Casas and Nigel Griffin (trans.), *A Short Account of the Destruction of the Indies* (London: Penguin, 1992), xxxv.

19 Ross Hassig, "The Collision of Two Worlds," in William H. Beezley and Michael C. Meyer (eds.), *The Oxford History of Mexico* (Oxford: Oxford University Press, 2010), p. 74, Kindle.

20 Williamson, *The Penguin History of Latin America*, pp. 16–17.

21 Schwaller and Nader, *The First Letter from New Spain*, p. 13.

22 Seed, "Exploration and Conquest," p. 77.

23 Williamson, *The Penguin History of Latin America*, p. 17; Elliott, *Empires of the Atlantic World*, p. 58; Hassig, "The Collision of Two Worlds," p. 75; Camilla Townsend, *Malintzin's Choices: An Indian Woman in the Conquest of Mexico* (Albuquerque: University of New Mexico Press, 2006), p. 37.

24 For more on Malintzin and her role, as well as the debates about her legacy, see Townsend, *Malintzin's Choices*; and Matthew Restall, *Seven Myths of the Spanish Conquest* (Oxford: Oxford University Press, 2003), chapter 5.

25 Schwaller and Nader, *The First Letter from New Spain*, p. 14.

26 Williamson, *The Penguin History of Latin America*, p. 43.

27 Schwaller and Nader, *The First Letter from New Spain*, p. 15.

28 See, for instance, Camilla Townsend, "Burying the White Gods: New Perspectives on the Conquest of Mexico," *American Historical Review* 108, no. 3 (2003): 659–87; John Charles Chasteen, *Born in Blood and Fire: A Concise History of Latin America* (New York: W. W. Norton, 2001), p. 49.

29 For a detailed and nuanced reading of the conquest and how it has been subsequently written about, see Inga Clendinnen, "'Fierce and Unnatural Cruelty':

Cortés and the Conquest of Mexico," *Representations*, no. 33, Special Issue: The New World (1991): 65–100.

30 Schwaller and Nader, *The First Letter from New Spain*, p. 15.

31 For more on the document that outlines this, see ibid.; also Elliott, *Empires of the Atlantic World*, pp. 3–4; John Tate Lanning, "Cortes and His First Official Remission of Treasure to Charles V," *Revista de Historia de América* 2 (1938): 5–29.

32 Hassig, "The Collision of Two Worlds," p. 77; Helen Nader, "The Spain That Encountered Mexico," in Beezley and Meyer, *The Oxford History of Mexico*, p. 38; Schwaller and Nader, *The First Letter from New Spain*, pp. 15–16.

33 Elliott, *Empires of the Atlantic World*, p. 4; Hassig, "The Collision of Two Worlds," pp. 80–83.

34 Hassig, "The Collision of Two Worlds," pp. 86–88.

35 Miguel León Portilla (ed.) and Angel María Garibay K. and Lysander Kemp (trans.), *The Broken Spears: The Aztec Account of the Conquest of Mexico* (Boston: Beacon Press, 1962), p. xix.

36 Hassig, "The Collision of Two Worlds," p. 88.

37 Hernan Cortés, "Second Letter to the Crown, 1522," in Pagden, *Hernan Cortes: Letters from Mexico*, pp. 101–4.

38 See, for instance, Alfred W. Crosby, *The Columbian Exchange: Biological and Cultural Consequences of 1492* (Westport, Conn.: Praeger, 2003); Charles C. Mann, *1493: Uncovering the New World Columbus Created* (New York: Vintage Books, 2012).

39 Nader, "The Spain That Encountered Mexico," p. 70.

40 Williamson, *The Penguin History of Latin America*, p. 19.

41 Seed, "Exploration and Conquest," p. 79.

42 Elliott, *Empires of the Atlantic World*, p. 5.

43 Hassig, "The Collision of Two Worlds," p. 90.

44 Ibid., p. 91.

45 Schwaller and Nader, *The First Letter from New Spain*, p. 17.

46 Hassig, "The Collision of Two Worlds," p. 102.

47 Williamson, *The Penguin History of Latin America*, p. 20.

48 Ibid.

49 The source was the Florentine Codex, compiled by Fray Bernardino de Sahagún, who started the project around 1529, when he arrived in Mexico. He asked indigenous people many questions about their culture and about the arrival of the Spanish. They often answered in their unique pictorial form of writing, which Sahagún then, with the help of many Nahua people, transcribed and translated. Although not without its problems—not least regarding translations and accuracy—the work remains one of the few surviving sources with indigenous voices. See also Portilla, *The Broken Spears*, pp. 92–93.

50 Seed, "Exploration and Conquest," pp. 79–80; Williamson, *The Penguin History of Latin America*, pp. 21–22.

51 MacLachlan, *Imperialism and the Origins of Mexican Culture*, pp. 21–22.

52 Susan Elizabeth Ramírez, "Institutions of the Spanish Empire in the Hapsburg Era," in Holloway, *A Companion to Latin American History*, pp. 106–7.

53 Mark Burkholder, *Spaniards in the Colonial Empire: Creole vs. Peninsulars?* (Chichester, West Sussex: Wiley-Blackwell, 2013), p. 9.

54 J. I. Israel, *Race, Class, and Politics in Mexico, 1610–1670* (Oxford: Oxford University Press, 1975), pp. 5–6.

55 MacLachlan, *Imperialism and the Origins of Mexican Culture*, pp. 198, 202.

56 Elliott, *Empires of the Atlantic World*, p. 119.

57 Jay Kinsbruner, *The Colonial Spanish-American City: Urban Life in the Age of Atlantic Capitalism* (Austin: University of Texas Press, 2005), p. 9.

58 Susan Schroeder, "The Mexico That Spain Encountered," in Beezley and Meyer, *The Oxford History of Mexico*, p. 71, Kindle.

59 Kinsbruner, *The Colonial Spanish-American City*, pp. 9–10; Nader, "The Spain That Encountered Mexico," p. 39.

60 Williamson, *The Penguin History of Latin America*, p. 81; for more detail on Spanish planning laws in the Americas see Kinsbruner, *The Colonial Spanish-American City*; Axel I. Mundigo and Dora p. Crouch, "The City Planning Ordinances of the Laws of the Indies Revisited. Part I: Their Philosophy and Implications," *Town Planning Review* 48, no. 3 (1977): 247–68.

61 MacLachlan, *Imperialism and the Origins of Mexican Culture*, p. 201.

62 Inga Clendinnen, *Ambivalent Conquests: Maya and Spaniard in Yucatan, 1517–1570* (Cambridge: Cambridge University Press, 1987), p. 47. See also Robert Ricard and Lesley Byrd Simpson (trans.), *The Spiritual Conquest of Mexico: An Essay on the Apostolate and the Evangelizing Methods of the Mendicant Orders in New Spain: 1523–1572* (Berkeley: University of California Press, 1966).

63 Mark Burkholder and Lyman Johnson, *Colonial Latin America*, 5th ed. (Oxford: Oxford University Press, 2004), p. 98.

64 Linda A. Curcio-Nagy, "Faith and Morals in Colonial Mexico," in Beezley and Meyer, *The Oxford History of Mexico*, p. 144.

65 MacLachlan, *Imperialism and the Origins of Mexican Culture*, pp. 204–5.

66 Clendinnen, *Ambivalent Conquests*, pp. 47–48.

67 Williamson, *The Penguin History of Latin America*, p. 102.

68 See, for instance, D. A. Brading, *Mexican Phoenix: Our Lady of Guadalupe—Image and Tradition Across Five Centuries* (Cambridge: Cambridge University Press, 2001).

69 Lawrence A. Clayton, *Bartolomé de Las Casas: A Biography* (Cambridge: Cambridge University Press, 2012), pp. 9, 14.

70 Ibid., pp. 20–21.

71 Ibid., p. 33.

72 Ibid., pp. 55–56.

73 Quoted in Lewis Hanke, *All Mankind Is One: A Study of the Disputation Between Bartolomé de Las Casas and Juan Ginés Sepúlveda in 1550 on the Intellectual and Religious Capacity of the American Indians* (De Kalb: Northern Illinois University Press, 1974), p. 4.

74 Clayton, *Bartolomé de Las Casas*, pp. 55–56.

75 *Historia de las Indias*, quoted in Parry and Keith, *New Iberian World*, vol. 2, pp. 291–300.

76 Ibid.; Clayton, *Bartolomé de Las Casas*, p. 70.

77 Charles Gibson, *Spain in America* (New York: Harper & Row, 1966), p. 40.

78 For more on the Requirement and its Islamic roots, see Patricia Seed, *Ceremonies of Possession in Europe's Conquest of the New World, 1492–1640* (Cambridge: Cambridge University Press, 1995), chapter 3.

79 Clayton, *Bartolomé de Las Casas*, pp. 80–81.

80 Ibid., p. 93.

81 Ibid., p. 95.

82 For more on the North African and Mediterranean roots of slavery, see chapter 4 of David Brion Davis, *Inhuman Bondage: The Rise and Fall of Slavery in the New World* (Oxford: Oxford University Press, 2008).

83 Toby Green, *The Rise of the Trans-Atlantic Slave Trade in Western Africa, 1300–1589* (Cambridge: Cambridge University Press, 2011), pp. 187–88.

84 Clayton, *Bartolomé de Las Casas*, pp. 102–3.

85 Ibid., p. 426.

86 See the Trans-Atlantic Slave Trade Database, http://www.slavevoyages.org/voyages/LffdfaeC (accessed January 3, 2018).

87 At this time, Seville still had around thirty thousand slaves, though this number included Muslims from North Africa as well as enslaved people from sub-Saharan Africa. See Carmen Fracchia, "Depicting the Iberian African in New Spain," in Jean Andrews and Alejandro Coroleu (eds.), *Mexico 1680: Cultural and Intellectual Life in the "Barroco De Indias"* (Bristol, U.K.: HiPLAM, 2007), p. 48.

88 Las Casas, *A Short Account of the Destruction of the Indies*, p. 10.

89 Ibid., p. 15.

90 Ibid., p. 24.

91 Pagden, "Introduction," p. xxvii.

92 William S. Maltby, *The Black Legend in England: The Development of Anti-Spanish Sentiment, 1558–1660* (Durham, N.C.: Duke University Press, 1971), p. 15.

93 Martine Julia Van Ittersum, *Profit and Principle: Hugo Grotius, Natural Rights Theories and the Rise of Dutch Power in the East Indies 1595–1615* (Leiden: Brill, 2006), p. 59.

94 Felipe II, however, did not take the title of Holy Roman emperor, which went instead to his uncle, Ferdinand I. See Elliott, *Empires of the Atlantic World*, p. 119.

95 Quoted in Irene Silverblatt, "The Black Legend and Global Conspiracies: Spain, the Inquisition, and the Emerging Modern World," in Margaret R. Greer, Walter D. Mignolo, and Maureen Quilligan (eds.), *Rereading the Black Legend: The Discourses of Religious and Racial Difference in the Renaissance Empires* (Chicago: University of Chicago Press, 2007), p. 99.

96 Las Casas, *A Short Account of the Destruction of the Indies*, pp. 12–13.

97 Van Ittersum, *Profit and Principle*, pp. 55, 63.

98 Clayton, *Bartolomé de Las Casas*, p. 347.

99 "Democrates Alter," in Parry and Keith, *New Iberian World*, vol. 1, pp. 323–24.

100 Ibid.

101 Clayton, *Bartolomé de Las Casas*, p. 353.

102 "In Defence of the Indians," in Parry and Keith, *New Iberian World*, vol. 1, pp. 67–68.

103 Ibid., p. 146.

104 Las Casas's manuscript and papers had been put in the care of the Dominicans, and by the early 1800s there was once again interest in publishing them, led in part by the Cuban historian José Antonio Saco. His efforts met with opposition by the Royal Academy of History, and this led Saco to criticize the organization for keeping the work—and its unflattering depiction of Spanish imperialism—buried. Saco won in the end, decades after his initial efforts, and publication began in 1875. For more on the long-running efforts to publish the manuscript,

see Clayton, *Bartolomé de Las Casas*, pp. 409–10; Lewis Hanke, *Las Casas, Historiador, Estudio Preliminar a La Historia de Las Indias* (Mexico **City,** Mexico: Fondo de Cultural Economica, 1951), pp. 54–56.

105 Worth, *Discovering Florida*, p. 18.

106 Weber, *The Spanish Frontier in North America*, p. 29.

107 Worth, *Discovering Florida*, p. 11.

108 Weddle, *Spanish Sea*, pp. 95–108.

109 Juan Ponce de León to the Spanish crown, February 10, 1521, translation in Worth, *Discovering Florida*, pp. 83–84.

110 For a discussion of the sixteenth-century sources on the Fountain of Youth, see Worth, *Discovering Florida*, p. 9.

111 Paul E. Hoffman, *A New Andalucia and a Way to the Orient: The American Southeast During the Sixteenth Century* (Baton Rouge: Louisiana State University Press, 1990), p. 8.

112 Ibid., p. 4.

113 Ibid., pp. 3–6, 42; Anna Brickhouse, *The Unsettlement of America: Translation, Interpretation, and the Story of Don Luis De Velasco, 1560–1945* (Oxford: Oxford University Press, 2015), p. 27.

114 Brickhouse, *The Unsettlement of America*, p. 27.

115 Paul E. Hoffman, *Florida's Frontiers* (Bloomington: Indiana University Press, 2002), p. 25; and Hoffman, *A New Andalucia and a Way to the Orient*.

116 Hoffman, *A New Andalucia and a Way to the Orient*, p. 54.

117 Lawrence S. Rowland, Alexander Moore, and George C. Rogers Jr., *The History of Beaufort County, South Carolina*, vol. 1, *1514–1861* (Columbia: University of South Carolina Press, 1996), p. 18.

118 Hoffman, *A New Andalucia and a Way to the Orient*, p. 61; Rowland et al., *The History of Beaufort County, South Carolina*, vol. 1, p. 19.

119 Rowland et al., *The History of Beaufort County, South Carolina*, vol. 1, p. 18.

120 Ibid.

121 Hoffman, *A New Andalucia and a Way to the Orient*, p. 71.

122 Ibid., p. 73.

123 Ibid., p. 76.

124 John Francis Bannon, *The Spanish Borderlands Frontier, 1513–1821* (New York: Holt, Rinehart and Winston, 1970), p. 22; Allman, *Finding Florida*, p. 20.

125 Weber, *The Spanish Frontier in North America*, pp. 30–31.

126 Worth, *Discovering Florida*, p. 20.

127 Milanich, *Laboring in the Fields of the Lord*, p. 63.

128 Ibid.

129 Weber, *The Spanish Frontier in North America*, p. 53; Robin Varnum, *Álvar Núñez Cabeza De Vaca: American Trailblazer* (Norman: University of Oklahoma Press, 2014), p. 61.

130 Varnum, *Álvar Núñez Cabeza De Vaca*, p. 61.

131 Ibid., p. 62.

132 Cyclone Covey (trans.), *Cabeza De Vaca's Adventures in the Unknown Interior of America* (Albuquerque: University of New Mexico Press, 1983), pp. 8–9.

133 Ibid., pp. 48–55.

134 Kathleen DuVal and John DuVal (eds.), *Interpreting a Continent: Voices from Colonial America* (Lanham, Md.: Rowman & Littlefield, 2009), p. 32; Covey, *Cabeza De Vaca's Adventures in the Unknown Interior of America*, pp. 55–60.

135 Nicolás Kanellos et al. (eds.), *Herencia: The Anthology of Hispanic Literature of the United States* (New York: Oxford University Press, 2002), p. 37.

136 Covey, *Cabeza De Vaca's Adventures in the Unknown Interior of America*, p. 64.

137 Ibid., pp. 125–26.

138 See Allman, *Finding Florida*, pp. 14–15, for more on the false legend of de Soto discovering the Mississippi.

139 Bannon, *The Spanish Borderlands Frontier, 1513–1821*, p. 23.

140 Covey, *Cabeza De Vaca's Adventures in the Unknown Interior of America*, p. 119.

141 Ibid., p. 12.

142 Milanich, *Laboring in the Fields of the Lord*, p. 69.

143 Hernando de Soto to officials in Santiago de Cuba, July 9, 1539, translated in Worth, *Discovering Florida*, pp. 151–53.

144 Varnum, *Álvar Núñez Cabeza De Vaca*, p. 83.

145 Milanich, *Laboring in the Fields of the Lord*, p. 69.

146 Weber, *The Spanish Frontier in North America*, p. 41.

147 Bannon, *The Spanish Borderlands Frontier, 1513–1821*, p. 23; Milanich, *Laboring in the Fields of the Lord*, p. 75.

148 Milanich, *Laboring in the Fields of the Lord*, p. 74.

149 Allman, *Finding Florida*, p. 13.

150 Weber, *The Spanish Frontier in North America*, p. 43.

151 Hoffman, *Florida's Frontiers*, p. 39.

152 Herbert Ingram Priestley (ed.), *The Luna Papers, 1559–1561*, vol. 1 (Tuscaloosa: University of Alabama Press, 2010), p. xxviii; Weddle, *Spanish Sea*, pp. 260–63.

153 Milanich, *Laboring in the Fields of the Lord*, p. 76.

154 Priestley, *The Luna Papers*, p. xxxv.

155 Ibid., p. xxxvi.

156 Priestly, *The Luna Papers*, pp. xl–xli; Weddle, *Spanish Sea*, p. 271.

157 Weddle, *Spanish Sea*, pp. 274–75.

158 Milanich, *Laboring in the Fields of the Lord*, p. 78; Weddle, *Spanish Sea*, pp. 276–77.

159 Charles Arnade, "The Failure of Spanish Florida," *Americas* 16, no. 3 (1960): 277.

160 Seed, "Exploration and Conquest," p. 76.

Chapter 2: St. Johns River, Florida

1 Weber, *The Spanish Frontier in North America*, p. 51.

2 Charles E. Bennett, *Laudonnière & Fort Caroline: History and Document* (Tuscaloosa: University of Alabama Press, 2001), pp. 6, 13.

3 Milanich, *Laboring in the Fields of the Lord*, p. 78.

4 John T. McGrath, *The French in Early Florida: In the Eye of the Hurricane* (Gainesville: University Press of Florida, 2000), pp. 50–51.

5 See ibid., chapter 4, for the detailed context of Ribault's world and the significance of his career trajectory.

6 Bennett, *Laudonnière & Fort Caroline*, p. 14.

7 Charles E. Bennett, *Three Voyages: René Laudonnière* (Tuscaloosa: University of Alabama Press, 2001), p. 23.

8 J. Michael Francis, Kathleen M. Kole, and David Hurst Thomas, "Murder and Martyrdom in Spanish Florida: Don Juan and the Guale Uprising of 1597," *Anthropological Papers of the American Museum of Natural History*, no. 95 (2011): 26.

9 Ibid., p. 27.

10 Milanich, *Laboring in the Fields of the Lord*, pp. 45–46.

11 See, for instance, John H. Hann, *Indians of Central and South Florida, 1513–1763* (Gainesville: University of Florida Press, 2003).

12 Patricia R. Wickman, "The Spanish Colonial Floridas," in Robert H. Jackson (ed.), *New Views of Borderlands History* (Albuquerque: University of New Mexico Press, 1998), p. 197.

13 Jerald T. Milanich, *The Timucua* (Oxford: Blackwell, 1996), pp. 95–97; Amy Turner Bushnell, "'None of These Wandering Nations Has Ever Been Reduced to the Faith,'" in James Muldoon (ed.), *The Spiritual Conversion of the Americas* (Gainesville: University Press of Florida, 2004), pp. 156–57; Wickman, "The Spanish Colonial Floridas," p. 201.

14 Randolf Widmer, "The Structure of Southeastern Chiefdoms," in Charles Hudson and Carmen Chaves Tesser (eds.), *The Forgotten Centuries: Indians and Europeans in the American South, 1521–1704* (Athens: University of Georgia Press, 1994), pp. 125–26; John H. Hann, "Political Leadership Among the Natives of Spanish Florida," *Florida Historical Quarterly* 71, no. 2 (1992): 188.

15 Hann, *Indians of Central and South Florida, 1513–1763*, pp. 78–79.

16 Rowland et al., *The History of Beaufort County, South Carolina*, p. 23.

17 Ibid., p. 24.

18 H. P. Biggar, "Jean Ribaut's Discoverye of Terra Florida," *English Historical Review* 32, no. 126 (1917): 266–67.

19 Ibid., p. 255; Rowland et al., *The History of Beaufort County, South Carolina*, p. 26.

20 Report translated in Lucy L. Wenhold, "Manrique De Rojas' Report on French Settlement in Florida, 1564," *Florida Historical Quarterly* 38, no. 1 (1959): 45–62.

21 Ibid., p. 54.

22 Ibid., p. 61.

23 Bennett, *Laudonnière & Fort Caroline*, p. 17.

24 Ibid., pp. 9–11.

25 Ibid., p. 21.

26 Ibid., p. 31.

27 Rowland et al., *The History of Beaufort County, South Carolina*, p. 27.

28 Eugene Lyon (ed.), *Pedro Menéndez De Avilés: Spanish Borderlands Sourcebooks* (New York: Garland, 1995), p. xvii.

29 Rowland et al., *The History of Beaufort County, South Carolina*, p. 26; Jean Parker Waterbury (ed.), *The Oldest City: St. Augustine Saga of Survival* (St. Augustine, Fla.: St. Augustine Historical Society, 1983), p. 24; Milanich, *Laboring in the Fields of the Lord*, p. 82.

30 Milanich, *Laboring in the Fields of the Lord*, pp. 82–83.

31 Ibid., p. 83.

32 Ibid., p. 84.

33 Waterbury, *The Oldest City*, p. 27.

34 Rowland et al., *The History of Beaufort County, South Carolina*, p. 27.
35 Milanich, *Laboring in the Fields of the Lord*, p. 84; Bennett, *Laudonnière & Fort Caroline*, p. 37.
36 Hoffman, *Florida's Frontiers*, p. 52.
37 Milanich, *Laboring in the Fields of the Lord*, p. 84.
38 Bennett, *Laudonnière & Fort Caroline*, pp. 9–11.
39 Weber, *The Spanish Frontier in North America*, p. 49.
40 Worth, *Discovering Florida*, pp. 31, 222–23.
41 Parts of his *memoria* were not published until 1722. See Worth, *Discovering Florida*, p. 223.
42 Gonzalo Solís de Merás translated in Worth, *Discovering Florida*, p. 245.
43 Ibid., p. 250.
44 Ibid., p. 251.
45 On the complex formation of the *casta* system, see, for instance, María Elena Martínez, *Genealogical Fictions: Limpieza De Sangre, Religion, and Gender in Colonial Mexico* (Stanford, Calif.: Stanford University Press, 2008).
46 Worth, *Discovering Florida*, p. 262.
47 Ibid., pp. 29–30.
48 Brickhouse, *The Unsettlement of America*, see chapter 4.
49 Translated "Memoria of Hernando de Escalante Fontaneda" in Worth, *Discovering Florida*, p. 207.
50 Rowland et al., *The History of Beaufort County, South Carolina*, pp. 29–30.
51 Weber, *The Spanish Frontier in North America*, p. 54.
52 Rowland et al., *The History of Beaufort County, South Carolina*, p. 31.
53 Ibid., pp. 31–32.
54 Milanich, *Laboring in the Fields of the Lord*, p. 89.
55 Lyon, *Pedro Menéndez De Avilés*, p. xix.
56 Rowland et al., *The History of Beaufort County, South Carolina*, p. 32.
57 "Fort San Juan," North Carolina History Project, http://www.northcarolinahistory.org/commentary/168/entry (accessed December 7, 2015).
58 McGrath, *The French in Early Florida*, pp. 157–60.
59 Milanich, *Laboring in the Fields of the Lord*, p. 95; Rowland et al., *The History of Beaufort County, South Carolina*, p. 33; McGrath, *The French in Early Florida*, pp. 157–63.
60 Lyon, *Pedro Menéndez De Avilés*, p. xxii.
61 Hoffman, *Florida's Frontiers*, p. 51.
62 Milanich, *Laboring in the Fields of the Lord*, pp. 88–89.
63 Rowland et al., *The History of Beaufort County, South Carolina*, p. 37; Francis et al., "Murder and Martyrdom in Spanish Florida," p. 24.
64 Rowland et al., *The History of Beaufort County, South Carolina*, p. 38; Milanich, *Laboring in the Fields of the Lords*, p. 105.
65 John H. Hann, *A History of the Timucua Indians and Missions* (Gainesville: University of Florida Press, 1996), pp. 41–42.
66 Hoffman, *Florida's Frontiers*, pp. 58–59; Hann, *A History of the Timucua Indians and Missions*, p. 53.
67 Rowland et al., *The History of Beaufort County, South Carolina*, p. 40.
68 Ibid.
69 Hoffman, *Florida's Frontiers*, pp. 67–68.

70 Ibid., p. 69.
71 Worth, *Discovering Florida*, pp. 23–24.
72 Ibid., p. 27.
73 Milanich, *Laboring in the Fields of the Lord*, p. 89.
74 Brickhouse, *The Unsettlement of America*, pp. 59–60.
75 Ibid., pp. 47–48.
76 Ibid., p. 98.
77 Ibid., p. 1; see also pp. 284–86 on the possibility of a connection to the Nahua term "Aztlán."
78 Ibid., p. 55.
79 Ibid., pp. 56–57.
80 Ibid., pp. 62–63.
81 Milanich, *Laboring in the Fields of the Lord*, p. 99. Also Weber, *The Spanish Frontier in North America*, pp. 54–55.
82 Seth Mallios, *The Deadly Politics of Giving: Exchange and Violence at Ajacan, Roanoke, and Jamestown* (Tuscaloosa: University of Alabama Press, 2006), pp. 54–55.
83 Milanich, *The Timucua*, p. 95.
84 Quoted in Brickhouse, *The Unsettlement of America*, p. 155.
85 Quoted in Ramón A. Gutiérrez, *When Jesus Came, the Corn Mothers Went Away: Marriage, Sexuality, and Power in New Mexico, 1500–1846* (Stanford, Calif.: Stanford University Press, 1991), p. 46; Weber, *The Spanish Frontier in North America*, p. 59.
86 Bushnell, "'None of These Wandering Nations Has Ever Been Reduced to the Faith,'" p. 149.
87 Milanich, *The Timucua*, pp. 95–97.
88 Ibid., p. 99.
89 Bonnie G. McEwan, "The Spiritual Conquest of La Florida," *American Anthropologist* 103, no. 3 (2001): 634.
90 Ibid., p. 635.
91 Jerald T. Milanich, "Tacatacuru and the San Pedro De Mocamo Mission," *Florida Historical Quarterly* 50, no. 3 (1972): 287.
92 Milanich, *The Timucua*, pp. 38–40.
93 Bushnell, "'None of These Wandering Nations Has Ever Been Reduced to the Faith,'" p. 156.
94 Quoted ibid., p. 163.
95 Milanich, *Laboring in the Fields of the Lord*, p. 33.
96 Ibid., p. 132.
97 A thorough account of this uprising can be found in Francis et al., "Murder and Martyrdom in Spanish Florida."
98 Ibid., pp. 13–14, 42.
99 Ibid., pp. 41–42.
100 Ibid., p. 42.
101 Ibid., p. 43.
102 Ibid., p. 47.
103 Ibid., pp. 132–33.
104 Ibid., p. 47.
105 Ibid., p. 145.

106 Ibid., p. 48.
107 Milanich, *Laboring in the Fields of the Lord*, p. 50.
108 Ibid., pp. 40–41.
109 Ibid., p. 27.

Chapter 3: Alcade, New Mexico

1 Colin G. Calloway, *One Vast Winter Count: The Native American West Before Lewis and Clark* (Lincoln: University of Nebraska Press, 2003), p. 132.
2 Weber, *The Spanish Frontier in North America*, p. 22.
3 Israel, *Race, Class and Politics in Mexico, 1610–1670*, p. 3.
4 Covey, *Cabeza De Vaca's Adventures in the Unknown Interior of America*, p. 141. As it happened, there were only six villages—not seven cities—in the Zuñi region. See Gutiérrez, *When Jesus Came, the Corn Mothers Went Away*, p. xxvi.
5 Gutiérrez, *When Jesus Came, the Corn Mothers Went Away*, p. 42.
6 Covey, *Cabeza De Vaca's Adventures in the Unknown Interior of America*, p. 141.
7 Quoted in Bannon, *The Spanish Borderlands Frontier, 1513–1821*, p. 16.
8 Later the Spanish used the term *cíbolo* to describe the bison they saw in the West. See Weber, *The Spanish Frontier in North America*, p. 36.
9 Kanellos et al., *Herencia*, p. 41.
10 Ibid., p. 45.
11 Ibid., p. 38.
12 Bannon, *The Spanish Borderlands Frontier, 1513–1821*, p. 17; Weber, *The Spanish Frontier in North America*, pp. 37, 61.
13 Calloway, *One Vast Winter Count*, p. 134.
14 Ibid.
15 Weber, *The Spanish Frontier in North America*, pp. 14–16.
16 Gutiérrez, *When Jesus Came, the Corn Mothers Went Away*, p. xxi; John L. Kessell and Rick Hendricks (eds.), *By Force of Arms: The Journals of Don Diego de Vargas, New Mexico, 1691–93* (Albuquerque: University of New Mexico Press, 1992), p. 3.
17 Ross Frank, "Demographic, Social, and Economic Change in New Mexico," in Jackson, *New Views of Borderlands History*, p. 44; Michael V. Wilcox, *The Pueblo Revolt and the Mythology of Conquest: An Indigenous Archaeology of Contact* (Berkeley: University of California Press, 2009), pp. 103–4.
18 James A. Brown, "America Before Columbus," in Frederick E. Hoxie (ed.), *Indians in American History* (Arlington Heights, Ill.: Harlan Davidson, 1988), pp. 35–36; Gutiérrez, *When Jesus Came, the Corn Mothers Went Away*, pp. 12–14.
19 Joseph L. Sánchez, Robert P. Spude, and Art Gómez (eds.), *New Mexico: A History* (Norman: University of Oklahoma Press, 2013), p. 10.
20 Gaspar Pérez de Villagrá, Miguel Encianas, et al. (eds.), *Historia de la Nueva México, 1610* (Albuquerque: University of New Mexico Press, 1992), p. xxxi.
21 Wilcox, *The Pueblo Revolt and the Mythology of Conquest*, p. 93.
22 Calloway, *One Vast Winter Count*, p. 135.
23 Gutiérrez, *When Jesus Came, the Corn Mothers Went Away*, p. 45.
24 Matthew F. Schmader, "'The Peace That Was Granted Had Not Been Kept': Coronado in the Tiguex Province, 1540-1542," in John G. Douglass and William M.

Graves (eds.), *New Mexico and the Pimería Alta: The Colonial Period in the American Southwest* (Boulder: University Press of Colorado, 2017), pp. 53–54.

25 Wilcox, *The Pueblo Revolt and the Mythology of Conquest*, p. 102; Calloway, *One Vast Winter Count*, p. 139.

26 Calloway, *One Vast Winter Count*, p. 140; Gutiérrez, *When Jesus Came, the Corn Mothers Went Away*, p. 45.

27 Weber, *The Spanish Frontier in North America*, p. 37.

28 Calloway, *One Vast Winter Count*, p. 142.

29 MacLachlan, *Imperialism and the Origins of Mexican Culture*, p. 5.

30 Marc Simmons, *The Last Conquistador: Juan De Oñate and the Settling of the Southwest* (Norman: University of Oklahoma Press, 1991), pp. 24–25; MacLachlan, *Imperialism and the Origins of Mexican Culture*, p. 228.

31 P. J. Bakewell, *Silver Mining and Society in Colonial Mexico: Zacatecas, 1546–1700* (Cambridge: Cambridge University Press, 1971), p. 14.

32 Robert W. Patch, "Indian Resistance to Colonialism," in Beezley and Meyer, *The Oxford History of Mexico*, p. 178.

33 Bakewell, *Silver Mining and Society in Colonial Mexico*, pp. 131–32.

34 Ibid., pp. 22–23.

35 Ibid., pp. 44–47.

36 Danna A. Levin-Rojo, *Return to Aztlan: Indians, Spaniards, and the Invention of Nuevo México* (Norman: University of Oklahoma Press, 2014), p. 80.

37 Simmons, *The Last Conquistador*, pp. 49–54.

38 Calloway, *One Vast Winter Count*, p. 143; Gibson, *Spain in America*, p. 185.

39 Simmons, *The Last Conquistador*, p. 55.

40 Pérez de Villagrá, *Historia de la Nueva México, 1610*, p. xxvi.

41 Calloway, *One Vast Winter Count*, p. 146.

42 Pérez de Villagrá, *Historia de la Nueva México, 1610*, p. xxvii.

43 Ibid., pp. xxvi–xxvii.

44 "Instructions to Don Juan de Oñate," October 21, 1595, originally in AGI Audiencia de México, Lejago 26, and translated in George P. Hammond and Agapito Rey (eds.), *Juan De Oñate: Colonizer of New Mexico, 1595–1628*, 2 vols., vol. 1 (Albuquerque: University of New Mexico Press, 1953); Gutiérrez, *When Jesus Came, the Corn Mothers Went Away*, p. 47.

45 Celia López-Chávez, *Epics of Empire and Frontier: Alonso De Ercilla and Gaspar de Villagrá as Spanish Colonial Chroniclers* (Norman: University of Oklahoma Press, 2016), p. 95.

46 Ibid., p. 92.

47 Jill Lane, "On Colonial Forgetting: The Conquest of New Mexico and Its *Historia*," in Peggay Phelan and Jill Lane (eds.), *The Ends of Performance* (New York: New York University Press, 1998), p. 53; Pérez de Villagrá, *Historia de la Nueva México, 1610*, p. 6.

48 Calloway, *One Vast Winter Count*, p. 146.

49 Pérez de Villagrá, *Historia de la Nueva México, 1610*, p. xxix.

50 Simmons, *The Last Conquistador*, p. 106; Pérez de Villagrá, *Historia de la Nueva México, 1610*, p. xxx.

51 Pérez de Villagrá, *Historia de la Nueva México, 1610*, p. xxxi.

52 Calloway, *One Vast Winter Count*, p. 147.

53 Pérez de Villagrá, *Historia de la Nueva México, 1610*, p. xxxvi.

54 Sánchez et al., *New Mexico: A History*, p. 35.

55 Calloway, *One Vast Winter Count*, p. 148; Sánchez et al., *New Mexico: A History*, p. 37.

56 Calloway, *One Vast Winter Count*, p. 148.

57 Ibid.; Weber, *The Spanish Frontier in North America*, pp. 63–64.

58 Calloway, *One Vast Winter Count*, p. 149; William B. Carter, *Indian Alliances and the Spanish in the Southwest, 750–1750* (Norman: University of Oklahoma Press, 2009), p. 146.

59 Calloway, *One Vast Winter Count*, p. 149; Pérez de Villagrá, *Historia de la Nueva México, 1610*, p. xxxix.

60 Sánchez et al., *New Mexico: A History*, p. 42. More on this site can be found at https://www.nps.gov/elmo/learn/historyculture/the-spaniards.htm.

61 Bannon, *The Spanish Borderlands Frontier, 1513–1821*, p. 40.

62 Calloway, *One Vast Winter Count*, p. 150.

63 López-Chávez, *Epics of Empire and Frontier*, p. 114.

64 Pérez de Villagrá, *Historia de la Nueva México, 1610*, p. 5; Lane, "On Colonial Forgetting," p. 284.

65 Bannon, *The Spanish Borderlands Frontier, 1513–1821*, p. 41.

66 Wilcox, *The Pueblo Revolt and the Mythology of Conquest*, p. 134.

67 Phillip O. Leckman, "Meeting in Places: Seventeenth-Century Puebloan and Spanish Landscapes," in Douglass and Graves, *New Mexico and the Pimería Alta*, p. 87.

68 Kessell and Hendricks, *By Force of Arms*, pp. 5–6; Gutiérrez, *When Jesus Came, the Corn Mothers Went Away*, p. 82.

69 Wilcox, *The Pueblo Revolt and the Mythology of Conquest*, p. 135.

70 Calloway, *One Vast Winter Count*, p. 153.

71 Leckman, "Meeting in Places," p. 87.

72 Carter, *Indian Alliances and the Spanish in the Southwest, 750–1750*, p. 158.

73 Calloway, *One Vast Winter Count*, p. 151.

74 Gutiérrez, *When Jesus Came, the Corn Mothers Went Away*, p. 81.

75 Quoted ibid., p. 12.

76 Baker H. Morrow (ed.), *A Harvest of Reluctant Souls: Fray Alonso De Benavides's History of New Mexico, 1603* (Albuquerque: University of New Mexico Press, 2012), pp. xi–xii.

77 Ibid., p. xviii.

78 Ibid., p. 15.

79 Ibid., p. 17.

80 Carter, *Indian Alliances and the Spanish in the Southwest, 750–1750*, p. 154.

81 Kessell and Henricks, *By Force of Arms*, p. 6.

82 J. Manuel Espinosa, *The Pueblo Indian Revolt of 1696 and the Franciscan Missions in New Mexico: Letters of the Missionaries and Related Documents* (Norman: University of Oklahoma Press, 1988), p. 28.

83 Kessell and Hendricks, *By Force of Arms*, p. 7.

84 Ibid., p. 8.

85 Espinosa, *The Pueblo Indian Revolt of 1696 and the Franciscan Missions in New Mexico*, p. 29.

86 James E. Ivey, "'The Greatest Misfortune of All': Famine in the Province of New Mexico, 1667–1672," *Journal of the Southwest* 36, no. 1 (Spring 1994): 82.

87 Ibid., p. 78.

88 Ibid., p. 83.

89 Calloway, *One Vast Winter Count*, p. 170.

90 Ann Ramenofsky, "The Problem of Introduced Infectious Diseases in New Mexico, AD 1540–1680," *Journal of Anthropological Research* 52, no. 2 (Summer 1996): 161–63. Ramenofsky points out that there are only two direct references to disease outbreaks in New Mexico in the historical sources between 1540 and 1680.

91 Carter, *Indian Alliances and the Spanish in the Southwest, 750–1750*, pp. 174, 187; Kessell and Hendricks, *By Force of Arms*, p. 6.

92 Quoted in Ivey, "The Greatest Misfortune of All," p. 76.

93 Weber, *The Spanish Frontier in North America*, pp. 100–1.

94 Calloway, *One Vast Winter Count*, p. 172.

95 Ibid., p. 173.

96 Espinosa, *The Pueblo Indian Revolt of 1696 and the Franciscan Missions in New Mexico*, p. 33; Calloway, *One Vast Winter Count*, p. 174.

97 Calloway, *One Vast Winter Count*, p. 173; Dedra S. McDonald, "Intimacy and Empire: Indian-African Interaction in Spanish Colonial New Mexico, 1500–1800," *American Indian Quarterly* 22, no. 1/2 (1998): 134–56.

98 Calloway, *One Vast Winter Count*, p. 174.

99 Antonio de Otermín to Francisco de Ayeta, September 8, 1680, in DuVal and DuVal, *Interpreting a Continent*, p. 253.

100 Calloway, *One Vast Winter Count*, p. 175; Espinosa, *The Pueblo Indian Revolt of 1696 and the Franciscan Missions in New Mexico*, pp. 34–35.

101 Carter, *Indian Alliances and the Spanish in the Southwest, 750–1750*, p. 197.

102 Calloway, *One Vast Winter Count*, p. 175.

103 Ibid., p. 176.

104 Matthew Liebmann, Robert Preucel, and Joseph Aguilar, "The Pueblo World Transformed: Alliances, Factionalism, and Animosities in the Northern Rio Grande, 1680–1700," in Douglass and Graves, *New Mexico and the Pimería Alta*, p. 143.

105 Kessell and Hendricks, *By Force of Arms*, p. 27; Liebmann et al., "The Pueblo World Transformed," p. 144.

106 Kessell and Hendricks, *By Force of Arms*, pp. 25–26.

107 Ibid., p. 389.

108 Ibid., pp. 397–98.

109 Calloway, *One Vast Winter Count*, p. 190; Kessell and Hendricks, *By Force of Arms*, p. 357.

110 Calloway, *One Vast Winter Count*, p. 191.

111 Carter, *Indian Alliances and the Spanish in the Southwest, 750–1750*, pp. 203–4; Calloway, *One Vast Winter Count*, p. 195.

112 Wilcox, *The Pueblo Revolt and the Mythology of Conquest*, chapter 5.

113 Gutiérrez, *When Jesus Came, the Corn Mothers Went Away*, p. 157; Wilcox, *The Pueblo Revolt and the Mythology of Conquest*, p. 159.

114 Gutiérrez, *When Jesus Came, the Corn Mothers Went Away*, pp. 150–51.

115 Ibid., p. 151.

116 James F. Brooks, "'This Evil Extends Especially . . . to the Feminine Sex': Negotiating Captivity in the New Mexico Borderlands," *Feminist Studies* 22, no. 2 (1996): 283.

117 Gutiérrez, *When Jesus Came, the Corn Mothers Went Away*, p. 149.

118 Frank, "Demographic, Social, and Economic Change in New Mexico," p. 51.

119 Calloway, *One Vast Winter Count*, p. 202.

120 Kevin Starr, *California: A History* (New York: Modern Library, 2005), p. 21.

121 Mozelle Sukut (ed.), *The Chronicles of California's Queen Calafia* (San Juan Capistrano, Calif.: Trails of Discovery, 2007), p. 17.

122 Ibid., p. 19.

123 Ibid., p. 43.

124 Starr, *California: A History*, p. 21.

125 Weber, *The Spanish Frontier in North America*, p. 34.

126 Starr, *California: A History*, p. 25.

127 Rose Marie Beebe and Robert M. Senkewicz (eds.), *Lands of Promise and Despair: Chronicles of Early California, 1535–1846* (Santa Clara, Calif.: Heyday Books, 2001), p. 39.

128 Starr, *California: A History*, pp. 26–27; Beebe and Senkewicz, *Lands of Promise and Despair*, p. 39.

129 Beebe and Senkewicz, *Lands of Promise and Despair*, pp. 39–41.

130 *Letter of Sebastián Vizcaíno Written from Monterey on December 28, 1602, and Sent to New Spain by the Almiranta* (Thomas W. Norris, 1949), Bancroft Library, University of California, Berkeley.

131 Starr, *California: A History*, pp. 29–31.

132 Gibson, *Spain in America*, p. 186; Thomas E. Sheridan, *Arizona: A History* (Tucson: University of Arizona Press, 2012), p. 41.

133 Calloway, *One Vast Winter Count*, pp. 183–84.

134 James Brooke, "Conquistador Statue Stirs Hispanic Pride and Indian Rage," *New York Times*, February 9, 1998, http://www.nytimes.com/1998/02/09/us/conquistador-statue-stirs-hispanic-pride-and-indian-rage.html.

135 The work was done by sculptor Jon Sherrill Houser. See Gregory Rodriguez, "El Paso Confronts Its Messy Past," *Los Angeles Times*, March 25, 2007, online, http://articles.latimes.com/2007/mar/25/opinion/op-rodriguez25.

136 Lee Goodwin, "Heritage and Change Through Community Celebrations: A Photographic Essay," *Western Historical Quarterly* 29, no. 2 (1998): 215–23.

137 See, for instance, http://www.elsantuariodechimayo.us/Santuario/Fiesta.html or https://www.espanolafiesta.org/

Chapter 4: Fort Mose, Florida

1 E. G. R. Taylor (ed.), *The Original Writings & Correspondence of the Two Richard Hakluyts*, vol. 2 (London: Hakluyt Society, 1935), pp. 211–13.

2 Elliott, *Empires of the Atlantic World.*, pp. 23–26.

3 "Charter to Sir Walter Raleigh: 1584," http://avalon.law.yale.edu/16th_century/raleigh.asp (accessed May 20, 2017).

4 Pedro de Zúñiga to Philip III, January 24, 1607, in Philip Barbour (ed.), *The Jamestown Voyages Under the First Charter, 1606–09*, vols. 1 and 2 (Cambridge: Cambridge University Press for the Hakluyt Society, 1969), vol. 1, pp. 65, 70.

5 Ibid., pp. 117–19.

6 Ibid., pp. 255–56.

7 Barbour, *The Jamestown Voyages Under the First Charter, 1606–09*, vol. 2, p. 292.

8 "Report of Francisco Fernández de Écija," ibid., pp. 293, 305, 309.

9 Ibid., p. 314.

10 Linda A Newson, "The Democgraphic Impact of Colonization," in Victor Bulmer-Thomas, John H Coatsworth, and Roberto Cortés-Conde (eds.), *The Cambridge Economic History of Latin America*, vol. 1 (Cambridge: Cambridge University Press, 2006), pp. 152-53.

11 Alan Taylor, *American Colonies: The Settling of North America* (New York: Penguin, 2001), p. 130.

12 Marilyn C. Baseler, *"Asylum for Mankind": America, 1607–1800* (Ithaca, N.Y.: Cornell University Press, 1998), p. 32.

13 Taylor, *American Colonies*, p. 136.

14 Elliott, *Empires of the Atlantic World*, pp. 81–83.

15 John Smith, "The Description of Virginia," in Edward Arber (ed.), *Capt. John Smith: Works* (Westminster, U.K.: Archibald Constable, 1895), pp. 56–63.

16 Ibid., pp. 62, 64.

17 Taylor, *American Colonies*, p. 129.

18 John Locke, *Two Treatises of Government* (London:Whitmore and Fenn, 1821), pp. 213–17.

19 Timothy Paul Grady, *Anglo-Spanish Rivalry in Colonial South-East America, 1650–1725* (London: Pickering & Chatto, 2010), p. 21. For more on the connections between Puritans and Catholics in the Americas, see Jorge Cañizares-Esguerra, *Puritan Conquistadors: Iberianizing the Atlantic, 1550-1700* (Stanford, Calif.: Stanford University Press, 2006).

20 Smith, "The Description of Virginia," p. 64.

21 Quoted in Elliott, *Empires of the Atlantic World*, p. 187.

22 Taylor, *American Colonies*, pp. 160–61.

23 Ibid., p. 137.

24 James E. McWilliams, *Building the Bay Colony: Local Economy and Culture in Early Massachusetts* (Charlottesville: University of Virginia Press, 2007), p. 9.

25 Elliott, *Empires of the Atlantic World*, p. 188.

26 Beezley and Meyer, *The Oxford History of Mexico*, p. 109.

27 Lawrence W. Kennedy, *Planning the City upon a Hill: Boston Since 1630* (Amherst: University of Massachusetts Press, 1992), p. 251.

28 Weber, *The Spanish Frontier in North America*, p. 74.

29 Jerald T. Milanich, "Franciscan Missions and Native Peoples in Spanish Florida," in Hudson and Chaves Tesser, *The Forgotten Centuries*, pp. 280–82.

30 Kathleen A. Deagan, "Mestizaje in Colonial St. Augustine," *Ethnohistory* 20, no. 1 (1973): 55; Weber, *The Spanish Frontier in North America*, p. 86.

31 Marvin T. Smith, "Aboriginal Depopulation in the Postcontact Southeast," in Hudson and Chaves Tesser, *The Forgotten Centuries*, pp. 265–66.

32 Deagan, "Mestizaje in Colonial St. Augustine," p. 58.

33 Grady, *Anglo-Spanish Rivalry in Colonial South-East America, 1650–1725*, pp. 22–23.

34 Taylor, *American Colonies*, p. 224.

35 Trans-Atlantic Slave Trade Database, http://www.slavevoyages.org/voyages/PrMJBIJq (accessed March 2, 2016).

36 Margaret Ellen Newell, "Indian Slavery in Colonial New England," in Alan Gallay (ed.), *Indian Slavery in Colonial America* (Lincoln: University of Nebraska Press, 2009), p. 33.

37 Ibid., pp. 34–35.

38 C. S. Everett, "'They Shalbe Slaves for Their Lives,'" in Gallay, *Indian Slavery in Colonial America*, pp. 69–70.

39 Alan Gallay, "South Carolina's Entrance into the Indian Slave Trade," in *Indian Slavery in Colonial America*, pp. 111, 135.

40 Grady, *Anglo-Spanish Rivalry in Colonial South-East America, 1650–1725*, p. 92.

41 Weber, *The Spanish Frontier in North America*, p. 91.

42 Gallay, "South Carolina's Entrance into the Indian Slave Trade," p. 118.

43 Ibid., p. 125.

44 Grady, *Anglo-Spanish Rivalry in Colonial South-East America, 1650–1725*, p. 63.

45 Galley, "South Carolina's Entrance into the Indian Slave Trade," p. 140.

46 Grady, *Anglo-Spanish Rivalry in Colonial South-East America, 1650–1725*, p. 55.

47 Ibid., pp. 57–58.

48 William C. Foster (ed.), *The La Salle Expedition on the Mississippi River: A Lost Manuscript of Nicolas De La Salle, 1682* (Austin: Texas State Historical Association, 2003), pp. xii, 6, 93.

49 Ibid., p. 8.

50 Taylor, *American Colonies*, p. 382.

51 See Weber, *The Spanish Frontier in North America*, pp. 110–12.

52 Ibid., p. 116.

53 Bannon, *The Spanish Borderlands Frontier, 1513–1821*, p. 102.

54 Allan Greer (ed.), *The Jesuit Relations: Natives and Missionaries in Seventeenth-Century North America* (Boston: Bedford/St. Martin's, 2000), pp. 1–19.

55 Ibid., pp. 187–88.

56 Thomas R. Hester, "Texas and Northwestern Mexico: An Overview," in David Hurst Thomas (ed.), *Columbian Consequences: Archaeological and Historical Perspectives on the Spanish Borderland West* (Washington, D.C.: Smithsonian Institution Press, 1989), pp. 197–98.

57 Calloway, *One Vast Winter Count*, p. 113.

58 Ibid., p. 207; Weber, *The Spanish Frontier in North America*, pp. 113–15.

59 Taylor, *American Colonies*, p. 384.

60 Grady, *Anglo-Spanish Rivalry in Colonial South-East America, 1650–1725*, p. 126.

61 Claudio Saunt, "'The English Has Now a Mind to Make Slaves of Them All': Creeks, Seminoles, and the Problem of Slavery," *American Indian Quarterly* 2, no. 1/2 (1998): 158.

62 Grady, *Anglo-Spanish Rivalry in Colonial South-East America, 1650–1725*, pp. 110, 115–18; Saunt, "'The English Has Now a Mind to Make Slaves of Them All,'" p. 163.

63 F. Todd Smith, *Louisiana and the Gulf South Frontier, 1500–1821* (Baton Rouge: Louisiana State University Press, 2014), p. 76.

64 Milanich, *Laboring in the Fields of the Lord*, p. 170; Smith, *Louisiana and the Gulf South Frontier, 1500–1821*, p. 76; Saunt, "'The English Has Now a Mind to Make Slaves of Them All,'" p. 161.

65 Milanich, *Laboring in the Fields of the Lord*, p. 190.

66 The settlement in this part of Louisiana was bound up in a scheme proffered by a Scot called John Law, who stoked land speculation in what became known as the "Mississippi bubble." For more on this, see Smith, *Louisiana and the Gulf South Frontier, 1500–1821*, pp. 78–83.

67 Juliana Barr, "Beyond Their Control: Spaniards in Native Texas," in Jesús F. de la Teja and Ross Frank (eds.), *Choice, Persuasion, and Coercion: Social Control on Spain's North American Frontiers* (Albuquerque: University of New Mexico Press, 2005), p. 158.

68 Weber, *The Spanish Frontier in North America*, p. 119.

69 Ibid., pp. 114, 120.

70 Ibid., p. 121.

71 Ibid., pp. 124–25.

72 Calloway, *One Vast Winter Count*, p. 209.

73 Thomas E. Chávez, "The Segesser Hide Paintings: History, Discovery, Art," *Great Plains Quarterly* 10, no. 2 (1990): 98; Calloway, *One Vast Winter Count*, p. 209. For more on Spanish-Ute relations, see Ned Blackhawk, *Violence over the Land: Indians and Empires in the Early American West* (Cambridge, Mass.: Harvard University Press, 2006).

74 See Weber, *The Spanish Frontier in North America*, pp. 110–12; Chávez, "The Segesser Hide Paintings," p. 99.

75 The story of this attack was painted on animal skins—probably bison or elk hides—by an unknown artist, giving a tapestry-like depiction of the fight between the Spanish and the French and Oto, Pawnee, Apache, and Pueblo Indians. There were other such skins and by the 1750s they fell into the possession of a Swiss Jesuit, Philipp von Segesser von Brunegg, who had spent time in Sonora. Today Segesser I and II are in the Palace of Governors/New Mexico History Museum in Santa Fe, New Mexico. See Chávez, "The Segesser Hide Paintings," p. 99; Calloway, *One Vast Winter Count*, pp. 210–11.

76 Weber, *The Spanish Frontier in North America*, pp. 114, 125.

77 Kanellos et al., *Herencia*, p. 60.

78 Weber, *The Spanish Frontier in North America*, pp. 144–45; Charles R. Porter Jr., *Spanish Water, Anglo Water: Early Development in San Antonio* (College Station: Texas A&M University Press, 2009), pp. 73–74.

79 Weber, *The Spanish Frontier in North America*, pp. 144–45.

80 Porter, *Spanish Water, Anglo Water*, pp. 70–73.

81 Antonio de Benavides to Madrid, November 2, 1725, Archivo General de Indias, Seville (hereafter AGI), Santo Domingo, Legajo 844.

82 Jane Landers, *Black Society in Spanish Florida* (Urbana: University of Illinois Press, 1999), p. 25. For more on the differences in the development of Anglo and Hispanic slavery, see Frank Tannenbaum, *Slave and Citizen: The Classic Comparative Study of Race Relations in the Americas* (Boston: Beacon Press, 1992).

83 Antonio de Benavides to Madrid, November 2, 1725, AGI, Santo Domingo, Legajo 844; Jane Landers, "Gracia Real de Santa Teresa de Mose: A Free Black Town in Spanish Colonial Florida," *American Historical Review* 95, no. 1 (1990): 15.

84 Landers, *Black Society in Spanish Florida*, pp. 26–27.

85 Antonio de Benavides, October 15, 1728, AGI, Santo Domingo, Legajo 844.

86 James Edward Oglethorpe, *A New and Accurate Account of the Provinces of South-Carolina and Georgia: With Many Curious and Useful Observations on the Trade, Navigation and Plantations of Great-Britain, Compared with Her Most Powerful Maritime Neighbours in Ancient and Modern Times* (London: J. Worrall, 1733), p. 31.

87 Weber, *The Spanish Frontier in North America*, p. 136.

88 Francisco del Moral Sánchez, March 2, 1736, AGI, Santo Domingo, Legajo 844.

89 Herbert Bolton (ed.), *Arredondo's Historical Proof of Spain's Title to Georgia: A Contribution to the History of One of the Spanish Borderlands* (Berkeley: University of California Press, 1925), p. 183.

90 Harvey Jackson, "The Darien Antislavery Petition of 1739 and the Georgia Plan," *William and Mary Quarterly* 34, no. 4 (1977): 619.

91 Landers, *Black Society in Spanish Florida*, p. 28.

92 DuVal and DuVal, *Interpreting a Continent*, pp. 179–80.

93 Landers, *Black Society in Spanish Florida*, pp. 29–30.

94 Rodney E. Baine, "General James Oglethorpe and the Expedition Against St. Augustine," *Georgia Historical Quarterly* 84, no. 2 (2000): 202.

95 Landers, *Black Society in Spanish Florida*, p. 35.

96 Ibid., p. 36.

97 Ibid., p. 37.

98 Landers, "Gracia Real De Santa Teresa De Mose," p. 20.

99 Landers, *Black Society in Spanish Florida*, p. 36.

100 Ibid., p. 38.

101 Weber, *The Spanish Frontier in North America*, p. 136.

102 Landers, *Black Society in Spanish Florida*, pp. 47–49.

103 Ibid., p. 50.

104 Ibid., p. 46.

105 Weber, *The Spanish Frontier in North America*, p. 137.

Chapter 5: New Madrid, Missouri

1 Weber, *The Spanish Frontier in North America*, p. 426.

2 For a more detailed breakdown on immigrants, see Bernard Bailyn, *The Peopling of British North America: An Introduction* (New York: Alfred A. Knopf, 1986); and Taylor, *American Colonies*.

3 Herbert S. Klein, *A Population History of the United States* (New York: Cambridge University Press, 2004), p. 64.

4 Magnus Mörner and Harold Sims, *Adventurers and Proletarians: The Story of Migrants in Latin America* (Pittsburgh, Pa.: University of Pittsburgh Press, 1977), p. 17. John Elliott puts sixteenth-century immigration at around 200,000 to 250,000; see Elliott, *Empires of the Atlantic World*, p. 52.

5 Herbert S. Klein and Ben Vinson III (eds.), *African Slavery in Latin America and the Caribbean* (Oxford: Oxford University Press, 2007), p. 273.

6   Gilbert C. Din, "Empires Too Far: The Demographic Limitations of Three Impe-
    rial Powers in the Eighteenth-Century Mississippi Valley," *Louisiana History: The
    Journal of the Louisiana Historical Association* 50, no. 3 (2009): 270.

7   Bannon, *The Spanish Borderlands Frontier, 1513–1821*, p. 172.

8   Ibid., p. 169.

9   Ibid., pp. 179–80.

10   A good starting point on the Bourbon reforms can be found in Gabriel B. Paquette,
    Enlightenment, Governance and Reform in Spain and Its Empire, 1759–1808 (Basingstoke,
    U.K.: Palgrave Macmillan, 2008).

11   David J. Weber, *Bárbaros: Spaniards and Their Savages in the Age of Enlightenment*
    (New Haven, Conn.: Yale University Press, 2005), p. 3.

12   Bannon, *The Spanish Borderlands Frontier, 1513–1821*, pp. 154–55.

13   Ibid., p. 182.

14   Quoted in Weber, *Bárbaros*, pp. 181–82.

15   Quoted ibid., p. 91.

16   Allan J. Kuethe, "The Development of the Cuban Military as a Sociopolitical
    Elite, 1763–83," *Hispanic American Historical Review* 61, no. 4 (1981): 696–701.

17   Ibid., pp. 697, 701; Barbara H. Stein and Stanley J. Stein, *Edge of Crisis: War and
    Trade in the Spanish Atlantic, 1789–1808* (Baltimore: Johns Hopkins University Press,
    2009), p. 6.

18   Baron de Montesquieu, *The Spirit of Laws* (Ontario: Batoche, 2001), ProQuest
    online access, p. 393.

19   Adam Smith and Jonathan B. Wight (ed.), *An Inquiry into the Nature and Causes of
    the Wealth of Nations* (Petersfield, U.K.: Harriman House, 2007), eBook Collec-
    tion, EBSCOhost, p. 369. For more on British thinking on Spain, see Gabriel B.
    Paquette, "The Image of Imperial Spain in British Political Thought, 1750–1800,"
    Bulletin of Spanish Studies 81, no. 2 (2004): 187–214.

20   Abbé Raynal and J. Justamond (trans.), *A Philosophical and Political History of the
    Settlements and Trade of the Europeans in the East and West Indies*, vol. 2, book 4
    (London: T. Cadell, 1776), p. 424.

21   Smith, *Louisiana and the Gulf South Frontier, 1500–1821*, p. 133.

22   Ibid., p. 131.

23   Ibid., p. 134.

24   Ibid., p. 133.

25   David Narrett, *Adventurism and Empire: The Struggle for Mastery in the Louisiana-Florida
    Borderlands, 1762–1803* (Chapel Hill: University of North Carolina Press, 2015), p. 35.

26   Ibid., p. 36.

27   Quoted ibid., p. 40.

28   Quoted ibid., pp. 41–42.

29   Deagan, "Mestizaje in Colonial St. Augustine," p. 60.

30   Anonymous, *Reflections on the Terms of Peace* (London: G. Kearsly, 1763), p. 8.

31   Landers, *Black Society in Spanish Florida*, pp. 66–67; J. Leitch Wright Jr., "Blacks in
    British East Florida," *Florida Historical Quarterly* 54, no. 4 (1976): 427.

32   Allman, *Finding Florida*, p. 51.

33   Patricia C. Griffin, "Blue Gold: Andrew Turnbull's New Smyrna Plantation,"
    in Jane Landers (ed.), *Colonial Plantations and Economy in Florida* (Gainesville:
    University Press of Florida, 2000), p. 40.

34 Andrew Turnbull to James Grant, July 1766, "A 'Greek Community' in British East Florida: Early Plans, Selecting a Site and Mosiquito [*sic*] Inlet, and Initaring [*sic*] the Smyrnea Settlement: Letters of Andrew Turnbull," http://www.unf.edu/floridahistoryonline/Turnbull/letters/2.htm (accessed August 7, 2014).

35 Andrew Turnbull to Sir William Duncan, St. Augustine, November 26, 1766, "A 'Greek Community' in British East Florida."

36 Griffin, "Blue Gold," p. 44.

37 Ibid., p. 45.

38 Ibid., pp. 39, 56.

39 Ibid., p. 58.

40 Ibid., p. 62.

41 Landers, *Black Society in Spanish Florida*, p. 68.

42 John Stuart to James Grant, August 4, 1769, "The Indian Frontier in British East Florida: Letters to Governor James Grant from British Soldiers and Indian Traders," http://www.unf.edu/floridahistoryonline/Projects/Grant/index.html (accessed March 7, 2016).

43 Claudio Saunt, *West of the Revolution: An Uncommon History of 1776* (New York: W. W. Norton, 2014), loc. 2746, Kindle version.

44 Anderson, *Imagined Communities*, p. 47.

45 Kathleen DuVal, *Independence Lost: Lives on the Edge of the American Revolution* (New York: Random House, 2015), loc. 1122, Kindle.

46 Ibid., loc. 368.

47 Antonia Sagredo, "Personal Connections Between Spaniards and Americans in the Revolutionary Era: Pioneers in Spanish-American Diplomacy," in *Legacy: Spain and the United States in the Age of Independence*, compiled by Smithsonian Institution (Madrid: Julio Soto Impresor, 2007), pp. 46–48.

48 Ibid., p. 49.

49 Benjamin Franklin to the Committee of Secret Correspondence, January 4, 1777, National Archives: Founders Online, https://founders.archives.gov/documents/Franklin/01-23-02-0066 (accessed May 24, 2017).

50 Reyes Calderón, "Spanish Financial Aid for the Process of Independence of the United States of America: Facts and Figures," in *Legacy*, p. 66.

51 Ibid., pp. 68, 71. Reyes estimates that the total could be as high as 37 million *reales*; see pp. 74–75.

52 The American Commissioners to the Committee for Foreign Affairs, October 7, 1777, National Archives: Founders Online, https://founders.archives.gov/?q=gardoqui&s=1111311111&sa=&r=12&sr= (accessed May 31, 2017).

53 DuVal, *Independence Lost*, loc. 2149.

54 Ibid., loc. 2290.

55 For more on the European context of the American Revolution, see Brendan Simms, *Europe: The Struggle for Supremacy, From 1493 to the Present.* (New York: Basic Books, 2014), chapter 3.

56 DuVal, *Independence Lost*, loc. 2376.

57 Quoted ibid., loc. 2462.

58 Ibid., loc. 2940–3076.

59 Ibid., loc. 3367–3802; Smith, *Louisiana and the Gulf South Frontier, 1500–1821*, p. 161.

60 Benjamin Franklin to the Conde d'Aranda, April 7, 1777, National Archives: Founders Online, https://founders.archives.gov/?q=franklin%20aranda&s=iiii3iiiii&sa=&r=ii&sr= (accessed May 31, 2017).

61 Quoted in Sagredo, "Personal Connections Between Spaniards and Americans in the Revolutionary Era," in *Legacy*, pp. 58–60.

62 Draft of Letter to John Jay, Explaining His Instructions, [October 17,] 1780, National Archives: Founders Online, http://founders.archives.gov/documents/Madison/01-02-02-0080 (accessed March 30, 2017); Sagredo, "Personal Connections Between Spaniards and Americans in the Revolutionary Era," in *Legacy*, p. 61.

63 Benjamin Franklin to John Jay, October 2, 1780, in Henry Johnston (ed.), *The Correspondence and Public Papers of John Jay, 1763-1781* (New York: G.P. Putnam's Sons, 1890), p. 432.

64 Instructions from Congress to Jay, February 15, 1781, ibid., p. 460; on Jay and West Florida, see Thomas E. Chávez, *Spain and the Independence of the United States: An Intrinsic Gift* (Albuquerque: University of New Mexico Press, 2004), p. 210.

65 The Definitive Treaty of Peace 1783, http://avalon.law.yale.edu/18th_century/paris.asp (accessed May 22, 2017).

66 DuVal, *Independence Lost*, loc. 4035–61.

67 "Dictamen reservado que el excelentísimo Señor Conde de Aranda dio al Rey sobre la independencia de las colonias inglesas después de haber hecho el tratado de paz ajustado en Paris el año de 1783," in Mario Rodriguez, *La revolución americana de 1776 y el mundo hispánico: ensayos y documentos* (Madrid: Editorial Tecnos, 1976), p. 64.

68 Maya Jasanoff, *Liberty's Exiles: American Loyalists in the Revolutionary World* (New York: Alfred A. Knopf, 2011), p. 99.

69 Ibid., p. 108.

70 Landers, *Black Society in Spanish Florida*, p. 69.

71 Ibid., pp. 74–75.

72 Ibid., pp. 76–80.

73 Calloway, *One Vast Winter Count*, pp. 347–52; Elliott, *Empires of the Atlantic World*, p. 305.

74 Calloway, *One Vast Winter Count*, p. 373.

75 Kevin T. Barksdale, *The Lost State of Franklin: America's First Secession* (Lexington: University Press of Kentucky, 2009), p. 18.

76 Ibid., p. 31.

77 Ibid., p. 21.

78 George Henry Alden, "The State of Franklin," *American Historical Review* 8, no. 2 (1903): 273; Barksdale, *The Lost State of Franklin*, p. 53.

79 Quoted in Barksdale, *The Lost State of Franklin*, p. 82.

80 Ibid., p. 146.

81 Ibid., p. 147.

82 Stephen Aron, *American Confluence: The Missouri Frontier from Borderland to Border State* (Bloomington: Indiana University Press, 2009), p. 78.

83 Quoted in Barksdale, *The Lost State of Franklin*, pp. 150–52.

84 Ibid., pp. 138–39, 154, 159.

85 Andro Linklater, *An Artist in Treason: The Extraordinary Double Life of General James Wilkinson* (New York: Walker, 2009), p. 72.

86 Ibid., p. 85.

87 Barksdale, *The Lost State of Franklin*, p. 155.

88 Gilbert C. Din, *Populating the Barrera: Spanish Immigration Efforts in Colonial Louisiana* (Lafayette: University of Louisiana at Lafayette Press, 2014), p. 51.

89 Barksdale, *The Lost State of Franklin*, pp. 155–56.

90 Linklater, *An Artist in Treason*, pp. 4, 88.

91 For more on Wilkinson, see Narrett, *Adventurism and Empire*.

92 Ibid., p. 120.

93 Ibid., pp. 104, 125.

94 David Narrett, "Geopolitics and Intrigue: James Wilkinson, the Spanish Borderlands, and Mexican Independence," *William and Mary Quarterly* 69, no. 1 (2012): 108.

95 Aron, *American Confluence*, p. 51.

96 Ibid., p. 3; "Report of the Various Indian Tribes Receiving Presents in the District of Ylinoa or Illinois, 1769," in Louis Houck (ed.), *The Spanish Regime in Missouri*, vol. 1 (Chicago: R. R. Donnelley, 1909), p. 44.

97 Aron, *American Confluence*, p. 81.

98 "First Spanish Detailed Statistical Report of St. Louis and Ste. Genevieve—Dated 1772," in Houck, *The Spanish Regime in Missouri*, vol. 1, p. 53.

99 "General Instructions of O'Reilly 17 February 1770," ibid., p. 78.

100 Aron, *American Confluence*, pp. 58–60.

101 Ibid., p. 61.

102 Ibid., p. 59.

103 "Report of Captain Don Francisco Rui to His Excellency Conde de O'Reilly Concerning the Settlement of Ylinois, and the Manner and Custom of Giving Presents to and Receiving the Indians," in Houck, *The Spanish Regime in Missouri*, vol. 1, p. 63.

104 Aron, *American Confluence*, p. 83.

105 DuVal, *Independence Lost*, loc. 5657, 5662,

106 Din, *Populating the Barrera*, p. 55.

107 "Protest of Governor Miró Against Grant to Col. George Morgan—Dated 1789," in Houck, *The Spanish Regime in Missouri*, p. 276.

108 Quoted in DuVal, *Independence Lost*, loc. 5670.

109 "Protest of Governor Miró Against Grant to Col. George Morgan—Dated 1789," p. 276.

110 Narrett, "Geopolitics and Intrigue," p. 110.

111 Aron, *American Confluence*, p. 83; Houck, *The Spanish Regime in Missouri*, p. 309.

112 Din, "Empires Too Far," p. 286.

113 Aron, *American Confluence*, p. 84.

114 "Statistical Census of New Madrid in 1797," in Houck, *The Spanish Regime in Missouri*, pp. 397–98.

115 Francis Baily, *Journal of a Tour in Unsettled Parts of North America in 1796 & 1797* (London: M. S. Rickerby, 1856), pp. 261–63.

116 Ibid., p. 264.

Chapter 6: Nootka Sound, Canada

1 James Cook and John Rickman, *Captain Cook's Last Voyage to the Pacific Ocean on Discovery* (London: E. Newbery, 1781), p. 233.

2 Ibid., p. 234.

3 Instructions, March 9, 1761, Archivo General De Simancas, Estado, Legajo 6618 (antiguo) in MSS Z-E 11, Bancroft Library, University of California, Berkeley.

4 Saunt, *West of the Revolution*, loc. 662.

5 Iris H. Engstrand, Robin Inglis, and Freeman M. Tovell (eds.) and Freeman M. Tovell (trans.), *Voyage to the Northwest Coast of America, 1792: Juan Francisco de la Bodega y Quadra and the Nookta Sound Controversy* (Norman: University of Oklahoma Press, 2012), p. 24; Weber, *The Spanish Frontier in North America*, p. 185.

6 Barry Gough, *Fortune's a River: The Collision of Empires in Northwest America* (Madeira Park, B.C.: Harbour, 2007), pp. 115–16.

7 Engstrand et al., *Voyage to the Northwest Coast of America, 1792*, pp. 25–26; Gough, *Fortune's a River*, p. 117.

8 Gough, *Fortune's a River*, p. 109; Howard V. Evans, "The Nootka Sound Controversy in Anglo-French Diplomacy 1790," *Journal of Modern History* 46, no. 4 (1974): 611.

9 Flores to Valdés, December 23, 1788, quoted in Warren L. Cook, *Flood Tide of Empire: Spain and the Pacific Northwest, 1543–1819* (New Haven, Conn.: Yale University Press, 1973), p. 130.

10 Gough, *Fortune's a River*, p. 112.

11 Ibid., p. 118.

12 Ibid., p. 119.

13 Ibid., p. 121.

14 Copy of the Memorial presented to the House of Commons, May 13, 1790, in John Meares, *Voyages Made in the Years 1788 and 1789 from China to the North West Coast of America* (London: John Meares, 1790), p. 450.

15 Engstrand et al., *Voyage to the Northwest Coast of America*, p. 27.

16 Flores to Valdés, December 23, 1788, quoted in Cook, *Flood Tide of Empire*, pp. 186–87.

17 Engstrand et al., *Voyage to the Northwest Coast of America, 1792*, p. 27.

18 Ibid.

19 Ibid., p. 28.

20 Cook, *Flood Tide of Empire*, p. 275.

21 Copy of the Memorial presented to the House of Commons, May 13, 1790, pp. 444–45.

22 Ibid., p. 451.

23 Frederick J. Turner, "English Policy Toward America in 1790–1791," *American Historical Review* 7, no. 4 (1902): 706–35.

24 Gough, *Fortune's a River*, p. 123.

25 Ibid., p. 124; Derek Pethick, *The Nootka Connection: Europe and the Northwest Coast 1790–1795* (Vancouver: Douglas & McIntyre, 1980), p. 23.

26 Flores to Valdés, December 23, 1788, quoted in Cook, *Flood Tide of Empire*, p. 247.

27 Engstrand et al., *Voyage to the Northwest Coast of America, 1792*, p. 25.

28 Ibid., p. 64.

29 Ibid., p. 66.

30 Ibid., pp. 86–87.

31 Weber, *The Spanish Frontier in North America*, p. 211.

32 Greg McLaughlin and Nancy H. Mayo (eds.), *The Mapping of California as an Island: An Illustrated Checklist* (Occasional Paper No 3, California Map Society, 1995), available online at http://collections.stanford.edu/bookreader-public/view.jsp?id=00021264#3; Vicente Virga and Ray Jones, *California: Mapping the Golden State Through History* (Guilford, Conn.: Morris Book, 2010), pp. 10–11.

33 Herbert Eugene Bolton (ed.), *Kino's Historical Memoir of Pimería Alta: A Contemporary Account of the Beginnings of California, Sonora, and Arizona, by Father Eusebio Francisco Kino, SJ, Pioneer Missionary Explorer, Cartographer, and Ranchman, 1683–1711*, vol. 1 (Cleveland: Arthur H. Clark, 1919), p. 55.

34 McLaughlin and Mayo, *The Mapping of California as an Island*.

35 See an example of maps at https://searchworks.stanford.edu/view/wy568jc7945 and https://searchworks.stanford.edu/view/hv371mq4870.

36 Saunt, *West of the Revolution*, loc. 127.

37 Starr, *California: A History*, p. 32.

38 David Hurst Thomas, "The Life and Times of Fr. Junípero Serra: A Pan-Borderlands Perspective," *Americas* 71, no. 2 (2014): 191–92.

39 Quoted in Beebe and Senkewicz, *Lands of Promise and Despair*, pp. 111, 114; Starr, *California: A History*, p. 34.

40 Starr, *California: A History*, p. 34.

41 Ibid., p. 35; Beebe and Senkewicz, *Lands of Promise and Despair*, p. 114.

42 "Searching for Monterey," in Beebe and Senkewicz, *Lands of Promise and Despair*, p. 128.

43 "A Beachhead at Monterey," ibid., p. 137; Starr, *California: A History*, p. 35.

44 Starr, *California: A History*, p. 36; "A Beachhead at Monterey," p. 137.

45 Junípero Serra to Juan Andrés, June 12, 1770, in Beebe and Senkewicz, *Lands of Promise and Despair*, p. 139.

46 Ibid., p. 140.

47 Lisa Conrad, "The Names Before the Names," in Rebecca Solnit (ed.), *Infinite City: A San Francisco Atlas* (Berkeley: University of California Press, 2010), pp. 11–12; Lowell J. Bean, "Indians of California: Diverse and Complex Peoples," *California History* 71, no. 3 (1992): 303.

48 Conrad, "The Names Before the Names," pp. 10–11.

49 Taylor, *American Colonies*, p. 455.

50 Conrad, "The Names Before the Names," p. 15.

51 Ibid., p. 16.

52 Taylor, *American Colonies*, p. 455.

53 Juan Crespí, "1769: The Santa Barbara Channel," in Beebe and Senkewicz, *Lands of Promise and Despair*, p. 121.

54 Conrad, "The Names Before the Names," p. 15.

55 Douglas Monroy, "The Creation and Re-Creation of Californio Society," *California History* 76, no. 2/3 (1997): 179.

56 Gregory Rodriguez, *Mongrels, Bastards, Orphans, and Vagabonds: Mexican Immigration and the Future of Race in America* (New York: Pantheon Books, 2007), p. 67;

Jack D. Forbes, "Black Pioneers: The Spanish-Speaking Afroamericans of the Southwest," *Phylon* 27, no. 3 (1966): 236.

57 Ibid., p. 237.

58 Ibid., pp. 239–40.

59 Taylor, *American Colonies*, p. 461.

60 Ibid., p. 462.

61 Ibid., p. 461.

62 Luis Jayme to Rafael Verger, October 17, 1772, in Beebe and Senkewicz, *Lands of Promise and Despair*, p. 156.

63 Vicente Fuster, "Rebellion at San Diego," in Beebe and Senkewicz, *Lands of Promise and Despair*, p. 186.

64 Vicente Fuster to Junípero Serra, 1775, ibid., p. 187.

65 Ibid., p. 191.

66 Starr, *California: A History*, p. 34.

67 "Adapting to the Governor's Regulations," in Beebe and Senkewicz, *Lands of Promise and Despair*, p. 217.

68 Charles N. Rudkin (trans.), *The First French Expedition to California: Lapérouse in 1786* (Los Angeles: Glen Dawson, 1959), p. 13.

69 Ibid., p. 55.

70 Ibid., p. 64.

71 Robert H. Jackson and Edward Castillo, *Indians, Franciscans, and Spanish Colonization: The Impact of the Mission System on California Indians* (Albuquerque: University of New Mexico Press, 1995), p. 83.

72 Ibid., pp. 74–75.

73 Fuster, "Rebellion at San Gabriel," pp. 247–48.

74 Steven Hackel, *Junípero Serra: California's Founding Father* (New York: Hill and Wang, 2013), p. 238.

75 "The Death of Junípero Serra," in Beebe and Senkewicz, *Lands of Promise and Despair*, p. 226.

76 Jackson and Castillo, *Indians, Franciscans, and Spanish Colonization*, p. 8.

77 Starr, *California: A History*, pp. 29, 39.

78 Ibid., p. 39.

79 For a much more detailed account of this expedition, see Saunt, *West of the Revolution*, loc. 1259-1451.

80 Starr, *California: A History*, pp. 41–42.

81 "1797: Treatment of the Indians at Mission San Francisco," in Beebe and Senkewicz, *Lands of Promise and Despair*, p. 260.

82 Frank, "Demographic, Social, and Economic Change in New Mexico," p. 66.

83 Gough, *Fortune's a River*, pp. 161–64.

Chapter 7: New Orleans, Louisiana

1 Smith, *Louisiana and the Gulf South Frontier, 1500–1821*, p. 85.

2 Emily Clark, "Elite Designs and Popular Uprisings: Building and Rebuilding in New Orleans, 1721, 1788, 2005," *Historical Reflections/Réflexions Historiques* 33, no. 2 (2007): 175.

3 Antonio María de Bucareli to Julian de Arriaga, April 1, 1767, AGI, Santo Domingo, Legajo 2542A.

4 Marques de Grimaldi to Julian de Arriaga, May 13, 1767, ibid.

5 Carlos Marichal and Matilde Souto Mantecon, "Silver and Situados: New Spain and the Financing of the Spanish Empire in the Caribbean in the Eighteenth Century," *Hispanic American Historical Review* 74, no. 4 (1994): 590–91.

6 Narrett, *Adventurism and Empire*, p. 47.

7 Antonio María de Bucareli to Julian de Arriaga. December 4, 1768, AGI, Santo Domingo, Legajo 2542A; Weber, *The Spanish Frontier in North America*, p. 150; Narrett, *Adventurism and Empire*, pp. 51–52.

8 Weber, *The Spanish Frontier in North America*, p. 150.

9 Report of August 18, 1769, *Records and Deliberations of the Cabildo: Book 1*, New Orleans Public Library City Archives, pp. 1–2.

10 Weber, *The Spanish Frontier in North America*, p. 151.

11 Bannon, *The Spanish Borderlands Frontier, 1513–1821*, p. 192.

12 Proclamation by O'Reilly regulating the establishment of inns, pool rooms, and taverns, September 21, 1769, Louisiana State Museum Archives, Record Group 4, Accession number 1890.1.

13 Jane Landers, "Rebellion and Royalism in Spanish Florida: The French Revolution on Spain's Northern Colonial Frontier," in David Barry Gaspar and David Patrick Geggus (eds.), *A Turbulent Time: The French Revolution and the Greater Caribbean* (Bloomington: Indiana University Press, 1997), p. 158.

14 Kimberly S. Hanger, "Conflicting Loyalties: The French Revolution and Free People of Color in Spanish New Orleans," ibid., p. 179.

15 Gilbert C. Din, *Spaniards, Planters, and Slaves: The Spanish Regulation of Slavery in Louisiana, 1763–1803* (College Station: Texas A&M University Press, 1999), p. 154.

16 Hanger, "Conflicting Loyalties," p. 180.

17 Ibid., p. 181.

18 Jean-Pierre Le Glaunec, "Slave Migrations in Spanish Louisiana and Early American Louisiana: New Sources and New Estimates," *Louisiana History* 46, no. 2 (2005): 188.

19 Ibid., pp. 195–96; Jack D. L. Holmes, "The Abortive Slave Revolt at Pointe Coupée, Louisiana, 1795," *Louisiana History: The Journal of the Louisiana Historical Association* 11, no. 4 (1970): 342.

20 Kimberly S. Hanger, "Patronage, Property and Persistence: The Emergence of a Free Black Elite in Spanish New Orleans," in Jane Landers (ed.), *Against the Odds: Free Blacks in the Slave Societies of the Americas* (London: Frank Cass, 1996), p. 57; Andrew McMichael, *Atlantic Loyalties: Americans in Spanish West Florida, 1785–1810* (Athens: University of Georgia Press, 2008), p. 17.

21 Din, *Spaniards, Planters, and Slaves*, p. 39.

22 Mary Williams, "Private Lives and Public Orders: Regulating Sex, Marriage, and Legitimacy in Spanish Colonial Louisiana," in Cécile Vidal (ed.), *Spanish Louisiana in Atlantic Contexts: Nexus of Imperial Transactions and International Relations* (Philadelphia: University of Pennsylvania Press, 2014), pp. 148–49.

23 Ibid., p. 152.

24 Carolyn Morrow Long, *A New Orleans Voudou Priestess: The Legend and Reality of Marie Laveau* (Gainesville: University Press of Florida, 2006), loc. 844, Kindle.

25 *Records and Deliberations of the Cabildo: Book 3*, June 1, 1786, New Orleans Public Library City Archives, pp. 105–12.

26 Rules issued by Baron de Carondelet quoted in Ned Sublette, *The World That Made New Orleans: From Spanish Silver to Congo Square* (Chicago: Chicago Review Press, Lawrence Hill Books, 2009), pp. 171–72.

27 Holmes, "The Abortive Slave Revolt at Pointe Coupée, Louisiana, 1795," pp. 342, 351–53; Ulysses S. Ricard, "The Pointe Coupée Slave Conspiracy of 1791," *Proceedings of the Meeting of the French Colonial Historical Society* 15 (1992): 118.

28 Narrett, *Adventurism and Empire*, p. 157; Holmes, "The Abortive Slave Revolt at Pointe Coupée, Louisiana, 1795," p. 357.

29 McMichael, *Atlantic Loyalties*, pp. 15–17.

30 Raymond A. Young, "Pinckney's Treaty—A New Perspective," *Hispanic American Historical Review* 43, no. 4 (1963): 530.

31 Gilbert C. Din, "Spanish Control over a Multiethnic Society: Louisiana, 1763–1803," in de la Teja and Frank, *Choice, Persuasion, and Coercion*, p. 64; Narrett, *Adventurism and Empire*, p. 231. See the full text of the treaty at http://avalon.law.yale.edu/18th_century/sp1795.asp.

32 James Madison to Thomas Jefferson, February 29, 1796, Founders Online: National Archives, http://founders.archives.gov/documents/Jefferson/01-28-02-0488 (accessed March 30, 2017).

33 Smith, *Louisiana and the Gulf South Frontier, 1500–1821*, p. 171.

34 James E. Lewis, *The American Union and the Problem of Neighborhood: The United States and the Collapse of the Spanish Empire, 1783–1829* (Chapel Hill: University of North Carolina Press, 1998), pp. 4, 8.

35 James Madison to Thomas Jefferson, March 6, 1796, Founders Online: National Archives, http://founders.archives.gov/documents/Madison/01-16-02-0167 (accessed March 30, 2017).

36 Weber, *Bárbaros*, p. 1; *American State Papers: Indian Affairs*, class II, vol. 1 (Washington, D.C.: Gales and Seaton, 1832), pp. 543–44.

37 Weber, *The Spanish Frontier in North America*, p. 212.

38 Aron, *American Confluence*, p. 107; Narrett, *Adventurism and Empire*, p. 264.

39 Lewis, *The American Union and the Problem of Neighborhood*, pp. 24–25, 28.

40 Jerry p. Sanson, "'Scour[ing] at the Mortar of the Constitution': Louisiana and the Fundamental Law of the United States," *Louisiana History: The Journal of the Louisiana Historical Association* 48, no. 1 (2007): 8–9.

41 Ibid., p. 10.

42 Quoted in Bernard Bailyn, *To Begin the World Anew: The Genius and Ambiguities of the American Founders* (New York: Vintage Books, 2004), p. 41.

43 Pedro Cevallos to Marques de Casa-Calvo, April 2, 1804, AGI, Papeles De Cuba, Legajo 2356.

44 Humboldt quoted in Narrett, "Geopolitics and Intrigue," p. 116.

45 Narrett, "Geopolitics and Intrigue," pp. 117–19.

46 Ibid., p. 121.

Chapter 8: Sabine River

1 Weber, *The Spanish Frontier in North America*, p. 216.

2 Linklater, *An Artist in Treason*, p. 244.

3 Narrett, "Geopolitics and Intrigue," pp. 123–27; Linklater, *An Artist in Treason*, p. 239.

4 Narrett, *Adventurism and Empire*, p. 265.

5 McMichael, *Atlantic Loyalties*, p. 76.

6 This deal is mentioned in Aaron Burr to Andrew Jackson, March 24, 1806, in Daniel Feller (ed.), *The Papers of Andrew Jackson Digital Edition* (Charlottesville: University of Virginia Press, Rotunda, 2015–), http://rotunda.upress.virginia .edu/founders/JKSN-01-02-02-0061 (accessed August 8, 2016).

7 McMichael, *Atlantic Loyalties*, pp. 152–53.

8 Jaime E. Rodríguez O., *The Independence of Spanish America* (Cambridge: Cambridge University Press, 1998), p. 53.

9 Elliott, *Empires of the Atlantic World*, p. 376.

10 Rodríguez O., *The Independence of Spanish America*, p. 2; Elliott, *Empires of the Atlantic World*, p. 375.

11 For more on this, see D. A. Brading, *The First America: The Spanish Monarchy, Creole Patriots and the Liberal State, 1492–1866* (Cambridge: Cambridge University Press, 1991).

12 Barbara H. Stein and Stanley J. Stein, *Crisis in an Atlantic Empire: Spain and New Spain, 1808–1810* (Baltimore: Johns Hopkins University Press, 2014), p. 328; Williamson, *The Penguin History of Latin America*, p. 212; Rodríguez O., *The Independence of Spanish America*, pp. 53–54.

13 Rodríguez O., *The Independence of Spanish America*, p. 61; Elliott, *Empires of the Atlantic World*, p. 378; Brian R. Hamnett, "Process and Pattern: A Re-Examination of the Ibero-American Independence Movements, 1808–1826," *Journal of Latin American Studies* 29, no. 2 (1997): 304.

14 Rodríguez O., *The Independence of Spanish America*, p. 8; Elliott, *Empires of the Atlantic World*, p. 379.

15 Rodríguez O., *The Independence of Spanish America*, pp. 79–80.

16 Ibid., p. 82; Elliott, *Empires of the Atlantic World*, p. 387; Michael P. Costeloe, *Response to Revolution: Imperial Spain and the Spanish American Revolutions, 1810–1840* (Cambridge: Cambridge University Press, 1986), p. 173, Costeloe puts the number at thirty people representing the American colonies when the Cortes convened, while the number of total American deputies was put at sixty-three in Brian R. Hamnett, *The End of Iberian Rule on the American Continent, 1770–1830* (Cambridge: Cambridge University Press, 2017), p. 194.

17 Stein and Stein, *Crisis in an Atlantic Empire*, pp. 658–59.

18 Ibid., p. 658.

19 John Lynch, *The Spanish American Revolutions, 1808–1826* (New York: W. W. Norton, 1986), p. 299.

20 Williamson, *The Penguin History of Latin America*, p. 215.

21 Elliott, *Empires of the Atlantic World*, p. 375.

22 Costeloe, *Response to Revolution*, pp. 21–22.

23 James Madison, Third Annual Message, November 5, 1811, American Presidency Project, http://www.presidency.ucsb.edu/ws/?pid=29453 (accessed June 26, 2017); J. C. A. Stagg, *Borderlines in Borderlands: James Madison and the Spanish-American Frontier, 1776–1821* (New Haven, Conn.: Yale University Press, 2009), p. 144.

24 Quoted in Jay Sexton, *The Monroe Doctrine: Empire and Nation in Nineteenth-Century America* (New York: Hill and Wang, 2012), p. 37; Vajda Zoltán, "Thomas Jefferson on the Character of an Unfree People: The Case of Spanish America," *American Nineteenth Century History* 8, no. 3 (2007): 273–92.

25 Thomas Jefferson to James Madison, April 19, 1809, Founders Online: National Archive, http://founders.archives.gov/documents/Madison/03-01-02-0143 (accessed March 15, 2016).

26 See, for instance, Thomas Norman DeWolf, *Inheriting the Trade: A Northern Family Confronts Its Legacy as the Largest Slave-Trading Dynasty in U.S. History* (Boston: Beacon Press, 2008); Stephen M. Chambers, *No God but Gain: The Untold Story of Cuban Slavery, the Monroe Doctrine, and the Making of the United States* (London: Verso, 2015).

27 See, for instance, Allan J. Kuethe, *Cuba, 1753–1815: Crown, Military, and Society* (Knoxville: University of Tennessee Press, 1986).

28 Gabriel Debien, "Les Colons de Saint-Domingue Réfugiés à Cuba, 1793–1815," *Revista de Indias* 13, no. 54–56 (1953): 559–605.

29 McMichael, *Atlantic Loyalties*, p. 159.

30 Ibid., p. 164.

31 Ibid., p. 165.

32 James Madison to Thomas Jefferson, October 19, 1810, Library of Congress, Manuscript/Mixed Material, https://www.loc.gov/item/mjm016177 (accessed March 16, 2016).

33 McMichael, *Atlantic Loyalties*, pp. 170–71.

34 Kenneth Wiggins Porter, "Negroes and the East Florida Annexation Plot, 1811–1813," *Journal of Negro History* 30, no. 1 (1945): 9.

35 J. C. A. Stagg, "George Matthews and John McKee: Revolutionizing East Florida, Mobile, and Pensacola in 1812," *Florida Historical Quarterly* 85, no. 3 (2007): 273.

36 Ibid.

37 Ibid.

38 Ibid., p. 278.

39 Ibid., p. 279.

40 Ibid., p. 284.

41 For a more detailed account of the Patriot War, see James G. Cusick, *The Other War of 1812: The Patriot War and the American Invasion of Spanish East Florida* (Gainesville: University Press of Florida, 2003).

42 Porter, "Negroes and the East Florida Annexation Plot, 1811–1813," p. 17.

43 James Madison to Thomas Jefferson, April 24, 1812, Founders Online: National Archives, http://founders.archives.gov/documents/Jefferson/03-04-02-0546 (accessed March 30, 2017).

44 Cusick, *The Other War of 1812*, pp. 6–7.

45 Barbara Tenenbaum, "The Making of a Fait Accompli: Mexico and the Provincias Internas, 1776–1846," in Jaime E. Rodríguez O. (ed.), *The Evolution of the Mexican Political System* (Wilmington, Del.: Scholarly Resources, 1993), p. 93.

46 Elizabeth Howard West, "Diary of Jose Bernardo Gutierrez De Lara, 1811–1812," *American Historical Review* 34, no. 1 (1928): 57.

47 Ibid., pp. 57–58.

48 Ibid., p. 71.

49 Ibid., p. 73.

50 David E. Narrett, "Liberation and Conquest: John Hamilton Robinson and U.S. Adventurism Toward Mexico, 1806–1819," *Western Historical Quarterly* 40, no. 1 (2009): 29; David E. Narrett, "José Bernardo Gutiérrez De Lara: 'Caudillo' of the Mexican Republic in Texas," *Southwestern Historical Quarterly* 106, no. 2 (2002): 208.

51 Narrett, "José Bernardo Gutiérrez De Lara," pp. 211–12.

52 Quoted ibid., p. 209.

53 Ibid., p. 194; Raúl Coronado, *A World Not to Come: A History of Latino Writing and Print Culture* (Cambridge, Mass.: Harvard University Press, 2013), pp. 248–50.

54 Quoted in Coronado, *A World Not to Come*, p. 414; Narrett, "José Bernardo Gutiérrez De Lara," pp. 214–16.

55 Bradley Folsom, *Arredondo: Last Spanish Ruler of Texas and Northeastern New Spain* (Norman: University of Oklahoma Press, 2017), pp. 85–86.

56 Andrew J. Torget, *Seeds of Empire: Cotton, Slavery and the Transformation of the Texas Borderlands, 1800–1850* (Chapel Hill: University of North Carolina Press, 2015), pp. 32–33.

57 Williamson, *The Penguin History of Latin America*, p. 214; Elliott, *Empires of the Atlantic World*, p. 386.

58 James F. King, "The Colored Castes and American Representation in the Cortes of Cadiz," *Hispanic American Historical Review* 33, no. 1 (1953): 57.

59 Jaime E. Rodríguez O., "The Process of Spanish American Independence," in Holloway, *A Companion to Latin American History*, p. 198; Elliott, *Empires of the Atlantic World*, p. 385.

60 Elliott, *Empires of the Atlantic World*, p. 388.

61 Lynch, *The Spanish American Revolutions, 1808–1826*, p. 296.

62 Quoted in Costeloe, *Response to Revolution*, p. 21.

63 Quoted ibid., p. 26.

64 Quoted ibid., pp. 34–35.

65 Gregory A. Waselkov, *A Conquering Spirit: Fort Mims and the Redstick War of 1813–1814* (Tuscaloosa: University of Alabama Press, 2009), see chapter 6; Robert V. Remini, *Andrew Jackson and the Course of American Empire, 1767–1821* (New York: Harper & Row, 1977), pp. 188–90.

66 Waselkov, *A Conquering Spirit*, p. 86.

67 See ibid., chapter 5; Remini, *Andrew Jackson and the Course of American Empire*, p. 191.

68 Remini, *Andrew Jackson and the Course of American Empire*, pp. 193–94.

69 Cusick, *The Other War of 1812*, p. 301.

70 Remini, *Andrew Jackson and the Course of American Empire*, pp. 206–16.

71 John Armstrong to Andrew Jackson, July 18, 1814, in Feller, *The Papers of Andrew Jackson Digital Edition*, http://rotunda.upress.virginia.edu/founders/JKSN-01-03-02-0055 (accessed August 8, 2016); Remini, *Andrew Jackson and the Course of American Empire*, p. 225, note 57.

72 Andrew Jackson to Mateo González Manrique, July 12, 1814, in Feller, *The Papers of Andrew Jackson Digital Edition*, http://rotunda.upress.virginia.edu/founders/ JKSN-01-03-02-0051 (accessed August 8, 2016).

73 Mateo González Manrique to Andrew Jackson, July 26, 1814, ibid., http://rotunda .upress.virginia.edu/founders/JKSN-01-03-02-0060 (accessed August 8, 2016).

74 Andrew Jackson to John Armstrong, August 25, 1814, ibid., http://rotunda.upress .virginia.edu/founders/JKSN-01-03-02-0076 (accessed August 8, 2016).

75 Cusick, *The Other War of 1812*, p. 303.

76 Andrew Jackson to Mateo González Manrique, November 6, 1814, in Feller, *The Papers of Andrew Jackson Digital Edition*, http://rotunda.upress.virginia.edu/ founders/JKSN-01-03-02-0115 (accessed August 8, 2016).

77 Mateo González Manrique to Andrew Jackson, November 6, 1814, ibid., http:// rotunda.upress.virginia.edu/founders/JKSN-01-03-02-0116 (accessed August 8, 2016).

78 Remini, *Andrew Jackson and the Course of American Empire*, p. 242.

79 Cusick, *The Other War of 1812*, p. 299.

80 Claudio Saunt, *A New Order of Things* (Cambridge: Cambridge University Press, 1999), p. 279; Allman, *Finding Florida*, p. 88.

81 Andrew Jackson to Mauricio de Zuñiga, April 23, 1816, in Feller, *The Papers of Andrew Jackson Digital Edition*, http://rotunda.upress.virginia.edu/founders/ JKSN-01-04-02-0013 (accessed August 8, 2016).

82 Mauricio de Zuñiga to Andrew Jackson, May 26, 1816, ibid., http://rotunda.upress .virginia.edu/founders/JKSN-01-04-02-0022-0002 (accessed August 8, 2016).

83 Ferdinand Louis Amelung to Andrew Jackson, June 4, 1816,ibid., http://rotunda .upress.virginia.edu/founders/JKSN-01-04-02-0022-0001 (accessed August 8, 2016).

84 T. Frederick Davis, "MacGregor's Invasion of Florida, 1817," *Florida Historical Society Quarterly* 7, no. 1 (1928): 3.

85 Ibid., p. 8; Caitlin Fitz, *Our Sister Republics: The United States in an Age of American Revolutions* (New York: Liveright, 2016), p. 110.

86 Davis, "MacGregor's Invasion of Florida, 1817," p. 14.

87 Ibid., p. 18.

88 Rafe Blaufarb, "The Western Question: The Geopolitics of Latin American Independence," *American Historical Review* 112, no. 3 (2007): 753.

89 Fitz, *Our Sister Republics*, p. 111.

90 Ibid.

91 Luis de Onís to John Quincy Adams, January 8, 1818, *Official Correspondence Between Don Luis de Onis and John Quincy Adams in Relations to the Florida and the Boundaries of Louisiana* (London: Effingham Wilson, 1818), pp. 60–61.

92 Ibid.; Fitz, *Our Sister Republics*, p. 112.

93 John Quincy Adams to Luis de Onís, January 16, 1818, *Official Correspondence Between Don Luis de Onis and John Quincy Adams in Relations to the Florida and the Boundaries of Louisiana*, p. 64.

94 Andrew Jackson to F. C. Luengo, April 6, 1818, University of West Florida, University Archives and West Florida History Center, Panton, Leslie and Company papers, Series No. 946, Reel 21.

95 Andrew Jackson to James Monroe, January 6, 1818, in Feller, *The Papers of Andrew Jackson Digital Edition*, http://rotunda.upress.virginia.edu/founders/JKSN-01-04 -02-0096 (accessed August 8, 2016).

96 Andrew Jackson to Headquarters, Division of the South, May 23, 1818, University of West Florida, University Archives and West Florida History Center, Panton, Leslie and Company papers, Series No. 946, Reel 21.

97 Andrew Jackson to Rachel Jackson, June 2, 1818, ibid.

98 Remini, *Andrew Jackson and the Course of American Empire*, p. 364; James Monroe to Andrew Jackson, July 19, 1818, in Feller, *The Papers of Andrew Jackson Digital Edition*, http://rotunda.upress.virginia.edu/founders/JKSN-01-04-02-0128 (accessed August 8, 2016).

99 Andrew Jackson to James Monroe, August 19, 1818, ibid., http://rotunda.upress .virginia.edu/founders/JKSN-01-04-02-0133 (accessed August 8, 2016).

100 Remini, *Andrew Jackson and the Course of American Empire*, pp. 371–74.

101 James Monroe to Andrew Jackson, July 19, 1818, in Feller, *The Papers of Andrew Jackson Digital Edition*, http://rotunda.upress.virginia.edu/founders/JKSN-01- 04-02-0128 (accessed August 8, 2016).

102 Blaufarb, "The Western Question," p. 751.

103 Luis De Onís to the Secretary of State, December 12, 1818, University of West Florida, University Archives and West Florida History Center, Panton, Leslie and Company papers, Series No. 946, Reel 21.

104 Cusick, *The Other War of 1812*, pp. 305–6. For the full text of the treaty, see "Treaty of Amity, Settlement, and Limits Between the United States of America and His Catholic Majesty, 1819," Avalon Project: Documents in Law, History, and Diplomacy, http://avalon.law.yale.edu/19th_century/sp1819.asp (accessed June 23, 2017).

105 Rodríguez O., *The Independence of Spanish America*, p. 194.

106 Ibid., pp. 195–96.

107 Fitz, *Our Sister Republics*, pp. 4–5.

108 Ibid., p. 163.

109 Ibid., p. 15.

110 Jaime E. Rodríguez O., *"We Are Now the True Spaniards": Sovereignty, Revolution, Independence, and the Emergence of the Federal Republic of Mexico, 1808–1824* (Stanford, Calif.: Stanford University Press, 2012), pp. 256–58.

111 Lynch, *The Spanish American Revolutions, 1808–1826*, p. 322.

112 Romeo Flores Caballero and Jaime E. Rodríguez O. (trans.), *Counterrevolution: The Role of Spaniards in the Independence of Mexico, 1804–38* (Lincoln: University of Nebraska Press, 1974), p. 63.

113 Virginia Guedea, "The Old Colonialism Ends, the New Colonialism Begins," in Beezley and Meyer, *The Oxford History of Mexico*, pp. 283–84; Costeloe, *Response to Revolution*, pp. 49, 191.

114 Christon I. Archer, "Fashioning a New Nation," in Beezley and Meyer, *The Oxford History of Mexico*, p. 299; Lynch, *The Spanish American Revolutions, 1808–1826*, p. 324.

115 Rodríguez O., *"We Are Now the True Spaniards,"* p. 322.

116 Sean Wilentz, *The Rise of American Democracy: Jefferson to Lincoln* (New York: W. W. Norton, 2005), pp. 222–23.

117 Lewis, *The American Union and the Problem of Neighborhood*, p. 216.

118 Sexton, *The Monroe Doctrine*, p. 3; Joseph Smith, *The United States and Latin America: A History of American Diplomacy, 1776–2000* (London: Routledge, 2005), p. 15.

119 James Monroe, from President James Monroe's seventh annual message to Congress, December 2, 1823, USHistory.org: Historic Documents, http://www .ushistory.org/documents/monroe.htm (accessed March 17, 2016).

120 Sexton, *The Monroe Doctrine*, p. 4.

121 J. Hector St. John de Crèvecoeur and Dennis D. Moore (ed.), *Letters from an American Farmer and Other Essays* (Cambridge, Mass.: Belknap Press of Harvard University Press, 2013), p. 307; this essay brought to my attention in Elliott, *Empires of the Atlantic World*, pp. 403–4.

122 Thomas Jefferson to Baron von Humboldt, December 6, 1813, Library of Congress: Manuscript/Mixed Material, https://www.loc.gov/item/mtjbib021586 (accessed March 17, 2016).

Chapter 9: San Antonio de Béxar, Texas

1 José María Sánchez, "A Trip to Texas in 1828," *Southwestern Historical Quarterly* 29, no. 4 (1926): 271.

2 Ibid.

3 Ibid.

4 Quoted in David J. Weber (ed.), *Foreigners in Their Native Land: Historical Roots of the Mexican-Americas* (Albuquerque: University of New Mexico Press, 2003), p. 102.

5 Alexis de Tocqueville, Harvey C. Mansfield, and Delba Winthrop (trans. and eds.), *Democracy in America* (Chicago: University of Chicago Press, 2000), p. 392.

6 Alan Taylor, "Remaking Americans: Louisiana, Upper Canada, and Texas," in Juliana Barr and Edward Countryman (eds.), *Contested Spaces of Early America* (Philadelphia: University of Pennsylvania Press, 2014), p. 220.

7 Ibid.

8 Torget, *Seeds of Empire*, p. 25.

9 More on Long and the expedition against him, ibid., p. 46.

10 Ibid., p. 68.

11 H. W. Brands, *Lone Star Nation: The Epic Story of the Battle for Texas Independence* (New York: First Anchor Books, 2005), p. 14; Torget, *Seeds of Empire*, p. 49.

12 Brands, *Lone Star Nation*, pp. 20–21.

13 Ibid., p. 101.

14 Narrett, *Adventurism and Empire*, p. 265.

15 J. H. Young, "New Map of Texas: with the Contiguous American & Mexican States" (Philadelphia: S. Augustus Mitchell, 1835), Library of Congress, http:// www.loc.gov/resource/g4030.ct002350/ (accessed April 9, 2015).

16 Rodriguez, *Mongrels, Bastards, Orphans, and Vagabonds*, p. 72.

17 Ibid., p. 74.

18 Quoted ibid., p. 73; see also Eugene C. Barker, "Native Latin American Contribution to the Colonization and Independence of Texas," *Southwestern Historical Quarterly* 46, no. 4 (1943): 328.

19 Arnoldo De León, *They Called Them Greasers: Anglo Attitudes in Texas, 1821–1900* (Austin: University of Texas Press, 1983), p. 6.

20 Joseph Smith, *The United States and Latin America* (London: Routledge, 2005), p. 27.

21 David Woodman Jr., *Guide to Texas Emigrants* (Boston: M. Hawes, 1835), p. 35.

22 Narrett, *Adventurism and Empire*, pp. 9, 51.

23 Richard Griswold del Castillo, *The Treaty of Guadalupe Hidalgo: A Legacy of Conflict* (Norman: University of Oklahoma Press, 1990), pp. 9–10.

24 Bannon, *The Spanish Borderlands Frontier, 1513–1821*, pp. 227, 238; Starr, *California: A History*, p. 45.

25 Starr, *California: A History*, p. 46.

26 Ibid.

27 Monroy, "The Creation and Re-Creation of Californio Society," p. 180.

28 Michael Gonzalez, "War and the Making of History: The Case of Mexican California, 1821–1846," *California History* 86, no. 2 (2009): 18; Jackson and Castillo, *Indians, Franciscans, and Spanish Colonization*, p. 77.

29 Starr, *California: A History*, p. 47.

30 Jackson and Castillo, *Indians, Franciscans, and Spanish Colonization*, p. 87.

31 Starr, *California: A History*, p. 49.

32 Ibid., pp. 46–47.

33 Ibid., p. 54.

34 Richard Henry Dana, *Two Years Before the Mast* (New York: Harper & Brothers, 1840), pp. 53–56, Kindle.

35 Ibid., p. 54.

36 Ibid., p. 56.

37 Ibid., p. 60

38 Ibid., p. 123.

39 Ibid.

40 Philip D. Curtin, *The Atlantic Slave Trade: A Census* (Madison: University of Wisconsin Press, 1969) p. 46; Rodriguez, *Mongrels, Bastards, Orphans, and Vagabonds*, p. 80.

41 Torget, *Seeds of Empire*, pp. 75–76.

42 Josefina Zoraida Vázquez and Michael M. Brescia (trans.), "War and Peace with the United States," in Beezley and Meyer, *The Oxford History of Mexico*, p. 326.

43 Ibid., p. 321.

44 Ibid., p. 325.

45 Brands, *Lone Star Nation*, p. 108; Taylor, "Remaking Americans," p. 222.

46 Eric R. Schlereth, "Voluntary Mexican: Allegiance and the Origins of the Texas Revolution," in Sam Haynes and Gerald D. Saxon (eds.), *Contested Empire: Rethinking the Texas Revolution* (College Station: Texas A&M University Press, 2015), p. 17.

47 Zoraida Vázquez, "War and Peace with the United States," p. 327.

48 Torget, *Seeds of Empire*, p. 122.

49 "Memoria en que el gobernador del estado libre de Coahuila y Tejas . . . January 2, 1834," University of Houston, Special Collections, Mexican Documents Collection, Box 1, Folder 32; Taylor, "Remaking Americans," p. 223.

50 Quoted in Zoraida Vázquez, "War and Peace with the United States," p. 328.

51 Taylor, "Remaking Americans," p. 223.
52 Paul D. Lack, "Slavery and the Texas Revolution," *Southwestern Historical Quarterly* 89, no. 2 (1985): 184.
53 Ibid.
54 Paul D. Lack, *The Texas Revolutionary Experience: A Political and Social History, 1835–1836* (College Station: Texas A&M University Press, 1992), pp. 6–7; "Address to Colonel José Antonio Mexia," June 13, 1832 (Turtle Bayou Resolutions), Texas State Library and Archives Commission, https://www.tsl.texas.gov/treasures/republic/turtle/turtle-1.html (accessed June 29, 2017).
55 Lack, *The Texas Revolutionary Experience*, pp. 7, 183.
56 Will Fowler, *Santa Anna of Mexico* (Lincoln: University of Nebraska Press, 2007), pp. 136–37.
57 Ibid., p. 145.
58 Smith, *The United States and Latin America*, p. 27; Lack, *The Texas Revolutionary Experience*, p. 5.
59 "Memoria en que el gobernador del estado libre de Coahuila y Tejas."
60 Brands, *Lone Star Nation*, p. 224.
61 Fowler, *Santa Anna of Mexico*, pp. 155–57.
62 Ibid., p. 161.
63 Torget, *Seeds of Empire*, p. 174.
64 Martín Perfecto de Cos to the Jefe Político del Departamiento de Nacogdoches, July 12, 1835, BANC MSS P-O 110, Alphonse Louis Pinart collection, Documents for the History of Texas, Bancroft Library, University of California, Berkeley, p. 1.
65 Both quoted in Schlereth, "Voluntary Mexican," p. 27.
66 "Proceedings of a Meeting of the Citizens of San Jacinto," August 8, 1835, BANC MSS P-O 110, Alphonse Louis Pinart collection, Documents for the History of Texas, Bancroft Library, University of California, Berkeley, p. 1.
67 Ibid., p. 6.
68 "Proceedings of a Meeting of the Citizens of Nacogdoches," September 21, 1835, BANC MSS P-O 110, Alphonse Louis Pinart collection, Documents for the History of Texas, Bancroft Library, University of California, Berkeley, p. 1.
69 Lack, *The Texas Revolutionary Experience*, p. 17.
70 Ibid., p. 18.
71 Stephen Austin to Mrs. Mary Austin Holley, August 21, 1835, in Eugene Barker (ed.), *The Austin Papers: October 1834–January 1837* (Austin: University of Texas Press, 1926), pp. 101–2.
72 Stephen Austin to David G. Burnet, October 5, 1835, ibid., pp. 160–61.
73 Lack, *The Texas Revolutionary Experience*, pp. 43–52.
74 Jose María Ortiz Monasterio to John Forsyth, October 28 and November 5, 1835, in Notes from the Mexican Legation in the U.S. to the Dept. of State, 1821–1906, NARA, Record Group 59, Microfilm 54, Roll 1, 1821–1835.
75 Government circular, 1835, Archivo General de la Nación (AGN, Mexico), Administración Pública: 1821–1910; Archivo de la Secretaria de Relaciones Exteriores, Secretaria de Guerra y Marina, Barker Transcripts, Dolph Briscoe Center for American History, University of Texas at Austin.

76 Fowler, *Santa Anna of Mexico*, p. 164; for more on Mexican connections to New Orleans, see, for instance, Linda K. Salvucci and Richard J. Salvucci, "The Lizardi Brothers: A Mexican Family Business and the Expansion of New Orleans, 1825–1846," *Journal of Southern History* 82, no. 4 (2016): 759–88.

77 Ray Suarez, *Latino Americans: The 500-Year Legacy That Shaped a Nation* (New York: Celebra, 2013), loc. 549–77, ebook.

78 Schlereth, "Voluntary Mexican," pp. 28–30.

79 Ibid., pp. 32, 35.

80 Sam W. Haynes, "'Imitating the Example of Our Forefathers': The Texas Revolution as Historical Reenactment," in Haynes and Saxon, *Contested Empire*, p. 53; Weber, *Foreigners in Their Native Land*, p. 105.

81 Quoted in Lack, *The Texas Revolutionary Experience*, p. xiv.

82 Quoted ibid., p. 86

83 "Proclama de Santa Anna," February 26, 1836, *Mercurio del Puerto de Matamoros*, accessed at Dolph Briscoe Center for American History, University of Texas at Austin, vol. 1, 2Q266.

84 Fowler, *Santa Anna of Mexico*, p. 165.

85 For more about Tejanos who sided with the centralists, see chapter 9 in Lack, *The Texas Revolutionary Experience*.

86 Richard R. Flores, "Private Visions, Public Culture: The Making of the Alamo," *Cultural Anthropology* 10, no. 1 (1995): 100.

87 Quoted in Brands, *Lone Star Nation*, p. 352.

88 Ibid., p. 359.

89 Fowler, *Santa Anna of Mexico*, p. 165.

90 Quoted in Weber, *Foreigners in Their Native Land*, p. 110.

91 Brands, *Lone Star Nation*, p. 367.

92 Ibid., p. 369.

93 Ibid., pp. 371–73.

94 Fowler, *Santa Anna of Mexico*, p. 166.

95 Brands, *Lone Star Nation*, pp. 378–79.

96 Timothy M. Matovina, *The Alamo Remembered: Tejano Accounts and Perspectives* (Austin: University of Texas Press, 1995), p. 4.

97 From the account of Francisco Antonio Ruiz, quoted ibid., pp. 43–44.

98 Fowler, *Santa Anna of Mexico*, p. 166.

99 *La lima de vulcano*, March 22, 1836, quoted in Michael p. Costelo, "The Mexican Press of 1836 and the Battle of the Alamo," *Southwestern Historical Quarterly* 91, no. 4 (1988): 537.

100 *La luna*, March 29, 1836, quoted ibid., pp. 539–40.

101 *Laws of the Republic of Texas*, 2 vols. (Houston: Office of the Telegraph, 1838), vol. 1, pp. 9, 19.

102 "Public Meeting at Nashville," *Telegraph and Texas Register*, February 20, 1836.

103 "Shall We Declare for Independence?" *Telegraph and Texas Register*, February 27, 1836.

104 "The Texas Declaration of Independence," March 2, 1836, http://avalon.law.yale.edu/19th_century/texdec.asp (accessed April 24, 2015).

105 Santa Anna to Colonel Nicolás de Portillo, quoted in Brands, *Lone Star Nation*, p. 399.
106 Stephen F. Austin to Andrew Jackson, April 15, 1836, in John Spencer Bassett (ed.), *Correspondence of Andrew Jackson* (Washington, D.C.: Carnegie Institution of Washington, 1926–35), http://www.loc.gov/resource/maj.01094_0049_0052 (accessed January 27, 2017).
107 Jose María Ortiz Monasterio to John Forsyth, November 19, 1835, Notes from the Mexican Legation in the U.S. to the Dept. of State, 1821–1906, NARA, Record Group 59, Microfilm 54, Roll 1, 1821–1835.
108 Fowler, *Santa Anna of Mexico*, p. 174; Lack, *The Texas Revolutionary Experience*, p. 114.
109 Schlereth, "Voluntary Mexican," p. 27.
110 Stephen F. Austin to Andrew Jackson, April 15, 1836, in Bassett, *Correspondence of Andrew Jackson*.
111 Fowler, *Santa Anna of Mexico*, pp. 167–72.
112 Ibid., p. 172.
113 Ibid., pp. 173–75.
114 Ibid., pp. 176, 183.
115 "Army of San Jacinto," *Pennsylvanian*, June 24, 1836, in University of Houston, Special Collections, Early Texas Document Collection, Box 1, Folder 201.
116 *Columbia Telegraph and Register*, April 4, 1837, quoted in Matovina, *The Alamo Remembered*, p. 2.
117 Torget, *Seeds of Empire*, p. 270.
118 Manuel Eduardo de Gorostiza to unknown official, July 12, 1836, AGN (Mexico), Administración Pública: 1821–1910; Archivo de la Secretaría de Relaciones Exteriores, Secretaria de Guerra y Marina, Barker Transcripts, Dolph Briscoe Center for American History, University of Texas at Austin.
119 Alcalde Galán to Stephen Austin, quoted in Lack, *The Texas Revolutionary Experience*, p. 206.
120 Lorenzo de Zavala, John Michael Rivera (ed.), and Wallace Woolsey (trans.), *Journey to the United States of North America* (Houston, Tex.: Arte Público Press, 2005), p. 6.
121 Ibid., p. 1.
122 Ibid., p. 79.
123 Ibid., p. 39.
124 Margaret Swett Henson, *Lorenzo de Zavala: The Pragmatic Idealist* (Fort Worth: Texas Christian University Press, 1996), pp. xi–xii.
125 De Zavala, *Journey to the United States of North America*, p. xxix.
126 Ibid., p. 195.
127 Amy S. Greenberg, *A Wicked War: Polk, Clay, Lincoln, and the 1846 U.S. Invasion of Mexico* (New York: Alfred A. Knopf, 2012), p. 10.
128 *Resolutions of the Legislature of Rhode Island, Against the Annexation of Texas to the United States*, April 17, 1838, 25th Cong., 2d Sess., SD281, Rice University, Woodson Special Collection, Americas Collection, Series III: Mexico, 1821–1865, and Series IV, United States 1823–1893, Box 3, Folder 16.
129 *Resolutions of the General Assembly of Tennessee, in Favor of the Annexation of Texas to the United States*, April 17, 1838, 25th Cong., 2d Sess., SD384, ibid.

130 J. L. Worley, "Diplomatic Relations of England and the Republic of Texas," *Quarterly of the Texas State Historical Association* 9, no. 1 (1905): 12.

131 Rodriguez, *Mongrels, Bastards, Orphans, and Vagabonds*, p. 84.

132 Zoraida Vázquez, "War and Peace with the United States," p. 336; Fowler, *Santa Anna of Mexico*, p. 225.

133 Sam W. Haynes, *Soldiers of Misfortune: The Somervell and Mier Expeditions* (Austin: University of Texas Press, 1990), pp. 3–4.

134 For more details on the Mier expedition, see ibid.

135 Fowler, *Santa Anna of Mexico*, pp. 226–27.

136 Greenberg, *A Wicked War*, p. 12.

137 Ibid.

138 "The Treaty of Annexation—Texas; April 12, 1844," http://avalon.law.yale .edu/19th_century/texan05.asp (accessed July 14, 2017).

139 Fowler, *Santa Anna of Mexico*, pp. 236–37.

140 Sexton, *The Monroe Doctrine*, p. 91.

141 Quoted in Greenberg, *A Wicked War*, p. 19; for more on the debates within Texas about slavery, see David E. Narrett, "A Choice of Destiny: Immigration Policy, Slavery, and the Annexation of Texas," *Southwestern Historical Quarterly* 100, no. 3 (1997): 271–302.

142 "Mr. Clay on the Texas Question," *National Intelligencer*, April 27, 1884, p. 3; Wilentz, *The Rise of American Democracy*, p. 568.

143 "The Treaty of Annexation—Texas; April 12, 1844."

144 James M. McPherson, *Battle Cry of Freedom: The Civil War Era* (New York: Oxford University Press, 1988), p. 47; Greenberg, *A Wicked War*, p. 59.

145 Wilentz, *The Rise of American Democracy*, pp. 575–76.

146 "Inaugural Address of James Knox Polk," March 4, 1845, http://avalon.law.yale .edu/19th_century/polk.asp#texas (accessed April 24, 2015).

147 Ibid.

148 "Annexation," *United States Magazine and Democratic Review* 17, no. 1 (July/August 1845): 5–9; Schama, *The American Future*, p. 256.

149 Rodriguez, *Mongrels, Bastards, Orphans, and Vagabonds*, p. 89; Fowler, *Santa Anna of Mexico*, p. 247.

150 Wilentz, *The Rise of American Democracy*, p. 582.

151 *El tiempo* (Mexico City), tomo 1, no. 12, AGI, Papeles de Cuba, Legajo 2265.

152 Fowler, *Santa Anna of Mexico*, p. 248.

153 Greenberg, *A Wicked War*, p. 102.

154 Robert W. Johannsen, *To the Halls of the Montezumas: The Mexican War in the American Imagination* (Oxford: Oxford University Press, 1985), p. 8; Greenberg, *A Wicked War*, p. 119.

155 "James K. Polk: Special Message to Congress on Mexican Relations," American Presidency Project, http://www.presidency.ucsb.edu/ws/?pid=67907 (accessed July 23, 2017).

156 Quoted in Greenberg, *A Wicked War*, p. 104.

157 Quoted in Steven Hahn, *A Nation Without Borders: The United States and Its World in an Age of Civil Wars, 1830–1910* (New York: Penguin, 2016), p. 137, Kindle. The Free-Soil movement had enough momentum for former Democratic president

Martin Van Buren to run for office again in 1848, but as a member of the Free-Soil Party. He received about 10 percent of the vote. For more on free soil, see Eric Foner, *Free Soil, Free Labour, Free Men* (Oxford: Oxford University Press, 1995).

158 Rodriguez, *Mongrels, Bastards, Orphans, and Vagabonds*, p. 91.

159 McPherson, *Battle Cry of Freedom*, pp. 53–54.

160 Laura E. Gómez, *Manifest Destinies: The Making of the Mexican American Race* (New York: New York University Press, 2007), p. 20.

161 Rosemary King, "Border Crossings in the Mexican American War," *Bilingual Review/La Revista Bilingüe* 25, no. 1 (2000): 66.

162 Fabiola García Rubio, *El daily Picayune de Nueva Orleans durante los años del conflicto entre Estados Unidos y México (1846–1848): su postura ante la guerra y su recepción en la prensa Mexicana* (Mexico: Instituto de Investigaciones Dr. José María Luis Mora, 2004), pp. 63, 70.

163 Johannsen, *To the Halls of the Montezumas*, pp. 186–88.

164 Prescott was nearly blind when he wrote it, and he needed assistants to dictate the sources to him and he composed the book on a device called a noctograph. It was also later translated into Spanish and widely read in Mexico. See William H. Prescott and Felipe Fernández-Armesto (ed.), *History of the Conquest of Mexico* (London: Folio Society, 1994), p. xxiii; Johannsen, *To the Halls of the Montezumas*, pp. 30, 245. See also chapter 3 in Eric Wertheimer, *Imagined Empire: Incas, Aztecs, and the New World of American Literature, 1771–1876* (Cambridge: Cambridge University Press, 1999).

165 Quoted in Johannsen, *To the Halls of the Montezumas*, p. 247. See also John E. Eipper, "The Canonizer De-Canonized: The Case of William H. Prescott," *Hispania* 83, no. 3 (2000): 416–27.

166 McPherson, *Battle Cry of Freedom*, pp. 49–50.

167 For more on the uprising and trial, see chapter 1 in Gómez, *Manifest Destinies*.

168 Starr, *California: A History*, pp. 67–68.

169 Ibid., p. 68; Hahn, *A Nation Without Borders*, p. 134.

170 Hahn, *A Nation Without Borders*, p. 134.

171 "Proclamation to the People of California from Stephen W. Kearny," March 1, 1847, Letters sent by the Governors and by the Secretary of State of California, 1847–1848, NARA, RG 94, Microfilm 94/07.

172 Chasteen, *Born in Blood and Fire*, p. 127.

173 Fowler, *Santa Anna of Mexico*, p. 254.

174 For more on these troops, including the debate about their composition, as well as anti-Catholicism, see John C. Pinheiro, "'Religion Without Restriction': Anti-Catholicism, All Mexico, and the Treaty of Guadalupe Hidalgo," *Journal of the Early Republic* 23, no. 1 (2003): 69–96; King, "Border Crossings in the Mexican American War."

175 Suarez, *Latino Americans*, loc. 632–47; Jesús de la Teja (ed.), *A Revolution Remembered: The Memoirs and Selected Correspondence of Juan N. Seguín* (Austin: Texas State Historical Association, 2002).

176 "Our Relations with Mexico," *American Review: A Whig Journal*, July 1846, pp. 3, 14.

177 Greenberg, *A Wicked War*, p. 111.

178 Ibid., p. 160.

179 Fowler, *Santa Anna of Mexico*, p. 263.

180 Quoted ibid., p. 255.

181 Johannsen, *To the Halls of the Montezumas*, p. 155; Greenberg, *A Wicked War*, p. 170.

182 "Proclamation Translated into Spanish from Winfield Scott in Veracruz," March 22, 1847, University of Houston, Special Collections, Mexican Documents Collection, Box 1, Folder 94.

183 Ibid.

184 Fowler, *Santa Anna of Mexico*, pp. 263–64.

185 Manuel Balbontín, *La Invasion Americana, 1846 a 1848: Apuntes del subteniente de artillería Manuel Balbontín* (Mexico: Tip de Gonzalo A. Esteva, 1883), p. 52.

186 Fowler, *Santa Anna of Mexico*, pp. 275–76.

187 Quoted in Johannsen, *To the Halls of the Montezumas*, p. 247.

188 Quoted ibid., p. 248.

189 Henry David Thoreau and John Wood Krutch (ed.), *Walden, and Other Writings* (New York: Bantam, 1981), p. 85; Greenberg, *A Wicked War*, p. 196.

190 Greenberg, *A Wicked War*, p. 128; Sexton, *The Monroe Doctrine*, p. 94; John Douglas Pitts Fuller, "The Movement for the Acquisition of All Mexico, 1846–1848," in *The Johns Hopkins University Studies in Historical and Political Science* (Baltimore: Johns Hopkins Press, 1936), p. 112.

191 Fuller, "The Movement for the Acquisition of All Mexico, 1846–1848."

192 Reginald Horsman, *Race and Manifest Destiny: The Origins of American Racial Anglo-Saxonism* (Cambridge, Mass.: Harvard University Press, 1981), pp. 2–3.

193 "Our Relations with Mexico," p. 14; Horsman, *Race and Manifest Destiny*, pp. 236–37.

194 John C. Pinheiro, *Manifest Ambition: James K. Polk and Civil-Military Relations During the Mexican War* (Westport, Conn.: Praeger Security International, 2007), p. 148.

195 Cong. Globe, Senate, 30th Cong., 1st Sess. (December 1846), pp. 53–54; Pinheiro, *Manifest Ambition*, p. 149.

196 *Speech of Mr. Calhoun, of South Carolina on His Resolutions in Reference to the War with Mexico*, January 4, 1848 (Washington, D.C.: J. T. Towers, 1848), pp. 9–10, https://babel.hathitrust.org/cgi/pt?id=hvd.32044024364713;view=1up;seq=5.

197 Cong. Globe, Senate, 30th Cong., 1st Sess. (December 1846), p. 54.

198 Pinheiro, *Manifest Ambition*, p. 149.

199 Albert Gallatin, *Peace with Mexico* (New York: Bartlett & Welford, 1847), p. 28.

200 Ibid., p. 27.

201 Pinheiro, *Manifest Ambition*, p. 149.

202 King, "Border Crossings in the Mexican American War," p. 66.

203 Griswold del Castillo, *The Treaty of Guadalupe Hidalgo*, p. 42.

204 McPherson, *Battle Cry of Freedom*, p. 50.

205 Quoted in Patricia Galeana, "Presentación," in Patricia Galeana (ed.), *Nuestra Frontera Norte* (México: Archivo General de la Nación, 1999), p. 8.

206 Ibid.

207 Balbontín, *La Invasion Americana, 1846 a 1848*, p. 136. See also Charles A. Hale, "The War with the United States and the Crisis in Mexican Thought," *Americas* 14, no. 2 (1957): 153–73.

208 *Apuntes para la historia de la guerra entre México y los Estados-Unidos* (Tip. De M
    Payno (hijo), México City, Mexico., 1848), p. 28.
209 James K. Polk: Fourth Annual Message, December 5, 1848, American Presidency
    Project, http://www.presidency.ucsb.edu/ws/?pid=29489 (accessed April 29,
    2015).
210 Ibid.
211 On the key generals who participated in the two conflicts, see introduction to
    McPherson, *Battle Cry of Freedom*.
212 Ulysses S. Grant, *Memoirs and Selected Letters: Personal Memoirs of U.S. Grant, Selected
    Letters 1839–1865* (New York: Library of America, 1990), p. 41.
213 Quoted in Brands, *Lone Star Nation*, pp. 352–53.
214 De la Teja, *A Revolution Remembered*, p. 73.
215 *Clarksville Standard*, March 4, 1887, quoted in Matovina, *The Alamo Remembered*,
    p. 48.
216 On the creation and importance of the commemoration of the niños heroes, see
    Enrique Plasencia de la Parra, "Conmemoración de la hazaña épica de los niños
    héroes: Su origen, desarrollo y simbolismos," *Historia Mexicana* 45, no. 2 (1995):
    241–79.

Chapter 10: Mesilla, New Mexico

1 José Angel Hernández, *Mexican American Colonization During the Nineteenth Century*
   (Cambridge: Cambridge University Press, 2012), p. 170.
2 Gómez, *Manifest Destinies*, p. 2.
3 Hernández, *Mexican American Colonization During the Nineteenth Century*, p. 72.
4 Quoted ibid., p. 69.
5 Ibid., p. 168.
6 Paula Rebert, *La Gran Línea: Mapping the United States–Mexico Boundary, 1849–1857*
   (Austin: University of Texas Press, 2001), p. 6.
7 St. John, *Line in the Sand*, p. 28.
8 Ibid., pp. 28–29; see also Sánchez et al., *New Mexico: A History*, p. 127; Rebert, *La
   Gran Línea*, pp. 7–8.
9 St. John, *Line in the Sand*, p. 24; McPherson, *Battle Cry of Freedom*, p. 11; Rebert,
   La Gran Línea, p. 12.
10 Allman, *Finding Florida*, p. 180.
11 St. John, *Line in the Sand*, pp. 40–41.
12 Fowler, *Santa Anna of Mexico*, p. 304.
13 St. John, *Line in the Sand*, pp. 22, 35, 46.
14 Ibid., p. 31.
15 Mesilla was also famous for its association with the outlaw Billy the Kid, as he
   was tried and sentenced in the town.
16 Schama, *The American Future*, p. 270.
17 Shirley Ann Wilson Moore, "'We Feel the Want of Protection': The Politics of
   Law and Race in California, 1848–1878," *California History* 81, no. 3/4 (2003): 99.
18 Ibid., p. 105.
19 Tomás Almaguer, *Racial Fault Lines: The Historical Origins of White Supremacy in
   California* (Berkeley: University of California Press, 1994), p. 26.

20 James L. Ord to Henry Cerruti, *Answers to Questions Concerning U.S. Conquest of California and Impressions of Events and People, as Surgeon with Company F, 3d U.S. Artillery, Landed, Jan. 27, 1847 at Monterey from U.S. Ship, Lexington*, BANC MSS C-E 63-65, Bancroft Library, University of California, Berkeley, p. 2.

21 Ibid., p. 4.

22 Christopher David Ruiz Cameron, "One Hundred Fifty Years of Solitude: Reflections on the End of the History Academy's Dominance on the Scholarship on the Treaty of Guadalupe Hidalgo," *Bilingual Review* 25, no. 1 (2000): 6.

23 "Proclamation to the People of California from Stephen W. Kearny," March 1, 1847, Letters sent by the Governors and by the Secretary of State of California, 1847–1848, NARA, RG 94, Microfilm 94/07.

24 Richard Barnes Mason to L. W. Boggs. June 7, 1847, ibid.

25 Richard Barnes Mason to William Blackburn, June 21, 1847, ibid.

26 Almaguer, *Racial Fault Lines*, pp. 14–15.

27 Quoted in Tamara Venit-Shelton, "'A More Loyal, Union Loving People Can Nowhere Be Found': Squatters' Rights, Secession Anxiety, and the 1861 'Settlers' War' in San Jose," *Western Historical Quarterly* 41, no. 4 (2010): 478.

28 Donald J. Pisani, "Squatter Law in California, 1850–1858," *Western Historical Quarterly* 25, no. 3 (1994): 290.

29 Ibid., p. 277; Venit-Shelton, "A More Loyal, Union Loving People Can Nowhere Be Found," p. 476.

30 Pisani, "Squatter Law in California, 1850–1858," pp. 282–83.

31 Ibid., p. 277.

32 Ibid., p. 288.

33 Griswold del Castillo, *The Treaty of Guadalupe Hidalgo*, p. 73.

34 Pisani, "Squatter Law in California, 1850–1858," p. 287.

35 Starr, *California: A History*, p. 105.

36 Pisani, "Squatter Law in California, 1850–1858," p.290-92.; Paul Kens, "The Frémont Case: Confirming Mexican Land Grants in California," in Gordon Morris Bakken (ed.), *Law in the Western United States* (Norman: University of Oklahoma Press, 2000), pp. 329–30.

37 Pisani, "Squatter Law in California, 1850–1858," p. 287; Starr, *California: A History*, p. 104. Pisani puts the number of confirmed grants at 553, while Starr says it is 604.

38 Venit-Shelton, "A More Loyal, Union Loving People Can Nowhere Be Found," p. 479.

39 Kanellos et al., *Herencia*, p. 111.

40 Quoted ibid.

41 Paul Bryan Gray, *A Clamor for Equality: Emergence and Exile of Californio Activist Francisco P. Ramírez* (Lubbock: Texas Tech University Press, 2012), pp. 1–14.

42 Robert M. Fogelson, *The Fragmented Metropolis: Los Angeles, 1850–1930* (Cambridge, Mass.: Harvard University Press, 1967), p. 1.

43 Gray, *A Clamor for Equality*, p. 15.

44 Daniel Lynch, "Southern California Chivalry: Southerners, Californios, and the Forging of an Unlikely Alliance," *California History* 91, no. 3 (2014): 60.

45 Venit-Shelton, "A More Loyal, Union Loving People Can Nowhere Be Found," pp. 483–84.

46 Lynch, "Southern California Chivalry," p. 61.

47 *El Clamor Publico*, October 30, 1855, no. 20, p. 2. Digitized editions of the newspaper are available at http://digitallibrary.usc.edu/cdm/search/collection/p15799coll70.

48 Stacey L. Smith, "Remaking Slavery in a Free State: Masters and Slaves in Gold Rush California," *Pacific Historical Review* 80, no. 1 (2011): 29.

49 Robert F. Heizer and Alan J. Almquist, *The Other Californians: Prejudice and Discrimination Under Spain, Mexico and the United States to 1920* (Berkeley: University of California Press, 1971), p. 124.

50 Moore, "We Feel the Want of Protection," p. 109; Heizer and Almquist, *The Other Californians*, p. 124.

51 Gray, *A Clamor for Equality*, pp. xvii, 17.

52 *El Clamor Publico*, July 24, 1855, no. 20, p. 2.

53 *El Clamor Publico*, December 31, 1859, no. 20, p. 2.

54 Ruiz Cameron, "One Hundred Fifty Years of Solitude," p. 4.

55 Quoted ibid., p. 4.

56 Griswold del Castillo, *The Treaty of Guadalupe Hidalgo*, pp. 54, 182.

57 Ibid., pp. 81–82.

58 Venit-Shelton, "A More Loyal, Union Loving People Can Nowhere Be Found," p. 474.

59 Frank H. Taylor, "Through Texas," *Harper's New Monthly Magazine*, October 1879, p. 713; De León, *They Called Them Greasers*, p. 27.

60 Martha Menchaca, "Chicano Indianism: A Historical Account of Racial Repression in the United States," *American Ethnologist* 20, no. 3 (1993): 586.

61 Heizer and Almquist, *The Other Californians*, p. 95; Donald E. Hargis, "Native Californians in the Constitutional Convention of 1849," *Historical Society of Southern California Quarterly* 36, no. 1 (1954): 4.

62 Rodriguez, *Mongrels, Bastards, Orphans, and Vagabonds*, p. 123.

63 Menchaca, "Chicano Indianism," p. 587; Moore, "We Feel the Want of Protection," p. 109.

64 Hahn, *A Nation Without Borders*, p. 171.

65 John Higham, *Strangers in the Land: Patterns of American Nativism, 1860–1925* (New Brunswick, N.J.: Rutgers University Press, 1988), p. 10.

66 Elliott West, "Reconstructing Race," *Western Historical Quarterly* 34, no. 1 (2003): 10–11.

67 Menchaca, "Chicano Indianism," p. 590.

68 Constitution ibid., p. 589.

69 Ibid., p. 589.

70 Statement of J. H. Watts to H. H. Bancroft, November 25, 1878, BANC MSS P-E 1-3, Bancroft Library, University of California, Berkeley, pp. 14–15.

71 Zaragosa Vargas, *Crucible of Struggle: A History of Mexican-Americans from Colonial Times to the Present Era* (Oxford: Oxford University Press, 2011), p. 151.

72 Case quoted in Ngai, *Impossible Subjects*, p. 53.

73 Menchaca, "Chicano Indianism," pp. 592–95.

74 Gómez, *Manifest Destinies*, pp. 43–44.

75 Moore, "We Feel the Want of Protection," p. 115.

76 Rodriguez, *Mongrels, Bastards, Orphans, and Vagabonds*, p. 102.

77 William D. Carrigan and Clive Webb, "The Lynching of Persons of Mexican Origin or Descent in the United States, 1848 to 1920," *Journal of Social History* 37, no. 2 (2003): 414.

78 Ibid., p. 416.

79 William D. Carrigan and Clive Webb, *Forgotten Dead: Mob Violence Against Mexicans in the United States, 1848–1928* (Oxford, Oxford University Press, 2013, p. 6.

80 Albert L. Hurtado, "Sex, Gender, Culture, and a Great Event: The California Gold Rush," *Pacific Historical Review* 68, no. 1 (1999): 4.

81 Ibid., p. 13.

82 Carrigan and Webb, "The Lynching of Persons of Mexican Origin or Descent in the United States, 1848 to 1920," p. 69.

83 Jerry Thompson, *Cortina: Defending the Mexican Name in Texas* (College Station: Texas A&M University Press, 2007), pp. 13–17.

84 Ibid., pp. 17–21.

85 Ibid., p. 23.

86 Quoted ibid., p. 30.

87 Ibid., pp. 40–41.

88 Suarez, *Latino Americans*, loc. 700–11; Rodriguez, *Mongrels, Bastards, Orphans, and Vagabonds*, p. 103.

89 Thompson, *Cortina*, pp. 228, 236, 245.

90 Wilentz, *The Rise of American Democracy*, p. 675.

91 From Shaler Papers and quoted in Lewis, *The American Union and the Problem of Neighborhood*, pp. 36–37.

92 Quoted in McPherson, *Battle Cry of Freedom*, p. 105; for more on this entire period, see Robert E. May, *The Southern Dream of Caribbean Empire, 1854–1861* (Gainesville: University Press of Florida, 2002).

93 McPherson, *Battle Cry of Freedom*, p. 105.

94 Ibid.

95 *Daily Crescent*, May 27, 1850, III, no. 72, p. 1.

96 "The Ostend Manifesto," October 18, 1854, online version at http://xroads.virginia.edu/~hyper/hns/ostend/ostend.html (accessed March 20, 2016).

97 Ibid.

98 William V. Wells, *Walker's Expedition to Nicaragua* (New York: Stringer and Townsend, 1856), p. 24.

99 Ibid., p. 25.

100 Juan Nepomuceno Almonte to William L. Marcy, December 21, 1853, Notes from the Mexican Legation in the United States to the Department of State, 1821–1906, NARA, RG 59, M0054, loc. 1/1/5, Mexico and the United States, Roll 3.

101 St. John, *Line in the Sand*, pp. 41–42.

102 Starr, *California: A History*, p. 113.

103 Donald S. Frazier, *Blood & Treasure: Confederate Empire in the Southwest* (College Station: Texas A&M University Press, 1995), pp. 4–5; McPherson, *Battle Cry of Freedom*, p. 683; see also May, *The Southern Dream of Caribbean Empire, 1854–1861*.

104 Sánchez et al., *New Mexico: A History*, p. 130.

105 Gómez, *Manifest Destinies*, p. 103; for more detail, see pp. 98–105.

106 Mark J. Stegmaier, "A Law That Would Make Caligula Blush? New Mexico Territory's Unique Slave Code, 1859–1861," in Bruce Glasrud (ed.), *African-American History in New Mexico: Portraits from Five Hundred Years* (Albuquerque: University of New Mexico Press, 2015), pp. 47–48.

107 Ibid., p. 59.

108 Sánchez et al., *New Mexico: A History*, pp. 131–32; Vargas, *Crucible of Struggle*, p. 128.

109 Sánchez et al., *New Mexico: A History*, p. 131.

110 Ibid., p. 134.

111 Jerry Don Thompson, *Vaqueros in Blue & Gray* (Austin, Tex.: Presidial Press, 1976), p. 81; Frazier, *Blood & Treasure*, pp. 40, 104.

112 Thompson, *Vaqueros in Blue & Gray*, pp. 5–6.

113 For more on this period, see Anne Eller, *We Dream Together: Dominican Independence, Haiti, and the Fight for Caribbean Freedom* (Durham, N.C.: Duke University Press, 2016).

114 Lynch, *The Spanish American Revolutions, 1808–1826*, p. 327.

115 Paul Vanderwood, "Betterment for Whom? The Reform Period: 1855–75," in Beezley and Meyer, *The Oxford History of Mexico*, pp. 352–53.

116 "The Fate of Mexico," *United States Democratic Review*, May 1858, pp. 340–41.

117 Karl Marx, "The Intervention in Mexico," *New York Daily Tribune*, November 23, 1861; also in Karl Marx and Friedrich Engels, *Marx and Engels: Collected Works*, vol. 19 (London: Lawrence & Wishart, 2010), pp. 71–78.

118 Vanderwood, "Betterment for Whom?" p. 358.

119 Hale, "The War with the United States and the Crisis in Mexican Thought," p. 169; Jasper Ridley, *Maximilian and Juárez* (London: Constable, 1993), chapter 2.

120 Leslie Bethell, "Brazil and 'Latin America,'" *Journal of Latin American Studies* 42, no. 3 (2010): 460; John Leddy Phelan, "Pan-Latinism, French Intervention in Mexico (1861–1867) and the Genesis of the Idea of Latin America," in Juan A. Ortega y Medina (ed.), *Conciencia y autenticidad históricas: escritos en homenaje a Edmundo O'Gorman* (México: UNAM, 1968), p. 279.

121 Phelan, "Pan-Latinism, French Intervention in Mexico (1861–1867) and the Genesis of the Idea of Latin America," pp. 279–81. For the development of the idea of "Latin America" see Michael Gobat, "The Invention of Latin America: A Transnational History of Anti-Imperialism, Democracy, and Race," *American Historical Review* 118, no. 5 (2013): 1345-75.

122 Vanderwood, "Betterment for Whom?" p. 358.

123 McPherson, *Battle Cry of Freedom*, p. 683.

124 M. M. Chevalier and W. Henry Hurlbut (trans.), *France, Mexico, and the Confederate States* (New York: C. B. Richardson, 1863), p. 6; Phelan, "Pan-Latinism, French Intervention in Mexico (1861–1867) and the Genesis of the Idea of Latin America," pp. 279–81.

125 Chevalier, *France, Mexico, and the Confederate States*, p. 7.

126 Andrew Rolle, *The Lost Cause: The Confederate Exodus to Mexico* (Norman: University of Oklahoma Press, 1965), p. 89. See chapter 10 for more on Sterling Price.

127 Letter from Sterling Price to Col. Thomas L. Snead, November 15, 1865, Rice University, Woodson Special Collection, Americas Collection MS 518, Series III and Series IV, Box 3, Folder 3.6.

128 Rolle, *The Lost Cause*, pp. 95–96.

129 Vanderwood, "Betterment for Whom?" p. 362.

130 Hahn, *A Nation Without Borders*, p. 391.

131 The emperor's death was depicted soon afterward in a series of paintings by the French artist Édouard Manet, https://www.nationalgallery.org.uk/paintings/edouard-manet-the-execution-of-maximilian.

132 Rolle, *The Lost Cause*, pp. x, 187; also see Robert E. May, "The Irony of Confederate Diplomacy: Visions of Empire, the Monroe Doctrine, and the Quest for Nationhood," *Journal of Southern History* 83, no. 1 (2017): 96–98.

133 Gregory P. Downs, "The Mexicanization of American Politics: The United States' Transnational Path from Civil War to Stabilization," *American Historical Review* 117, no. 2 (2012): 387.

134 Mark Wahlgren Summers, "Party Games: The Art of Stealing Elections in Late-Nineteenth-Century United States," *Journal of American History* 88, no. 2 (2001): 431.

135 "What Is 'Mexicanisation'?" *Nation*, December 21, 1876, p. 365.

136 Ibid.

137 Summers, "Party Games," p. 431.

138 "What Is "Mexicanisation?" p. 366.

139 McPherson, *Battle Cry of Freedom*, p. 450.

140 St. John, *Line in the Sand*, p. 67.

141 Willa Cather, *Death Comes for the Archbishop* (New York: Alfred A. Knopf, 1927), loc. 152, Kindle.

142 For more on the "copper borderlands" and the rise of the mining industry in the Southwest, see Samuel Truett, *Fugitive Landscapes: The Forgotten History of the U.S.-Mexico Borderlands* (New Haven, Conn.: Yale University Press, 2006).

143 McPherson, *Battle Cry of Freedom*, p. 818.

144 St. John, *Line in the Sand*, p. 63.

145 Ibid., pp. 91–94.

146 Ibid., p. 85.

147 Ibid., p. 77.

148 Griswold del Castillo, *The Treaty of Guadalupe Hidalgo*, pp. 80–81; Sánchez et al., *New Mexico: A History*, p. 176.

149 David V. Holtby, *Forty-Seventh Star: New Mexico's Struggle for Statehood* (Norman: University of Oklahoma Press, 2012), p. 6.

150 David L. Caffey, *Chasing the Santa Fe Ring: Power and Privilege in New Mexico* (Albuquerque: University of New Mexico Press, 2014), pp. xiii–xv.

151 Ibid., p. 42.

152 Ibid., p. 16.

153 David L. Caffey, *Frank Springer and New Mexico: From the Colfax County War to the Emergence of Modern Santa Fe* (College Station: Texas A&M University Press, 2006), pp. 25–26; John M. Nieto-Phillips, *The Language of Blood: The Making of Spanish-American Identity in New Mexico, 1880s–1930s* (Albuquerque: University of New Mexico Press, 2004), p. 61; Holtby, *Forty-Seventh Star*, p. 78.

154 Caffey, *Frank Springer and New Mexico*, pp. 48–49.

155 Ibid., pp. 65–70.

156 Much of this explanation about the Maxwell grant case comes from Nieto-Phillips, *The Language of Blood*, p. 61; Holtby, *Forty-Seventh Star*, p. 78.
157 Rodriguez, *Mongrels, Bastards, Orphans, and Vagabonds*, p. 103; Anselmo Arellano, "The People's Movement: Las Gorras Blancas," in Erlinda Gonzales-Berry and David Maciel (eds.), *The Contested Homeland: A Chicano History of New Mexico* (Albuquerque: University of New Mexico Press, 2000), pp. 59–83.
158 Arellano, "The People's Movement," p. 66.
159 Report to Samuel D. King, Surveyor General for California, from Leander Ransom, September 28, 1852, NARA RG 49: Records of the Bureau of Land Management, Special Act Files, 1785–1926, no. 124 (1860), United States–California Boundary, Box 27.
160 Charles F. Lummis, *The Spanish Pioneers and the California Missions* (Chicago: A. C. McClurg, 1936), p. 304.
161 Thomas G. Andrews, "Towards an Environmental History of the Book: The Nature of Hubert Howe Bancroft's Works," *Southern California Quarterly* 93, no. 1 (2001): 36.
162 Ibid., p. 39.
163 Ibid., p. 42.
164 *Proceedings of the Society of California Pioneers in Reference to the Histories of Hubert Howe Bancroft* (San Francisco: Sterett, February 1894).
165 María Amparo Ruiz de Burton, and Beatrice Pita and Rosaura Sánchez (eds.), *The Squatter and the Don* (Houston: Arte Público Press, 1997), Kindle. For more oral histories, see Rosaura Sánchez, *Telling Identities: The Californio Testimonies* (Minneapolis: University of Minnesota Press, 1995); Marissa López, "The Political Economy of Early Chicano Historiography: The Case of Hubert H. Bancroft and Mariano G. Vallejo," *American Literary History* 19, no. 4 (2007): 874–904. For more on the life of women in Mexico and early American California, see Miroslava Chávez-García, *Negotiating Conquest: Gender and Power in California, 1770s to 1880s* (Tucson: University of Arizona Press, 2004).
166 María Amparo Ruiz de Burton to Platón Vallejo, April 23, 1859, in Rosaura Sánchez and Beatrice Pita (eds.), *Conflicts of Interest: The Letters of María Amparo Ruiz De Burton* (Houston: Arte Público Press, 2001), pp. 157–58.
167 Ruiz de Burton, *The Squatter and the Don*, loc. 1114.
168 Ibid., loc. 1290.
169 Helen Hunt Jackson, *Ramona, Translated and with an Introduction by José Martí*, in Gonzalo de Quesada (ed.), *Obras completas de Martí*, no. 57 (La Habana: Editorial Trópico, 1994), p. 12.
170 Ibid., p. ix.
171 James J. Rawls, "The California Mission as Symbol and Myth," *California History* 71, no. 3 (1992): 347.
172 Jackson, *Ramona*, p. 350.
173 Ibid., p. 387.
174 Lummis, *The Spanish Pioneers and the California Missions*, p. 295.
175 Starr, *California: A History*, p. 148.
176 Barbara A. Wolanin, *Constantino Brumidi: Artist of the Capitol* (Washington, D.C.: Featured Senate Publications 103d Congress, 1998), p. 164.

177 Montgomery C. Meigs to Emanuel Leutze, February 8, 1857, quoted ibid., p. 149.

178 Francis V. O'Connor, "The Murals by Constantino Brumidi for the United States Capitol Rotunda, 1860–1880," in Irma B. Jaffe (ed.), *The Italian Presence in American Art, 1860–1920* (New York: Fordham University Press, 1992), pp. 87–88.

179 Special thanks to Andrés Bustamante for drawing my attention to the frieze as well as the influence of William Prescott's work on U.S. troops during the Mexican-American War.

180 Frederick Jackson Turner, *The Frontier in American History* (New York: Holt and Company, 1920), p. 1, Kindle.

Chapter 11: Ybor City, Florida

1 Juan González, *Harvest of Empire: A History of Latinos in America*, rev. ed. (New York: Penguin Books, 2001), p. 238.

2 Luis Martínez-Fernández, "Political Change in the Spanish Caribbean During the United States Civil War and Its Aftermath, 1861–1878," *Caribbean Studies* 27, no. 1/2 (1994): 56.

3 Ulysses S. Grant: Seventh Annual Message, December 7, 1875, American Presidency Project, http://www.presidency.ucsb.edu/ws/?pid=29516 (accessed March 21, 2016); Louis A. Pérez Jr., *Cuba and the United States: Ties of Singular Intimacy* (Athens: University of Georgia Press, 1997), p. 53.

4 Pérez, *Cuba and the United States*, p. 54.

5 Laird W. Bergad, "Toward Puerto Rico's Grito De Lares: Coffee, Social Stratification, and Class Conflicts, 1828–1868," *Hispanic American Historical Review* 60, no. 4 (1980): 641–42.

6 Martínez-Fernández, "Political Change in the Spanish Caribbean During the United States Civil War and Its Aftermath, 1861–1878," p. 55.

7 Ibid., p. 54.

8 Ibid.

9 Louis A. Perez, "Vagrants, Beggars, and Bandits: Social Origins of Cuban Separatism, 1878–1895," *American Historical Review* 90, no. 5 (1985): 1094–98.

10 Ibid., p. 1098.

11 Louis A. Pérez Jr., "Cubans in Tampa: From Exiles to Immigrants, 1892–1901," *Florida Historical Quarterly* 57, no. 2 (1978): 129.

12 Lisandro Pérez, "Cubans in the United States," *Annals of the American Academy of Political and Social Science* 487, no. 1 (1986): 128.

13 José Martí, Philip Foner (ed.), and Elinor Randall (trans.), *Our America: Writings on Latin America and the Struggle for Cuban Independence* (New York: Monthly Review Press, 1977), p. 249.

14 Paul J. Dosal, *Tampa in Martí / Tampa En Martí* (Matanzas: Ediciones Vigía, 2010), p. 21.

15 Gerald E. Poyo, "Tampa Cigarworkers and the Struggle for Cuban Independence," *Tampa Bay History* 7, no. 2 (Fall/Winter 1985): 103; Yoel Cordoví Núñez, *La emigración cubana en los Estados Unidos: Estructuras directivas y corrientes de pensamiento, 1895–1898* (Santiago de Cuba: Editorial Oriente, 2012), p. 32.

16 Cordoví Núñez, *La emigración cubana en los Estados Unidos*, p. 44.

17 Gerald Horne, *Race to Revolution: The United States and Cuba During Slavery and Jim Crow* (New York: Monthly Review Press, 2014), p. 159.

18 Martí, *Our America*, p. 93.

19 César Jacques Ayala, *American Sugar Kingdom: The Plantation Economy of the Spanish Caribbean, 1989–1934* (Chapel Hill: University of North Carolina Press, 2003), pp. 25–26.

20 Philip S. Foner, *The Spanish-Cuban-American War and the Birth of American Imperialism, 1895–1902* (New York: Monthly Review Press, 1972), p. 164.

21 Pérez, *Cuba and the United States*, pp. 56–57.

22 Ayala, *American Sugar Kingdom*, pp. 56–57.

23 Pérez, *Cuba and the United States*, pp. 57–58.

24 Ibid., p. 62.

25 Ibid., p. 71; César Brioso, *Havana Hardball: Spring Training, Jackie Robinson, and the Cuban League* (Gainesville: University Press of Florida, 2015), p. 1.

26 Louis A. Perez, "Between Baseball and Bullfighting: The Quest for Nationality in Cuba, 1868–1898," *Journal of American History* 81, no. 2 (1994): 505.

27 Ibid., p. 511.

28 Ibid., p. 504.

29 Suarez, *Latino Americans*, loc. 3906.

30 George Marvin, "Puerto Rico, 1900–1903," *Puerto Rico Herald*, August 1, 1903, no. 105.

31 Tom Dunkel, *Color Blind: The Forgotten Team That Broke Baseball's Color Line* (New York: Grove/Atlantic, 2013), p. 53.

32 Leslie Bethell, *Cuba: A Short History* (Cambridge: Cambridge University Press, 1993), p. 28.

33 Horne, *Race to Revolution*, p. 158.

34 *Colored American*, August 13, 1898, quoted ibid.

35 Horne, *Race to Revolution*, pp. 147–48.

36 Ibid., p. 149.

37 Ayala, *American Sugar Kingdom*, p. 58.

38 Memorial to the Secretary of State, May 17, 1897, quoted in Foner, *The Spanish-Cuban-American War and the Birth of American Imperialism, 1895–1902*, p. 213.

39 Henry Cabot Lodge, "Our Blundering Foreign Policy," *Forum* 19 (March 1895): 17–18.

40 Piero Gleijeses, "1898: The Opposition to the Spanish-American War," *Journal of Latin American Studies* 35, no. 4 (2003): 686–707.

41 Quoted ibid., p. 704. For more on Afro-Cuban participation in the independence movement, see Ada Ferrer, *Insurgent Cuba: Race, Nation, and Revolution, 1868–1898* (Chapel Hill: University of North Carolina Press, 1999).

42 Carmen Diana Deere, "Here Come the Yankees! The Rise and Decline of United States Colonies in Cuba, 1898–1930," *Hispanic American Historical Review* 78, no. 4 (1998): 732.

43 Evan Thomas, *The War Lovers: Roosevelt, Lodge, Hearst, and the Rush to Empire, 1898* (New York: Little, Brown, 2010), p. 200.

44 Quoted ibid., p. 204.

45 Quoted ibid., p. 209.

46 "The Maine Disaster," *New York Times*, February 17, 1898, p. 1.

47 Thomas, *The War Lovers*, pp. 210–11.

48 "William McKinley: War Message," Digital History, http://www.digitalhistory .uh.edu/disp_textbook.cfm?smtID=3&psid=1373 (accessed March 22, 2016).

49 Ibid.

50 Pérez, *Cuba and the United States*, p. 95.

51 "William McKinley: War Message."

52 Stephen Kinzer, *The True Flag: Theodore Roosevelt, Mark Twain, and the Birth of the American Empire* (New York: Henry Holt, 2017), p. 38, Kindle.

53 Deere, "Here Come the Yankees!" p. 732; Pérez, *Cuba and the United States*, p. 96.

54 Quoted in Louis Pérez Jr., *Cuba Between Empires, 1878–1902* (Pittsburgh: University of Pittsburgh Press, 1983), p. 95.

55 For an examination of how Cuban participation after the United States arrived was either denigrated or ignored, see chapter 4 in Louis A. Pérez, *The War of 1898: The United States and Cuba in History and Historiography* (Chapel Hill: University of North Carolina Press, 1998).

56 Ferrer, *Insurgent Cuba*, p. 187; Pérez, *The War of 1898*, p. 83.

57 Quoted in Ferrer, *Insurgent Cuba*, p. 188.

58 Quoted ibid.

59 Philip Hanna to J. B. Moore, June 21, 1898, Center for Puerto Rican Studies, Hunter College, Microfilm Collection, U.S. Consuls in Puerto Rico, San Juan, reels covering 1898–99, Roll 21.

60 *New York Journal*, August 13, 1898.

61 Albert J. Beveridge, "March of the Flag," September 16, 1898, Voices of Democracy: U.S. Oratory Project, http://voicesofdemocracy.umd.edu/beveridge-march-of -the-flag-speech-text/ (accessed January 20, 2017).

62 Ibid.

63 W. E. B. Du Bois and Nahum Dimitri Chandler (ed.), "The Present Outlook for the Dark Races of Mankind (1900)," in *The Problem of the Color Line at the Turn of the Twentieth Century* (New York: Fordham University Press, 2014), p. 118.

64 For more on the anti-imperialism movement more widely in the United States in this period, see Michael Patrick Cullinane, *Liberty and American Anti-Imperialism, 1898–1909* (New York: Palgrave Macmillan, 2012).

65 Thomas McCormick, "From Old Empire to New: The Changing Dynamics and Tactics of American Empire," in Alfred McCoy and Francisco Scarano (eds.), *Colonial Crucible: Empire in the Making of the Modern American State* (Madison: University of Wisconsin Press, 2009), chapter 3.

66 Sexton, *The Monroe Doctrine*, pp. 213–14; Kinzer, *The True Flag*, p. 66.

67 Quoted in Kinzer, *The True Flag*, pp. 170–71.

68 Ibid., p. 171.

69 Quoted in Pérez, *The War of 1898*, p. 23.

70 Ibid., p. 33; Pérez, *Cuba Between Empires*, pp. 186, 277.

71 General William Ludow to the New York Chamber of Commerce, quoted in Pérez, *Cuba Between Empires*, p. 307.

72 Pérez, *Cuba Between Empires*, pp. 310–11.

73 Deere, "Here Come the Yankees!" p. 737.

74 Pérez, *The War of 1898*, pp. 33–34.

75 Pérez, *Cuba and the United States*, pp. 121–22; Pérez, *Cuba Between Empires*, p. 363.

76 Louis A. Perez, "Insurrection, Intervention, and the Transformation of Land Tenure Systems in Cuba, 1895–1902," *Hispanic American Historical Review* 65, no. 2 (1985): 234.

77 Ibid., p. 240.

78 Ibid., p. 252.

79 Deere, "Here Come the Yankees!" p. 742.

80 Pérez, *Cuba and the United States*, p. 122.

81 Philip Hanna to J. B. Moore, June 21, 1898, Center for Puerto Rican Studies, Hunter College, Microfilm Collection, U.S. Consuls in Puerto Rico, San Juan, reels covering 1898–99, Roll 21.

82 Picó, *History of Puerto Rico*, p. 239.

83 Sam Erman, "Meanings of Citizenship in the U.S. Empire: Puerto Rico, Isabel Gonzalez, and the Supreme Court, 1898 to 1905," *Journal of American Ethnic History* 27, no. 4 (2008): 10.

84 "The New Governor," *Puerto Rico Herald*, August 15, 1903, no. 107.

85 Suarez, *Latino American*, loc. 1155; José A. Cabranes, "Citizenship and the American Empire: Notes on the Legislative History of the United States Citizenship of Puerto Ricans," *University of Pennsylvania Law Review* 127, no. 2 (1978): 392.

86 Leonard Wood, William Taft, Charles H. Allen, Perfecto Lacoste, and M. E. Beale, *Opportunities in the Colonies and Cuba* (London: Lewis, Scribner, 1902), pp. 279, 290.

87 Ibid., pp. 316–17.

88 Ibid., p. 369.

89 Ibid., p. 280.

90 "Porto Rico Not Prospering Under United States Rule," *New York Times*, October 4, 1903.

91 Picó, *History of Puerto Rico*, p. 144; Vicki L. Ruiz and Virginia Sánchez Korrol, *Latinas in the United States: A Historical Encyclopedia* (Bloomington: University of Indiana Press, 2006), p. 591.

92 Picó, *History of Puerto Rico*, pp. 243–44.

93 Erman, "Meanings of Citizenship in the U.S. Empire," p. 6.

94 Ibid., p. 11.

95 Ibid.

96 Ibid., p. 12.

97 Ibid.

98 Ibid., p. 13.

99 Ibid., p. 15.

100 Ibid., p. 23.

101 Suarez, *Latino Americans*, loc. 1259.

102 Quoted in César J. Ayala and Rafael Bernabe, *Puerto Rico in the American Century: A History Since 1898* (Chapel Hill: University of North Carolina, 2007), p. 57; Harry Franqui-Rivera, "National Mythologies: U.S. Citizenship for the People of Puerto Rico and Military Service," *Memorias: Revista digital de historia y arqueología desde el Caribe* 10, no. 21 (2013): 8.

103 Nancy Morris, *Puerto Rico: Culture, Politics, and Identity* (Westport, Conn.: Praeger, 1995), pp. 31–33.

104 Franqui-Rivera, "National Mythologies," p. 14.

105 Ibid.

106 Ibid., p. 15.

107 Truman R. Clark, "Governor E. Mont. Reily's Inaugural Speech," *Caribbean Studies* 11, no. 4 (1972): 106–8.

108 E. Mont. Reily to Warren Harding, August 31, 1921, E. Mont. Reily Papers, 1919–23, New York Public Library MSS and Archives Division, 1919, Folders 1.1–1.4, 1919 to June 1923.

109 Juan B. Huyke to Warren Harding, September 22, 1921, ibid.

110 E. Mont. Reily to Warren Harding, March 22, 1922, and Juan B. Huyke to Warren Harding, September 22, 1921, both ibid.

111 Clark, "Governor E. Mont Reily's Inaugural Speech," pp. 106–8.

112 For more on the history of the Panama Canal, see Matthew Parker, *Panama Fever: The Battle to Build the Canal* (London: Hutchinson, 2007).

113 Theodore Roosevelt, Fourth Annual Message to Congress, December 6, 1904, http://www.presidency.ucsb.edu/ws/?pid=29545 (accessed March 22, 2016).

114 Ibid.

115 Ibid.

116 Linda Noel, "'I Am an American': Anglos, Mexicans, *Nativos* and the National Debate over Arizona and New Mexico Statehood," *Pacific Historical Review* 80, no. 3 (2011): 432–33.

117 Holtby, *Forty-Seventh Star*, p. 34.

118 John M. Nieto-Phillips, "Spanish American Ethnic Identity and New Mexico's Statehood Struggle," in Gonzales-Berry and Maciel, *The Contested Homeland*, p. 105.

119 Private note to Stephen B. Elkins, May 22, 1874, Washington, D.C., MS 0033, Box 1, Folder 2, A&M no. 53, Stephen B. Elkins Papers, Archives and Manuscripts Section, West Virginia Collection, West Virginia University Library, accessed in Archives and Special Collections Department, New Mexico State University Library, Stephen B. Elkins Papers, Rio Grande Historical Collection.

120 *New Mexico: Its Resources and Advantages*, Territorial Bureau of Immigration, 1881, New Mexico history collection, Center for Southwest Research, University Libraries, University of New Mexico, MSS 349, BC, Box 11, Folder 11.

121 Ibid.

122 Speech of Hon. Casimiro Barela in the [Colorado] State Senate, Upon the Joint Memorial to the President and Congress, Praying for the Admission of New Mexico into the Union, February 8, 1889, New Mexico History Collection, Center for Southwest Research, University Libraries, University of New Mexico, Thomas B. Catron Papers, 1692–1934, MSS 29, BC, Series 102, Box 2, Folder 5.

123 Prince quoted in Nieto-Phillips, "Spanish American Ethnic Identity and New Mexico's Statehood Struggle," pp. 117–18.

124 Nieto-Phillips, *The Language of Blood*, p. 1.

125 Miguel Otero, *My Nine Years as the Governor of the Territory of New Mexico, 1897–1906* (Albuquerque: University of New Mexico Press, 1940), p. 35.

126 Ibid., p. 36.
127 Ibid., p. 50.
128 Sánchez et al., *New Mexico: A History*, p. 180.
129 Otero, *My Nine Years as the Governor of the Territory of New Mexico*, p. 200.
130 John Braeman, "Albert J. Beveridge and Statehood for the Southwest 1902–1912," *Arizona and the West* 10, no. 4 (1968): 313; Beveridge, "March of the Flag."
131 Otero, *My Nine Years as the Governor of the Territory of New Mexico*, p. 212.
132 Ibid., p. 216.
133 For more on English-language education, see Erlinda Gonzales-Berry, "Which Language Will Our Children Speak? The Spanish Language and Public Education Policy in New Mexico, 1890–1930," in Gonzales-Berry and Maciel, *The Contested Homeland*, p. 173; Otero, *My Nine Years as the Governor of the Territory of New Mexico*, p. 214.
134 Braeman, "Albert J. Beveridge and Statehood for the Southwest 1902–1912," p. 318.
135 Nieto-Phillips, "Spanish American Ethnic Identity and New Mexico's Statehood Struggle," p. 122.
136 Orville Platt to Stephen Elkins, February 5, 1889, New Mexico History Collection, Center for Southwest Research, University Libraries, University of New Mexico, Thomas B. Catron Papers, 1692–1934, MSS 29, BC, Series 102, Box 2, Folder 5.
137 Braeman, "Albert J. Beveridge and Statehood for the Southwest 1902–1912," p. 322.
138 Theodore Roosevelt, Fifth Annual Message, American Presidency Project, http://www.presidency.ucsb.edu/ws/?pid=29546 (accessed October 5, 2016).
139 Noel, "'I Am an American,'" pp. 435, 450; see also Linda C. Noel, *Debating American Identity: Southwestern Statehood and Mexican Immigration* (Tucson: University of Arizona Press, 2014); Braeman, "Albert J. Beveridge and Statehood for the Southwest 1902–1912," p. 327; Sheridan, *Arizona: A History*, p. 181.
140 Noel, "I Am an American," p. 434.
141 *La Voz del Pueblo*, February 25, 1911, quoted in Noel, "I Am an American," p. 445.
142 For more detail on this, see Nieto-Phillips, "Spanish American Ethnic Identity and New Mexico's Statehood Struggle," pp. 123–24.
143 "Taft Rebukes New Mexicans: Sharply Answers Speakers Who Utter Doubts on Statehood Promises," *New York Times*, October 17, 1909.
144 For more on this marginalization, see Noel, "I Am an American," pp. 461–65.
145 Holtby, *Forty-Seventh Star*, pp. 231–32.
146 Ibid., p. xiii.

Chapter 12: Del Rio, Texas

1 This photo is reproduced in Carole Nagger and Fred Ritchin (eds.), *México: Through Foreign Eyes / Visto Por Ojos Extranjeros, 1850–1990* (New York: W. W. Norton, 1993), pp. 138–39. See also Claire F. Fox, *The Fence and the River: Culture and Politics at the U.S. Mexico Border* (Minneapolis: University of Minnesota Press, 1999), pp. 81–85.
2 Fox, *The Fence and the River*, p. 81.
3 For a starting point for much more detail about the Mexican Revolution in the English-language literature, see Alan Knight, *The Mexican Revolution*, vol. 1,

Porfirians, Liberals and Peasants, and vol. 2, *Counter-Revolution and Reconstruction* (Lincoln: University of Nebraska Press, 1990).

4 Fox, *The Fence and the River*, p. 69.

5 See chapter 2 in Gilbert M. Joseph and Jürgen Buchenau, *Mexico's Once and Future Revolution: Social Upheaval and the Challenges of Rule Since the Late Nineteenth Century* (Durham, N.C.: Duke University Press, 2013).

6 John Tutino, *From Insurrection to Revolution in Mexico: Social Bases of Agrarian Violence, 1750–1940* (Princeton, N.J.: Princeton University Press, 1986), pp. 258–67.

7 Ibid., pp. 269–70.

8 Ibid., pp. 283–84; John Womack, "The Mexican Revolution, 1910–1920," in Leslie Bethell (ed.), *The Cambridge History of Latin America* (Cambridge: Cambridge University Press, 1984), vol. 5, p. 82.

9 Tutino, *From Insurrection to Revolution in Mexico*, pp. 289, 298.

10 John Mason Hart, "The Mexican Revolution," in Beezley and Meyer, *The Oxford History of Mexico*, pp. 409–10.

11 Quoted in Chasteen, *Born in Blood and Fire*, p. 194.

12 Hart, "The Mexican Revolution," p. 409; Knight, *The Mexican Revolution*, vol. 1, p. 46.

13 Joseph and Buchenau, *Mexico's Once and Future Revolution*, pp. 35–36.

14 Ibid., pp. 34–35. See extracts in English at Document #4: "Plan de San Luis de Potosí," Brown University Library, Center for Digital Scholarship, https://library .brown.edu/create/modernlatinamerica/chapters/chapter-3-mexico/primary - documents-with-accompanying-discussion-questions/document-4-plan-de-san -luis-de-potosi-francisco-madero-1910/; or in Spanish at http://www.bibliotecas .tv/zapata/1910/plan.html (accessed October 18, 2016).

15 Knight, *The Mexican Revolution*, vol. 1, p. 181.

16 Ibid., p. 184.

17 For a detailed account of Zapata and Morelos during the revolution, see John Womack Jr., *Zapata and the Mexican Revolution* (London: Penguin, 1972).

18 Joseph and Buchenau, *Mexico's Once and Future Revolution*, pp. 42–43.

19 Womack, "The Mexican Revolution, 1910–1920," p. 84.

20 Ibid., p. 85.

21 Hart, "The Mexican Revolution," p. 412.

22 Knight, *The Mexican Revolution*, vol. 1, pp. 202–18.

23 Joseph and Buchenau. *Mexico's Once and Future Revolution*, pp. 42–43.

24 Ibid., pp. 49–51; Hart, "The Mexican Revolution," p. 413.

25 Hart, "The Mexican Revolution," p. 415.

26 Joseph and Buchenau, *Mexico's Once and Future Revolution*, p. 52.

27 Ibid., p. 53.

28 Ibid., p. 56; Hart, "The Mexican Revolution," p. 419.

29 Joseph and Buchenau, *Mexico's Once and Future Revolution*, p. 59.

30 Ibid., p. 60; St. John, *Line in the Sand*, p. 132.

31 Nancy Brandt, "Pancho Villa: The Making of a Modern Legend," *Americas* 21, no. 2 (1964): 155.

32 Rodriguez, *Mongrels, Bastards, Orphans, and Vagabonds*, pp. 137–38.

33 St. John, *Line in the Sand*, pp. 122–23.

34 Ralph S. Connell to Albert B. Fall, July 29, 1913, Albert B. Fall family papers, MS 0008, New Mexico State University Library, Archives and Special Collections Department, MS 8, Box 7, Folder 15.

35 Albert Fall to Ralph S. Connell, August 16, 1913, ibid.

36 Hart, "The Mexican Revolution," p. 421.

37 Telegraph from W. H. Austin to T. B. Catron, April 23, 1914, New Mexico History Collection, Center for Southwest Research, University Libraries, University of New Mexico, Thomas B. Catron Papers, 1692–1934, MSS 29, BC, Series 501, Box 6, Folder 1.

38 Letter from Thomas B. Catron to William Jennings Bryan, April 23, 1914, ibid.

39 Frank McLynn, *Villa and Zapata: A Biography of the Mexican Revolution* (London: Jonathan Cape, 2000), pp. 214–15; Womack, "The Mexican Revolution, 1910–1920," p. 99.

40 St. John, *Line in the Sand*, p. 131; McLynn, *Villa and Zapata*, pp. 219–20.

41 Hart, "The Mexican Revolution," p. 422; McLynn, *Villa and Zapata*, p. 220.

42 Hart, "The Mexican Revolution," pp. 422–24; St. John, *Line in the Sand*, p. 131.

43 Joseph and Buchenau, *Mexico's Once and Future Revolution*, pp. 60–61.

44 Hart, "The Mexican Revolution," p. 425.

45 Womack, "The Mexican Revolution, 1910–1920," p. 106.

46 Hart, "The Mexican Revolution," p. 423; Womack, *Zapata and the Mexican Revolution*, pp. 296–301.

47 Joseph and Buchenau, *Mexico's Once and Future Revolution*, pp. 63–64; McLynn, *Villa and Zapata*, p. 261.

48 Joseph and Buchenau, *Mexico's Once and Future Revolution*, pp. 63–65.

49 Womack, *Zapata and the Mexican Revolution*, pp. 303–5.

50 Ibid., p. 306.

51 Womack, "The Mexican Revolution, 1910–1920," p. 113.

52 L. W. Mix to Frederick Simpich, January 29, 1916, NARA, RG 59, Records of the Department of State, Relating to Internal Affairs of Mexico, 1910–1920, M274, Roll 190.

53 Langston Hughes, *The Big Sea* (New York: Hill and Wang, 2015), pp. 39–40, Kindle.

54 McLynn, *Villa and Zapata*, p. 399.

55 Oscar J. Martínez, *Fragments of the Mexican Revolution: Personal Accounts from the Border* (Albuquerque: University of New Mexico Press, 1983), p. 248.

56 Ibid., pp. 254–55.

57 Charles H. Harris III and Louis R. Sadler, *The Plan De San Diego: Tejano Rebels, Mexican Intrigue* (Lincoln: University of Nebraska Press, 2013), p. 1.

58 Carrigan and Webb, *Forgotten Dead*, p. 85.

59 Harris and Sadler, *The Plan De San Diego*, pp. 1–5.

60 Martínez, *Fragments of the Mexican Revolution*, p. 146.

61 Vargas, *Crucible of Struggle*, p. 185; Harris and Sadler, *The Plan De San Diego*, p. 19.

62 David Montejano, *Anglos and Mexicans in the Making of Texas, 1836–1986* (Austin: University of Texas Press, 1987), pp. 122–25.

63 Ibid., p. 119; Carrigan and Webb, *Forgotten Dead*, p. 86.

64 Harris and Sadler, *The Plan De San Diego*, p. 27; Montejano, *Anglos and Mexicans in the Making of Texas*, p. 117.

65 Joseph and Buchenau, *Mexico's Once and Future Revolution*, p. 73; Hart, "The Mexican Revolution," p. 428.

66 Womack, "The Mexican Revolution, 1910–1920," p. 121; Hart, "The Mexican Revolution," p. 436.

67 Tutino, *From Insurrection to Revolution in Mexico*, pp. 337–39.

68 Harris and Sadler, *The Plan De San Diego*, p. 6.

69 James Sandos, "Pancho Villa and American Security: Woodrow Wilson's Mexican Diplomacy Reconsidered," *Journal of Latin American Studies* 13, no. 2 (1981): 300.

70 Martínez, *Fragments of the Mexican Revolution*, pp. 250–53.

71 Hart, "The Mexican Revolution," p. 431.

72 Martínez, *Fragments of the Mexican Revolution*, pp. 178–79.

73 Sandos, "Pancho Villa and American Security," p. 295.

74 Ibid., p. 293.

75 Martínez, *Fragments of the Mexican Revolution*, p. 182.

76 Narrative Report, 13th U.S. Cavalry, Concerning the Part the Regiment Took in the Punitive Expedition, U.S. Army, into Mexico, from March 15, 1916, to June 2, 1916, March 16, 1916, NARA, RG 395: Records of the U.S. Army Overseas Operations and Commands, 1898–1942, Box 1, NM-94, E-1201, HM 1999.

77 Sandos, "Pancho Villa and American Security," p. 303.

78 Joseph and Buchenau, *Mexico's Once and Future Revolution*, p. 78.

79 Zimmermann Telegram, NARA, RG 59, General Records of the Department of State, 1756–1979, available online at https://www.archives.gov/education/lessons/zimmermann/#documents.

80 For more on Germany's involvement in Mexico, see Friedrich Katz, *The Secret War in Mexico: Europe, the United States, and the Mexican Revolution* (Chicago: University of Chicago Press, 1981).

81 Quoted in Joseph and Buchenau, *Mexico's Once and Future Revolution*, pp. 8–83, 92; Womack, "The Mexican Revolution, 1910–1920," p. 130; Tutino, *From Insurrection to Revolution in Mexico*, p. 340. For a full text of the current Mexican constitution, see https://www.oas.org/juridico/mla/en/mex/en_mex-int-text-const.pdf.

82 Hart, "The Mexican Revolution," p. 434.

83 Joseph and Buchenau, *Mexico's Once and Future Revolution*, pp. 84–85.

84 Ibid., pp. 92–95.

85 St. John, *Line in the Sand*, pp. 143–45.

86 Monica Muñoz Martinez, "Recuperating Histories of Violence in the Americas: Vernacular History-Making on the U.S.-Mexico Border," *American Quarterly* 66, no. 3 (2014): 667–69.

87 Carrigan and Webb, *Forgotten Dead*, p. 64.

88 Ibid., pp. 85–86.

89 Muñoz Martinez, "Recuperating Histories of Violence in the Americas," pp. 667–69; Carrigan and Webb, *Forgotten Dead*, pp. 124–25.

90 Timothy Henderson, *Beyond Borders: A History of Mexican Migration to the United States* (Oxford: Wiley-Blackwell, 2011), pp. 32–33; St. John, *Line in the Sand*, p. 182.

91 Richard Delgado, "The Law of the Noose: A History of Latino Lynching," *Harvard Civil Rights–Civil Liberties Law Review* 44 (2009): 305.

92 Starr, *California: A History*, p. 169.

93 Ibid., p. 170.

94 Sánchez et al., *New Mexico: A History*, p. 181.

95 Ibid., p. 182.

96 Ibid., pp. 182–83.

97 Sheridan, *Arizona: A History*, p. 216.

98 Starr, *California: A History*, p. 170; Sheridan, *Arizona: A History*, p. 212.

99 Sheridan, *Arizona: A History*, p. 214.

100 Montejano, *Anglos and Mexicans in the Making of Texas, 1836–1986*; see chapter 5.

101 This decline was later compounded by Japanese internment during the Second World War. See Kelly Lytle Hernández, *Migra! A History of the U.S. Border Patrol* (Berkeley: University of California Press, 2010), pp. 22–23.

102 Ibid., p. 37; St. John, *Line in the Sand*, pp. 103–4.

103 St. John, *Line in the Sand*, p. 97.

104 Ibid., p. 99.

105 Ibid.

106 Ibid., p. 163.

107 Ibid., pp. 151–53.

108 Ibid., pp. 156–57, 160.

109 Ibid., p. 110.

110 Ibid., pp. 166, 172–73.

111 Katherine Benton-Cohen, "Other Immigrants: Mexicans and the Dillingham Commission of 1907–1911," *Journal of American Ethnic History* 30, no. 2 (2011): 33.

112 For the full text of the legislation, see http://library.uwb.edu/static/USimmigration/39%20stat%20874.pdf (accessed July 15, 2016); Benton-Cohen, "Other Immigrants," p. 37.

113 Henderson, *Beyond Borders*, p. 25.

114 Benton-Cohen, "Other Immigrants," p. 37.

115 Ibid., p. 38.

116 Henderson, *Beyond Borders*, p. 31.

117 Ibid.

118 Karl De Laittre, "The Mexican Laborer and You," *Nation's Business* 18 (November 1930). For more on the idea of the Mexican as being a "temporary" worker, see Noel, *Debating American Identity*.

119 Montejano, *Anglos and Mexicans in the Making of Texas*, pp. 181–82, 228.

120 St. John, *Line in the Sand*, p. 186.

121 Quoted in Hernández, *Migra!* p. 35.

122 Ibid., pp. 53–55.

123 Ibid.

124 Julie M. Weise, "Mexican Nationalisms, Southern Racisms: Mexicans and Mexican Americans in the U.S. South, 1908–1939," *American Quarterly* 60, no. 3 (2008): 749.

125 Ibid., p. 754.

126 Ibid., pp. 755, 758.

127 Ibid., p. 772.

128 WPA Tampa Office Records 1917–1943, University of South Florida Special Collections, 1929, p. 241.

129 Ibid.

130 Evelio Grillo and Kenya Dworkin y Méndez (intro.), *Black Cuban, Black American: A Memoir* (Houston, Tex.: Arte Público Press, 2000), loc. 192, Kindle.

131 Ibid., loc. 200.

132 Ibid., loc. 216.

133 Natalia Molina, "'In a Race All Their Own': The Quest to Make Mexicans Ineligible for U.S. Citizenship," *Pacific Historical Review* 79, no. 2 (2010): 168, 176.

134 Ibid., pp. 178–80.

135 Jovita González Mireles and María Eugenia Cotera (ed.), *Life Along the Border: A Landmark Tejana Thesis* (College Station: Texas A&M University Press, 2006), p. 6.

136 Priscilla Solis Ybarra, "Borderlands as Bioregion: Jovita González, Gloria Anzaldúa, and the Twentieth-Century Ecological Revolution in the Rio Grande Valley," MELUS 34, no. 2 (2009): 175–89.

137 González Mireles and Cotera, *Life Along the Border*, p. 41.

138 Ibid.

139 Ibid., p. 113. González later married and worked as a teacher in Corpus Christi and died in 1983. She also cowrote two novels, *Dew on the Thorn* and *Caballero: A Historical Novel*, with Eve Raleigh, but the manuscripts were not discovered until her papers were donated to the library at Texas A&M University–Corpus Christi in 1992. They have since been published.

140 Julián Juderías, *La leyenda negra* (Madrid: Editorial Swan, 1986), p. 28.

141 Ibid.

142 Weber, *The Spanish Frontier in North America*, p. 245.

143 Michael Kammen, *The Mystic Chords of Memory: The Transformation of Tradition in American Culture* (New York: Vintage Books, 1993), p. 55.

144 Flores, "Private Visions, Public Culture: The Making of the Alamo," p. 99.

145 Ibid.

146 Ibid., p. 101.

147 Ibid., p. 103.

148 Kenneth Baxter Ragsdale, *The Year America Discovered Texas: Centennial '36* (College Station: Texas A&M University Press, 1987), p. 1.

149 James Early, *Presidio, Mission, and Pueblo: Spanish Architecture and Urbanism in the United States* (Dallas, Tex.: Southern Methodist University Press, 2004), p. 210.

150 Kammen, *The Mystic Chords of Memory*, p. 47.

151 Carey McWilliams, and Dean Stewart and Jeannine Gendar (eds.), *Fool's Paradise: A Carey McWilliams Reader* (Santa Clara, Calif.: Santa Clara University, 2001), p. 4.

152 Monroy, "The Creation and Re-Creation of Californio Society," pp. 73–195.

153 Phoebe S. Kropp, *California Vieja: Culture and Memory in a Modern American Place* (Berkeley: University of California Press, 2006), p. 28.

154 Richard Amero, "The Making of the Panama-California Exposition, 1909–1915," *San Diego Historical Society Quarterly* 36, no. 1 (1990).

155 Christopher Reynolds, "How San Diego's, San Francisco's Rival 1915 Expositions Shaped Them," http://www.latimes.com/travel/california/la-tr-d-sd-sf-1915-panama-expos-20150104-story.html (accessed December 10, 2015).

156 Harral Ayres, "Building of Old Spanish Trail as Thrilling as the Romance of Its Padres and Conquistadores," 1929, Briscoe Center for American History, 978 AY22B.

157 James W. Travers, *From Coast to Coast Via the Old Spanish Trail* (San Diego, Calif.: 1929).

158 Benny J. Andrés Jr., "La Plaza Vieja (Old Town Alburquerque): The Transformation of a Hispano Village, 1880s–1950s," in Gonzalez-Berry and Maciel, *The Contested Homeland*, p. 243.

159 Ibid., pp. 252–56.

160 Ibid., p. 240.

161 Ibid., pp. 252–56.

162 Patricia Galloway, "Commemorative History and Hernando de Soto," in Patricia Galloway (ed.), *The Hernando De Soto Expedition: History, Historiography, and "Discovery" in the Southeast*, pp. 419, 421.

163 Annelise K. Madsen, "Reviving the Old and Telling Tales: 1930s Modernism and the Uses of American History," in Judith A. Barter (ed.), *America After the Fall: Painting in the 1930s* (Chicago: Art Institute of Chicago, 2016), p. 93; Galloway, "Commemorative History and Hernando de Soto," p. 422.

164 David J. Weber, "Turner, the Boltonians, and the Borderlands," *American Historical Review* 91, no. 1 (1986): 69; Albert L. Hurtado, "Bolton and Turner: The Borderlands and American Exceptionalism," *Western Historical Quarterly* 44, no. 1 (2013): 6.

165 John Francis Bannon, "Herbert Eugene Bolton—Western Historian," *Western Historical Quarterly* 2, no. 3 (1971): 268; Helen Delpar, *Looking South: The Evolution of Latin Americanist Scholarship in the United States, 1850–1975* (Tuscaloosa: University of Alabama Press, 2008), p. 28.

166 Hurtado, "Bolton and Turner," pp. 9–10; Delpar, *Looking South*, pp. 41–42.

167 Herbert Eugene Bolton, *The Spanish Borderlands: A Chronicle of Old Florida and the Southwest* (New Haven, Conn.: Yale University Press, 1921). Bolton's work today—when it is discussed—comes under fire for what it does not do and who it does not include, particularly indigenous people. Despite its shortcomings, Bolton did influence and develop the idea of borderlands, Latin American, and hemispheric studies.

168 "The Epic of Greater America," in John Francis Bannon (ed.), *Bolton and the Spanish Borderlands* (Norman: University of Oklahoma Press, 1964), p. 302. Also on Bolton, the frontier, and borderlands, see Jeremy Adelman and Stephen Aron, "From Borderlands to Borders: Empires, Nation-States, and the Peoples in Between in North American History," *American Historical Review* 104, no. 3 (1999): 814–41.

169 Franklin D. Roosevelt, Inaugural Address, March 4, 1933, American Presidency Project, http://www.presidency.ucsb.edu/ws/?pid=14473 (accessed October 10, 2016).

170 Susannah Joel Glusker, *Anita Brenner: A Mind of Her Own* (Austin: University of Texas Press, 1998), pp. viii–27.

171 Ibid., p. 26.

172 Anita Brenner and George R. Leighton (photos), *The Wind That Swept Mexico: The History of the Mexican Revolution of 1910–1942* (Austin: University of Texas Press, 2008), p. 4.

173 "Anita Brenner, Wrote on Mexico: Author and Journalist Dies—Detailed Life of Indians," *New York Times*, December 3, 1974.

Chapter 13: New York

1 Mitchell Codding, "Archer Milton Huntington, Champion of Spain in the United States," in Richard L. Kagan (ed.), *Spain in America: The Origins of Hispanism in the United States* (Chicago: University of Illinois Press, 2002), p. 147.

2 Mike Wallace, "Nueva York: The Back Story: New York City and the Spanish-Speaking World from Dutch Days to the Second World War," in Edward J. Sullivan (ed.), *Nueva York, 1613–1945* (New York: Scala and New-York Historical Society, 2010), pp. 59–61.

3 James D. Fernández, "The Discovery of Spain in New York, circa 1930," in Sullivan, *Nueva York, 1613–1945*, p. 220.

4 Richard L. Kagan, "Blame It on Washington Irving: New York's Discovery of the Art and Architecture of Spain," in Sullivan, *Nueva York, 1613–1945*, pp. 162–64; Fernández, "The Discovery of Spain in New York, circa 1930." See also Kagan, *Spain in America*.

5 "City's Spanish Colony Lives in Its Own Little World Here," *New York Times*, March 23, 1924.

6 Ibid.

7 Wallace, "Nueva York," p. 59.

8 Ibid.

9 Ibid., pp. 62–63.

10 Ana Maria Varela-Lago, "Conquerors, Immigrants, Exiles: The Spanish Diaspora in the United States (1848–1948)" (PhD diss., University of California, San Diego, 2008), pp. 65–69.

11 Federico García Lorca, Christopher Maurer (ed.), and Greg Simon and Steven F. White (trans.), *Poet in New York* (New York: Penguin Classics, 2002), p. 202.

12 Fernández, "The Discovery of Spain in New York, circa 1930," p. 225.

13 García Lorca, *Poet in New York*, p. 11.

14 Ibid., p. 189.

15 Ibid., p. 212; Fernández, "The Discovery of Spain in New York, circa 1930," pp. 226–27.

16 Gabriel Haslip-Viera, "The Evolution of the Latino Community in New York City: Early 19th Century to the 1990s," in Claudio Iván Remeseira (ed.), *Hispanic New York: A Sourcebook* (New York: Columbia University Press, 2010), p. 37.

17 Jonathan Gill, *Harlem: The Four Hundred Year History from Dutch Village to Capital of Black America* (New York: Grove Press, 2011), pp. 211–18.

18 *Club Cubano Inter-Americano, Inc. Records*, New York Public Library Schomburg Center for Research in Black Culture, 1945, Manuscript and Rare Books Division, Box 1, Folder 1, "Proyeto de Reglamento," November 1945.

19 Haslip-Viera, "The Evolution of the Latino Community in New York City," p. 37; Wallace, "Nueva York," p. 64; Peter Kihss, "Flow of Puerto Ricans Here Fills Jobs, Poses Problems," *New York Times*, February 23, 1953; David F. García, "Contesting That Damned Mambo: Arsenio Rodríguez and the People of El Barrio and the Bronx in the 1950s," in Miriam Jiménez Román and Juan Flores (eds.), *The Afro-Latin@ Reader: History and Culture in the United States* (Durham, N.C.: Duke University Press, 2010), p. 190.

20 Exhibition: "Shaping Puerto Rican Identity: Selections from the DivEdCo Collection at Centro Library & Archives," accessed November 2014, Centro de Estudios Puertorriqueños, Hunter College, City University of New York.

21 Ibid.

22 González, *Harvest of Empire*, p. 63.

23 Haslip-Viera, "The Evolution of the Latino Community in New York City," p. 37.

24 Gill, *Harlem*, p. 219.

25 Armando Rendon, "El Puertorriqueño: No More, No Less," *Civil Rights Digest* 1, no. 3 (Fall 1968): 30.

26 Ibid.

27 Judith Ortiz Cofer, *The Line of the Sun* (Athens: University of Georgia Press, 1989), pp. 171–72.

28 Rafael Angel Marín to Israel Weinstein, October 22, 1947, Oscar García Rivera Collection, Hunter Centro de Estudios Puertorriqueños, New York, 1947, Series IV: Subject Files, Box 2, Folder 9.

29 Jorge Duany, "Transnational Migration from the Dominican Republic: The Cultural Redefinition of Racial Identity," *Caribbean Studies* 29, no. 2 (1996): 254.

30 Bernardo Vega, "Al Margen de la Lucha," *Alma Boricua* (New York), October 1934, p. 8.

31 Julia Alvarez, *How the Garcia Girls Lost Their Accents* (New York: Plume, 1992), p. 139.

32 Ed Morales, *The Latin Beat: Rhythms and Roots of Latin Music from Bossa Nova to Salsa and Beyond* (New York: Da Capo Press, 2003), p. xviii.

33 Ruth Glasser, "From 'Indianola' to 'Ño Colá': The Strange Career of the Afro-Puerto Rican Musician," in Jiménez Román and Flores, *The Afro-Latin@ Reader: History and Culture in the United States*, p. 157.

34 Gill, *Harlem*, p. 324.

35 Gustavo Pérez Firmat, *The Havana Habit* (New Haven, Conn.: Yale University Press, 2010), p. 51.

36 Ibid., pp. 55–56.

37 Morales, *The Latin Beat*, pp. 5–6.

38 Pérez Firmat, *The Havana Habit*, p. 60.

39 Glasser, "From 'Indianola' to 'Ño Colá,'" p. 170.

40 Morales, *The Latin Beat*, pp. 34–35.

41 Pérez Firmat, *The Havana Habit*, pp. 103–5.

42 García, "Contesting That Damned Mambo," p. 187.

43 For more on "latune," see Pérez Firmat, *The Havana Habit*, pp. 53–55.

44 For more on "mamboid," see ibid., pp. 110–11.

45 Ibid., pp. 116–17.

46 Juan Flores, "Boogaloo and Latin Soul," in Jiménez Román and Flores, *The Afro-Latin@ Reader*, p. 190.

47 Ed Morales, "The Story of Nuyorican Salsa," in Remeseira, *Hispanic New York*, p. 367.

48 Ibid., p. 367.

49 Ayala and Bernabe, *Puerto Rico in the American Century*, p. 105.

50 Augusto Espíritu, "American Empire, Hispanism, and the Nationalist Vision of Albizu, Recto, and Grau," in Alyosha Goldstein (ed.), *Formations of United States Colonialism* (Durham, N.C.: Duke University Press, 2014), pp. 158, 165, Kindle.

51 Ayala and Bernabe, *Puerto Rico in the American Century*, p. 105.

52 Espíritu, "American Empire, Hispanism, and the Nationalist Vision of Albizu, Recto, and Grau," p. 105.

53 Pedro Albizu Campos, "Puerto Rican Nationalism," in Robert Santiago (ed.), *Boricuas: Influential Puerto Rican Writings—An Anthology* (New York: One World, 1995), pp. 28–29.

54 Picó, *History of Puerto Rico*, p. 256.

55 González, *Harvest of Empire*, p. 85.

56 José Trías Monge, *Puerto Rico: The Trials of the Oldest Colony in the World* (New Haven, Conn.: Yale University Press, 1997), pp. 96–97.

57 José Acosta Velarde to Charles West, Acting Secretary of the Interior, June 12, 1936, NARA, RG 126, Office of Territories and Classified Files, 1907–1951, Box Number 933, File 9-8-78.

58 James L. Dietz, *Economic History of Puerto Rico: Institutional Change and Capitalist Development* (Princeton, N.J.: Princeton University Press, 1986), p. 169.

59 Blanton Winship to Harold Ickes, Secretary of the Interior, June 1, 1936, NARA, RG 126, Office of Territories and Classified Files, 1907–1951, Box Number 933, File 9-8-78.

60 Lorrin Thomas, *Puerto Rican Citizen: History and Political Identity in Twentieth-Century New York City* (Chicago: University of Chicago Press, 2010), p. 119.

61 Ibid.

62 "Report on the Commission of Inquiry on Civil Rights in Puerto Rico," May 22, 1937, p. 10.

63 Ibid., p. 12.

64 Ibid., pp. 17, 21.

65 Ibid., pp. 28–29.

66 Ernest Gruening, Director of the Division of Territories & Islands, to Blanton Winship, April 5, 1937, NARA, RG 126, Office of Territories and Classified Files, 1907–1951, Box Number 933, File 9-8-78.

67 John W. Wright, Colonel, 65th Infantry, to Ernest Gruening, Director of the Division of Territories & Islands, March 24, 1937, ibid.

68 "Report on the Commission of Inquiry on Civil Rights in Puerto Rico," p. 15.

69 Ibid., p. 28.

70 Jorge Rodríguez Beruff, "From Winship to Leahy: Crisis, War, and Transition in Puerto Rico," in McCoy and Scarano, *Colonial Crucible*, pp. 435–36.

71 Congressional Record 84, 1939, p. 4063. Extracts also available in Annette T. Rubinstein (ed.), "I Vote My Conscience: The Debates, Speeches, and Writings of Congressman Vito Marcantonio, May 11, 1939," http://www.vitomarcantonio.org/chapter_9.php#76th_8 (accessed October 27, 2016).

72 Ibid.

73 Monge, *Puerto Rico*, p. 98.

74 Ayala and Bernabe, *Puerto Rico in the American Century*, p. 98.

75 Ibid., p. 137.

76 Luis Muñoz Marín to Franklin D. Roosevelt, November 28, 1940, Materials from the Franklin Delano Roosevelt Library relating to Puerto Rico, Reel 1, Selected Documents Concerning Puerto Rico, Center for Puerto Rican Studies, Hunter College.

77 Ayala and Bernabe, *Puerto Rico in the American Century*, p. 148.

78 Ibid., p. 149. See Nelson A. Denis, *War Against All Puerto Ricans: Revolution and Terror in America's Colony* (New York: Nation, 2015); see chapters 11 and 17.

79 William D. Leahy to Dr. Rupert Emerson, Director of the Divisions of Territories & Island Possessions, July 18, 1940, NARA, RG 126, Office of Territories and Classified Files, 1907–1951, Box Number 933, File 9-8-78.

80 Memorandum for the Secretary from the U.S. Department of the Interior, December 24, 1943, ibid.

81 Rexford Tugwell, *The Stricken Land: The Story of Puerto Rico* (Garden City, N.Y.: Doubleday, 1947), pp. 42–43, quoted in Monge, *Puerto Rico*, pp. 97–98.

82 Ayala and Bernabe, *Puerto Rico in the American Century*, p. 157.

83 Rexford Tugwell to Harold Ickes, May 28, 1943, Materials from the Franklin Delano Roosevelt Library relating to Puerto Rico, Reel 2, Rexford Tugwell Papers, Center for Puerto Rican Studies, Hunter College.

84 J. Edgar Hoover to Harry L. Hopkins, July 17, 1943, Materials from the Franklin Delano Roosevelt Library relating to Puerto Rico, Reel 3, Hopkins Papers, Center for Puerto Rican Studies, Hunter College.

85 J. Edgar Hoover to Harry L. Hopkins, September 15, 1943, ibid.

86 Dietz, *Economic History of Puerto Rico*, pp. 206–10.

87 Ayala and Bernabe, *Puerto Rico in the American Century*, p. 181.

88 Ibid.; Dietz, *Economic History of Puerto Rico*, p. 238.

89 Katherine T. McCaffrey, *Military Power and Popular Protest: The U.S. Navy in Vieques, Puerto Rico* (New Brunswick, N.J.: Rutgers University Press, 2002), p. 30.

90 Ibid., p. 32.

91 Ibid., pp. 35–36.

92 Ayala and Bernabe, *Puerto Rico in the American Century*, p. 159.

93 Ibid., p. 158

94 Ibid., p. 160.

95 Ibid., p. 164.

96 Monge, *Puerto Rico*, p. 114.

97 Ayala and Bernabe, *Puerto Rico in the American Century*, p. 165.

98 Pedro A. Malavet, *America's Colony: The Political and Cultural Conflict Between the United States and Puerto Rico* (New York: New York University Press, 2004), p. 92.

99 Ayala and Bernabe, *Puerto Rico in the American Century*, p. 165.

100 Malavet, *America's Colony*, p. 92.

101 Arthur Krock, "In the Nation: The Tragedy in Pennsylvania Avenue," *New York Times*, November 2, 1950.

102 Ayala and Bernabe, *Puerto Rico in the American Century*, p. 167.

103 Ibid., p. 168.

104 Ibid.

105 Clayton Knowles, "Five Congressmen Shot in House by 3 Puerto Rican Nationalists: Bullets Spray from Gallery," *New York Times*, March 2, 1954.

106 Ibid.

107 Irene Vilar, *The Ladies' Gallery: A Memoir of Family Secrets* (New York: Vintage, 1998), p. 99.

108 Ibid., p. 88.

109 Ibid., p. 72.

110 Ibid., p. 117.

111 Ibid., p. 96.

112 For more detail on Albizu, the nationalist struggle, and the United States' operation against it, as well as Albizu Campos's imprisonment, see Denis, *War Against All Puerto Ricans*.

113 Picó, *History of Puerto Rico*, p. 277.

114 Hunter S. Thompson, *The Rum Diary: The Long Lost Novel* (New York: Bloomsbury, 2015), pp. 42–43, Kindle.

115 Frederick E. Kidder to Alan Cranston, January 22, 1979, U.S. Senator for California, NARA, RG 204, Office of the Pardon Attorney, Entry #P3: Security-Classified Pardon Case Files: 1951–1991, Container #3.

116 Department of Justice Press Release, September 6, 1979, ibid.

117 Kenneth H. Neagle, Warden of Alderson Federal Correctional Institution, to Norman A. Carlson, Director, Bureau of Prisons, September 10, 1979, ibid.

118 Tony Schwartz, "2 Freed Puerto Rican Nationalists Say They Can't Rule Out Violence," *New York Times*, September 12, 1979.

119 Joseph Egelhof, "2 Puerto Ricans Tell of U.S. Offer to Deal," *Chicago Tribune*, September 12, 1979, p. 16.

120 Wayne King, "4 Nationalists Are Welcomed as Heroes in Puerto Rico," *New York Times*, September 13, 1979.

121 Ed Pilkington, "'I'm No Threat'—Will Obama Pardon One of the World's Longest-Serving Political Prisoners?" *Guardian*, October 16, 2016, https://www.theguardian.com/world/2016/oct/16/obama-pardon-mandela-puerto-rico-oscar- lopez-rivera- (accessed March 28, 2018).

122 "Filiberto Ojeda Ríos," *Economist*, September 29, 2005. https://www.economist.com/node/4455267 (accessed April 3, 2018); Abby Goodnough, "Killing of Militant Raises Ire in Puerto Rico," *New York Times*, September 28, 2005. https://www.nytimes.com/2005/09/28/us/killing-of-militant-raises-ire-in-puerto-rico.html (accessed April 3, 2018).

Chapter 14: Los Angeles, California

1 Kropp, *California Vieja*, p. 211.

2 William D. Estrada, "Los Angeles' Old Plaza and Olvera Street," *Western Folklore* 58, no. 2 (1999): 110.

3 Ibid., pp. 110–13.

4 Quoted in Jean Bruce Poole and Tevvy Ball, *El Pueblo: The Historic Heart of Los Angeles* (Los Angeles: Getty Conservation Institute and J. Paul Getty Museum, 2002), p. 43.

5 Quoted ibid., p. 48.
6 Estrada, "Los Angeles' Old Plaza and Olvera Street," p. 116.
7 Quoted ibid., p. 117.
8 Kropp, *California Vieja*, pp. 228–29.
9 Quoted in Estrada, "Los Angeles' Old Plaza and Olvera Street," p. 115.
10 Quoted in Poole and Ball, *El Pueblo*, pp. 50–51.
11 *Los Angeles Times*, February 25, 1924, quoted in Gustavo Arellano, *Taco USA: How Mexican Food Conquered America* (New York: Scribner, 2012), pp. 54–56.
12 Quoted in Poole and Ball, *El Pueblo*, p. 75.
13 Quoted ibid., p. 77.
14 Quoted in Sarah Schrank, *Art and the City: Civic Imagination and Cultural Authority in Los Angeles* (Philadelphia: University of Pennsylvania Press, 2009), p. 49.
15 Leslie Rainer, "The Conservation of América Tropical: Historical Context and Project Overview," presented at The Siqueiros Legacy: Challenges of Conserving the Artist's Monumental Murals, Getty Center, Los Angeles. October 16, 2012, http://www.getty.edu/conservation/publications_resources/pdf_publications/pdf/historical_context.pdf (accessed April 2, 2018.)
16 Estrada, "Los Angeles' Old Plaza and Olvera Street," p. 116.
17 Helen Delpar, *The Enormous Vogue of Things Mexican: Cultural Relations Between the United States and Mexico, 1920–1935* (Tuscaloosa: University of Alabama Press, 1992), p. 55.
18 Ibid., p. 55; James Krippner, *Paul Strand in Mexico* (Singapore: Fundación Televisa/Aperture, 2010), p. 18.
19 Johnston McCulley, *The Mark of Zorro: The Curse of Capistran* (2009), p. 9, Kindle.
20 Ibid., p. 3.
21 Krippner, *Paul Strand in Mexico*, p. 17.
22 Ibid., pp. 37, 69.
23 Ibid., pp. 42–43.
24 Moreno Figueroa and Tanaka, "Comics, Dolls and the Disavowal of Racism," pp. 187–90. Contributing significantly to the *mestizaje* movement was an influential essay, *La raza cosmica*, by José Vasconcelos in 1925. He went on to be Mexico's education minister and also promoted the development of public murals. His legacy and that of his idea of Mexicans as a blended "cosmic race" have come under scrutiny in more recent years and been criticized for their inherent racism, for example the exclusion of indigenous people, among others.
25 Katherine Ware, "Photographs of Mexico 1940," in Krippner, *Paul Strand in Mexico*, pp. 267–68.
26 Lawrence Cardoso, *Mexican Emigration to the United States, 1897–1931* (Tucson: University of Arizona Press, 1980), pp. 91–94.
27 Henderson, *Beyond Borders*, p. 51.
28 Starr, *California: A History*, p. 204.
29 Ibid., p. 205.
30 Henderson, *Beyond Borders*, p. 54.
31 Ibid., p. 56.
32 Zaragosa Vargas, "Tejana Radical: Emma Tenayuca and the San Antonio Labor Movement During the Great Depression," *Pacific Historical Review* 66, no. 4 (1997): 556.

33 Alan Knight, "Mexico, c. 1930–46," in Bethell, *The Cambridge History of Latin America*, vol. 7, pp. 3–5.

34 Joseph and Buchenau, *Mexico's Once and Future Revolution*, p. 124.

35 Knight, "Mexico, c. 1930–46," pp. 19–20.

36 Ibid., pp. 43–48; Joseph and Buchenau, *Mexico's Once and Future Revolution*, pp. 132–33.

37 St. John, *Line in the Sand*, p. 189.

38 Starr, *California: A History*, p. 179; Kropp, *California Vieja*, p. 231.

39 Henderson, *Beyond Borders*, p. 45; Francisco E. Balderrama and Raymond Rodríguez, *Decade of Betrayal: Mexican Repatriation in the 1930s* (Albuquerque: University of New Mexico Press, 1995), p. 59.

40 Balderrama and Rodríguez, *Decade of Betrayal*, p. 55.

41 Rodriguez, *Mongrels, Bastards, Orphans, and Vagabonds*, p. 163; Carlos K. Blanton, "George I. Sánchez, Ideology, and Whiteness in the Making of the Mexican American Civil Rights Movement, 1930–1960," *Journal of Southern History* 72, no. 3 (2006): 569–604; Balderrama and Rodríguez, *Decade of Betrayal*, p. 195.

42 F. Castillo Nájera to Cordell Hull, September 26, 1940 NARA, RG 59: General Records of Department of State, Decimal File, from 811.4 to 811.4016/449, Box 3804, Folder 1: 811.40/7-811.4016/299, File 811.4016/272.

43 Culbert L. Olson to Sumner Welles, April 11, 1941, ibid.

44 Geraldo L. Cadava, *Standing on Common Ground: The Making of a Sunbelt Borderland* (Cambridge, Mass.: Harvard University Press, 2013), p. 21, Kindle.

45 Ibid., p. 23.

46 Suarez, *Latino Americans*, loc. 1679.

47 Richard Griswold del Castillo, "The Los Angeles 'Zoot Suit Riots' Revisited: Mexican and Latin American Perspectives," *Mexican Studies/Estudios Mexicanos* 16, no. 2 (2000): 367.

48 Mauricio Mazón, *The Zoot Suit Riots: The Psychology of Symbolic Annihilation* (Austin: University of Texas Press, 1984), p. 20.

49 Luis Alvarez, *The Power of Zoot: Youth Culture and Resistance During World War II* (Berkeley: University of California Press, 2008), p. 2.

50 Suarez, *Latino Americans*, loc. 1664.

51 Starr, *California: A History*, pp. 230–34.

52 Griswold del Castillo, "The Los Angeles 'Zoot Suit Riots' Revisited," p. 370; Mazón, *The Zoot Suit Riots*, p. 2.

53 Quoted in Alvarez, *The Power of Zoot*, p. 155.

54 Henry S. Waterman to Secretary of State, June 11, 1943, NARA, RG 59: General Records of Department of State, Decimal File, from 811.4016/450 to 811.4016/637, Box 3805, File 811.4016/560.

55 Ibid.

56 Griswold del Castillo, "The Los Angeles 'Zoot Suit Riots' Revisited," p. 369.

57 Quoted ibid., p. 386.

58 *El Nacional* (Mexico City), June 17, 1943, in NARA, RG 59: General Records of Department of State, Decimal File, from 811.4016/450 to 811.4016/637, Box 3805, File 811.4016/568.

59 Griswold del Castillo, "The Los Angeles 'Zoot Suit Riots' Revisited," p. 379.

60 Ibid., pp. 369, 382.

61 McWilliams, Stewart, and Gendar, *Fool's Paradise*, p. 206.

62 Carlos Kevin Blanton, "The Citizenship Sacrifice: Mexican Americans, the Saunders-Leonard Report, and the Politics of Immigration, 1951–1952," *Western Historical Quarterly* 40, no. 3 (2009): 300.

63 Steven H. Wilson, "Brown over 'Other White': Mexican Americans' Legal Arguments and Litigation Strategy in School Desegregation Lawsuits," *Law and History Review* 21, no. 1 (2003): 154.

64 Rodriguez, *Mongrels, Bastards, Orphans, and Vagabonds*, p. 157.

65 Blanton, "The Citizenship Sacrifice," p. 300.

66 Neil Foley, *Mexicans in the Making of America* (Cambridge, Mass.: Belknap Press of Harvard University Press, 2014), p. 97.

67 Suarez, *Latino Americans*, loc. 1522.

68 Foley, *Mexicans in the Making of America*, p. 97.

69 Ibid.

70 Ibid., p. 100.

71 Ibid., pp. 101–2.

72 Ibid., p. 117.

73 Thomas H. Kreneck, "Dr. Hector P. García: Twentieth Century Mexican-American Leader," in Donald Willett and Stephen J. Curley (eds.), *Invisible Texans: Women and Minorities in Texas History* (Boston: McGraw-Hill, 2005), p. 207.

74 See, for instance, Steve Rosales, "Fighting the Peace at Home: Mexican American Veterans and the 1944 GI Bill of Rights," *Pacific Historical Review* 80, no. 4 (2011): 597–627.

75 Kreneck, "Dr. Hector P. García," p. 208.

76 Ibid., pp. 208–9.

77 Molina, "'In a Race All Their Own,'" p. 192.

78 Ibid., pp. 199–200.

79 Roberto R. Treviño, "Facing Jim Crow: Catholic Sisters and the 'Mexican Problem' in Texas," *Western Historical Quarterly* 34, no. 2 (2003): 141.

80 Alonso Perales, "Lista que contiene los nombres de las poblaciones en Texas en donde se les ha negado servicio a los mexicanos," University of Houston, Special Collections, Alonso S. Perales Papers, Box 8, Folder 5. 1944. Also available at http://digital.lib.uh.edu/collection/perales/item/65.

81 William P. Blocker to Cordell Hull, February 27, 1940, "Transmitting Results of a Confidential Survey of the Problem of Racial Discrimination Against Mexican and Latin American Citizens in Texas and New Mexico," NARA, RG 59: General Records of Department of State, Decimal File, from 811.4 to 811.4016/449, Box 3804, Folder 3: 811-4106/337-360.

82 Ibid.

83 Ibid.

84 For more detail, see Thomas A. Guglielmo, "Fighting for Caucasian Rights: Mexicans, Mexican Americans, and the Transnational Struggle for Civil Rights in World War II Texas," *Journal of American History* 92, no. 4 (2006): 1212; Foley, *Mexicans in the Making of America*, p. 79.

85 Foley, *Mexicans in the Making of America*, pp. 83–84.

86 Guglielmo, "Fighting for Caucasian Rights," pp. 1220–30.

87 Rosie Escobar to Hector García, October 29, 1951, Texas A&M University Corpus Christi, Mary and Jeff Bell Library, Hector Garcia Collection, Box 215, Folder 10.
88 Rodriguez, *Mongrels, Bastards, Orphans, and Vagabonds*, p. 163.
89 Suarez, *Latino Americans*, loc. 1657.
90 Henderson, *Beyond Borders*, pp. 78–79.
91 Ibid., pp. 62–63.
92 Blanton, "The Citizenship Sacrifice," p. 299.
93 Ibid., p. 303.
94 Lyndon B. Johnson to Hector García, October 13, 1949, Texas A&M University Corpus Christi, Mary and Jeff Bell Library, Hector García Collection, Box 223, Folder 5.
95 *What Price Wetbacks?* 1953, Arizona State University, Hayden Library, Department of Archives and Special Collections, Chicano Research Collection CHI NM-37, p. 1.
96 Ibid., p. 5.
97 Michelle Hall Kells, *Héctor P. García: Everyday Rhetoric and Mexican American Civil Rights* (Carbondale: Southern Illinois University Press, 2006), p. 132.
98 Henderson, *Beyond Borders*, p. 58; Albert M. Camarillo, "Mexico," in Mary C. Waters, Reed Ueda, and Helen B. Marrow (eds.), *The New Americans: A Guide to Immigration Since 1965* (Cambridge, Mass.: Harvard University Press, 2007), pp. 508–9.
99 Henderson, *Beyond Borders*, pp. 72, 85.
100 Ibid., pp. 74–76.
101 Ngai, *Impossible Subjects*, p. 258; Elizabeth Hull, *Without Justice for All: The Constitutional Rights of Aliens* (Westport, Conn.: Greenwood Press, 1985), p. 24.
102 Ngai, *Impossible Subjects*, p. 261.
103 Henderson, *Beyond Borders*, p. 102; Ngai, *Impossible Subjects*, p. 261.
104 Don Parson, *Making a Better World: Public Housing, the Red Scare, and the Direction of Modern Los Angeles* (Minneapolis: University of Minnesota Press, 2005), p. 164; Ronald López, "Community Resistance and Conditional Patriotism in Cold War Los Angeles: The Battle for Chavez Ravine," *Latino Studies* 7, no. 4 (2009): 459.
105 Ibid.
106 Parson, *Making a Better World*, p. 165.
107 Ibid., p. 167.
108 López, "Community Resistance and Conditional Patriotism in Cold War Los Angeles," p. 460.
109 Quoted ibid., p. 467.
110 Parson, *Making a Better World*, pp. 164–71.
111 Ibid., p. 172
112 Ibid., p. 173.
113 Ibid., p. 174; López, "Community Resistance and Conditional Patriotism in Cold War Los Angeles," p. 457.
114 Parson, *Making a Better World*, p. 174.
115 Ibid., p. 177.
116 Nick Wilson, *Voices from the Pastime: Oral Histories of Surviving Major Leaguers, Negro Leaguers, Cuban Leaguers, and Writers, 1920–1934* (Jefferson, N.C.: McFarland, 2000), p. 138.

117 Ibid., pp. 141–42.

118 Brioso, *Havana Hardball*, p. 70.

119 Wilson, *Voices from the Pastime*, pp. 138–39.

120 Ibid., p. 141.

121 Adrian Burgos Jr., "An Uneven Playing Field: Afro-Latinos in Major League Base-ball," in Jiménez and Flores, *The Afro-Latin@ Reader: History and Culture in the United States*, p. 129.

122 Wilson, *Voices from the Pastime*, p. 139.

123 Brioso, *Havana Hardball*, p. 82.

124 Wilson, *Voices from the Pastime*, p. 140.

125 Ibid., p. 141.

126 Burgos, "An Uneven Playing Field," pp. 131–32.

127 Ibid., pp. 133–34.

128 Mark Armour and Daniel R. Levitt, "Baseball Demographics, 1947–2012," Society for American Baseball Research, http://sabr.org/bioproj/topic/baseball-demographics-1947-2012 (accessed May 27, 2015).

129 Robert B. Fairbanks, "The Failure of Urban Renewal in the Southwest: From City Needs to Individual Rights," *Western Historical Quarterly* 37, no. 3 (2006): 303.

130 Ibid., pp. 305–6.

131 Ibid., p. 406.

132 Robert B. Fairbanks, "Public Housing for the City as a Whole: The Texas Experience, 1934–1955," *Southwestern Historical Quarterly* 103, no. 4 (2000): 429.

133 Ibid., p. 409.

134 Ibid., p. 423.

135 Fairbanks, "The Failure of Urban Renewal in the Southwest," p. 312. On these sorts of later schemes, see, for instance, Lydia Otero, *La Calle: Spatial Conflicts and Urban Renewal in a Southwest City* (Tucson: University of Arizona Press, 2010), regarding the case of Tucson.

136 James W. Loewen, *Sundown Towns: A Hidden Dimension of American Racism* (New York: New Press, 2005), p. 4.

137 Ibid., pp. 75–76.

138 Declarations of Restrictions: Homeowners Estates, Phoenix, AZ, 1950, Chicano Research Collection, Hayden Library, Arizona State University, ME CHI LC-3.

139 Cadava, *Standing on Common Ground*, p. 13.

140 Ibid., p. 82.

141 David G. Gutiérrez, *Walls and Mirrors: Mexican Americans, Mexican Immigrants, and the Politics of Ethnicity* (Berkeley: University of California Press, 1995), p. 2.

142 Michael E. Martin, *Residential Segregation Patterns of Latinos in the United States, 1990–2000: Testing the Ethnic Enclave and Inequality Theories* (London: Routledge, 2007), pp. 8, 42–43.

143 Menchaca, "Chicano Indianism," p. 598.

144 David Torres-Rouff, "Becoming Mexican: Segregated Schools and Social Scientists in Southern California, 1913–1946," *Southern California Quarterly* 94, no. 1 (2012): 127.

145 Menchaca, "Chicano Indianism," pp. 597–98.

146 Torres-Rouff, "Becoming Mexican," p. 96.

147 George I. Sánchez, *Forgotten People: A Study of New Mexicans* (Albuquerque: University of New Mexico Press, 1940), pp. 17, 32.

148 Ibid., pp. 13–14.

149 Wilson, "Brown over 'Other White,'" p. 155; Menchaca, "Chicano Indianism," p. 598; Torres-Rouff, "Becoming Mexican," p. 107.

150 San Miguel Guadalupe, "The Struggle Against Separate and Unequal Schools: Middle Class Mexican Americans and the Desegregation Campaign in Texas, 1929–1957," *History of Education Quarterly* 23, no. 3 (1983): 344.

151 "Before 'Brown v. Board,' Mendez Fought California's Segregated Schools," http://www.npr.org/blogs/codeswitch/2014/05/16/312555636/before-brown-v-board-mendez-fought-californias-segregated-schools (accessed January 18, 2015).

152 Menchaca, "Chicano Indianism," pp. 598–99.

153 Gary Orfield, Erica Frankenberg, Jongyeon Ee, and John Kuscera, *Brown at 60: Great Progress, a Long Retreat and an Uncertain Future*, Civil Rights Project UCLA. May 15, 2014, https://civilrightsproject.ucla.edu/research/k-12-education/integration-and-diversity/brown-at-60-great-progress-a-long-retreat-and-an-uncertain-future/Brown-at-60-051814.pdf (accessed April 3, 2018).

154 Wilson, "Brown over 'Other White,'" p. 148.

155 Sheridan, *Arizona: A History*, p. 296.

156 Gill, *Harlem*, pp. 353–54.

157 Wilson, "Brown over 'Other White,'" pp. 181–82.

158 Ibid., p. 183.

159 "School Desegregation in Corpus Christi, Texas," May 1977, Texas A&M University Corpus Christi, Mary and Jeff Bell Library, Hector García Collection, Box 30, Folder 10.

160 Draft of the Texas Advisory Committee's Proposed Publication, October 22, 1976, Texas A&M University Corpus Christi, Mary and Jeff Bell Library, Hector García Collection, Box 9, Folder 16.

161 González, *Harvest of Empire*, pp. 170–71.

162 Ibid., p. 171.

163 Kreneck, "Dr. Hector P. García," p. 210.

164 Wilson, "Brown over 'Other White,'" p. 174.

165 Raymond Telles to Hector García, April 2, 1966, Texas A&M University Corpus Christi, Mary and Jeff Bell Library, Hector García Collection, Box 195, Folder 48.

166 Miriam Pawel, *The Crusades of Cesar Chavez: A Biography* (New York: Bloomsbury, 2014), p. 13.

167 Ibid., p. 15.

168 Rodriguez, *Mongrels, Bastards, Orphans, and Vagabonds*, p. 206.

169 Quoted in Pawel, *The Crusades of Cesar Chavez*, p. 2.

170 Rodriguez, *Mongrels, Bastards, Orphans, and Vagabonds*, p. 203.

171 Ibid.

172 David R. Mariel and Juan José Peña, "La Reconquista: The Chicano Movement in New Mexico," in Gonzales-Berry and Maciel, *The Contested Homeland*, p. 270.

173 Andrés Bustamante, "American Aztlán: Cultural Memory After the Mexican-American War," presentation given at Legacies of Conquest conference, April 11, 2017, http://www.crassh.cam.ac.uk/events/26941.

174 Rodriguez, *Mongrels, Bastards, Orphans, and Vagabonds*, p. 203.
175 Gutiérrez, *Walls and Mirrors*, p. 185.
176 Lorena Oropeza and Dionne Espinoza (eds.), *Enriqueta Vasquez and the Chicano Movement: Writings from el Grito del Norte* (Houston: Arte Publico, 2006), pp. 86–87.
177 Nieto-Phillips, *The Language of Blood*, p. x.
178 Ibid., p. xi.
179 Ibid.
180 Joseph A. Rodríguez, "Becoming Latinos: Mexican Americans, Chicanos, and the Spanish Myth in the Urban Southwest," *Western Historical Quarterly* 29, no. 2 (1998): 166–67.
181 Rodriguez, *Mongrels, Bastards, Orphans, and Vagabonds*, p. 212.
182 Mariel and Peña, "La Reconquista," p. 280.
183 Ibid., p. 283.
184 Quoted in Robert Urias, "The Tierra Amarilla Grant, Reies Tijerina, and the Courthouse Raid," *Chicano-Latino Law Review* 16, no. 141 (Winter 1995): 148.
185 FBI Memorandum, June 16, 1964, New Mexico History Collection, Center for Southwest Research, University Libraries, University of New Mexico, Reies López Tijerina Papers, 1954–2003, MSS 654 BC, Box 2.
186 Alianza pamphlet, n.d., MSS 628 BC, Oversized drawer C9, Alianza Federal de Pueblos Libros Collection, 1963–1997, New Mexico History Collection, Center for Southwest Research, University Libraries, University of New Mexico.
187 Urias, "The Tierra Amarilla Grant, Reies Tijerina, and the Courthouse Raid," pp. 144–45; Lorena Oropeza, "Becoming Indo-Hispano: Reies López Tijerina and the New Mexican Land Grant Movement," in Goldstein, *Formations of United States Colonialism*, p. 184.
188 Oropeza, "Becoming Indo-Hispano," p. 185.
189 Ibid., p. 193.
190 Urias, "The Tierra Amarilla Grant, Reies Tijerina, and the Courthouse Raid," p. 150.
191 Mora, *Making Hispanics*, p. 4.
192 Pablo Guzmán, "Before People Called Me a Spic, They Called Me a Nigger," in Jiménez Román and Flores, *Afro-Latin@ Reader*, pp. 235–36.
193 Robert M. Utley, *Changing Courses: The International Boundary, United States and Mexico, 1848–1963* (Tucson, Ariz.: Southwest Parks and Monuments Association, 1996), p. 100.
194 Ibid., p. 101.
195 Ibid., p. 109.

Chapter 15: Miami, Florida

1 Louis Pérez Jr., "Between Encounter and Experience: Florida in the Cuban Imagination," *Florida Historical Quarterly* 82, no. 2 (2003): 178.
2 Ibid.
3 Ibid.
4 Ibid.
5 Ibid., p. 179.

6 Ibid., p. 186.

7 Ibid., pp. 179–80.

8 Ibid., pp. 179–80, 189; Pérez, "Cubans in the United States," p. 128.

9 C. N. Rose, "Tourism and the Hispanicization of Race in Jim Crow Miami, 1945–1965," *Journal of Social History* 45, no. 3 (2011): 736.

10 Ibid.

11 Pérez, *Cuba and the United States*, p. 245.

12 "Impide el departamento de estado la salida de los Cubanos de su territorio," *Noticias de Hoy*, February 1, 1961, p. 1.

13 "Llegan a nuestra patria repatriados cubanos perseguidos en los Estados Unidos," *Noticias de Hoy*, March 15, 1961, p. 11.

14 Jack Kofoed, "Miami Already Has Too Many Refugees," *Miami Herald*, October 5, 1965.

15 Ibid.

16 Pérez, *Cuba and the United States*, p. 254.

17 María de los Angeles Torres, *In the Land of Mirrors: Cuban Exile Politics in the United States* (Ann Arbor: University of Michigan Press, 2001), pp. 85, 100–101.

18 Brendan I. Koerner, *The Skies Belong to Us: Love and Terror in the Golden Age of Hijacking* (New York: Crown, 2013), p. 35.

19 Ibid., p. 37.

20 Ibid., p. 50.

21 Ibid., p. 45.

22 Ibid., p. 48.

23 Pérez, *Cuba and the United States*, p. 255.

24 Ibid.

25 María Cristina García, "Central American Migration and the Shaping of Refugee Policy," in Dirk Hoerder and Nora Faires (eds.), *Migrants and Migration in Modern North America: Cross-Border Lives, Labor Markets, and Politics* (Durham, N.C.: Duke University Press, 2011), p. 354.

26 David M. Reimers, *Other Immigrants: The Global Origins of the American People* (New York: New York University Press, 2005). See chapter 5 on Central and South America.

27 García, "Central American Migration and the Shaping of Refugee Policy," p. 356.

28 Joseph and Buchenau, *Mexico's Once and Future Revolution*, pp. 156–57, 172–75.

29 Henderson, *Beyond Borders*, p. 99.

30 "Statistical Portrait of Hispanics in the United States," Pew Research Center Hispanic Trends, http://www.pewhispanic.org/2016/04/19/statistical-portrait-of-hispanics-in-the-united-states-key-charts/ (accessed November 6, 2016); "Estimates of the Unauthorized Immigrant Population Residing in the United States: January 2010, Office of Immigration Statistics, Department of Homeland Security," February 2011, https://www.dhs.gov/xlibrary/assets/statistics/publications/ois_ill_pe_2010.pdf (accessed August 29, 2017).

31 Starr, *California: A History*, p. 312.

32 Ibid.

33 Pérez, *Cuba and the United States*, p. 269.

34 Joan Didion, *Miami* (New York: Simon and Schuster, 1987), p. 65.

35 Milton Weiss, "Letter to the Editor: Pre-Cuban Miami Was a Good Place to Live," *Miami Herald*, October 15, 1990.

36 Anzaldúa, *Borderlands/La Frontera*, p. 75.

37 Starr, *California: A History*, p. 315.

38 Hector Tobar, "Tucson School Board Lifts Ban on Latino Studies Books," *Los Angeles Times*, October 25, 2013, http://articles.latimes.com/2013/oct/25/entertainment/la-et-jc-tucson-school-board-latino-studies-books-20131025 (accessed January 19, 2015).

39 James C. McKinley, "Texas Conservatives Win Curriculum Change," *New York Times*, March 12, 2010, http://www.nytimes.com/2010/03/13/education/13texas.html?_r=0 (accessed March 31, 2016); Gail Collins, "How Texas Inflicts Bad Textbooks on Us," *New York Review of Books*, June 21, 2012.

40 Cindy Casares, "A Textbook on Mexican Americans That Gets Their History Wrong? Oh, Texas," *Guardian*, May 31, 2016, https://www.theguardian.com/commentisfree/2016/may/31/texas-textbook-mexican-american-heritage-public-schools-us-history?CMP=share_btn_fb (accessed November 7, 2016).

41 U.S. Census 2000: Chapter 8: Language, p. 124, report available at https://www.census.gov/population/www/cen2000/censusatlas/pdf/8_Language.pdf (accessed November 6, 2016).

42 Ibid., p. 125.

43 María de Los Angeles, "¿Qué Pasa, U.S.A.? Gets a Modern Update for the Miami Stage," *Miami New Times*, December 18, 2017, http://www.miaminewtimes.com/arts/que-pasa-usa-at-arsht-center-may-17-to-may-19-9903994 (accessed January 20, 2018).

44 Suarez, *Latino Americans*, loc. 3408–31.

45 Sheridan, *Arizona: A History*, p. 391.

46 Ibid.

47 Mora, *Making Hispanics*, p. 2.

48 "Measuring Race and Ethnicity Across the Decades: 1790–2010," United States Census Bureau, http://www.census.gov/population/race/data/MREAD_1790_2010.html (accessed March 28, 2016).

49 Ibid.

50 Grace Flores-Hughes, *A Tale of Survival: Memoir of an Hispanic Woman* (Bloomington, Ind.: Author House, 2011), pp. xviii, 222.

51 Ibid., p. 226.

52 Ibid., p. 227.

53 Ibid.

54 "Special Report: America's Hispanics: From Minor to Major: A Suitable Box to Tick," *Economist*, March 14, 2015, p. 6.

55 "Measuring Race and Ethnicity Across the Decades: 1790–2010"; Painter, *The History of White People*, loc. 6351–65.

56 Laura E. Gómez, "The Birth of the 'Hispanic' Generation: Attitudes of Mexican-American Political Elites Toward the Hispanic Label," *Latin American Perspectives* 19, no. 4 (1992): 46; Gómez, *Manifest Destinies*, p. 150.

57 "'Mexican,' 'Hispanic,' 'Latin American' Top List of Race Write-Ins on the 2010 Census, Pew Research Center," http://www.pewresearch.org/fact-tank/2014/04/04/

mexican-hispanic-and-latin-american-top-list-of-race-write-ins-on-the-2010
-census/ (accessed September 1, 2017).

58 Mora, *Making Hispanics*, p. 167. See the 2010 census form at https://www.census
.gov/schools/pdf/2010form_info.pdf (accessed November 18, 2016).
59 Alex Wagner, "The Americans Our Government Won't Count," *New York Times*,
April 1, 2018, Opinion, https://www.nytimes.com/2018/03/30/opinion/sunday/
united-states-census.html (accessed April 2, 2018).
60 Mora, *Making Hispanics*, pp. 4–5.
61 "Special Report: America's Hispanics," p. 4.
62 Mora, *Making Hispanics*, p. 153.
63 Marilyn Halter, *Shopping for Identity: The Marketing of Ethnicity* (New York:
Schocken Books, 2000), p. 51.
64 Arellano, *Taco USA*, p. 90.
65 Ibid., p. 93.
66 David E. Hayes-Bautista, *Cinco de Mayo: An American Tradition* (Berkeley: University
of California Press, 2012), chapters 3 and 6.
67 Frances Negrón-Muntaner, Chelsea Abbas, Luis Figueroa, and Samuel Robson,
The Latino Media Gap: A Report on the State of Latinos in U.S. Media, Columbia
University, 2014, p. 1.
68 "Hollywood Fails to Represent U.S. Ethnic Diversity, Says Study," theguardian
.com, August 5, 2014, http://www.theguardian.com/film/2014/aug/05/
hollywood-fails-to-represent-ethnic-diversity-study-usc (accessed January 20,
2015).

Chapter 16: Tucson, Arizona

1 See the full text, for instance, at https://www.washingtonpost.com/news/
post-politics/wp/2015/06/16/full-text-donald-trump-announces-a-presidential
-bid/ (accessed January 21, 2018).
2 Ioan Grillo, "Why Did Peña Nieto Invite Trump to Mexico?" *New York Times*,
September 1, 2016, http://www.nytimes.com/2016/09/02/opinion/why-did
-pena-nieto-invite-trump-to-mexico.html (accessed November 11, 2016).
3 Pew Research Center Hispanic Trends, "Latino Voters in the 2012 Election," http://
www.pewhispanic.org/2012/11/07/latino-voters-in-the-2012-election/ (accessed
January 19, 2015).
4 About SVREP, http://svrep.org/about_svrep.php (accessed September 1, 2017).
5 Jeremy Schwartz and Dan Hill, "Silent Majority: Texas' Booming Hispanic Population Deeply Underrepresented in Local Politics," *Austin American-Statesman*,
October 21, 2016, http://projects.statesman.com/news/latino-representation/
index.html (accessed November 7, 2016); Pew Research Center Hispanic Trends:
"Latinos in the 2016 Election: Texas," http://www.pewhispanic.org/fact-sheet/
latinos-in-the-2016-election-texas/ (accessed August 29, 2017).
6 "The Status of Latinos in California: An Analysis of the Growing Latino
Population, Voting Trends and Elected Representation, 2015," http://
leadershipcaliforniainstitute.org/sites/all/files/Status%20of%20Latinos%20
Report%20Preview.pdf. Also http://latinocaucus.legislature.ca.gov/

news/2015-07-09-report-despite-recent-gains-california-latinos-continue-be
-underrepresented-every-le (accessed January 21, 2018).

7 Adam Nagourney and Jennifer Medina, "This City Is 78% Latino, and the Face of a New California," *New York Times*, October 11, 2016, http://www.nytimes.com/2016/10/12/us/california-latino-voters.html?hp&action=click&pgtype=Homepage&clickSource=story-heading&module=second-colum&_r=0 (accessed November 7, 2016).

8 Rafael Bernal, "Latino Representation in Congress Record High, but Far from Parity," *Hill*, September 14, 2017, http://thehill.com/latino/350673-latino-representation-in-congress-at-record-high-but-far-from-parity (accessed January 21, 2018).

9 González, *Harvest of Empire*, p. 256; Josefina Zoraida Vázquez and Lorenzo Meyer, *México frente a Estados Unidos: un ensayo histórico, 1776–2000* (Mexico, D.F.: Fondo de Cultura Económica, 2013), p. 215.

10 González, *Harvest of Empire*, p. 257.

11 Joseph and Buchenau, *Mexico's Once and Future Revolution*, p. 181.

12 Zoraida Vázquez and Meyer, *México frente a Estados Unidos*, p. 234.

13 Henderson, *Beyond Borders*, p. 123.

14 González, *Harvest of Empire*, p. 266.

15 Ibid., p. 269.

16 Ibid., p. 258; Henderson, *Beyond Borders*, pp. 93–94.

17 Mark Weisbrot, Stephan Lefebvre, and Joseph Sammut, "Did NAFTA Help Mexico? An Assessment After 20 Years," *Center for Economic and Policy Research* (2014), p. 1.

18 Azam Ahmed and Elisabeth Malkin, "Mexicans Are the Nafta Winners? It's News to Them," *New York Times*, January 4, 2017, https://www.nytimes.com/2017/01/04/world/americas/mexico-donald-trump-nafta.html?hp&action=click&pgtype=Homepage&clickSource=story-heading&mod&_r=0 (accessed September 1, 2017).

19 Weisbrot et al., "Did NAFTA Help Mexico?" p. 1.

20 "NAFTA 20 Years Later: PIIE Briefing No 14-3," Peterson Institute for International Economics (2014), p. 4.

21 Shawn Donnan, "Renegotiating Nafta: 5 Points to Keep in Mind," *Financial Times*, January 1, 2017, https://www.ft.com/content/4c1594c6-e18d-11e6-8405-9e5580d6e5fb (accessed September 1, 2017).

22 González, *Harvest of Empire*, p. 200.

23 Ibid., p. 201.

24 Ibid., p. 203.

25 Nora Caplan-Bricker, "Who's the Real Deporter-in-Chief: Bush or Obama?" *New Republic*, April 18, 2014, https://newrepublic.com/article/117412/deportations-under-obama-vs-bush-who-deported-more-immigrants (accessed March 29, 2016); Brian Bennett, "High Deportation Figures Are Misleading." *LA Times*, April 1, 2014, http://www.latimes.com/nation/la-na-obama-deportations-20140402-story.html (accessed March 27, 2018).

26 Julia Preston and Randal C. Archibold, "U.S. Moves to Stop Surge in Illegal Immigration," *New York Times*, June 21, 2014, http://www.nytimes.com /2014/06/21/us/us-plans-to-step-up-detention-and-deportation-of-migrants.html?_r=1&asset-Type=nyt_now (accessed January 19, 2015).

27 Richard Fausset and Ken Belson, "Faces of an Immigration System Overwhelmed by Women and Children," *New York Times*, June 6, 2014, https://www.nytimes.com/2014/06/06/us/faces-of-an-immigration-system-overwhelmed-by-women-and-children.html (accessed January 21, 2018).

28 "Southwest Border Unaccompanied Alien Children," United States Customs and Border Protection, http://www.cbp.gov/newsroom/stats/southwest-border-unaccompanied-children/fy-2015 (accessed January 19, 2015).

29 Preston and Archibold, "U.S. Moves to Stop Surge in Illegal Immigration."

30 "Transnational Organized Crime in Central America and the Caribbean," United Nations Office on Drugs and Crime, 2012, https://www.unodc.org/documents/data-and-analysis/Studies/TOC_Central_America_and_the_Caribbean_english.pdf (accessed January 20, 2015).

31 Editorial, "America's Test at the Border," *New York Times*, July 21, 2014, https://www.nytimes.com/2014/07/21/opinion/Americas-Test-Children-at-the-Border.html (accessed January 21, 2018).

32 Editorial, "A Tale of Two Migration Flows," *New York Times*, August 1, 2016, http://www.nytimes.com/2016/08/01/opinion/a-tale-of-two-migration-flows.html; U.S. Customs and Border Protection, https://www.cbp.gov/newsroom/stats/southwest-border-unaccompanied-children/fy-2016 (accessed November 12, 2016).

33 "A Tale of Two Migration Flows"; Kirk Semple, "Fleeing Gangs, Central American Families Surge Toward U.S." *New York Times*, November 12, 2016, http://www.nytimes.com/2016/11/13/world/americas/fleeing-gangs-central-american-families-surge-toward-us.html?_r=0 (accessed November 13, 2016). For FY 2017 U.S. Border Patrol figures, see https://www.cbp.gov/sites/default/files/assets/documents/2017-Dec/USBP%20Stats%20FY2017%20sector%20profile.pdf (accessed April 4, 2018).

34 Patrick J. McDonnell, "Mexico Rejects U.S. Plan to Deport Central Americans to Mexico," *Los Angeles Times*, February 24, 2017, http://www.latimes.com/politics/washington/la-na-essential-washington-updates-mexico-rejects-u-s-plan-to-deport-1487988401-htmlstory.html (accessed September 1, 2017).

35 Colleen Shalby, "Parents Ask: What Happens to My Child If I'm Deported?" *Los Angeles Times*, March 22, 2017, http://www.latimes.com/politics/la-na-questions-trump-immigration-20170322-htmlstory.html (accessed September 1, 2017).

36 Sabrina Siddiqui and Oliver Laughland, "Trump Plans to Greatly Expand Number of Immigrants Targeted for Deportation," *Guardian*, February 21, 2017, https://www.theguardian.com/us-news/2017/feb/21/donald-trump-immigration-deportation-guidelines-homeland-security (accessed September 1, 2017).

37 Elliot Spagat, "Immigration Judges to Be Sent to Border Detention Centers," Associated Press, March 18, 2017, https://apnews.com/5b824828b2d647e589c004afd43ec858/immigration-judges-be-sent-border-detention-centers (accessed September 1, 2017).

38 Miriam Jordan, "Trump Administration Says That Nearly 200,000 Salvadorans Must Leave," *New York Times*, January 8, 2018, https://www.nytimes.com/2018/01/08/us/salvadorans-tps-end.html (accessed March 27, 2018. Miriam Jordan and Manny Fernandez. "Judge Rejects Long Detentions of Migrant Families, Dealing Trump Another Setback." *New York Times*, July 9, 2018, https://

www.nytimes.com/2018/07/09/us/migrants-family-separation-reunification
.html (accessed July 20, 2018).

39 María DeGuzmán, *Spain's Long Shadow: The Black Legend, Off-Whiteness, and Anglo-American Empire* (Minneapolis: University of Minnesota, 2005), p. xxvii.

40 Pew Research Center, "5 Facts About Illegal Immigration in the U.S.," April 27, 2017, http://www.pewresearch.org/fact-tank/2017/04/27/5-facts-about-illegal-immigration-in-the-u-s/ (accessed September 1, 2017).

41 Janet Adamy and Paul Overberg, "Immigration Source Shifts to Asia from Mexico," *Wall Street Journal*, September 7, 2016, http://www.wsj.com/articles/immigration-source-shifts-to-asia-from-mexico-1473205576 (accessed November 12, 2016).

42 Ibid.

43 Ana Gonzalez-Barrera, "More Mexicans Leaving Than Coming to the U.S.," Pew Research Center, November 19, 2015, http://www.pewhispanic.org/2015/11/19/more-mexicans-leaving-than-coming-to-the-u-s/ (accessed March 29, 2016).

44 Jens Manuel Krogstad, "Key Facts About How the U.S. Hispanic Population Is Changing," Pew Research Center, http://www.pewresearch.org/fact-tank/2016/09/08/key-facts-about-how-the-u-s-hispanic-population-is-changing/ (accessed September 1, 2017).

45 Ibid.

46 See, for instance, Michael Deibert, *In the Shadow of Saint Death: The Gulf Cartel and the Price of America's Drug War in Mexico* (Guilford, Conn.: Lyons Press, 2014), p. 233.

47 Christopher Ingraham, "Legal Marijuana Is Finally Doing What the Drug War Couldn't," *Washington Post*, March 3, 2016, https://www.washingtonpost.com/news/wonk/wp/2016/03/03/legal-marijuana-is-finally-doing-what-the-drug-war-couldnt/ (accessed November 12, 2016). FY 2016 figures at https://www.cbp.gov/sites/default/files/assets/documents/2017-Jan/USBP%20Stats%20FY2016%20sector%20profile.pdf.

48 Ibid.

49 See Department of State: Merida Initiative, https://www.state.gov/j/inl/merida/ (accessed November 13, 2016).

50 Harel Shapira, *Waiting for José: The Minutemen's Pursuit of America* (Princeton, N.J.: Princeton University Press, 2013), p. 3; Foley, *Mexicans in the Making of America*, ch 8.

51 Shapira, *Waiting for José*, p. 13.

52 Ibid., p. 2.

53 James Marcus, "Easy Chair: Beyond a Boundary," *Harper's*, June 2014, p. 5.

54 Sheridan, *Arizona: A History*, p. 392.

55 Ibid.

56 Mari Herreras, "All Souls All Community," *Tucson Weekly*, November 6–12, 2014, p. 11.

57 Jeremy Harding, "The Deaths Map," *London Review of Books*, October 20, 2011, pp. 7–13.

58 See http://www.humaneborders.org/wp-content/uploads/deathpostercumulative_letter16.pdf. Also, the charity provides a searchable map for deceased migrants at http://www.humaneborders.info/app/map.asp.

59 Miriam Jordan, "Desert Castaways Get Second Life in Art Exhibition," *Wall Street Journal*, January 17, 2008.

60 Marcus, "Easy Chair," p. 5; U.S. Border Patrol, Sector Profile, FY 2015, CBP FY15 Border Security Report: Department of Homeland Security, December 22, 2015, p. 3, https://www.cbp.gov/sites/default/files/documents/USBP%20Stats%20FY2015%20sector%20profile.pdf (accessed March 29, 2016).

61 Bob Davis, "The Thorny Economics of Illegal Immigration," *Wall Street Journal*, February 9, 2016, online edition, http://www.wsj.com/articles/the-thorny-economics-of-illegal-immigration-1454984443 (accessed March 29, 2016); also see http://www.migrationpolicy.org/data/unauthorized-immigrant-population/state/AZ.

62 Sheridan, *Arizona: A History*, p. 394.

63 Harding, "The Deaths Map," pp. 7–13; Jude Joffe-Block, "Ahead of Arizona Primary, Business Community Fears Trump Will Inspire Backlash," NPR, March 16, 2016, http://www.npr.org/2016/03/19/471000171/ahead-of-arizona-primary-business-community-fears-trump-will-inspire-backlash (accessed September 1, 2017).

64 Julie Hirschfeld Davis and Maggie Haberman, "Trump Pardons Joe Arpaio, Who Became Face of Crackdown on Illegal Immigration," *New York Times*, August 25, 2017, https://www.nytimes.com/2017/08/25/us/politics/joe-arpaio-trump-pardon-sheriff-arizona.html (accessed September 1, 2017).

65 William Finnegan, "Sheriff Joe," *New Yorker*, July 20, 2009, http://www.newyorker.com/magazine/2009/07/20/sheriff-joe (accessed January 19, 2015).

66 Ibid.

67 Jaques Billeaud, "Taxpayer Costs of Sheriff Joe Arpaio's Profiling Case: Another $13M on Top of $41M," Associated Press, May 12, 2016, https://www.azcentral.com/story/news/local/phoenix/2016/05/12/taxpayer-costs-sheriff-joe-arpaios-profiling-case-another-13m-top-41m/84293950/ (accessed September 1, 2017).

68 Julia Preston, "Tension Simmers as Cubans Breeze Across U.S. Border," *New York Times*, February 12, 2016, https://www.nytimes.com/2016/02/13/us/as-cubans-and-central-americans-enter-us-the-welcomes-vary.html. (accessed April 27, 2018); Tom Dart, "Cuban Immigrants Face Resentment in Texas over 'Preferential Treatment,'" *Guardian*, March 14, 2016, http://www.theguardian.com/us-news/2016/mar/14/cuban-immigrants-texas-resentment-us-policy (accessed March 29, 2016).

69 González, *Harvest of Empire*, p. 281.

70 Ibid.

71 Ibid., pp. 282–84.

72 Lizette Alvarez, "Economy and Crime Spur New Puerto Rican Exodus," *New York Times*, February 9, 2014, https://www.nytimes.com/2014/02/09/us/economy-and-crime-spur-new-puerto-rican-exodus.html (accessed January 21, 2018).

73 Mary Williams Walsh, "A Surreal Life on the Precipice in Puerto Rico," *New York Times*, August 6, 2016, http://www.nytimes.com/2016/08/07/business/dealbook/life-in-the-miasma-of-puerto-ricos-debt.html (accessed November 15, 2016).

74 Mary Williams Walsh, "Puerto Rico Declares a Form of Bankruptcy," *New York Times*, May 2, 2017, https://www.nytimes.com/2017/05/03/business/dealbook/

puerto-rico-debt.html?hp&action=click&pgtype=Homepage&clickSource=story
-heading&module=first-column-region&region=top-news&WT.nav=top-news
(accessed September 1, 2017).

75 Ayala and Bernabe, *Puerto Rico in the American Century*, p. 293.

76 Jens Manuel Krogstad, "Historic Population Losses Continue Across Puerto Rico,"
Pew Research Center Fact Tank, March 24, 2016, http://www.pewresearch.org/
fact-tank/2016/03/24/historic-population-losses-continue-across-puerto-rico/
(accessed November 15, 2016).

77 Patricia Mazzei and Nicholas Nehamas, "Florida's Hispanic Voter Surge Wasn't
Enough for Clinton," *Miami Herald*, November 9, 2016, http://www.miamiher-
ald.com/news/politics-government/election/article113778053.html (accessed
November 15, 2016).

78 Ed Pilkington, "Puerto Rico Governor to Take Statehood Case to Washington
but Faces US Snub," *Guardian*, June 12, 2017, https://www.theguardian.com/
world/2017/jun/12/puerto-rico-governor-washington-statehood-us (accessed
September 1, 2017).

79 Frances Robles, Kenan Davis, Sheri Fink, and Sarah Almukhtar, "Official Toll in
Puerto Rico: 64. Actual Deaths May Be 1,052," *New York Times*, December 9, 2017,
https://www.nytimes.com/interactive/2017/12/08/us/puerto-rico-hurricane
-maria-death-toll.html?_r=0 (accessed January 21, 2018).

80 Kyle Dropp and Brendan Nyhan, "Nearly Half of Americans Don't Know Puerto
Ricans Are Fellow Citizens," *New York Times*, September 26, 2017, https://www
.nytimes.com/2017/09/26/upshot/nearly-half-of-americans-dont-know-people
-in-puerto-ricoans-are-fellow-citizens.html?mcubz=1 (accessed January 21, 2018).

81 Rebecca Spalding, "Puerto Rico to Lose Tax Advantages Under GOP Plan, Expert
Says," *Bloomberg*, December 16, 2017, https://www.bloomberg.com/news/
articles/2017-12-16/puerto-rico-to-lose-tax-advantages-under-gop-plan-expert
-says (accessed January 21, 2018).

Epilogue: Dalton, Georgia

1 Interview with Beth Jordan, Dalton, Georgia, June 25, 2015.

2 Interview with Jennifer Phinney, Dalton, Georgia, June 2, 2015.

3 "Georgia Project," *The New Georgia Encyclopedia*, September 25, 2009, http://
www.georgiaencyclopedia.org/articles/education/georgia-project (accessed
November 22, 2015).

4 Miriam Jordan, "Georgia Town Is Case Study in Immigration Debate," *Wall Street
Journal* (online) (accessed January 20, 2015).

5 See figures from Pew Research Center Hispanic Trends, http://www.pewhispanic
.org/states/county/13313/ (accessed November 14, 2016).

6 Interview with Esther Familia-Cabrera, Dalton, Georgia, March 24, 2015.

7 Samuel p. Huntington, "The Hispanic Challenge," *Foreign Policy*, no. 141 (2004):
31.

8 Toni Morrison, "Mourning for Whiteness," *New Yorker*, November 21, 2016,
http://www.newyorker.com/magazine/2016/11/21/aftermath-sixteen-writers
-on-trumps-america (accessed November 13, 2016).

9 "Hispanic Population Growth and Dispersion Across U.S. Counties, 1980–2014," Pew Research Center Hispanic Trends, September 6, 2016, http://www.pewhispanic .org/interactives/hispanic-population-by-county/ (accessed November 18, 2016).

10 Huntington, "The Hispanic Challenge," p. 32.

11 Walter D. Mignolo, "Afterward," in Greer et al., *Rereading the Black Legend*, p. 324.

12 Edna Ferber, *Giant* (New York: Perennial Classics, 2000), pp. 74–75.

13 Richard Simon, "Little-Remembered Revolutionary War Hero a Step Closer to Citizenship," *Los Angeles Times*, July 10, 2014, http://www.latimes.com/nation/ nationnow/la-na-nn-honorary-citizen-galvez-20140710-story.html (accessed March 31, 2016).

14 The following section draws from Cadava, *Standing on Common Ground*, chapter 6, Kindle.

15 Ibid., p. 244.

16 "Remains of Lost Spanish Fort Found on South Carolina Coast," *New York Times*, July 26, 2016. For more on the Luna settlement, see http://uwf.edu/cassh/ departments/anthropology-and-archaeology/luna-settlement/.

Index